Palestine and International Law

Palestine and International Law

Essays on Politics and Economics

Edited by SANFORD R. SILVERBURG

McFarland & Company, Inc., Publishers
Jefferson, North Carolina, and London

> The present work is a reprint of the library bound edition of Palestine and International Law: Essays on Politics and Economics, *first published in 2002 by McFarland.*

LIBRARY OF CONGRESS CATALOGUING-IN-PUBLICATION DATA

Palestine and international law : essays on politics and economics / edited by Sanford R. Silverburg.
    p.   cm.
Includes bibliographical references and index.

ISBN 978-0-7864-4248-5
softcover : 50# alkaline paper ∞

1. West Bank — International status.   2. Gaza Strip — International status.
3. West Bank — Economic conditions.   4. Gaza Strip — Economic conditions.
5. Arab-Israeli conflict —1993–   I. Silverburg, Sanford R.
KZ4282.P35   2009
341.2'9 — dc21   2001007858

British Library cataloguing data are available

©2002 Sanford R. Silverburg. All rights reserved

No part of this book may be reproduced or transmitted in any form or by any means, electronic or mechanical, including photocopying or recording, or by any information storage and retrieval system, without permission in writing from the publisher.

Cover imgae ©2008 Shutterstock.

Manufactured in the United States of America

McFarland & Company, Inc., Publishers
  Box 611, Jefferson, North Carolina 28640
    www.mcfarlandpub.com

To David, my first, my oldest, my…

Acknowledgments

I extend my appreciation to the following publishers who have kindly granted me permission to reprint materials originally appearing in their respective publications. Please note that any errors, omissions, or emendations that have occurred in the reprint of these articles are my responsibility and not that of the original publishers.

The *Tulsa Journal of Comparative and International Law* for permission to reprint "Diplomatic Recognition of States *in statu nascendi:* The Case of Palestine" by Sanford R. Silverburg (6 *Tulsa J. Comp. & Int'l Law* 21 [1998]).

Texas International Law Journal for permission to reprint "Israel and the Creation of a Palestinian State" by Joseph H. Weiler (17 *Texas Int'l Law J.* 287 [1982]).

Muwatin of Ramallah, Palestine, for permission to reprint "From Liberation to State Building in South Africa: Some Constitutional Considerations for Palestine" by Adrien Katherine Wing, which appeared in *Liberation, Democratization and Transitions to Statehood in the Third World*, edited by May Jayussi (1998).

Israel Law Review for permission to reprint "Aspects of Foreign Relations Under the Israeli-Palestinian Agreements on Interim Self-Government Arrangements for the West Bank and Gaza" by Joel Singer (28 *Israel Law Review* 268 [1994]).

Case Western Law Review for permission to reprint "Peace and Political Imperative of Legal Reform in Palestine" by George E. Bisharat (31 *Case W. Res. J. Int'l Law* 253 [1999]) and portions of "Foreign Private Investment in Palestine Revisited: An Analysis of the Revised Palestinian Investment Law" by David Fidler (31 *Case W. Res. J. Int'l Law* 293 [1999]).

Fordham International Law Journal for permission to reprint

"Palestinian Economic Progress Under the Oslo Agreements" by Mel Levine (19 *Fordham Int'l Law J.* 1393 [1996] and "Legal and Structural Hurdles to Achieving Political Stability and Economic Development in the Palestinian Territories" by Keith C. Molkner (19 *Fordham Int'l Law J.* 1419 [1996]).

Contents

Acknowledgments	vii
Introduction	1

Part I: Political Issues

1. Diplomatic Recognition of States *in statu nascendi:* The Case of Palestine. *Sanford R. Silverburg.* — 9

2. Palestine: The Issue of Statehood. *John Quigley.* — 37

3. Israel and the Creation of a Palestinian State: The Art of the Impossible and the Possible. *Joseph H. Weiler.* — 55

4. Palestine and the World of Law: A Structural Analysis. *Sanford R. Silverburg.* — 160

5. Aspects of Foreign Relations Under the Israeli-Palestinian Agreements on Interim Self-Government Arrangements for the West Bank and Gaza. *Joel Singer.* — 174

6. From Liberation to State Building in South Africa: Some Constitutional Considerations for Palestine. *Adrien Katherine Wing.* — 199

7. Peace and the Political Imperative of Legal Reform in Palestine. *George E. Bisharat.* — 214

8. Mandate Ways: Self-Determination in Palestine and the "Existing Non-Jewish Communities."
   John Strawson. 251

9. Palestine and the United Nations.
   Neri Sybesma-Knol. 271

10. From Ostracism to a Leading Role — Spain's Foreign Policy Towards the Middle East Since 1939. *Juan Bautista Delgado.* 299

Part II: Economic Issues

11. Palestinian Economic Development in the Era of Globalization. *David P. Fidler and Fadi G. Harb.* 331

12. Legal and Structural Hurdles to Achieving Political Stability and Economic Development in the Palestinian Territories. *Keith C. Molkner.* 367

13. Palestinian Economic Progress Under the Oslo Agreements. *Mel Levine.* 395

Selected Bibliography 419
Contributors 425
Index 427

Introduction

Conflict in any of its forms is a regular component of human behavioral interaction, whether it occurs between two or more individuals or, similarly, among groups. The very nature of conflict is a divergence of perspectives on some common element of varying value as held by any one of the individuals or groups. In the organized political world of the contemporary global structure, this phenomenon is often violent. Hence under these conditions, the give and take of relations between states often renders less than its potential benefit, and the ability to reach the optimal level or range of benefits that reflect the full worth of any commodity found in a stable political order is commensurately decreased.

Violent conflict has been, historians have shown us, if not commonplace in the Middle East then certainly a fairly regular element in the unfurling of human development in the region. In order to provide an alternative to the violent resolution of conflict, nations have developed regularized rules of conduct between and among states—what we call international law.[1] Over time the recognition of international law as a diplomatic tool for the furtherance of state interest has served the statesman well. Its continued operation, along with the expected changes in rules and application, continues to widen with every new state and transnational political configuration that emerges. We must also be aware that politics, when it has become intertwined with international law, has often blurred the distinction between the two approaches to human organization—those approaches being (a) political organization and (b) a legal regimen—adding to the continued inability of political and legal bodies to act out of the same script.

Whether at the global or the individual level, law requires interpretation regardless of the care and effort afforded to the language of any accord or agreement. But international politics most often involves individual and state political actors who, when acting rationally, prioritize their goals and behavior in order to generate the greatest good as they define it. Their actions may not comport with established legal conventions. The notion of law operating in some sort of a vacuum maintained by logic is certainly offset by the involvement of external actors to political conflict who, for reasons of their own, often project a position combining law with political virtue. This is the case, interestingly, not only for political actors but international law specialists as well. Some couch their beliefs in the rhetoric of legal argument because it is what they believe the law calls for. Others seek to maintain, perpetuate and even instigate a political position via the law, often assuming the role of a political activist or even a crusader.[2] In between is a contemporary and growing genre, offered by political scientists and lawyers, applying international relations theory to international legal arguments.[3]

The numerous political and legal conflicts involving Palestine and Israel — leaving aside for the moment the relationship between the two — have evolved along with the terminology setting out their classification. Hence, in the latter part of the 19th century and early part of the 20th century, one would read about the Zionists and Arabs in a collectivity of provinces of the disaggregating Ottoman Empire. Once the European allies won military victory over the German monarchy and its Near Eastern ally in World War I, a western dominated international organization imbued with its civilized notions of law and order superimposed its paradigm of conflict resolution on the region, and since that time it has become commonplace to refer to "the Arab-Israeli conflict." The issue of western state-centric politics and Palestinian Arab identification, with less than a specifically defined territory, has allowed for the ambiguity that serves as the basis for misunderstanding among regional actions — a misunderstanding that has often escalated to violent conflict.[4] What is in evidence is an assumed framework of analysis, the foundation of which, while plausible, is without much clear historical support. It is, specifically, the lack of a universal adhesion of particular ideas to definite terms of reference accepted by the different cultures resident in and around Palestine that allows for differing viewpoints.

The Palestinians, although clearly always a prime political actor at the geographic core, rarely received political recognition during the period of Ottoman suzerainty for reasons that can only be explained by an examination of the administrative procedures adopted in the Empire at the time. The transfer of governing authority to western European Christians, while not accomplished with the approval of native folk, was done in point of fact. It is at this chronological juncture that obfuscation emerges in much that has been written on the mix of historical events. The situation has also allowed for a variety of both normative and empirical arguments, with commensurate calls for action. A western legal system, based upon its own particular cultural roots and preaching respect for the individual and communal order, became the basis for a completely new regional political system. The issue presented here is that if the legal system imposed upon a people is based on a foundation different from their own, how can its application operate to their benefit?[5]

The resurgence of Jewish nationalism and its embodiment in political Zionism added to the already complex and nuanced political features of a European "mandate" in a Muslim region. Now introduced was a voice that was familiar with western language and which could, thereby, proceed with its goal less impeded. The interests of the Palestinians, on the other hand, at least while they were advanced through force of arms directed first against Jewish Zionists and British occupation forces and later against the Israeli state, under international law could only be properly pressed by the armed forces of national patrons of the region. Once Israel was established the Palestinian community responded through the efforts of the Palestine Liberation Organization (PLO) and an array of other insurgent elements, certainly operating diplomatically but overwhelmingly employing irregular warfare and terrorism. Politically over time, the Palestinians assumed an ever-increasing public persona that ultimately produced the newly accepted rubric, "the Palestinian-Israeli conflict."

Many students of international political affairs and Middle East politics are agreed that new times bring new realities and Palestinian political affairs are today more in the hands of Palestinian nationals than ever before. There remains, however, considerable variance, with the "is" and the "ought," on the direction, suitability, and perhaps even desirability of much of this new course of events. The essays in this collection tackle Palestinian affairs along two primary and real dimensions, political and economic. Material on Palestinian politics would fill a small library. Substantive treatment of the economic aspects of the national community under the various organizational administrations is far more sparse.[6]

At the age of 25 the brilliant mathematician Kurt Gödel, working at the University of Vienna in 1931, postulated the "Impossibility Theorem." Although Gödel's thought related to an arithmetical system; it can be applied to a social scientific understanding and interpretation of political conflict. No matter how much we study a subject, the cumulative effect can never be a *complete* explanation. There are differences in interpretation of facts, which are not concrete phenomena but mental constructions. We must, I would argue, keep in mind a paraphrase of the German philosopher George Hegel's aphorism: history teaches us nothing; historians do. With all of this in mind, the reader has the opportunity to contemplate, in the context of international law, a variety of views on a timely, contentious, and relevant political experiment unraveling continuously.

Part I covers political issues. In the opening chapter I examine efforts by the organized Palestinian political authority to gain diplomatic support for a potentially independent Palestinian state. Next, Professor John Quigley takes up the issue of the nature of Palestinian statehood, its historical complexity as affected by international law and the efforts by both states and international organizations to effect change. Professor Weiler then takes to task those who argue that the establishment of an independent Palestinian state is sufficient to bring the Arab-Israeli conflict to an end. Conditions of mutual recognition and acceptance must be established in addition. Weiler proposes a phased model, envisioning a regional economic community.

In the next chapter I argue that the Palestinian Basic Law, as presently framed, is insufficient to guide a proposed state to pursue its international legal obligations. Joel Singer, a diplomat and an active participant in peace negotiations between Israel and the Palestinians, then gives the reader an insider's view of what is an unofficial but accurate perspective of the Israeli position on what it believes are the limits of the Palestinian Authority (PA) to move from autonomy to sovereignty. Professor Adrien Wing, a long time advocate of universal human rights, next provides a comparative analysis of the South African experience and its transition to a more popular democracy and simultaneous dismantling of apartheid. She suggests that the PA could learn from this development when, in an attempt to protect the civil liberties of its citizens, it develops a national constitution.

Professor George Bisharat calls for the PA to establish a fully independent judiciary and to respect fully the civil and human rights of Palestinians under its control. He urges the United States to alter its foreign policy towards the region in general and Palestine in particular, leaning on the PA if and when it shirks its responsibility to move toward a more democratic stance.

Professor John Strawson examines the contemporary setting in which the Palestinian Question was formed, the League of Nations–created "mandate" with Great Britain as the supervisory power. Professor Neri Sybesma-Knol looks at the legal question of *ius standi* and the Palestinian position at the international level before the United Nations. Finally, Professor Juan

Delgado closes Part I with a review of Spanish foreign policy towards the Middle East and, specifically, Spain's approach towards Israel and the Palestinians.

Part II deals with economic issues. Professor David Fidler, working with Fadi Harb, revises and updates his analysis of the Palestinian economy published in an earlier effort,[7] and now focuses on the potential for economic development in a proposed Palestinian state within the context of "globalization." Dr. Keith Molkner — who was one of the first economic analysts to take notice of Palestinian economic development — establishes the position that any furtherance of economic fortunes is tied to the political "peace process." In the final essay Mel Levine, another early contributor to an analysis of the Palestinian economy, calls for the liberalization of restrictions on that economy's expansion — including those imposed, intentionally or not, by the Israeli government. Furthermore, he sees as necessary the infusion of financial support from international institutions such as the World Bank.

Notes

1. The philosophical underpinnings are examined in an erudite manner in RICHARD TUCK, THE RIGHTS OF WAR AND PEACE (1999).

2. In general see LAW AND MORAL ACTION IN WORLD POLITICS (Cecelia Lynch and Michael Loriaux eds., 2000).

3. See for example FRANCIS ANTHONY BOYLE, WORLD POLITICS AND INTERNATIONAL LAW (1985) and ANTHONY C. AREND, LEGAL RULES AND INTERNATIONAL SOCIETY (1999).

4. This theme is dealt with in depth in GILLIAN YOUNG'S INTERNATIONAL RELATIONS IN A GLOBAL AGE: A CONCEPTUAL CHALLENGE (1999).

5. A subject taken up in RONEN SHAMIR, THE COLONIES OF LAW: COLONIALISM, ZIONISM AND LAW IN EARLY MANDATE PALESTINE (2000) and in what may be considered a subsequent phase by LAWS OF THE POSTCOLONIAL (Eve Darian-Smith and Peter Fitzpatrick eds., 1999).

6. Interested readers might look at HAIM BEN SHAHAR ET AL., ECONOMIC STRUCTURE AND DEVELOPMENT PROSPECTS OF THE WEST BANK AND GAZA STRIP (1971).

7. *Foreign Private Investment in Palestine Revisited: An Analysis of the Revised Palestinian Investment Law*, 31 CASE WEST. RES. J. INT'L. L. 293–309 (1999). *See also* D. Fidler, *Peace Through Trade? Developments in Palestinian Trade Law During the Peace Process*, 39 VA. J. INT'L L. 155–190 (1998).

Part I
Political Issues

1

Diplomatic Recognition of States in statu nascendi: *The Case of Palestine*

Sanford R. Silverburg

When I ask the Palestinians if they'll stamp my passport, they say "Burhureyya" ("with Independence"). Palestine is still not a state.[1]

I. Introduction

It was a concluding observation, made with some degree of prescience, that "we can only wait and observe the way the international political system, but more particularly the West, adapt to a rearrangement of national dominance with the U.N. and a shift in the emphasis of supporting norms and values."[2] The argument, as previously outlined, is now extended here to wit: the character of the contemporary international political system has lent itself to the expansion of recognized acceptable subjects of international law to what is, for lack of an accepted term, a latent and tentative territorial unit, an "entity." Because the state, as the traditional political actor at the international system level, is now complemented by other styles of authoritative organizations that conduct affairs that at least resemble interstate business, a recognition of what is in fact occurring, is a basis for decisions by states and international organizations and merits concern and attention.

In particular, the emergence of an *autonomous* Palestinian entity (*al-kiyan al-filastini*) without *sovereignty*,[3] resulting from the multilateral negotiations begun at the Madrid Conference (1991) continuing through the Hebron Agreement (1995), presents an opportunity to witness a unique development in international law.[4] There is adequate evidence in place to indicate that a process of institutionalized state-building[5] has been put into place at least since the most recent Palestine Declaration of Independence.[6] All these developments bear witness to, if for no other reason than the ambivalence exhibited by the international political community, the issue of an acceptable non-state actor role in the international community of states. Therefore, the recognized referent, as the observer must make, is that it is an imperfect system. It is sometimes, perhaps even frequently, disheartening to jurists to observe change occur particularly if it is directed by or from non-western sources. According to one court, "to interpret various human rights documents as imposing legal duties on nonstates like the PLO would require both entering a new and unsettled area of international law and finding there an exception to international law's general rule."[7] Certainly, following both World War I and World War II, other territories and colonies that came under mandatory jurisdiction evolved into states.[8] The political process as practiced in the post-World War II era, focusing on the phenomenon of decolonization and the concomitant increased demand for national self-determination, rests on a belief that as long as states exist and evolve *in forma*, new criteria for bringing them into existence may be introduced. But as has been apparent, all new proposals are based upon the existence of already existent sovereign entities or at least a formally established and separate territorial element recognized as distinctive. The issue of the legitimacy of any act of recognition of such political units may, of course, come subsequently.

As stated, Palestine, while appreciating the dangers of the assertion as a self-fulfilling prophecy, is a state *in statu nascendi*,[9] something in the process of becoming but which hitherto has not received either the attention or the formal international legal support generally reserved for traditional subjects of international law.[10] The legal maxim *nasciturus pro jam nato habetur*[11] applies in this instance and carries a set of recognized strictures. According to Brownlie, whose approach is close to political expediency, the position is that "[f]or certain legal purposes it is convenient to assume continuity in a political entity and thus to give effect, after statehood has been attained, to legal acts occurring before independence."[12] Even after statehood is assumed, "it is justifiable, both legally and practically, to assume the retroactive validation of the legal order during a period prior to general recognition as a state, when some degree of effective government existed."[13] There is from his approach an understanding that political events occur with a frequency that outpace any commanding legal authority. Realizing the need though to maintain a relationship of law to politics, a principle of continuity is given heavy weight or value.

Therefore, left aside is the intriguing but necessarily entangling idea of a two-state or a binational option in the region, let alone within an historic Palestine.[14] But if, as has been asserted by Palestinians as a historical fact, Palestine is an integral whole then any dismemberment, conceivably, violates the Declaration on the Granting of Independence to Colonial Countries and Peoples.[15] However, the argument put forth here is that there has never been a state of Palestine and, therefore, there is no territorial integrity to violate.

Actually, the process of Palestinian state development is a continuation after an interregnum of close to 50 years of a combination of interrelated historical dynamics. The League of Nations was succeeded, politically at least, by the United Nations which in its collective judgment recommended the partition of mandatory Palestine into an Arab state and a Jewish state.[16] The Arab state members of the United Nations, but not an organized Palestinian body, "responding to the will of the Palestine Arab majority, rejected the Partition Plan." [17] In the ensuing hostilities between the Palestinians, supported and abetted by their allied and neighboring Arab states, and the newly declared State of Israel, the latter never occupied *completely* mandatory Palestine. Presumably then, whatever portion of mandatory Palestine was not under control by Israel became available for reconstitution.[18] In fact, in September 1948, in an attempt to maintain a legitimate claim of governance, an Arab Government of All-Palestine, now defunct, was formed by the Arab League (without the compliance of Jordan) in Gaza. This political act was done on behalf of all Palestinians, ostensibly to govern the West Bank and Gaza Strip. However, little was to come from this development since the West Bank was annexed by Jordan in 1950 and Egypt "supervised" as a trustee an independent government in Gaza in 1959.[19]

While the forecasted outcome of a political development is certainly speculative,[20] the nature of diplomatic recognition, it is argued, concretizes the status of the targeted organization by virtue of the nature of interstate exchange. The formal action taken by states and international organizations afforded the Palestine National Authority (PNA) is such that the political body, while it is recognized as less than a sovereign state, is certainly more than a completely dependent colonial enterprise.

There are two areas of concentration in this current exposition: diplomatic recognition and economic trade relations. In both instances, the emblematic nature of the nation state in a state-centric system is to be seen as transitory. The expansion in the number of states combined with an increased awareness of the global extent of issues that affect humanity, sometimes with grave consequences, has spurred an intent in creating conditions that lessen tensions while simultaneously providing human benefits. Trade and investment have been essential characteristics of industrial regions and drive pacific state relations. In order for economic relations to develop and produce positive results, political stability must serve as a foundation. A world in which liberal economies foster stability in due course encourages acceptance of reasonably viable political units. In writing about new international relations theory or new states in a chain of developments, one commentator has noted "that the contemporary global system of sovereign states has emerged out of an earlier Eurocentric system of 'civilized' and before that 'Christian' states." The evolutionary process, the author goes on to claim, has retained its constancy "because the underlying imperatives of independence are still the same,"[21] but the context of the process has moved on to greater complexity.

II. Palestine as a Political Concept

The nation-state system or the Westphalian system developed in Europe as a western and predominantly Christian, political organization which was subsequently superimposed on the remaining extent of the globe through imperial and colonial exploits.[22] The limitation of a people's political expression was set by the sole tangible quality of geographic borders. The manner of acceptance in the "civilized" world was also to no small degree conditional upon adherence to European cultural norms of existence, at least up through the middle of the 20th century.[23] In the Islamic world, the concept of "the state" has existed but with a distinguishably different heritage and orientation from its Christian counterpart.[24] Hence, for Palestinians, for many generations at least, the sense of peoplehood was present providing substance but without, however, the form of a western state present.[25] This condition occurred not because of a lack of intent to do otherwise. Essentially, the regional culture was not susceptible to the acculturation process necessary to adjust in the time period as presented to the non–Western people resident there. Additionally, the western understanding of the modern state as it developed in the contemporary period requires an industrial base. With the superimposition of a modern capitalist system, many scholars of nationalism hold that there is a tendency that serves as a demolishing instrument of traditional societies; i.e., preindustrial or agriculturally based societies. Thus any organic nature of Palestinian political organization was rendered subservient to an industrially oriented competitor, in this case European-based and acculturated Zionists. The Arab — Palestinian and other —

opposition to political Zionism from its inception took on the character of a mantra for fear and threat perception of cultural and dispossessive foreign imposition.[26]

There are many plausible explanations diachronically for the varied declarations and understandings of cultural groups' self-awareness. The effect of modernity on either Arab nationalism or Palestinian nationalism, assuming *arguendo* there is a difference, has not reduced the anxiety of the subject peoples but has placed contemporary generations in a cognitive position whereby their frame of reference is current and thus the standard of evaluation is different from that which was dominant in the predecolonization period.

In the case of the Palestinians, when their perception is blended with similarly situated people who may have emerged with a recognized political structure because of a preexisting territorial setting, their factual support pales. Contextually some theorists hold that nationalism is not necessarily "modern." Rather it is subject to a series of historical developmental forces that allies itself to cultural coherence, which places the controversy over Palestinian nationalism in still more of a controversial focus.[27]

In the contemporary period, Palestine[28] was an amorphous geopolitical territory within the Ottoman Turkish Empire. As one Palestinian scholar and expert on Palestinian nationalism notes, "there was no political unit known as Palestine" in the Ottoman Empire.[29] Even in the premier examination of the development of Palestinian nationhood, one can find no formal setting beyond a "sense" of place, "a sort of sacred — if not yet a national — space."[30] Following World War I and as a result of that conflagration, the Ottoman Turkish Empire was despoiled by the victorious European alliance, and the Arab territories were divided into zones of occupation. The British military presence in Jerusalem and its environs, early in December 1917, placed its government in a preeminent position to claim belligerent occupant rights. The British succeeded. Although the initial military administration established was meant to be transitional,[31] the following year an Occupied Enemy Territory Administration-South (O.E.T.A.-South) was created. The principle of *postliminium* with regard to the dismantling of Turkish Near and Middle East territories in accordance with a peace treaty, had to be held in abeyance until the French were assuaged which was done at the Inter-Allied Conference at San Remo in April 1920.[32] Again, following the European tradition and experience, the nation-state organizational form was extended by the western creation, the League of Nations, and operating as a formal political-legal agent of the major western powers, demarcated Palestine and made Great Britain the mandatory power.[33] It should be noted with great importance that it is only at this point in time and because of the action taken by the League of Nations in conjunction with Great Britain that the factor of territoriality was attached to what Palestinians understood then and now to exist *in situ*, but in point of fact only existed in another cultural and hence legal context. Palestine was never considered *terra nullius* because there was no such legal body before its creation by externally regional diplomatic negotiations. The beginnings of what *could* evolve into a state, as understood in western political and legal parlance, originated as a mandate and was never an "old state" or an "original state" interrupted by historical forces to become a "new state."[34] The act of creating a mandate in the generally recognized region of ancient Palestine, in effect, lent a modicum of juridical personality to the territory, thereby legitimizing the governing authority and in turn setting into motion a historic process whereby the components of statehood *could* become established. International legal authorities, who for reasons of their own support the Palestinian cause and demand for political self-determination, support the notion that there was *a Palestine* in the past, that is prior to 1917. To complicate the history of "modern Palestine," and to indicate its pure anomalous nature requires an examination of how and why Trans-Jordan was diplomatically excised from mandatory Palestine in 1922 and anointed with statehood.[35]

However, the gravamen is clearly as stated above that a Palestine within the western political understanding of the term, simply never existed.[36] Indeed, the failure to establish a western-based territorial element in a rhetorical frame of reference had done much for years to cloud discussion over relevant issues but more importantly made the arguments for such a condition a *non sequitur*.[37] On a more positive note, from this temporal point forward the conflict of interests between Palestinians and Jewish Zionists operates with a great deal more symmetry, even if there are significant differences in strategies and approaches to their respective political goals and ideologies.

The argument put forth here then is that a people in the Arab world with a self-identity as Palestinian were a settled folk during the period of Ottoman Turkish control in some demarcated portion thereof. As outlined above, a Palestine was ultimately created, albeit not by Palestinians, and almost immediately subject to violent contention. Years of sporadic low-intensity conflict between Israel and Palestinians was followed by the creation of the Palestine Liberation Organization (PLO) in 1964. By 1968 the PLO was clearly an organization that was committed to debilitating the State of Israel. In 20 years, this strategy moved to a two-state solution, while the current peace process holds out the possibility of Palestinian autonomy. Characterizing this ideological development is an anecdote from a meeting of the PLO's Central Committee in Tunis, held on October 10, 1993, where Mahmoud Abbas (aka "Abu Mazen"), a Palestinian diplomat who helped frame the Oslo Accords, told Chairman Arafat that "it was now 'time to take off the uniforms of the revolution and put on the business suits of the nascent Palestinian state.'"[38]

Rightfully so, the nature and status of political autonomy in the annals of international law is unique, to be sure. On this point Benvenisti points out two forms: internal and international. Internal autonomy exists as a political unit within a sovereign state while international autonomy involves multinational administration. The autonomy established by the Cairo Agreement is for a territory, the extent of which is yet to be negotiated.[39] Even if the territorial element of a state is present there are other factors to consider as well which for our purpose here take primacy in the evaluation of the argument presented. While the Palestinians have no sovereign title to territory, there is an established governing authority that maintains an ability to insure relative internal order and as pointed out, conducts regular diplomatic relations with states and international organizations. These conditions can not be claimed by all other established states.[40]

III. SUBJECTS OF INTERNATIONAL LAW

The issue here is limited to those elements and issues that most directly affect the present theme. Therefore, a state, for purposes of a positivistic approach to public international law, is the primary subject for purposes of *locus standi*. Accordingly, the demanded status requires four well known and recognized elements: 1) "a permanent population"; 2) "a defined territory"; 3) a "government"; and 4) the "capacity to enter into relations with the other states" of the international political system.[41] In the opinion of one jurist, territoriality is the primary characteristic of the state and an absolute necessary characteristic for its existence.[42] Although it could be argued, as has been in some quarters, that a "political community" may be more important.[43] The notion of a geographically fixed presence for the governing authority lends itself to predictable outcomes. However, the state is an artificial creation for some functional purposes in place and time. As the required function of organization realigns with conditions of a changing world, so has the legal system adapted commensurately.[44] The expansion of general categories of subjects of international law was to occur in 1949 when the International Court of Justice recognized the United Nations as an international person for purposes of juridical status.[45] Briggs suggests that "absence of one or more of these criteria over relatively long periods has not been regarded by other States as depriving such States of legal capacity under international law."[46] However, he conflates two completely different categories of states in support of his argument. For example, Albania, which could be said was a configured territory prior to admittance to the League of Nations, and Israel, which emerged from a completely different political arrangement, serve to reduce the acceptability of Briggs' assertion. Therefore, his position does not serve us well in establishing any formal rule to follow.

Controversial but nevertheless applicable to the argument presented here generally and specifically is the realistic acceptance of insurgent groups and national liberation movements under the umbrella of the laws of war and humanitarian intervention.[47] Since the early 1970s, many such organizations received favorable, and even preferential, treatment by the United Nations General Assembly, which by this time had greatly expanded to include many former colonies.[48] The affinity of the greater number of like situated states with similarly historical backgrounds coalesced particularly on political issues such as self-determination. Current international *opinio juris* does not, unfortunately, provide sufficient clarification regarding any movement away from traditional approaches of how any people is expected to gain an organic structure of authority. For example, in a recent German case, the court rendered a decision reserving an opinion held by the European Court of Human Rights[49] obliging Austria not to deport a defendant to Somalia where it was suspected he would be subject to violation of Article 3 of the European Convention on Human Rights because of the lack of state control over nonstate agents.[50]

Clearly beginning in 1974, the United Nations saw the eventual creation of a Palestinian state as a necessary condition to fulfill the growing acceptance of the norm of national self-determination.[51] Since the General Assembly operates with plenary voting, the body gave numerous "liberation movements" from developing areas "observer status" to its subgroups. In the case of the PLO, that status was even elevated to the General Assembly itself.[52] The alacrity of the decolonization process along with the actual numbers of newly emergent states and concomitant concern for humanitarian issues, and given the voting weight from raw membership, all together increased the overall concern for the respective populations. The practical realities of international politics and relations may demand from time to time that strict adherence to acceptance of the state as the sole beneficiary of international juridical personality be set aside in favor of de factoism. In the words of one preeminent international legal scholar, Oliver Lissitzyn:

> We must ... be on guard against attaching too much significance to the characterization of a particular entity such as a "State." Indeed, depending on one's preference, certain entities which are not regarded as independent but which seem to participate in treaty relations can be described either as "dependent States" or as entities which though not "States," possess a degree of international personality.[53]

In international political economics, particularly in the post–World War II era, the transition from GATT (General Agreement on Tariffs and Trade) to the WTO (World Trade Organization) has, while not necessarily subverting state sovereignty, offered a transnational alternative and thus has added weight to the importance of transborder economic relations and agreements.[54] The argument put forth frequently is that transnational organizations permit a freer exchange of capital, greater flexibility in organizational style, and fewer limitations on individual behavior. The interesting development in political relationships on a global level is perhaps the manner of dispute resolution which is, in the context of the WTO, handled through an organizational body though its decisions ultimately affect members' operability on an international scale.[55] The WTO now provides for trade dispute resolution by an international organization rather than permitting unilateral state action. The relevance of this discussion is to bring attention to the growing acceptance of economics and related organizational structures that impact on what has for so many years been an exclusively political sphere of activity. The globalization of economics does not have full consensus, however. It is recognized by some to be a reversible trend and a choice made by national political leaders.[56] But also the argument presented here assumes, inter alia, that the growing globalization of trade economics and liberal belief that trade leads to stability and order undergirds much of the desire of states to support the institutional framework of the PNA.

IV. Diplomatic Recognition

Traditionally in international law, acceptable subjects determine the parameters for choices available to states' governments to accept similarly situated others into their midst which has effectively been de facto or de jure recognition of either governments or states. As indicated above, the international political system is a model of structural change and many argue for international law to follow the changes accordingly. One major school of modern thought on recognition in international law is the declaratory doctrine which emphasizes the political nature of the exercise and while not derogating legal responsibility, nevertheless presents a formal obligation for it.[57] That states and international organizations have chosen to enter into negotiations and formulate political and economic agreements with the PNA is an indicator of an appreciation of a putative state ability to engage in interstate relations and thus conduct itself in a regularized manner in the international political community. Professor Brownlie is instructive here when he opines that "[t]he legal consequence accorded by governments and foreign courts to the acts of governments recognized *de facto* provide evidence for the views" of the process of an entity assuming statehood.[58] The PNA as a recognized governing authority is expected to maintain *effective control* over territory allocated it pursuant to diplomatic negotiations. How effective its control is, internally, has not had a deleterious effect on recognition of its institutional basis.[59] The general precursor to the PNA and the public body whose heritage present day recognition is attributable to is the PLO. The process and pattern of recognition of the PLO lays the ground for similar and succeeding action for the PNA. While recognition of the PLO, either as a representative of the Palestinian people per se[60] or as a diplomatic representative of the Palestinian cause,[61] the manner of acceptance is probably less salient than the act itself. Indeed, statehood may not require recognition from others in the world community.[62] The United States has accepted "state" action by entities that have not enjoyed the luxury of diplomatic recognition.[63]

All of this is to note that given the nature of the PNA's status and the sensitivity of the Arab-Israeli conflict, state interaction is not frequently subject to public notice.[64] Nevertheless, the subtleties of diplomacy can be seen operating in the matter of interaction with the PNA. Hence, without full and complete recognition, there can not truly be embassies or consulates with the appropriate ambassadors and consular officials. Some states, therefore, maintain legations in Gaza from which business is conducted as a circumlocution of an otherwise absent official diplomatic premise. Representatives of those states that maintain a presence in Gaza, it has been observed, tend to have preferential status with regard to gaining access to PNA officialdom.

There is a frequent claim that the political world has already given recognition to the Palestinians, first to the PLO and then to its successor, the PNA. There has been little investigation, however, into the nature or substance of this assertion. Professor de Waart, for example, boldly holds that "Palestine has been recognized as a state by a great majority of members of the United Nations. Western states, however, are still conspicuous by their absence under the pretext of legal or political arguments."[65] He goes on to proffer that the 1993 Declaration of Principles (DOP) and 1994 Israeli-PLO Agreement gave "international lawyers much food for thought with respect to the legal status of Palestine under international law," all the while recognizing that the PLO "*is neither a state nor an international organization.*"[66] Additionally, on November 15, 1988, the Palestine National Council (PNC) declared at its 19th Extraordinary Session in Algiers, the establishment "of the State of Palestine in the Land of Palestine with its capital at Jerusalem."[67] The Declaration while a grandiloquent rhetorical statement, was made without effective control over a territory. The PNC's action, in any case, was followed in December in the United Nations General Assembly with formal statements of recognition reportedly by at least 100 states.[68]

The contention advanced here is that the structure of the international political system is not fixed and is subject to change. The emergence of transnational political actors and relations is matched by new forms of political organization which are recognized by existing states to be effective bargaining units in diplomatic relations. Some would argue that international personality and its expansion remains a fixture of statehood for determination.[69] Moreover, recognition may not necessarily proceed from states issuing a formal statement but it may be implied by formal acts of state such as engaging in diplomatic interaction and concluding an agreement even below the level of a treaty.[70] Now, admittedly, to permit nonstates the degree of recognition that has been accorded states would only permit greater confusion. Proceeding with the focus at this point thus leads to economic ties which states and international organizations have sought either to enter into or to maintain with the PNA as a major indicator of the potential viability of a sovereign Palestinian body but also a willingness of states to recognize such. Great Britain, for example, conducts its diplomacy with regard to recognition of governments without being tied to some standardized or formal set of guidelines, although its policy towards states remains substantially unaltered.[71]

A. Political

Pursuant to the Gaza-Jericho Agreement in May 1994 and the subsequent Further Transfer Protocol of September 1995,[72] a Palestinian National Authority, was created as a transitional body by the PLO according to the first agreement, while the authority set out was then extended to portions of Gaza and the West Bank by the second.[73] But the nonstate status of the PNA precludes its ability to extend its legitimacy in ways that are reserved for states. In addition, as signatory to the Gaza-Jericho Agreement,[74] the PNA is constrained from engaging in a number of actions in foreign relations, the attention to which has been brought to light by Israeli concerns. A litany of charges raised by Israel illustrates the contentiousness of the PNA's ability to enjoy an international political status of some note. The Agreement makes clear that following the DOP,[75] the PNA, as distinct from the PLO, "will not have powers and responsibilities in the sphere of foreign relations."[76] With regard to the conduct of foreign affairs, Article IX(5)(a) indicates that the PNA is that of "an autonomous and not an independent entity." Having said that, there is an implicit understanding that following the precedent set out in the Gaza-Jericho Agreement, if the PNA was to operate with even a modicum of effectiveness, it would have to have "a mechanism ... to enable some dealings with regard to specific matters between the Palestinian side and foreign states or international organizations."[77] Therefore, the PLO *not* the Palestinian National Council was to conduct negotiations and sign agreements with states or international organizations.[78] It was noted by Israeli officials that the Palestinian representative in Egypt is designated as a PNA official, a violation of Article VI(2)(a). It was also noted that the PLO representative in Moscow signed a protocol on security cooperation with Russia in the name of the PNA, and that the PNA joined the International Airport Council as the PNA, both in violation of Article VI(2)(b). Noted in addition was that Morocco has a "liaison" office in Gaza, a violation of Article VI(2)(c).[79]

The distinction between the PLO and the PNA is an important one as set out in the Agreement. The PLO became in the mid–1960s the public representative of the Palestinians and received the accolades forthcoming for any movement whose objective was satisfaction of the demand for self-determination. But with any public body that enjoys juridical credibility, there is the concomitant obligation to assume responsibility for its collective behavior. In the case of the PLO, there is the haunting historical corpus of terrorism, acts for which the body might be held accountable after statehood if it becomes the constitutional government. The PNA, however, has been designated as the authorized governing body, regardless of how transparent the transition appears. To supplement Israeli authority, specifically to ban the PNA and the PLO from conducting foreign relations,[80] Israel legislated a formal exclusion of Palestinian sources in Jerusalem from conducting foreign affairs.

B. Economic

The interest here is to provide a cursory examination of a spectrum of states and international organizations that maintain commercial contact with the PNA, through the PLO, or otherwise, as an indicator of a phenomenon. More concentrated efforts on this subject have already been made[81] and hence the topic will not be examined any more thoroughly here.

It is instructive to follow such developments in the area of economic relations and statements that emanate from such meetings as took place on February 18, 1998, at the head offices of the Palestinian Ministry of International Cooperation in the al–Ram section of northern Jerusalem. At this meeting were representatives from the European Union, Israel, Norway, the PNA, the United States, and the World Bank. The group met to work out difficulties between Israel and the PNA that were standing in the way of further economic development in those areas on the West Bank and Gaza controlled by the PNA. Perhaps more important was the announcement of a planned signing of two protocols by France and the PNA worth $20 million. It was pointed out by the Palestinian representative that the "protocols fall within the framework of French action to bolster the establishment of the Palestinian state.... France does not sign such agreements except with fully independent countries; Palestine is the only country [sic] that is not totally independent with whom France has signed this kind of agreement."[82]

1. Australia. Australia, which recognizes the Palestinians' right to self-determination and has publicly noted its expectation of the emergence of a Palestinian state has also provided funds for the development of "the rural sector in the Occupied Palestinian Territories."[83]

2. Canada. Canada has been active in establishing free trade agreements with the United States and Israel[84] and has begun to enter into a trade relationship with the PNA[85]. In February 1997, the Canadian Minister of International Trade set into motion a commercial and investment effort[86].

3. China. The Chinese government has discussed the possibility of extending a $12 million loan for the construction of a Chinese medical facility on both the West Bank and in Gaza[87].

4. European Union (EU). The EU relationship with the Palestinians[88], it can be said, began in 1971 when it contributed to the operation of the United Nations Relief and Works Agency for Palestine refugees (UNRWA). In 1980, the EU released the Venice Declaration[89] expressing support for the general principle of Palestinian self-determination. The EU has been the single largest financial contributor to the PNA for development projects with contributions of just under 1.7 billion ECU (3.4 DM billion) between 1993 and 1997, and for the establishment of democratic institutions[90]. The EU clearly sees a role to play in the economic development of those areas under the jurisdiction of the PNA[91]. The EU, in its attempt to foster regional stability, is actively supporting the peace process[92]. There is also a realistic understanding that in order for the EU to play the constructive role so eagerly sought, it would have to take Israeli concerns into consideration. In this case, an antiterrorist stance would be taken. To this end, the EU maintains a "special advisor" to the PNA[93]. Somewhat related is the EU's financial support for the Ex-Detainees Rehabilitation Program, an effort to reintegrate Palestinians who have spent at least a year in an Israeli prison[94].

5. Finland. In January 1996, Finland announced it would provide the PNA, over some undetermined period of time, economic assistance totaling 10 million Finnish Marks ($10 million US)[95].

6. Germany. Germany was the first state following the signing of the DOP to open a Representative Office in Jericho with the PNA. Its interest in the peace process was also a motivation in providing substantial financial assistance to various sectors of the Palestinian economy[96].

7. Great Britain. British assistance represents self-proclaimed contributions to multilateral programs, underwriting the EU's efforts and subsidizing UNRWA's assistance to Palestinian refugees. Beginning in 1994, British bilateral aid was preferred and increased during the following year[97].

8. Japan. In October 1997 Japan agreed with the PNA to provide the latter with $17.5 million for education in the Gaza Strip. The importance of the grant is that it added to the total of $312 million since 1994 and at a time when the Japanese foreign aid budget planned cuts up to 10 percent[98].

9. Jordan. Jordan has gone so far as to establish formal trade relations with the PNA in an attempt to keep its historic commitment to the Palestinians[99].

10. The Netherlands. The Netherlands' interest in Palestinian politics and economic development is in support of the peace process. There is a strong financial contribution for the construction of an airfield and a seaport in the Gaza Strip, amounting to about 40 million guilders in 1997[100].

11. South Africa. The relationship of the South African Government today to the PNA is to some degree a result of the regime's pedigree. Since the ruling administration is an outgrowth of the efforts of the African National Congress (ANC), a fellow national liberation movement to the PLO[101], there is an affinity towards the Palestinians and their political efforts which appear to mirror those of the ANC.

12. Spain. During 1996, Spain provided $119,048 (US) in humanitarian assistance to the PNA Ministry of Health. The money was made available for local purchase by Palestinians in need of pharmaceuticals[102].

13. Sweden. For an 18-month period during 1995–96, the Swedish International Development Cooperation Agency (SIDA) allocated 216,600

MSEK, and 120,000 MSEK for 1997, for such varied activities as childrens' health, health rehabilitation, and police training.[103] SIDA along with the Institute for Further Education of Journalists in Sweden (FOJO) also supports financially the Birzeit University Journalist Training Project.[104]

14. United States. The United States has appreciated throughout the peace process the importance of the West Bank to any Palestinian aspiration for political self-control. During the administration of George Bush the Elder, a presidential determination was made to allocate funds for economic development of the area, presumably to aid the bulk of the residents in the area who were Palestinian.[105] In an attempt to insure compliance with the Oslo agreement, particularly the demand that the PNA crack down on terrorist activity, amend its National Covenant, and negotiate in good faith, the Congress passed legislation providing the Palestinians with $100 million of annual aid.[106] In September 1994, the United States signed a treaty with the PLO for the encouragement of investments which it was believed would strengthen the Palestinian economy permitting greater autonomy to commit to a peaceful resolution of conflict.[107] Since the United States was signatory to a free trade agreement with Israel, goods imported from Palestinian autonomous areas were at a commercial price disadvantage with Israeli-produced goods. To offset this advantage, presumably as an overall diplomatic package, the United States, in April 1995, applied its General System of Preferences (GSP) to cover Palestinian goods.[108] To supplement this action and firm up relations with the Palestinians, President Clinton signed H.R. 3074 into law on October 2, 1996,[109] but it was not promulgated until November.[110]

15. World Bank. On October 18–19, 1995, in Paris, representatives of the PNA, Israel, and the World Bank, along with 29 donor states and international organizations, convened for the express purpose of developing an assistance program for the Palestinian territories.[111] The meeting was a follow-up to the Taba Agreement, reached a few weeks previously following progress in the peace process.[112]

The World Bank's Consultative Group decided at a meeting in mid–December 1997 in Paris to pledge $900 million in grants and loan guarantees for the first of a three-year development plan for the Palestinian territories.[113]

V. Conclusion

The evolutionary nature of international politics has included the emergence of Palestine as a nonstate actor which because of its importance in a major geographical region has given credence to the de facto acceptance of a structural change in the international political system that is in the process of being defined. In sequence, the political development of Palestine, while not complete enough to satisfy the standard requirement for statehood in international law, has been recognized in more than a courtesy manner by virtue of financial investment, economic venture capital grants, and subtle diplomatic interaction by donor states and international organizations. Recognition of states, in the expressed opinion of Hans Kelsen, can be and often is a political — as distinguished from a legal — act but in this instance "presupposes the legal existence of a state or government to be recognized,"[114] while simultaneously having no legal effect, nor does the act in and of itself create an obligation on the part of either the recognizing state or government or the recipient of its political largess. On a higher plane, the observed practice of some states acting as if in formal compliance with international norms adds a new dimension to our understanding of the Westphalian system, assuming it still exists. It may be a more cogent assertion to claim that there has been a fundamental reconfiguration of the system with respect to a model of rule.

It might be said that the more staid understanding of the rules and norms of public international law was at one time and until recently a fixture of western-dominated state practice. The contemporary era has become global not only in presence but in function also, first politically and eventually economically as private commercial enterprise operates in the form of multinational corporations and transnational actors in the international economic system.

The important issue here with regard to Palestine is that unlike the mandatory period in which internecine family conflict and a general lack of social and political cohesion set forth the conditions in which the Palestinians confronted a western, socially based competitor for territory, the Zionists, the political cohesion now exhibited is visibly accepted by a broad section of the Palestinian community. Having failed to achieve their political objectives in the past, the Palestinians have organized, but now along western political lines, first as the PLO and now in the form of the PNA, with support from major western states all who ostensibly seek to stabilize the Middle East and reap some economic benefit therefrom. In order to accomplish this, it would be necessary to satisfy the Palestinians' demand for political self-determination while simultaneously providing the necessary satisfaction for their nemesis, Israel, of its primary objective, its national security.

The current peace process has done much to move an unorganized and unaffiliated people to real political status, to autonomy, and in time what appears to be a sovereign entity. Both the current status of the PNA and the process that brought the conditions of its operation into evidence have lent to this organization some sort of legal personality. If international personality can be denied by virtue of nonrecognition, does the obverse portend furtherance of an anomaly? I suggest that the Palestinian situation is a case in the making for the study of the relationship of political dynamics to the inertia of international legal development.

Notes

1. Daniel Jacobs, *Researching Gaza: An Author's Diary*, No. 2 ROUGHNEWS 7 (1997).

2. Sanford Silverburg, *The Palestine Liberation Organization in the United Nations*, 12 ISRAEL L. REV. 365, 392 (1977).

3. The selection of the descriptor "entity" is borrowed from the research of MOSHE SHEMESH, *THE PALESTINIAN ENTITY 1959–1974* (1996). See also Samir Anabtawi, *The Palestinians as a Political Entity*, 60 THE MUSLIM WORLD 47 (1970), and Julius Stone, *Peace and the Palestinians*, 3 N.Y.U.J. INT'L L. & POL. 247 (1970).

4. For a discussion of the Madrid Peace Conference see 2 DISPATCH 775 (1991), *id.*, at 806–810; 2 PUB. PAPERS PRES. US: GEORGE BUSH 1308 (1992), *id.*, at 1352, 1362–1364; Jorge Dezcallar de Mazarredo. *Conferencia de Madrid para la Paz en Oriente Media in* LA PAZ EN ORIENTE MEDIO: SEMINARIO CELEBRADO EN LA ESCUELA DIPLOMÁTICA LOS DÍAS 20 A 23 DE FEBRERO DE 1995, at 27–48 (1996). For a general collection of documents relating to the "peace process," see <http://www.israel-mfa.gov.il/peace/palest.html>. It is worth noting that all the "agreements" reached between Israel and the Palestinians, while commendable as an approach to develop regional stability, fall short of "international agreements," which must be "concluded between states." Vienna Convention on the Law of Treaties, May 23, 1969, 1155 U.N.T.S. 331, reprinted in 8 I.L.M. 679 (1969). For an argument contra see John Quigley, *The Israel-PLO Interim Agreements: Are They Treaties?* 30 CORNELL INT'L L.J 717 (1997).

Oslo I consists of the following: The Declaration of Principles on Interim Self-Government Arrangements (DOP), Sept. 13, 1993, Isr.-P.L.O., 32 I.L.M. 1525 (1993)(Declaration of Principles); Israel-Palestine Liberation Organization Agreement on the Gaza Strip and the Jericho Area, May 4, 1994, Isr.-P.L.O., 33 I.L.M. 622 (1994) (Cairo Agreement); Protocol on Economic Relations Between Israel and the P.L.O., 33 I.L.M. 696 (1994) (which was later included as an appendix to the Cairo Agreement). Together the DOP and Cairo Agreements constitute Phase 1 of an interim agreement. The Camp David Agreements were to establish a Palestinian "self-governing authority" which would lead to a final solution to the Arab-Israeli conflict, including peaceful resolution of outstanding issues and to be sure, territory. Camp David Agreements, Sept., 17, 1978, Egypt-Isr.-U.S., 17 I.L.M. 1466. Following actions were: Agreement on Preparatory Transfer of Powers and Responsibilities, Aug. 29, 1994, Isr.-P.L.O., 34 I.L.M. 455 (1994) (Erez Agreement); The Protocol on Further Transfer of Powers and Responsibilities, Sept. 28, 1995, UN Doc. A/51/889 (1995)(Further Transfer Protocol).

Arab League: Final Communiqué of the *Cairo Summit Conference on Mideast Peace* and Decisions on *New Institutions*, 35 I.L.M. 1280 (1996).

Oslo II: The Israeli-Palestinian Interim Agreement on the West Bank and Gaza Strip, Sept. 28, 1995, Isr.-P.L.O., 36 I.L.M. 551 (1997).

Taba Agreement: Israel and the Palestine Liberation Organization, Joint Communiqué on the Permanent Status Negotiations, Taba, Egypt, May 5–6, 1996, Isr.-P.L.O., <http://www.israel-mfa.gov.il/peace/taba596/html>.

Hebron Agreement: Israel-Palestine Liberation Organization: Agreement on the *Temporary International Presence in the City of Hebron (TIPH)* and the Memorandum of Understanding Between Denmark, Italy, Norway, Sweden, Switzerland and Turkey on the *Establishment of TIPH*, 36 I.L.M. 547 (1997).

Israel-Palestine Liberation Organization: Protocol Concerning the *Redeployment in Hebron* and Note for the Record, 36 I.L.M. 650 (1997). For the text of a Letter of Assurance to Israel by the American Secretary of State, Warren Christopher, January 15, 1997, see *New York Times*, Jan. 17, 1997, at A31 and 3 ISRAEL AFF. 343–344 (1997). For Secretary Christopher's letter and the Israeli Cabinet's "Communique" of January 16, 1997 see 26 PAL. STUD. 139–140 (1997). For a version of Israeli and Palestinian interpretation of the various agreements *see* SAMUEL SEGEV. CROSSING THE JORDAN: RABIN'S ROAD TO PEACE at chap. 12 (1998).

5. MOHAMMED AL-AZAR, DEMOCRATIC TRANSFORMATION AND THE POLITICAL SYSTEM IN PALESTINE. (1996); HILLEL FRISCH. COUNTDOWN TO STATEHOOD: PALESTINIAN STATE FORMATION IN THE WEST BANK AND GAZA (1998); GLENN ROBINSON. BUILDING A PALESTINIAN STATE (1997); THE PALESTINE COUNCIL: STRUCTURE, POWER AND RESPONSIBILITIES (1996); Francis Boyle. "The Creation of the State of Palestine," 1 EUR. J. INT'L L. 301 (1990) and his *Create the State of Palestine!* 7 SCAND. J. DEV. ALTERNATIVES 25 (1988); James Crawford. "The Creation of the State of Palestine," *id.*, at 307; Mark Heller. *Towards a Palestinian State*, 39 SURVIVAL 5 (1997); Ann Lesch. *Transition to Palestinian Self-Government*, 22 J. PAL. STUD. 46 (1993); and Kathryn McKinney. *The Legal Effects of the Israeli-PLO Declaration of Principles: Steps Toward Statehood for Palestine*, 18 SEATTLE U.L.REV. 93 (1994); David Newman and Ghazi Falah. *Small State Behavior: On the Formation of a Palestinian State in the West Bank and Gaza Strip*, 39 CAN. GEOG. 219 (1995). Menachem Mautner has suggested that a Palestinian political organization with a status more than autonomous but less than sovereign was the best solution to the Arab-Israeli conflict. See *West Bank and Gaza: The Case for Associate Statehood*, 6 YALE STUD. WORLD PUB. ORD. 297 (1981).

6. Palestine National Council, Declaration of Independence, 43 GAOR, Annex 3, Agenda Item 37, 13, UN Docs. A/48/827 and S/20278 (1988) *reprinted in* 27 I.L.M. 1688 (1988). *See generally* Maurice Flory. *Naissance d'un état palestinien*, 93 G. GÉN INT'L PUB. 389 (1989). The first Declaration of [Palestinian] Independence was issued on October 1, 1948. The text is *reprinted in* 4 PAL. Y.B. INT'L L. 294 (1987/88).

Mr. Khalil Tufakji was commissioned by the Palestine National Authority (PNA) to produce an "official map" of Palestine showing the "Palestinian State," comprising the entirety of the West Bank, the Gaza Strip, Israel, and some of Jordan. *See* <http://www.palestine-net.com/geography/gifs/palmap.gif>. Mr. Tufakji, it might be interested to learn, has been similarly commissioned by the PNA to design and locate a capitol building, to be located on the Mount of Olives (or as it is known in Arabic, Ras al-Amud, which also includes the neighborhood of Mitzpe Daniel) in Jerusalem.

7. Tel-Oren v. Libyan Arab Republic, 726 F.2d 774, 806 (1984).

8. *See* Appendix 2, JAMES CRAWFORD. THE CREATION OF STATES IN INTERNATIONAL LAW 426–428 (1979).

9. For a general treatment of this concept see id., at 391–398; IAN BROWNLIE. PRIN. OF PUB. INT'L L. 82 (1973); Friedrich von der Heydte, *Rechtssubject und Rechtperson im Völkerrecht*, *in* GRUNDPROBLEME DES INTERNATIONALEN RECHTS 237 (D. Constantopoulous et al. eds., 1957) and M. Vorster, *The International Legal*

Personality of Nasciturus States, 4 S. AFR. Y.B. INT'L L. 1 (1978). See also ANTONIO CASSESE. SELF-DETERMINATION OF PEOPLES 346–348 (1995). For an older version of the phenomenon see R. Erich. *La Naissance et la reconnaissance de états*, RECUEIL DES COURSE, 1926, III, at 431.

10. The interest here is specific, particular and completely within an international legal context. For the concept *see* MUSA MAZZAWI. PALESTINE AND THE LAW: GUIDELINES FOR THE RESOLUTION OF THE ARAB-ISRAELI CONFLICT 291–295 (1997). A more political tone can be inferred from other commentaries. See for example Katherine Meighan. *Note. The Israel-PLO Declaration of Principles*, 34 VA. J. INT'L L. 435 (1994) and especially at 467 and *contra* Justus Weiner. *Hard Facts Meet Soft Law — The Israel-PLO Declaration of Principles and the Prospect for Peace*, 35 VA. J. INT'L L. 931 (1995).

11. Literally, "Those who are about to be born shall be considered already born." DAVID WALKER, THE OXFORD COMPANION TO LAW 133 (1980). The notion emanates from Roman law. See for example, G. INST. 1.147; DIG. 1.5.7. (Paulis); DIG. 1.5.26 (Salvus Julianus); DIG. 38.16.7 (Juventius Celsus); DIG. 50.16.231 (Paulianus). An analogy to the juristic personality of an individual, according to the French Civil Code, is where an infant not yet born is subject to the rights of inheritance *when viable*. C.CIV. §§725, 906.

12. BROWNLIE *supra note* 9, at 66.

13. Id., at 82.

14. Some proponents of Palestinian statehood have argued that pursuant to United Nations resolutions, "there is continuing authority for the establishment of two states in Palestine." W. THOMAS MALLISON AND SALLY MALLISON. THE PALESTINE PROBLEM IN INTERNATIONAL LAW AND WORLD ORDER 206 (1986). Chairman Arafat proposed a "two-state solution" initiative in the U.N. General Assembly in Geneva on December 13, 1988. UN Doc. A/453/PV.78 (1988).

15. G.A. Res. 1514, 15 U.N. GAOR, Supp. 16, at 66, UN Doc. A/4684 (1961).

16. G.A. Res. 181 (II), 2 U.N. GAOR, Resolution 131, 132, U.N. Doc. A/519 (1947).

17. Nabil Elarby, *Some Legal Implications of the 1947 Partition Resolution and the 1949 Armistice Agreements*, 33 LAW & CONTEMP. PROBS. 97, 103 (1968). It should also be noted that the Arab Higher Committee, the only recognized "national" Palestinian political body, rejected the Resolution on November 30, 1947. See ISSA KHALAF. POLITICS IN PALESTINE 169 (1991).

18. Professor van de Craen argues that "the juridical status of the remaining Palestinian territory can only be made by the use of the concept of 'sovereign vacuum,'" permitting the Palestinians to enter a claim at some subsequent point in time. Frank L.M. van de Craen. *The Territorial Title of the State of Israel to "Palestine": An Appraisal in International Law*, 14 REVUE BELGE DE DROIT INTERNATIONAL 500, 505 (1978/79). Presumably in the case under review here, because of a consideration that the Israeli presence in those areas of mandated Palestine not allocated by the United Nations Partition Plan could be labeled as belligerent occupation, any territorial sovereignty that could similarly be sought by some Palestinian political authority yet to be established must be rejected. Indeed, the disposition of the territory under review after 1949 was determined by armistice agreements and not any treaty of peace.

19. For a discussion of the perfunctory efforts to maintain an illusion of Palestinian governing authority during the years immediately after the establishment of Israel see HUSSEIN HASSOUNA, THE LEAGUE OF ARAB STATES AND REGIONAL DISPUTES, at Ch. 11, Sec. 2 (1975).

20. From polling data we can derive that among Israelis there is a growing belief that a conterminous Palestinian state is evolving.

Date	Percentage
1990	37%
1991	48%
1994	74%

ASHER ARIAN, ISRAEL SECURITY AND THE PEACE PROCESS: PUBLIC OPINION IN 1994, at 6 (1994).

21. ROBERT JACKSON, QUASI-STATES: SOVEREIGNTY, INTERNATIONAL RELATIONS, AND THE THIRD WORLD 79 (1993).

22. From a positivist perspective, the initiation of the state system emerged from Christian civilization, at least in the period prior to Westphalia. See the canon law interpretation given by Hostiensis. G. Le Bras. *Théologie et droit romain dans Henri de Suse*, in ÉTUDES HISTORIQUE À LA MÉMOIRE DE NOEL DIDIER 195 (1960). It was not until 1856 and the organization of the Concert of Europe, that a non–Christian state, in this case Ottoman Turkey, was admitted into a European qua Christian political system. TRAVERS TWISS. LE DROIT DES GENS 83 (1887).

23. J.A. Andrews. *The Concept of Statehood and the Acquisition of Territory in the Nineteenth Century*, 94 L.Q. REV. 408 (1978).

24. See generally CHRISTINE HELMS. ARABISM AND ISLAM: STATELESS NATIONS AND NATIONLESS STATES (1990) [McNair Papers No. 10]. For a general understanding of the development of the Islamic political community see MOHAMMAD AL GHUNAIMI. THE MUSLIM CONCEPTION OF INTERNATIONAL LAW AND THE WESTERN APPROACH 61–70 (1968). For a thoroughly exacting examination of the idea of the Islamic state, from the perspective of a non–Muslim historian, see R. Serjeant. *The Constitution of Medina*, 8 ISLAMIC Q. 3 (1964) and *The 'Sunnah Jam'ah' Pacts with the Yathrib Jews, and the 'Tahrim' of Yathrib*, 41 BULL. SCH. ORIENTAL & AFR. STUD. 1 (1978).

25. For an examination of the formation of the Palestinian national self see Sari Nusseibeh. *Personal and National Identity: A Tale of Two Wills* in PHILOSOPHICAL PERSPECTIVES ON THE ISRAELI-PALESTINIAN CONFLICT 205–220 (Tomie Kapitan ed., 1997).

26. For a survey see Sami Zubaidi. "Theories of Nationalism" in POWER AND THE STATE 52–71 (Gary Littlejohn *et al.* eds., 1978). See also Wolfgang Mommsen. *The Varieties of the Nation State in Modern History* in THE RISE AND DECLINE OF THE NATION STATE 210–226 (1990).

27. See *for example* Anthony Smith. *The Myth of the 'Modern Nation' and the Myths of Nations*, 11 ETHNIC & RACIAL STUD. 1 (1988). As the theme is connoted within an Islamic context, see SAMI ZUBAIDA. ISLAM, THE PEOPLE AND THE STATE chap 6 (1989). For a specific characterization of the Palestinian economy from 1917 to 1945 see Bernard Wasserstein. *The British Mandate in Palestine* in MIDDLE EASTERN LECTURES NUMBER ONE, at 29, 37 (1995).

28. For a general treatment of the nature of the territory in historic texts see SUSAN ROLEF. THE POLITICAL GEOGRAPHY OF PALESTINE: A HISTORY AND DEFINITION (1983)[Middle East Review Special Studies, no. 3]; Louis Feldman. *Some Observations on the Name of Palestine*, 61 HEBREW UNION COLL. ANN. 1 (1990); Haim Gerber. *"Palestine" and Other Territorial Concepts in the 17th Century*, 30 INT'L J. MIDDLE EAST STUD. 563 (1998); Bernard Lewis. *Palestine: On the History and Geography of a Name*, 11 THE INT'L HIST. REV. 1 (1980). The history of ancient Palestine is covered in such basic works as GOSTA AHLSTRÈOM. THE HIST. OF ANCIENT PALESTINE (1993); DAVID FIENSY. THE SOCIAL HIST. OF PALESTINE IN THE HERODIAN PERIOD (1991); MOSHE GIL. A HIST. OF PALESTINE, 634–1099 (1992);

A. AL-KAYYALI. PALESTINE [1978]; ISMAIL SHAMMOUT. PALESTINE (1972); and ROBERT WILKEN. THE LAND CALLED HOLY (1992). On the relationship of ancient Israel to ancient Palestine *see* Marit Skjeggestad. *Ethnic Groups in Early Iron Age Palestine*, 6 SCAN. J. OLD TEST. 159 (1992) and Thomas Tompson. *Palestine Pastoralism and Israel's Origins*, id., at 1.

29. MUHAMMAD MUSLIH. THE ORIGINS OF PALESTINIAN NATIONALISM 12 (1988).

30. RASHID KHALIDI. PALESTINIAN IDENTITY 29 (1997). There is no equivalent in English to Khalidi's for the treatment of the development of a Palestinian consciousness in a political realm.

31. BERNARD WASSERSTEIN. THE BRITISH IN PALESTINE 18 (1978).

32. Perhaps the most salient development within the cultural context of the region to the creation of an Arab Palestine was in 1830 when the Ottoman Porte united the Empire's three *sanjaqs,* Jerusalem, Nablus, and Acre into one administrative unit. GREAT BRITAIN. PARLIAMENTARY PAPERS, 1920, Misc. No. 11, Cmnd. 675.Alexander Schölch. *Jerusalem in the 19th Century (1831–1917 A.D.)* 238 (K. J. Kasali ed., 2000). As a result, the territory east of the Jordan River was separated from Syria (*Bilad al–Sham*) and meant to be incorporated in the Palestine Mandate under British supervision. Many Palestinians demonstrated a nationalistic response in terms of Palestine being a part of southern Syria (*Suriyya al–Janubbiyya*). *See* Yehoshua Porath. *The Political Organization of the Palestinian Arabs Under the British Mandate, in* PALESTINIAN ARAB POLITICS 8–9 (Moshe Maoz ed., 1975).

33. Terms of the British Mandate for Palestine Confirmed by the Council of the League of Nations, July 24, 1922, 3 LEAGUE OF NATIONS O.J. 1007 (1922) (entered into force Sept. 29, 1923).Even the geographical title, Palestine, was a British contribution reached by the British Geographical Committee for Names, operating under the control of the Royal Geographical Society. MERON BENVENISTI. SACRED LANDSCAPES: THE BURIED HISTORY OF THE HOLY LAND SINCE 1948, at 12–13 (2000). Both the British military and provisional governing authority during the period of occupation up to the acquiring of mandatory authority included what is in the present day The Hashemite Kingdom of Jordan. With the Mandate for Palestine, a separate state of Trans-Jordan was unilaterally created by the British. Art. 2 id. refers to the area east to the Jordan river as "Trans-Jordan," an entity understood to be administered under the control of the Amir 'Abdullah. The final conclusion of belligerency was only completed by the Treaty of Lausanne (1923), 117 BFSP 543, which followed the negotiations over the Treaty of Sèvres (1920), 113 BFSP 652, an agreement that was unratified. One commentator discussing the role of the United Nations as a forum to bless the Palestinian Declaration of Independence, refers to Palestine "as one of *the territories* detached from the Turkish Empire." Vera Gowlland-Debbas. *Collective Responses to the Unilateral Declarations of Independence of Southern Rhodesia and Palestine*, 61 BRIT. Y.B. INT'L L., 1990, at 135, 197 (1991) (emphasis added).

34. The distinction between "old" and "new" states was made by the delegate from Ceylon at a meeting of the Sixth Committee (Legal) of the UN General Assembly, at the time dealing with a Report of the Int'l Comm'n on Succession of States and Governments in Respect of Treaties, in October 1968. U.N. Doc. A/C 6/SR 1036 (1968).

35. Yitzhak Gil-Har. *The Separation of Trans-Jordan from Palestine in* THE JERUSALEM CATHEDRA 284–313 (Lee Levine ed., 1981).

36. We can read notable specialists such as Professor John Quigley who claims: "From the sixteenth century until World War I, Palestine was ruled by the Ottoman Empire." *Judicial Autonomy in Palestine: Problems and Prospects*, 21 U. DAYTON L. REV. 698, 700 (1996). Sometimes, Professor Quigley's characterizations are hyperbolic,

to wit: "For as long as history records, the Palestinians have been the majority population in Palestine." *The Oslo Accords: More Than Israel Deserves*, 12 AM. U. J. INT'L L. & POL'Y 285 (1997). For a fuller treatment of relevant issues by Professor Quigley *see* PALESTINE AND ISRAEL (1990).

37. Perhaps one example will suffice:
On April 20, 1920, the Supreme Allied Council allocated the Palestinian Mandate to Great Britain. In March of 1921, the British detached all territory east of the Jordan River from Palestine — this territory had historically been a part of Palestine since before the arrival of the Hebrews led by Moses — and established the emirate of Transjordan. M. Cherif Bassiouni and Eugene Fisher. *The Arab-Israeli Conflict — Real and Apparent Issues*, 44 ST. JOHN'S L. REV. 399, 438 (1970).

38. SEGEV supra *note* 4, at 285.

39. Eyal Benvenisti. *The Status of the Palestinian Authority* in THE ARAB-ISRAELI ACCORDS: LEGAL PERSPECTIVES 60 (Eugene Cotran and Chibli Mallat eds., 1996).

40. The point here is to highlight the near-anarchic state conditions found presently in Afghanistan, Liberia, Somalia, and the former Yugoslavia in each of which nations has been seen to implode. One United States court has held at least that "any government, however violent and wrongful in its origin, must be considered a *de facto government* if it was in full and actual exercise of sovereignty over territory and people large enough for a nation." Ford v. Surget, 97 U.S. (7 Otto) 594, 620 (1878)(Clifford, J. concurring) (emphasis added). Having said this, it should also be stated that non-state actors are not widely recognized for purposes of a cause of action in U.S. courts. See Sanchez-Espinoza v. Reagan, 770 F.2d 202 (D.C. Cir. 1985); Linder v. Calero Portocarrero, 747 F.Supp. 1452, 1462, 1469 n. 8 (S.D. Fla. 1990); Carmichael v. United Technologies Corp., 835 F.2d 109, 113 (5th Cir. 1988).

41. Art. 1, Montevideo Convention on Rights and Duties of States of 1933, 165 L.N.T.S. 19. Related and expanded is the statement found in THE RESTATEMENT (THIRD) ON THE FOREIGN RELATIONS LAW OF THE UNITED STATES, at §201 (1987) which requires inter alia that an entity "engages in, or has the capacity to engage in formal relations with other such entities." See also National Petrochemical Co. of Iran v. M/T Stolt Sheaf, 860 F.2d 551, 553 (2d Cir. 1988), *cert. denied* 489 U.S. 1081 (1989) and Texas v. White, 74 U.S. (7 Wall.) 700, 720 (1868).

42. Island of Palmas Case (United States v. Netherlands), 2 U.N. Rep. Int'l Arb. Awards 829, 839 (1928) (separate opinion of Judge Huber). Taking various historical and cultural factors into consideration the issue of territorial sovereignty can be found in the decisions of the Legal Standard of Eastern Greenland (Norway v. Denmark), 1933 P.C.I.J. (ser. A/B) No. 53; the Anglo-Norwegian Fisheries (United Kingdom v. Norway) 1951 I.C.J. 116; and the Minquiers and Ecrehos cases (France v. United Kingdom) 1953 I.C.J. 47. Professor Quigley, as a renowned advocate of Palestinian self-determination and an acute observer of the changing character of statehood in the world today, has this to say on point: "Even without control of territory *in the usual sense*, however, the PLO exercised considerable powers in the Gaza Strip and West Bank through its control of various organizations carrying out quasi-governmental functions." Supra note 4 at 724. *Emphasis added.*

43. North Sea Continental Shelf Case (Judgment), 1969 I.C.J. 3, 32.

44. The classic approach to this theme is, of course, John Herz. *Rise and Demise of the Territorial State*, 9 WORLD POL. 473 (1957) followed by his *The Territorial State Revisited*, 1 POLITY 11 (1968). From a purely economic perspective *see*: JEAN-MARIE GUÉHANNO. THE END OF THE NATION-STATE (1995) and KENICHI OHMAE. THE END OF THE NATION STATE (1995). For a discussion on the impact of global economic issues *see* Peter Evans. *The Eclipse of the State?* 50 WORLD POL. 62 (1997).

See generally DAVID J. ELKINS. BEYOND SOVEREIGNTY (1995); DAVID HELD. DEMOCRACY AND THE GLOBAL ORDER (1995); HENRIK SPRUYT. THE SOVEREIGN STATE AND ITS COMPETITORS (1995); WALTER WRISTON. THE TWILIGHT OF THE SOVEREIGNTY (1992); Thomas Forsberg. *Beyond Sovereignty, Within Territoriality*, 31 COOPERATION AND CONFLICT 355 (1996); Barry Hindess. *Power and Rationality*, 17 ALTERNATIVES 149 (1992); David Kanin. *The State, Its Dysfunction, and Ours*, 34 INT'L POL. 355 (1997); Assa Lindbeck. *The Changing Role of the Nation State*, 28 KYKLOS 23 (1975); Oscar Schachter. *Is the State Withering Away?* 24 CAN. COUNCIL INT'L L. PROC. 184 (1995); Christoph Schreuer. *The Waning of the Sovereign State*, 4 EUR. J. INT'L L. 447 (1993); Mihály Simai. *The Changing State System and the Future of Global Governance*, 11 GLOBAL SEC. 141 (1997); *Symposium on the Decline of the Nation State and Its Effects on Constitutional and International Economic Law*, 18 CARDOZO L. REV. 903 (1996); Bruce Trigger. *The Archaeology of Government*, 6 WORLD ARCHAEOLOGY 95 (1974).

45. Reparation for Injuries Suffered in the Service of the United Nations, 1949 I.C.J. 174, 179.

46. THE LAW OF NATIONS: CASES, DOCUMENTS, AND NOTES 66 (Herbert Briggs ed., 1952).

47. See generally AZIZ HASBI. LES MOUVEMENTS DE LIBERATION NATIONALE ET LE DROIT INTERNATIONAL (1981); ABDELWAHAB HECHICHE. L'AUTODETERMINATION PALESTINIENNE ENTRE LE DROIT ET LA FORCE (1991); CHRISTOPHER QUAYLE. LIBERATION STRUGGLES IN INT'L L. (1990);and Malcolm Shaw. *The International Status of National Liberation Movements*, 5 LIVERPOOL L. REV. 19 (1983). See esp. Yezid Sayigh. *Armed Struggle and State Formation*, 36 J. PAL. STUD. 17 (1997).

48. For a discussion of the growing United Nations see Tullio Treves. *The Expansion of the World Community and Membership of the United Nations*, 4 FINN. Y.B. INT'L L. 248 (1995).

49. Ahmed v. Austria, 24 Eur. Ct. H.R. (Ser. B) at 278 (1996).

50. Case 9 C 38.96 BVerfGE, *reprinted in* INFORMATIONSBRIEF AUSLÄNDERRECHT 1997, No. 9, at 341.

51. See for example G.A. Res. 3236, 29 U.N. GAOR, Supp. 31, at 4, UN Doc. A/9631 (1974). The role of self-determination is emphasized in: THE RIGHT OF SELF-DETERMINATION OF THE PALESTINIAN PEOPLE, UN Doc. ST/SG/SER/F/3 (1979). While a widely accepted idea as evidenced by state practice, there are still those with strong reservations. See Tal Becker. *Self-Determination in Perspective: Palestinian Claims to Statehood and the Relativity of the Right to Self-Determination*, 32 ISRAEL L. REV. 301 (1998) and Sanford Silverburg. *In Perpetuation of Myth: National Self-Determination* de lege ferenda, 2 GLENDALE L. REV. 273 (1978) or as Professor Yoram Dinstein has written, "one should beware of an anachronistic application of legal norms in temporarily wrong settings," *Arab-Israeli Conflict in International Law*, 43 U.NEW BRUNS. L.J. 301, 3154 (1994).

52. The PLO was accorded "observer" status by the UN by G.A. Res. 3237, id. Observer status was elevated in the summer 1998, by GA A/RES/52/250 (1988), to an unprecedented level when the General Assembly voted to permit the PLO to participate actively in the general debates within the chamber, as well as other procedural accommodations. For a fuller description see Press Release GA 9427, U.N. GAOR, 52d Sess., 89th mtng. (1998). The Security Council had permitted the organization to participate in its deliberations when the debate directly involved it. U.N. SCOR, 44th Sess., 2841st mtg., U.N. Doc. S/PV. 2841 (1989) contrary to the body's rules as set out in Security Council, *Provisional Rules of Procedure*, Rule 14, U.N. Doc. S/96/Rev. 4 (1946).

53. Oliver J. Lissitzyn. *Territorial Entities in the Law of Treaties*, RECUEIL DES COURS, III, 1968, at 1, 13 (1970).

54. See generally Roy Goode. *Usage and its Reception in Transnational Commercial Law*, 46 INT'L & COMPL. L.Q. 1 (1997) and Ernst-Ulrich Petersmann. *The Transformation of the World Trading System Through the 1994 Agreement Establishing the World Trade Organization*, 6 EUR. J. INT'L L. 161 (1995). Still another distinctive development is the Multinational Agreement on Investment (MAI), currently being negotiated within the OECD (Organization for European Co-operation), a free-standing international treaty open to signature to all OECD members, the European Community, and all nonmembers able to meet the required obligations. See <http://www.oecd.org/daf/cmis/mai/MAIRAP97.HTM>.

55. *World Trade Organization (WTO) Dispute Settlement Review Commission Act: Hearing Before the Comm. on Finance, United States Senate*, 104th Cong., 1st Sess. (1996); ASIF QURESHI. THE WORLD TRADE ORGANIZATION (1996); and Steven Corley and John Jackson. *WTO Dispute Procedures, Standards of Review, and Deference to National Governments*, 90 AM.J.INT'L L. 1993 (1996).

56. See for example the discussion in Eric Helleinen, *From Bretton Woods to Global Finance: A World Turned Upside Down in* POLITICAL ECONOMY AND THE CHANGING GLOBAL ORDER 163–175 (Richard Stubbs and Geoffrey R.D. Underhill eds., 1994).

57. See IAN BROWNLIE. PRIN. OF PUB. INT'L L. 94 (1973). See also JOE VERHOEVEN. LE RECONNAISSANCE INTERNATIONALE DANS LA PRATIQUE CONTEMPORAINE 721 (1975).

58. Id. at 82.

59. An interesting albeit complicating factor here is the contentious status of the City and District of Jerusalem which, of course, has been under effective control of Israel since June 1967.

60. G.A. Res. 3210, 29 U.N. GAOR Supp., No. 31, at 3, U.N. Doc. A/L 736/Add. 1,2 (1974).

61. *See* MARIA LÄHTEENMÄKI. THE PALESTINE LIBERATION ORGANIZATION AND ITS INTERNATIONAL POSITION: UNTIL THE PALESTINE NATIONAL COUNCIL OF ALGIERS IN NOVEMBER 1988 (1994); David Gilmour. *The Creation and Evolution of the Palestine Liberation Organization in* PRESSURE GROUPS IN THE GLOBAL SYSTEM 46, 56–59 (Peter Willetts ed., 1982); and Anis Kassim. *The Palestine Liberation Organization's Claim to Status*, 9 DEN. J. INT'L L. & POL'Y 1 (1980). But see William O'Brien. *The PLO in International Law*, 2 BOSTON U. INT'L L.J. 349, 372–395 (1984).

62. THE RESTATEMENT (THIRD) ON THE FOR. RELS. OF THE UNITED STATES, at §202 cmt. 6.

63. United States v. Insurance Cos., 89 U.S. (22 Wall.) 99, 101–103 (1875); Thorington v. Smith, 75 U.S. (8 Wall.) 1, 9–12 (1868); Carl Zeiss Stiftung v. VEB Carl Zeiss Jena, 433 F.2d 686, 699 (2d Cir 1970) *cert. denied*, 403 U.S. 965(1971).

64. See generally KARIN AGGESTAM. TWO-TRACK DIPLOMACY: NEGOTIATIONS BETWEEN ISRAEL AND THE PLO THROUGH OPEN AND SECRET CHANNELS (1996)[Davis Papers on Israel's For. Pol'y, No. 53].

65. PAUL DE WAART. THE LEGAL STATUS OF PALESTINE UNDER INTERNATIONAL LAW 5 (1996)[Birzeit University Law Center Encounters]. See the list of states supplied by the PLO official news organization WAFA in February 1989. 18 J. PALESTINE STUD. 175–176 (1989). For a detractive commentary on the value of implicit recognition by virtue of a vote total for a U.N. General Assembly Resolution see Patrick Travers. *The Legal Effect of United Nations Action in Support of*

the PLO and National Liberation Movements in Africa, 17 HARV., INT'L L.J. 561 (1976).

66. Id., at 6 (emphasis added). Much of the remarks here are prefatory to his general format as laid out in DYNAMICS OF SELF-DETERMINATION IN PALESTINE: PROTECTION OF PEOPLE AS A HUMAN RIGHT (1994).

67. For the text see supra *note 6*. It was not lost on Chairman Arafat that the Declaration was issued *in Algeria*, as was clearly indicated by his address during the opening ceremony for the 50th anniversary of the 1948 *al–Nakhba* (the Catastrophe). AL QUDS (Jerusalem), Feb. 13, 1998, at 1. The Declaration was not acceptable as "official" by Australia, Canada, Norway, Spain, and the United States, according to letters to the Director-General of the WHO. WHO Doc. A42/INF Doc./3, May 1989. See Japanese sentiment expressed in UN Doc. A/43/PV. 82, at 8 (1989) and the US position in id., at 47 as well as its address to the 43d World Health Assembly. WHO Doc. A43/VR/8, at 3–4 (1989).

68. The United Nations took note of the Declaration in G.A. Res. 43/177, U.N. GAOR, 43d Sess., Supp. No. 49 at 62, U.N. Doc. A/43/49 (1989); 34 KEESING'S RECORD OF WORLD EVENTS 36321 (1988).

69. F.A. Mann. *International Corporations and National Law*, 42 BRIT. Y.B. INT'L L. 147, 153 (1969).

70. Manfred Lachs. *Recognition and Modern Methods of International Co-operation*, 35 BRIT. Y.B. INT'L L. 252, 253 (1960).

71. 983 PARL. DEB., H.C. (5th Ser.) 277–9 (1980). See also Colin Warbrick. *The New British Policy on Recognition of Governments*, 30 INT'L & COMP. L. Q. 568 (1981).

72. Supra *note 4*.

73. For a discussion and listing of ministers see <http://www.arts.mcgill.ca/MEPP/PDIN/pdpa.html>.

74. Supra *note 4*.

75. Id.

76. Id., Art VI(2)(a).

77. Joel Singer. *The West Bank and Gaza Strip: Phase Two*, JUSTICE, No. 7, at 5, 13 (1995).

78. See Art. IX(5)(b).

79. *Middle East Peace Process: Hearing Before House Comm. on Int'l Rels.*, 104th Cong., 1st Sess. 288–289 (1996).

80. Israel. Law Implementing the Agreement on the Gaza Strip and the Jericho Area (Restriction on Activity), 1994, S.H. 85–6, popularly known as "The Orient House Law." Orient House was the main office of Faysal al–Husseini, appointed by PNA Chairman Yasir Arafat as minister without portfolio to head Jerusalem Affairs for it. A number of official PNA functions, to include diplomatic, were conducted at the Orient House. For an overall examination see Nadav Shragei. *Security Course: Palestinian Institutions' Activity Intended to Undermine Israel's Sovereignty in Jerusalem*, HA'ARETZ (Tel Aviv), Feb. 20, 1997, at A4.

81. David Fidler. *Peace Through Trade? Developments in Palestinian Trade Law During the Peace Process*, 39 VA. J. INT'L L. 155 (1998) and Keith Molkner. *Legal and Structural Hurdles to Achieving Political Stability and Economic Development in the Palestinian Territories*, 19 FORDHAM INT'L L.J. 1419 (1996). The most thorough listing of donor assistance can be gleaned from the quarterly monitoring reports of the PNA's Ministry of Planning and International Cooperation (MOPIC) which maintains its own website. See <http://www.pna.net/reports/aid_reports/150698/150698.htm>.

82. AL-AYYAM (Ramallah)(Internet version), Feb. 19, 1998. (In Arabic as translated by FBIS/WNC.)

83. AUSTRALIAN AGENCY FOR INTERNATIONAL DEVELOPMENT. MEDIA RELEASES & HOT TOPICS, AA72, *Aid for Occupied Palestinian Territories* (Dec. 5, 1997) *reprinted in* <http://www.ausaid.gov.au/media/reslease/ab72.html>.

84. For the text of the Canadian-Israel Free Trade Agreement (CIFTA) see <http://www.dfait-maeci.gc.ca/ENGLISH/GEO/AFRICA/cda-isr.htm> and *see* <http://www.dfait-maeci.gc.ca/english/news/newletr/disweek/1997/fev24.htm>.

85. <http://www.dfait-maeci.gc./english/news/press_~1/96_press/96_180E.HTM>. Mr. Art Eggleton, Canada's Minister for International Trade is noted to have remarked that CIFTA would serve as a sort of platform "to extend benefits to goods produced in the West Bank and Gaza." Most pointedly, he went on to declare: "We are examining ways to best achieve this in co-operation with the Palestinian Authority." *Notes for an Address by the Honorable Art Eggleton, Minister for International Trade, on the Occasion of the Signing of the Canada-Israel Free Trade Agreement*, Jul. 31, 1996, as cited in Randall Hofley and Jason Gudovsky. *The Canada-Israel Free Trade Agreement: Leveling the Playing Field*, 31 J. WORLD TRADE L. 153, 154, n7.

86. Press Release No. 31, Canada. Department of Foreign Affairs and International Trade, Feb. 16–23, 1997. The direction was indicated by an intent to sign a Memorandum of Understanding or Protocol with the PLO, but on behalf of the PNA, to achieve freer trade as well as closer Canada-Palestinian trade and investment. <http://www/dfait-meci.gc.ca/english/geo/africa/delegation-e.htm>. For more extensive treatment see the Canadian International Development Agency (CIDA) Home Page at <http://www.acdi-cida.gc.ca/>.

87. AL-AYYAM (Ramallah)(Internet version), Feb. 24, 1998. (In Arabic as translated by FBIC/WNC.)

88. *See generally* EUROPEAN UNION. THE EUROPEAN UNION AND THE PALESTINIANS (1995); IP/96/406, <http://www.ce.pt/textos/IP6406/html>.

89. *A Very Successful European Summit Meeting*, EUROPEAN COMMUNITY NEWS, No. 21/1980, June 16, 1980.

90. Andreas Middel. *Europea dringt auf mehr Einfluss im Nahen Osten*, DIE WELT (Internet Version), Jan. 20, 1998. <http://www.welt.de/archiv/1998/01/20/0120au02.htm>. To its credit, the EU has supplied 50 percent of the development aid to the Palestinian territories and has been the recipient of 50 percent of Israel's exports. For a general discussion of a development aid program to the Palestinians see <http://www.arts.mcgill.ca/MEPP/PDIN/pdoverview.html> and <http://europa.eu.int/en/comm/dg1b/en/cisjordan.htm>.

91. Proposal for a Council Decision Concerning the Conclusion by the European Community of a Euro-Mediterranean Interim Association Agreement on Trade and Cooperation Between the European Community and the PLO for the Benefit of the Palestinian Authority of the West Bank and the Gaza Strip, COM(97) 51 final.

92. See generally Communication From the Commission to Council and Parliament on Future European Union Economic Assistance to the West Bank and the Gaza Strip, <http://europa.eu.int/en/comm/dg16/en/cisjordan.htm>; Communication from the Commission. The Role of the European Union in the Peace Process and its Future Assistance to the Middle East, COM/97/0715/FIN. (Also known as the [Manual] "Marin Memorandum.") This report was followed by a formal visit to the region by EU President Jacques Santer during the first week in February 1998. LE SOIR (Brussels), Feb. 19, 1998, at 7.

93. LA LIBRE BELGIQUE (Brussels), Feb. 11, 1998, at 6.

94. Alessandra Antonelli. *From Jail to a New Life*, PALESTINE REPT., Mar. 13, 1998. <http://www.birzeit.edu/jmcc/weekly/980313pr.html>. Financial support for this effort is also provided by Italy and Switzerland.

95. Ministry for Foreign Affairs of Finland. Press Releases: "Finland Supports the Middle East Peace Process and Doubles Economic Aid for the Palestinians," Jan. 9, 1996. See also <http://www.mofile.fi/fennia/um/803/htm>.

96. Communication from Allam Jayyusi, Project Managter of the Aid Coordination Department, Palestinian Ministry of Planning and International Cooperation supported by the German Technical Cooperation Agency (GTZ), on the West Bank and Gaza. Mar. 10, 1998. <allam@nmopic.pna.net>.

97. <http://www.fco.gov.uk/current/1996/jan/09/hanley_statement_aid-to-palestinians.txt>.

98. AL QUDS (Jerusalem), Oct. 27, 1997 at 1, 19.

99. Hashemite Kingdom of Jordan. Treaty of Cooperation on Trade Between the Kingdom of Jordan and the Palestine National Authority [Amman, 1995] (copy on file with the author); Hashemite Kingdom of Jordan. Revised Text of the Treaty of Cooperation on Trade Between the Kingdom of Jordan and the Palestine National Authority [Amman, 1995] (copy on file with the author); Hashemite Kingdom of Jordan. Joint Jordanian-Palestinian Committee. Report [Amman, 1995] (copy on file with the author).

100. NRG HANDELSBLAD (Rotterdam), Feb. 6, 1998, at 4.

101. *Mandela Calls for International Support to Restructure the ANC*, JERUSALEM POST, Feb. 28, 1990, at 1 and Asher Walfish. *ANC Visitors Stress Ties with the PLO*, id., Jan. 25, 1993, at 12. See also ARYE ODED. AFRICA, THE PLO AND ISRAEL (1990)[Leonard Davis Inst. for Int'l Rels., Pol'y Stud. No. 37].

102. Donor Humanitarian Assistance Database. <http://www.reliefweb.int/fts/donor-db/spa96gaw.html>.

103. <http://www.sida.se/eng/bistand/sidaworld/gaza/numbers.html>.

104. <http://home1.swipnet.se/~w-10358/JLD/Birzeit.html>.

105. Pres. Determination No. 89–22, 54 Fed Reg. 34,475 (1989).

106. Pub. L. No. 103–125, 107 Stat. 1309, known as the 1993 Middle East Peace Facilitation Act (MEDPFA) the terms of which were extended by Pub. L. No. 103–166, 107 Stat. 1978.

107. See T.I.F. 212 (1997); Hein's No. KAV 4032. See also "Executive Briefing," 18 MIDDLE EAST EXEC. REPTS. 4 (1995) and S. Miles. *Gaza: Foreign Investment: OPIC Loan Opens Up Investment Opportunities*, 2 MIDDLE EAST COM. L. REV. A19 (1996).

108. PUB. PAPERS OF PRES. WILLIAM J. CLINTON. BK. I, 1995 at 395 (1996); Proclamation 6778, 60 Fed. Reg. 15,455 (1995). See also H. REP. NO. 104–495 (1996) reprinted in 1996 U.S.C.C.A.N. 3485 and S. REP. 104–270 (1996); *Economic Development and U.S. Assistance in Gaza/Jericho: Hearing Before the Subcomm. on Near East and South Asian Aff. of the Sen. Comm. on For. Rels.*, 104th Cong., 1st Sess. (1995). The EU has a preferential trade agreement with the PNA covering the West Bank and Gaza. Israel and the PNA signed an Economic Protocol in April 1994 in Paris covering trade arrangements between the two.

109. Pub. L. No. 104–234, 110 Stat. 3058 amending the United States-Israel Free Trade Agreement Implementation Act of 1985 to provide the President with additional proclamation authority with respect to articles of the West Bank or Gaza Strip or a qualifying industrial zone, 19 U.S.C. 2112, n.1.

110. Proclamation No. 6955, 61 Fed Reg. 58,761–58,765 (1996).

111. See generally Torunn Laugen. *The World Bank and the UN in the Occupied Territories*, 29 SECURITY DIALOGUE 63 (1998) and Barbara Balaj. *Nouvelles approaches pour le développement économique et social de la Cisjordanie et de la bande de Gaza*, 62 POLITIQUE ÉTRANGÈRE 335 (1997).

112. THE WORLD BANK GROUP. PRESS RELEASE, *International Community Reaffirms Support For Palestinian Development*, Dec. 15, 1997. <http://worldbank.org/html/extdr/extme.1215pr.htm>.

113. THE JERUS. TIMES, Jan. 23, 1998, at 10.

114. Hans Kelsen. *Recognition in International Law: Theoretical Observations*, 35 AM. J. INT'L L. 605 (1941).

2

Palestine: The Issue of Statehood
JOHN QUIGLEY

A leitmotif of the Israeli-Palestinian dialogue through the 1990s was the question of Palestinian statehood. After declaring a Palestine state in 1988, the Palestinian side announced a plan to repeat the declaration in the 1998 run-up to negotiations with Israel. This announcement prompted a threat from Israel to annex Palestinian territory. Under pressure from Israel and others in the international community, the Palestinian side put the plan on hold, only to take it up again in 2000.

Throughout the episode, Israel, which occupied the territory claimed for a Palestine state, acted as if it were its decision whether such a state would come into being. The Palestinian side, to the contrary, insisted that Israel had no say in the matter. Other states weighed in on the issue, some recognizing Palestine as a state, others urging the Palestinians to put the issue aside. When in 2000 the Palestinians renewed the campaign to declare a state, Israel's response was more subdued, but the matter was not settled.

The statehood issue bore both a political and a legal aspect. It raised the question of what, at base, statehood means, and how statehood comes about in international practice. In the particular situation, was it up to the Palestinians to decide upon their statehood? Was Palestine statehood a matter to be negotiated with Israel?

An additional, and complicating, factor was the possibility that the matter did not rest solely with the Palestinian, or even the Palestinian and Israeli parties. The international community as a whole weighed in on the issue in a variety of ways, giving rise to a third possibility, namely, that the issue of Palestine statehood depended in the final analysis on a collective international decision.

The issue of Palestine statehood cannot be analyzed solely on the basis of the positions taken on it during the last decade of the 20th century. It is an issue with a past, and that past must first be briefly explored.

I. Palestine Statehood Before World War II

The issue of Palestine statehood was not new in the 1990s. Palestine became a territory with international status when the Ottoman Empire was dismembered after World War I. Great Britain occupied Palestine in 1918, and in 1922 the League of Nations gave Britain a mandate to administer it.[1] The League's Covenant, in its Article 22, forbade states that had occupied territories during World War I to hold them as colonies. By that same article, a state occupying such a territory whose people were "not yet able to stand by themselves under the strenuous conditions of the modern world" was required to promote the "well-being and development of such peoples." The mandate system was premised on "a rejection of the notion of annexation."[2] The mandatory power did not hold sovereignty.[3] The League of Nations Permanent Mandates Commission, which monitored compliance by administering powers, "consistently challenged on every possible occasion any policy or legal text that seemed to imply directly or indirectly that the mandatory state possessed or could possess sovereignty."[4]

Sovereignty in mandate territories resided in the community of persons being administered, which enjoyed an international status. "Communities under mandate," said the Institute of International Law in 1931, were "subjects of international law" since they held "a patrimony distinct from that of the Mandatory State."[5]

Palestine under Britain's mandate was a subject of international law capable of treaty relations, despite the control exercised by Britain as the administering power. Palestine had its own citizenship, separate from British citizenship.[6] Palestine under the mandate became a party in its own name to treaties.[7] It adhered to multilateral treaties on topics ranging from taxation to intellectual property.[8] It concluded bilateral treaties with regional and European states, for example, extradition and trade treaties with Egypt,[9] and treaties on postal services with France,[10] Greece,[11] Italy,[12] Switzerland,[13] and Great Britain.[14] These bilateral treaties were registered with the League of Nations and published in its treaty series.

Article 22 aimed at making the communities under mandate "capable of self-determination."[15] The phrase "not yet able to stand by themselves" indicated that the territories were entitled to self-determination, which would mean independence if that were the will of the population.[16] As explained by a leading British journal, the expectation was "that the mandates would find their natural and only conclusion in the attainment of independence by the mandated territory."[17]

The communities under mandate, the International Court of Justice would later say, "were admitted" to "possess a potentiality for independent existence on the attainment of a certain stage of development: the mandates system was designed to provide peoples 'not yet' able to manage their own affairs with the help and guidance necessary to enable them to arrive at the stage where they would be 'able to stand by themselves.'"[18] The Court said that the "ultimate objective" of the mandate system was the "self-determination and independence of the peoples concerned."[19] The practice of the League of Nations Permanent Mandates Commission, which supervised the mandates, "consistently upheld the theory of ultimate independent sovereignty." It "assumed that sovereign independence, and not merely 'self-government' and 'autonomy,' was intended by the Covenant."[20]

Even while acknowledging a right to eventual independence for the population of Palestine, the League of Nations urged the creation in Palestine of a "Jewish national home." That aim potentially conflicted with the self-determination of Palestine's inhabitants, although it was not clear from the mandate instrument whether "Jewish national home" meant a sovereign Jewish state in a part of Palestine, or some concept of "home" short of sovereignty. Quincy Wright, who visited Palestine at that period, expressed concern over the potential conflict, writing that "the Palestine Mandate, in recognizing the Jewish people as entitled to a national home in Palestine ... [was a] political decision ... difficult to reconcile with the claim of the Arab population to self-determination."[21]

II. Palestine Statehood after World War II

The United Nations Charter, adopted in 1945, recognized and confirmed the international status of mandate populations and of their right to independence. Article 80 of the United Nations Charter, included in the Charter's trusteeship chapter, states that "nothing in this Chapter shall be construed in or of itself to alter in any manner the rights whatsoever of any states or any peoples or the terms of existing international instruments to which Members of the United Nations may respectively be parties."

The U.N. Charter, in addition, declared self-determination to be a legal right. Article 1, paragraph 2, referred to self-determination as a "principle" in its Chinese, Spanish, English, and Russian texts, leading some commentators to view the Charter version of self-determination as aspirational only.[22] However, the French text of Article 1, paragraph 2, does not use the term "principle" but rather the term "right" (*droit d'autodétermination*). This use of the term "right" in the French text suggests that "principle" was being used here in the Chinese, Spanish, English, and Russian texts in the sense of a principle that has attained the status of law.

Such a construction is consistent with the standard approach to reading treaty texts composed in more than one official language. When the texts vary, they must be reconciled if possible. The presumption is that treaty terms have the same meaning in each language.[23] Thus, "principle" and "right" must be read as having the same meaning. The term "principle," moreover, is often used in treaties in a normative sense.[24] The prohibition in U.N. Charter Article 2, paragraph 4, against use of force, a prohibition understood as mandatory, is indicated by that article to be a "principle."

In 1947 the United Nations General Assembly's Special Committee on Palestine characterized the League's mandate instrument for Palestine as having been violative of self-determination. The Special Committee stated that self-determination "was not applied to Palestine, obviously because of the intention to make possible the creation of the Jewish National Home there." The Committee said that "the Jewish National Home and the *sui generis* Mandate for Palestine run counter to that principle."[25]

In 1947 the United Nations General Assembly recommended the establishment in Palestine of two states, one to be designated as "Arab" and the other "Jewish," in borders suggested in a resolution of the General Assembly.[26] The Arab authorities in Palestine did not act to implement the recommendation, however, because they considered that the recommendation anticipated an unfairly truncated Palestine as the Arab state. The Arab Higher Committee by a resolution of November 30, 1947, rejected Resolution 181.[27] The General Assembly recommendation would have given the Jewish state 57 percent of Palestine, though Jews constituted less than one third of its population. The unfairness of the recommendation was highlighted, in the view of the Arab authorities, by the fact that the proposed Arab state would have had an almost entirely Arab population, whereas the proposed Jewish state would have had an approximately equal number of Arabs and Jews.[28] Nonetheless, the General Assembly, by proposing the establishment of the two states, affirmed that it considered that there should be a Palestine state.

In 1948 in Palestine, a Jewish state was declared and established, called Israel, and it extended its control to 80 percent of the territory of Palestine.[29] Speaking on behalf of the Jewish Agency for Palestine, the body that declared Israel, Abba Eban told the United Nations on May 22, 1948, that self-determination was the basis for the Jewish claim to territory in Palestine.[30] This territorial claim was based on the existence of a Jewish kingdom in a portion of Palestine in ancient times. Ancient occupation is not recognized as giving entitlement to territory.[31] By late 1948, Israel occupied all Palestine except for the West Bank of the Jordan River (held by Jordan) and the Gaza Strip (held by Egypt). On October 1, 1948, the Arab Higher Committee, which represented the Arab population of Palestine, declared a Palestinian state.[32] A Government of All Palestine was formed at the same time, but it was unable to assume control of any territory.[33] Egypt and Jordan viewed Palestine as continuing to be a state with a valid claim to the territory of mandate-era Palestine.

Israel's view of Palestine's status was ambiguous. Israel did not regard itself as a successor state to Palestine, rather, it regarded itself as a new state.[34] This was so despite the fact that statutory law of the mandate period was continued in force pending its modification, and judicial precedents from the courts of the mandate period continued to be regarded as valid. In a report to the United Nations in 1950, Israel's foreign ministry provided a list of treaties to which Palestine was a party.[35] Israel specified that it did not deem itself to be bound by them since, in its view, Israel was a new state. It recited, "the Government of Israel reached the conclusion that it could be said that on the basis of the generally recognized principles of international law, Israel, which was a new international personality, was not automatically bound by the treaties to which Palestine had been a party and that its future treaty relations with foreign Powers were to be regulated directly between Israel and the foreign Powers concerned."[36]

In the 1960s, the Palestine Liberation Organization formed and claimed to represent the people of Palestine, and from the 1970s the United Nations recognized this representation.[37] The United Nations granted the P.L.O. observer status at the United Nations in 1974.[38] The Security Council has treated the P.L.O. as a state for the purpose of admitting it to participation in Security Council sessions. Only a "state" is entitled to participate in Security Council sessions.[39]

III. Palestine Statehood in the 1990s

On November 15, 1988, the Palestine National Council proclaimed the establishment of the state of Palestine in a document denominated a Declaration of Independence. The Council's Declaration recited: "when in the course of modern times a new order of values was declared with norms and values fair for all, it was the Palestinian Arab people that had been excluded from the destiny of all other peoples by a hostile array of local and foreign powers." The Declaration referred to "the historical injustice inflicted on the Palestinian Arab people resulting in their dispersion and depriving them of their right to self-determination."[40]

The Palestine National Council thus relied on the right of self-determination as its legal basis. As its factual basis, it relied on the fact that the Arab population of Palestine had been in occupation of that territory continuously since ancient times. Indeed, before immigration of Jews began from Europe in the late 19th century, the Arabs constituted nearly the entire population of Palestine, with Jews accounting for only about two percent.

Recognition of a putative state by other states serves an evidentiary function. It indicates that other states find that the putative state satisfies the criteria for statehood. "[T]he attitude of single States acquires considerable weight as evidence for or against the existence of new legal subjects," writes one authority on the issue.[41] After the Palestine National Council declared statehood in 1988, over 100 states recognized it. There is no numerical minimum in the law of nations, but since there are fewer than 200 states in the world, this number of recognitions was substantial. Most European states declined at that time to recognize Palestine; some declined on the grounds that they wanted a more definite indication of Palestine's positive attitude towards Israel, such as an explicit act of recognition of Israel. French President François Mitterand of France said at the time, "Many European countries are not ready to recognize a Palestinian state. Others think that between recognition and non-recognition there are significant degrees; I am among these."[42]

Even though they did not give immediate recognition, the European states made clear within a few years that they deemed there to be an entitlement to a Palestinian state. In 1999, the European Union issued a statement in which it indicated that the European states anticipated recognizing Palestine as soon as the P.L.O. negotiations with Israel led to the establishment of actual Palestinian control of territory. The statement read:

> The European Union reaffirms the continuing and unqualified Palestinian right to self-determination, including the option of a State, and looks forward to the early fulfillment of this right. It appeals to the parties to strive in good faith for a negotiated solution on the basis of the existing agreements, without prejudice to this right, which is not subject to any veto. The European Union is convinced that the creation of a democratic, viable and peaceful sovereign Palestinian State on the basis of the existing agreements and through negotiations would be the best guarantee of Israel's security and Israel's acceptance as an equal partner in the region. The European Union declares its readiness to consider the recognition of a Palestinian State in due course in accordance with the basic principles referred to above.[43]

Once a Palestinian National Authority was established under the 1993 Oslo agreement, states of the world began to deal with it.[44] A number of states established missions in Ramallah, the West Bank town that became the PNA's administrative center. These states typically referred to their missions by names other than "embassy," a fact that suggested some uncertainty about the character of the PNA and whether it was the government of a Palestine state.

This caution was open to the interpretation that these states did not consider Palestine to be a state. On the other hand, it was open to the interpretation that the states in question were uncertain about the status of the PNA, rather than about the status of Palestine as a state. The PNA was the authority on the ground, hence the authority with which these states were maintaining relations. The PNA, however, was a creature of a bilateral agreement with Israel, which, moreover, continued to control the territory and the activity of the PNA. As a consequence, states may have understandably been reluctant to regard the PNA as an entity with which they could maintain normal interstate relations. Palestine, even if a state, was not a party to international conventions on a diplomatic and consular status, a fact that had to leave the character of foreign-state missions in some doubt.

Beyond unilateral actions by other states, collective action by the United Nations was taken on the issue of Palestine statehood in the 1990s. In 1998, the U.N. General Assembly voted by resolution to reshape the P.L.O.'s observer status at the United Nations in a way that made it appear to be something quote close to a state.[45] The 1998 resolution recited ways in which the P.L.O. was carrying out governance in the Gaza Strip and West Bank and thus was exercising functions normally associated with sovereignty. The 1998 resolution provided that the P.L.O. was entitled to participate in General Assembly debates on all issues, rather than, as previously, only on issues related to it. Further, the term "Palestine" was used instead of "P.L.O." as the official designation.[46] This change suggested that the entity in question was not a national liberation organization, but a state.

IV. PALESTINIAN STATEHOOD AND THE ISSUE OF TERRITORY

The claim of statehood for Palestine confronted two conceptual hurdles. First, Israel occupied the territory claimed for the Palestine state. Second, given that Palestinian authorities did not control territory, the territorial extent of a purported Palestinian state was in some doubt. It remains to examine these issues.

The first potential impediment to Palestine statehood was the fact that Israel was in occupation of the territory that was apparently being claimed as Palestine. A normal requisite of statehood is control over a population in a territory. By the generally accepted definition, a "state" is "an entity that has a defined territory and a permanent population, under the control of its own government, and that engages in, or has the capacity to engage in, formal relations with other such entities."[47]

During the early 1990s, the Palestine National Council enjoyed the political support of the majority population in the West Bank and Gaza Strip, and the Palestine Liberation Organization even played a significant role in the life of the population, providing a variety of quasi-governmental services. Nevertheless, the P.L.O. did not exercise control over the West Bank or Gaza Strip in a military sense. It did not control borders.

Certain entities that do not control territory have, however, been regarded as states by the international community. The International Labor Organization and Food and Agriculture Organization both admitted the United Nations Council for Namibia as a member state, even though it controlled no territory.[48] Like the Palestine National Council, the United Nations Council for Namibia was recognized as enjoying a right to statehood, and on that basis it was treated as a state.

The United Nations General Assembly for many years accepted the credentials of the Taiwan government as representing China, even though it did not control China. The Assembly accepted the credentials of the Khmer Rouge government as representing Kampuchea, even after it lost power in 1979 and no longer controlled Kampuchea. Viewing the existing government of Kampuchea as having come to power by aggression, the

General Assembly opted to accept the credentials of what it found to be the government with a claim of legitimacy.[49]

In all these situations, the attitude taken was based not on control of territory but on a view regarding legitimacy. The entity claiming recognition was seen to be entitled to the territory it claimed, even though it was not in control. That factor doubtless played a significant role in the response of states, both individually and collectively, to Palestine's claim of statehood.

Moreover, if states view a claimant to statehood as not so entitled, they typically so indicate. A claim of statehood by one entity in territory controlled by another is potentially a circumstance affecting the international peace. If a claim is made that is deemed improper, the international community is likely to act to discourage the claim before it causes difficulty. Significantly, there was no international denunciation of the 1988 Palestinian declaration as a violation of the rights of Israel or of any other state or people. Thus, there was no expression of international sentiment that there was no entitlement to a Palestinian state. That lack of denunciation contrasts sharply with the response, five years earlier, to a declaration of statehood in Cyprus. On November 15, 1983, statehood was declared for a Turkish Republic of Northern Cyprus.

The international community found this declaration invalid, on the ground that Turkey had occupied this territory militarily and that the putative state was its creation. The U.N. Security Council pronounced the independence declaration illegal. In a resolution the Security Council declared that it was "[c]oncerned at the declaration by the Turkish Cypriot authorities issued on 15 November 1983 which purports to create an independent State in northern Cyprus." The Council continued, "Considering ... that the attempt to create a 'Turkish Republic of Northern Cyprus' is invalid, [the Security Council] [c]onsiders the declaration referred to above as legally invalid and calls for its withdrawal; ..."[50]

The international community obviously did not regard the 1988 Palestine claim the same way it regarded the 1983 northern Cyprus claim. The consistent view of the international community, and even, as indicated, of Israel itself, was that Israel had no claim to Gaza and the West Bank. Thus, a claim of Palestinian statehood did not threaten any pre-existing recognized interest. The claim of statehood for northern Cyprus, to the contrary, threatened the well-recognized claim of Cyprus to sovereignty throughout the island of Cyprus.

If the international community had deemed the Palestinian declaration illegitimate, it could have said so. It did not. To the contrary, as indicated, it moved in the 1990s to give the P.L.O. a status that was hard to distinguish from that of a state.

The legitimacy issue was particularly pertinent because the state in control, Israel, did not claim sovereignty. It was in belligerent occupation, having taken the territory during the 1967 hostilities. It neither claimed sovereignty nor was recognized as enjoying such. Indeed, the U.N. Security Council had called on it to withdraw from that territory.[51]

A state that occupies territory during hostilities, as Israel did with the Gaza Strip and West Bank, holds it under a legal regime called belligerent occupation. This legal regime recognizes the occupant's control but limits the occupant to temporary possession pending a peace treaty. The state that held sovereignty at the commencement of the occupation continues to do so, even though it does not exercise control. Israel acknowledges that its status in the West Bank and Gaza is that of a belligerent occupant, even after the agreements with the P.L.O. The Legal Adviser to Israel's Ministry of Foreign Affairs explained that the West Bank and Gaza Strip remain under belligerent occupation during the interim period contemplated by the 1993 Declaration of Principles: "notwithstanding the transfer of a large portion of the powers and responsibilities currently exercised by Israel to Palestinian hands, the status of the West Bank and Gaza Strip will not be changed during the interim period."[52]

The international community as well continued to regard Israel's status as that of a belligerent occupant, even after the 1993 agreements. In a 1996 resolution, the United Nations General Assembly "reaffirm[ed] that the Geneva Convention relative to the Protection of Civilian Persons in Time of War, of 12 August 1949, is applicable to the occupied Palestinian territory, including Jerusalem."[53]

With belligerent occupation, the state holding sovereignty normally is deemed by the international community to continue to exist, and its government is deemed to represent it.[54] Belligerent occupation does not negate the statehood of the state whose territory is occupied.[55] "An entity does not necessarily cease to be a state even if all of its territory has been occupied by a foreign power or if it has otherwise lost control of its territory temporarily."[56]

"The legal (*de jure*) sovereignty still remains vested where it was before the territory was occupied, although obviously the legal sovereign is unable to exercise his ruling powers in the occupied territory."[57] Thus, when Iraq occupied Kuwait in 1990 and purported to incorporate it into Iraq, Kuwait's status as a state was unaffected: "Kuwait remained a state notwithstanding its occupation and putative annexation by Iraq in 1990."[58] The international community continued to recognize it as a state, and to recognize its government as the government of Kuwait. The U.N. Security Council, by resolution, "decide[d] that annexation of Kuwait by Iraq under any form and whatever pretext has no legal validity, and is considered null and void; ... [and] demand[ed] that Iraq rescind its actions purporting to annex Kuwait."[59] This was so despite the fact that the government of Kuwait did not control Kuwait's territory. As stated by one authority, this Security council resolution "reaffirmed the basic tenet of the law of occupation, the inalienability of sovereignty through the use of force."[60]

As applied to the Gaza Strip and West Bank, the analysis is more complex, since sovereignty over these two areas was not clear at the commencement of Israel's occupation. Egypt had held the Gaza Strip since 1948 but had not incorporated it and did not claim sovereignty. Egypt considered Gaza to be part of Palestine.[61] Egypt's view was that it was holding the territory pending the emergence of a Palestine state. In a constitution adopted for Gaza by Egypt in 1962, Article 1 stated: "The Gaza Strip is an indivisible part of the land of Palestine."[62] Article 73 of the same constitution made it clear that Egypt contemplated the eventual re-emergence of Palestine: "This constitution shall continue to be observed in the Gaza Strip until a permanent constitution for the state of Palestine is issued."

The West Bank had been held by Jordan since 1948. Jordan had incorporated the West Bank in 1950, claiming sovereignty, but subject to a proviso. Jordan's parliament specified that in incorporating the West Bank into Jordan, it acted "without prejudicing the final settlement of Palestine's just case within the sphere of national aspirations, inter–Arab cooperation and international justice."[63] Thus, Jordan's claim of sovereignty was subject to the eventual emergence of a Palestinian state.

Jordan deemed itself a provisional sovereign. "One might thus conclude, it seems," said one analyst, "that the Palestinians are only *provisionally* placed under Jordanian sovereignty."[64] In 1988, after the Palestine National Council declared statehood for Palestine, Jordan renounced its sovereignty claim in the West Bank in favor of Palestine's claim.[65] Jordan's King Hussein declared, "The independent Palestinian state will be established on the occupied Palestinian land after its liberation."[66]

There is no reason why sovereignty in occupied territory might not change during the period of occupation. If, for example, a state whose territory was occupied decided to merge with another state (not the occupant), there is no reason it could not do that. As regards the Gaza Strip and West Bank, there was not so much a change in sovereignty, however, as a clarification of sovereignty, since Egypt never claimed sovereignty, and Jordan did so only provisionally, and since, as indicated, a Palestinian state was close to being recognized after the mandate period.

Israel disputed the conclusion that the P.L.O. holds sovereignty in the West Bank and Gaza during the interim period, even though Israel does not claim sovereignty for itself. It takes the position that the fact that belligerent occupation continues negates any possibility of P.L.O. sovereignty. It says that, given belligerent occupancy,

> the Palestinian Council will not be independent or sovereign in nature, but rather will be legally subordinate to the authority of the military government. In other words, operating within Israel, the military government will continue to be the source of authority for the Palestinian Council and the powers and responsibilities exercised by it in the West Bank and Gaza Strip.[67]

This conclusion confuses control and sovereignty. Israel continues to exercise control to the extent determined in the interim agreements, but control is a matter separate from sovereignty. With belligerent occupation, there is always a separation between control and sovereignty.

A related difficulty for a Palestine state as of the early 1990s was that since it was not in control of territory, there was ambiguity about its borders. With most claimed states, there is general acceptance of their borders. The Declaration of Independence recites that the Palestine National Council "hereby proclaims the establishment of the State of Palestine on our Palestinian territory with its capital Jerusalem." The Declaration was silent as to the territory claimed for the state, however. It referred to the General Assembly's partition resolution of 1947 as a document that "still provides the conditions for international legitimacy that guarantees the right of the Palestinian Arab people to sovereignty on their homeland." However, it did not claim the borders proposed for the Arab state in that resolution. It cited the resolution solely as a source of legitimation.[68]

Some states cited the lack of claimed borders in their reactions to the Declaration of Independence, because that lack made it unclear precisely what the PNC was asking recognition for. The U.S.S.R., for example, announced that it acknowledged the Declaration of Independence, but did not recognize the state, citing the fact that the Palestine National Council had not defined its borders.[69]

The matter of borders was addressed in a Statement of the Palestine National Council, issued at the same time as the Declaration.[70] The Statement called for United Nations supervision over the West Bank and Gaza Strip and said that an international conference should be convened based on United Nations Security Council Resolution 242.[71] That resolution, adopted in 1967, called on Israel to withdraw from the Gaza Strip and West

Bank. These were the two segments of mandate-era Palestine that Israel had not occupied in 1948, but which it did occupy in 1967.

The Final Statement called on Israel to withdraw from the Gaza Strip and West Bank, "including Arab Jerusalem." It thus appeared that the territory being claimed in the Declaration was the West Bank and Gaza Strip.[72] However, the ambiguity about borders was not definitively resolved.

Nonetheless, ambiguity of borders is not normally an impediment to recognition. Many states have unclear claims to borders, and the territory occupied by many states is claimed by others. A state must have a claim to some piece of territory. However, for a state to exist, it is not necessary that its territorial extent be clearly fixed. A state may have a border dispute with neighboring states, such that each of the two claims a particular piece of territory.

China's longstanding claim to areas of Siberia taken by Russia in the 19th century provides an example. The fact that both China and Russia claimed the same piece of territory in Siberia did not cast doubt on the statehood of either China or Russia.

A claim of borders has not always been deemed necessary for recognition. When the Jewish Agency declared statehood as the state of Israel in 1948, it did not specify borders. The Declaration of the Establishment of the State of Israel was silent on the question. It used the term "Eretz-Israel," which was construed variously as meaning what is generally regarded as Palestine, though by others as including as well what is now the state of Jordan.

The United Nations admitted Israel to membership despite the fact that it had claimed no borders.[73] Since, under Article 4 of the U.N. Charter, only states may be admitted to the United Nations, this act reflected a conclusion that Israel was a state. The territorial extent of Israel, however, was not clear at the time, and the General Assembly and Security Council considered there was no need for clarity on Israel's territorial extent in order to deem it a state.

To date Israel has made no claim of borders. Where it has been necessary in Israeli legislation to refer to the territory within which Israeli law is applicable, the Knesset (parliament) has delegated to the government the power to designate the territory. When it incorporated Arab Jerusalem in 1967, for example, the Knesset adopted a law stating that "the law, jurisdiction and administration of the state" of Israel "shall extend to any area of Eretz Israel designated by the Government by order."[74] The term "Eretz Israel" thus is still used, though the territory it includes is unclear.

One possibility was that the view of the United Nations was that Israel had a valid claim to the territory anticipated for a Jewish state in Resolution 181, representing 53 percent of the territory of mandate-era Palestine. Recognition of even that territory is questionable, however, because Resolution 181 was a recommendation only. Moreover, Resolution 181 was premised on fair treatment by a putative Jewish state of the Arabs inhabiting its territory, and on fair treatment by a putative Arab state of the Jews inhabiting its territory. After the Jewish Agency declared a state, that state (Israel) declined to recognize the citizenship of its Arab inhabitants, except for those who were continuously present from 1948 to 1952.[75] This represented only a small minority of the Arabs of the territory that Israel came to occupy. Thus, arguably, the Israeli state did not satisfy the criteria for recognition by the United Nations of its sovereignty over the territory recommended for a Jewish state in Resolution 181.

As for the territory of the city of Jerusalem, Resolution 181 did not include it in the territory of either a putative Jewish state or a putative Arab state. As a result, arguments based on Resolution 181 do not provide a basis for recognition of the territory of Jerusalem as being within the Israeli state.

Of possible relevance is Security Council Resolution 242, adopted after the June 1967 war, during which Israel occupied the portions of mandate-era Palestine it had not taken in 1948. Resolution 242 calls on Israel to withdraw from the territory it occupied in 1967. It has been considered by some analysts that this call for withdrawal represented an implicit recognition of Israel's sovereignty over the territory it had held since 1948. That view of Resolution 242, however, is open to serious objection. First, the international community, even after 1967, considered the status of the territory of the city of Jerusalem to be unresolved, meaning that it did not deem any part of the city of Jerusalem to be territory of Israel, including the western sector of Jerusalem, which had been under Israel's control since 1948. Since the international community did not, after 1967, deem the western sector of Jerusalem to be Israel's territory, Resolution 242 apparently did not have the effect of recognizing as Israeli territory all that it held as of 1948.

Second, and more generally, Resolution 242 was adopted in the aftermath of the June 1967 war, and thus its call for Israel to withdraw from the 1967 occupied territory did not necessarily imply recognition of any other territory as appertaining to Israel. To be sure, Resolution 242 did contemplate an overall settlement between Israel and its neighbors, as reflected in its provision that the Arab states should discontinue their states of belligerency with Israel. Nevertheless, it would be a strained reading of Resolution 242 that would conclude that out of an effort at an overall settlement one can infer recognition of specific territory as being that of Israel. Resolution 242, both with respect to Jerusalem and more generally, did not settle territorial issues between Israel and Palestine. It was understood in the Security Council during the adoption of Resolution 242 that the line between Israel and the West Bank of the Jordan River was an armistice line only, as set between Israel and Jordan in 1949, and not an international border.[76]

In 1993, Israel and the Palestine Liberation Organization agreed to determine the issue of borders by bilateral negotiation, to be based on Resolution 242. Since, however, Resolution 242 did not provide a ready solution of that issue, the reference to Resolution 242 did not settle the matter.

V. PALESTINE AS A STATE

Statehood is a legal construct, and while territory is relevant, the entity claiming statehood need not always be in control of territory. An entity claiming statehood must have a valid claim to some territory, although the scope of its claimed territory may be unclear.

The Palestine National Council's declaration in 1988, coupled with the recognition accorded that declaration, resulted in a strong claim of sovereignty for a Palestine state.[77] The claim was reinforced by the prior recognition of the P.L.O. as the representative of the Palestinian people, and the prior recognition of the people of Palestine as entitled to independence during the period of Britain's mandate in Palestine, despite its lack of physical control.

An additional factor reinforcing the claim was the fact that no other state claimed sovereignty in the territory concerned. Despite Israel's occupation of that territory, Israel, as the belligerent occupant, had no claim to sovereignty and had not asserted one. Egypt had never made a sovereignty claim to the Gaza Strip. For the West Bank, Jordan had renounced its sovereignty claim, which in any event had been of a provisional character.

The issue of Palestinian statehood became beclouded in the mid–1990s when the P.L.O. indicated an intent to declare statehood anew. That effort had more to do with implementing than with declaring anew. However, the effort made it appear that the P.L.O. itself might not deem there to be a Palestine state.

The controversy over a Palestinian state that emerged as a political issue in the mid–1990s was unnecessary. Had there been clarity on the legal position, all concerned might have agreed that there was a Palestinian state.

What was being contested under the guise of an argument about statehood was the implementation of Palestinian statehood, not its existence.

Notes

1. Mandate for Palestine, Permanent Mandates Commission no. 466, League of Nations Doc. C.529.M.314.1922.VI and C.667.M.396.1922.VI,8 LEAGUE OF NATIONS O.J. 1007(1922), *reprinted in* TERMS OF LEAGUE OF NATIONS MANDATES: REPUBLISHED BY THE UNITED NATIONS, U.N. Document A/70 (1946).

2. Legal Consequences for States of the Continued Presence of South Africa in Namibia (South West Africa) Notwithstanding Security Council Resolution 276 (1970), 1971 I.C.J. 30.

3. International Status of South-West Africa (Advisory Opinion), 1950 I.C.J. 131.

4. DUNCAN HALL, MANDATES, DEPENDENCIES AND TRUSTEESHIPS 81 (1948).

5. James Brown Scott, *The Two Institutes of International Law*, 26 AM. J. INT'L L. 91 (1932).

6. Norman Bentwich, *Nationality in Mandated Territories Detached from Turkey*,7 BRIT. Y.B. INT'L L. 102 (1926).

7. J[acob]. L[andau]., *The International Status of Palestine*, 90 JOURNAL DU DROIT INTERNATIONAL 964 (1963).

8. 138 L.N.T.S.149 (taxation, Mar. 30, 1931); 109 L.N.T.S. 121 (health, May 20, 1926); 1 L.N.T.S. 59 (patents/copyrights, June 30, 1920); 1 L.N.T.S. 83 (legal procedures, March 18, 1904); 9 L.N.T.S. 415 (status of women, March 31, 1922); 7 L.N.T.S. 35, 65 (water transport, April 20, 1921); 186 L.N.T.S. 301 (mass media, Sept. 23, 1936).

9. 36 L.N.T.S. 343 (extradition, Aug. 7, 1922); 80 L.N.T.S. 277 (commerce, June 6 & 21, 1928).

10. 172 L.N.T.S. 17 (June 19, 1936).

11. 170 L.N.T.S. 145 (March 28, 1936).

12. 139 L.N.T.S. 59 (Dec. 16, 1931).

13. 95 L.N.T.S. 395 (May 15, 1929).

14. 13 L.N.T.S. 9 (Jan. 23, 1922).

15. QUINCY WRIGHT, MANDATES UNDER THE LEAGUE OF NATIONS 499 (1930).

16. W. OFUATEY-KODJOE, THE PRIN. OF SELF-DETERMINATION IN INT'L L. 89 (1977); Comments by Rouhollah K. Ramazani, *in Self-Determination and Settlement of the Arab-Israeli Conflict*, 65 PROC. AM. SOC. INT'L L. 51 (1971).

17. *Termination of the British Mandate for Palestine* (editorial comment), 2 INT'L L.Q. 57 (1948).

18. Legal Consequences for States of the Continued Presence of South Africa in Namibia (South West Africa) Notwithstanding Security Council Resolution 276 (1970), 1971 I.C.J. 28–29.

19. Id., 31.

20. Supra note 4, at 81.

21. Quincy Wright, *The Palestine Conflict in International Law*, in MAJOR MIDDLE EASTERN PROBLEMS IN INT'L L. 26 (M. Khadduri, ed., 1972).

22. Eugene V. Rostow, *Palestinian Self-Determination: Possible Futures for the Unallocated Territories of the Palestine Mandate*, 5 YALE STUD. WORLD PUB. ORD.153–154 (1978).

23. Vienna Convention on the Law of Treaties, art. 33, para. 3 U.N. Doc. A/CONF.39/27 (1969), in 8 I.L.M. 679 (1969).

24. Wolfgang Benedek, *Progressive Development of the Principles and Norms of International Law Relating to the NIEO: The UNITAR Exercise*, 36 ÖSTERREICHISCHE ZEITSCHRIFT FÜR ÖFFENTLICHES RECHT UND VÖLKERRECHT 307–311 (1986).

25. Report of the United Nations Special Committee on Palestine, U.N. General Assembly Official Records, 2d session, Supplement No. 11, p. 35 (para. 176), Sept. 3, 1947, U.N. Document A/364.

26. U.N. General Assembly Resolution 181, Nov. 29, 1947, U.N. General Assembly Official Records, 2d session, Resolutions, p. 131, U.N. Document A/519 (1947).

27. 6 KEESING'S CONTEMP. ARCH. 8979 (1946–1948).

28. U.N. General Assembly Official Records, 2d session, p. 304, U.N. Document A/AC.14/32, Annex I (1947).

29. *Declaration of the Establishment of the State of Israel*, 1 LAWS OF THE STATE OF ISRAEL 3 (1948).

30. U.N. Security Council Official Records, 3d session, Supplement No. 72, p. 31, U.N. Document S/PV.302 (1948).

31. R. Y. JENNINGS, THE ACQUISITION OF TERRITORY IN INT'L L. 16–35 (1963).

32. Declaration, in 4 PAL. Y.B. INT'L L. 294 (1987/88).

33. Provisional Charter of the Government of All Palestine, Oct. 1, 1948, in id.

34. Declaration of the Establishment of the State of Israel, supra note 30.

35. *Replies from Governments to Questionnaires of the International Law Commission*, U.N. Document A/CN.4/19, in Y.B. INT'L L. COMM'N 209–210 (1950, part 2).

36. Id., at 215.

37. U.N. General Assembly Resolution 3236, Nov. 22, 1974, U.N. General Assembly Official Records, 29th session, Supplement No. 31, p. 4, U.N. Document A/9631 (1974).

38. U.N. General Assembly Resolution 3237, Nov. 22, 1974, U.N. General Assembly Official Records, 29th session, Supplement No. 31, p. 4, U.N. Document A/9631 (1974).

39. Security Council, *Provisional Rules of Procedure*, Rule 14, U.N. Document S/96/Rev.4 (1946).

40. Palestine National Council, *Declaration of Independence*, Nov. 15, 1988, U.N. Document A/43/827, S/20278, Nov. 18, 1988, in 27 I.L.M. 1668 (1988).

41. ANTONIO CASSESSE, INT'L L. IN A DIVIDED WORLD 79(1986). 79.

42. Maurice Flory, *La Naissance d'un État Palestinien*, 93 REVUE GÉN. DE DROIT INT'L PUB. 401 (1989).

43. Commission of the European Communities, March 26, 1999, Presidency conclusions: Berlin European Council 24 and 25 March 1999 (available on NEXIS).

44. Sanford R. Silverburg, *Diplomatic Recognition of States* in statu nascendi: *The Case of Palestine*, supra chapter 1.

45. Barbara Crossette, "Palestinians' U.N. role widened; a U.S. 'no' vote is overwhelmed," *New York Times*, July 8, 1998, at A1.

46. *Participation of Palestine in the Work of the United Nations*, U.N. General Assembly Resolution 52/250, U.N. Document A/RES/52/250 (1998).

47. American Law Institute, Restatement (Third) of the Foreign Relations Law of the United States, §201 (1987).

48. Ebere Osieke, *Admission to Membership in International Organizations: The Case of Namibia*, 51 BRIT. Y.B.INT'L L. 208–219 (1980).

49. *New York Times*, Oct. 21, 1983, at A11.

50. U.N. Security Council Resolution 541, U.N. Security Council Official Records, 38th session, Resolutions & Decisions, p. 15, U.N. Document S/INF/39 (1984).

51. U.N. Security Council Resolution 242, U.N. Security Council Official Records, 22d session, Resolutions & Decisions, p. 8, U.N. Document S/INF/22/Rev.2 (1967).

52. Joel Singer, *The Declaration of Principles on Interim Self-Government Arrangements*, 1 JUSTICE 6 (1994)(International Association of Jewish Lawyers and Jurists).

53. U.N. General Assembly Resolution 50/29B, Feb. 5, 1996.

54. GERHARD VON GLAHN, THE OCCUPATION OF ENEMY TERRITORY 31–37(1957).

55. JAMES CRAWFORD. THE CREATION OF STATES IN INT'L L. 58 (1979).

56. Restatement (Third) of the Foreign Relations Law of the United States, §201, Comment b.

57. MORRIS GREENSPAN. THE MODERN LAW OF LAND WARFARE 217(1959).

58. LOUIS HENKIN, RICHARD PUGH, OSCAR SCHACHTER & HANS SMIT, INT'L L.: CASES AND MATERIALS 247(1993).

59. U.N. Security Council Resolution 662, U.N. Security Council Official Records, 45th session, U.N. Document S/RES/662 (1990), in 29 I.L.M.1327 (1990).

60. EYAL BENVENISTI. THE INT'L L. OF OCCUPATION 151(1993).

61. Carol Farhi, *On the Legal Status of the Gaza Strip*, in 1 MIL. GOVT. IN THE TERRITORIES ADMINISTERED BY ISRAEL 1967–1980, at 75 (1982).

62. *Republican Decree Announcing Constitutional System of Gaza Sector*, March 9, 1962, art. 1, in 17 MIDDLE EAST J. 156 (1963).

63. Albion Ross, "Amman Parliament Vote Unites Arab Palestine and Transjordan," *New York Times*, April 25, 1950, at A1.

64. G. Feuer, *Les accords passés par les gouvernements jordanien et libanais avec les organisations palestiniennes (1968–1970)*, 16 ANN. FRAN. DE DROIT INT'L 177, 189 (1970) [translation by author].

65. John Kifner, "Hussein Surrenders Claims on West Bank to the P.L.O.," *New York Times*, August 1, 1988, at A1.

66. "Excerpts from Hussein's address on abandoning claims to the West Bank," *New York Times*, Aug. 1, 1988, at A4.

67. Supra note 52, at 6.

68. Ghassan Bishara, "'Soon in Jerusalem, Our Capital,' Palestinians in Algiers Wished Each Other When State Was Declared," AL–FAJR, Nov. 2, 1988, at 4.

69. Maher Abukhater, "Palestinian Diplomacy, An Outcome of the Algiers Resolutions, Continues to Win International Support," AL–FAJR, Nov. 28, 1988, at 1.

70. *Political Communiqué*, U.N. Document A/43/827, S/20278, Nov. 18, 1988, Annex II, in 27 I.L.M. 1661 (1988).

71. U.N. Security Council Resolution 242, U.N. Security Council Official Records, 22d session, Resolutions & Decisions, p. 8, U.N. Document S/INF/22/Rev.2 (1967).

72. Edward W. Said, "Palestine Agenda," NATION, Dec. 12, 1988, at 638.

73. U.N. Security Council Resolution 69, U.N. Security Council Official Records, 4th session, Resolutions & Decisions, p. 11, U.N. Document S/INF/3/Rev.1 (1949).

74. Law and Administration Ordinance (Amendment No. 11) Law, 21 LAWS OF THE STATE OF ISRAEL 75 (1967).

75. Nationality Law, art. 3, 6 LAWS OF THE STATE OF ISRAEL 50 (1952).

76. MUSA MAZZAWI, PALESTINE AND THE LAW: GUIDELINES FOR THE RESOLUTION OF THE ARAB-ISRAEL CONFLICT 209–212 (1997).

77. Eugene Cotran, *Some Legal Aspects of the Declaration of Principles: A Palestinian View*, in THE ARAB-ISRAELI ACCORDS: LEGAL PERSPECTIVES 73 (E. Cotran & E. Mallat eds., 1996).

3

Israel and the Creation of a Palestinian State: The Art of the Impossible and the Possible

JOSEPH H. WEILER

INTRODUCTION

Few international events have provoked as much legal comment as the Arab-Israeli conflict. This derives in part from the conflict's long duration; it has spanned the entire century. More profound reasons lie, however, in the strategic and economic importance of the Middle East and in the intractable moral issues that seem to defy intellectual consensus. Legal literature abounds with scholarly works addressing all aspects of the interminable struggle between Israel and its neighbors. Every phase of the conflict has ushered forth immense commentary. The Balfour Declaration, the subsequent League of Nations Mandate, the United Nations Partition Resolution and the actual creation of Israel stand as major landmarks of the past.[1] Countless events of aggression, terror and reprisal, war, armistice and peacemaking have also inspired scholarly comment. More recently, the status of the Palestinians regarding their claim to a right of self-determination, statehood and title over the West Bank and the Gaza Strip and their relations with the State of Israel—the subject of this Article—present equally troubling legal and political problems.[2]

Despite the abundance and diversity of contributions, there is a common trait unifying much of the legal scholarship. With some notable exceptions,[3] legal writers and lawyers have tended to address past events with a view toward determining legal rights and wrongs. Thus, law and legal scholarship have been used primarily to conduct a normative evaluation of the parties' political acts and claims. This tendency of scholarly commentary derives from the very nature of the discipline. Municipal legal scholarship and law, especially in the common-law world, have long been dominated by a judicial process whose main purpose has been to adjudicate between conflicting parties to determine their legal rights and duties. This post facto determination is meant, of course, to have ramifications for the future, as it is through adjudication that parties resolve their conflicts—wrongs must be undone and rights must be vindicated. And yet, overemphasis of this dimension of the legal process conceals certain dangers that undermines some of the societal functions of law.

Judicial policymakers are becoming increasingly aware that the traditional adversary proceeding—unquestionably useful in determining rights and wrongs regarding past conduct—may be at odds with the future relations of the litigating parties. This problem is particularly acute when parties are constrained to continue living together by external factors such as family, working or residence circumstances. The legal profession's renewed interest in alternative dispute resolution methods such as conciliation, arbitration, lay justice and neighborhood courts illustrates this concern and disillusionment with the traditional adversary process.[4] In the international sphere, the problem appears in more subtle ways.

The international order has moved to the other extreme. Here, dispute resolution concerning matters regarded by one or more of the disputants as vital to their national interest takes place completely outside legal frameworks; negotiation and conciliation substitute almost entirely for any judicial process of adjudication.[5] This development results from the peripheral role of formal adjudication in international matters, the weak or voluntary nature of obedience to public international law, and the absence of direct enforcement mechanisms.

Although legal scholarship in this area has not been instrumental in the emplacement of frameworks within which conciliation and negotiation might take place, it has served two other functions. The first has been to translate agreements made in the political arena into technical terminology. No harm results from this function as long as one remembers that a dispute regarding such translation may have to be resolved *de novo* by nonlegal methods. The second function of legal scholarship has been to introduce lawyers and legal arguments into the process of negotiation. This contrasts with some municipal analogues where once an "alternative," nonjudicial framework for resolution has been emplaced, legal argument is often discouraged. This second function may not always be constructive, because an interest dressed up as a legal right loses its flexibility and receptiveness to compromise. Thus, a potentially dangerous consequence of adversary legal arguments concerned exclusively with the determination of rights and wrongs but without the final authority of a court might result not merely in rendering difficult the continued peaceful coexistence of the parties after a settlement but in actually impeding resolution.[6] One obvious explanation of the relative abandonment by legal scholars of suggesting legal constructs as a basis for settlement is the subsidiary potential that is attributed to public international law as a system or framework that might evoke compliance. Dinstein has masterfully encapsulated this legal-political conundrum in the context of the Middle East conflict:

> Public international law has no reply to the practical problems which arise in a situation of conflict between equal or competing rights of self-determination which are bestowed simultaneously on several people.... In [Palestine] sit two nations ... the Jewish nation and the Arab nation. Each of these nations is entitled — in accordance with public international law — to self determination. But each of these nations aspires to self-determination over all of [Palestine] and in fact denies — entirely (in the case of the Arabs) or partially (in the case of the Jews — the right of self determination of the other person. In these circumstances only partition of the territory could resolve the conflicting rights of both peoples, but it is difficult to arrive at a division that would satisfy both parties. Since [the 1947 Partition Plan — rejected by the Arabs] a redeeming formula has not been found.[7]

International law thus remains important in providing the fundamental normative legal imperative of a solution, namely division. Its failure lies in its inability to find a reply to the "practical problems" of construing ("a division that would satisfy both parties"). This practical failure, the roots of which will be dealt with below, partially explains the subsidiary potential attributed to public international law in the context of the conflict. This article examines the potential relevance of "supranationalism"—a concept politically connoting a specific arrangement of transnational relations between states and peoples and legally straddling international law and municipal (constitutional) law — to these problems of a division that must satisfy both Israelis and Palestinians. This article further attempts to open a new line of inquiry based on this concept towards finding the elusive "redeeming formula." Supranationalism and supranational law are not suggested as a substitute to traditional public international law, but as a legal-political, practical superstructure to be imposed upon the normative public international law foundation.

Part I of this article analyzes the dynamics of the conflict in broad political, sociological and ideological terms, as well as the entrenched legal positions of both the current Israeli government and the Palestine Liberation Organization (PLO). The principal purpose is to highlight the elements contributing to the apparent 'p' radical difficulties, as seen by both parties, of a solution based on the partition apparently required by public international law.

Part II provides an overview of the European Common Market, in which supranational legal structures and political processes were pioneered. Part III suggests the potential application of these supranational elements to the Arab-Israeli conflict as a means for overcoming the difficulties of partition set out in Part I.

The "tragic" dimensions of the Israeli-Palestinian conflict are rooted in the mutual exclusivity by which each party perceives its own position and subsequent refusal to accord any legitimacy — moral or legal — to the claims of the other. This entrenchment is at least partially due to the deep fear that a solution based on division evokes in the two camps. Further, even assuming a political breakthrough by which some form of mutual recognition were established between Israel and the Palestinian leadership — a possibility that the Lebanese war may, paradoxically, produce and at which the Fez Summit[8] already hints— there is a danger that the political follow-up to such a breakthrough will falter because of the practical difficulties created by a partition solution. Suggestions of legal political constructs for regulating future relations and generating public debate regarding these constructs are thus justified, because they may serve as an element in enlisting the political will to break the fear of mutual acceptance (and the partition-based solution that mutual acceptance inevitably implies) and may prevent the dissipation of the political will should a breakthrough occur if the problems of partition do, indeed, appear insuperable.

PART I. THE DYNAMICS OF THE CONFLICT

A. The Deadlock

The peace process in the Middle East seems to have stalled while the thorny issue of the Palestinians' political fate is debated. The Palestinian problem is inextricably linked with the destiny of the occupied territories, principally the West Bank and the Gaza Strip. Disagreement over the destiny of the Palestinians, reflected in the debates concerning the nature of autonomy, is as strong as ever.

The war in Lebanon has provided a fresh reminder of the centrality of the Palestinians to the entire architecture of the region, and the recent American and Fez peace initiatives underlie the urgency with which both friends and foes of Israel regard the situation. The present impasse over the issue of autonomy and its stalemating effect on negotiations has have hampered United States attempts to improve relations with the principal oil-producing Arab States east of the Suez. The United States' complete support for Presidents Sadat and Mubarak may, in this context, be embarrassing, if not damaging, unless a breakthrough is achieved. For their part, several of the key Arab states, principally Saudi Arabia, have become increasingly aware that a struggle against Israel is at present unlikely to succeed and that the menace posed by Israel pales in comparison to the threat represented by events in Afghanistan and Iran.[9] The net result may be that the United States will place greater pressure on Israel to make fundamental policy concessions and that some of the Arab States will pressure the PLO to make equally fundamental concessions. There is a potential, then, for a qualitative change of negotiating premises. To date,[10] however, there have been no signs of official changes of heart by either side.

Israel's official rejection of the Saudi and Fez plans and its insistence on the principles regarding the nature of powers to be devolved on the local inhabitants clearly demonstrate the limited autonomy any Palestinian entity would have. Such an entity would be no more than a protectorate, in a most restricted sense, with little substantive legislative power. The constitutional source of power would remain vested in the Israeli legal order, and the Parliamentary enactment by which it is created — always subject to repeal or amendment — would be the essential element of the autonomy institutions and the source of their competences. Whereas the Egyptian-Israeli Peace Treaty[11] and the preceding Camp David Accords are neutral on the eventual evolution of the projected five-year interim period,[12] one cardinal Israeli principle is clear: "Autonomy" must not be allowed to lead to the creation of a Palestinian state in the occupied territories.[13] For the Egyptians, currently the only Arab partner actively participating in the negotiations, autonomy must do just that — provide the means for the gradual establishment of a Palestinian state, whether or not as a partner with the Kingdom of Jordan. The local Palestinians have shown little enthusiasm for the Israeli plan and their largest representative organization, the PLO, has not, at this time, modified its attitude toward Israel.

Two basic, antithetical hypotheses prevail regarding future relations between Israel and the Palestinians. The first excludes the creation of an independent Palestinian state in any form. The second considers the creation of a Palestinian state fundamental to solving any conflict.

In Israel, for several reasons to be explored in this Article, there is widespread consensus supporting the first hypothesis. The introduction of an independent Palestinian state, inevitably to be led by the PLO or its delegates, is regarded as guaranteed to precipitate the conflict rather than solve it. Under this hypothesis, a Palestinian independent state is rejected, and a variety of other means of accommodating the Palestinians under Israeli, Jordanian or joint rule are contemplated. This framework might give the Palestinians a larger or smaller measure of self-rule, but not independence. Although this model is likely to be favored by Israel and several other states, within and outside the region, it has been totally rejected by the PLO. However, it is not the purpose of this article directly to address these models.

The second basic hypothesis derives from the view that the political forces affecting the conflict, especially the Palestinian national movement and the PLO, have developed to the point that the establishment of a Palestinian state is a necessary condition to a solution.[14] This article is concerned with the problems raised by this assumption. To suggest that the establishment of a Palestinian state is a necessary condition to a solution is not to suggest that it is a sufficient condition. Perhaps both hypotheses are correct, resulting in two incompatible necessary conditions: (1) it is not possible to move toward a solution without the establishment, or at least the clear prospect of the establishment, of a Palestinian state; and (2) such an entity will lead to a precipitation of the conflict. This may result from the belligerent and uncompromising posture that a Palestinian state might adopt toward Israel and even Jordan. The increased Soviet presence in the Middle East stemming from the avowed Marxist orientation of some factions of the PLO might also precipitate conflict. Israel fears that an independent Palestinian state will strive to replace rather than peacefully coexist with Israel, and official PLO pronouncements reinforce this fear.[15] If both propositions prove correct, the prospect for a peaceful solution will be virtually eliminated. An exploration of ways to bridge the two hypotheses is therefore essential.

Those committed to the first hypothesis seek models of governance that, despite falling short of granting independent statehood, may be acceptable to the Palestinians and their leadership.[16] This article is concerned with outlining an alternative view that a Palestinian state can be established through means that reduce the real and apparent dangers to a level acceptable even to Israel. The theory by which the second hypothesis may become acceptable to the parties is grounded in the realization that the classic concept of the sovereign independent state is obsolete.

A critical reason for the apparent incompatibility of the current Israeli and Palestinian approaches is that the conceptual framework underlying the present negotiations is based on traditional notions of statehood, nationalism and sovereignty. Couched in these terms, proposed solutions that suggest the simple coexistence of the State of Israel[17] with a Palestinian state have drawn persistent resistance from successive Israeli governments. But it is not the Israeli Government alone that rejects the solution; the main organized political organs of the Palestinians[18] share this opposition, as do broad sections of both Israeli and Palestinian society.[19] This widespread and deeply felt resistance derives from a variety of political, social and psycho ideological factors that permeate the two societies. Mutual acknowledgement by Israel and a Palestinian state of each other's right to exist appears to threaten vital interests and, at a deeper level, to threaten the very foundation of their relatively young national movements. As long as mutual nonacceptance persists, little prospect of enduring peace exists.

It has been suggested that the autonomy plan may serve as an intermediate phase to draw the parties closer together. But the Israeli plan for autonomy explicitly excludes eventual statehood; the policy of encouraging settlement in Gaza and the West Bank is the practical manifestation of this exclusion. Thus, even if the Israeli autonomy plan, as presently defined, is accepted, it might lead to a deterioration in negotiations.[20] Palestinian resistance would be likely to increase, and rejection of the plan by the Arab nations will follow. These signs might, in turn, confirm to many in Israel the danger of moving towards accepting Palestinian self-determination and statehood. Their reaction — for example, increased settlement of the West Bank — may silence the few Palestinian voices disposed to recognize Israel. Thus, the mutual nonacceptance gap would widen even further.

Conditions under which mutual recognition may become acceptable to both parties must be suggested to break this vicious cycle. A framework that expresses the legitimate desires of both parties for statehood, while eliminating the factors that have caused both parties to regard their claims to statehood as necessarily exclusive, should be proposed. Further, the proposal is insufficient if it merely outlines a final acceptable settlement; it must also suggest ways to implement and safeguard the plan. This is particularly important for Israel, because establishing a Palestinian state represents an irreversible political development.

This article considers a number of plans that over the years have suggested federal or confederal proposals as a solution to the problem of division.[21] The traditional weaknesses of these solutions are well known. Federalism, or at least the federal state,[22] seems to leave too little space for the continued existence of "unique" peoples exercising national self-determination and is thus inappropriate for the Middle East, where a strong emphasis on national identity is a cardinal political and societal desideratum. Confederal arrangements suffer from the precariousness of their political structures, the limitations of their social impact and the fragility of their very existence.[23] Against this background, the employment of a supranational model might be profitable, because it represents a combination of federal and confederal elements that in some senses mitigate the weaknesses of the two systems when taken alone. Supranational structures leave independent states largely intact in the decision-making process of the transnational organs whereas, in the operation of the policies adopted by these organs, they resemble full-fledged federal states. Further, in the idea of a supranational common market there is room for arrangements which Part III of this Article illustrates, and which may help overcome some of the fears that the prospect of partition now evokes. Finally, the very nature of the arrangement makes it a particularly promising framework for a situation as complex as that in the Middle East.[24] In the balance between the sovereign member states and the supranational institutions, the arrangement affords a degree of fluidity that preserves the option to make certain changes the structure of the basic arrangement without threatening the entire entity. Such a supranational framework would also serve as an organizational basis other states in the region could join; it might eventually evolve into a powerful vehicle for regional socioeconomic development.

To the extent this article proposes a future Middle East political order, its purpose is not to suggest a blueprint for peace, but to suggest some principles for a possible peaceful solution to current hostilities. This article concentrates more on the sociopolitical and constitutional aspects of a new regime; the economic aspects will be merely touched upon, because a fuller treatment is not within the scope of this work.

To appreciate how a common market framework might be of significance in closing the nonacceptance gap, it is necessary to understand the motives for the mutual rejection of the framework by Israel and the Palestinians. It is also necessary to appreciate features of the European experience. This article addresses both these issues, and then, with due attention to the hazard of transplanting institutions to widely differing situations, suggests how certain elements of the European model may be adapted to fashion a solution for the Israeli-Palestinian conflict.

B. Mutual Nonacceptance: The Israeli Dilemma

On its face, a solution calling for Israel's return of the West Bank and Gaza, land from which a Palestinian state would be created, in exchange for recognition[25] and security guarantees, seems eminently sensible. This is the type of solution that is now being advocated or suggested by friends of both parties to the conflict. In pressing for this solution, the international community may be concerned more with ensuring the long-term supply of oil than with protecting the survival of Israel or vindicating the rights of the Palestinians. Whatever the motive, the pressures on Israel to accept this framework are likely to increase, and the international support it now receives is likely to diminish as it continues to reject the possibility of Palestinian statehood. The current catastrophic state of Israel's economy suggests a weak position from which to continue resisting such pressure.[26] Yet, to date, despite international and limited internal pressure, and despite the economic considerations favoring peaceful settlement,[27] the present government and opposition — following in the footsteps of former governments—continue to resist the very idea of a Palestinian state. In the past, many observers thought that this resistance front was a tactical rejection permitting Israel to show as strong a hand as possible at the negotiating table. But recent events tend to disprove this theory.[28] The continuing policy of establishing settlements in Gaza and the West Bank indicates that the rejection of a Palestinian state has actually become an article of faith for Israel.

The reasons for rejecting Palestinian independence fall into two categories: (1) the Israeli authorities and most Israeli Jews fear that the establishment of a new Palestinian state — even one that would formally recognize and accept Israel — would threaten the very existence of the State of Israel; and (2) many Israelis do not wish to make what they consider definite sacrifices by yielding the West Bank and Gaza.

1. The Security Problem. The security issue is undoubtedly the most serious and potent problem facing the Israelis. The Jewish citizenry of modern Israel live in the shadow of the Holocaust, in the wake of a long history of persecution and in a country whose brief independent history has seen considerable warfare and strife. The subjective national concern for security must be accepted as an objective factor in any Middle East peace plan. Solutions that seem eminently sensible to outsiders may be received with skepticism or even cynicism by a people that has been mortally threatened three times in its short, modern history and endlessly in its long diaspora.

Thus, security safeguards proposed to Israel must not only be objectively suited to govern the transition from belligerency to peace, but must also take account of subjective Israeli concerns and sensibilities. Regarding the West Bank — the principal territory to be discussed[29] — the Israeli security argument is as simple as it is powerful. Israeli withdrawal and the establishment of an independent Palestine are, it is argued, simply inconsistent with vital Israeli security needs. Is Israel to exchange a strategic territory bordering and enclosing its main center of population and industry, its soft underbelly, for a paper peace treaty? Israel feels it cannot allow the establishment in that zone of an independent Palestinian state when the official policy objective of the largest Palestinian organization is the dismantling of the State of Israel[30] and when that organization is currently engaged in a vicious terror campaign against it.

The PLO has agreed to take over any part of Palestine that becomes liberated from the Israelis.[31] They insist, for the moment, that a mini–Palestine would be regarded as a mere step towards eventual liberation of Palestine in its entirety.[32] Israel's concern is that PLO recognition of Israel might represent a mere tactical ploy rather than a strategic change of objectives. Merely recognizing the State of Israel would not satisfy the skeptics who believe an independent Palestinian state would subsequently disregard such recognition. Israel would then be in an untenable security position.

Given that Israelis are currently reluctant to yield the West Bank to a people it perceives as set on destroying the State of Israel, it has become clear that the status quo is not itself devoid of security risks. The continuous terror campaign in Israel or in the West Bank and Gaza provides sufficient evidence of this fact. Some form of accommodation would appear profitable, but the principles that may lead to such an accommodation seem to produce a subsequent vicious cycle.[33]

Let us isolate the security problem from all other factors that inhibit Israeli acceptance of a Palestinian state. Israeli rejection is linked to their notion of peace. If "real peace"[34] could be ensured, there would be little objection from the strict security point of view to giving up the occupied territories and even to establishing a Palestinian state. In any event, the risk would be outweighed by the economic and social advantages that peace would yield. Because the Israelis perceive "real peace" as difficult to guarantee, and in fact unlikely, they would demand extremely tight security guarantees prior to relinquishing rule over the territories. Given its mistrust of the international community, Israel would demand a role in implementing these guarantees. The West Bank's proximity to central Israel dictates, as part of these measures, the limited presence of Israeli troops and personnel on the West Bank and the denial of any defense and military capability to any Palestinian political entity. Such a security measure is, however, inconsistent with classical notions of independence.

Thus, the means that Israel would choose to secure peace are locked in irreconcilable conflict with the attributes of an independent Palestinian state. By infringing symbolically and materially on the independence of the other party, relations between Israel and the Palestinian quasi-state would deteriorate and the prospect of a durable settlement would become illusory.[35] To the policymaker, the problem lies in devising a system of security guarantees within the geopolitical limitations of the West Bank[36] that will be effective, but will not deteriorate and become a destabilizing factor. In other words, the objective is to break the cycle created by the wish for "real peace" and the need for special security guarantees[37] that, as presently conceived, prevents the realization of peace.

2. The Historical Attachment. Security considerations alone do not shape Israel's rigid position regarding the West Bank. Indeed, in many instances, the security rationale serves to veil the much deeper feelings and aspirations that bind part of Israeli society to the occupied territories. This attachment—less objective in nature—is probably even less acceptable to outside observers than the acute security sensitivity described above. Nonetheless, it is important to trace the roots and gain an understanding of the diverse Israeli societal attitudes toward the West Bank. These attitudes determine crucial social and political factors, which in turn explain some of the steps taken by the present government and impose certain constraints on any proposed solutions. Jewish-Israeli attitudes regarding the issue of attachment differ dramatically. At one end of the spectrum stand the small and largely noninfluential anti–Zionist groups who hold a socialist-secular point of view and express little or no sentimental attachment to the land of Israel or to the Zionist State of Israel. Consequently, they claim no exclusive or historically based right to the West Bank.[38] At the other end of the spectrum stand sections of Israeli society represented by, for instance, the influential Bloc of the Faithful (Gush-Emunim) and its political arm, the Tehiya Party, which command significant political power and popular influence despite a relatively small membership.[39] Their ideological position is rooted in both Jewish and Zionist fundamentalism and historical nationalism. To them, the West Bank—Judea and Samaria—represents an inalienable part of Israel's ancestral land: Eretz-Yisrael. Thus, they not only support a right to occupation, but feel a positive duty to settle this land.[40] Although some notable Zionists regard their policies of militant settlement in the West Bank as a betrayal of traditional "non-revisionist" Zionism,[41] they are regarded by others—and this accounts for some of their support—as resembling the ideals of the early prestate pioneers.

In contrast to the radicalism of the Bloc of the Faithful are the more traditional Zionists of the center and center-left, who superficially support attachment and, in some cases, claim a right to the West Bank, and actually favor far-reaching territorial compromise supported by sufficient security safeguards. This faction is motivated by a variety of forces, including a genuine concern for the rights of the Arabs and the desire to preserve the democratic and humanistic fabric of Israeli society.[42] Many of these moderate Zionists agree that there is a Jewish right to the West Bank but feel that neither justice nor the interests of Israel would be served if such right were exercised. Nevertheless, few members of this group would favor the establishment of an independent Palestinian state. While the attitudes of the extremists and many moderates regarding the attachment issue are relatively easy to conceptualize, for many Israelis who occupy the middle ground—possibly the largest group—the issues of historical attachment and security lie in a state of complete confusion. Political Zionism has always had a strong historical current, a major aspect of which is the link to the land of Israel.[43] This theme has united Zionists of different shades and has bridged the gap between secular and religious Zionists. To many people whose Jewish religious convictions have dissipated,[44] the link to the land and to the early Jewish history that took place on the land has become the main internal reference point for national Jewish identity. The significance of the Land of Israel in Jewish and Zionist lore has transcended its religious importance[45] so that those who no longer practice traditional Judaism still feel a strong attachment to Jerusalem and Zion.

Historical Zionism also advances a moral justification for establishing a modern State of Israel at the expense of displacing part of the indigenous population. Present Israeli society feels a strong geographical and historical link to the land, and many aspects of Israeli life are designed to reinforce this attachment. Thus, it is natural that the prospect of withdrawing from the West Bank should be traumatic for the majority of Israelis. On the ideological level, it is claimed that the division between the West Bank and the rest of Israel is artificial, from both a historical and geographical point of view. Besides the genuine attachment to such historical West Bank sites as Judea and Samaria, years of conflict have conditioned many Israelis to believe that giving these lands back to the Palestinian enemy would eventually result in a denial of access to these territories.[46]

On a more profound level, territorial compromise and recognition of a Palestinian right to self-determination arguably threaten some of the moral foundations of historical Zionism. Fundamental Zionists argue that *if* the right to Hebron is conceded, the right to Jaffa would be correspondingly undermined,[47] as both are part of the same ancestral land.

Further, if the Palestinian people are recognized as comprising a nation of separate and distinct identities, it is feared that this will give them at least equal national rights to the territory of the State of Israel. The powerful security arguments discussed in the previous section of this article are buttressed by an attachment to the territories that is determined by equally strong and complex historical and psycho ideological factors.

3. Arguments for Withdrawal. Despite the numerous arguments supporting continued Israeli presence and rule, there are some factors that even from an Israeli-Zionist perspective mandate withdrawal from the West Bank. This article has already rioted the argument linked to the notion of peace.[48] Continued Israeli rule over an alien population is arguably inconsistent with long-term peace. The autonomy plan demonstrates that even the present Israeli government accepts this fact. It has already been argued that autonomy without more will not alter the current situation. Thus, to the extent that peace is an objective of Israeli policy, eventual withdrawal becomes imperative. Moderate Israelis, despite their feelings concerning historical attachment, would be willing to make territorial sacrifices if real peace could be attained and the security of the country could be guaranteed.[49] Moreover, continued rule over the Palestinians denying them the right to self-governance would contravene the very democratic values fundamental to Israeli society and Zionism itself. Military occupation, however benign, would lead to an embarrassing compromise of fundamental human rights.[50] Full annexation, coupled with a grant of complete political rights might satisfy the exigencies of democracy but would weaken the Jewish nature of the Zionist State. One can already see an unhealthy socioeconomic stratification of Arab manual workers in the occupied territories from the Israeli employer class. In short, continued rule in any form would endanger basic Zionist values.[51]

Acute as these dangers may be, no ready solution is available, for evacuation of the territories, as noted above,[52] creates an unacceptable security risk. The security rationale, as evidenced so often in history, provides an escape from the moral dilemma. For those who consider attachment to the land a supreme value, this rationale provides a happy way out; to others it is a painful but necessary choice. The large numbers of Israelis in the middle find it a convenient way to eschew a difficult moral choice.

4. Conclusions. The internal dilemma of Israel consists of a series of interlocking conflicts:

(1) The desire for real peace conflicts with the skepticism, generated by years of hostility and by numerous official Palestinian declarations, that peace can ever be realized; and

(2) The strong historical and ideological attachment to the Land of

Israel (Eretz-Yisrael) including the West Bank (Judea and Samaria) which has been reinforced by 15 years of occupation conflicts with the moral problems that result from ruling the people (Palestinians) who inhabit that land.

Externally, these conflicts manifest themselves as follows:

(1) Insistence on continued, indefinite Israeli presence in all or part of the territories as the only effective guarantee for Israeli security;

(2) The concomitant, absolute rejection of Palestinian independence based on the view that this would be inconsistent with the objective of peace and security;

(3) The desire to preserve access to Judea and Samaria in a manner that would be impossible under a traditional international relationship; and

(4) A willingness to grant the Palestinians a measure of independence short of statehood.

This article considers Palestinian statehood to be a necessary condition for peace. The current Israeli position, deriving from its fundamental security and ideological concerns, would appear to offer little in the way of a solution. Yet the above analysis does suggest that if Palestinian statehood could be made consistent with Israel's security needs and if a degree of territorial access higher than that pertaining to traditional internation and interstate relations could be guaranteed, the ideological conflict might be diffused, and the current position might change. Israel would stand to gain the best of all worlds: a long-desired peace coupled with necessary security guarantees, and a measure of access to the disputed territories without the need to rule over and deny national rights to the Palestinian population.

C. Mutual Nonacceptance. The Palestinian Dilemma[53]

1. Historicity. United Nations Security Council Resolution 242 of November 22, 1967, alluded to the Palestinians by referring to the "refugee problem."[54] Whatever the situation in 1967, there is little doubt today about the national identity of those refugees; the political force behind their main institutionalized organ, the PLO, is well known. Any plan for peace in the Middle East will have to accommodate the national aspirations of the Palestinians. Principal among these aspirations is the desire for political self-determination and its expression in statehood. It is not entirely surprising that a measure of parallelism and symmetry runs throughout the official positions of both the PLO and Israel. The current official Palestinian view does not recognize the State of Israel as the national home of the Jewish People.[55] The Palestinian Covenant calls for the liberation of all Palestine, the displacement of certain categories of Jewish citizens, and the establishment of a unified state in which those Jews who will be allowed to remain can enjoy equal rights.[56] In this vision, based on a simplistic and unempirical notion of Jewishness,[57] there can be no place for Jewish nationalism or expression through statehood in Palestine. The Palestinian position not only seeks to deny the Jews as a nation the very right to self-determination, but also advocates a proposal that is pragmatically unable to command confidence and which suffers from certain logical defects. The Covenant proposes a unified, progressive, democratic and nonsectarian Palestine in which Christian, Moslem and Jew will worship, work, live peacefully and enjoy equal rights.[58] The first problem with this proposal arises in attempting to square the denial of national self-determination to the Jews in Israel with the notion of a democratic state. The current Palestinian position suffers from a conflict between reliance on their own sense of unique self-identity and a denial of the same to the Jewish-Israeli population. The traditional Palestinian claim that Jewishness may have no unique national expression is just as untenable as similar Israeli claims regarding Palestinianism.[59]

Many Palestinians have for some reason, regarded the advent of Zionism and its geopolitical expression in the State of Israel as nothing more than a colonial adventure.[60] This view, when properly utilized, serves a powerful national unifying and motivating role in their liberation struggle. But one must realize that three decades in exile and the changing demographic nature of the conflict may have demonstrated to the Palestinians the relativity of historical claims to exclusive title over ancestral land.[61] Paradoxically, the Palestinians' own plight may become the catalyst for tolerating, if not accepting, the moral force of political-existential Zionism.[62] Purely pragmatic considerations may also lead to a shift in political and moral evaluations. While accepting Israel simply because it is a fait accompli could well be regarded as moral capitulation; indefinite rejection of Israel may condemn the Palestinians to a lengthy existence of suffering and sacrifice. This destiny itself would become morally questionable if a workable solution — Palestinian statehood alongside Israel — were to exist.

Although it is submitted that Palestinian statehood could in the foreseeable future come about only if the Palestinians openly and unequivocally accept the State of Israel, they find it difficult, even after their plight in Lebanon, openly to modify their position. The reasons for this rejection resemble an equivalent Israeli rationale. The Palestinians feel a strong attachment to the land of Palestine; it is a cornerstone of Palestinian national ideology. Returning home to regain the land taken from them represents a fundamental principle of Palestinian nationalism. Perhaps more than anything else, the "Catastrophe" of exile has forged this Palestinian nationalism. This has become the primary motivating instrument in the Palestinians' continuous struggle and a yardstick of the dedication and commitment of the Palestinian leadership to the Palestinian ideal. Politically, it restricts the space in which a moderate leadership may show signs of flexibility. But the attachment to the land of Palestine and concentration on the events that led to exile are not derived solely from the psychology of Palestinian nationalism. They are also, in symmetry with Zionism, linked to its ideological core. Palestinian nationalism, like other Arab national movements, is characterized by a strong measure of dualism; a dualism of Arab universalism and Palestinian particularism.[63] In their language, culture and history, the Palestinians in part belong to the Arab nation at large. Their particularism was dramatically reinforced and found a major expression through the politics of exile and the territoriality of Palestine. The Palestinians' desire to emphasize their unique identity within the Arab world is achieved by emphasizing their unique recent history and their territorial attachment. Interestingly, the attachment is becoming increasingly historical because to the majority of Palestinians, Palestine is a historic motherland rather than a real one. This historicity is demonstrated by the reference in the Palestinian Covenant to a "right of return."[64] Even if attachment loses a sense of immediacy and becomes, like Jewish attachment, more historical in nature, its immense force is not reduced. Recognition of Israel's 1949 (Armistice) boundaries would spell a final concession of treasured, exclusive rights to those territories. It would signal final acceptance of their historical displacement. The difficulties of Palestinian acceptance of Israel are thus no less formidable than those confronting Zionism.[65]

2. Practical Considerations. A different problem inhibiting recognition of Israel's 1949 boundaries concerns the pragmatic aspects of a putative Palestinian state. Accepting Israel would necessarily mean that a Palestinian state would be limited in size and resources. The economic viability of such a reduced state must be guaranteed to make the proposition acceptable. Although various studies[66] suggest that a state on the West Bank and Gaza could be economically viable, it would undoubtedly face serious difficulties, at least in its first years. These initial gloomy prospects are yet another reason explaining the lack of enthusiasm to accept a solution based on partition. One solution would be to merge the new Palestinian state with the Kingdom of Jordan. It is doubtful that the Hashemite House would voluntarily give up its control in any such union. King Hussein's reaction to Palestinian desires in the 1960s is probably too painful and recent to convince Palestinians otherwise. It is unlikely that the Palestinians would agree to anything more than some form of confederal link with Jordan. A plan that offers the prospect of independence within the occupied territories and provides a framework for establishing economic viability would be a minimum prerequisite to Palestinian acceptance of Israel. The prospect of a viable and prosperous economy may well attract the support of Palestinian individuals despite official PLO censure.[67] Such a reaction could pressure the leadership to change its policy. Structuring economic links with Israel might be another means to overcome the economic problems facing the future Palestinian state, but the political problems of this solution appear, at first sight, to be even greater than these resulting from a link with Jordan.[68]

3. Conclusions. Recognizing Israel would be painful to a Palestinian leadership that has sought the country's elimination for so long. In addition to the political and ideological problem is the economic unattractiveness of partition that would inevitably follow. At the same time, it will become increasingly difficult to continue rejecting Israel if statehood in the occupied territories becomes available. If such an offer were coupled with a program of economic development directed at ensuring a measure of prosperity, resistance would become even more difficult. The Palestinians' conflicting interests are clearly as potent as those of Israel.

D. General and Regional Programs

The prospect of a Palestinian state's economic cooperation with Israel gives rise to further problems of a more general nature. A Palestinian national movement characterized by a strong Third World concept of nationalism and sovereignty would be likely to regard newly acquired independence with extreme suspicion. The prospect of economic or any other type of cooperation with their previous oppressors is likely to create fears of neocolonial subjugation; the unequal level of economic development exacerbates this problem. Furthermore before accepting the creation of a Palestinian state, Israel will insist on a wide range of security guarantees inconsistent with Palestinian independence. One way to persuade Israel to relax its insistence on security guarantees would be to promote a tangible process of normalization manifested by economic, technological and scientific ties. Thus, a major problem that would exist is the reconciliation of the new Palestinian state's fear of Israeli neocolonialism with Israel's need for Security guarantees.

A second general problem concerns the political architecture of the region as a whole. Although this article focuses principally on the requisite conditions for Israeli and Palestinian mutual acceptance, a framework that included the cooperation of all parties to the Arab-Israeli conflict would be even more viable. It is not necessary that all Arab States give their immediate blessing to whatever solution is adopted but the opportunity for them to express their approval should remain open.[69] In fact, a framework that promises distinct tangible benefits to other states, giving them an incentive to participate in the process, would be quite advantageous.

E. Israel Palestine and the West Bank: The Legal Dimension

The above analysis of political interests and social and ideological motivations discloses a curious symmetry of positions which in turn produces a seemingly unbridgeable chasm. If the interests of both parties are to be respected in a situation of mutually exclusive claims, the only possible solution is some form of compromise between these claims. The apparently tragic character of the conflict is rooted in the fact that this midway position — the creation and the continued existence, side by side, of a Palestinian state and Israel — seems, not without reason, unacceptable and unfeasible to both parties.

Not surprisingly, the uncompromising attitude of both parties is reflected in the legal arguments each employs to support its respective positions. This article's analysis of these legal positions follows the subjective and reductionist method used earlier in examining the sociopolitical issues. This article first outlines the subjective Israeli and Palestinian legal positions and then highlights their respective shortcomings. From this analysis, the objective international law position should emerge which accords with partition, mutual self-determination and statehood, and peaceful coexistence. It is at this point that the political and legal analyses will fuse. For, if indeed the requirement of objective, normative and legal analyses is mutual recognition and partition, the practical political problems of such a normative requirement to which public international law has no reply will remain. The scene will be set to examine the possible contribution of supranational structures.

1. Legal Issues: An Israeli View. Israel's restrictive view of autonomy and objection to the establishment of a Palestinian state in any form derive from the political and ideological reasons discussed above. The sovereignty issue serves as the Israeli legal basis for justifying a policy that goes beyond the strict requirements of belligerent occupation and for a rejection of adversary territorial claims. If Israel could establish a valid title to the West Bank, any legal obligation to evacuate the area would be greatly diluted. The Palestinian legal claim to self-determination, riddled as it is with complexities, would be considerably weakened should sovereignty over the West Bank actually vest in Israel. Although Israel has not officially annexed the West Bank, and although in certain nonbinding texts it is referred to as an "administered territory," Israel has not conceded sovereignty over the West Bank.[70] The government-sponsored settlement policy, which disregards the customary and conventional international law of belligerent occupation,[71] demonstrates that Israel considers its status above that of a belligerent occupant.[72] Professor Blum in an influential article provides the theoretical foundation for this position.[73] Blum proceeds from the premise that when a mandatory regime is terminated, sovereignty does not merely disappear.[74] Thus, when the British withdrew their forces from the Mandate of Palestine, the territory, Blum argues, did not become *res nullius* subject to the rules of international law governing the territorial acquisition of *res nullius*.[75] It follows that the Jordanian acquisition of the West Bank in 1948 was contrary to article 2(4) of the United Nations Charter and was therefore incapable of vesting title to the area in the Kingdom of Jordan. Professor Blum further submits that the illegal Jordanian occupation was not cured by the 1949 Armistice Agreements because they contain specific "no prejudice" clauses.[76] Because Jordan's annexation of the West Bank must therefore be regarded as void under international law, the rights of a legitimate sovereign could not inure to Jordan.[77] Blum concludes his argument by stating that after 1967

> [T]he legal standing of Israel ... became that of a State which is lawfully in control of territory in respect of which no other State [has] a better title ... [Since in the present view no State can make out a legal claim that is equal to that of Israel, this relative superiority of Israel may be sufficient under international law to make Israel's possession of Judea and Samaria virtually indistinguishable from an absolute title, to be valid *erga omes*.[78]]

One major weakness of Blum's argument—of which Gerson is the major advocate[79]—lies in his curt dismissal of the possibility that sovereignty may vest in the *inhabitants* of the territory in question.[80] Blum cites Judge McNair's separate opinion in the *International Status of South West Africa* case in support of his position.[81] Actually, McNair's opinion, which in any event is only of persuasive value, establishes the principle of trusteeship in favor of the inhabitants.[82] Under this view, when the Mandate ceases to exist, the Mandatory power relinquishes its role as trustee; but the problem of determining in whom sovereignty vests still remains. Two scenarios could explain why sovereignty correctly vested in Jordan: Jordan continued as trustee after the British departed,[83] or the inhabitants acquiesced to annexation, thus fusing their sovereignty with that of Jordan.[84]

Israel would he "trustee occupant"[85] under the former view, or a belligerent occupant in the latter view, and sovereign title simply would not vest.[86] Even under the first view, which is somewhat novel in international law, one could not deduce an absolute Israeli title valid *erga omnes.*

Other difficulties exist with Blum's view, however. Much reliance is placed on the fact that only two states, Pakistan and the United Kingdom, overtly recognized the "annexation" of the West Bank by Jordan. This, however, disregards de facto recognition by the international community in the periods both before and after the 1967 occupation.[87] If there were reservations regarding Jordanian title, these concerned her relationship to the indigenous population and their eventual rights to independence.[88] The virtual unanimity among UN members in condemning the settlement policy of Israel endorses this view of the attitude of the international community.[89] Thus, to the extent that international recognition may be considered probative or even constitutive in relation to the legal obscurity surrounding the status of the West Bank, the evidence points towards recognition of Jordanian sovereignty subject to the rights of the local inhabitants.

In similar fashion, Blum strongly rejects the possible claim that Israel's own *silence* and lack of protest of the Jordanian annexation can preclude Israel from claiming sovereignty.[90] There can be no question that silence cannot, without more, be interpreted as consent. But Israel's international policy regarding peace with its neighbors in the period 1948–1967, the main plank of which was a constant call for full-fledged peace and mutual recognition of neighbors on the basis of slightly modified 1949 frontiers, can hardly be called silence.[91] Israel's policy in those years is not surprising. First, the sincerity at that time of Israel's desire for peace cannot be seriously questioned. Second, from the legal point of view, a similar question mark could be placed over her permanent title to territorial acquisitions made before the final armistice. In particular, West Jerusalem was problematic because Israeli rule over the city did not receive widespread formal recognition at the time.

The significance of the 1949 Armistice Agreements is also less clear than Blum seems to suggest. To be sure, article 11(2) of the Jordanian-Israeli General Armistice Agreement of April 3, 1949,[92] is a general "no prejudice" clause. But in the absence of consensus among the parties in regard to territorial modifications, the actual demarcation coupled with the strong proscription against the use of force contained in the Agreements arguably rendered them constitutive of an international frontier.[93] The frontiers may have acquired a validity that would have become independent of the Agreement as a whole.

Finally, there remains the matter of Security Council Resolution 242, which has been accepted as binding by all states party to the conflict. The reference in the Resolution to territories from which Israel must withdraw rather than to "the" territories was intentional — to allow security-motivated changes. But to suggest, as the present Israeli Government has, that it does not apply to the entire West Bank over which Israel has sovereignty and hence is not a belligerent occupant is, in the language of Feinberg, a thesis "without a firm legal foundation ... unconvincing, not helpful to peace and one that does not add honor to Israel."[94] Indeed, no acceptable legal construction could deny application of the Resolution to the West Bank and Gaza.

2. Legal Issues: A Palestinian View. Despite the setback suffered in the Lebanese war, the PLO has refused to give an unequivocal statement recognizing the legitimacy of Israel's existence. The writings of Henry Cattan, a noted jurist, have supplied the Palestinians with the theoretical legal foundation for this refusal.[95] Although Cattan attempts to justify nonrecognition and nonacceptance of Israel on grounds of both international law and principles of justice, he shows a certain preference for the latter. The reasons he provides for proffering legal arguments based on principles of justice are the following:

> The concept of justice is universal and, unlike international law, is less subject to divergences of opinion or interpretation. Moreover, the concept of justice suffers no lacunae and recourse can be made to it to resolve any given situation, whereas international law, being largely based on practice and precedents, does not necessarily cover all situations.[96]

Although one may doubt the validity or utility of this distinction,[97] Cattan is profoundly correct in suggesting that "justice must be a condition of any solution of the Arab-Israeli conflict ... [because] without justice no settlement could endure."[98] This statement would not be correct if based simply on moral conviction; history has repeatedly demonstrated the durability of unjust solutions founded on mere political expediency.[99] It does, however, seem correct because it reflects a realistic assessment of the high measure of Palestinian and Israeli national consciousness, political organization and the respective power to undermine solutions regarded by the parties as patently unjust. By contrast, a solution that appears just has a good chance of gaining popular support, perhaps in the face of leadership opposition, while a solution that clearly appears unjust cannot hope to gain such legitimacy. This article takes the position that objective justice is not necessarily a condition to solving the Arab-Israeli conflict, although there is some measure of it evident in the positions of both parties.[100] Subjective justice, on the other hand, is a precondition to a lasting solution. The trouble with Cattan's notion of a just solution is that it hardly induces durability. Cattan argues that "justice requires [inter alia] the dismantling of the Zionist racist political structure set up in Palestine."[101] In other words, Cattan calls for the elimination of the State of Israel. Cattan's approach and conclusion are off the mark, for they result from trying to convince theoreticians, politicians and others of the evils of Zionism. The better posture is to understand that both parties are motivated by a strong belief in the justice of their respective causes and that a prerequisite to attaining a durable solution is respect for those conceptions of justice.

Cattan's just solution may be questioned on another ground. He advocates *restitutio in integrum* as a means of redressing the alleged injustices committed against the Palestinians, a principle that also underlies the Palestinian Covenant.[102] This approach, while suited to certain types of private law transactions, is inappropriate and dangerous in an international context. First, it fails to take account of temporal factors that affect the dynamics of the conflict. *Restitutio in integrum* would create a renewed refugee problem, because more than half the Israeli Jewish population has known no home other than Israel. Uprooting them in an attempt to turn back the clock would surely evoke moral outrage as intense as that felt by supporters of the Palestinians. Second, *restitutio in integrum*, while formally redressing past wrongs, fails to consider the parties' future interests. There is little value in a solution that will literally foment the next dispute. If a solution is to resolve a dispute as well as redress a wrong, a variety of restitutionary measures must be explored.[103] The true key to solving this brutal conflict lies in some innovative compromisary or pluralistic solution.

Cattan has examined all major junctures in the evolving Arab-Israeli conflict. The Balfour Declaration, the Mandate, the United Nations Partition Resolution and the subsequent establishment of the state of Israel as well as Israeli actions vis-à-vis her neighbors after independence[104] are all condemned as being illegal. It will serve no purpose to examine these arguments comprehensively and systematically; this has been done in a convincing legal challenge by Nathan Feinberg.[105] This article focuses instead on one episode, the Balfour Declaration and its material incorporation in the League of Nations Mandate, not only because in this episode both legal and moral claims come sharply into focus, but also because Cattan himself regards the purportedly illegal mandate to constitute the basis of the Arab-Israeli conflict.[106] Moreover, Cattan's legal view of the Mandate is shared by a substantial number of Arab jurists.[107]

Concerning the Balfour Declaration itself, Cattan challenges Britain's ability to give away something it did not own.[108] Feinberg considers this a moot point, commenting that the British promise was not intended to create an *erga omnes* obligation. Legal force was given to the Declaration only in the terms of the League of Nations Mandate. The legality of this incorporation is challenged by Cattan as well.[109] Cattan offers three principal grounds for the Mandate's invalidity. First, he states that inclusion of the Balfour Declaration in the Mandate violated Palestine inhabitants' right to "sovereignty ... and their natural rights of independence and self-determination."[110] Second, he argues that the Mandate was beyond the scope of article 22 of the League of Nations Covenant. By providing a national home for another people it contradicted the principle embodied in article 22 that "the well-being and development of such [indigenous] peoples [should] form a sacred trust of civilization and that securities for the performance of this trust should be embodied in this Covenant."[111] Cattan further claims that, in granting the Mandatory power legislative jurisdiction, the Council went beyond the League intention that the Mandate, in the case of ex–Turkish territories, should be limited to an administrative function. Finally, Cattan argues that granting the Mandate to Britain was contrary to the wishes of the inhabitants, which were to be "a principal consideration in the selection of the Mandatory."[112] Cattan also argues that by changing the demographic nature of Palestine through the acceptance of Jewish immigrants the Mandate's implementation violated its terms.[113]

Responses to the alleged illegality of the Mandatory regime can be made at several levels. On strict legal and textual grounds it has been pointed out that article 22 gave the "Council of the League the ultimate power of determining the texts of the Mandates.[114] Thus, their decisions would have original constitutive power. Further, the reference to ex–Turkish territories is not absolute; article 22(4) refers to "certain" territories, and Palestine is not specifically included. Feinberg rightly recalls the decision of the International Court of Justice (ICJ) in 1950 in the South West Africa[115] case, which considered Mandatory regimes and held that the interests of humanity constituted a part of the general purpose of the applicable Mandate. The establishment of a national home for the Jewish people could fall within that broad purpose. Article 22 thus seems to have given more scope to the League Council than Cattan maintains. It is extremely doubtful that the ICJ could have declared the matter illegal.[116] It is also questionable whether the Mandate's incorporation of the Balfour Declaration conflicted with the protection and development of the Arab people in the region. Significantly, Cattan states that the "natural rights" of independence and self-determination[117] were violated by the Mandate's provisions for the establishment of a Palestinian home for the Jewish People. While modern positive international law might permit a sufficiently precise definition of the rights of a home to a people in a land in which another people already lived, when this issue arose, the right to self-determination was not incorporated into positive international law. Incorporation of the Declaration into the Mandate, therefore, could not have violated the legal norms operative at that time. Cattan thus resorts to the elusive concept of "natural rights." He ignores, however, the possibility that the Jewish people may also have had "natural rights." To talk of the Mandate as impairing or destroying the rights of the "original" inhabitants is misleading.[118] Not only does such an argument fail to define the concept and identity of "original inhabitants," but it also neglects the *fact* that, until the Mandate, Turkey, and not the inhabitants, had sovereignty over Palestine.

Cattan's prescription for redress parallels that of the hard-line Palestinians: "[J]ustice requires the dismantling of the Zionist racist political structures Set up in Palestine... ." The issues surrounding the Mandate constitute, according to Cattan, the basis of the conflict. On strict legal grounds, Cattan's arguments are wanting. But on moral grounds as well can it be said that the establishment of a national home for the Jews in Israel—and the concomitant incorporation of the obligation in the Mandate—constituted an injustice? In the implementation stage, it is true that Palestinian Arabs have suffered substantially. Under current positive international law, their right to self-determination, though problematic, is probably valid.[119] It is not clear, however, that the idea of granting Jews rights in Israel is unjust. If two national homes could exist in Palestine (sovereignty over which, as noted above, was vested in Turkey), the acceptance of the idea by the Council of the League cannot on its own be regarded as an injustice. The Mandatory regime and the incorporation of Jewish rights were not conclusively illegal or unjust. The same can be said of Cattan's other arguments regarding the Partition Resolution and the legality of the actual State of Israel.[120]

F. Mutual Nonacceptance: Need for a New Approach

The arguments of Cattan and Blum and the official positions they reflect are symmetrical not only in their counter affirmations and negations, but also in their respective failures to consider some of the processes of legal change in the international arena. As Quincy Wright affirms, "All systems of law provide means ... by which situations which originated in illegality become moot or acquire a legal status. The principle *jus ex injuria non orilur* ... must be balanced by the principle *ex factis jus oritur* ... especially in the society of nations which is often unable to rectify wrongs and is faced by a general interest that disputes be terminated.[121]

An analysis of public international law shows that a total denial of the legal legitimacy of Israel is juridicially unfounded and morally questionable. On the other hand, Israeli claims to sovereignty over the West Bank, which would effectively deny Palestinian statehood, are equally open to challenge. This affirmation is confirmed not only by a per se analysis of these specific issues but also by their general acceptance by the international community. Thirty-five years after the UN Partition Resolution, the international legal cycle closes again with apparently the same imperative. In fact, its modern trend is to indicate this solution despite theoretical difficulties. Based on the principle of self-determination, traditional public international law suggests, and perhaps requires, the establishment of a Palestinian state,[122] the character of which would be based upon the classical model of the European nation-state.[123] Under this model, a Palestinian state would be fully Sovereign and independent and would be bound in its relations with other states only by the rules of the Law of Nations. Application of this model of statehood and interstate relations to a Palestinian state, however, is met with disfavor. Disfavor of the European model is largely responsible for Israel's refusal to accept a Palestinian state as a solution to the conflict and is likewise partly responsible for Palestinian nonacceptance of Israel. Under the theory of international law, distrust of the creation of a Palestinian state based on the classical model is unjustified, for the same international rules that direct the establishment of "the new state" also direct its behavior in the international community of states. International law would require, for example, that the new state not use force in resolving disputes. If these rules were observed by the new state, no reason to fear its establishment would remain.

Traditional international law, however, exhibits weakness in providing effective guarantees of observance and remedies for breach[124] of its rules governing interstate behavior. The failure of the rule of law in international relations is well illustrated by the history of the region since 1947; while the placement of blame is arguable, it is clear that the repeated failure of the international legal system is partially responsible for the present impasse.

Thus, in a situation characterized by mutual suspicion based on decades of hostility, any solution resting solely on traditional public international law and its classical model for creation of an independent state is severely weakened by ineffective control over the behavior of the state once established. Acceptance of such a solution will require construction of a novel politico legal order that offers a nonclassical model of interstate relationships and ensures control of the new state's behavior in the international community of states. International law alone will not suffice.

The current Israeli and Palestinian positions are revealing not only in terms of the nonviability of their strict legal arguments, but also in their representation of certain prevailing societal attitudes. Thus, Cattan explicitly and Blum implicitly are not concerned merely with striking a legal claim; their submissions are intended as a model for future relations between the two peoples. Application of the attitudes reflected in their legal contentions as a basis for a resolution of the conflict leads to discouraging results. The modern psychology of dispute resolution [125] distinguishes between competitive conflicts and dispute processes on the one hand, and cooperative conflicts and dispute processes on the other. In a study that "translates" this theory into its psychopolitical dimension in the context of the Middle East conflict,[126] these terms were defined as follows:

> Conflicts which take place in competitive contexts are marked by actions which aim at maximizing one's own gains regardless of losses to the other. They occur when goals are perceived such that one cannot gain unless the other loses, or that one party's loss is automatically another's gain.... Competitive resolution denotes either a sense of gain for one party and loss for the other or mutual dissatisfaction.... Cooperative processes are characterized by actions which aim at mutually satisfying outcomes. Cooperative conflict resolution occurs when issues are resolved such that all parties feel at least somewhat satisfied.[127]

The cooperative and competitive models are further distinguished by the extent to which there is an "accordance of some degree of legitimacy to each other's interest versus attributions of total malignancy," and the degree to which there are "beliefs about the need for collaborative versus unilateral problem-solving."[128] Not surprisingly, under the competitive model, "mutually satisfying outcomes are difficult or impossible to envision."[129]

The positions of Blum and Cattan, which generally represent the respective positions of Israel and the PLO, clearly fit within the competitive model. Admittedly, the competitive model in theory generally ignores the actual process of international dispute resolution,[130] in which unacceptable strategic solutions are often adopted as tactical bargaining positions. But it is precisely for this reason that the Blum and Cattan positions are instructive — perhaps to a greater extent than official positions. For, in their writings they indicate a certain political desideratum and reflect an important societal attitude. To a lesser or larger extent these attitudes influence or reinforce actual policy making or both. They express the strategic aims unambiguously and these aims, by virtue of their "competitive" nature, cannot serve as a basis for a durable solution. Not only new legal tools, but also a fundamental change of approach must be adopted.

G. Towards a Solution: Interim Conclusions

The foregoing analysis confirms the basic premise of this article: statehood is indispensable to the expression and focus of the national feelings of both peoples. Progress toward peace in the Middle East, however, would not be significantly advanced by suggesting as a solution to the conflict the creation of a Palestinian state led by the PLO,[131] even if that state would recognize and accept Israel.[132] This proposal, *without more,* is defective in two respects. First, the bistate solution implies mutual acceptance, yet is strongly resisted by both parties for subjective reasons. Second, the historical failure of traditional international law in the region suggests that the bistate solution would present objective problems as well. How then, is the need for a bistate solution to be reconciled with its apparent impracticality? Squaring this vicious circle will be the focus of the remainder of this article.

If the bistatal solution is to become a workable arrangement, it must overcome, or at least substantially mitigate, the subjective concerns of the parties. In addition, it must solve the objective problems that would arise from the introduction of a new Palestinian state to the region. At a minimum, the arrangement must meet the following principal requirements:

1. Parity and Reciprocity. The arrangement must strive for parity in the fulfillment of the basic political aspirations of both parties. At present, the balance is tilted strongly in favor of Israel, the existence of which satisfies so many interests of its Jewish citizens. Establishment of a Palestinian state will do much to restore the balance. As previously noted, the establishment of a Palestinian state will ideally require a reduction of the traditional sovereign independence of the parties. The principle of parity must be accompanied by the principle of reciprocity in the execution of the peace arrangements. While there may be transitional periods in which nonreciprocity of limitations on the partners is deliberately provided, these periods must be limited in time, and the prospect of full reciprocity must be clear.

2. The Security Risk. The security risk to Israel inherent in the creation of a potentially belligerent state so sensitively positioned must be minimized. Therefore, the arrangement must preclude the possibility of a massive attack by the Palestinian state on Israel and should further require that armed conflict will not reach a level higher than that which prevails at present. Although absolute guarantees of peace are impossible in any interstate or intersociety arrangement, Israel could accept a risk that:

    a) was no higher than that inherent in the continuation of the conflict between Israel and all but one of its neighbors; and

    b) offered possible elimination of the dispute or settlement of one of its primary causes; and

    c) would not cause Israel to lose all in the case of failure.

3. Economic Viability and Prosperity. The arrangement must ensure the Palestinian State's economic viability and prospects for prosperity while guarding against the perils of neocolonial subjugation.

4. Mutual Attachment. The attachment of both peoples to the land comprising Israel/Palestine must be recognized and addressed.

5. Particularism. The need—resulting, in part, from the current intensity of the respective national moods and the problem, in respect of both peoples, of defining with precision their uniqueness—for a high measure of national particularism must be given expression within the framework of the bistate solution.

A Palestinian state created in the mold of the old European nation-states and its modern day Third World counterparts clearly fails to meet these requirements. The traditional dynamics of modern statehood—a fierce, if unrealistic, quest for "independence," emphasis on acquisition and consolidation of military power, and suspicion of offers of aid from the industrialized countries—all seem to militate against mutual acceptance of this classical model. The nondemocratic traditions of some Arab States in the region further exacerbate the problem. Moreover, the lack of internal democracy and a weakness of the rule of law within a state substantially reduce its international credibility, especially where long-term, security-sensitive pacts are concerned.

Possibly the only promising means by which these apparent problems can be solved is the establishment of a different model of governance and interstate relations. The model should replace, conceptually, institutionally and substantively, the classical model of independent statehood and interstate relations with one based on partnership, cooperation and integration in some form of transnational, federal or confederal arrangement.

As mentioned above, many "federal" approaches to the Middle East conflict have been suggested over the years. The models of federalism are almost endless.[133] Federalism expresses an approach to relationships rather than the mechanics of statecraft. Choice of the precise model depends on the results desired and above all of the specific conditions and preparedness of the partners for the federal experience. A wrong choice of model may contribute to the failure of federal experiments.[134] Traditionally, in categorizing federal arrangements a distinction is made between two basic prototypes—the American style federation (and its variants) and the confederation of states.[135] Recently, the form of federacy/associated state federalism has been identified. Most major variants have been suggested as solutions to the Arab-Israeli conflict. The ideal solution would allow the independent existence of a Palestinian state, coupled with some form of association and cooperation with Israel. The ideal solution therefore excludes an American style federation. It also excludes those solutions which, although federal in nature, do not envisage equality of partners.[136] Thus, within the traditional categories, a form of confederacy offers certain promise. Mere categorization achieves little, however, for the federal arrangements suggested in the final part of this article defy precise classification; they are inspired by the experience of the *sui generis* phenomenon of European integration, which is characterized by its fluidity, flexibility and adaptability to changing circumstances. By learning from the successes and failures of the European experience and borrowing, with suitable adaptation, from among the most promising European institutions, there may evolve a framework of transnational ties that may satisfy the essential requirements and thus provide a suitable and acceptable solution to the Israeli-Palestinian imbroglio. This article will focus primarily on an arrangement between Israel and Palestine because of the need for simplicity and the need to maintain, at least initially, parity in the proposed transnational institutions of the two States. Israel is unlikely to accept transnational institutions in which there is a higher degree of Arab representation. Jordanian involvement, which is virtually imperative in any settlement concerning the West Bank, need not be excluded by this fact, however, for the transnational Israeli-Palestinian entity may establish a variety of contacts and associations to ensure Jordanian involvement. Alternatively, the Arab partner in the transnational solution may be a joint Palestinian-Jordanian entity. These possibilities will be further explored in later portions of this article.

The main purpose of this article is to suggest direction and principles for a possible solution to the Middle East conflict. The details of implementing the solution must be a matter for interparty negotiation. In the long run, participation of other states in the region as full members in the transnational arrangement may be possible and even desirable.

Part II. The European Community — A Model

The reconciliation and spectacular rejuvenation of the Western European states after World War II is the general vision from which this article's model is drawn. Particularly inspiring is the rehabilitation, of which the European Community's Common Market is a major facet, that brought former enemies together in a regional joint venture. A central question at the outset is the comparability of this article's diverse subjects of analysis. As well as the different set of opposed political and social forces characterizing the European and Middle East arenas, the different temporal settings must be considered. Some of the major events in the modern history of European integration took place in the 1950s and 1960s in a political and economic climate distinctly different from the late 1970s and 1980s. Thus, for example, the first two and a half decades after World War II were characterized in the West by a continuous period of economic growth and by a certain disenchantment with the classic notion of the nation-state. This attitudinal change, in addition to the advent of the Cold War, created a favorable climate for political and legal integration. The 1970s and, in all likelihood, the 1980s present a picture of economic stagnation and persistent recession. Many states, in a reaction to the harsh economic climate, have indulged in a certain revival of national protectionism.

It is unrealistic, then, to suggest indiscriminate application of European solutions to the very different Middle East constellation. A note of caution introduced in a different context by an eminent comparativist that "no serious student of comparative law could deny the profound difficulties in seeking to tear institutions away from their legal culture and plant them in foreign soil"[137] becomes painfully acute in this context. The envisaged Middle Eastern "transplantation" concerns not only the constitutional structure of one state and of a state-to-be, but also the reconciliation of profound political, ideological and sociological differences. At the same time, "informed analysis of basic institutional models can be extremely useful in confronting problems which, after all, are common to most societies. Solutions adopted elsewhere can suggest fresh ideas for reform."[138] The purpose of this part of the article is to examine some of these common problems with a view to identifying fresh ideas suitable for a possible resolution of the Israeli-Palestinian conflict.

First, a discussion is proposed to detail the objections to the comparability of the European model to the Middle East conflict. This will be done with a view to both revealing common problems and noting promising features of the EEC which have contributed to solving those problems in the European context. The article will then specifically focus on some of the features which offer promise in the Middle East context. Finally, the article will review, albeit synoptically, certain trends in the theory of European integration with a view once again to establishing parameters of comparability and transplantability.

A. *The European Common Market: Failure or Success?*

To some, the present day European Community displays signs of strain that seem to bring into question its viability and that create doubts about its utility as an effective model for transnational and regional cooperation and integration. The Community now faces a wide range of institutional, political and legal crises. The institutional crisis is characterized by a marked decline in the status [139] and efficiency [140] of the Community organs, an incapacitation of its Council of Ministers [141] and a general feeling of purposelessness and lack of direction. Some have gone so far as to suggest that the Community today faces a "remarkable institutional failure," the "dismal failure of its institutional ventures" and the prospect of facing not a crisis but, even worse, "irrelevance." [142]

This institutional crisis is coinciding with an equally troubling political crisis, which is stretching the cohesion of the member states to its limits. The European Monetary System, in itself a pale shadow of a full economic and monetary union,[143] commenced inauspiciously with only eight out of the then nine partners partaking in this joint venture. Similarly, the debate over Britain's net transfer to the Community Budget has introduced a strain in member state relations unprecedented since the days of President de Gaulle. The strain is symptomatic of Britain's uneasy integration into the Community structure. Within the Community itself, the Parliament gave expression to popular resentment by rejecting the Community's 1980 budget. Worse still, that vote may have represented a dangerous revival of national interests and alliances in the European Parliament. Direct elections to the Parliament, which were meant in large part to canvass popular support for the European venture, were a disappointment.[144] Constitutionally and legally, the Community is facing perhaps the most fundamental challenge: an emerging pattern of member state noncompliance with their obligations under the Treaty. [145]

Disturbing as these developments may be, they do not detract substantially from the overall achievements of the European Community. The Community is accustomed to periodic crises, some of which have been no less grave than the present one. Similar disappointment was expressed in the 1960s over the rejection of Great Britain's application for membership[146] and over the majority vote crisis which led to the 1966 Luxembourg Accord.[147] The Community has a history of resilient responses to crises. The disruption caused by sectoral secessions still would not equal the trauma caused by Community disbandment. Grave as the present crisis may be, certain solutions will undoubtedly be found. An apparent weakness may thus become an illustration of the flexibility, adaptability and resilience of the Community. The current disillusionment with the Community may also be attributed to unrealistic conceptions and expectations of its objects and limitations. The purpose of the present analysis is not, however, to assess the crises of the European Community, but to examine the Community's original political objectives and their pertinence to the Middle Eastern conflict. The origins and early political evolution of the Community are well known and ably described elsewhere.[148] It will suffice for our purposes to reconsider the principal elements of the Community's development.

Despite the narrow, sectoral nature of the European Coal and Steel Community and the explicit economic nature of the European Economic Community, the origins of the EEC were rooted in a political assessment of international relations. The issues were succinctly set out in the declaration made by M. Robert Schuman, the French Foreign Minister, on May 9, 1950.[149] Schuman introduced the plan for the Coal and Steel Community by emphasizing the ultimate objective of consolidating the postwar peace process. Specifically, he focused on the key issue, namely "the elimination of the age-old opposition of France and Germany."[150] Under this conception the only method of consolidating peace and of eliminating the age-old enmity was through "concrete achievements which would first create a *de facto* solidarity."[151] Specifically, the first step would be the placing of "Franco-German production of steel and coal under a Common High Authority."[152] The theoretical analysis of European integration in this and later phases will be discussed below. For now, it is important to emphasize the political objective and its methods of achievement — solidarity, cooperation and integration — as the main motives of the Community experience. Thus, in terms of the initial desire of the founders "never to see a repetition of those horrible three decades from 1914 to 1945...,"[153] the Community story is, to date, no mean success.

The Treaty of Paris[154] must be regarded as a main part, if not the main part, of the framework for consolidating the peace process in post–1945 Western Europe. Despite Germany's defeat and partition and the clearly articulated Soviet threat to the Federal Republic, there was still much mistrust, even fear, of Germany by her former Western enemies. The Treaty of Dunkirk, the Saar Crisis and French objections to American demands for the rearmament of West Germany served as reminders fostering an atmosphere of unease.[155] The Schuman declaration represented a radical departure from the previous history of European international cooperation. It suggested a pattern of interstate cooperation through an international multiparty treaty which differed substantially from previous attempts at long-term dispute resolution.

There were three main components to Schuman's Declaration. One was the idea of placing coal and steel output under the Franco-German High Authority, which other States could join. In the words of Schuman's Declaration, the objective of the scheme was to make future armed conflict between Germany and France not only "unthinkable but materially impossible."[156] This objective would not realistically be achieved through joint control of these strategic industries. The effect was, rather, symbolic. The principle underlying this aspect of the Schuman Declaration and representing a new departure from French foreign and defense policy in particular and international relations in general was the idea that in certain circumstances interaction was a better device for eliminating the risks of war than was the exclusive reliance on power politics.

The second component of the Schuman Declaration, the theoretical foundations of which may be found in the now obsolete theories of functionalism and neofunctionalism,[157] was the belief that a more general process of political union could begin by the integration of critical areas of national economies. The dreams of the founders of a "United States of Europe" are now recognized for what they were. Equally, the theoretician's "spill over" was to be more of a trickle than a watershed. Nevertheless, these hindsight realizations do not detract from one fundamental truth: integration could best be initiated by focusing on limited economic sectors, that is, by creating sectoral, as opposed to geographic, condominia. Success here would be a major step towards peace regardless of further political continuity. The final revolutionary component of the Schuman Plan was an autonomous High Authority which would have the power to make decisions binding on the member states, breaking away from the traditional pattern of international organizations.

The intellectual and pragmatic driving force of the new scheme was Jean Monnet, and the scheme was developed from a profound rejection and mistrust of earlier instruments of international dispute resolution. The traditional instrument of dispute resolution used by earlier generations of Europeans was the classic international peace treaty. Peace treaties were characterized by the following features:

1. Their terms reflected the balance of power as it existed at the termination of hostilities. One this balance changed, the terms could be rendered obsolete or even destructive.

2. Traditional peace treaties often sought to impose conditions on the vanquished which would unilaterally impede the vanquished's capacity to wage a new war. These measures included territorial annexation or, in modern peace treaties, unilateral limitations on state functions such as defense. Many treaties penalized the vanquished for the damage caused by the war.

3. Peace treaties concerned relations between governments. The binding nature of the treaties relied on the principles of public international law. Effectiveness depended largely on the power of the victor to enforce the terms. When this power disappeared, so would the effective binding power of the treaty.

The patent failure of World War I peace treaties to prevent World War II and, as some would argue, the treaties' contribution to the causes of World War II, weighed heavily in the minds of Schuman and his associates.[158] Although the United Nations Organization was set up after World War II, the lack of success of earlier pacificatory international organizations did not inspire much confidence in the efficacy of such organizations. These organizations were characterized by the following features:

1. The organization operated exclusively at intergovernmental level.

2. Member states were not strictly bound by the terms of the organization's bylaws.

3. The organization lacked any effective machinery for adjudicating disputes, and implementation of policies was left to the member states themselves.[159]

Their inefficiency is a matter of history.

The Schuman Plan and the European Community represent a radical departure from the traditional pattern. Before examining how the doctrine was instituted, it is necessary to look at the sociopolitical conditions that made it possible and to ask whether comparable conditions exist in the Middle East.

B. The Conditions for European Integration

The political origins of the European Community offer some parallels to the Palestinian-Israeli situation in terms of attaining "real peace" between two or more ex-belligerents. The differences between the two political situations should not be overlooked. For example, the legitimacy of German statehood was never in question after the world wars. In fact, there existed strong incentives, such as the Soviet threat, to encourage integration of the former enemies.[160] Nevertheless, important as these differences may be, a comparison of the two situations is helpful.

Israel and the Creation of a Palestinian State

The prospect of Palestinian statehood is becoming more rapidly accepted. Further, as the Sadat "historical mission" so dramatically proved, the states' attitudes may be more volatile, even in the Middle East, than commonly thought. A Palestinian volte-face vis-à-vis Israel cannot be ruled out;[161] a Palestinian Government may be eager to create a positive relationship with Israel if such a relationship is perceived as a useful lever for consolidation of the new state. Finally, the Soviet invasion of Afghanistan and the subsequent Moslem reaction is not unlike the 1950s' Cold War. Differences may, therefore, be less rigid and subject to change. In any case, the peace problem remains the basis of a comparative analysis between the post–World War II European situation and the current Palestinian-Israeli situation. The European solutions represented an institutional, legal and substantive departure from previous methods of long-term peace consolidation. Cooperation and integration among former enemies substituted for the traditional concept of power control. The question here is whether the conditions exist for a similar approach in the Middle East. Europe, after all, is one of the few areas where a real measure of transnational integration has been achieved since World War II, and it may be that unique conditions enabled this success. In a lucid synthesis of various analyses, one researcher isolated four elements of the process of European integration in particular and political integration in general.[162]

First, certain "structural characteristics" encourage a successful integrational enterprise: geographical propinquity, a common cultural background,[163] a roughly comparable level of economic development, a similar set of economic and political values, and compatible political systems."[164] These characteristics, however, serve only as rough indications of potential success in integration.

The European Community may be said only with hindsight to have had certain structural conditions favorable to integration. Thus,

> [i]t is true, for instance that the European States shared a common cultural heritage — but this was characterized by many divisive elements, including religious sectarianism; it was true that they were at much the same level of economic development — but it was precisely because of this that France feared being overtaken by a revived Germany. It is doubtful if, even after the war, Italy and France could be characterized as sharing the same level of economic development. They also shared similar economic and political values — though the prevailing values were being challenged by significant political forces in several of the countries concerned; and they had similar political institutions, though in three of the major countries these

> had only recently been established ... they constituted neither a natural geographical unit nor corresponded to any recent political unit. For a great deal of their history the peoples involved had been in conflict with one another, and in the more recent past the two main countries, France and Germany, had through bitter experience come to regard each other with intense suspicion and hostility. And, although the new Community gave itself the name "European" it was in fact a mini–Europe; a truncated, partial realization of the old dream of unity. It is hardly surprising, therefore, that the problem of relations with its neighbors in Western Europe — particularly Britain — came to assume such importance, and proved to be so serious a source of stress within the group. [165]

Reading the Middle East sociopolitical map in light of the five structural characteristics reveals an equally mixed and confused picture. Israel is larger than a potential Palestine, but it is difficult to assess whether this difference is critical. Participation by Jordan and other states in any form of transnational arrangement would, in any event, tend to restore a measure of equilibration in addition to the obvious geographical propinquity.[166] Compatibility of the cultural backgrounds is equally difficult to define: are the semitic origins of both peoples not as close as, say, the common cultural background of the citizens of Naples and Amsterdam? Can one gauge the effect, negative or positive, of the Israeli population, a large number of whom emigrated from Arab countries? It may be true, as one leading theorist argues, that

> [i]ntegration .. requires a very high degree of integration of the social fabric. Communication theory will tell us that without having much in common in memories, mutual signals will not be understood.... . [S]ocial fabrics, the social system, the social and political cultures are to a large extent the devices which serve societies for communication channels, for decoding, and for memory interpretation.[167]

Social/political culture is not an easily measurable factor. For example, the evidence of interaction between Israeli Jews and Arabs is mixed[168] and may be interpreted differently. Indications of cultural compatibility are perhaps no worse than those which existed in postwar Europe. In any event, the indications are sufficiently compatible not to preclude an attempt at association, cooperation and integration.

Another difference between postwar Europe and the contemporary Middle East is that in the former, certain antinationalist feelings resulted from a reaction to the nationalism perceived to be a cause of the war. Israel and Palestine are, respectively, a young state and a state-to-be. A new Palestine might wish powerfully to assert statehood. At the same time, however, it has been argued that this very fact, namely that the Middle East does not have a strong tradition of nation states, would therefore render nationalist tendencies easier to overcome.[169]

The second factor necessary for successful integration is "political will," a much more subjective factor. The incentive to cooperate should result in a political will that encourages integration. In analyzing how "political will" could affect the Middle East, two basic distinctions may be made. One distinction is between initial "static" and evolutionary "dynamic" will. The other distinguishes between political will deriving from a desire to integrate per se and that deriving from the utility of integration as perceived by the parties (affective-utilitarian).[170]

In the European Community, initial political will emanated from elite groups and spread. In the Community's early history, there existed a strong initial integrational will of the affective type. This will is particularly evident in certain groups and individuals in the political elites of the original member states. Widespread integration, however, is more a result of "negative utilitarian will" initially prompted by "the threat of renewed conflict between France and Germany" and from "the expectations of benefits to be derived from union ... namely, security (internal and external) and welfare."[171]

Particularly interesting in the Community experience has been the *evolution* of political will (and objections) despite the virtual disappearance of the Franco-German problem. This persistence may be attributed to a certain dynamism resulting from the process of integration itself. The commercial and economic mobility, resulting from the success of the EEC customs union with the benefits of the slow emergence of Europe as a power in world international economic and noneconomic relations, generated incentives and political will supporting continued integration. Demands of individual member states, interest groups within the states, such as farmers-consumers, and transnational interests have not always converged and, indeed, occasionally have conflicted with formal Community policies. As the Community developed and defined its policies, the likelihood of sectoral clashes and contradictory demands increased, putting pressure on the Community's unity. This dialectic resulted in a series of gradual approximations and syntheses of the conflicting interests. The same unity that prompted the clash of interests also reflected an ability to accommodate the tensions and reconcile the differences.

In the Middle East one discovers equally perplexing indications of a potential "political will." The initial static will is largely absent. However, basic societal needs for security (internal and external) and welfare do exist and indicate a potential for cooperation demands. Political shifts, such as the emerging Egyptian-Israeli alliance, may transform the potential into a strong political will to cooperate if the two societal needs for security and welfare could be satisfied by the success of a cooperative venture.

In this context, we should consider the issue of a "European Political Union." Originally, this concept reflected the ideal of true political integration in the context of a federal "United States of Europe." This was a prime "positive" factor in the political outlook of the "Founding Fathers."[172] However, such a vision would be clearly inappropriate for the Middle East. In the delicate dialectics of integration and particularism, this would tip the scales too far in favor of the former. Yet, was the goal of complete political integration a critical factor in the evolution of the Community, and if so, does the lack of such a vision in the Israeli-Palestinian scene seriously undermine its integrational prospects? The failure of the European Defense Community and of the European Political Community would suggest that the idea of complete union never became a true common vision. Of course, the federalist voice had a positive influence in maintaining the momentum of lesser integrational concepts. The Treaty of Rome[173] may have been a step toward "pragmatic" integration, but was also a step away from the notion of true union. Although the Treaty pays lip service to the concept of political union, it was, in effect, an "attempt to save faltering European supranationalism by utilizing and expanding the economic goals set forth in the Schuman Plan."[174] De Gaulle's famous "Europe of States" speech,[175] which appeared to some the nadir of European integration, reflects in retrospect not only the present political situation but also an equilibrium that, paradoxically, may have contributed to the resilience of the Community.[176] The assertion, "I do not believe that Europe can have any living reality if it does not include France and its Frenchmen, Germany and its Germans, Italy and its Italians and so forth,"[177] was in de Gaulle's strategy only a justification to arrest supranationalism. His strategy was far from successful, however, because supranationalism took some of its greatest steps forward during de Gaulle's term. Nevertheless, the echoes of de Gaulle's speech may still be heard today as a powerful expression of the need to preserve national identity. Europe's choice was clearly pluralistic, involving a range of cooperative and integrative arrangements. Despite the pluralism of the member states, a high measure of integration was achieved which translated the Schuman (and Monnet) vision into a living reality. The European model may appeal to many Middle Eastern analysts, because it does not suggest a structure in which the parties would forego too many essentials of statehood (or at least not initially unless by express choice). Even a federal political union need not be an initial primary goal or even an option. Integration may be conceived at a variety of economic and other levels to achieve the goals of security and prosperity.

Two other elements necessary for successful integration are patterns of support and political leadership.[178] While "political will" concerns the integrational demands made by various sectors in the system, in relation to patterns of support, a successful integration venture necessitates a broad support for Community institutions to enable them to develop despite recurring crises. This support was, in the European model, generated by the rewards that the Community seemed to offer. Closely linked was the role played by political leadership. The role of individuals and elite groups in launching the concept of the Community and steering it through difficult periods is well known. Leadership helped launch the Community idea and canvassed the support of pressure groups and policy makers. "Technocratic leadership" became a cardinal factor of the evolution of the Community in the early years.[179] Diplomatic skills were needed not only to habituate national administrations to new Community procedures, but also to maintain a momentum of *acquis communautaire* by elaborating programs, setting timetables and keeping the entire machine working. There has been a decline in the maintenance of Community achievement that can be partly attributed to a decline in leadership. The Community has been fortunate to have experienced in its initial years and afterwards a period of excellent national leadership. This has been particularly important in recent years when national leaders have had to contend with the strains imposed by enlargement and a changed economic climate.

Thus, widespread patterns of support for the Community and effective political leadership were strong contributory factors to the success of European integration. Unlike the structural elements and the existence of integration demands, they are factors that created themselves in the process of integration and could not be initially postulated, because it is hazardous to predict the future behavior of existing political leaders or the reaction of the public to new political arrangements. In considering the prospects of a Middle East common market, we should not look for the initial existence of patterns of support (as distinguished from demands) nor even to the "quality" of leadership; rather, the crucial nature of these factors should be recorded to encourage the evolution of both factors.

This brief analysis is not meant to discredit attempts at scientific definitions of the conditions for a successful integrative transnational venture. Rather, it points to the difficulties of relating, in an a priori fashion, political and social fact to integration theory. We can neither prove nor disprove that the reality of the Middle East is conducive to a successful venture; but in the face of the alternative, continued impasse and a cycle of conflict, it is at least worth maintaining serious discussion about the advantages that such a venture might have for the Israeli-Palestinian scenario. Before engaging in this exercise, one must examine more closely the legal structure and political process of the European Common Market to understand this particular model of transnational organization.

C. Patterns of Integration — Legal Structure and Political Process of the European Model

By their nature, all federal and confederal arrangements are characterized by a tension between whole and parts, between central "common" institutions and constituent "particularist" segments and between centripetal and centrifugal forces. Whether we categorize any "federal" model by the allocation of its constitutional, legislative and administrative powers and by the location of the formal authority to resolve disputes over competences or alternatively by an approach that looks at the actual process of governance and decision making (or indeed by both), the tension between whole and parts will remain a constant feature of the model. The European Community is a fascinating phenomenon in this respect. Its continued cohesion, 30 years after inception, can be explained by various factors. The ongoing perception of the member states (or at least most of them) of the external and internal advantages that lie in continued Community existence and the measure of integration already achieved — economic and political — are but two of many factors. Undoubtedly, however, a key factor must be the equilibrium achieved in the Community between a powerful representation of the interests of the member states on the one hand and the Community interest on the other. This balance may seem particularly promising and relevant to a prospective arrangement between Israel and Palestine inasmuch as it expresses one of the paradoxes of the European Community: the paramountcy of the member states coupled with a continued cohesion and a high measure of integration of the Community.

To understand this crucial balance one must examine one of the key concepts in the Community experience: supranationalism.

D. Supranationalism[180]

The European Community is said to be supranational — that is, "over or above individual States"[181] – but this concept is neither clear nor static, because it is a term derivative of the very experience of the phenomenon it seeks to explain. Thus, in gauging it one may be tempted merely to list the unique features of the Community system, rather than to attempt a clear-cut definition.[182] This still leaves a margin for dispute over the precise enumeration of these distinguishing features.[183] A further source of confusion is the all-embracing nature attributed to the term "supranationalism," as if it could explain *all* that is not intergovernmental in the Community system. A sharp distinction must be drawn between two facets of supranationalism — normative supranationalism and *decisional* supranationalism.

Normative supranationalism defines the hierarchical relationship between Community policies and legal measures on the one hand, and competing policies and legal measures of the member states on the other. Decisional supranationalism relates to the institutional framework and processes by which Community policies and measures are initiated, debated, formulated and ultimately promulgated. The measure of supranationalism is not fixed in relation to each one of these facets. A high measure of normative supranationalism will denote in general a hierarchy in which Community measures will take *effective precedence* over national ones. A high measure of decisional supranationalism will denote — in the Community context — a process in which decisions are taken and policies formulated and promulgated:

a) by Community institutions deliberately *communautaire*, rather than intergovernmental, in composition and mode of operation; or

b) by traditionally intergovernmental Community institutions whose decision-making process — e.g., majority voting — is not strictly that of intergovernmental diplomacy; or

c) by a combined process of the two types of institutions (pluri-institutional decision making), but in which the role of the nonintergovernmental institution is crucial.

E. The Dynamics of Normative and Decisional Supranationalism: Divergence and Balance

Examination of the European Community's evolution in the last three decades reveals the apparently paradoxical emergence of two conflicting trends.

On the one hand exists a nearly continuous process of *approfondissement* of normative supranationalism, whereby the relationship between the legal order of the Community and that of the member states resembles increasingly a full-fledged federal system. On the other hand exists a nearly continuous process of diminution of decisional supranationalism, stopping, in some respects, only short of traditional intergovernmentalism. The possible meaning of these trends and their relevance to the Middle East situation will be discussed below. A more detailed examination of the two facets of supranationalism will lead to both a clearer understanding of their meaning and an illustration of their respective evolutionary processes.

F. The Approfondissement of Normative Supranationalism

The primary innovation of the Treaty of Paris and the first hallmark of supranationalism in its early European Coal and Steel Community days was the power vested in the Community's main supranational institution, the High Authority, to give directly binding orders to individual coal and steel undertakings formerly subject only to national law.[184] In relation to the Treaty of Rome,[185] the European Court of Justice further developed this notion of direct effect during the 1960s and 1970s.[186] It first held that self-executing provisions of the Treaty of Rome could bestow enforceable rights between individuals and the member states. Implicit in this decision was the notion that the member states' international treaty obligations bound their *internal legal orders*. In other words, breach of international obligations— at least those which were self-executing and materially capable of bestowing rights on individuals— became a matter of internal law and subject to the vigilance and efficiency of the new guardian of international obligations— the individual.[187] Since that 1963 decision, the doctrine of direct effect has been extended, deepened and elaborated. Important steps in its evolution have been its extension to create directly enforceable Treaty rights between individuals *inter se*[188] and application of the Treaty to secondary Community legislation directed to member states, which does not suggest, on its face, the possibility of bestowing rights and duties on individuals.[189]

The doctrine of supremacy encapsulates the normative essence of full-fledged federal systems by establishing a clear hierarchy of norms: Community law, primary or secondary, in its sphere of application is superior to member state law, even if the latter is subsequently enacted or is of a constitutional nature.[190] Acceptance of this view amounts to a quiet revolution in the legal orders of the member states. With respect to any matter within the competence of the Community,[191] the legal *Grundnorm* must be effectively shifted, placing Community norms at the top of the legal pyramid. The slow evolution of the doctrine of supremacy has not ended to date, because full reception of this fundamental rule of Community law depends on its incorporation in the legal orders of the member states and acceptance by their courts, a process which has been met with mixed— although, generally, ultimately successful— reaction.[192]

With respect to fields in which the Community has competence, the member states are not only precluded, by virtue of the doctrine of supremacy, from enacting legislation contradictory to Community law, but are also preempted from taking any action at all. Before the full ripening of the preemption doctrine [193] occurred, the European Court of Justice achieved this objective by forbidding the disguise of national laws through their reinstatement in community regulations. In subsequent applications of a more mature preemption theory, the Court appears to be striving to attain an equilibrium between the need to consolidate the policymaking capacity of the Community and the necessity of member state regulation in fields in which the Community has competence, but in which it has not been able to evolve comprehensive policies. An apparent evolution from a pure preemption policy to a recognition of concurrent member state competence[194] might suggest a retardation of the scope of the doctrine in the Community legal order. Yet, the *approfondissement* of preemption is revealed in the evolution of the doctrine from a crude statement of pure principle to a relatively sophisticated doctrine sensitive to Community needs, particularly in recognition of the inappropriateness of pure preemption when Community institutions are not yet ready to assume decision-making functions. Furthermore, preemption is spreading from one substantive field of Community law to another and now affects sectors such as external relations, fisheries, competition policy and agriculture.

G. The "All-or-Nothing Effect":
The Rule of Law in the Supranational System

It is helpful here briefly to outline the "all-or-nothing effect" in the European Community. Whereas member states retain the ultimate political option of withdrawing from the Community and thereby disengaging from their obligations of membership, as long as they opt for membership they are largely unable to practice selective application of Community obligations. Thus, the doctrines of direct effect, supremacy and preemption are given their full effect. Although certain lacunae in the full realization of the "effect" remain, it has evolved into a fundamental distinguishing characteristic of the Community. The key to achieving the all-or-nothing effect is the functional division of adjudicatory tasks in the Community.

The Community system of judicial review has been thoroughly described elsewhere and need not be discussed in detail here.[195] For our purposes it is important to recall that the Community features a double-limbed system of judicial review, subjecting both Community acts and national acts to scrutiny for conformity with the Treaty obligations. One limb, enabling the Commission and member states to bring an action against another member state for failure to fulfill its obligations under the Treaty,[196] sets the Community apart from most other international organizations. At the same time, the "intergovernmental" character of the process and the consequent limitations on its efficacy are clear enough.[197] Yet, these weaknesses are remedied to a large extent by the review of both judicial limbs at the national level—the second limb—a process made possible by Treaty article 177's functional division of judicial tasks between the European Court of Justice and national courts. This multifunctional article provides, inter alia, that when a question concerning either the interpretation of the Treaty or the validity and interpretation of acts of the institutions of the Community is raised before national courts, the latter may (and in the case of courts of final instance, must) refer the issue for a preliminary ruling by the European Court of Justice. Once this ruling is made it will be remitted to the national court, which will give, on the basis of the ruling, the decision in the case pending before it. The national courts and the European Court of Justice are thus integrated into a unitary system of judicial decision making.[198] What is crucial is that it is *the national court* acting in tandem with the European Court that gives the final formal decision on the compatibility of the national measure with Community law. The result of this procedure is the binding effect and enforcement value that such a decision will have on a member state, as opposed to the effect of a similar decision by the European Court of Justice wearing its intergovernmental hat.[199]

H. The Diminution of Decisional Supranationalism

Thus, the doctrines of direct effect, supremacy and preemption, coupled with the functional division of judicial review, form the core attributes not only of supranationalism but also of full-fledged federal systems. Whither then, the acknowledged paramountcy of the member states in the Community system?

First, it should be remembered that the Community remains, functionally, a *multisectoral condominium*. The Community legal order applies only to those fields in which the Community has competence. Admittedly, the evolution of European integration from the limited spheres of the Coal and Steel Community to the "Common Market" and further, within the Common Market, far beyond what a literal reading of the Treaties might suggest, indicates a tremendous increase in the breadth of the sectoral condominium. Yet many fields, such as defense, fiscal and monetary policy, and education remain outside the official Community sphere. In these fields the member states exercise their traditional functions by traditional mechanisms of governance. The crucial nature of these fields is one factor preserving the member state as the nucleus even within the Community order.

The second feature explaining the paramountcy of the member states is the decline of decisional supranationalism. Decisional supranationalism and its expression in the evolution of decision making in the Community is, for several reasons, less easy to analyze and trace than is normative supranationalism. Strangely, the Treaties are rather cryptic in their institutional provisions, giving little guidance on the functioning of the institutions and only a formal indication of their competences. Inevitably, an enormous gap arises between these formal competences and the actual *Realpolitik* manifestation of power in Community life. Furthermore, the judicial process, so crucial to the development of normative supranationalism, enjoys a high measure of transparency, which facilitates the task of the Community observer. By contrast, the process of political decision making and policy formulation appears much more obscure;[200] its evolution is marked less by clear-cut landmarks, although some critical ones exist, than by a subtle process of institutional interplay.[201]

The tension between "whole and parts" is a constant feature of the decisional field as well. It manifests itself in two sometimes converging axes: 1) Community versus member states; and, within the Community, 2) less supranational versus more supranational institutions. It would be far too simplistic to suggest that decision making may be explained by simple reference to these axes. The evolution of Community policies is a complicated and multiphased process, and the duality of axes manifests itself at almost every stage.[202] At the same time, if a global view is adopted — one corresponding to that adopted in relation to normative supranationalism — a fairly clear evolutionary line emerges in decisional supranationalism: its decline. This decline is apparent in all three criteria used above to describe decisional supranationalism. To understand this decline we must first describe briefly the theoretical institutional balance and then turn to the decision-making process.

The main European Community institutions, the Commission and the Council of Ministers, are sufficiently well known and do not need detailed description.[203] Also clear is the general role assigned to both organs. For our purposes, it is sufficient to recall that, in theory, the tandem of the Commission — charged with policy initiative, selected secondary legislation[204] functions and execution and supervision tasks — and the Council—charged with policy decision making and actual legislation and representing directly the interests of the member states— was meant to achieve the balance in the decision-making process between Community and member States. The real story has been very different, its main theme being the ever-increasing strength of the Council and member states and a corresponding decline of the Commission.

1. The Commission. In the first years of the Coal and Steel Community, the High Authority (Commission) enjoyed a large measure of autonomy within a highly limited sphere of responsibility. The effect of High Authority activity on the member states was *ex hypothesis* rather limited, and did not emerge politically as a serious focal point of real power. Yet, with the conclusion of the Treaty of Rome, the sphere of activities of the Communities received an enormous qualitative and quantitative boost. Thus, since 1958, Community decisions have had a much greater effect on national life. One could expect an *a priori* greater interest and involvement of the member states in the Community process. Further problems were bound to develop: the emergence of the Community "democracy deficit," a function of the lack of any democratic element in, or control over, the Community legislative process,[205] and the disinterest of the Court in pursuing a bold judicial review policy.[206] Despite these two factors, both of which would seem to suggest an inevitable increase in the importance of the Council of Ministers, the eclipse of the Commission was not immediately apparent.[207] Given that the Commission's main task was the execution of explicit policies in the Treaty—principally the establishment of the customs union—it did not come into major policy conflicts with the Council. Once these first tasks were substantially accomplished, the process of erosion of the Commission's position became more transparent. The signs of the Commission decline are clear enough; they are discussed ably elsewhere[208] and need little further discussion here. The rise of the Committee of Permanent Representatives (COREPER) as a powerful intermediary between the Commission and Council and the initial exclusion and subsequent toleration of the Commission in the new extra—Treaty policy-shaping European body—the European Council—were important signs of this erosion. The rise of COREPER meant that Commission initiatives were subject to intergovernmental influence at an extremely early stage in their formulation, thereby detracting from the Commission's role of representing the *Community* vision.[209]

2. The Council of Ministers. The Council of Ministers itself has experienced a decline in supranational characteristics. The emergence of the European Council has been noted previously. This, it is submitted, is an indication of the failure of the Council of Ministers' "First Eleven"—

the foreign ministers—to assert themselves as an institutional body capable of giving direction to the Community and solving its problems. The need to resort to old-style, loosely structured summitry is a clear regression in the role of the Council of Ministers qua Community body.

The second, and perhaps more important, landmark in the decline of decisional supranationalism was the retreat by the Council of Ministers from majority voting. This move, precipitated by France and at first only grudgingly accepted by the other five member states in the legally dubious Accord of Luxembourg,[210] became an accepted Community norm with the accession of the three new member states.[211] Thus, one of the truly outstanding supranational features of the Council's procedure was undermined.[212] The veto power has not resulted in a paralysis of the decision-making process, but has effectuated a move toward "package deal" decision making with compromise being sought not only in regard to each policy, but also among various policies. This development was no doubt instrumental in the emergence of the European Council as a forum for this high-powered political horse trading, although the Council of Foreign Ministers could have assumed this function.

I. The Reasons for Decline

Reasons for this erosion in the position of the Commission and the general decline of decisional supranationalism include the following:

a) The need to evolve a "second generation" of Community policies, positive rather than negative, imposed a much more delicate and politically sensitive task on the Commission. The power of "initiative" now called for was no longer formal and technical—giving legislative form to explicit Treaty obligations—but wide, reflective and more "value" prone. It was questionable if the Commission, more technocratic in nature, was in fact suitable for this task. In the absence of any other body, the Council was the obvious alternative.

b) The need for "second generation" policies brought the democracy deficit to the fore. Further, with the widening of Community activities, national parliaments felt threatened by a process that would wrest even more power from them. The Commission, having little formal democratic legitimacy, became an easy target for attack.

c) The Commission itself has put on much bureaucratic fat. This is evident not only in the growth of its numerical staff, but also in the evolution of traditional bureaucratic ailments that have significantly reduced its internal efficiency.[213]

d) Finally, the process of *approfondissement* of normative supranationalism itself may have had a negative effect on decisional supranationalism. Both in the Council-Commission relationship and within the member states, perception of the development of normative supranationalism as an inescapable broadening and deepening of Community policies may have triggered insistence on control over Community decision making, even to the extent of a veto. Thus, the correlation between the *approfondissemeni* of normative supranationalism and the decline of decisional supranationalism may be partially causal rather than accidental.

J. Diverging Trends — An Assessment

What meaning can be given to this divergence in the evolution of normative and decisional supranationalism, and what lessons may be learned in attempts to conceptualize an Israeli-Palestinian Common Market? These diverging trends and their balanced outcome represent that which is special, and perhaps even unique, in the Community formula to oscillate between whole and part, centripetal and centrifugal. Perhaps this is the key to the Community equilibrium that has enabled the continuation of a process characterized by seemingly irreconcilable factors. The result is a surprisingly large and effective measure of integration with, at the same time, the preservation of strong, unthreatened member states. The deeper roots of this success have been sought in the earlier analysis of the common interests and compatibilities, where extant, among the member states. Here one can see the instrumentalities of structures and process whereby this venture was put into operation.

K. The Europe of Today: Aims and Policies

The analysis of the Community experience has thus far emphasized its reductionist aspects — the way in which, in its early European Coal and Steel Community days, it served the purpose of postwar peace consolidation in Europe, and the manner in which its institutional and legal machinery may be viewed as a model for cooperation and integration. The substantive concrete aims and policies of the Community were alluded to only in passing. The reason is clear: if it is difficult to transplant legal and political institutions, mechanisms and procedures from one society to another, it is doubly difficult in relation to the substantive content of policies dictated by the more specific economical, geographical and social conditions of any given place. What purpose would be served by describing the policies of Coal and Steel, when these vital minerals do not exist in the region under discussion? Analysis of the substantive achievements can be useful, however, in dispelling certain myths about the Common Market and indicating its current direction. Merely reading the treaties would not be conclusive in this context. The Treaty of Rome, for example, honors the myth of the Customs Union and Common Market. Undoubtedly a singular achievement of the EEC and a cornerstone in its evolution, the customs union today represents only *one*, albeit important, aspect of Community life. The classic theory that envisaged a progression from customs union through common market to economic (and monetary) union and finally arriving at total economic integration has been seriously discredited.[214] If the customs union — as an agent of market integration — and the economic theory upon which it was based have been shown to be both naive and simplistic,[215] the notion of the Common Market in its strict sense as indicating a precise state in economic progression has been shown to be simply wrong.[216] The Treaty and the accompanying theory placed too much reliance on the effect of removal of barriers in achieving market integration. Two things have happened in the reality of the last ten years. Market integration in the shape of an economic and monetary union, not to mention political union, has been to all intents and purposes abandoned. In addition, it was realized in achieving the limited original aims of a common market (namely customs union coupled with the free movement of workers, services and capital, and a competition policy), that little progress would be gained without the evolution of common positive policies. This development was accompanied by a general realization of the wider aims and purposes of the Community that transcended the narrow vision of customs union-common market evolution and eschewed the grandiose idea of political union. The realization and maturation of the Community has aptly been called "*alliance politics.*"[217] In substance, alliance politics stem from the realization by the partners that certain issues, because of their transnational nature, cannot be effectively fielded by a single government. These issues may be new and "neutral," such as the protection of the environment. They may, however, be issues, such as control of trade and business transactions, that traditionally were the concern of governments in the modern industrial state but which, by virtue of the internationalization of transactions, manage to escape public control.[218] "Reassertion of public control"[219] is achieved by matching the institutions and mechanisms of control to the expanding phenomenon. The creation of the Framework for Political Cooperation is a classic outward manifestation of alliance politics — not always successful — in the traditional foreign relations field.[220] The evolution of Community embryonic policies in the fields of consumer protection and the environment, fields which pose transnational problems and call for transnational solutions, is an inward manifestation. The list is much longer. This is particularly pertinent for our comparative vision, for even if it be contested that the Israeli-Palestinian-Jordanian situation is not suitable for customs union-based integration, the notion of *alliance politics*— trimmed to the specific needs of the region —cannot thus be discarded.

L. The European Experience— Conclusions

The brief survey of the European experience is not meant simply as a source of inspiration for a similar venture in the Middle East. Through analysis of its structural and procedural components— principally, normative and decisional supranationalism and the system of compliance encapsulated in the all-or-nothing effect — the Community offers a model that is distinct from both federal and confederal international organization arrangements. Indeed, it is the union of the normative (federal) and decisional (confederal) facets, with their unequal weighting, coupled with the "all-or-nothing" effect, that illustrates this systemic differentiation.

In many international organizations, including the United Nations, a high measure of decisional supranationalism exists. This is manifest in the voting rules of the Assembly and even, with the known exceptions, the Security Council, as well as in the role of the Secretary General. What is crucially lacking is any real measure of normative supranationalism. By contrast, a treaty among monist states with self-executing provisions may display a measure of normative supranationalism, but will not have decisional characteristics. Thus, it is the union of the two that distinguishes the Community order from other classical international organizations and confederations. If we turn to federal states, the differentiation lies in the weight allowed the two facets. In federal states there is, by contrast to the Community model, an *ex hypothesi* high measure of decisional supranationalism that is a result of the independent and distinct tier of the federal government that enjoys its own democratic legitimacy and functional allocations of tasks. In relation to the all-or-nothing effect, it is clear that most international organizations lack "all" mechanisms to ensure systematic compliance, whereas, in the federal state, the ultimate freedom encapsulated in the "nothing" option is missing.

The final section of this article attempts to explain the manner in which common market structures may solve some of the problems analyzed in the earlier discussion of the dynamics of the conflict. It is possible in this exercise to draw many "micro-lessons" from the European Community experience. Two examples of such lessons are the following:

1. It would clearly be in the interest of an Israeli- Palestinian common

market to progress rapidly and tangibly in its initial stages, even if in narrow sectors, in order to give the entire venture momentum. Progress is more likely to result if the execution of the venture is entrusted to some kind of autonomous body (such as the Commission) rather than to an organ such as the Council, which displays many of the difficulties of traditional intergovernmental bodies. Whereas any constitutional treaty setting up a common market should be wide, flexible and open-ended enough to give room for future evolution and development, should that be desired, the initial programs should be delineated with sufficient precision to solve the main policy problems and to enable an activist-oriented body to make progress. The distinction between first generation and second generation policies is thus an example of a European feature that may be useful in the Middle East.

2. *Approfondissement* of normative supranationalism, one of the two limbs upon which the European structure stands, was largely a result of judicial activity, principally by the European Court of Justice and to a lesser extent by the main body of national courts that accepted the novel doctrines. The European Court was not obliged to choose that particular route; it could have adopted a less integrationalist approach that would have resulted in a very different outcome. Some kind of dispute resolution forum — a Court — would certainly be a necessary organ in an Israeli-Palestinian common market. An adjudicatory, supervisory and review body that seems essential in a framework envisaging autonomous lawmaking (within the framework of an enabling constitutional treaty) could be the source of a variety of disputes. Much will depend on the judicial astuteness and creativity of such a court. First of all, however, the structuring of judicial tasks to make effective the decisions of such a court must be considered. Tandem decision making with national courts creating something like the "all-or-nothing effect," could be considered an important feature in any future Israeli-Palestinian common market.

Given that a low measure of decisional supranationalism is probably the realistic product of current political possibilities in the Middle East, it would seem essential to guarantee the creation of a high measure of normative supranationalism. It would be too risky to leave these particular issues to the common market Court. First, there is the danger that it simply would not establish these principles — a phenomenon not unknown in other transnational ventures. Second, its ruling may be challenged and resented, given the inevitably political nature of the decisions in question. Thus, it would seem preferable that the principles of normative supranationalism be made explicit in the constitutional treaty. In this sense, one would be replicating not from the European constitutive treaties but from their subsequent interpretation by the Court. Admittedly one could argue that had the European member states been required to sign a treaty with explicit reference to the principles of normative supranationalism, they would not have done so. In the case of the Middle East, it would seem that the pressure to conclude the Treaty in a manner ensuring the attainment of its goals would be strongest at the initial stages, when this conclusion would be perceived as crucial to the entire peace process. It is possible that at that early phase there will be a willingness to accept the proposed normative engagement.

The main lesson, however, is the overall, structural one. The supranational model offers the potential for a high measure of effective and binding transnational cooperation and integration — a fact that is crucial to this article's construct of a future Israeli-Palestinian scenario — while not threatening the essential independence of the participating nations. In addition, in its substantive dimension, the nature of "alliance politics" underscores the open-endedness and flexibility of the structure. These, then, are the two essential elements favoring consideration of the supranational model in the Middle East.

Part III. Is a Common Market in the Common Interest?

A. The Vision

The evolution of the European Common Market, by which a large measure of integration has been achieved without a significant loss in national identity and political force, it is proposed, may serve as a model for a framework within which the coexistence of Israel and a Palestinian state could be acceptable to both parties.[221] Certainly more research will be needed for the political, institutional, legal and economic specifics of applying supranational principles to a Palestinian-Israeli transnational arrangement. At this stage, one of the prerogatives of those who try to gaze into the crystal ball of political potentials in the Middle East is that of suggesting ideas and possibilities without having to be either comprehensive or absolutely precise. The term "common market" is a code for a flexible arrangement of diverse methods of association, cooperation and integration that transcend the purely economic sphere. It is suggested that a plan in which Israel and Palestine associate in a supranational framework to overcome the current problems of bistate solutions may be of some promise.

In general terms, the common market envisaged is one in which the two states would associate through a "constitutional treaty" in a wide range of joint enterprises. Some of these would remain on an intergovernmental level, while others would be supranational in nature, to be administered by suitable institutions. The general framework would be agreed upon in the initial, or even "pre-initial," stages of formal recognition and mutual acceptance, and would be a condition of recognition and acceptance. The evolution of the common market would be phased, leading through predetermined target dates, to a final structure of complex, intimate and widespread integration on the individual enterprise and national levels. The beginnings may be modest in selected areas where close integration may be expected to yield relatively rapid benefits and thus generate momentum for other sectors. The final objectives need not be overly optimistic, suggesting full political union as a final objective would not be necessary.

In the wake of initial sectoral achievements, a measure of social interaction would be expected to follow the economic process. It may be encouraged by certain judicially controlled, supranationally inspired initiatives. This new common market will have self-generating economic and social momentum that may, however, be supplemented by massive, externally supplied and supranationally administered, financial incentives. The common market would, it is hoped, resist the inevitable disintegrative pressures it will face. The framework should be sufficiently flexible to allow the incorporation, at a given stage in its evolution, of other states in the region, as well as the political and constitutional development of a closer form of union should that become desirable. At the same time, this process should not preclude, once a certain level of interaction is achieved, the option of allowing a continuation at that level without further dramatic evolution, while at the same time retaining the potential for development into new areas of integrational activity.

It is envisaged that the member states and their governments will play a leading role, as they do in Europe, in the governance of this transnational entity. Further, there is nothing in the European experience that suggests that the unique national identities of the partners could not be given adequate expression and protection. In short, here, as in Europe, the fundamental objectives of the common market would be making war not only unthinkable, but impossible, and furthering the prosperity of the peoples involved.

A detailed offering of institutions designed to solve the organizational problems of a common market will not be attempted here. Nor will an attempt be made to analyze at any length the substantive areas with which such a common market might deal.[222] Rather, ways shall be demonstrated in which a common market may obviate the difficult problems associated with the bistate solution.

B. *The Problem of Security*

Of all the problems associated with the creation of a Palestinian state (the critical element in the bistate solution), the issue of security is, undoubtedly, the most acute and intractable. It is the single most important factor contributing to the Israeli consensus opposing the establishment of Palestine. Israel's security concerns are most sharply directed toward the West Bank, which is strategically close to the main population and industrial centers of Israel. Israeli concern over the control of this territory is reflected in the words of an eminent Israeli scholar who avers that in any future solution "the West Bank ... should be in a situation in which under no circumstances can [it] again become [a place] for heavy armaments and attacks on Israel, because with modern warfare we cannot allow that. This touches on the very future of Israel."[223]

In the eyes of most, but not all, Israelis, the establishment of a Palestinian state would be inconsistent with nonnegotiable Israeli military and security needs. According to this view, the Palestinian state could serve as a staging base for large-scale military and guerilla operations. The Begin Government's position is that the only effective guarantee against both security risks is the continued permanent control by Israel of the entire area of the West Bank, and that this is to be accomplished by a network of urban and agrarian Jewish settlements (subject to Israeli law) and Israeli army bases in the disputed area. This is tantamount to precluding the creation of a Palestinian state if the word "state" is to be given its normal meaning. An analysis of the West Bank security problem and the various options for its solution will be facilitated by considering separately the two strategic problems which most concern the Israelis: large-scale military attack and guerrilla operations from the West Bank.

1. Preventing a Massed Armor Attack. The first option is the Begin Government's view, shared by the Israeli senior military staff, which calls for control of the entire West Bank area through civilian settlements and army presence. This view, however, has been sufficiently discredited to lose much of its force, and is shared neither by the Labor opposition nor by the leading military experts that belong to Labor's front bench.[224] The Elon-Moreh case, recently decided by the Israeli Supreme Court, seriously undermined the military and security bona fides of this view.[225] Consequently, it is not likely to be followed by any subsequent Israeli government. The security rationale is employed in this context to divert attention from other political and ideological desiderata. Therefore, the proposal for complete Israeli control of the West Bank will not be considered in the Security context. Responses to the other nonsecurity Israeli needs will be treated below in a discussion of the historical attachment of the Jewish people to the West Bank area.

The second option is Israeli control of the Jordan Valley. This limited objective, which received world attention with the publication of the Allon Plan,[226] has far greater strategic merit. According to this view, a belt of civilian settlements along the Jordan Valley serving as "a dividing line" could, in the words of Professor Weitz, ensure "that the West Bank will not be, under any circumstances, a staging ground for an attack on Israel...."[227] The settlements would "ensure that in the long run the West Bank will be demilitarized permanently."[228] Presumably, the primary function of the belt would be to prevent heavy armor from crossing the Jordan River into the West Bank. This could be achieved by: (a) channeling any clandestine crossing to easily observable points; (b) providing a base from which to repel such channeled crossing; or (c) establishing an initial buffer from which to repel any overt multipoint crossing. Weitz echoes the sentiments of most Israelis by adding that "on that I will not rely on paper, verbal or any other solemn promises...."[229] The need for permanent demilitarization of the West Bank and the insistence on an Israeli belt of civilian settlements along the Jordan Valley to guarantee this demilitarization is a widely held belief among moderate Israelis. To some, a Palestinian state may be acceptable within this plan.[230]

Either goal of this plan, however, faces the same intractable problem. The success of the security belt concept depends upon the further permanent annexation of West Bank territory. Permanent, forced demilitarization also entails a fixed nonreciprocal encroachment on the sovereignty of the entity governing the West Bank. Historical analogies are notoriously dangerous. The history of international dispute resolution would suggest, however, that both of these elements— nonreciprocity and sovereign limitation — touching as they do on the sensitive issue of Palestinian sovereignty, would in all likelihood remain a continuous source of conflict. The combination of these elements in this situation is particularly dangerous. The issue thus turns on the guarantee that a belt of civilian settlements will provide protection from attacks issuing from the West Bank.

The indispensability of the Jordan Valley settlement belt may be questioned on several grounds. Three critical questions are the following:

(1) Can a belt of civilian settlements ensure the envisaged demilitarization?

(2) Are the settlements the only means by which this may be accomplished? Are other solutions not involving annexation available to achieve the same objective at a reduced political risk?

(3) Even if demilitarization is necessary, need it be stipulated, a priori, that it should be permanent?

These questions are posed to minimize those factors within the security measures which may undermine any eventual peace settlement.

The likelihood that the settlement belt will ensure demilitarization may be seriously dubbed. Assume for a moment that the West Bank authorities (the government of Palestine) decide, in breach of a demilitarization pact, to introduce heavy armor into the demilitarized zone. Modern means of air transport would enable them to introduce a full range of armored weaponry, including main battlefield tanks, thus completely circumventing the need to cross the Jordan River. The central problem in this scenario is not that of finding a military solution to an armed buildup in contravention of a demilitarization agreement. Rather, the difficulty lies in invoking the political will and possessing the strategic readiness to regard such a buildup as a legitimate casus belli, and then acting accordingly. The reaction of the international community in such hostilities would be equally important.

Thus, it is not certain that the existence of a belt of settlements on territory annexed for this purpose would prevent in all circumstances the introduction of armor in the West Bank. The difficult decision will be political; that is, whether or not to regard such a crossing as a cause for taking military action. Further dangers to be considered are attempts by the Palestinians to transfer armor clandestinely into the West Bank, or to mount a surprise attack from the Jordan Valley to gain quick passage across the West Bank and into central Israel. In both scenarios the civilian settlements could do no more than warn of the impending invasion. In both cases the only effective Israeli response, in the event of failure of diplomatic efforts, would be armed retaliation. The presence of civilian settlements might in such circumstances become a military liability.

It seems, then, that the settlements alone would not perform any indispensable military or security function. Modern intelligence technology will detect an armored crossing. The detection stations, manned by military personnel (if necessary, from both Israeli and Palestinian forces or from other nations), need not be located in any occupied or annexed territory. Security considerations might require the positioning of Israeli army units in the proposed belt. The settlements alone, as noted above, would have a very limited military function, if any. On the other hand, it may be possible to station Israeli troops (or forces consisting of troops from an independent nation, or of such troops and Israeli forces) along the belt without establishing settlements in annexed territory. Thus, security would be provided for without the necessity of settlement. Admittedly, Palestinian authorities in the West Bank could still call for the pullback of troops in adjacent Israeli territory. This would raise again the undoubtedly difficult casus belli dilemma. Yet, as has been noted, this dilemma may arise even if a settlement belt is created. Assuming that a troop stationing arrangement were agreed upon by the Israelis and the Palestinians, the duration of the arrangement would still present problems. As has been noted, an a priori insistence on permanent demilitarization of the West Bank and its corollary, the permanent stationing of Israeli troops along the Jordan Valley, might threaten the peace process as much as permanent Israeli annexation of disputed territory. The potentially permanent nature of this security measure and its nonreciprocal character would presumably continue to cause Palestinian discontent. Although an initial period of unilateral demilitarization would be necessary, the prospect of its eventual termination would facilitate Palestinian acceptance of its nonreciprocal, transitory nature. It should be noted at this point that demilitarization is required to reinforce the mutual agreement on neighborly relations which would, *ex hypothesi,* accompany any peace settlement.

Israeli-supervised, permanent demilitarization is insisted upon as the guarantee of a pacific undertaking for which no "paper, verbal or any other solemn promises"[231] would be sufficient. The problem may thus be redefined as one of finding guarantees for pacific undertakings that would be more than promises. They must instead promise reciprocity and must not encroach indefinitely on sensitive sovereign rights.

A third option relies on the common market. The primary purpose of the common market model is to substitute, in a predetermined, visible way, tangible "peace facts" for verbal promises. Indeed, a possible weakness of the Israeli-Egyptian peace negotiations is that "normalization" has become a negotiating process that requires re-establishing a consensus at every juncture. Apart from the establishment of certain basic conditions of normalization, the process is dependent on mutual governmental goodwill that may be withdrawn at any time.[232] A cardinal principle of a common market is that the ultimate, long-term and durable guarantees of peaceful relations lie in normalization, even "hypernormalization", but, crucially, this process of normalization would be an automatic part of the process. The tangibles that give substance to promises of peace are a wide measure of socioeconomic lateral integration, and commercial, financial, cultural, scientific and educational ties among both citizens and governments.

To an extent these tangibles can be planned and developed; certain theorists even suggest that they may be measured.[233] Critical target dates can be assigned. If an acceptable level of "pragmatic integration" is attained, the necessity for "special" security measures that encroach on traditional sovereign powers of either party will diminish. In other words, Israeli withdrawal and the gradual development of a Palestinian state would be complemented by an equally tangible normalization process. Even a measure of military integration may be contemplated, though this would not be essential. Several related considerations illustrate this model of integration: the principle of "normalization" and governmental and societal integration as factors appertaining to the security analysis; the potential of common market organization to plan, facilitate, and perhaps measure the level of integration; and the ability to develop interrelated timetables linking steps in the "integration" process with the phasing out of "special" security guarantees.

This last factor deserves some elaboration. In the EEC, years and sometimes decades were required to attain Community goals.[234] The adjustment of diverse economies necessitated a phased program of transitional periods. The greater the diversity, the more complex and time-consuming the adjustment.[235] In the model suggested here, a common market transition period characterized by the dismantling of security apparatuses is envisaged. The initial transitional period may therefore be characterized by the presence of large concentrations of Israeli armed forces at key strategic points in the West Bank and a stipulation of general demilitarization in the area. As the goals for each transitional period are attained, it will be possible to reduce the level of West Bank security forces.[236] The presence of the security forces will perhaps reassure Israel more than serve as real protection from a Palestinian threat. As the common market evolves, the belt will gradually demilitarize and eventually, at least theoretically, disappear. It will later be argued that the actual dismantling of the settlements may not be necessary. If an Israeli-Palestinian common market establishes a "supranational right of establishment," these settlements may be included within a regime albeit, significantly, under Palestinian sovereignty. They may be protected by judicially guaranteed supranational nondiscrimination provisions.

Ideally, the regime of transitional periods and phased withdrawals of security forces should be designed to enable the Israelis to halt reductions in West Bank forces should the Palestinians again become belligerent. It may be suggested that certain sophisticated weapons may be procured by Palestine only at an advanced stage of the common market's evolution. Thus, even a shift to a more hostile position by the Palestinians would not subject Israel to immediate large-scale attack, and would still allow her the flexibility of exercising various military options.

The likelihood that the peace framework would be disrupted in one of the final stages of the transition period, or even after the accomplished transition, is diminished by the institutionalized community practices that would encourage cooperative settlement of disputes. Common market systems should be designed to ensure that at the end of the transitional periods a level of cooperation and integration is achieved that discourages or penalizes dramatic shifts in national policy disruptive of community order. The interlocking transitional period and security dephasing could be arranged in such a way that even if such a shift in Palestinian policy or attitude occurred, the strategic force to translate such a change of attitude into a feasible threat would be lacking. The interrelated transition periods and reductions of armed forces should be structured to deny the Palestinians the military means to mount an attack should their attitudes toward the Israelis become more belligerent. In such a case, the Palestinians would require a period of time to marshal their forces. This may raise the issue of a legitimate casus belli. The possible need to face difficult decisions in the future whether or not to use force to prevent Palestinian threats of attack should not, however, dissuade Israel from endorsing and participating in peace plans which risk dissolution. Moreover, it is likely that the hypothetical shift to belligerence will occur, if at all, at an earlier stage in the period of transition when Israeli security forces will be present in large numbers. Finally, it should be noted that the focus of the treatment of the large-scale attack issue thus far has been on the perceived threat of a Palestinian state situated strategically near to Israel. Yet, in the words of an eminent Palestinian writer, "[i]f Tel-Aviv is 15 miles from the West Bank, the West Bank is the same distance from Tel-Aviv.... [a]ny PLO leadership would take the helm in a Palestinian state with few illusions about the efficacy of revolutionary armed struggle in any direct confrontation with Israel."[237]

2. Low-Level Military Operation. The problem of low-level guerilla military actions by Palestinian forces may be dealt with more briefly. Presently, Israel's direct rule over the West Bank does not prevent Palestinian commando units from mounting raids within Israel from the disputed territory; indeed, it is partly a catalyst of Palestinian discontent. The bistate solution for resolving the present hostilities requires *ex hypothesi,* a halting of the PLO terror campaign. It is likely that splinter terrorist groups will continue their struggle against Israel, but these forces could be confronted by both states as members of a single community. Any splinter group that rejected peace solutions of the Palestinian members of the common market would represent a threat to the Palestinian authorities and the stability of their government. Continued resistance by these groups would indicate their rejection of the Palestinian leadership that accepted peace terms. An identity of interests could thus possibly develop between Israel and Palestine. If a terror campaign sponsored overtly or covertly by Palestine should continue, the progress towards a full common market and the disengagement of Israeli special security forces would naturally be impeded. If a Palestinian state is established in a common market framework, the prospects for acceptable solutions that will eliminate motives for terror attacks will outweigh the probabilities of increased Palestinian raids, or at least make it vastly more difficult to carry out such attacks.

3. The Problem of Security — Substantive Steps. Some suggestions for integrational objectives may now be offered. The suggestions are meant to be illustrative only. For this purpose it is perhaps best to use two progression tables. The first suggests steps for the reduction of security forces; the second illustrates the progressive evolution of *acquis communautaire*. For now, a precise scheme integrating the two will not be attempted. Both tables assume formal mutual recognition and the adaptation of a common market approach.

PROGRESSION TABLE 1— DEPHASING OF "SPECIAL SECURITY MEASURES"

1. Under the status quo there is effective Israeli rule according to the law of belligerent occupation. Security is maintained by the following:
    a) Army units are spread in a network throughout the occupied territory.
    b) Regular military training is carried out in the territory.
    c) Regular static controls[238] are maintained.
    d) Regular active controls (patrols) are carried out.
    e) A network of civilian and paramilitary settlements is established throughout the territory and protected by the army.
    f) There is a general prohibition on any armed Palestinian force.
    g) The secret services freely operate in the territory.
2. Steps in an agenda for the progressive elimination of "special Security measures" are the following:
    a) Israeli army bases are concentrated.
    b) Israeli forces are no longer being trained in occupied territory.
    c) Active Israeli control is restricted to border areas and to control of the airspace over the territory (except in "hot pursuit").

d) Joint static controls are established.
   e) New settlements cease to be constructed pending the establishment of a policy of reciprocal "freedom of establishment."
   f) A Palestinian armed police force is created.
3.
   a) Concentration of Israeli bases is primarily in the Jordan Valley.
   b) Border control is maintained exclusively by electronic surveillance and joint patrols.
   c) Joint static controls cease.
   d) The Israeli rights of control of the airspace and of hot pursuit continue.
   e) Nonborder settlements are dismantled or placed under the administration of local law, which is subject to the nondiscrimination provisions of a transnational bill of rights.
   f) A Palestinian militia is created.
4.
   a) Joint static controls are eliminated.
   b) Civilian border (Jordan Valley) settlements are dismantled or brought under the administration of local law. Military bases and paramilitary settlements are maintained.
   c) The amount of heavy armor and other sophisticated weaponry in the Palestinian army arsenal is tightly restricted. (It may be, even if unlikely, that a new Palestinian state would choose to limit its armed forces to a militia. This agenda should be regarded as provisional, not imperative.)
5. Israeli military forces are completely withdrawn. Settlements are brought under Palestinian rule. Palestinian army is restricted.[239]

PROGRESSION TABLE 2—STEPS IN AN AGENDA FOR THE CREATION OF A COMMON MARKET

The task of drawing a blueprint of a common market is complicated by the potentially wide range of common market activities. The success of the plan will depend to a great degree upon which sectors are integrated. Areas which have been suggested in the past and which seem promising now include the following:
1) The construction of irrigation projects.
2) The production and distribution of energy.
3) The production and marketing of agricultural resources.
4) The promotion of tourism.

5) Transport — internal and external.
6) The development of international trade.

Initial common organizations within supranational sectorial condominiums may develop to coordinate these activities. In addition, the classical common market activity — a comprehensive customs union incorporating a free trade area and a common external tariff — might be sine qua non for any meaningful, comprehensive economic integration. A description of the program of transition leading to the adjustment and alignment of the Israeli and Palestinian economies is beyond the scope of this article. Applications to the Middle East of "freedoms" allowed in the EEC — freedom of movement and the right of establishment and the freedom to provide services — are discussed elsewhere in this article in relation to the Historical Attachment.

For the moment, the following steps are suggested to accomplish the integration of the abovementioned economic sectors:
a) The ratification by both states of the Constitutional Treaty and its procedures.
b) The establishment of transnational institutions.
c) The promulgation of common policies and the planning for appropriate sectorial transition periods.
d) Monitoring the compliance of implemented integration schedules with policy goals.

C. Common Market — Incentives and Disincentives

The EEC experience has firmly established the principles of supremacy, direct effect and preemption as the necessary tools of Community integration. Refusal by a European member state to fulfill its obligations would clearly violate the treaties establishing the Community; persistence in such a refusal is technically inconsistent with continued membership. The European Community has depended for its success on the diligent observance of the rule of law. The special judicial system of the EEC permits, in some cases, judicial review of the conformity of state action with Community law in the courts of the allegedly violating state. This makes it virtually impossible for a member state to disregard the ruling.[240]

Despite the independence accorded member states, the rule of European Community law is, ultimately, an expression of a political fact. In cases of sufficient importance, member states may choose to withdraw from the Community,[241] and thus escape their treaty obligations. Therefore, the ultimate sanction against actions or positions of a member state contrary to EEC policies is not legal, but political. Legal sanctions serve to prevent significant day-to-day violations. Political sanctions against withdrawal, however, are different, and may be explained on several levels. The disruptive effects on the Community of the withdrawal of a member state would be a severe blow to European and Western unity. The benefits of continued Community participation outweigh the hardships and compromises which cooperation often entails. If this balance in favor of the EEC is seriously threatened, the cohesion of the Community could be seriously shaken despite the organization's impressive supranational structure.

No guarantee exists that a Middle East common market would experience the same kind of successful EEC evolution. There are certain practices which may, however, enhance the probability that the Israelis and the Palestinians will also find that the benefits of continued cooperation in a common market outweigh the costs of compromise and concession.

D Integral-Internal Factors

The adoption of common policies and the administration of them by supranational institutions are likely to create two disincentives for dissolution. First, the logic of economic integration dictates that pooling resources and planning on a scale that disregards artificial boundaries maximizes benefits to all in the Community. Indeed, some economic studies of the viability of a Palestinian state in the West Bank clearly indicate the advantages to the Palestinians of cooperation.[242] Integration is conceived, therefore, not only as an intrinsically effective means of achieving peaceful coexistence, but also as a way of achieving tangible benefits for the participant. As economic and social ties are developed, the potentially vast losses to be suffered from a disintegration of joint export plans, trade flows and mutual water and energy development programs should act as cogent disincentives to renunciation of the common market. Second, dissolution would seriously jeopardize the entire peace process, of which the common market is the centerpiece. A demise of the common market raises the specter of regression in normalization and an increase in political tensions.

E. External Incentives and Disincentives — "New Federalism"

The countries of the Middle East receive a large amount of international aid. The United States subsidizes a substantial part of Israel's budget, and the Palestinians, the PLO and Jordan receive aid from oil-rich Arab states as well as the United Nations and other international agencies.

Much of this money is currently used by both sides, directly and indirectly, for military purposes. A shift in the use of this aid could clearly contribute to the success of the common market venture. Foreign aid could fund the operation of transnational institutions in the early years, before they attained financial independence. If such institutions were forced to rely solely upon subsidies from member states, the common market formation process might be retarded. Funds spent to establish and maintain the institutions would be diverted from the types of investments in sectoral industries which invigorate national, and ultimately, community economies. Substantial funding of common market transnational institutions by foreign sources would facilitate integration, bestow immediate tangible benefits on the parties and discourage narrow national interests from affecting community policies. It may be safely predicted that if a common market calmed the hostilities between the Arabs and the Jews, increased financial support from nations interested in the region's stability would follow.

F. Neocolonialism

A major predicament resulting from the dynamics of the Israeli-Palestinian conflict was envisaged in the first part of this Article. First, it was regarded as imperative that the right of a Palestinian state to economic independence and viability be recognized. This condition, essential to the survival of any state, is particularly significant in the circumstances of this conflict. Economic crisis could encourage those opposed to the common market scheme to blame the difficulties on the formation of a new Palestinian state. Economic problems would increase the general potential for political instability and undermine the institutions of the new state. An obvious method of promoting industrial and agricultural development in Palestine is to secure the aid and cooperation of Israel. Israel's proven expertise in the very type of economic activity from which a Palestinian state could benefit-principally, the creation of an agro-industrial infrastructure-makes cooperation an obvious possibility. Yet, the Palestinians, who have for so long demanded independence from Israeli rule, are unlikely initially to accept any direct offers of aid from Israel. To the Palestinians, the specter of neocolonialism is second only to the menace of direct subjugation.[243]

A neocolonial relationship between the two states is thought to be a threat in two ways. First, some economic dependence may result from Israeli Government loans, grants and technical assistance. Second, there is a threat of "blinder" market subjugation, which may result from the disparity in levels of economic development of the two states. To avoid this predicament, the Palestinians certainly could obtain aid from friendly Third World sources such as the Soviet Union or China,[244] as well as from Arab OPEC States. Continued relations with these countries may, however, as they have in the past, undermine an Israeli-Palestinian rapprochement. This possibility is a significant reason that Israel has, and may still, resist the idea of an independent Palestinian state.

It is possible that a supranational common market, which would eliminate national barriers in certain economic spheres, could also have the unintended effect of straining Arab-Israeli relations. The elimination of barriers to the movement of goods, labor and services and the creation of a common economic market might, in the absence of comparable national economic capacities lead to the following phenomenon: manufactured goods would flow from Israel to Palestine, stifling the latter's industrial development. If; in return, a flow of cheap labor were to enter Israel from Palestine, the labor market in a relatively small country like Israel could be overburdened. At present, there are already many signs of this very scenario. Their continuation in a post-independence era would obviously be unacceptable. The alternative-mutual economic rejection- is, for the reasons developed at length in Part I, politically unacceptable. Thus, a common market may create a problem that it was designed to dispel.

Despite the tensions that might arise from dependencies developed between unequal national economies, it is submitted that the current, graver differences are more likely to be solved by institutionalized cooperation and coordination than by a continuation of the status quo. The common market seems to offer particular promise. The common market model introduces an "insulation layer" ensuring that development-aid does not merely become unidirectional, economically unbalanced and politically loaded transactions flowing from Israel to Palestine. This "insulation" will be achieved in two principal ways. First, the foundation of the common market will be its Constitutional Treaty. The Treaty will outline the spheres of cooperation and integration and the intergovernmental and supranational legal regimes applicable to the various common organizations and sectoral condominia. The Treaty will designate the initial projects over which the Israelis and Palestinians will have joint sovereignty. It should be possible in the Treaty to permit the use of Israeli expertise in development and aid projects while mitigating the disproportionate effects of trade between economically distinct entities. Palestinian representatives (principally the PLO) will *ipso jure* be parties to the negotiating and drafting teams. In this way legitimate Palestinian concerns and interests would be incorporated into the document constituting the framework for economic cooperation. A method of fashioning a balancing of interests would be to compensate the Palestinians for the benefits to Israeli industry from a Palestinian market, which could be deluged with manufactured and consumer goods, by planning sectoral and regional projects that primarily benefit Palestine. Barriers to common market sectoral programs will be eliminated by phases. This slow regime of integration can be modified, permitting quicker entry to some markets than others to account for unequally developed local economies.

The second insulating device, which is of possibly greater importance, lies in the institutional framework. Joint development projects and the integration of certain economic sectors will be executed and supervised by supranational institutions, the composition of which will ensure political parity and whose objective will be the furtherance of the integration process rather than the advancement of national interests. Thus, the recruitment of personnel for and the financing and implementation of development projects will be the responsibility of neutral bodies who will owe allegiance to neither of the former protagonists. This operational insulation, coupled with integrating mechanisms provided for in the constitutive Treaty, could help to ensure cooperation and integration without either subjugation or the appearance thereof.

Finally, the common market model would seem to offer other advantages. It institutionalizes close cooperation and integration in economic activities, but does not prevent each state from maintaining present ties with other nations. Admittedly, if and when a common external tariff is imposed by a customs union, the independent external economic relations of both parties would be subject to the customs union's common rules. The same would be true for other common market sectors whose products or services are traded beyond the Israeli and Palestinian borders. In most areas of foreign relations, however, the two partners would be free to pursue unilateral policies. Given the foreign sources of some of the Palestinians' and Israel's current military and political support, such a prospect might appear to be alarming. It is probable, however, that in the event of a solution to the present conflict, Israel's almost exclusively Western-oriented foreign policy will end and evolve instead towards a broad base of foreign relations. The PLO has in recent years been trying to broaden its own foreign posture. A peace solution will probably promote this tendency. Thus, it is possible that both states' foreign policies will tend to converge, and that the policy of each will include a bettering of relations with its former adversary.

G. Historical Attachment

A supranational common market with common institutions and common policies will not, in all likelihood, adequately embody the sense of attachment that both the Palestinians and the Israelis feel for the disputed land. The accomplishment of peace per se by adoption of a common market scheme will not grant each state the sort of sovereignty over land which has historically exemplified a people's attachment with the land. The common market model could, however, secure a high measure of mobility and a guaranteed right of access within the territory of both states. Such a model might also engender the feeling that mobility and access are rights, not privileges, to be exercised by citizens of one of the two states. The rights of mobility granted the common market citizens should approach the similar rights enjoyed by citizens within their national boundaries.

In a federal system, the solution lies in a common federal citizenship that bestows automatic *state* rights on all "federal citizens."[245] Public international law, on the other hand, does not require a state to admit the citizens of another state. Clearly, then, a common market regime is appropriate in these circumstances. Although the historical attachment was not a problem that faced the founders of the EEC, a body of instruments designed for another purpose may indicate a solution of the problem at hand. The European conception of a common market envisaged the free circulation of goods, labor, services and capital. Although the idea of the free movement of capital was partially abandoned, the European Community developed a comprehensive regime for the movement of goods and workers and for the freedom to provide services. Although it is clearly beyond the scope of this study to outline the substantive law on these issues,[246] the following points seem pertinent. Under the Community regime, migrants retain their national citizenship, but are given the right of free movement within the Community to take new work, and, on a more limited basis, to seek new work. Their families are allowed to follow them and, within the host state, the migrants are not to be discriminated against on the basis of national origin. Likewise, self-employed migrants enjoy the right to establish their businesses (within defined limits) and not to be discriminated against in the Community. These rights, however, do not encompass full political assimilation. For example, the migrant worker has no automatic Community right to vote in national or local elections. Migrants are subject to the law of the countries in which they are guests. Further, a member state may still require migrants to comply with its immigration policies. Member states may, according to the Treaty and its implementing legislation, exclude undesirable Community nationals. Thus, for example, in regard to the free movement of the workers, article 48(3) provides that limits on migrant worker immigration may be imposed on the grounds of public policy, security or health. In addition, secondary legislation elaborates the means to be given to this clause.[247] Similar provisions apply to freedom of establishment,[248] In regard to freedom of establishment of undertakings, the Council of Ministers was given the power to exclude activities from the scope of the regime.[249]

It is not suggested that these freedoms should be applied fully or partially, with no more, to the Israeli-Palestinian common market. Economic and political conditions may militate against their immediate application to a Middle Eastern common market. Palestine would not wish to see an exodus of its labor force, any more than Israel would wish to accept those workers. The provisions of the common market treaty concerning migrant worker movement should create a regime that allows some measure of supranationally guaranteed mobility but at the same time does not disregard traditional attributes of national citizenship and allows member states in the protection of the national interest to monitor and control the movement of nonnationals across their borders. Unlike some practices permitted in classical international law, however, the protection of the national interest cannot be arbitrary and discriminatory and must follow a common market concept of what constitutes public policy. The European experience teaches that the member states retain a wide measure of control over their borders.[250] Without prejudging the issue of the suitable means for economic integration in the Middle East, within a common market framework a special regime that ensures free access within the territory of the common market may be established. Thus, for example, Israelis and Palestinians would initially have the right to cross the other state's frontiers to visit in that state, subject only to the admitting state's justified limits on entrance for public policy and security reasons. Derogation from this right would be subject to judicial review.

As economic parity is achieved, the right of free access may be extended. Within this context a solution may be found to the problem of Israeli settlements in the West Bank. Agricultural and other settlements may be included under a regime which allows citizens of both states freely to establish themselves in the nation of their choice. The regime would not ensure automatic mobility, because the marketplace would determine land availability. To the extent that each state has sovereign authority over its land, when it releases new land for development and settlement it must consider all applications without discriminating between Palestinians and Israelis. New citizens would of course be subject to the laws of the state concerned; under this proposal, they too would have the right to be dealt with under the law in a nondiscriminatory fashion. Such a regime would benefit not only Israelis but also Palestinians settling Israel and Israeli Arabs migrating to the new Palestinian state. Of course, many details would have to be settled before such a regime could be fully implemented. The common market institutions and its court would first have to prove their efficacy.

H. The Problem of Institutions

European Community institutions are characterized by a diminution in their supranational character-increasingly so in the last decade of EEC activity. Although this development is perceived as an arrest in the process towards achieving political union or a "higher" form of federalization, it corresponds to the integrational potential of the region. The Israeli-Palestinian model conceived in this Article is one that, like the EEC, must recognize the importance, even primacy, of the member states. In the Middle East Community, as in the European Community, this primacy does not exclude supranational decision making on certain levels, nor does it exclude a high level of normative supranationalism.

If a body of supranational law applied with direct effect is to evolve, the need for a supreme adjudicatory forum-a "Supreme Court"-becomes imperative. By necessity, the Court should be charged with the adjudication of a variety of disputes: between supranational authorities, between those authorities and the member states (particularly on the delicate questions of respective competences), between member states concerning the duties flowing from the Constitutional Treaty, between individuals and enterprises and the supranational authorities, and between individuals and a state when supranational law is concerned. The Supreme Court posited should ensure that it is supreme in all matters concerning supranational law. The European Community may serve as a model for a Middle East common market, although the task of creating a community of two nations presents far fewer problems than those faced by the Europeans. A particularly promising feature of the EEC is the functional division of its adjudicatory tasks. The interplay of national courts and the European Court has far-reaching integrational consequences. National courts, the main "dispensers of Community law," play a central role in the process of integration. By shifting the major adjudicatory forum into the national legal system, where, traditionally, the rule of law is far stronger, the prospects for observance of community law are heightened.

I. Decisional Supranationalism

The power to legislate is a hallmark of the autonomy and viability of the Supranational organization. Executive and legislative bodies should therefore be created to operate within the jurisdiction of the common market. It is equally necessary, indeed inevitable, that the member states have a veto power over any new legislation. Undoubtedly, individual governments will represent, at least initially, their own national interests in the common market legislative body. Eventually, it is hoped that a split will occur between the legislative functions of the individual governments, acting as a single common market institution, and an elected parliament with ultimate power to block or pass legislation. It is unlikely, of course, that such a power, characteristic of the authority of a federal state legislative body, will be accepted by the member states in the initial stages of development. The danger exists that a common market legislative body which passes laws disagreeable to some member states, and thereby compels them to veto or ignore community legislation, would slow the progress of the common market. The EEC experience teaches that a range of tasks of an administrative body should be defined in the Constitutional Treaty. The supranational administrative authority should have sufficient power and competence to perform these tasks without the need to secure the agreement of the legislative body. The latter's task will commence in the second or third phase of the common market development process, after the initial organizational regimes have been established. Creation of a parliament and a system of checks and balances would occur at a later stage.

The institutional complexity of a common market may also influence, to an extent, the initial number of member states. Each member state will, of course, insist on equal representation in each of the three "branches." This is to be expected with respect to the legislative body. Although the Court and the supranational administrative authority in their decision-making powers would be independent of member state review, initially, it is likely that individual governments will nevertheless demand representative parity in the appointments to the two bodies. As an example, incorporation of Jordan into the common market would interfere with the bistate balance, with the likely result that Israel would refuse to be outnumbered by a two-thirds Arab majority. A possible solution is to give all member states veto power in the community legislative body (which, in any event, they would enjoy in a bistate structure). It would be potentially damaging to the organizational Structure, however, to give the member states veto power over decisions of the Court and administrative bodies, whose duties are to disregard narrow national interests and, instead, to represent and consider the community interest. A bistate community would necessarily obviate these problems, because there would be a parity of appointments to key positions in all of the bodies, and the possibility of majority voting in the non-legislative organs. If for political reasons it is thought that Jordanian membership is necessary in the early stages, such involvement could be achieved in three ways:

a) Jordan and the Palestinians are represented as one negotiating entity (implying an eventual high measure of integration of Jordan and Palestine).

b) Jordan "associates" with the Israeli-Palestinian common market in economic and other areas in joint interest.

c) Jordan becomes a partner in certain sectoral condominia without participating in the common market permanent institutions. Jordan is represented in the specific bodies which have administrative power over the sector.

All of these proposals would provide for Jordan's participation without, however, threatening the initial need for national parity in community institutions.

J. The Problem of Democracy

Two problems fall under this general heading. The first concerns the basic idea of an association of two states that voluntarily accept "self-imposed rules of conduct governing the exercise of [their] sovereignty...."[251] This is the essence of both the European model and the proposed system for the Middle East. The efficiency of such a system depends to an extent on a high level of observance of the rule of law by and in the member states. The observance of the rule of law and the evolution of the common market would, according to this view, depend on the democratic nature of the member states. In a nondemocratic state, the societal effects of the "federal" arrangement would not evolve nor would the Constitutional Treaty arrangement be regarded as sufficiently solid. In the Middle East, the Arab states have unevenly demonstrated their allegiance to democratic practices and their observance of the rule of law (as these concepts are understood in the West). Certain regimes, although authoritarian, do boast a record of political stability. The Arab states, particularly those surrounding Israel, have shown uneven records of political stability as well as of fealty to democratic norms. The Israelis legitimately fear that a Palestinian state would reflect this pattern of development in other Arab states and fail to observe diligently the community rule of law. Indeed, the same reason is aired in relation to the general reliability of a future Palestinian state as a partner to any international treaty.

The second problem relates to the democratic nature of the Middle East common market in general. The indispensability of supranational executive/administrative organs to implement the common market substantive program and policies has been noted. It has also been shown that, initially, rapid progress and tangible success are important to provide the new entity with momentum. Furthermore, to prevent the common market from being weakened by disputes between member states, legislative and administrative powers should be delegated to central institutions. When the first decision is made that is not agreeable to Israel or Palestine, charges concerning the undemocratic nature of the common market system will probably be raised. Although, as shall be argued, it is possible to show that the two problems relating to the democratic structure of the common market are less troublesome than would at first appear, their ultimate solutions lie in seeing the possible connection between the two.

As far as the first problem is concerned, the democratic character of the states cannot, of course, ensure the cohesion of the transnational arrangement. By the same token, an authoritarian regime is not necessarily fatal to the cohesion of a transnational scheme. The Comecon,[252] with its many defects, is still a viable regional organization. It may even be argued that a strong, central Palestinian Government committed to the peace process and the common market, though not dedicated to democratic principles, would be preferable to a weak, democratic government with no interest in the structure. This last hypothesis fails ultimately to take into consideration that one of the main functions of the proposed common market is to promote the peace process. The purpose of creating popularly motivated support for, and self-interest in, the common market and its institutions is to place constraints on the political options of governments. An authoritarian regime — even one that supported the common market idea-would be inconsistent with the concept of a community system with broad-based support. Similarly, if the common market idea is to evolve and adapt adequately to the changing circumstances of the region, and if its institutions are to remain politically legitimate, a measure of internal "direct democracy" (not, however, the sort that is exercised indirectly through governmental representation in a community legislature) would be important.

There are several ways to enhance the expression of democratic values in the common market and its institutions. A parliament composed of members from both national legislatures or of delegates who are directly elected by the citizens of both nations is one method. The differences in size of the Israeli and Palestinian populations would require that such a parliament not have exclusive legislative competence for some time. "National interests," as enunciated by national governments, would during this initial period have to be respected in some measure if common market policies are truly to be arrived at democratically. Nonetheless, the very existence of a community parliament as a forum in which transnational policies are debated and to which the common market administrative organs are accountable may well contribute to the process of integration. The detailed structure and the precise powers of such a body need not be dealt with here. It is the necessity of its existence that must be emphasized. Nevertheless, it may not in fact be needed in the early stages. The transnational institutions will at first enjoy the legitimacy bestowed upon them by the Constitutional Treaty. When the first concrete practices are begun and the common market becomes a living fact, however, some form of transnational parliament must be established. Not only will it lend legitimacy to a potentially expanding field of transnational activity, but, through the regular elections of its delegates, it may also encourage the growth of democratic practices in the member states. Should a Palestinian state reject the policies of the common market, a security rather than a purely political problem will confront the two countries.[253]

K. *Tactics and Strategy — Diplomacy and Timetables*

Acceptance of a common market by Israel and the PLO[254] will require that each state make fundamental and probably difficult changes in its policies concerning the other. In Part I of this Article, some of the substantive causes that impede such acceptance were outlined. Another possible cause, related to the negotiation process, must now be mentioned. Mutual recognition and acceptance are issues that presently touch upon the political strategy of both parties. Even if the parties are persuaded to change their present positions, such acknowledgments will be predicated upon the extraction of concessions from the other party, and other states as well. Unilateral recognition and acceptance, without more, would not be likely. Neither Israel nor the Palestinians would recognize the other without requiring the same of its adversary; to do so would sacrifice an essential element of the initial bargaining position. Implicit in this proposition is an assumption that both parties are willing to negotiate. Although there have been intractable difficulties in reaching a consensus thus far, it is hoped that a forum for the resolution of these conflicts may be created without compromising in advance the bargaining position of either state.[255]

One method of achieving a climate favorable to discussion is the conditional recognition.[256] A state would offer less than full recognition of the other on condition that the recognized party fulfill certain requisites and respond in kind. The conditional recognition offers two potential advantages: (a) it may yield significant political benefits due to the recognizing state's improved image in the international community; and (b) therefore would increase the pressure on the recognized state to reciprocate. It is hoped that full acceptance of each state by the other would follow, leading to negotiations for the creation of a common market. There are, however, corresponding drawbacks to these advantages. The conditional acceptance is a potentially irreversible decision, for it is a grant to the other party, albeit subject to conditions, of a high measure of legitimacy from a former antagonist. The recognized party may try to reject the conditions of acceptance, yet retain the benefits of its newly conferred legitimacy, and emerge in a better bargaining position without having to recognize its opponent in return. The greater the pressure from the recognized state's leadership and citizenry and from other nations to recognize the other state in turn, the less likely this maneuver will succeed. On the other hand, the more onerous the conditions of acceptance, the less likely they are to create the sorts of external and internal pressures on the recognized state to return the gesture and the more likely they are to enable the other party to reap the benefits without making a corresponding measure.

The "Autonomy Exercise" illustrates this point. Israel, in the Camp David Agreement,[257] made a significant formal policy concession on the Palestinian issue. To this concession, however, were attached several onerous conditions regarding the issue of sovereignty over the territories of the West Bank and the nature of any rights of autonomy to be given the Palestinians. The failure of the Palestinians to agree among themselves whether to adopt the plan is well known.[258] Israel, however, now finds itself committed to negotiations in a specific direction related to its initial concession without having gained any benefits from that step. The Palestinians could find themselves in the same dilemma. Their long-held position has been to deny Israel's legitimacy. If they were unilaterally to offer to accept an Israeli withdrawal to the 1947 United Nations Partition boundaries, their overture would likely be met with the same derision that greeted the Israeli proposal for autonomy. On the other hand, acceptance by one state of the other's validity with the understanding that certain conditions which are not onerous are to be fulfilled in return, would weaken the negotiating position of the accepting state. Thus, unilateral Israeli acceptance of Palestinian independence or unilateral Palestinian acceptance of Israel's 1949 boundaries would probably appear to each state as too great a concession before the actual commencement of negotiations.

A second disadvantage of the conditional acceptance is rooted in the psychology of the negotiating process. The difficulties in assessing the impact of unilateral conditional acceptance were discussed above. In the current belligerent climate, each party may feel that such a voluntary act would be interpreted by the other as a sign of weakness. If a party's resolve appears to bend, it is thought that this will only encourage the other state to assume an uncompromising stance.

The deadlock caused by the state of mutual distrust may be overcome by the covert diplomatic efforts of a third party. If a peace initiative is offered by persons not party to the conflict, the danger of misinterpreting the proposal as a sign of weakness is diminished. A measure of protracted negotiation might be possible, freeing the Israeli and Palestinian leaderships from the effects of popular internal pressures and the possibility of loss of face. A third party proposition of negotiating terms may then have some chance of acceptance.

A public third party initiative, on the other hand, invites public responses that may subvert the careful balance of obligations and rights in the peace plan proposal. Past successful Middle East negotiations have been characterized by a combination of secret and public third party conciliation efforts. A final assessment of the most dramatic breakthrough, the historic visit of President Sadat to Jerusalem in 1977, must be reserved. Sadat's successful efforts, however, attest to the viability of a proposal of unilateral conditional acceptance in promoting a forum for negotiations.

Conclusions

In breaking the impasse concerning the creation of a Palestinian state, an initial foundation for mutual acceptance may best be established by secret initiatives in connection with public pressures by third parties to accept the proposals. Once the initial framework or discussion has been completed, negotiations may proceed based upon the model of conditional acceptance. In the context of the model offered in this Article, the following negotiating phases are envisaged. In the first phase, the Israelis and the Palestinians, aided by the secret, mediative efforts of third parties, are each convinced to accept conditionally the right of the other to exist. The common market model advocated would, for example, return Israel to its 1949 boundaries and provide for a mutually acceptable framework for the phase-out of security measures. Once agreement, even if not public, is reached, the constitutional treaties are negotiated. This phase may take place during the Camp David "autonomy" period. "Autonomy" will, of course, acquire a substantially different character, because it is now regarded as a transition stage to eventual statehood. The third phase signals the beginning of the transition Stages leading to the creation of a common market, the number and length of which stages will have been decided in the second phase.

In the third phase, both Palestinian national institutions (still subject to special security measures) and common market supranational institutions function. As envisaged in this Article, the evolution of these latter entities triggers the dismantling of special security measures and at the same time complements the development of the Palestinian state within the guidelines of the supranational framework.

It may be that the Arab-Israeli conflict may be solved without dealing with the thorny issues of Palestinian self-determination and statehood. It may also be possible that negotiations can proceed without the participation of the PLO. Recent events, including the near collapse of the Camp David initiative and the unprecedented, PLO-inspired unrest in the West Bank suggest that these possibilities have little chance of success. This Article has suggested certain modalities on the assumption that a PLO-endorsed plan for Palestinian statehood is a necessary condition to any successful peace plan. Whether the ideas presented here are reasonable and practicable is left to the reader's judgment; even should they be found promising, this would not by itself presage a Middle East peace. States do not necessarily act reasonably. The many reasonable peace plans previously formulated and rejected attest to this unfortunate fact. This Article will have accomplished its purpose if it stimulates thought and discussion in the current search for new approaches to Middle East conflict resolution.

Notes

1. See generally H. CATTAN, PALESTINE AND INTERNATIONAL LAW (1st ed. 1973); A.GERSON, ISRAEL, THE WEST BANK AND INTERNATIONAL LAW (1978).

2. For a monumental collection of readings tracing the evolving legal commentary on the dispute, see J. NORTON-MOORE, THE ARAB-ISRAELI CONFLICT (1974).

3. Some outstanding exceptions are given in J. NORTON-MOORE, id at vol.11. In particular, the articles by Rosenne, id at 777, Stone, id at 801, Wright, id at 828, Blum, et al at 840, and Cattan, id at 936, are worth careful study. Opinions on proposed solutions are as diverse as the appraisals of the normative character of the conflict. In general, however, proposals are made in a nonlegal context. See J. NORTON-MOORE, id at 1001-144; see also 7 BULL. OF PEACE PROPOSALS 291-334 and M. NITZAN, A REVIEW OF PROPOSALS FOR FEDERAL SOLUTIONS IN THE PERIOD 1917-1977 (1978). Nitzan points out the dearth of scientific research, id at 23. In regard to peace solutions with a federal aspect, he suggests that "the lion's share were proposals by politicians, statesmen, and bureaucrats." The proposals are often made "for tactical purposes only" id.

4. See, e.g., ACCESS TO JUSTICE AND THE WELFARE STATE (M. Cappelletti ed. 1981), particularly Galanter, *Justice in Many Rooms,* id at 147–82; Johnson,

The Judicial System of the Future. Four Scenarios/or the Twenty-First Century, id at 183–216.

5. The reliance on negotiation, mediation and conciliation is well illustrated in STUDY GROUP OF THE DAVID DAVIES MEMORIAL INSTITUTE OF INTERNATIONAL STUDIES REPORT, INTERNATIONAL DISPUTES: THE LEGAL ASPECTS 57–177 (1972).

6. Thus, F.C. Ilké, in his influential HOW NATIONS NEGOTIATE (1964), suggests that in negotiations a "way of expressing firmness is to maintain that one's position accords with legal or scientific principle." Indeed, "this is the *principal function* of legal and scientific arguments; for you do not usually make your proposal more attractive to your opponent by telling him that what you are proposing is in accordance with scientific fact or international law. However, if you make your opponent believe that you think your proposal is grounded on such principles, you may have conveyed to him that your proposal is firm." id at 202 (first emphasis added).

7. 5 Y. DINSTEIN, THE NON-STATAL [sic] INTERNATIONAL LAW 149 (1979).

8. See "Text of Final Declaration at Arab League Meeting," *New York Times,* Sept.10, 1982, at A8, col. 1; "Arabs Adopt Plan/or Mideast Peace at Morocco Talks," *New York Times,* Sept.10, 1982, at Al, col. 1.

9. The declaration of Crown Prince Fahd that "[t]he war with Israel damages everyone" and his recent peace plan are indications of this new awareness. See Elon, "Diplomacy of /Destruction," HAARETZ, May 30, 1980, at 13, col. 5. (All references to *Haaretz* in this study, if not otherwise indicated, will refer to the weekly international Hebrew edition.) According to one view, already "[t]here appears to be a consensus among all the major Arab states (with the possible exceptions of Libya and South Yemen) that the PLO must curb its dreams and work through essentially peaceful means for the achievement of a small Palestinian state in the West Bank, East Jerusalem and Gaza." Hudson, *The Palestinians Retrospect and Prospects,* 78 CURRENT HIST. 22, 41 (1980). This view seems to have been confirmed at the recent Fez Summit, supra note 8.

10. In discussing any questions of contemporary international affairs, and particularly the Arab-Israeli conflict, one runs the risk of being out of date at the time of publication. The main themes in this paper relating to long-term trends and principles should, despite the volatility of events in the region, remain relevant for some time to come.

It is too early to assess fully the ramifications of the three calamitous events that took place in summer 1982. As noted above, the Lebanese war has underscored the centrality of the Palestinian issue to any peace move. Israel's military victory has, even from her point of view, only tackled (at immense disproportionate cost) a symptom rather than the root problem.

The American initiative, although on its face still contrary to the establishment of an independent Palestinian state, comes close to this proposition and thus raises many of the issues with which this Article seeks to grapple.

As for the Fez Summit, supra note 8, it is difficult to tell if the concluding declaration, which implies a muted recognition of Israel, signifies a mere tactical ploy or a real, strategic change of heart. One must also wait and see whether the declaration will be endorsed by the Palestinian movement once it has had time to reorganize after its military defeat. But even the most optimistic assumptions regarding Fez face the dilemma outlined in the concluding paragraph of the introduction to this article: a political breakthrough might be doomed because its operational details seem unacceptable. The solution of this dilemma may be regarded as a key objective of this article.

11. Egypt-Israel: Treaty of Peace, Mar.26, 1979, 18 I.L.M. 362 (1979).

12. The "Framework for Peace in the Middle East Agreed at Camp David" provides, in regard to the West Bank and Gaza, the following: "Egypt and Israel agree that ... there should be transitional arrangements for the West Bank and Gaza for a period not exceeding five years." It is that period, which is to commence only after the inauguration of the Administrative Council in the West Bank and Gaza, for which autonomy is specifically provided. Negotiations for a final settlement are to commence within the five-year period. On the one hand, the Agreement foresees that these negotiations will be based on UN Security Council Resolution 242, which accords the Palestinians only refugee status. 22 U.N. SCOR (1382d mtg.) Supp. (1967) at 8, U.N. Doc. S/INF/22/Rev. 2 (1968). On the other hand, the Agreement affirms that "[t]he solution from the negotiations must also recognize the legitimate rights of the Palestinian people and their just requirements." Likewise, in the preamble to the Agreement, the parties declare that "[t]he provisions of [the UN charter and] other accepted norms of international law and legitimacy ... provide accepted standards for the conduct of relations among all states." The tension between the insistence on "states" (rather than peoples) and "legitimacy" reflects the same ambiguity as to any eventual solution at the end of the transitional period.

In principle, the autonomy plan which, as confirmed in a joint letter of March 26, 1979, from Begin and Sadat to Carter (see also Agreed Minutes: Article VI (2)), was perceived as a transitional measure, could be renewed as a permanent solution after the five-year period. The Agreement does not, however, preclude more radical solutions. By recognizing the legitimate rights of the Palestinians, Israel seems to have conceded, in law, more than her current political position would suggest. On the binding effect of the Camp David Framework Agreement and its relation to the subsequent Peace Treaty, see Lapidoth, *The Relation between the Camp David Frameworks and the Treaty of Peace-Another Dimension,* 15 ISR. L. REV. 191, 192–93 (1980). The joint Begin-Sadat letter and the Agreed Minutes have been published in 25 KITVEH AMANAH 872 (1980) and 25 KITVEH AMANAH 869 (1980), respectively. The Camp David Agreement was published in 17 I.L.M. 1463 (1978) [hereinafter cited as Camp David Agreement].

13. See A. SHALAV, AUTONOMY: THE PROBLEMS AND POSSIBLE SOLUTIONS 62–66 (1979).

14. A leading Palestinian scholar comments that only "a sovereign, independent Palestinian state" (within the 1967 frontiers—subject to slight amendments) would win the endorsement of the PLO. Khalidi, *Thinking the Unthinkable: A Sovereign Palestinian State,* 56 FOREIGN AFF. 695, 701 (1978). The evolving attitude of the member states of the European Community, as well as the Community attitude as such, is instructive in this connection. An early analysis suggests a measure of caution in the attitudes of the member states and the Community as a whole. See Yaniv, *The European Community and the Palestinians,* in THE PALESTINIANS AND THE MIDDLE EAST CONFLICT, 291, 291–314 (G. Ben-Dor ed. 1979). A recent London *Times* appraisal recalls that "[a]s long ago as January 1976 France voted for a draft resolution in the Security Council which affirmed 'that the Palestinian people should be enabled to exercise its inalienable right of self-determination, including the right to establish an independent State in Palestine." Britain and Italy abstained. Further, it is recalled that West Germany and Italy have consistently spoken of the Palestinian right of self-determination and that in the September 1979 session of the United Nation General Assembly, "Mr. Michael O'Kennedy speaking on behalf of the Nine, demanded respect for the right of the Palestinian people 'through its representatives' to play its full part in the negotiations Mr. O'Kennedy later referred explicitly to the PLO and emphasized

that Security Council Resolutions 242 and 338 should be the basis for negotiations. These resolutions, naturally, accept the right of Israel to peaceful existence. Lord Carrington, Foreign Secretary of the United Kingdom, indicated that Resolution 242 should be supplemented to include the political rights of the Palestinians, including their rights to a "homeland." Ireland, on February 10, 1980, recognized the central role of the PLO and explicitly called for the establishment of a Palestinian state alongside Israel. Current British thinking would support this while emphasizing the need for the PLO to recognize and accept Israel. "Europe and the Palestinians," the *Times* (London), Mar. 11, 1980, at 13, col. 1. See also, Stebbing, *The Creation of a Palestinian Arab State as Part of a Middle East Settlement,* 6 INT'L REL. 507 (1978); La Republica, Mar. 9–10, 1980, at 10, col. 1. America's cautious endorsement of the Fahd plan makes the second hypothesis mentioned in the text a more likely future scenario. See "Two-Month-Old Saudi Peace Plan Is Gaining New Attention in US," *New York Times,* Oct.31, 1981, at 1, col. 2. See generally "Saudi Arabia's Peace Plan and Text of Resolution 242," NEW YORK TIMES, Oct.31, 1981, at 6, col. 1.

15. See infra notes 32 and 33. See also Halkin, infra note 65, at 27, 30. A durable settlement without PLO endorsement is unlikely. The official position of PLO and the Palestinian National Council vis-à-vis Israel and the particularly blind anti–Israeli terror campaign, coupled with Israel's no less uncompromising attitude vis-à-vis the PLO, create a sad chicken-and-egg cycle. The problems of breaking the cycle are touched upon in Part III infra. It should be emphasized that even if Israel and/or the PLO were to shift their actual position — unilaterally or bilaterally — a credibility gap would still remain.

16. All students of the Middle East conflict and its potential for federal solutions will be indebted to the pioneering and seminal work of Professor D. Elazar of Bar Ilan University and President of the Institute for Federal Studies, Jerusalem. In two important books, FEDERALISM AND POLITICAL INTEGRATION (1979) and SELF RULE/SHARED RULE (1979) (hereinafter cited as SELF RULE), edited by, and with contributions from, Elazar, many of the complexities and problems of federal solutions are analyzed, as well as their promising features. Elazar, who favors the Israel-Jordan condominium solution, adopts basically the first premise, which excludes the creation of a Palestinian state. Despite the fact that the present study departs radically from Elazar's prescriptions, his contributions remain an indispensable source.

17. Essentially in 1949 (pre–June 1967) boundaries.

18. This is not only the present official position of the PLO [see, e.g., Ma'oz, *New Attitudes of the PLO Regarding Palestine and Israel?,* in THE PALESTINIANS AND THE MIDDLE EAST CONFLICT 545, 545–51 (G. Ben-Dor ed. 1979)], but it is also a view shared by militant Palestinian leaders on the West Bank who follow the PLO line. Should the PLO reformulate its position to accept Israel, however, this shift would not cause traumatic tremors on the West Bank. More likely, opposition would come from the extreme "rejection front" Palestinian organizations.

19. With several notable exceptions, this represents Israeli consensus. Palestinian popular opinion under military occupation is less easy to assess accurately. It would probably be more difficult for an Israeli leader to accept the concept of a Palestinian state than it would be for a Palestinian to accept Israel if this were connected with the establishment of a Palestinian state.

20. See Kaplowitz, *Psychopolitical Dimensions of the Middle East Conflict,* 20 J. CONFLICT RESOLUTION, 279, 311 (1976). West Bank Palestinians, the very subjects of the exercise, have received the "autonomy" with abject coolness.

21. Nitzan, in his bibliography of federal solutions, lists no fewer than 59 of these plans. NITZAN, supra note 3. See also Peretz, *A Binational Approach to the Palestine*

Conflict, in THE MIDDLE EAST CRISIS: TEST OF INTERNATIONAL LAW (J. Halderman ed. 1969).

22. The term "federal" in the wide sense connotes a principle and an approach rather like a specific system of governance. Thus, Elazar usefully reminds us that the origins of the term lie

> first in the biblical term *brit,* then the Latin *foedus* (literally 'covenant'), from which the modern 'federal' is derived. Elaborated by the Calvinists in their federal theology, the concept formed the basis for far more than a form of political organization .... [The original use of the term deals with contractual linkages that involve power sharing — among individuals, among groups, among states. This usage is more appropriate than the definition of modern federation, which represents only one aspect of the federal idea and one application of the federal principle.

SELF RULE supra note 16, at 3. In this wide sense, supranationalism may justly be characterized as a manifestation of the federal idea, hence the juxtaposition to federal *states.*

23. The classic "confederal option" is analyzed in Amit, *A Confederal Solution to the Palestinian Problem: Chances and Dangers,* in IS THERE A SOLUTION TO THE PALESTINIAN PROBLEM? ISRAELI POSITIONS 111, 230 (A. Hareven ed., 1982).

24. In their detailed analysis of the various possible federal solutions, Elazar and Irkansky single out the common market model (as part of Sectoral Federal Arrangements) for its flexibility. It is suggested that this flexibility, which would enable limited projects, may be suitable for the first stages of cooperation. SELF RULE, supra note 16, at 258–59. For reasons of space, this article's analysis will be confined to Israel and Palestine alone, although the suggested framework could be a basis for other arrangements including Jordan and other states.

25. "Recognition" is an ambiguous term. Nonrecognition of a regime or a state does not necessarily imply an immediate threat of war. Likewise, recognition as such does not preclude war. In this article, unless otherwise indicated, "recognition" will not be used in its narrow legal meaning, but *rather* as an indication of acceptance in the wider political and social sense.

26. Israel requested in 1982 an aid package from the United States totaling $2,585 million. The TIMES (London), Aug. 6, 1982, at 4, col. I. This economic dependence places inevitable restrictions on the policy latitudes of the Israeli Government, although it is hardly conceivable that the United States will use its economic grip in a *direct* manner to extract political concessions.

27. It is difficult to keep up with the pace of economic developments in Israel. In an article that seeks to establish the constants in the relationship between Israel's political situation (vis-à-vis the Arab-Israeli conflict) and internal social and economic plight, it has been argued that "[a]s long as the [Israeli] nation remains in this state of siege, it seems unlikely that any Israeli government, of the Right or the Left, will alter the current economic policies significantly." The policies at issue are those which maintain full employment but also hyperinflation. Crittenden, *Israel's Economic Plight,* 57 FOREIGN AFF. 1005, 1012 (1979).

28. This was reaffirmed recently by Israel's flat rejection of both the Reagan and Fez initiatives. See the TIMES (London) Sept. 11, at I, col. 5.

29. Jerusalem, probably the most emotive issue in the conflict, will not be dealt with; I subscribe to the "Jerusalem last" thesis, which holds that once all other issues are settled, the climate will be conducive to solving this problem as well.

The Gaza Strip does not raise the range of emotive, ideological, historical or even security issues as does the West Bank. Thus, it is likely that the fate of the Gaza Strip, if it is not eventually returned to Egypt, will be linked to the more complex issue of the West Bank. On the security issue, some regard the Gaza Strip as posing a threat equal to that of the West Bank. See SELF RULE, supra note 16, at 215.

30. The Palestinian National Covenant (often referred to as the Charter), which expresses the official political and ideological platform of the PLO, provides, inter alia, that the 1947 partition and the establishment of Israel are acts void *ab initio* (article 19); that Zionism has no legitimacy as a national movement (article 22); and that Jews may not be recognized as a people (article 20). PALESTINIAN NATIONAL COVENANT, reprinted in L. KADI, BASIC POLITICAL DOCUMENTS OF THE ARMED PALESTINIAN RESISTANCE MOVEMENT 137 (1969). It further provides that the only Jews who may have rights, qua Palestinians, are those who themselves, or whose ancestors, habitually lived in Palestine before the Zionist invasion (article 6). For a sharp articulation of the fear that the State of Israel will be dismantled, see infra note 65. At the same time, one must not overestimate the political and operative significance of the dated Covenant. Like many historical documents, it may be overtaken by events. Professor Kasher, an influential Israeli "dove," suggests that "one can understand from sources identified with the PLO that [should] negotiations commence the Covenant will go in the way of all ancient manifestos and ideologies." 2341 HAOLAM HAZEH July 14, 1982, at 21, 22.

31. The origins of the "step-by-step" program for the liberation of Palestine and establishment of independence in any part that will be liberated may be found in the Resolution of the 12th meeting of the National Palestinian Council in Cairo in June 1974. For the text of the Resolution, see THE ARABS AND ISRAEL Nos. 3–4, 219 (Y. Harkabi ed. 1975) and 3 J. PALESTINIAN STUD. 224 (1974). The program was consolidated in the Council's 13th meeting in March 1977. See 6 J. PALESTINIAN STUD. 188 (1977). See also *1974 Tripartite Palestinian-Egyptian-Syrian Communique*, 4 J. PALESTINAN STUD. 164, 165 (1975).

32. Ma'oz describes this as a pragmatic-tactical position which favors a separate and independent Palestinian state as a basic condition for a political settlement, but without compromising on the principle of Palestinian sovereignty over the whole of Palestine.... [I]t should be emphasized that this pragmatic-tactical attitude of the PLO by no means represents an essential change in the basic position of its leaders, let alone the rank and file. Even the most 'moderate' PLO spokesmen maintain that their ultimate goal is one Palestinian Arab State, throughout Palestine." Ma'oz, supra note 18, at 549–50. This is the dilemma that faces Israelis in trying to evaluate Arafat's apparent concurrence with the Fez declaration.

33. Perhaps one may, in this international context, borrow from Professor Calabresi the term "tragic choice." G. CALABRESI & P. BOBBITT, TRAGIC CHOICES (1978). The tragic Israeli choice is rooted in the knowledge that continued occupation of the territories will forever preclude a final settlement, whereas evacuation and establishment of a Palestinian state would also seem to preclude such a settlement. If one is to follow the Calabresi terminology, the "scarce resource," the allocation of which causes the apparently tragic choice, is sovereignty over Eretz Yisrael-Palestine. The scarcity derives from the conviction of both parties that outright and durable partition would be too risky, would spell defeat and simply would not work.

This article, then, is designed to dispel the "tragedy" from the "choice" by suggesting a different type of resource allocation or by suggesting that the resource is not scarce.

34. For a lucid statement of the problem of "real peace," see Hoffman, *A New Policy for Israel*, 53 FOREIGN AFF. 405 (1975). Hoffman argues that in Israel every piece of conquered territory is important, especially the West Bank:

"And yet, there is also a perfectly genuine willingness to return almost everything in exchange for 'real peace.'

But 'real peace' is conceived in terms that make it unrealistic. For what is called 'real peace' is a set of attitudes and modes of behavior that would normally *follow* from peace rather than precede it...."

Id. at 428. Although there has certainly been a hardening in the position of Israel and the Israelis toward the return of the territories, the confusion about "real peace" remains.

35. For the psychological analogue of the mutually reenforcing nature of the conflict, see Kaplowitz, supra note 20, at 299.

36. The size of the West Bank and the density of its population, as well as its proximity to Israeli centers of population, rule out buffer zones.

37. In this article, "normal" security measures will designate the traditional apparatus and means a state takes for its defense: the maintenance of an army during peace time and its reinforcement and deployment on its borders in situations of tension. "Special" security measures will refer to measures that encroach upon the traditional sovereignty and independence of the potential enemy. The possibility of "special" security measures is contemplated in the Camp David Framework Agreements, supra note 12, although, significantly, on the basis of reciprocity.

38. Large sections of the Arab population share the same anti-Zionist premises. The Israeli Communist Party is a strong focal point for anti-Zionist feeling. It is generally accepted that the strong attraction to the Party of a sizeable percentage of Arab voters in Israel is based on its anti-Zionist stance rather than its Communist (Moscow-oriented) ideology. See generally, SELF RULE, supra note 16, at 29. The *moral* untenability of the historical claim is strongly argued in A. YEHOSHUA, BETWEEN RIGHT AND RIGHT 85–89 (1981). Despite the strong argument of Yehoshua, with whose conclusions I agree, the strong historical feeling of both parties is a subjective factor with which one must reckon.

39. Several explanations have been given for the discrepancy between the small number of actual Gush-Emunim activists and their importance in Israeli political and social life. At the social level, against a background of the profound materialism with which Israeli society is currently afflicted, the Gush settlers are depicted as latter-day "pioneers" *(Haluzim)* reviving the most venerated tradition in political Zionism. See the excellent book by A. RUISENSTEIN, FROM HERTZL TO GUSH-EMUNIM AND BACK 111–33 (1980). In this way they are able to appeal both to Jewish Orthodox sectors, to some of whom the settlement of Eretz Yisrael is a sacred value, as well as to nonreligious Jews, to whom settling the land is regarded as a per se Zionist value. For both groups the Gush activists have become proxies for ideological praxis. The manner and even the objects of the Gush are, in my view, a travesty of classical Zionism, which, in its origins, was based, like other national movements, on respect for the individual, human rights and the rights of other national movements. See J. Talmon, "The Pairia Imperiled," HAARETZ, Mar.31, 1980, at 15, col. 1. At the political level, Gush-Emunim represents to many the conscience of the Likud movement and is thus supported by many Likud back-benchers. Some of these have recently established a new political party (the Tehiya) to the right of Likud. A final factor in Gush-Emunim's strength is open and often defiant support from Cabinet Ministers.

40. Contrary to a common misimpression, rabbinical disagreement exists on the religious duty to settle the West Bank in present political conditions. The two Israeli chief rabbis differ on this issue as do leading rabbis in the Diaspora. See, for example, the moderate views of Rabbi Jakobowits, Chief Rabbi of Great Britain and the Commonwealth, in the TIMES (London), June 25, 1980, at I, col. 5. Even if there is a gen-

eral duty to settle, this may in the view of some rabbinical authority be disregarded if it imperils the well-being and security of the state.

41. See Talmon, supra note 39; RUBENSTEIN, supra note 39. See also, Goldmann, *Zionist Ideology and the Reality of Israel,* 57 FOREIGN AFF. 70 (1978).

42. The "Peace Now" movement is the best organized group of this persuasion. Thus, if the typology of Jewish-Israeli society is to be reduced to two principal groups, Gush Emunim and Peace Now may be regarded as the focal points of the dichotomy. The former is

> convinced that in the face of an international conspiracy to establish a PLO and lackey of the Soviet Russian State, which would seek to destroy the State of Israel, it is a supreme imperative to hurry and expand settlements [in the Occupied Territories] and to maintain determined and uncompromising policies and to develop daring activism as the only way to prevent a calamity,

whereas the latter group

> believes that a unique opportunity for peace with [Israel's] neighbors has occurred and that the efforts to spread and consolidate by force [Israeli] rule over the population of the Territories will lead to the losing of any chance for a peace settlement and will open the way to unimaginable dangers.

Talmon, supra note 39 (author's translation).

43. In the political history of Zionism, several geographical alternatives to Israel were advocated at one time or another — notably the Uganda solution supported by Hertzl himself. See A. ELAN, HERTZL, 424 (1975). The defeat of all such suggestions is testimony to the inextricability of Zionism and Zion.

44. For an analysis, albeit controversial, of the "syndrome" in relation to a renowned Zionist leader, see HEBREW ENCYCLOPEDIA 678–80 (Supp. 1967). Cf Avi-hai, *David Ben Gurion's Political Philosophy,* ENCYCLOPEDIA JUDAICA 88 (1973).

45. It is estimated that certainly no more than a third of (Jewish) Israelis may be regarded as religious in the sense of placing religious law as above secular national law in the hierarchy of norms. Cf Elazar, *Towards a Jewish Definition of Statehood,* 49–50 PETAHIM 58, 74 n.4 (1980).

46. This was demonstrated very clearly in relation to the Agreement over Sinai with Egypt, Treaty of Peace, March 26, 1979, Egypt-Israel, annex I app., Protocol Concerning Israeli Withdrawal and Security Arrangements, Organization of Movements in the Sinai, reprinted in 18 I.L.M. 367 (1979). Although probably far less animosity and fear exist vis-à-vis the Egyptians, and although the Agreements envisioned continuation of tourism, the formal signing and the planned evacuation of Sinai led to wide scale vandalism and looting of the coral treasures along the Red Sea. The motivation was, at least in part, the fear that handing over these territories to Egypt would impede further Israeli access. Evidently the very concept of peace is still difficult to grasp.

47. Thus, Dr. Israel Eldad, one of the main ideologues of the Israeli right, argues that "at the moment I forego the basis for our rights to [Hebron] and [East] Jerusalem I forego the basis for living [anywhere in Israel] and for returning here." Eldad, "To Write in Haaretz," HAARETZ, Feb.28, 1980, at 9, col. 1. Significantly, the same point was made recently very forcefully by General Eitan, the Chief of Staff of the Israel Defense Forces. See MAARIV, Apr. 3, 1980. Chief-of-staff statements traditionally reflect at best the political consensus in Israel and at worst the official government line. See also interview with Eitan in BEMAHANEH (special overseas ed.), July, 1982, at 4–7.

48. See supra text accompanying notes 25–27.

49. This is the official policy of the main Labor Opposition Party in Israel.

50. Assessment of the degree to which human rights are violated by Israel in the occupied territories is extremely difficult. Inevitably, objectivity is sacrificed in the interests of the continuous propaganda war. Extremely damaging reports were made by the SUNDAY TIMES (London) Insight Team. See "Israel and Torture," the SUNDAY TIMES (London), June 19, 1977, at 17, col. I. For the official Israeli reply, see the JERUSALEM *Post*, July 4, 1977. For reports characterized by a high degree of restraint, see the prestigious Annual Reports of Amnesty International. See also the disturbing accounts in F. LANGER, WITH MY OWN EYES: ISRAEL AND THE OCCUPIED TERRITORIES 1967–1973 *(1975)* and F. LANGER, THESE ARE MY BROTHERS (1979).

51. See Talmon, supra note 39; see Kaplowitz, supra note 20 at 302, 310. See also Goldmann, supra note 41 and J. LEIBOWITZ, JUDAISM, JEWISH PEOPLE AND THE STATE OF ISRAEL 418–22 (1976).

52. See supra text accompanying notes 29–37.

53. The literature on the Palestinians, even in English, is already vast. Researchers face the problem of sifting the scholarly and objective from the ideological and emotive. A useful, even if slightly dated, political background account is that of Rouleau, *The Palestinian Ouest*, 53 FOREIGN AFF. 264 *(1975)*. Two recent studies are E. SAID, THE QUESTION OF PALESTINE (1979) and THE PALESTINIANS AND THE MIDDLE EAST CONFLICT, supra note 14. Other sources that merit study include the following: R. EL-RAYYIS & D. NAHAS, GUERRILLAS FOR PALESTINE (1976); D. HIRST, THE GUN AND THE OLIVE BRANCH: THE ROOTS OF VIOLENCE IN THE MIDDLE EAST (1977); W. KAZZIHA, PALESTINE FOR PALESTINIANS (1976); S. MISHAL, WEST BANK/EAST BANK (1978); THE PALESTINIANS IN PERSPECTIVE (G.E. Gruen ed. 1982); Y. PORATH, THE EMERGENCE OF THE PALESTINE-ARAB NATIONAL MOVEMENT, 1918–1929 (1974); THE TRANSFORMATION OF PALESTINE: ESSAYS ON THE ORIGIN AND DEVELOPMENT OF THE ARAB-ISRAELI CONFLICT (I. Abu-Lughod ed. 1971); R. WARD, D. PERETZ & E. WILSON, THE PALESTINE STATE: A RATIONAL APPROACH (1977).

54. 22 U.N. SCOR (1382d mtg.) Supp. (1967) at 8, U.N. Dcc. S/INF/22/Rev. 2 (1967).

55. See, e.g., PALESTINIAN NATIONAL COVENANT arts. 19, 20, 22 and 23, reprinted in L..5. KADI, supra note 30. Speaking of the PLO and rank and file Palestinians, Ma'oz comments that "none of them are willing to compromise with the Zionist or Jewish character of Israel—that is to say, the right of self-determination of the Jewish population in Israel." MA'OZ, supra note 18, at 550. See also H. CATTAN, PALESTINE AND INTERNATIONAL LAW 241 (2d ed. 1976). There have been many "nonofficial" PLO statements expressing a more moderate position, but it is always difficult to assess their political significance. The Covenant proves extremely embarrassing to moderate Palestinians.

56. This, it is submitted, is the only meaningful way of understanding article 6 of the Palestinian National Covenant in conjunction with articles 7 and 5. See Y. HARKABI, THE PALESTINIAN COVENANT AND ITS MEANING 42–61 (1979).

57. Article 20 of the Palestinian National Covenant provides, inter alia, that "Judaism being a divine religion is not an independent nationality. Nor do Jews constitute a single nation with an identity of its own: they are citizens of the States to which they belong." Id at 78–80.

58. See Rasheed, *Towards a Democratic State in Palestine*, in MIDDLE EAST RESEARCH AND INFORMATION PROJECT (1971). See also Y. HARKABI, supra note *56*, at 50–57.

59. The conceptual refutation by Israeli politicians of Palestinian nationalism in the late 1960s and early 1970s is notorious. Palestinians have focused on one aspect of "Jewishness" (the religious aspect) to the exclusion of all others. In this way they blind themselves to Jewish nationalism. Many Israelis (especially in the past) used to focus on the "Arabism" of Palestinians to the exclusion of their national particularism. This is but one of many parallels in the Israel-Palestine equation. For a recent study of the Palestinian movement since the establishment of the State of Israel, see Y. HARKABI, THE PALESTINIANS: FROM QUIESCENCE TO AWAKENING (1979). See also Hirst, supra note 53, at chs. 6–7.

60. See M. RODINSON, ISRAEL: A COLONIAL-SETTLER STATE? 75–78 (1973).

61. Approximately 47.9 percent of Israelis as of 1973 were born in Israel. MINISTRY OF INFORMATION, FACTS ABOUT ISRAEL (1975) (hereinafter cited as FACTS ABOUT ISRAEL). Over 50 percent of Palestinians (especially under the wide definition of the Covenant, article 5) were born outside Israel. AMERICAN ENTERPRISE INST. FOR PUBLIC POLICY RESEARCH, ISRAEL AT THE POLLS 83 (H. Penniman ed. 1979).

62. A powerful expression of "existential" Zionism is that of the Israeli Oz:

> I am a Jew and a Zionist. In defining the nature of my identity, I do not rely on religion, for I stand outside it... A Jew, in my vocabulary, is someone who regards himself as a Jew, and also someone who is forced to be a Jew.
>
> I am a Zionist because I will not and cannot exist as a splinter of a symbol in the consciousness of others. Not as the symbol of a shrewd, gifted vampire who deserves compensation and atonement. Therefore there is no place for me in the world other than in the country of the Jews. That does not make me circumvent my responsibility as a Jew, but it saves me from the nightmare of being a symbol in the mind of strangers.
>
> The country of the Jews could not have come into existence anywhere than [in Israel]. Not in Uganda and not in Ararat and not in Birobidjan. Because this is the country the Jews have always looked to and longed for. Because there is no other part of the world to which the Jews would have come to in their quantities to establish a Jewish country. And on this point I commit myself to a severe distinction between the inner motives of the return to Zion and its justification to others. The longings are a motive but no justification. Our justification in respect of the Arab inhabitants cannot base itself on our age-old longings. We have no other justification than that of one who is drowning and grasps at the only plank he can: and let me anticipate here. There is a difference between the man who grasps a plank and makes room by pushing others on one side and the man who pushes the others into the sea. This is the difference between making Jaffa or Nazareth Jewish and making Ramallah or Nablus Jewish.
>
> ... I am a Zionist in all that concerns the redemption of the Jews, but not when it comes to the redemption of the Holy Land. We have come here to live as free men, not to free the land that groans under the desecration of a foreign yoke, Jerusalem or Galilee or Samaria or Gilead or Aram up to the Euphrates. I was not born to blow trumpets or to liberate a heritage that has been violated by strangers. I do not regard myself as a Jew merely by virtue of "race" or a "Hebrew" by Virtue of having been born in the land of Canaan. I choose to be a Jew. As a Jew, I would not and cannot live anywhere but in a Jewish State,

and this could only come into being in the land of Israel. That is as far as my Zionism goes.

Oz, *To be or not to be a Jew* 352–54, ADAM INT'L REV. 59, 59–61 (1971). See also A. YEHOSHUA, supra note 38, at 95–104. For a critique, see HAARETZ, Sept. 10, 1979, at 10, especially the article by Professor Engelrad.

63. See PALESTINIAN NATIONAL COVENANT arts. 12–15, reprinted in L. KADI, supra note 30. See also W. KAZZIHA, supra note 53.

64. See PALESTINIAN NATIONAL COVENANT arts. 4, 5, reprinted in L. KADI, supra note 30, and Y. HARKABI, supra note 56, at 40–42.

65. The following hypothesis acutely encapsulates this problem:

> Suppose... [the Palestinians] succeeded in establishing an independent state in Palestine; suppose that this state were composed of two discontiguous pieces of roughly twice the size of Luxembourg; ... suppose that it had practically no natural resources to speak of, and could barely support its own rapidly reproducing population, much less absorb the millions of ... "diaspora" countrymen whose problem it was supposed to solve; suppose, once the first flush of enthusiasm for a passport and flag ... had worn off frustration and disillusionment set in; and suppose that at the same time the overall balance of power between Israel and the Arab states kept tilting in favor of the Arabs, surfeited with oil, petrodollars, and arms ... [would the Palestinians] accept the fact that the Jews have permanently gotten away with the more richly endowed three-quarters of Palestine ... and resolve to be good neighbors with them? Or [would they] obey ... irredentist emotions, trusting that considerations of *Realpolitik* will sooner or later make the world force Israel to return still more of [Palestinian] stolen homeland or even acquiesce in the destruction of the Jewish state entirely once Arab strength has made this possible?

Halkin, *Whose Palestine?* 69 COMMENTARY 21, 26–27 (1980). Halkin's fears are not frivolous, but they do not necessarily lead to a conclusion that precludes the establishment of a Palestinian state. Thus, for example, it is possible that consideration of *Realpolitik* will make the world even more disposed to acquiesce in the destruction of the Jewish state once Arab strength has made this possible — if a Palestinian state is *not* established. A more constructive approach, attempted in this study, is that which would minimize the potential for "frustration and disillusionment" by reducing the importance of boundaries and by finding solutions to the lack of natural resources which is not, after all, a problem unique to the putative Palestine. The population is going to reproduce rapidly regardless of the establishment of a Palestinian state and unless some meaningful political solution is found — one which will take cognizance of the strength of the Palestinian National Movement — the security threat will merely manifest itself in another form.

66. See, e.g., V. BULL, THE WEST BANK — IS IT VIABLE? (1975). Bull in fact points to the economic advantages of some form of integration of the West Bank with Jordan and/or Israel. Id at 243. See also A. PLASCOV, A PALESTINIAN STATE? EXAMINING THE ALTERNATIVES, 163 ADELPHI PAPERS 34 (1981), and R. WEITZ, WHERE ARE WE HEADED? (private publication, on file at European University Institute, Florence, 1976). But see E. TUMA & H. DARIN-DRABKIN, THE ECONOMIC CASE FOR PALESTINE 103–12 (1978), whose authors are skeptical about the need or even desirability of integration to ensure economic viability of the West Bank. They are particularly concerned with "Free Trade Imperialism." Id. at 108. Part III of this article deals with this problem.

67. See Kaplowitz, supra note 20, at 302.

68. See infra text accompanying note 244.

69. Relations between an independent Palestinian state, should it emerge, and the Kingdom of Jordan would be problematic. Formal relations between the PLO and the Hashemite House were long at a low point, although they have improved since the Camp David Agreement. The close socioeconomic links between the two regions are such that some form of linkage would appear essential. At the same time there is a strong measure of mutual suspicion between the Palestinians and the Hashemites. The model suggested in this article is confined to Israel and Palestine for institutional reasons that will be discussed below. This does not preclude close ties with Jordan.

70. See, e.g., FACTS ABOUT ISRAEL, supra note 61, at 57. See also A. SHALAV, supra note 13, at 63.

71. For a modern incisive treatment of the law of belligerent occupation in the context of human rights, see Dinstein, *The International Law of Belligerent Occupation and Human Rights,* 8 ISR. Y.B. HUM. RTS. 104 (1978).

72. For a brief review of the different theories on the status of the area (as well as the connected question of the internal legal system), see Drori, *The Legal System in Judea and Samaria: A Review of the Previous Decade with a Glance at the Future,* 8 ISR. Y.B. HUM. RTS. 144, 145–46 (1978). See also DRORI, THE LEGISLATION IN THE AREA OF JUDEA AND SAMARIA 23–31(1975).

73. Blum, *The Missing Reversioner: Reflections on the Status of Judea and Samaria,* 3 ISR. L. REV. 279 (1968). See also Blum, The Jurisdiction Status of Jerusalem, in 2 J. OESTERREICHER & A. SINAI, JERUSALEM 108 (1974); and Y. BLUM, SECURE BOUNDARIES AND MIDDLE EAST PEACE 61–110(1971). Cf. Shamgar, *The Observance of International Law in the Administered Territories,* I ISR. Y.B. HUM. RTS. 262(1971) and J. STONE, No PEACE No WAR IN THE MIDDLE EAST (1969).

74. Blum, *The Missing Reversioner. Reflections on the Status of Judea and Samaria,* 3 ISR. L. REV. 279, 283 (1968).

75. On these rules, see generally R. JENNINGS, THE ACQUISITION OF TERRITORY IN INTERNATIONAL LAW (1963).

76. Blum, supra note 74, at 287.

77. Id at 288–89. Blum further points out that only two states, the United Kingdom and Pakistan, accorded recognition to this annexation. Id at 290. While this is factually correct, it affords perhaps too little weight for implicit recognition, and preclusion from denying it, by most states in the world. Cf. R. JENNINGS, supra note 75. While it is possible that Israeli silence in relation to Jordanian annexation should not be considered acquiescence, Blum, supra note 74, other states have engaged in a variety of activities, statements and resolutions that would be inconsistent with non-recognition. These states may, of course, feel that with the evolution of Palestinian nationalism the latter's right to self-determination should be assertable in respect of the West Bank; or alternatively, that Jordanian annexation was subject to that right in the first place. In relation to Israel, Blum relies on the 1949 Israel-Jordan General Armistice Agreements which contained "no prejudice" clauses in respect of boundaries. Id at 292. This argument can, of course, be turned against Israel in respect of territories acquired by Israel in 1948–49 and extending beyond the 1947 Partition Resolution boundaries. For this and other illuminating remarks, see Kuttner, *Israel and the West Bank, Aspects of the Law of Belligerent Occupation,* 7 ISR. Y.B. HUM. RTS. 166, 177 (1977). The essence of Blum's thesis formed part of respondent's submission in the Elon Moreh case, Judgment of Oct. 22, 1979, High Court of Justice, Israel, reprinted in 19 I.L.M. 148,162 (1980). Justice Landau (Acting President), id at 165, in the main judgment reiterated his opinion from a previous petition that "[w]e are not required

to consider this problem in this petition and this demurrer joins therefore the group of demurrers ... which remain as open questions in this Court." Beit-El Case HC 606/78; 610/78 1979, 33 *Pskei Din* (2) 113,165 (Mar. 13. 1974).

Elsewhere in his judgment, Justice Landau referred to the argument which Israel puts forward in the international arena "... [which is] based *on the fad* that [in 1967, the occupied territories were] not occupied by any sovereign whose occupation had won general international recognition." Id at 164 (emphasis added). The text should not be read as an acceptance by the court of this alleged "fact" of nonrecognition of Jordanian sovereignty.

78. Blum, supra note 74, at 294, 295 n.60.
79. See Gerson, *Trustee-Occupant: The Legal Status of Israel's Presence in the West Bank,* 14 HARV. INT'L L.J. 1(1973).
80. Kuttner, supra note 77, at 176.
81. Blum, supra note 74, at 282–93.
82. Cf. Kuttner, supra note 77, at 175–76.
83. Id.
84. Kuttner states that if indeed Jordan's annexation became legally valid by local acquiescence and international de facto recognition this "would deny the validity of any claim by the Palestinian National Congress or its constituent parts to sovereignty in Palestine." Id. This view might be too inflexible, particularly in regard to the effect of emergent Palestinian nationalism and possible rights of self-determination.
85. See Gerson, supra note 79.
86. Strictly speaking, if sovereignty had vested in Jordan, it would not be for Israel to attempt to change the status of the territories by consenting to the establishment of a Palestinian state. Naturally, Jordan would have to be party to any negotiations concerning the West Bank's ultimate status. Cf Camp David Agreements, 17 I.L.M. at 1467–68. Section A (West Bank and Gaza) foresees such Jordanian participation in the decision as to final destiny. Id.
87. See A. GERSON, supra note 1, at 78.
88. Blum correctly cites the negative reaction of the Arab League itself to the Jordanian annexation. But as Gerson explains, in the language of the Arab League Resolution itself, this opposition was intended to ensure "that the country would be handed over to its [local Palestinian] owners to rule in the way they like." Id.
89. See, e.g., G.A. Res. 32/5, U.N. Doc. A/32/PV.51, at 925 (1977). By a vote of 131 to 1 (Israel), with 7 abstentions, the Assembly considered that Israeli measures to change the legal status, geographic nature and demographic composition of the territories were not valid and constituted a "serious obstruction" to a just peace. Id.
90. Blum, *The Legal Status of Judea and Samaria,* in THE GREATER ISRAEL BOOK 121, 128 (A. Ben-Ami ed. 1977).
91. See, e.g., statement by Mr. Eban, 4 U.N. SCOR (433d mtg.) at 9 (1949).
92. U.N. Doc. S/I 302/Rev.I. Article 11(2) provides that "no provision of this Agreement shall in any way prejudice the rights, claims and positions of either Party thereto in the ultimate peaceful settlement of the Palestine question, the provisions of this Agreement being dictated exclusively by military considerations." For full text of all Armistice Agreements, see 42 U.N.T.S. 251, 287, 303, 327.
93. S. Rosenne, a former legal adviser to the Israeli Ministry of Foreign Affairs and a signatory to some of the Armistice Agreements, develops the following reasoning: First, he argues that the Agreements "were not intended merely as affording temporary respite from hostilities, but rather as definite steps forward in the direction of permanent peace." He then recalls the aforementioned article 11(2), which is common to all the Armistice Agreements concluded between Israel and her Arab neighbors, but

points out that the Egyptian Agreement included an additional, more severe reservation, namely that the "[t]he Armistice Demarcation Line is not to be construed in any sense as a political territorial boundary (Article V of the Egyptian-Israeli Armistice Agreement.) He then asks whether the presence of this clause in the Egyptian Agreement and its absence in all others produces any juridical consequences. His conclusion is that "in the other Agreements the armistice demarcation line is equivalent to an international frontier, i.e., that it may be construed there as a political or territorial boundary." His view is based on a coincidence of the demarcation lines with previous international lines which would seem as though he himself does not raise the doubt — to exclude the frontier with Jordan. But he also suggests that this coincidence is subject to "the demographic situation subsisting at the time of negotiation." This also might explain why the pre-1967 frontier with Jordan would have assumed a higher status than an armistice line. S. ROSENNE, ISRAEL'S ARMISTICE AGREEMENTS WITH THE ARAB STATES 41–48 (1951). But see Rosenne, *Directions for a Middle East Settlement — Some Underlying Legal Problems,* in THE MIDDLE EAST CRISIS: TEST OF INTERNATIONAL LAW 44, 51–55 (J. Halderman ed. 1969).

94. N. FEINBERG, ESSAYS ON JEWISH ISSUES OF OUR TIME 216 (1980). Cf id. at 217–23.

95. See generally H. CATTAN, PALESTINE, THE ARABS AND ISRAEL: THE SEARCH FOR JUSTICE (1969); H. CATTAN, supra note 1; Cattan, *The Arab-Israeli Conflict and the Principles of Justice,* 28 REVUE EGYPTIENNE DE DROIT INTERNATIONAL 44 (1972).

96. Cattan, *The Arab-Israeli Conflict and the Principles of Justice,* 28 REVUE EGYPTIENNE DE DROIT INTERNATIONAL 44, 45 (1972).

97. Cattan's sharp dichotomy between international law and justice raises several questions and tends to beg others. It is one thing to suggest the universal existence of a metaphysical and vague concept of justice; establishing criteria for concrete application of this universal concept in order to make moral judgments is quite another. A brief glance at any anthology of moral philosophy is sufficient to call into question Cattan's statement that the concept of justice is less subject to divergence of opinion or interpretation. See, e.g., THEORIES OF ETHICS (P. Foot ed. 1967). Further, it is not at all clear, as Cattan contends, that international law "being largely based on practice and precedents, does not necessarily cover all situations." Cattan, supra note 96. The problem that arises also in municipal law is jurisprudentially unsettled. See, e.g., H. HART, THE CONCEPT OF LAW 121–32 (1961). For a view that denies "gaps" in international law, see I P. GUGGENHEIM, TRAITE DE DROIT INTERNATIONAL PUBLIC 292 (1967). Finally, of most importance, the distinction that Cattan makes raises the prospect of a conflict between international law and justice. Cattan relies, in part, on the order in which article I of the United Nations Charter speaks of "principles of justice and international law" to solve the potential conflict. He suggests a clear "choice of principle" rule, namely, that justice must prevail. While one must applaud the moral conviction behind this rule, several remarks must be made. First, it should be recalled that article I of the Charter mentions as the first purpose of the United Nations the maintenance of "international peace and security." Cattan's laudable rule is based on his earlier characterization of the principle of justice as not only universal, but also clear and less open to divergence of opinion. If, as has been suggested, this is not the case, Cattan's "choice rule" may become extremely dangerous because it will create a legitimate excuse for those actors claiming to adhere to the principles of justice. In the constant tension between the function of law as a normative explication of justice and its other function as a system to ensure order, there can be no easy self-evident solutions as Cattan implies.

98. Cattan, supra note 96.

99. The Indians in the United States are one such example. Most states have their own crosses to bear.

100. See, e.g., Talmon, *Haaretz*, Nov. 3, 1973, at 11; *Haaretz*, Dec. 7, 1973, at 15, cot. 1. See also A. YEHOSHUA, supra note 38.

101. H. CATTAN, supra note 1, at 164.

102. THE PALESTINIAN NATIONAL COVENANT, arts. 2, 3, 9, 15–20, reprinted in L.S. KADI, supra note 30, at 137–41.

103. The difficulties of *restitutio in integrum* are prominent in private law as well. Courts will often refuse an injunction that will turn back the clock if the cost to the allegedly offending party will far outweigh the benefits to the wronged party. See, e.g., Redland Bricks Ltd. v. Morris, 1970 A.C. 652. The concern for the future relations between the disputants as a consideration in the process of adjudicating past disputes is one reason that has prompted the interest in conciliation as a formally recognized method of dispute resolution. See Cappelletti & Garth, *Access to Justice The Worldwide Movemeni to Make Rights Effedive A General Report*, in I ACCESS TO JUSTICE 59–64 (M. Cappelletti & B. Garth eds. 1978). Cappelletti and Garth point out that "[c]onciliation is extremely useful for many types of claims and parties, especially as we learn the importance of mending long-term relationships rather than simply judging parties right to wrong." Id. at 64.

104. See generally H. CATTAN, supra note 1; A. GERSON, supra note I.

105. N. FEINBERG, STUDIES IN INTERNATIONAL LAW 515–611 (1979).

106. Cattan, supra note 96, at 46–47.

107. See INST. FOR PALESTINE STUDIES, THE PALESTINE QUESTION 62–72 (1968). This work is the product of a meeting of Arab jurists who met in July 1967 in Algiers to discuss the legal aspects of the Arab-Israeli conflict.

108. H. CATTAN, supra note 1, at 11–21; Cattan, supra note 96, at 46.

109. H. CATTAN, supra note I, at 33.

110. Id. at 30.

111. LEAGUE OF NATIONS COVENANT art. 22.

112. H. CATTAN, supra note 1, at 30–33.

113. Id at 33.

114. N. FEINBERG, supra note 105, at 451–59.

115. International Status of South West Africa, 1950 I.C.J. 128 (Advisory Opinion of July 11).

116. The General Assembly of the United Nations defeated such a suggestion in 1947. See H. CATTAN, supra note I, at 29. The *travaux preparatoires* of the United Nations Charter, article 80, confirm, according to Feinberg, that there was not widespread support for the view that regarded the Palestine Mandate as illegal. N. FEINBERG, supra note 105, at 457.

117. H. CATTAN, supra note 1, at 30.

118. Id. at 33.

119. But see, Rostow, *"Palestinian Self Determination": Possible Futures for the Unallocated Territories of the Palestine Mandate*, 5 YALE STUD. IN WORLD PUB. ORD. 147 (1979).

120. See Cattan, supra note I, and N. FEINBERG, supra note 105, at 515–611.

121. Wright, *Legal Aspects of the Middle East Situation*, in THE MIDDLE EAST CRISIS: TEST OF INTERNATIONAL LAW 12 n.42 (J. Halderman ed. 1969).

122. As I have postulated independence and statehood as necessary political conditions for resolution of the Palestinian conflict, it is not strictly necessary to discuss the legal problem of self-determination. The issue, despite numerous United Nations

reiterations, is far from unambiguous. As late as the last decade there were those who doubted the absorption of self-determination into positive customary international law. See Gross, *The Right of Self Determination in International Law in New States,* in NEW STATES IN THE MODERN WORLD (M. Kilson ed. 1975). Gross states that "the 'principle' of self-determination in Article 1(2) of the charter has not been transformed into a right to self-determination and that, independently of the charter, no such right has become part of customary international law..." Id. at 156. To the extent that self-determination has crystallized into a binding rule of public international law, especially in light of United Nations practice, the application of this rule to the Palestinians remains unsettled. See R. HIGGINS, THE DEVELOPMENT OF INTERNATIONAL LAW THROUGH THE POLITICAL ORGANS OF THE UNITED NATIONS 101-06 (1963). The concept of self-determination is defined in the following three United Nations General Assembly Resolutions: G.A. Res. 1514, 15 U.N. GAOR Supp. (No.16) at 66, U.N. Doc. A/4684 (1960); G.A. Res. 2105, 20 U.N. GAOR Supp. (No.14) at 3, U.N. Doc. A/6014 (1965); and G.A. Res. 2189, 21 U.N. GAOR Supp. (No.16) at 5, U.N. Doc. A/6316 (1966). Each definition is notoriously unclear on whether self-determination is adopted for the benefit of the peoples or of the territories. There is, however, little doubt that in colonial situations the indigenous population should enjoy a right of self-determination, but, at least in respect to the West Bank, the better view is to regard Israel as a belligerent occupant rather than a colonizing power. A more profound difficulty, connected to the previous one, relates to the identity of the Palestinian people as distinct from the Jordanians. In the definitions of self-determination there has always been a constant duality of the right to freedom from colonial subjugation but an equally strong imperative against the secession from states. See, e.g., G.A. Res. 1514, supra.

For an extremely useful general discussion of this aspect of self-determination, see Emerson, *Self-Determination,* 65 AM. J. INT'L L. 459, 462-66 (1971). See also 5 Y. DINSTEIN, supra note 7.

123. As Emerson indicates, in principle even the United Nations envisaged the possibility that "a legitimate outcome of self-determination [be] not only independence but also association or *integration with an independent state* or the emergence into any other political status freely accepted by a people." Emerson, supra note 122, at 470 (emphasis added). Emerson adds, however, that "the deep-rooted preference for independence generally shines out undisguised." Id. at 470 n.24.

124. See, e.g., I. BIBO, THE PARALYSIS OF INTERNATIONAL INSTITUTIONS AND THE REMEDIES 1-8 (1976); G. SCHWARZENBERGER & E. BROWN, A MANUAL OF INTERNATIONAL LAW 148-49 (1976).

125. See generally M. DEUTSCH, THE RESOLUTION OF CONFLICT 17, 20-32 (1973).

126. Kaplowitz, supra note 20.

127. Id. at 280-81.

128. Id. at 281.

129. Id.

130. On the different formal processes of dispute resolution, see DAVID DAVIES MEMORIAL INST. OF INT'L STUDIES, INTERNATIONAL DISPUTES: THE LEGAL ASPECTS (1972). For an analysis of the political process of international negotiations, see F. IKLE, HOW NATIONS NEGOTIATE (1964). Negotiation as Ikle defines it "is a process in which explicit proposals are put forward ostensibly for the purpose of reaching agreement on an exchange or on the realization of a common interest where conflicting interests are present." Id. at 3-4.

131. Negotiating with the PLO and the prospect of a PLO state are among the most emotive issues in Israel. It is, however, unrealistic to imagine that a settlement

could be achieved in the face of direct PLO opposition. It would be less unrealistic to hope for a modification in the PLO position once negotiations commenced. While on the legal level it would appear strange and indeed illegal that the UN has accorded official status to an organization (the PLO), the official policy of which calls for the dismantling of a member of the UN. On the political level one may wonder if now, at the PLO's hour of defeat, it is not the time for an act of magnanimous statesmanship on Israel's part. It will remain a pertinent, if moot, historical question whether a less intransigent Israeli policy after the 1967 "Six Day War" would have changed the course of subsequent belligerency and conflict. See J.LEIBOWITZ, supra note 51, at 419.

132. Recognition and acceptance of Israel would necessitate, naturally enough, a formal amendment of the Palestinian National Covenant. Whether this should be done before or as a result of negotiations is a matter adverted to in Part III of this article.

133. See Elazar, *The Ends of Federalism,* in FEDERALISM AND POLITICAL INTEGRATION, supra note 16.

134. For interesting studies in the failure of a confederal arrangement, see Hazelwood, The End of the East African Community. What Are the Lessons for Regional Integration *Schemes?* 18 J. COMMON MKT. STUD. 40 (1979); and Y. GHAI, REFLECTIONS ON LAW AND ECONOMIC INTEGRATION IN EAST AFRICA (Research Report No.36, 1976).

135. Dinstein observes that the confederation exists today more in theory than in practice. In the case of the three best-known confederations (United States, Federal Republic of Germany and Switzerland), there was an evolution to federal structures. As a result, perhaps, of these and other precedents that tend to associate confederalism with an automatic evolution to federalism, Dinstein concludes that the ancient objectives of confederations (characterized by the retention of independent statehood) are now achieved by international organizations. Had the EEC been established in the last century, Dinstein suggests it would have been called a confederation. 5 Y. DINSTEIN, supra note 7, at § 754.

136. See, e.g., Elazar's innovative idea of an Israeli-Jordanian condominium. SELF RULE, supra note 16, at xvi.

137. 2 CAPPELLETTI & WEISNER, ACCESS TO JUSTICE v–vi (1979).

138. Id.

139. See Report on European Institutions presented by the Committee of the Three of the European Council (§IV) (Brussels, European Communities, 1979) [hereinafter cited as Three Wise Men Report].

140. See PROPOSALS FOR REFORM OF THE COMMISSION OF THE EUROPEAN COMMUNITIES AND ITS SERVICES (report made at the request of the Commission by an Independent Review Body under the Chairmanship of Mr. Dirk Spierenburg) (Brussels, European Communities, 1979) [hereinafter cited as Spierenburg Report].

141. THREE WISE MEN REPORT, supra note 139, § III.

142. Dahrendorf, *A Third Europe?* Jean Monnet Lecture delivered at the European University Institute (1979).

143. In October 1970, a committee under the Prime Minister of Luxembourg presented a plan, endorsed by the Hague Summit of that year, designed to attain full economic and monetary union with a common currency. EUROPEAN COMMUNITIES COMMISSION, STEPS TO EUROPEAN UNITY 42 (1980).

144. Generally, it is considered that the turnout was rather disappointing, especially in those countries in which resentment of the Community was, in any event, high. The overall turnout was about 62 percent. Turnout was as low as 31 percent in the United Kingdom. *The European Parliamentary Election,* 4 EUR. L. REV. 145 (1979).

145. We must distinguish among several types of Community law infractions by states. Most common are inadvertent prelitigation legislative or administrative violations, and less common are deliberate evasions (e.g., 1981 French-Italian wine war). Effective judicial remedy in respect of both is usually available. Postlitigation defiance may consist of dilatory compliance by the member states, e.g., In Re Export Tax on Art Treasures: E. C. Commission v. Italy, 1968 E. Comm. Ct. J. Rep. 2729, [1969] Comm. Mkt. L.R. I, or even outright defiance, e.g., In Re Export Restrictions on Imports of Lamb: E.C. Commission v. France, 1979 E. Comm. Ct. J. Rep. 2729, [1980] Comm. Mkt. L.R. 418; In Re Restrictions on Imports of Lamb (No.2): E. C. Commission v. France, 1980 E. Comm. Ct. J. Rep. 1319, [1981] Comm. Mkt. L.R. 25. National courts may apply Community law evasively, e.g., Regina v. Secretary of State for the Home Department, Ex Parte Santillo, [1981] W. L. R. 355, 362, or even deliberately defy it, e.g., Judgment of Dec.22, 1978, Conseil d'état, Fr., 1979 Recucil des decisions du Conseil d'état [1979 Lebon] 524. The cases of deliberate judicial and executive defiance are, of course, most troublesome. See *The Mutton and Lamb Story. Isolated Incident or the Beginning of a New Era?* 17 COMMON MKT. L. REV. 311. See also THE INDIVIDUAL MEMBER STATES' COMMUNITY OBLIGATION: FAITHFUL IMPLEMENTATION OR REALIZATION OF UNILATERAL GOALS (mimeograph) (H. Rasmussen ed. 1981).

146. See generally U. KITZINGER, DIPLOMACY AND PERSUASION (1973).

147. In a leading text the Luxembourg crisis is referred to as "the most serious political-institutional crisis experienced by the Communities." E. STEIN, P. HAY & M. WAELBROECK, EUROPEAN COMMUNITY LAW AND INSTITUTIONS IN PERSPECTIVE 63 (1976). In any event,

> for years the Community has been described as being in crisis. But when crises exist permanently, merely changing their immediate causes, it should be asked if they really are crises, that is to say exceptional conflict situations. It is rather more likely that the conflicts the Community has so far experienced are significant of tensions inherent in the integration process itself.

Everling, Possibilities and Limits of European Integration, 17 J. COMMON MKT. STUD. 217 (1980).

148. The literature on European integration is vast. For a relatively recent bibliography, see K. KUJAH, BIBLIOGRAPHY ON EUROPEAN INTEGRATION (1977). History and policy may be found in § 2.4.1.

149. The text of the Schuman Declaration may be found in R. PRYCE, THE POLITICAL FUTURE OF THE EUROPEAN COMMUNITY 97 (1962). Schuman's opening paragraph clearly sets the political tone of the entire declaration: "World peace cannot be safeguarded without constructive efforts proportionate to the dangers which threaten it." Id. See also W. DIEBOLD, THE SCHUMAN PLAN (1959); R. DUCCI & B. OLIVI, L'EUROPA INCOMPIUTA 156–60 (1970); H. RIEBEN, DES ENTENTES DE MAITRES DE FORGES AU PLAN SCHUMAN 314–536 (1954). These sentiments are expressed almost verbatim in the Preamble to the Treaty of Paris. Treaty Instituting the European Coal and Steel Community, Apr. 18, 1951, 261 U.N.T.S. 140, 143 [hereinafter cited as Treaty of Paris].

150. R. PRYCE, supra note 149.

151. Id.

152. Id.

153. Dahrendorf, supra note 142.

154. Treaty of Paris, supra note 149.

155. The language of the Dunkirk Treaty, concluded as late as March 1947 between

the United Kingdom and France, is most revealing. Treaty of Dunkirk, Mar. 4, 1947, France United Kingdom, 1947 Gr. Brit. T.S. No.73 (Cmnd. 7217), 9 U.N.T.S. 187. Phrases such as:

"In the event of any threat to the security of either (of the Parties) arising from the adoption by Germany of a policy of aggression ...," id art. 1, or "should either of the High Contracting Parties become again involved in hostilities with Germany ...," id art. 2, abound. On Franco-German relations as a background to the signing of the Treaty of Paris, see P. KAPTEYN & P. VERLOREN VAN THEMAAT, INTRODUCTION TO THE LAW OF THE EUROPEAN COMMUNITIES 4–5 (1973).

156. R. PRYCE, supra note 149.

157. For an excellent account of the evolution of the theory of European Integration, see Greilsammer, *Theorizing European Integration in its Four Periods*, 2 JERUSALEM J. INT'L REL. 129 (1976).

158. For a brief but lucid account of the terms imposed on Germany after World War I and their contributory function on the road to World War II, see P. CALVO-CORESSI & G. WINT, TOTAL WAR (1974).

159. P. KAFTEYN & P. VERLOREN VAN THEMAAT, supra note 155.

160. Some authors tend to see the Soviet threat as a cardinal feature and incentive for European integration. See, e.g., D. WYATT & A. DASHWOOD, THE SUBSTANTIVE LAW OF THE EEC 3 (1980).

161. Even within the PLO there is no homogeneity. Arafat, characterized as a moderate, has shown some flexibility in his reaction to the Fahd plan.

162. R. PRYCE, THE POLITICS OF THE EUROPEAN COMMUNITY 28–51 (1973).

163. On the importance of the cultural background, see Deutsch, *Between Sovereignty and Integration*, in BETWEEN SOVEREIGNTY AND INTEGRATION 182 (G. Ionescu ed. 1974). But Alexandre Marc argues that "[t]here can be a Very good, Very efficient federation without real understanding between different peoples of the federation in the field of psychology and culture." SELF RULE, supra note 16, at 105.

164. R. PRYCE, supra note 162, at 30.

165. Id. at 31.

166. A full-fledged, regional common market must be regarded as a very long-term plan, however. The actual number of units in the transnational entity is in itself of importance. On one hand, a small number of partners may indicate a correspondingly small number of interests to square and a higher potential to accord. Puchala's model of decision making illustrates the variety of interests that have to be squared in reaching concordance between just *two* states. Puchala, *Of Blind Men, Elephants and International Integration*, 10 J. COMMON MKT. STUD. 267, 277–84 (1972). On the other hand, a multiunit entity reduces the power of each individual member state. The prospect of clear-cut and permanent alliances and enmities is less likely to arise. There will be a fluidity of groupings of interest depending on the issues and the possibility of "package deal" compromises. In the EEC the Paris-Bonn axis is still paramount, each of these partners being probably the only two indispensable member states. For a view that rejects the possibility of a two-party association, see Pentland & Soberman, *Forms of Economic Association* (to be published by the Institute of Intergovernmental Relations, Queen's University in its series of Discussion Papers on the "Future of the Canadian Communities").

167. Deutsch, supra note 163, at 182.

168. See generally SELF RULE, supra note 16, at 15–42.

169. Id. at 108; but see id., at 103–04.

170. For a recent variation on this theme, see D. MARQUAND, THE EURO-

PEAN PARLIAMENT 1–10 (1979). Marquand uses the terms integrationist and pragmatic. See also Deutsch, supra note 163.

171. R. PRYCE, supra note 162, at 32–34.

172. The *locus classicus* is J. MONNET, LES ETATS-UNIS D'EUROPE ONT COMMENCÉ: DISCOURS ET ALLOCUTIONS 1952–1954 (1955).

173. Treaty Establishing the European Economic Community, Mar. 25, 1957, 298 U.N.T.S. 11 [hereinafter cited as Treaty of Rome].

174. Willis, *Origins and Evolution of the European Communities*, 440 ANNALS 1, 6 (1978).

175. Address by President de Gaulle, reprinted in R. DUCCI & B. OLIVI, supra note 149, at 411–16.

176. It is possible that, without the de Gaulle formula, Europe would not have advanced in its integration plans, but rather would have collapsed as a result of a member state backlash.

177. Address by President de Gaulle, supra note 175. See also R. MOWAT, CREATING THE EUROPEAN COMMUNITY 154–89 (1973).

178. R. PRYCE, supra note 162, at 35–51.

179. Id. at 43.

180. For a full analysis of this concept and its evolution in the last 30 years, see Weiler, *The Community System: The Dual Character of Supranationalism*, 1981 Y.B. EUR. L. 267.

181. Robertson, *Legal Problems of European Integration*, 91 COLLECTED COURSES OF THE HAGUE ACADEMY 105, 143 (1957).

182. This is, strangely perhaps, characteristic of common-law lawyers. "The pursuit of definitions has never appealed much to lawyers because they are aware that the concepts they employ have been rough-hewn by history and stoutly resist philosophical formulation." Pollock, *The Distinguishing Mark of Crime*, 22 MOD. L. REV. 495 (1959).

183. For a useful collection of different points of view, see E. STEIN, P. HAY & M. WAELBROECK, supra note 147, at 17–29.

184. Treaty of Paris, supra note 149, art. 15.

185. Treaty of Rome, supra note 173.

186. The literature on the doctrine is immense. For a lucid, up-to-date statement, see J. USHER, EUROPEAN COMMUNITY LAW AND NATIONAL LAW 17–30 (1981); D. WYATT & A. DASHWOOD, supra note 160, ch. 3 (1980). For earlier studies that foreshadowed and perhaps even influenced developments, see Bebr, *Directly Applicable Provisions of Community Law. The Development of a Community Concept*, 19 INT'L & COM P. L.Q. *257* (1970); Waelbroeck, *Effects Internes des Obligations Imposees—l'Etat*, in 2 MISCELLANEA W.J. GANSHOF VAN DER MEERSCH 573 (1972).

187. Van Gend en Loos v. Nederlandse Belastingsadministratie, 1963 E. Comm. Ct. J. Rep. 10, [1963] Comm. Mkt. L.R. 128. The process of constitutionalization implies a combined and circular process by which the treaties were interpreted using techniques associated with constitutional documents rather than by multipartite treaties and in which the treaties both as cause and effect assumed the higher law attributes of a constitution. For a systematic analysis of the process, see Stein, *Lawyers, Judges, and the Making of a Transnational Constitution*, 75 AM. J. INT'L L. 1(1981). See also, *The Emerging European Constitution*, 1978 PROC. AM. SOC'Y INT'L L. 166–97. The German Federal Constitutional Court has actually said that "[t]he European Economic Community Treaty is, as it were, the constitution of this Community." Id. at 168, quoting Judgment of Oct. 18, 1967, Bundesverfassungsgericht, I Senate, W. Ger., 22 Bundesverfassungsgericht [BVerfG] 293 (1967).

188. In Belgische Radio en Televisie v. S.A.B.A.M., 1974 E. Comm. Ct. J. Rep. 51, [1974] Comm. Mkt. L.R. 238, the European Court held that articles 85 and 86 of the EEC were capable of bestowing rights and duties on individuals *inter se*. It should be noted, however, that these treaty articles themselves involved actions of individuals. Cf Bosch G.m.b.H. v. Kleding-Verkoopbedrijf de Geus en Uitdenbogerd, 1962 E. Comm. Ct. J. Rep. 51, [1962] Comm. Mkt. L.R. 1, in which this development is already anticipated. The doctrine was further developed in a subsequent case that concerned the general principle embodied in article 7 of the EEC (non-discrimination on grounds of nationality) and which, unlike *SA.B.A.M,* did not necessarily involve individuals. Even the usually very integrationalist-minded Commission doubted whether this treaty principle should be given horizontal effect. The Court took the radical position and held that the Treaty could indeed bestow rights and duties on individuals *inter se,* Walrave and Koch v. Association Union Cycliste Internationale, 1974 E. Comm. Ct. J. Rep. 1405, [1975] Comm. Mkt. L.R. 320. See also Defrenne v. SABENA, 1976 E. Comm. Ct. J. Rep. 455, [1976] Comm. Mkt. L.R. 98.

189. It is not proposed to discuss here the well-known distinction between direct applicability and direct effect. See, e.g., USHER, supra note 186, at 18, 26–30; Winter, *Direct Applicability and Direct Effect — Two Distinct and Different Concepts in Community Law,* 9 COMMON MKT. L. REV. 425 (1972). The step-by-step extension of direct effect to directives has been remarkable. Cases signaling this evolution are Van Duyn v. Home Office, 1974 E. Comm. Ct. J. Rep. 1337, [1975] Comm. Mkt. L.R. I (direct effect of a substantive provision of a directive, but one which elaborated a substantive right bestowed by the Treaty of Rome — vertical effect); Verbond van Nederlandese Ondernemngen v. Inspecteur der Invoerrechten en Accijnzen, 1977 E. Comm. Ct. J. Rep. 113, [1977] Comm. Mkt. L.R. 413 (direct effect of a substantive provision of directive concerning an obligation not directly bestowed by the Treaty of Rome and against which a national implementing measure was reviewed — vertical effects). Cf Delkvist v. Anklagemyndighen, ex parte Landsnaevnet for Omnibuskrsel, 1978 E. Comm. Ct. J. Rep. 2327, [1979] Comm. Mkt. L.R. 372 (directive as source of judicial review). On the possible extension of horizontal direct effect to directives, see Easson, *Can Directives Impose Obligations on Individuals?,* 4 EUR. L. REV. 67 (1979). But see Pubblico Ministero v. Ratti, 1979 E. Comm. Ct. J. Rep. 1629, [1980] Comm. Mkt. L.R. 96; Usher, *The Direct Effect of Directives,* 4 EUR. L. REV. 268 (1979).

190. Costa v. ENEL, 1964 E. Comm. Ct. J. Rep. 585, [1965] Comm. Mkt. L.R. 425. The following are the main operative elements in the judgment:

> By contrast with ordinary international treaties, the EEC Treaty has created its own legal system which, on the entry into force of the Treaty, became an integral part of the legal system of the Member States and which their courts are bound to apply. By creating a Community of unlimited duration, having its own institutions, its own personality, its own legal capacity and capacity of representation on the international plane and, more particularly, real powers stemming from a limitation of sovereignty or a transfer of powers from the States to the Community, the Member States have limited their sovereign rights, albeit within limited fields, and have thus created a body of law which binds both their nationals and themselves. The integration into the laws of each Member State of provisions which derive from the Community, and more generally, the terms and the spirit of the Treaty, make it impossible for the States, as a corollary, to accord precedence to a unilateral and subsequent measure over a legal system accepted by them on a basis of reciprocity. Such a measure cannot therefore be

inconsistent with that legal system. The executive force of Community law cannot vary from one State to another in deference to subsequent domestic laws without jeopardizing the attainment of the objectives of the Treaty set out in article 5(2) and giving rise to the discrimination prohibited by article 7. Id. at 593–94.

191. Here, of course, we have one of the most intractable problems of Community law. The Treaty of Rome is fairly general in many of its provisions, lending itself to expansive teleological interpretation by the court. This, coupled with certain elastic clauses, e.g., Treaty of Paris, supra note 149, art. 235, gives a wide measure of latitude to the policymaking organs to extend the boundaries of Community competence. Often this meets with national resistance. Cf Close, *Harmonization of Laws: Use or Abuse of the Powers Under the EEC Treaty?* 3 EUR. L. REV. 461(1978).

192. In some member states this caused little problem; in others, courts accepted the doctrine with reservations regarding the possible incompatibility of Community law with fundamental human rights. This was the case in Germany and Italy. See Judgment of May 29, 1974, Bundesverfassungsgericht, II Senate, W. Ger., 37 BVerfG 271; Judgment of Dec. 27, 1973, Corte Const., Italy, 1974 Foro Italiano [Foro It. I] 314. For a useful discussion on the implications of this case, see H. SCHERMERS, JUDICIAL PROTECTION IN THE EUROPEAN COMMUNITIES 92–97 (1979). Note that the German Federal Constitutional Court was concerned with constitutional safeguards in regard to legislation; the supremacy challenge was only indirect. Otherwise, the German Federal Constitutional Court has fully accepted the supremacy of Community law even over subsequent national law. See Judgment of June 9, 1971, Bundesverfassungsgericht, II Senate, W. Ger., 31 BVerfG 145. The German Federal Constitutional Court also rejected the possibility of *Vefassungsbeschwerde* (constitutional complaints) against acts of the Community authorities, limiting this type of recourse to action by German public authorities. See Judgment of Oct. 18, 1967, Bundesverfassungsgericht, I Senate, W. Ger., 22 BVerfG 293, 5 COMMON MKT. L. REV. 483 (1967–1968) note J. Frowein. It should be underlined that, although from the point of view of the European Court of Justice the principle of supremacy was established in one specific decision, the process of *approfondissement* may be seen in the gradual acceptance of the doctrine by the highest courts of the member states. The French Cour de cassation (Chambre mixte) accepted the doctrine in the celebrated case, Administration des Douanes v. Societe "Cafes Jacques Vabie" et J. Weigel et Cie. S.a.r.l., Judgment of May 24, 1975, Cass. ch. mixte, Fr., 1975 Recueil Dalloz-Sirey [D.S. Jur.] 497, [1975] 2 Comm. Mkt. L.R. 336. The Court relied, however, on article 55 of the French Constitution, which gives treaty provisions (subject to certain conditions, especially reciprocity) a force higher than French statutes, even those subsequently enacted. This reasoning does not amount, then, to full acceptance of the shift in the *Grundnorm*. It should be noted that Procureur General Touffait had explicitly requested, in relation to article 55 of the French Constitution, that the Court should not "mention it and instead base its reasoning on the very nature of the legal order instituted by the Rome Treaty." Id at 504, [1975] 2 Comm. Mkt. L.R. at 363. This the Court implicitly declined to do. In a subsequent case, however, Judgment of Dec. 15, 1975, Cass. civ. III chambre, Fr., 1976 D.S. Jur. 33, the third civil chamber arguably "did take the plunge...," Hunnings, *Rival Constitutional Courts. A Comment on Case 106/77*, 15 COMMON MKT. L. REV. 483, 484 (1978), and accepted the doctrine without reference to article 55 of the French Constitution. The criminal chamber of the Cour de cassation has also been Community-minded. See Judgment of Oct.22, 1970, Cass. crim., Fr., 1971 D.S. Jur. 221; Judgment of Nov. 10, 1970, Cass. crim., Fr., 1971 D.S. Jur. 509. By contrast, the Conseil d'état has, basing itself on somewhat antiquated notions of separation of powers, refused the

acceptance of the supremacy principle as applied to parliamentary. The doctrine would probably apply to governmental decrees. Cf Judgment of Dec.22, 1978, Conseil d'état, Fr., 1979 Lebon 524. See Judgment of Mar. 1,1968, Conseil d'état, Fr., 1968 D.S. Jur. 285. *See also* Judgment of Oct.12, 1979, Conseil d'état, Fr., 1979 Lebon 373. On the ambiguous position of the French Constitutional Court, see Mitchell, *what Happened to the Constitution on 1st January 197'?*, 2 CAMBRIAN L. REV. 69,78–79(1980). See also Kovar & Simon, Some *Reflections on the Decision of the French Constitutional Council of December 30, 1976*, 14 COMMON MKT. L. REV. 525 (1977).

Ireland actually introduced a Constitutional amendment. Article 29, third amendment to Irish Constitution of 1972, quoted in Lang, *Legal and Constitutional Implications for Ireland of Adhesion to the EEC Treaty*, 9 COMMON MKT. L. REV. 167 (1972). The Danish Constitution in article 20 already provided for delegation of powers to international organizations. But see Due & Gulmann, *Constitutional Implications of the Danish Accession to the European Communities*, 9 COMMON MKT. L. REV. 256, 265–67 (1972), which analyzes the debate over the possibility of Danish compliance with the principle of supremacy, especially vis-à-vis constitutional provisions.

In relation to the United Kingdom, a particularly interesting case because of the resemblance of its constitutional order to that of Israel, a question remains concerning the theoretical possibility of a shift in the *Grundnorm* of the type discussed above. See Winterton, *The British Grundnorm. Parliamentary Supremacy Re-examined*, 92 L.Q. REV. 591(1976). But even in the United Kingdom the courts have indicated a halfway house acceptance of the supremacy of Community law.

A leading authority summarizes the situation in Britain thus:

(1) While the European Communities Act 1972 remains in force, existing directly applicable or effective Community law will be the law in the United Kingdom, notwithstanding any legislation prior to the Act which is inconsistent with such directly applicable or effective law;

(2) Community law which is not directly applicable or effective will have no force in the United Kingdom until given effect by Act of Parliament or by order or regulation enacted pursuant to powers given by the European Communities Act 1972 or other legislation;

(3) Directly applicable or effective Community law will take effect in the United Kingdom, notwithstanding any legislation prior to the 1972 [European Communities] Act, or even after the Act but prior to the coming into effect of the Community rule;

(4) A subsequent Act of Parliament which is inconsistent with a rule of Community law will be read subject to the rule of construction in S. 2(4) 50 that Community law can take effect notwithstanding the Act, at any rate if the Court is satisfied that the subsequent inconsistent legislation is not intended, expressly or impliedly, to repeal 5.2(1) or (4) of the 1972 [European Communities] Act; but

(5) Any subsequent Act of Parliament inconsistent with the European Communities Act 1972, including one which repeals the latter in whole or in part and one which is intended to limit the application of 5.2(1) and (4), will be given effect by the United Kingdom courts.

L.COLLINS, EUROPEAN COMMUNITY LAW IN THE U.K. 25–26 (1 980). But see supra, note 166.

193. See Waelbroeck, *The Emerging Doctrine of Community Pre-emption — Consent and Re-delegation*, in COURTS AND FREE MARKETS § 48 (K. Sandalow & E. Stein eds. 1982).

194. See Geddo v. Ente Nazionale Riss, 1973 E. Comm. Ct. J. Rep. 865, [1974] Comm. Mkt. L.R. 230.

195. On the system of judicial review generally, see, e.g., the erudite treatment

by L. NEYILLE BROWN & F. JACOBS, THE COURT OF JUSTICE OF THE EUROPEAN COMMUNITIES (1977); H. SCHERMERS, supra note 192; G. VANDERSANDEN & A. BARAY, CONTENTIEUX COMMUNAUTAIRE (1977). Naturally, this Article's treatment will sketch only the bare limbs of the complex system.

196. For a description of the emergence of this higher law, see Cappelletti, *The Mighty Problem of Judicial Review,* 2 LEGAL ISSUES EUR. INTEGRATION 1 (1979).

197. Four weaknesses are particularly glaring. First, political considerations will often influence the decision of the Commission and/or member states to bring an action against an alleged violation by another member state; the Commission might not wish to risk a political crisis that may be precipitated by a Court decision on a sensitive issue. Thus, the Commission has apparently decided not to bring an action against France in the wake of the decision of the Conseil d'éat in Cohn-Bendit, Judgment of Dec.22, 1978, Conseil d'état, Fr., 1979 Lebon 524, although a clear violation had taken place. See Isaac, *L'affaire Cohn-Bendit,* 15 C. DE D. EUR. 265 (1979). The Commission may fear that bringing an action might give the impression of interfering with the independence of the French judiciary. Second, effective supervision will depend on the ability of the Commission to monitor the implementation of Community law. Given the vast range of Community measures, this becomes an impossible task. See Commission observations in the Italian Animal Slaughter Case, E. C. Commission v. Italy, 1978 E. Comm. Ct. J. Rep. 1307, [1977-1978 Transfer Binder] COMMON MKT. REP. (CCH) ¶ 8498. Third, the type of action which is likely to be brought will relate largely to abject member state failure to *implement* a national measure required by Community law or to a national measure that is in clear violation of Community law. It will be far less suited to review of the *application* by member states of Community obligations, especially as they affect individuals. That type of violation normally becomes transparent only through cases and controversies affecting individuals. Even if alleged violations were brought to the attention of the Commission, it is unrealistic to expect them to take up all but the most flagrant violations. Finally, given the intergovernmental character of this process, a member state found to have failed to fulfill an obligation may simply disregard the judgment against it. This is what happened in the *Art Treasures* case, 168 E. Comm. Ct. J. Rep. 2729, [1969] Comm. Mkt. L.R. 1, and the Lamb Meat case, 1979 E. Comm. Ct. J. Rep. 2729, [1980] Comm. Mkt. L.R. 418.

198. The two limbs of judicial review exist on this level as well. A referral to the Court on the *validity* of acts of institutions is clearly a mode for judicial review of Community acts at the instance of individuals. One will note that the question of *locus standi* from the point of view of the European Court of Justice does not arise. Thus, it may even be possible for an individual to be denied standing in a direct challenge before the European Court, but have the act reviewed if he or she has standing in accordance with national procedural law. The individual will be able to challenge the Community act in the national courts (Community law being, of course, part of the law of the land), whereupon it will be remitted to the European Court of Justice for an interpretation on validity and returned back to the national Court for pronouncement. See Koninklijke Scholten-Honig N.V. v. Council and Commission, 1977 E. Comm. Ct. J. Rep. 797, [1977-1978 Transfer Binder] COMM. MKT. REP. (CCH) ¶ 8473. This may of course introduce a nonuniform measure of judicial protection because the remedy for the individual will depend on the vagaries of national procedural law on standing. Taking judicial review of Community measures as a whole, the trend, in respect to individual challenges, is one of a restrictive attitude to actions brought directly before the European Court with a shift to national courts as the forum for adjudication, using, when necessary, the preliminary reference for an interpretation on *validity.*

Turning to the second limb concerning the judicial review of national measures for conformity with Community law, the European Court has made astute use of the part of article 177 that provides for references to the "interpretation" of Community law. On its face, the purpose of the procedure is to guarantee uniform application of Community law in all ten member states. The normal factual situation in which it arises, however, is when a litigant pleads in the national court that a rule or measure of national law or administrative practice should not be applied because it contradicts Community law. The European Court then renders its interpretation of Community law in the factual context of the case before it. Theoretically, a division exists in the adjudicatory tasks of the two courts: the European Court states the law, and the national court applies it, using, of course, the principle of supremacy when necessary, to the case in hand. As Rasmussen states:

> It is no secret, however, that in practice, when making preliminary rulings the Court has often transgressed the theoretical borderline . . . it provides the national judge with an answer in which questions of law and of fact are sufficiently interwoven as to leave the national judge with only little discretion and flexibility in making his final decision.

Rasmussen, *Why is Article 173 Interpreted Against Private Plaintiffs?* 5 EUR. L. REV. 112, 125 (1980).

199. The above analysis helps to express the four main limitations and lacunae in the "all-or-nothing effect." First, it is clear that not all issues involving alleged violations of member states' Community obligations can become cases and controversies involving individuals. Many obligations do not produce direct effect and rest in the province of intergovernmental relations, violations of which remain a matter for the Commission and member states. Second, even in matters potentially involving individuals, there will exist inevitable "access-to-justice" barriers to overcome. Ignorance of the European rights, the increased cost and time that the two-tier litigation involves (the procedural price of the system of compliance) and the fragmentary diffuse character of the rights that might entail a very low stake for any one individual (in Costa v. ENEL, 1964 E. Comm. Ct. J. Rep. *585,* [1964] Comm. Mkt. L.R. 425, the controversy involved a sum of approximately two United States dollars) are the more obvious barriers. Third, the use of article 177 as a method for judicial review of member state compliance will depend on the acceptance by national courts of the utility and/or duty to make references. The practice in this respect, although encouraging, is not complete. Finally, once preliminary rulings have been received by the referring court, they must be followed both by that court and the national administration. Here, as well, the system displays certain breaches either overt as in the case of the Conseil d'état or of a more subtle kind. But, even if incomplete, the existing "all-or-nothing effect" is a singular distinguishing feature of the Community in comparison to other international organizations and one of its most promising integrating tools.

It is not proposed to discuss here all the various differences brought about by the two-level system and the advantages and disadvantages that each system entails. For example, it has been pointed out that the article 177 procedure for judicial review of member state actions does not allow the member states sufficient facilities to air their arguments before the Court. See *United Kingdom House of Lords Select Committee on the European Communities,* 23d Rep., 1979–1980 Sess. See generally Rasmussen, supra note 198, and bibliography in note 6 therein.

200. This is not to imply that the court's role is apolitical. In fact, the court has shown a high degree of political acumen in, say, changing course on the question of human rights. It also has played an important role in demarcating the division of competences between different European Community Institutions. See generally A. GREEN,

POLITICAL INTEGRATION BY JURISPRUDENCE (1969); C. MANN, THE FUNCTION OF JUDICIAL DECISION IN EUROPEAN INTEGRATION (1972).

201. See generally S. HENIG, POWER AND DECISION IN EUROPE (1980); POLICY-MAKING IN THE EUROPEAN COMMUNITIES (H. Wallace, W. Wallace & C. Webb eds. 1977); C. SASSE, E. POULLET, D. COOMBES & G. DEPREZ, DECISIONMAKING IN THE EUROPEAN COMMUNITIES (1977).

202. See H. Wallace, National Bulls in the Community China Shop. The Role of National Governments in Community Policy Making, in POLICY-MAKING IN THE EUROPEAN COMMUNITIES, supra note 201, at 33; Webb, *Introduction Variations on a Theoretical Theme,* in POLICY-MAKING IN THE EUROPEAN COMMUNITIES, supra note 201, at 1.

203. For a recent treatment of this issue, see Lasok, *The Institutional Framework of the Community,* in THE EUROPEAN COMMUNITIES IN ACTION 87 (D. Lasok & P. Soldatos eds. 1981).

204. A certain terminological confusion exists regarding "secondary" legislation. Regulations and directives are often referred to as secondary legislation. The better view, it is submitted, is to regard them as primary legislation. For if we view the Treaty as being the Constitution of the European Communities, the legislation thereunder, by analogy to national systems, would be primary. Perhaps the power of legislation entrusted to the Commission under enabling regulations of the Council may be characterized as "secondary."

205. The following remarks by a leading commentator are instructive in this context. "All Member States have organized their policy-making in such a way as to promote their own national interests... These efforts to keep the formation and implementation of Community rules under national control are sustained by the fact that the organs of the European Communities still lack a democratic legitimation of their own.... To date, the control of European policy through national parliaments is at any rate comparably weak and is at most exerted via a detour — that is, through the control of governments." Sasse, *The Control of the National Parliaments of the Nine over European Affairs,* in PARLIAMENTARY CONTROL OVER FOREIGN POLICY 147 (A. Cassesse ed. 1980).

206. The Court originally pursued a narrow formalistic approach to judicial review, e.g., Friedrich Stork & Co. v. High Authority of the European Coal and Steel Community, 1959 E. Comm. Ct. J. Rep. 17. The Court later learned that the process of integration would be enhanced by a bold judicial review. See Cappelletti, supra note 196.

207. The democracy deficit did not immediately come to the foreground both because of the proximity in time to the ratification of the Treaty of Rome and because the EEC was seen as confined to the operative parts of the Treaty.

208. E.g., Three Wise Men Report, supra note 139, at 49–53. See also S. HENIG, supra note 201, at 51–63, 105–17.

209. On this effect of COREPER, the Three Wise Men commented that the Commission "should not, as so often happens now, be drawn into negotiating with [national experts, etc.] to find a supposedly acceptable form of the [policy] measure." They also commented that "[t]he Commission must frame its proposals in a more *independent* manner." Three Wise Men Report, supra note 139, at 54. At the same time, given this decline in decisional supranationalism, the COREPER does, of course, facilitate the actual arrival at consensus in an intergovernmental way, and thus prevents a complete blocking of the system. Cf. Noel & Etienne, *The Permanent Representatives Committee and the "Deepening" of the Communities,* 6 GOV'T & OPPOSITION 422 (1971). But see Tizzano, NOVISSIMO DIGESTO ITALIANO, II app. COREPER 819 (1981).

210. Arrangement Regarding Collaboration, Jan.31, 1966, reprinted in 5 I.L.M. 315 (1966). For text and brief commentary, see II "Liberum veto"-conférence de presse du Président de Gaulle, September 9, 1965; I Cinque Soli-Dichiarazione del Consigho dci Ministri delle CEE, Bruxelles, Oct.26, 1965; Vincitori e Vinti—Communiqué de presse surles accords de Luxembourg, 29 janvier 1966. R. Ducci & B. OLIVI, supra note 149, at 411–22.See also P. KAPTEYN & VERLOREN VAN THEMAAT supra note 155, 143–46.

211. The three new member states joining on January 1, 1973, were Great Britain, Denmark and Ireland. Treaty of Accession of Denmark, Ireland and the United Kingdom, Jan.22, 1972, 2 COMMON MKT. REP. (CCH) ¶ 7011.

212. Majority voting itself is not entirely exceptional. It is the lawmaking power of the Council and the effect of that law as expressed in the concept of normative supranationalism which made the prospect of majority voting unique.

213. See Spierenburg Report, supra note 140.

214. For a devastating critique of the classic economic theories of integration, see Pelkmans, *Economic Theories of Integration Revisited,* 18 J. COMMON MKT. STUD. 333 (1980).

215. Id. at 7.

216. Id. at 25.

217. A. SHONPIELD, EUROPEAN INTEGRATION IN THE SECOND PHASE: THE SCOPE AND LIMITATION OF ALLIANCE POLITICS (1974).

218. Id. at 7, 9–11.

219. Id.

220. Concerning the Framework for Political Cooperation, see TEXTS RELATING TO THE EUROPEAN POLITICAL COOPERATION (1977). See also von der Gablentz, *Luxembourg Revisited or The Importance of European Political Cooperation,* 16 COMMON MKT. L. REV. 685 (1979).

221. Inspiration may be found in a source that precedes the European experience and even that of the Partition Resolution, which in section D provided for an Economic Union of the two states, G.A. Res. 181, U.N. Doc. A/310, at 131(1947). Martin Buber, writing in 1947 on potential solutions to the conflict, suggested the following:

> Equally important for the intended agreement is the precedence of the intranational principle over the international one. Prevailing Zionist policy hitherto adhered to the axiomatic view that international agreement had to precede, nay, determine the intranational agreement with the Arabs. It is imperative to reverse this order: it is essential to arrive at an intranational agreement, which is later to receive international sanction. This order will recommend itself also to the Arabs, even if today their political leaders refuse to admit it, because the Palestinian State they aim at will, in the present international situation, only come about if demanded jointly by Jews and Arabs—that is, only after Jewish-Arab agreement will have been established.
>
> In the present state of world politics, the intranational principle tends more and more to assume a constructive role, whilst it remains for the international principle only to sanction the results of the former. In other words: as a consequence of agreements between nations, supernational structures will of necessity come into being, based, from without, upon common economic interests and joint economic action, and cemented inwardly by the singleness of purpose in the cultural and social domains. Within this common concern of two or more nations, economically unified and culturally diverse, the political activities will partly be the

> joint action of all and partly the result of the separate action of each group; but all this diversity of effort will be molded into a whole, by a great vision, shared by all and creative. Finally, these new social structures will be fitted into a super-territorial pattern, corresponding without present "international" principle, but more vital and more active.
>
> In the Middle East, no such larger integration will come about without a genuine agreement between Jews and Arabs and its international sanctioning. In the same manner, the essential Jewish demands can only be realized by way of such an agreement. Only if the Jews are able to offer the world the peace of the Middle East — as far as this depends upon them — will the world concede those demands to Jewry. For, one thing is certain: not only this or that Great Power needs a peaceful Middle East, but the nations of the world at large.

Buber, *The Bi-National Approach to Zionism,* in TOWARDS UNION IN PALESTINE I 1-12 (M. Buber, J. Magnes & E. Simon eds. 1947).

222. In order to form a concrete plan, the tentative ideas presented here would have to be elaborated, taking into consideration, inter alia, the following "critical functional areas": "Foreign relations; Police; Military; Internal taxation; Customs; Control of banking and currency; Definition of citizenship and control of immigration; Education; Religious sites and services; Ports; Transportation; Posts and telecommunications; Electric power; Water; Tourism; Health; Environmental protection; Economic development; Regulation of commerce and industry." Elazar and Sharkansky, *Alternative Federal Solutions to the Problem of the Administered Territories,* in SELF RULE, supra note 16, at 244. It should be noted that this sophisticated check list is geared more towards a federal or geographical condominium type of arrangement in which all of these issues would, ipso facto, have to be resolved. In the common market model there can be a selection of functional areas which would be integrationally promising or necessary from, say, the point of view of security.

223. SELF RULE, supra note 16, at 215.

224. See, *e.g.,* the views of General Weitzman, former Defense Minister in Begin's Cabinet, as reported in HAARETZ, Mar. 7, 1980, at 9, col. I. Talmon brings to this issue the broad historical strategic argument.

> The whole of history shows that security or its absence are not a function of secure or insecure borders but of enemy motivation. If the enemy is determined ... to go to war, it will not be borders which will [prevent him] from attacking. At most one can speak of borders which obstruct the aggressor, which give the attacked party more time and more room for maneuver. From this point of view strategic depth can constitute an asset in uninhabited areas like Sinai. Its effectiveness is doubtful in densely inhabited areas with an alien and belligerent population such as Judea and Samaria.

Talmon, *The Danger of Destruction,* HAARETZ, Dec. 7, 1973, at 15, col. 6.

225. Elon Moreh, Settlement in the Occupied West Bank, H.C.J. 390/79 (Oct.22, 1979), reprinted in 19 I.L.M. 148 (1980). See Note, *Digest Recent Legislation and Cases,* 15 IS. L. REV. 131(1980). A most sophisticated analysis attempting to prove the indispensability of continued Israeli full control of the West Bank (especially Samaria) is that of Neeman, *Foundation for the Security of Israel,* 6 MAARACHOT 273-74 (1980). Neeman is skeptical of all military warning devices that would prevent a surprise crossing of the Jordan and is equally dismissive of demilitarization and other devices that can be eroded, in his opinion, in "salami" fashion (slice by slice). He thus also rejects the Allon Plan, infra note 226, or any of its variants.

Naturally, one may question Neeman's military assessment of alternatives to continued control (and annexation) and, in particular, his curt dismissal of the dynamics of peace. Id. at 10–11. It is clear from the latter part of Neeman's article that at least part of his motivation is strongly politicohistorical based on an ideological commitment to Jewish rule over the West Bank. On the general issue of Israel's boundaries and their bearing on her defense, see D. HOROWITZ, ISRAEL'S CONCEPT OF DEFENSIBLE BORDERS (1975).

226. See Y. COHEN, THE ALLON PLAN (1972).

227. SELF RULE, supra note 16, at 215.

228. Id.

229. Id.

230. Id.

231. Id.

232. Cf interview with Professor Arens in his capacity as Chairman of the Knesset's Foreign Affairs and Security Committee, BEMAHANEH (overseas edition) September 1980, 14, 52.

233. See J. NYE, PEACE IN PARTS 21–54 (1971).

234. Cf Willis, supra note 174.

235. The Community had transitional periods that extended up to twelve years. See, e.g., Treaty of Paris, supra note 149, art. 8.

236. There is a certain paradox here. It is unlikely that a real threat would emanate from Palestine immediately after its establishment, whereas with its evolution its strategic strength would increase. The security measures would be dephased in a contrary trend. The regime proposed here would, from the Israeli point of view, be important not only symbolically but also in preventing an immediate threat from outside forces.

237. Khalidi, *Thinking the Unthinkable: A Sovereign Palestinian State*, 56 FOREIGN AFF. 695, 712, 713 (1978).

238. Static control at strategic points throughout the territory.

239. It is possible to envision a variety of restrictions in terms of quality and quantity of arms which Palestine may be permitted to have in any transitional arrangements. Israeli settlements would also have to come under Palestinian rule protected, however, by supranational guarantees.

240. See supra Part II.

241. Regardless of legal theory, see Akehurst, *Withdrawal from International Organizations,* 32 CURRENT LEGAL PROB. 143, 150–52 (1979), it is clear that legal sanctions alone would not explain the continued adhesion to, nor prevent the withdrawal of a member state from, the Community (and, for that matter, from any other international organization). Cf R. PRYCE, supra note 162, at 54.

242. See V. BULL, *supra* note 66.

243. "[A] Palestinian state in the West Bank and the Gaza strip would be a disaster... since it would become a mini-State at the mercy of Jordan and Israel.... [T]he Palestinian Arabs will become a reservoir of manpower for Israel industry Ma'oz, *New Attitudes of the PLO Regarding Palestine and Israel?,* in THE PALESTINIANS AND THE MIDDLE EAST CONFLICT, 595, 550 (G. Bendor ed. 1979). Professor Akzin sees the danger from the Israeli perspective:

> I would suggest that we in Israel, even if we want a regional confederation very much, should not day and night speak about our desire for it.
>
> The reason is that there exists among the Arabs a feeling-I think an unjustified feeling-that if we, the Jews of Israel, don't want territorial expansion, we certainly want economic, cultural and technological

domination or influence over them, that kind of influence which is now known in the world as neo-colonialism."
SELF RULE, *supra* note 16, at 199–200.
Akzin strongly objects to the creation of a Palestinian state for two main reasons: (1) it would be "bent on expansion and war," *id* at 196, and (2) if a federal arrangement is proposed as a solution it would "[f]rom the point of view of the Arab world ... be an extension of Israeli sovereignty ... [which] would be a very deep disappointment for all Arab forces within that state and in the Arab world generally." *Id.* at 197. One may wonder if the Israeli-Jordanian condominium, which Akzin favors, would be any less disappointing to these forces. For a different view on the posture of a Palestinian state, see Khalidj, *supra* note 237.

244. The European Community may now also be regarded as competing as champion of Third World interests through its development and cooperation policy.

245. For an analysis of this issue in the United States, see Rosberg, *Free Movement of Persons in the United States*, in COURTS AND FREE MARKETS 275 (T. Sandalow & E. Stein eds. 1982).

246. A recent study is that of Hartley, *EEC Immigration Law*, in 7 EUROPEAN STUDIES IN LAW (1978).

247. *See, e.g.*, Council Directive on the Coordination of Special Measures Concerning the Movement and Residence of Foreign Nationals which are Justified on Grounds of Public Policy, Public Security or Public Health, 7 J.O. COMM. EUR. 850 (1964); 7 O.J. EUR. COMM. 117(1963–1964). *See* Hartley, supra note *246*, at 145–81 and Note, *Free Movement of Workers in the European Economic Community: The Public Policy Exception*, 29 STAN. L. REV. 1283 (1977).

248. Treaty of Rome, *supra* note 173, art. 56.

249. *Id.*, art. 55.

250. *See* Van Duyn v. Home Office, 1974–1978 E. Comm. Ct. J. Rep. 1337, [1975 Transfer Binder] COMMON MKT. REP. (CCH) ¶ 8283.

251. R. PRYCE, *supra* note 162, *at 55*.

252. The Council for Mutual Economic Assistance (Comecon or CMEA) is the socialist bloc's forum for economic cooperation, headquartered in Moscow. *See* K. PÉCSI, THE FUTURE OF SOCIALIST ECONOMIC INTEGRATION (1981).

253. See *supra* text accompanying notes 223–37.

254. It must be emphasized again that, in the opinion of this writer, no lasting arrangements could be achieved without the cooperation of the PLO.

255. This section is not meant as a substitute for a more profound "game theory" analysis of the various possible gambits and outcomes, *Cf.* E. GILBOA, SIMULATION OF CONFLICT AND CONFLICT RESOLUTION IN THE MIDDLE EAST (1980).

256. This, reputedly, was suggested by Gen. A. Yariv who served as an Israeli national security adviser. The possibility that Israel should make a conditional acceptance was said to have caused a serious debate in PLO ranks.

257. Camp David Agreement, *supra* note 12.

258. *See* sources cited *supra* note 58.

4

Palestine and the World of Law: A Structural Analysis
Sanford R. Silverburg

I. Introduction

The emergence of a state onto the international political scene in the contemporary world, that is from the end of the Second World War to date, is no longer a particularly noteworthy event. The process of a political group's achievement of independence with a distinctive organizational configuration, in essence the extent of its sovereignty, is a topic that depends a great deal on the perspective of the observer. To be sure, while alternatives to the nation-state are increasingly gaining credibility, the prime political and legal actor remains the systemic status quo as it has been for three hundred plus years.[1] Since the state is the preeminent political actor in the international political system, its ability to exist at this level must be conducive to the conditioned arrangements that custom has found over time to serve the needs of the vast majority of similarly situated political organs of the globe. It also requires *de minimus* the fulfillment of its expected functions as a state, according to international law, on the same international level.

The contention exhibited here is that the present constitutional format of the Palestine Authority (PA), the Basic Law, operating as it does as the legislative body of the Palestine Liberation Organization (PLO) in those areas of the West Bank and Gaza Strip in which it maintains autonomous control, is substantially overvalued because of its avoidance to support a diplomatic agenda as a part of its political system's operation at the international level. This essay will take this focus and deliberately review: (a) the Palestinian Basic Law, (b) its relational component parts to foreign affairs and, (c) will provide a comparative analysis of a constitution as it affects the establishment of a democratic state. In order to do so, some background is offered, examining relevant political factors, especially foreign affairs, the status of Jerusalem, and the modern concept of the state. An argument will be presented, modest in scope, that essentially represents an additional element of reform to those set out in a prestigious report prepared by the Council on Foreign Relations. The findings of that review dealt with the Palestinian political system and had as a primary goal, to recommend policies that "will bring about improvements in the running of the Palestinian Authority and the quality of life of the Palestinian people."[2] While not addressing the need for an institutionalized structure and process to conduct diplomatic and politicoeconomic affairs, there was a keen recognition for the need to maintain a structure that was sensitive to the demands of external funding sources. Hence the Task Force notes that the PA has to create more efficient operational institutions in order to comply "with General Agreement on Trade and Tariffs/World Trade Organization (GATT/WTO) criteria to ensure external market entry."[3] Taking a stand vicariously, it has been suggested elsewhere that if economic issues would be considered first, then it would be easier to create a regional trade regimen that would bring about an accompanying security condition;[4] one can then be led to conclude, of course, that regional security will solve the issue of legitimate Palestinian political activity at the international level. There certainly is observable evidence of attention paid to attracting investment capital and related strategies to induce economic development. Less visible are efforts at establishing a diplomatic regime and therefore it has the appearance of lesser importance.

II. POLITICAL FACTORS

The ability of a state to interact with other states and multistate organizations on the international level presumes that for a working arrangement there must be an ability to extend policy outward from a domestic governing system. This condition operates for purposes of reciprocity and so as not to merely react to other states' diplomatic gestures or be a recipient of another state's largesse.[5] The option, of course, does remain allowing the state to relegate the conduct of its foreign relations to another state[6] while not ceding its independence in any real sense.[7] One would think, also, in the case at hand where the achievement of sovereignty is a paramount goal, the inability to project a policy at the international level not only diminishes the state's capacity to act but also perpetuates the image and status of dependency. To the extent a state engages in international relations peacefully, it is said that the state is abiding by the established rules of international law; whether that is intended or not is subject to an additional determination. Nevertheless, it has become increasingly more incumbent upon new states that adopt new constitutions by design and interpretation to publicly espouse its familiarity with the accepted rules of conduct established by international law.[8] In the set of circumstances under review here, there is admittedly a unique set of criteria whereby a territorial entity has been afforded considerable attention and political recognition, prior to obtaining sovereign status. The complexity of irrigating contemporary international law with normative values in congruence with the appearance of nonstate actors is a situation clearly on the rise. "The lack of a generalized, normative, and procedural framework has also reinforced inevitable tendencies of major states to react in different ways to different claims, not for principled universal reasons but for particularist reasons reflecting the special interests of major states and decision-makers."[9] We thus can witness states from all regions of the globe rushing in to invest in the fledgling Palestinian polity for any number of reasons. Some aid providers do so for humanitarian purposes while others probably seek to position themselves for future benefits that may accrue. All the diplomacy that is in evidence and that is essentially externally initiated, adds to importance for the Palestinians to establish the mechanics and politics of a constitutional framework for interstate behavior. What political good will the Palestinians enjoy today results from its familiarity with the standard procedures of diplomacy. But there is little to indicate a guaranteed continuation in any positive direction. The risk of a possible reduction in favorable relations can be lessened, however, by establishing a predictable manner of interstate relations.

Realizing that the current period of political development for Palestine is an "interim" one,[10] there is an expectation on the parts of all participants in the current "peace process" to proceed to a further negotiated permanent status. Declaratory statements reflective of a proposed position in the world, nonetheless, can only serve a higher purpose by encouraging respect for the world of law with explicit stipulations. The PA has the semblance of a foreign ministry and diplomatic interaction has been in evidence. It is strongly suggested here that a policy statement be placed on record by Palestinian authorities indicating what would appear in a revised or amended constitution that would support a foreign policy process.[11]

III. Foreign Affairs

One Palestinian legal scholar, Omar Dajani,[12] offers an interesting argument along with commensurate insight with regard to the current status of the PLO and the PA vis-à-vis Palestine, to wit: there is a presumption, that begins with the Montevideo Convention of 1933 as being authoritative, demanding that a *state* in order to enjoy that elevated status "have the capacity to enter into relations with other states."[13] Beyond this stated point, reliance for the execution of authority in binding relations rests largely on scholars' interpretations. It is also noted to be sure that the two major schools of diplomatic recognition of states, constitutive and declaratory theories, include certain factors as discussed above as essential.[14] The logical order of argument it seems is that while states have been traditionally the only public bodies recognized by international law,[15] newer forms of political organization have widened the perspective, now to include some forms of nonstate actors.[16] Accordingly, a nonstate actor may legitimately engage in what otherwise would be considered interstate relations if that body maintains reasonably independent control over its governing capacity.[17] On the issue of political independence, Dajani concedes that "Palestine, as a nation and territorial unit, does not have the capacity to engage independently in international relations."[18] This is an important point. Aside from the fact that the Declaration of Principles (DOP), to which the Palestinians are signatory, constricts their organizational ability to conduct foreign relations,[19] the diplomatic function has been hampered, at least officially, pursuant to formally entered into agreements. But this approach is incomplete since the Interim Agreement, [20] and in particular Art. IX, para. 5, sets out that the (Legislative) Palestine National Council has authority in foreign affairs but is relegated to what is laid out in para. 5(b)[21] and what is specifically denied in foreign affairs[22] by para. 5(a) including the diplomatic functions of establishing embassies, consulates or diplomatic missions *outside* the West Bank and Gaza Strip. Interestingly, the PLO[23] may involve itself by formal agreement with foreign powers and international organizations in those areas of activities stipulated in para. 5(a).

IV. Jerusalem

Jerusalem is a unique municipality whose importance is such that it is jointly and simultaneously claimed as the capital city of Israel and the proposed Palestinian state. Jerusalem as an issue in the peace process was deliberately postponed until sometime after the interim period was concluded but no later than the third year of the interim period.[24] To begin with, the Israeli Knesset, for its part, in 1980 enacted a "basic law" that designated "Jerusalem united in its entirety" as the capital of Israel.[25] The Palestinians have also made attempts to establish some sort of a formal presence in Jerusalem, notably at this time in the eastern sector,[26] but not without observed opposition.[27] According to a study conducted by an Israeli security office, there are 20 Palestinian institutions, either official ministries of the PA or having some other connection with it, but otherwise operating in violation of the Oslo Accords.[28] Whether the observer considers the action of the PA a negotiating tactic, an open attempt to circumvent restrictions placed on its freedom of activity by the Israelis, or a sincere measure of diplomacy, the fact is that it has maintained an official *presence* in (East) Jerusalem. In particular, since 1991 the Orient House has been maintained not only as the headquarters of the Palestinian negotiating team with Israel but also, less openly, to protect Palestinian and Muslim affairs in the Holy City which is sought as the capital of any independent state.

The Palestine National Council (PNC) adopted a Declaration of Independence at its 19th session in Algiers in November 1988, seeking a "State of Palestine on our Palestinian territory *with its capital Holy Jerusalem.*"[29] The Orient House,[30] which is associated with the PA and the Legislative Council, was the domicile of the PA's Minister for Jerusalem Affairs, Faisal al-Husseini.[31] Although the Palestinians are expected to refrain from conducting international relations in Jerusalem,[32] Husseini met with foreign consuls general at the Orient House, generally negotiating economic development programs.

By late March 1999, Israel, balancing its negotiating position with the need for a display of strength prior to national elections, revoked the travel permits and special travel privileges to three Palestinians for their conduct of diplomacy at the Orient House.[33] The following month, and as the Israeli election campaign intensified, orders were issued to close three Palestinian offices at the Orient House for what were considered to be illegal activities.[34] While the Israeli security cabinet issued a closure order, Palestinian legal authorities threatened to petition the Israeli Supreme Court for a staying order.[35] The official response was one of caution as the Internal Security Minister offered a suspension to the closure order in return for a show cause action why the government should not proceed.[36]

When the matter reached the Israeli High Court, a temporary injunction was issued enjoining the Internal Security Ministry from enforcing the closure order at least until after the elections, thereby thoroughly intertwining politics with a judicial decision.[37] Following the elections, however, the State Attorney's Office again went before the High Court of Justice arguing that the matter held in abeyance should be resumed.[38]

The contentiousness of the activities ongoing at the Orient House is even more heavily burdened by its venue, the City of Jerusalem. So fearful are all parties of endangering the overall peace process that the composite issue of Jerusalem was not included fully in the DOP but held in abeyance for the permanent status negotiations which are to take place following the interim period, ending May 4, 1999. From the Palestinian perspective, "[t]he agreement does not explicitly prohibit the activities of the Palestinian National Authority in Jerusalem. It only excludes Jerusalem and other subjects postponed for final status negotiations from the jurisdiction of the Palestinian Council."[39]

V. THE STATE AS A NATIONAL ACTOR

The overall capability of a state to behave accordingly is derived in no small part by the nature and extent of its sovereignty — as distinct from autonomy. The state as a political unit is dependent on the existence of a government that symbolizes territorial control to the geographical extent of its proclaimed borders. Furthermore, democracy demands that the government be legitimate, or that popular consent be evident in some reasonable manner. Whether the government can deal externally without the cloud of dependency is largely a matter of perception and to some extent empirical reference. Palestine lacks capacity, in this regard, given the legal circumstances of its political existence, particularly because of the artificial character, historically and diplomatically, of its origins.

Sovereignty can be limited in any significant manner without damaging its inherent nature; there may be a reduction in an entity's ability to exercise authority that a full-fledged state exercises without hesitation or debility. While it could be shown that the PA's ability to conduct foreign relations, *mutatis mutandis*, is a state of affairs that exists,[40] the manner of its legitimacy can not be established without serious reservation or even opposition. A putative exercise of authority may under some circumstances be recognized as a valorous attempt to join the comity of nations, but without complete satisfaction of the requirements of statehood, it remains something less than actual international relations.

VI. Basic Law

A. General

The Palestinian constitution is a prime indicator of Palestinian political development in an organized fashion, with a definite political end, but proceeding in a manner unlike the preceding efforts at armed conflict. To be sure, the Palestinian National Covenant — the Charter of the PLO — calls for "[a]rmed struggle" as "the only way to liberate Palestine."[41] But that is clearly not in evidence in the Basic Law, at least not in its current form.

B. Foreign Affairs

The nature of authority to conduct foreign affairs is found in Chapter Seven of the Basic Law, the Conclusion and Transitory Provisions, and in particular Article 117. The PLO in this article is recognized as the sole representative of the Palestinian people, unaffected by the transitory authority of the PA. Hence, it remains the power of the PLO "to represent the Palestinian people in foreign affairs and international relations and relations with foreign governments and international organizations."[42] The haziness of the current legal standing of the PLO with the PA standing in the wings is further obfuscated when reviewing the position of the former on foreign relations. Thus, Article 19 of the PLO Constitution orders its Executive Committee to:

> establish close relations and coordinate activities between the Organization and all Arab and international Organizations, federations, and institutions which agree with its aims, or which help in the realization of the Organization's objectives.[43]

We can hereby see that even the precursor to the Basic Law was limited in scope and objectives with regard to the world outside of "Palestine."

VII. Constitutions

The nature of a constitution is probably as variable as the political institution to which it applies. In the case of Palestine, the primary official document is the Basic Law, clearly understood to be a temporary guide[44] for a political system in transition; thus what is presently available for review is something to operate in the interim.[45] This condition and understanding certainly is not new, especially for the American reader whose colonial experience with its first constitution, the Articles of Confederation, was similarly as pragmatic. Under the Articles of Confederation, the United States, pursuant to authority established in the early constitution, did conduct diplomacy, albeit limited.[46] The United States, even in its earliest phase — under the Articles of Confederation — was recognized by other states.[47]

Considerable concern by legal scholars has already been addressed to the domestic side of constitutionalism in Palestine,[48] or what may be referred to in a comparative perspective as *Rechtsstaatlichkeit*. There has been little concern, however, for the manner in which foreign affairs will proceed in the future. The degree to which a constitution places constraints on a state's role in international affairs can be deduced from its adherence to principles of international law, recognition of international organizations, and general acceptance of peaceful relations, whatever that conjures up. One notable example for this condition would be the Preamble to the French constitution that holds:

> The French Republic, faithful to its traditions, shall abide by the rulesof international public law. It shall not undertake wars of conquestand shall never use force against the freedom of any people.
> On conditions of reciprocal terms, France shall accept the limitations of Sovereignty necessary to the organization and defense of peace.[49]

It is also instructive to examine, comparatively, other states' constitutions with regard to their position on acceptable interstate behavior. Henc van Maarseveeen and Ger van der Tang studied 142 constitutions against 233 variables.[50] Their findings, relevant to this discussion, are below in Table 1.

Table 1

Variable No.	Topic	Response
79	Provisions permitting international legislation, i.e., treaties and other agreements	Y(es) N=118 83.1% N(o) N=24 16.9%
80	With respect to the relationship between domestic legislation and international law, there is significantly less	Y(es) N=44 31.0% N(o) N=98 69.0%
81	The constitution recognizes international law	Y(es) N=36 25.4% N(o) N=106 74.6%
82	When some stipulation is mentioned when treaties are at variance with the constitution:	

Variable No.	Topic	Response
	Treaty is valid	N=7 4.9%
	Not valid	N=13 9.2%
	No stipulation	N=2 1.4%
	Not ascertainable	N=14 9.9%
	No statement	N=105 74.6%
83	Constitution mentions international organizations	Y(es) N=53 37.3% N(o) N=89 62.7%
136	Does the constitution refer to (promotion of) peace among nations?	Y(es) N=80 56.3% N(o) N=62 43.7%

The message implied by the data is mixed. While an overwhelming number of states recognize international agreements as the primary instrument of international interchange, the reverse is the case for the acceptance of a single legal system of order. What is overwhelmingly evident though is the inclusion of statements directly or indirectly formally linking the state to the traditional rules governing international behavior among states.

VIII. A Structural Analysis

The state, as a social creation at some point in time, necessarily occupies global space and combines people and its organizations. Since the key to an understanding and appreciation of man as a group being is organizations, we employ the notion of structure, or the formal composition of government with its designation of roles and functions, as the theoretical format to filter our information and to speculate on potential for adaptation. Abstract conditions of statehood, or the ability to function unencumbered must be complemented by the norms according to which it governs itself if the state is to be viewed as a serious political actor. In a larger context, the accepted complex of rules most widely accepted *and adhered to over time*, simultaneously benefits in the maintenance of the free standing of the state and contributes to a stable world order.

Recognizing that a political society is in large part determined by its institutionalized structure, there is a need for a Palestinian body to set out a prospective in anticipation of any fuller development of increased political authority beyond autonomy, particularly in the area of foreign affairs. If we assume that the structure of the state, as it is most commonly observed in the world, is a peculiarly western concept in origin, dedicated to some degree to the maintenance of the values and culture of the West, then those states falling outside this ambit face a challenge of integration. Foreign relations for an Arab state, if it is not completely committed to being an Islamic state, takes on an uncompromising burden of deciding on the character of its governing principles. Emerging as it is, arguably a secular, democratic state, Palestine must yet accommodate itself with the various hues of Islamic thought, the Palestinian Christian community, and its potential relationship to a neighboring Jewish state. Palestinians must also consider its role within the Arab World and North Africa, then the remaining developing world, and ultimately the source of real economic and political power, the West, Europe and the United States.[51]

At this point there is a serious question to be resolved: does the current Middle East peace process, whether one dates it from Madrid or Oslo, alter the status of the PLO as a negotiating body in any way? Or does the diplomatic recognition accorded to that organization, *prior to its acquisition of autonomy on the West Bank and Gaza Strip*, add to its legal capacity in spite of any subsequent set of negotiations? In other words, has there been a seamless thread of incrementally accumulated accomplishments and achievements?

For purposes of the current peace process, the opening phase must begin with the DOP which explicitly states in Article VII (5) that the authority to conduct "foreign relations" is excluded from Palestinian purview as constituted by the PA. There was an allowance for the obvious need for an infusion of foreign investment into the autonomous areas, hence the access of the PA to the PLO's Palestinian Economic Council for Development and Reconstruction (PERDAR),[52] without the inclusion of traditional diplomatic activities. Activities, which are to benefit the areas under the PA's jurisdiction, are to be handled by the PLO.

The development of the necessary infrastructure of any future sovereign Palestinian entity has occurred, according to at least one set of observers,[53] in two phases. Initially from July 1994 to January 1996, the PLO sought to consolidate its dominance during the transitory period. The second phase came after elections were held for its leadership in those areas controlled by the PNA, which was an effective determinant of legitimacy. While creating a responsive and responsible governing system is necessary to satisfy the demands for a domestic society, there similarly needs to be an institutionalized structure guided by a publicly stated and officially mandated guidance order. The preference here would be for its inclusion in the final ratified version of a Palestinian constitution.

A negotiated process may be necessary to meld the PLO's authority to conduct foreign relations and the judicial personality and standing of the PA. The Israeli desire to maintain some sort of a separation between two clearly developed Palestinian political bodies that have similar if not identical capabilities to conduct foreign relations is understandable as a negotiating position in "the peace process" and a policy to mollify some domestic constituents. It may be propitious for forward thinking Palestinians to prepare a position that would take into account facts already established; i.e., diplomatic recognition of Palestine, foreign investment programs in existence and promised, foreign diplomatic representatives in Palestine, and PLO representatives around the globe. The Israelis might reject such a proposal out of hand without a security option to offer as a counterbalance. Nevertheless, I would argue, in an effort of such considerable worth, in order to assuage the international political community, the Palestinians must, in a way that is more detailed than the present character of the Basic Law, create a foreign policy outlook commensurate with the attention that has been given to the protection of civil liberties.

Notes

1. Excluded here is notably Antarctica and whatever nonself-governing territories exist.
2. MICHAEL ROCARD ET AL., STRENGTHENING PALESTINIAN PUBLIC INSTITUTIONS at x (1999). [An Independent Task Force Report]. Available at: <http://www.foreignrelations.org/public/pubs/palinstfull.html>.
3. Id. at 61.
4. Jack Garvey, *Regional Free Trade Dispute Resolutions as Means for Security in the Middle East Peace Process*, 47 AM. J. COMP. L. 147, 184 (1999).
5. Convention on Rights and Duties of States, Dec. 26, 1933, art. 1, 165 U.N.T.S. 19.
6. RESTATEMENT (THIRD) OF FOREIGN RELATIONS LAW OF THE UNITED STATES § 201, cmt. E (1987).
7. BROWNLIE, PRINCIPLES OF PUBLIC INT'L L. 75 (1990).
8. Vladlen Vereshchetin, *New Constitutions and the Old Problem of the Relationship Between International Law and National Law*, 7 EUR. J. INT'L L. 29, 39 (1996).
9. Benedict Kingsbury, *Claims by Non-State Groups in International Law*, 25 CORNELL INT'L L. J. 481, 508 (1992).
10. Sanford Silverburg, *Diplomatic Recognition of States* in statu nascendi: *The Case of Palestine*, supra ch. 1.
11. What is called for in this instance has, in fact, been voiced by Mahmoud Abbas (Abu Mazen), a member of the PLO Executive Committee, who called for inter alia: the establishment of "strong political, social and cultural ties" with Arab states, "strong relations with states around the world," and "relations with the State of Israel." *The Palestine National Authority: Its Tasks and Responsibilities* in THE PALESTINE NATIONAL AUTHORITY: A CRITICAL APPRAISAL: A SPECIAL REPORT 31 (1995).
12. Omar Dajani, *Stalled Between Seasons: The International Legal Status of Palestine During the Interim Period*, 26 DENV. J. INT'L L. & POL. 27 (1997).
13. Supra note 3.
14. See generally P.K. MENNON, RECOGNITION IN INTERNATIONAL LAW; THEORETICAL OBSERVATIONS 4–5 (1990). The constitutive theory, its critics aside, best applies to the positivisitic manner in which Palestine is emerging as a legal entity.

15. Supra note 5, at 79. Further support is given as Myres McDougal et al., *The World Constitutive Process of Authoritative Decision*, 19 J. LEGAL EDUC. 253, 262, n. 8 (1967) and J.D. van der Vyver, *Statehood in International Law*, 5 EMORY INT'L L. REV. 9, 12 (1991).

16. Id., with support from Erik Suy, *The Status of Observers in International Organizations*, 160 ACADEMIE DE DROIT INTERNATIONALE 84, 100–01 (1978).

17. Dajani relies here, again, on a secondary authority, JAMES CRAWFORD, THE CREATION OF STATES IN INTERNATIONAL LAW 47 (1979).

18. Supra note 7, at 87.

19. Joel Singer was a member of the Israeli negotiating team and has provided an in-depth perspective on the *traveaux preparatoires* to the relevant materials. See generally Joel Singer, *Aspects of Foreign Relations Under the Israeli-Palestinian Agreements on Interim Self-Government Arrangements for the West Bank and Gaza*, 28 ISRAEL L. REV. 268 (1994).

Annex II (3)(6), Declaration of Principles on Interim Self-Government Arrangements, Sept. 13, 1993, Isr.-PLO, reprinted in 32 I.L.M. 1525 (entered into force Oct. 13, 1993) [hereafter cited as the DOP] along with the Israel-Palestine Liberation Organization Agreement on the Gaza Strip and the Jericho Area, May 4, 1994, Isr.-P.L.O., reprinted in 33 I.L.M. 622 (1994). See also Kathyrn McKinney, *The Legal Effects of the Israeli-PLO Declaration of Principles: Steps Toward Statehood for Palestine*, 18 SEATTLE U.L. REV. 93 (1994) and James Prince, *The International Legal Implications of the November 1988 Palestinian Declaration of Statehood*, 25 STAN. J. INT'L L. 681 (1989).

20. The Interim Agreement, Isr.-Pal. Interim Agreement on the West Bank and the Gaza Strip, Wash., D.C. (Sept. 28, 1995), reprinted in 36 ILM 551.

21. Id. at 36 ILM 551, 561.

22. Id.

23. According to a letter from Israeli Prime Minister Yitzhak Rabin to PLO Chairman Yasser Arafat, for purposes of the peace process, Israel recognized the PLO as the legitimate representative of the "Palestinian people." 13 ISRAEL'S FOREIGN RELATIONS: SELECTED DOCUMENTS, 1992–1994 at 307 (Meron Medzini, ed. 1995).

24. Pursuant to Arts. V(2) and V(3) of the DOP and Arts. XI(2) and XXI(5) of the Interim Agreement.

25. The Basic Law: Jerusalem Capital of Israel. 34 LAWS OF THE STATE OF ISRAEL, Authorized Translation 209 (5740–1979/80), reprinted in THE JERUSALEM QUESTION AND ITS RESOLUTION: SELECTED DOCUMENTS 322 (Ruth Lapidoth & Moshe Hirsch eds., 1994).

26. Professor Cassese has argued that "sovereign rights over Eastern Jerusalem ... should be granted to the legitimate representative of the Palestinian people." Antonio Cassese, "Legal Considerations on the International Status of Jerusalem," 3 PAL. Y.B. INT'L L. 13, 39 (1986).

27. For a discussion of legal perspectives emanating from official Israeli sources see D. Herling, "The Court, the Ministry and the Law: *Awad* and the Withdrawal of East Jerusalem Residence Rights," 33 ISRAEL. L. REV. 67 (1999).

28. Israel. Government Press Office. *Twenty PA Institutions, Including 11 "Ministries," Operate Illegally in Jeruslam: Oslo Accords Prohibit PA Activity in the Capital.*" (Sept. 9, 1998) <http://www.israel.org/mfa/go.asp?MFAH0d840>; Nadav Shragai, "Security Sources: Palestinian Authority Institutions' Activity Intended to Undermine Israel's Sovereignty in Jerusalem," HA'ARETZ, at A4 (Feb. 12, 1997).

29. Declaration of Independence, reprinted in U.N. Doc. A/432/827, at para. 10 (1988) (emphasis added).

30. Orient House was originally built as a private residence in 1897 by Ismail

Musa al–Husseini, representing one of the most respected Palestinian Jerusalemite families. Historically, the home was used for diplomatic receptions, at one time serving to host the German Emperor Kaiser Wilhem II when he paid an official visit to the city in 1898.

31. The house, since it was built by the Husseini, family remains family property and is, also then, a private residence. Faisal al–Husseini held the Jerusalem affairs ministerial portfolio in each of President Arafat's three cabinets.

32. Jerusalem as an issue subject to negotiation is postponed for final status negotiations.

33. JERUSALEM POST, March 19, 1999.

34. Id., April 5, 1999.

35. Id., April 25, 1999.

36. Id., April 28, 1999.

37. Id., May 12, 1999.

38. Id., June 8, 1999.

39. Riziq Shuqar. "Jerusalem: Its Legal Status and the Possibility of a Durable Settlement," 17 (October 1996)[Palestinian National Authority Official Website; Special Report]. <http://www.pna.net/report/alhaq_jerusalem.htm> (emphasis added).

40. There are at present five Arab, six European, two Asian, and one African state representative offices to the PA in Palestine; ten consulates general in [East] Jerusalem to handle Palestinian affairs; and 70 states that recognize a Palestinian passport for travel purposes. But perhaps most telling is the reality that the PA maintains diplomatic missions to 17 Arab states as well as to the Arab League and the Organization of the Islamic Conference (OIC), 13 missions to Asian and Oceanic states, 11 missions to African states, 25 missions to European states, with an office allocated to UNESCO in Paris and a Permanent Observer of Palestine to the UN Office at Geneva, ten mission to states in North and Latin America, as well as a permanent mission established at the United Nations Headquarters in New York. See generally various documents compiled by Dr. Baker Abdel Munem at <http://www.cyberus.ca>.

41. Article 9. BASIC POLITICAL DOCUMENTS OF THE ARMED PALESTINIAN RESISTANCE MOVEMENT 137, 138 (Leila S. Kadi, ed. 1969). A faction of the Palestinian political community, the Palestinian National Liberation Movement, "Fateh," continues to play a role in Palestinian political dynamics urging armed struggle against what it sees as a colonial interloper and threat to the Muslim character of Palestine. See this group's constitution at <http://www.fateh.org/e_public/constitution.htm>.

42. BASIC LAW FOR THE NATIONAL AUTHORITY IN THE TRANSITIONAL PERIOD 26 (Jerusalem Media & Communication Centre, 1996). See for example the Euro Mediterranean Interim Association Agreement on Trade and Cooperation Between the European Community and the PLO, entered into on behalf of the PA. 1997 O. J. (L 187) 3–135. The PLO, acting as *porte-parole* for the PA, was also a signatory to the Declaration On the Principles Guiding Relations Among the CICA (Conference on Interaction and Confidence) Member States, signed at Almaty, Kazakhstan, September 14, 1999. <http://www.pna.net/faffairs/cica_principles.htm>.

43. The PLO's Constitution was amended and ratified at their Fourth Session in Cairo, July 10–17, 1968. <http://wu-israel.org/jsource/Peace/plocon.html>.

44. The Palestinian Authority's Legislative Council created a draft and submitted it to Yasir Arafat, as President, for his signature that has not been forthcoming. Meanwhile, the PA has created a Constitutional Drafting Committee that met in Cairo and drafted an actual constitution of six chapters that will be submitted to the PLO Central Council for review. PALESTINE REPT. (June 11, 1999) as reported by Rex

Brynen <cyr6@MUSICA.MCGILL.CA>, June 10, 1999, and AL-SHARQ AL-AWSAT (London), July 5, 2000, at 5, via FBIS/WNC. At a meeting of the PLO's Central Council (PCC) in April 1999, a constitution committee was formed to continue to study and work on the constitution for an eventual Palestinian state. Assisting in this effort is the legal committee of the Arab League, emphasizing the role of international law. 29 J. PAL. STUD. 109 (1999).

45. For a discussion on the temporally linear development of the Basic Law see G. MAHLER, CONSTITUTIONALISM AND PALESTINIAN CONSTITUTIONAL DEVELOPMENT, at ch. 3 (1996), Nathan Brown, *Constituting Palestine: The Effort to Write a Basic Law for the Palestinian Authority,"* 54 MIDDLE EAST J. 25 (2000); Gary Hengstler, *First Steps Towards Justice,* 80 A.B.A. J. 52 (1994); John Strawson, *Palestine's Basic Law: Constituting New Identities Through Liberating Legal Culture,* 20 LOY. L. A. INT'L & COMP. L. J. 411 (1998), and Adrien Wing, *The Palestinian Basic Law: Embryonic Constitutionalism,* 31 CASE W. RES. J. INT'L L. 383 (1999).

46. See generally THE REVOLUTIONARY DIPLOMATIC CORRESPONDENCE OF THE UNITED STATES (Francis Wharton ed., 1889), 6 VOLS.; DIPLOMATIC CORRESPONDENCE OF THE UNITED STATES OF AMERICA FROM THE SIGNING OF THE DEFINITIVE TREATY OF PEACE, SEPTEMBER 10, 1783, TO THE ADOPTION OF THE CONSTITUTION, MARCH 4, 1789 (1837), 3 VOLS.; A. DARLING, OUR RISING EMPIRE (1940); F. MARKS, INDEPENDENCE ON TRIAL: FOREIGN AFFAIRS AND THE MAKING OF THE CONSTITUTION (1973).

47. Which was the first state to recognize the United States and when is a debate. The City of Dubrovnik, then known as the Republic of Ragusa, claims to be the first; the city museum has a permanent exhibit detailing this act; Barbara W. Tuchman claims it was the Dutch. FIRST SALUTE 5–17 (1988); Jerome Weiner claims it was Morocco. "Foundations of U.S. Relations With Morocco and Barbary States," 20–21 HESPÉRIS-TAMUDA 163 (1982–83).

48. See e.g., George E. Bisharat, *Peace and the Political Imperative of Legal Reform in Palestine,* 31 CASE W. RES. J INT'L L. 253 (1999) and Adrien Katherine Wing, supra note 44.

49. CONSTITUTIONS AND CONSTITUTIONAL TRENDS SINCE WORLD WAR II: AN EXAMINATION OF SIGNIFICANT ASPECTS OF POSTWAR PUBLIC LAW WITH PARTICULAR REFERENCE TO THE NEW CONSTITUTIONS OF WESTERN EUROPE 232, 233 (Arnold J. Zurcher ed., 1975).

50. HENC VAN MAARSEVEEN AND GER VAN DER TANG, WRITTEN CONSTITUTIONS: A COMPUTERIZED COMPARATIVE STUDY 79–82, 95 (1978).

51. This theme is taken up and discussed more elegantly by the Palestinian intellectual Edward Said. *Visions of National Identity in Palestine and Lebanon, in* SMALL STATES IN THE MODERN WORLD 125–142 (Peter Worsley and Paschalis Kitromilides eds., 1979).

52. DOP, Art. VI, Cairo Agreement, para. 2(a).

53. Yossi Shain and Gary Sussman, *From Occupation to State-Building: Palestinian Political Society Meets Palestinian Civil Society,* 33 GOVT. & OPPOSITION 283–284 (1998).

5

Aspects of Foreign Relations Under the Israeli-Palestinian Agreements on Interim Self-Government Arrangements for the West Bank and Gaza

JOEL SINGER

I. INTRODUCTION

In each one of the three main agreements which Israel has concluded to date with the PLO as part of the current peace process,[1] the issue of foreign relations has received special treatment. This reflects the fact that, while the transfer of a number of spheres of authority to the Palestinian autonomous entity has serious practical ramifications, the treatment of the sphere of foreign relations has an added effect on the very nature of the autonomous entity itself, because full capacity to conduct foreign relations is one of the accepted indicia of sovereignty and statehood. Any arrangements reached with regard to the sphere of foreign relations are, therefore, of critical significance.

In approaching the issue of foreign relations in connection with the self-government arrangements for the West Bank and the Gaza Strip, this article will first consider the principles of international law that have a bearing on the subject. These fall into three categories: first, as already indicated, is the question of the significance of the authority to conduct foreign relations in the context of statehood. Second, this article reviews the extent to which such authority can be exercised by an autonomous entity. Third, and no less important in the context of the West Bank and the Gaza Strip, is the question of the nature of foreign relations authority with regard to occupied territory. Having considered the international law framework, the article will review the approach taken by the negotiating parties to the issue of foreign relations, first in the autonomy negotiations conducted pursuant to the Framework for Peace in the Middle East agreed at Camp David, dated September 17, 1978 ("the Camp David Agreement"),[2] and second in the current Israel-Palestinian negotiations.

II. INTERNATIONAL LAW ASPECTS

A. Foreign Relations as an Element of Statehood

The capacity to enter into foreign relations has traditionally been regarded as one of the four fundamental criteria of statehood. Thus, Article I of the Montevideo Convention on the Rights and Duties of States[3] provides:

The State as a person of international law should possess the following qualifications:
- a) a permanent population;
- b) a defined territory;
- c) a government; and
- d) *capacity to enter into relations with the other States* (emphasis added).

It has been argued that the fourth criterion established in the Montevideo Convention does not accurately reflect customary international law, and should in fact be "independence from foreign rule."[4] The reason for this criticism is that the constitution of a state may grant the constituent elements of that state the capacity to enter into limited relations with other states, without granting independence to the constituent elements. Clearly, in such a case these elements cannot be considered states.[5] At the same time, even if the criterion of "capacity to enter into foreign relations" is too narrowly stated, it is evident that in its absence an area cannot be considered an independent state.

Significantly, the criteria of statehood were recently considered by a United States federal court in the context of the PLO. The family of the late Leon Klinghoffer, murdered in the course of the hijacking of the Achille Lauro Cruise Liner in 1985, filed a claim for damages against owners of the vessel and other defendants, including the PLO. Amongst the arguments raised by the PLO in its defense was a claim, based on its purported "Declaration of Independence" of 1988, that, as a sovereign state, the PLO was immune from suit.[6] The United States court rejected this argument, basing its decision on the definition of statehood:[7]

> [T]his court has limited the definition of "state" to entit[ies] that ha[ve] a defined territory and a permanent population, [that are] under the control of [their] own governments, and that *engage[d] in, or ha[ve] the capacity to engage in formal relations with other such entities* (emphasis added).

In considering each of these elements of statehood in turn, the court found that the PLO satisfied none of the criteria. The court concluded that, despite the aspiration of the "Declaration of Statehood" to have a defined territory, no such defined territory existed.[8] The court further concluded that since it did not have a defined territory, the "State of Palestine" could not have a permanent population.[9] The court also held that the PLO was unable to demonstrate that its "state" was under the control of the State of Israel.[10] Finally, the court held that, despite the fact that a number of states had recognized the PLO, the PLO "does not have the capacity to enter into genuine formal relations with other nations."[11]

The establishment of self-governing arrangements in the West Bank and the Gaza Strip should not affect this conclusion; because, among other things, as demonstrated below, under these arrangements the Palestinian autonomous entity lacks the authority to conduct foreign relations, and thus lacks independence from foreign rule.

B. Foreign Relations as an Element of Autonomy

Research conducted for the U.S. State Department by Hurst Hannum and Richard B. Lillich on the subject of the Theory and Practice of Governmental Autonomy suggests that the lack of authority to conduct foreign relations, including the competence to enter into international agreements, is one of the two conspicuous characteristics of autonomies, the other being the lack of authority in relation to external security.[12]

Nevertheless, on the basis of their analysis of a wide variety of autonomies, Hannum and Lillich conclude that, in certain cases, a limited authority to conduct foreign relations is granted to the autonomous body. The transfer of authority to conduct foreign relations can take many forms. Frequently, the autonomous entity is authorized to enter into international agreements only within specific spheres of competence. Hannum and Lillich note that "such treaty-making power is most often restricted to economic, cultural, social and similar matters (as opposed to political or military agreements)."[13]

A more limited authority is contained in the Danish statute granting autonomy to Greenland. While the statute provides that Greenland's foreign relations are to be conducted by Denmark, it permits Greenland to participate, with Denmark's consent, in the conduct of negotiations relating to international agreements with foreign states on issues which are "of special importance for Greenland's commercial life."[14]

The economic interests of the Netherlands Antilles, a Dutch autonomy, are similarly protected in the Charter for the Kingdom of the Netherlands. Under this charter, where the central Dutch Government wishes to enter into or denounce an international economic or financial agreement which would be binding on the Netherlands Antilles, it may not do so without the consent of the Netherlands Antilles and, when requested, it must cooperate with the latter in concluding such an agreement, "unless this would be inconsistent with the partnership of the Country in the Kingdom."[15]

In the cases of the association of New Zealand with the Cook Islands and Niue, the relevant constitution acts provide that, while these territories will be self-governing, "Her Majesty the Queen in right of New Zealand" will retain responsibility for "external affairs and defense." The responsibility of New Zealand in the area of external affairs is qualified, however, by a duty to consult the associates before exercising this responsibility.[16]

While treaty-making authority is most frequently granted to autonomies in the economic sphere, there are instances where treaty-making power is transferred for cultural purposes. Such a power is evident in the Basque autonomy where treaty-making power is limited to the establishment of cultural relations with states having Basque-speaking communities. The Basque authorities are empowered to implement international agreements affecting matters within their local jurisdiction, but such treaties or agreements may not affect the fundamental attributes or authority of the autonomous community without a local referendum.[17]

In sum, it can be generally stated that, where latitude is given to an autonomous region in the realm of foreign relations, this is most often done in order to enable it to enter into commercial, and occasionally cultural, agreements. It should also be noted, however, that there exist a number of instances of nonindependent entities being permitted to participate in international organizations, though this almost only occurs in cases of associate statehood. Thus, the Netherlands Antilles is a member of the Universal Postal Union and the World Meteorological Association, while the Saar Territory, under League of Nations administration was a member of the Universal Postal Union and the Universal Telegraphic Convention.[18] Cases of relations between autonomies which are not associate states and international organizations are rare, though the Aland Islands are members of the Nordic Council, and, while Denmark is a member of the European Community, Greenland left the community, and the Faroe Islands, autonomous areas under Danish sovereignty, never became a member.[19]

C. Foreign Relations and Occupied Territory

In the context of the Israel-PLO negotiations, the issue of foreign relations, as with many other issues, is complicated by the fact that the territories in which autonomy is being established — the West Bank and the Gaza Strip — are not considered sovereign territory of Israel, but rather territories under the control of an Israeli military government, though Israel has a claim to sovereignty over these areas.[20]

Since the source of authority of the Palestinian autonomous body in the West Bank and the Gaza Strip is rooted in the Israeli military government, which continues to exercise some powers during the interim period,[21] it follows that, during the interim period, neither the Palestinian autonomous body nor the Israeli military government, either individually or collectively, can be vested with more extensive powers and responsibilities in the sphere of foreign relations (or in any other sphere) than those possessed by the military government prior to the interim period.

The basic principle governing the exercise of authority by the military government established by an occupant is that laid down in Article 43 of the Hague Regulations:[22]

> The authority of the power of the State having passed de facto into the hands of the occupant, the latter shall do all in his power to restore, and ensure, as far as possible, public order and safety, respecting at the same time, unless absolutely prevented, the laws in force in the country.

Since Article 43 places no limitation on the scope of the authority passing to the occupant, it may be assumed that all the authority formerly exercised by the State — including authority with regard to foreign relations — now passes de facto to the occupant. However, while the scope of the authority is not limited, Article 43 limits the exercise of this authority for the purposes of restoring and maintaining public order, safety and the well-being of the local population. As Greenspan notes:[23]

> In general, since [the occupant] is legally only temporarily in possession of the territory for the purposes of the war he should exercise only the power necessary for those purposes, plus the maintenance of order and safety, and the proper administration of the area.

Von Glahn, Greenspan and others suggest that the purposes identified by Article 43 are too narrow to be practicable, particularly in the context of a long-term occupation. Specifically, this view has been expressed with regard to the power to legislate. Article 43 permits the occupant to change the laws in force only in cases of military necessity. However, there may be many instances in which a genuine need to enact or amend legislation does not arise from strictly military necessity. As Von Glahn observes:[24]

> It has to be remembered that the secondary aim of any lawful military occupation is the safeguarding of the welfare of the native population, and this secondary and lawful aim would seem to supply the necessary basis for such new laws as are passed by the occupant for the benefit of the population and are not dictated by his own military requirements.

This principle has been applied by analogy to the question of the application of treaties to occupied territory. In considering this question, Theodor Meron states his acceptance of the view "that the occupant may take measures affecting local laws not only when required to do so for reasons of military necessity but also when such changes are required in the interest of the welfare of the population,"[25] and concludes that "international labor conventions, as distinguished from the labor laws of a particular country, are evidence of generally agreed labor standards and may, therefore, be regarded as being in the interests of the population of an occupied territory."[26]

However, the position that treaties should be applied by the occupant to occupied territory when they are in the interest of the local population frequently conflicts with a political concern of contracting states, or the international community, not to be seen to condone the state of occupation. One instance in which a related issue has arisen in the context of the West Bank and the Gaza Strip is the approach taken by the Committee for the Elimination of Racial Discrimination to the reports submitted by Israel under the International Convention on the Elimination of all Forms of Racial Discrimination.[27] For many years, this committee espoused the view that reports submitted by Israel concerning the implementation of Convention provisions should be limited to the territory of Israel, and exclude the areas of the West Bank and the Gaza Strip, since the inclusion of these areas might be construed as legitimizing Israel's claim to sovereignty. In recent years, however, the Committee has moved away from this political concern and given greater weight to the interests of the population by requiring that such reports cover the West Bank and the Gaza Strip.[28]

Beyond the question of treaty application, it is generally accepted that the occupant has the authority to regulate all aspects of international trade. The point is noted by Von Glahn:[29]

> The occupant possesses a right, based on logic, to regulate all trade between an occupied area and the outside world. This privilege extends even to a complete suspension of all foreign trade if conditions were to make such a step appear desirable. Should the occupant so choose, trade could be permitted under certain conditions.

Although it appears that this principle is universally accepted, its basis is unclear. Von Glahn, in this passage, declares that the occupant's right to regulate trade is "based on logic," but he leaves open the question whether this right can be used by the occupant at its will, in the same way as the occupant's usufructuary rights, or whether, as with other powers, it must be exercised for the interests of the local population. Whatever the basis for regulating international trade is, it is clear that such regulation must involve the exercise of foreign relations authority.

In conclusion, it seems that the full scope of foreign relations authority with regard to occupied territory is vested in the occupant, but that these powers may only be exercised for the purpose of maintaining public order and safety, and, according to most opinions, for other purposes in the interest of the local population.

III. Foreign Relations in the Framework of the Middle East Peace Negotiations

A. Treatment of Foreign Relations in the Autonomy Negotiations Conducted Pursuant to the Camp David Agreement

The notion that the Palestinian body designated to administer the autonomous government in the West Bank and the Gaza Strip would lack, among other things, authority in foreign relations emerged many years before the Declaration of Principles was concluded. This view was shared by the delegations of Egypt, Israel and the United States during their negotiations on an autonomy agreement conducted between 1979 and 1982 pursuant to the Camp David Agreement. While the Camp David Agreement itself did not spell out this principle, it stated that "[t]he parties will negotiate an agreement which will define the powers and responsibilities of the self-governing authority to be exercised in the West Bank and Gaza." When, during the course of the autonomy negotiations, the three delegations presented their positions with regard to the powers and responsibilities that should be transferred to the Palestinian self-governing authority (administrative council),[30] they all, either explicitly or implicitly, expressed their opinion that responsibility for foreign relations should not be so transferred.

Thus, on September 3, 1980, the United States delegation presented the two other parties with a proposed Memorandum of Understanding ("MOU").[31] With regard to foreign relations, the U.S. draft stated:

> The elected body will not ... conduct foreign relations or enter into international agreements, subject to the final autonomy agreement.

In response, the Israeli delegation submitted a draft MOU, dated September 21, 1980, to the delegations of Egypt and the United States. This draft MOU stated that "[i]n addition to other principles and limitations to be agreed upon, the SGA(AC) will, in particular, not ... conduct foreign relations." A few weeks later, the Egyptian delegation presented its own draft MOU, dated October 13, 1980, which included a long list of powers and responsibilities to be transferred to the SGA(AC); this list did not include foreign relations.

On November 4, 1980, the United States delegation submitted a revised draft MOU to the Israeli and Egyptian delegations, which attempted to bridge the gap between the Israeli and Egyptian MOUs. This revised U.S. draft MOU adopted the language included in the Israeli draft MOU of September 21, 1980, regarding foreign relations.

In June 1982, the United States delegation presented the two other delegations with a draft Progress Report of the Working Team to the Ministerial Level. This document attempted to provide a status report on the agreements and disagreements between the delegations of Israel and Egypt. This report stated as follows with regard to foreign relations:

> Egypt and Israel agree that, in accordance with the Camp David framework, the SGA(AC) will not be allocated powers and responsibilities which can reasonably be considered indicia of sovereignty or which are unnecessary for full autonomy during the transitional period. They also agree that powers and responsibilities which are not exercised by the SGA(AC) will be handled in a manner which will not prejudge the final status of the West Bank and Gaza. Egypt maintains that the powers and responsibilities which will not be exercised by the SGA(AC) are

> foreign affairs, *strictu sensu*, and that these powers and responsibilities should be held in abeyance or exercised, if necessary, through agreed arrangements.
>
> Israel maintains that this category should include additional items, such as international communications and transportation, currency, postage and travel documents.
>
> Israel maintains that the current situation should continue with regard to these powers and therefore that Israel shall hold these powers, although it may not exercise some of them.

Shortly after the submission of this draft report, the post–Camp David autonomy negotiations were suspended indefinitely.

In sum, during the course of these negotiations, the delegations of Egypt, Israel and the United States shared the view that the Palestinian autonomous body would not have any powers or responsibilities in the sphere of foreign relations. There was, however, a distinction between the Israeli view, which favored the retention by Israel of these powers and responsibilities, and the Egyptian view, which preferred to hold such powers and responsibilities in abeyance during the transitional period.[32]

When the Government of Israel launched its Peace Initiative of May 14, 1989, it again reiterated its longstanding position with regard to foreign affairs.[33]

> "During the transitional period ... Israel will continue to be responsible for ... foreign affairs ..."

B. Treatment of Foreign Relations in the Current Israeli-Palestinian Autonomy Negotiations

1. Treatment of Foreign Relations in the Declaration of Principles. With regard to the issue of foreign relations, the Declaration of Principles effectively took over where the Camp David autonomy negotiations left off. Unlike the Camp David Agreement, however, the Declaration of Principles did specify that the sphere of foreign relations would not be transferred to the Palestinian Authority to be established in the Gaza Strip and the Jericho Area. Thus, the Declaration of Principles stated that the agreement to be concluded in relation to the Gaza Strip and the Jericho Area would include, among other things:[34]

> Structure, powers and responsibilities of the Palestinian authority in these areas [of transferred authority], except: external security, settlements, Israelis, foreign relations, and other mutually agreed matters [emphasis added].

While the Declaration of Principles did not assert clearly that this authority would be vested in Israel, it did effectively vest the sphere of foreign relations in Israel, along with all other powers not specifically transferred to the Palestinians, by providing, in the Agreed Minute to Article VII(5), that:

> The withdrawal of the military government will not prevent Israel from exercising the powers and responsibilities not transferred to the Council.

2. Treatment of Foreign Relations in the Cairo Agreement. The translation of this principle into more detailed arrangements in the Cairo Agreement required that consideration be given to a number of factors. Thus, during the negotiations on the Cairo Agreement, the PLO argued that Israel had never (since 1967) actually represented the residents of the West Bank and the Gaza Strip internationally, either in its relations with foreign states or by its representation at the United Nations; nor had Israel entered into international agreements on their behalf. The PLO added that, in these circumstances, it was unreasonable that Israel should take advantage of the opportunity of the establishment of autonomy in order to grasp authorities that it had never actually exercised.

In addition, over the years the PLO has developed a network of international connections, including observer status in United Nations agencies[35] and missions in various countries, variously labeled "embassies," "general delegations" or "information offices."[36]

In the course of the Gaza-Jericho negotiations, the PLO requested that Israel recognize these facts and agree that, during the period of the autonomy, the PLO would continue to conduct foreign relations on behalf of the Palestinian Authority. Israel objected to this proposal. As a compromise, the PLO suggested that the agreement should provide that the Palestinian Authority would not conduct foreign relations, and that the agreement would remain silent on the issue of foreign relations conducted by the PLO. Israel opposed this proposal, concerned that, in the absence of a specific provision dealing with the issue, over time members of the Palestinian Authority would gradually begin engaging in the conduct of foreign relations, especially since many of them also fulfill functions within the PLO.

However, Israel recognized that, notwithstanding its concerns regarding the granting of powers and responsibilities pertaining to foreign relations to the autonomy, in order to ensure that the Palestinian Authority could function viably, there was a genuine need to enable some Palestinian interaction with foreign states and international organizations in specific spheres. Specifically, Israel felt that in the realm of economic assistance to the Gaza Strip and the Jericho Area it was essential that the assistance be channeled directly to the Palestinian Authority and that it not require Israeli intervention. Israel therefore agreed that an organ of the PLO, the Palestinian Economic Council for Development and Reconstruction (PECDAR), be given responsibility for the channeling of foreign economic assistance.[37] As noted above, the inclusion of some exceptions to the rule that an autonomous body should not conduct foreign relations is in accordance with international practice.

It was with these considerations in mind that Israel and the PLO agreed to the inclusion of the following provisions dealing with foreign relations in Article VI of the Cairo Agreement:

> 2.a. In accordance with the Declaration of Principles, the Palestinian Authority will not have powers and responsibilities in the sphere of foreign relations, which sphere includes the establishment abroad of embassies, consulates or other types of foreign missions and posts, or permitting their establishment in the Gaza Strip or the Jericho Area, the appointment of or admission of diplomatic and consular staff, and the exercise of diplomatic functions.
> b. Notwithstanding the provisions of this paragraph, the PLO may conduct negotiations and sign agreements with states or international organizations for the benefit of the Palestinian Authority in the following cases only:
> (1) economic agreements, as specifically provided in Annex IV of this Agreement;
> (2) agreements with donor countries for the purpose of implementing arrangements for the provision of assistance to the Palestinian Authority;
> (3) agreements for the purpose of implementing the regional development plans detailed in Annex IV of the Declaration of Principles or in agreements entered into in the framework of the multilateral negotiations; and
> (4) cultural, scientific and educational agreements.
> c. Dealings between the Palestinian Authority and representatives of foreign states and international organizations, as well as the establishment in the Gaza Strip and Jericho Area of representative offices other than those described in subparagraph 2.a above, for the purpose of implementing the agreements referred to in subparagraph 2.b above, shall not be considered foreign relations.

In considering the implications of these provisions, a number of points should be kept in mind:

> a. Paragraph VI(2)(a) quoted above contains an absolute prohibition on the conduct of "foreign relations" by the Palestinian Authority. The paragraph goes on to give examples of such conduct,

including the establishment of embassies abroad and so on. The prohibition is not limited to these examples however, but extends to the entire spectrum of activity customarily considered to fall within the conduct of foreign relations, including, for example, representation in international organizations, and negotiating and signing international agreements.

b. In addition to the prohibition on the establishment of new embassies, consulates, etc. abroad, Paragraph VI(2)(a) also contains a specific prohibition on the appointment of diplomatic or consular staff and the exercise of diplomatic functions. Accordingly, the prohibition contained in this paragraph also covers any attempt by an existing PLO office to exercise diplomatic and consular functions which the Palestinian Authority is itself prohibited from exercising. Similarly, such an office is prohibited from acting in practice as, or presenting the appearance of, a representative mission of the Palestinian Authority. Any attempt to confer on such an office the title or functions of a representative mission of the Palestinian Authority in addition to its existing title or functions is therefore prohibited by this paragraph.

c. The prohibition contained in Paragraph VI(2)(a) not only covers activity conducted by the Palestinian Authority outside the Gaza Strip and the Jericho Area, but also activities conducted by foreign states and international organizations within the Gaza Strip and the Jericho Area. Thus, the paragraph not only prohibits the Palestinian Authority from establishing missions and posts abroad, but also from "permitting their establishment" in these areas.[38] The implications of this prohibition were set out in internal guidelines prepared by the Israeli Ministry of Foreign Affairs for briefing foreign missions. The general rule was stated in these guidelines as follows:[39]

> The Palestinian Authority may neither permit the opening of diplomatic or consular missions in the Gaza Strip or the Jericho Area, nor conduct foreign relations with representatives of States or international organizations.

d. As an exception to the general rule, the PLO (but not the Palestinian Authority) is permitted to enter into agreements in certain limited *spheres for the benefit of* the Palestinian Authority.[40] The use of the phrase "for the benefit of" is significant. A phrase such as "on behalf of" would imply that the Palestinian Authority has authority to enter into such agreements and that the PLO is merely acting as its agent. In fact, the Palestinian Authority has no such authority—

it is the PLO which is exercising its own authority for the Palestinian Authority's benefit.[41]

e. The four spheres in which, as an exception to the general rule, the PLO is permitted to enter into agreements for the benefit of the Palestinian Authority are clearly specified. Thus, subparagraph (1) of paragraph VI(2)(b) does not provide a blanket permission covering all economic agreements, but rather is limited to those economic agreements "specifically provided in Annex IV," i.e., in the Protocol Concerning Economic Relations. Similarly, subparagraph (2) provides that agreements with donor countries may only be concluded "for the purpose of implementing arrangements for the provision of assistance to the Palestinian Authority." The agreements referred to in subparagraph (3) are limited to those agreements "for the purpose of implementing the regional development plans detailed in Annex IV of the Declaration of Principles or in agreements entered into in the framework of the multilateral negotiations." The regional development plans described in Annex IV of the Declaration of Principles—the Economic Development Program for the West Bank and the Gaza Strip and the Regional Economic Development Program—are in fact synonymous with the programs developed in the context of the multilateral negotiations. The final category of agreements, listed in subparagraph (4), includes "cultural, scientific and educational agreements." The reason for the inclusion of this category was the fact that, prior to the signing of the Cairo Agreement, the PLO had signed a memorandum with the United Nations Educational, Cultural and Scientific Organization (UNESCO), on December 9, 1993. The inclusion of this paragraph was seen as a way of retroactively bringing the arrangements included in this memorandum into the framework of the Cairo Agreement.

f. Article VI, as its title states, sets out the "Powers and Responsibilities of the Palestinian Authority"—not those of the PLO. Thus, in the realm of foreign relations, affairs conducted by or for the benefit of the Palestinian Authority are governed by the article. The foreign relations of the PLO, as with all of its other powers, fall outside the scope of the Cairo Agreement, which is concerned only with the establishment and functioning of the Palestinian Authority. Only where the PLO purports to conduct foreign relations for the benefit of the Palestinian Authority does it fall within the purview of the Agreement, and in such cases the PLO's authority to conduct negotiations and sign agreements is limited to the four categories of agreements listed in Paragraph VI(2)(b).

Moreover, this paragraph does not establish the PLO's authority in this regard; it merely recognizes the fact that the PLO engages in activity that includes relations with foreign states and international organizations[42] and sets limits for this activity.

g. Where an agreement has been negotiated and signed by the PLO, acting for the benefit of the Palestinian Authority in accordance with Paragraph VI(2)(b), the activity of the Palestinian Authority for the purpose of implementing that agreement, including dealing with representatives of foreign states and international organizations, is not considered to be a contravention of the Cairo Agreement. This provision, incorporated in paragraph VI(2)(c), reflects Israel's willingness to accommodate the requirements of the Palestinians. Israel felt that, while the PLO may effectively conduct negotiations concerning such agreements on an international level, their actual implementation must be done in full participation with the relevant branches of the Palestinian Authority responsible for the implementation of these agreements.

h. For the purpose of implementing such agreements, Paragraph VI(2)(c) also permits the establishment of "representative offices" in the Gaza Strip and the Jericho Area. The essential differences between these representative offices and foreign missions, such as embassies or consulates, the presence of which in the Gaza Strip and the Jericho Area is prohibited by the Agreement, were outlined in the Israel Ministry of Foreign Affairs' internal guidelines:[43]

> States and international organizations which have entered into agreements with the PLO for the benefit of the Palestinian Authority as described above, may open representative offices in the Gaza Strip and the Jericho Area, provided that such states maintain diplomatic relations with Israel.
>
> Such offices will be technical offices only, intended to facilitate due implementation of the agreement concerned, such as for the purpose of coordinating the assistance or developmental services provided by that state or organization pursuant to the agreement. They will not have any diplomatic, consular or other political status for functions. Such offices may be established in the Gaza Strip and the Jericho Area only, and not outside these areas.
>
> Such offices shall, in their operation and physical appearance, maintain their technical nature. For example, only the name and function of each office should be displayed outside its premises.

These guidelines also make it clear that foreign staff manning such offices will not have diplomatic or consular status. In practice, the coordination of the activities of the representative office will often be effected by a member of an embassy or consulate accredited to Israel. In this regard the guidelines note:[44]

> States may appoint a member of an Embassy or Consulate accredited to Israel whose function will be, in addition to those official functions performed within that Embassy or Consulate, to coordinate the activities of its representative office in the Gaza Strip or the Jericho Area. Such a person shall be stationed in the Embassy or Consulate, and not in the technical office.
>
> Israel will enable such a member of an Embassy or Consulate as referred to in paragraph 7 above to travel without restriction between Israel and the Gaza Strip and the Jericho Area. Israel will not be able to guarantee enjoyment in the Gaza Strip or the Jericho Area of diplomatic or consular privileges or immunities enjoyed by such persons in Israel.

The Cairo Agreement contains a further provision with implications in the sphere of foreign relations. Article I(6) of Annex III (Protocol Concerning Legal Matters) contains a specific provision relating to Israel's role in the relation between foreign citizens detained in prisons in the Gaza Strip or the Jericho Area and foreign consuls in Israel, as follows:

6.a. Tourists in transit to or from Israel through the Gaza Strip or the Jericho Area, who are present on the Lateral Roads or on the main North-South Road crossing the Jericho Area (Route No. 90), may be arrested and questioned only by the Israeli authorities which shall notify the Palestinian Authority. Where the Israeli authorities conclude that an offense under the prevailing law has been committed, and that further legal proceedings in respect of the tourist are required, such proceedings shall be taken by the Palestinian Authority.

b. Where such a tourist present outside these areas is detained or arrested by the Palestinian Authority, it shall notify the Israeli authorities immediately and shall enable them at the earliest opportunity to meet the detainee and to provide any necessary assistance, including consular notification, requested by the detainee.[45]

Though the above-quoted Article I(6) uses the phrase "tourist," it is clear from the Cairo Agreement that this phrase includes all foreigners, i.e., anyone who is neither Israeli nor Palestinian. Where such a foreigner is arrested by the Palestinian Authority, the responsibility for providing "any necessary assistance, including consular notification" remains with Israel. Thus, although, as regards issues of internal security, i.e., the continued detention of the suspect and consequent judicial process, the foreigner falls within the responsibility of the Palestinian Authority, the responsibility for establishing the connection between the foreigner and the relevant consul, for the purpose of consular access and other consular assistance, remains with Israel. Such a provision was imperative since no foreign consulates are allowed to be opened in the West Bank and the Gaza Strip. Consequently, only foreign consular staff located in Israel can provide foreigners present in the Gaza Strip and the Jericho Area with consular services and assistance, as has been the case since 1967. This provision is reflected in the Israeli Ministry of Foreign Affairs' internal guidelines:[46]

> Consular activity with regard to foreign nationals detained by the Palestinian police in the Gaza Strip or the Jericho Area, will be coordinated through the Foreign Nationals Branch of the Israel Police which will coordinate such matters directly with the Palestinian police.

3. Treatment of Foreign Relations in the Preparatory Transfer Agreement. Pursuant to the Declaration of Principles, following the implementation of the Cairo Agreement, Israel and the PLO negotiated the Preparatory Transfer Agreement, signed on August 29, 1994. This Agreement provides for the initial transfer of powers and responsibilities to the Palestinian Authority throughout the West Bank in six specific spheres: education and culture, health, social welfare, tourism, direct taxation and value added tax. Additional agreed spheres may subsequently be transferred in a phased manner. Since many of the spheres transferred are ones with regard to which states normally negotiate and conclude international agreements, it was important that this Agreement should also contain a specific provision governing the conduct of foreign relations with regard to these spheres. Accordingly, Article III(3) of the Agreement provides:

> The transfer of powers and responsibilities under this Agreement does not include powers and responsibilities in the sphere of foreign relations, except as indicated in Article VI(2)(b) of the Gaza-Jericho Agreement.

It should be noted that, as outlined above, under Paragraph VI(2) of the Cairo Agreement, the Palestinian Authority is authorized to permit the establishment of certain representative offices in the Gaza Strip and the Jericho Area in order to implement agreements entered into by the PLO for its benefit. Under the Preparatory Transfer Agreement, however, the Palestinian Authority has no such authority. Its power to engage in foreign relations is restricted to Paragraph VI(2)(b), which deals only with the negotiating and signing of agreements for its benefit by the PLO in four specified spheres. Foreign representative offices may not, therefore, be opened in the West Bank, except for the Jericho Area.

4. Prohibition on the Conduct by Palestinians of Foreign Relations in Jerusalem. Detailed discussion on the issue of opening foreign representative offices, or conducting any other foreign relations activity, in East Jerusalem exceeds the scope of this article, though mention should be made of some of the ramifications that the Israel-PLO agreements have in this regard.

The Government of Israel has repeatedly refused to permit the opening of foreign representative offices in East Jerusalem. Furthermore, it has also objected to the maintenance of any official contacts between members of the Palestinian Authority and foreign diplomats in East Jerusalem. Such meetings have taken place occasionally, in particular in the Orient House building in East Jerusalem. Israel's objections to the conduct of such activity in Jerusalem are based on the fact that the Declaration of Principles excludes Jerusalem from the autonomy arrangements. In Article V(3) of the Declaration of Principles, Jerusalem is listed as one of the issues to be discussed in the permanent status negotiations, while the Agreed Minute to Article V(4) provides that "[j]urisdiction of the Council will cover West Bank and Gaza Strip territory, except for issues that will be negotiated in the permanent status negotiations", indicating that the jurisdiction of the Council will not include Jerusalem. It should be noted that, although this provision relates to restrictions on the jurisdiction of the elected Council, these restrictions similarly apply to the Palestinian Authority in the Gaza Strip and the Jericho Area. This is evident from the General Understandings and Agreements contained in the Agreed Minutes to the Declaration of Principles, which provide:

> Any powers and responsibilities transferred to the Palestinians pursuant to the Declaration of Principles prior to the inauguration of the Council will be subject to the same principles pertaining to Article IV, as set out in these Agreed Minutes below.

Furthermore, as regards the offices of the Palestinian Authority, Paragraph 5 of Annex II of the Declaration of Principles states:

> The offices responsible for carrying out the powers and responsibilities of the Palestinian authority under this Annex II and Article VI of the Declaration of Principles will be located in the Gaza Strip and in the Jericho area pending the inauguration of the Council.

The principle embodied in this paragraph prohibits the functioning of the Palestinian Authority in areas located outside the Gaza Strip and the Jericho Area, including in Jerusalem.

These provisions of the Declaration of Principles are not intended to obstruct the operation of Palestinian institutions already in existence in Jerusalem and serving the Palestinian population of Jerusalem. It was made clear in a letter dated October 11, 1993, sent by Israeli Foreign Minister Shimon Peres to the Foreign Minister of Norway Johan Jorgen Holst that these institutions have an important role to play in the economic, social, educational and cultural life of the Palestinians of Jerusalem. The letter stressed that "all the Palestinian institutions of East Jerusalem, including the economic, social, educational and cultural, and the holy Christian and Moslem places, are performing an essential task for the Palestinian population," and concluded:

> Needless to say we will not hamper their activity: on the contrary, the fulfillment of this important mission is to be encouraged.

It should be stressed, however, that this letter underlines the need to preserve the existing institutions in Jerusalem, and the performance of their existing functions. Any attempt, during the interim period, to establish new institutions operated by the Palestinian Authority, or to expand the functions exercised by existing institutions by turning them into an apparatus of the Palestinian Authority, is clearly prohibited by the provisions of the Declaration of Principles, as noted above.

The Israeli Knesset recently enacted legislation in order to implement the Cairo Agreement internally. This legislation was prepared pursuant to paragraph 12 of the exchange of letters, dated May 4, 1994, accompanying the Cairo Agreement, which reads:

> The Government of Israel and the Palestinian Authority shall pass all necessary legislation to implement the Agreement.

One of these laws, the Law Implementing the Agreement on the Gaza Strip and the Jericho Area (Restriction on Activity) 1994,[47] deals specifically with the prohibition on the exercise of powers and responsibilities by the Palestinian Authority outside the Gaza Strip and the Jericho Area. Section 3 of this Law provides:

(a) The Palestinian Authority shall not open or operate a representative mission, and shall not hold a meeting, within the area of the State of Israel unless written permission for this has been given by the State of Israel or by someone authorized by it to do so. For the purpose of this paragraph, "the Palestinian Authority" includes any person acting on its behalf or under its auspices or using its name.

(b) The Minister of Police may, by means of an order, prohibit the opening or operation of a representative mission of the Palestinian Authority, order its closure, or prevent the holding of a meeting, if permission has not been obtained in accordance with sub-paragraph (a).

(c) Orders referred to in sub-paragraph (b) shall be served, insofar as possible, on the owner of the premises, or the occupier, or the organizers, or whoever it seems to the Minister of Police is responsible for the activity which is the subject of the order. Where it is not possible to serve the order as aforesaid, the Minister of Police shall give instructions for its publication in a manner which he shall establish. A notice concerning the giving of the order shall be published in the Official Gazette.

The aim of this provision is to ensure adherence to the principle established in the Cairo Agreement that all offices of the Palestinian Authority should be situated in the Gaza Strip or the Jericho Area. It should be noted that "representative mission" and "meeting" are given broad definitions, being defined as including any "institution, office or branch", and any "march, assembly or congress," respectively.[48]

The provisions of the law concerning activity of the PLO are less stringent than those relating to the Palestinian Authority. Rather than providing that the establishment of offices, the holding of meetings, etc. by the PLO within the area of the State of Israel is prohibited unless permission has been obtained, it provides that, as a general rule, such activity is permitted and may only be prevented exceptionally by the Government of Israel. Thus, section 4(a) provides:

> The Government may, by means of an order, prohibit the opening or the operation of a representative mission of the PLO, order its closure, or prevent the holding of a meeting on behalf of the PLO or under its auspices within the area of the State of Israel.

The intention of the Law is explained in section 1 which provides:

> The purpose of this law is to ensure compliance with the undertaking of the Palestinian Liberation Organization (hereinafter "the PLO") concerning the restriction on the activity of the Palestinian Authority to the areas of Gaza and Jericho in accordance with the Agreement and to prevent activity of a political or governmental nature or other similar activity within the area of the State of Israel which does not accord with respect for the sovereignty of the State of Israel by the Palestinian Authority or the PLO, without the agreement of the State of Israel.

Under the provisions of the Law, a closure order may not be granted for a period exceeding six months.[49] Any decision for such an order is subject to an appeal to the Supreme Court sitting as the High Court of Justice.

The fact that neither the Palestinian Authority nor the Council, once it is established, is authorized to conduct official business, including contacts with foreign representatives, in Jerusalem, was recognized in a recent United States appropriation act provision dealing with "Restrictions Concerning the Palestinian Authority,"[50] which provides:

(a) None of the funds appropriated by this Act may be obligated or expended to create in any part of Jerusalem a new office of any department or agency of the United States government for the purpose of conducting official United States Government business with the Palestinian Authority over Gaza and Jericho or any successor Palestinian governing entity provided for in the Israel-PLO Declaration of Principles: Provided, That this subsection shall not apply to the acquisition of additional space for the existing Consulate General in Jerusalem.

(b) Meetings between officers and employees of the United States and officials of the Palestinian Authority, or any successor Palestinian governing entity provided for in the Israel-PLO Declaration of Principles, for the purpose of conducting official United States Government business with such authority should continue to take place in locations other than Jerusalem. As has been true in the past, officers and employees of the United States Government may continue to meet in Jerusalem on other subjects with Palestinians (including those who now occupy positions in the Palestinian Authority), have social contact, and have incidental discussions.

Although technically a violation of the Israel-PLO agreements, Israel has raised no objection to meetings between foreign diplomats accredited to Israel or visiting Israel and members of the Palestinian Authority even where the subject of such meetings exceeded the four exceptions set out in paragraph VI(2)(b) of the Cairo Agreement, provided that such meetings take place in the Gaza Strip or the Jericho Area.

IV. Conclusion

In sum, Israel, in its agreements with the PLO, agreed to relinquish authority over a limited number of aspects of foreign relations relating to the Gaza Strip and the West Bank, mainly in the areas of foreign trade and economic assistance. This was done with a view to enabling the Palestinian Authority to function effectively. Consistent with international practice regarding autonomies, these are only exceptions—the general rule is that the Palestinian Authority lacks the authority to conduct foreign relations.

These arrangements, therefore, are indicative of the intention of the parties to establish autonomy, and not an independent entity, in the Gaza Strip and the West Bank.

Notes

1. The three main agreements concluded thus far between Israel and the PLO are as follows:

    1. The Declaration of Principles on Interim Self-Government Arrangements, signed at Washington on September 13, 1993 ("the Declaration of Principles"). This agreement sets out a framework for Israeli-Palestinian negotiations during an interim period of five years until the implementation of the outcome of permanent status negotiations between the two parties;

    2. The Agreement on the Gaza Strip and the Jericho Area, signed at Cairo on May 4, 1994, ("the Cairo Agreement"). This agreement gives effect to the provisions of the Declaration of Principles dealing with the withdrawal of Israeli military forces from the Gaza Strip and the Jericho Area and the transfer of powers from the Israeli military government and its Civil Administration to a Palestinian Authority established in these areas; and

    3. The Agreement on Preparatory Transfer of Powers and Responsibilities, signed at Erez on August 29, 1994 ("the Preparatory Transfer Agreement"). This agreement implements the provisions of the Declaration of Principles requiring a functional transfer of authority from the Israeli authorities to the Palestinians in a number of specific civilian spheres throughout the West Bank.

Each of these Agreements has been published by the Information Division, Israeli Ministry of Foreign Affairs. In addition, the Declaration of Principles and the Cairo Agreement have been distributed by the United Nations General Assembly as documents A/48/486–S/26560 (annex) of October 11, 1993 and A/49/180–S/1994/727 (annex) of June 20, 1994 and published in 32 I.L.M. 1525 (1993) and 33 IIAM. 622 (1994).

2. Framework for Peace in the Middle East agreed at Camp David, September 17, 1978, 11 I.L.M. 1466–74 (1978); 25 *KS* 857.

3. Convention on the Rights and Duties of States, 1933, 28 AM. J. INT'L L. (supp.) 75 (1934).

4. See YORAM DINSTEIN, INT'L L. AND THE STATE 98 (1971, in Hebrew).

5. Under the Federal Constitution of the Swiss Confederation of 1874, for example, alliances and treaties "of a political character: between cantons are prohibited (Article VII), but agreements with foreign nations "on matters of public economy and neighbourship and police relations" are permitted, as long as they do not "contain anything prejudicial to the Confederation or the rights of other Cantons" (Article IX). For the text of the Constitution, see 131 B.F.S.P. 713–740 (1929 part II).

6. For the background and content of the Palestinian "Declaration of Independence," see 27 I. L. M. 1660 (1988).

7. *Klinghoffer v. Achille Lauro*, 937 F.2D 44, 47 (2nd Cir., 1991).

8. Id.

9. Id., at 48.

10. Id.

11. Id.

12. Hurst Hannum and Richard B. Lillich, *The Concept of Autonomy in International Law*, 74 AM J. INT'L L. 858–889, at 872 (1980). Also published in MODELS OF AUTONOMY 215–254 (Yoram Dinstein ed., 1981).

13. Hannum and Lillich, supra note 12, at 874.
14. Section 16, the Greenland Home Rule Act, Act No. 577 November 29, 1978. See U.N. Doe E/CN.4/199242 Add. 1 pp. 109–116. See also Isi Foighel, *A Framework for Local Autonomy: The Greenland Case*, in Yoram Dinstein, supra n. 12, at 37.
15. Charter for the Kingdom of the Netherlands, Articles 24 (1), 26 and 27, 15 NETH. INT'L L.R. 107–118 (1958). The Charter also provides for the appointment of a special representative to participate on behalf of the Netherlands Antilles in deliberations of the Government of the Netherlands in matters of foreign relations affecting the Netherlands Antilles. Where this representative has serious objections to the preliminary opinion of the Government, he may request further deliberations (Charter, Article 12).
16. Cook Islands Constitution Act 1964, Articles 3 and 5; Niue Constitution Act 1974, Articles 3, 7 and 8, quoted in Menachem Mautner, *West Bank and Gaza: the Case for Associate Statehood*, 6 YALE STUD. WORLD PUB. ORDER 297–360, n. 80 (1980).
17. See Hannum and Lillich, supra note 12, at 875.
18. Id.
19. See Ruth Lapidoth, *Autonomy: Potential and Limitations*, 1 INT'L J. ON GROUP RIGHTS 269–290 (1994).
20. Although Israel has undertaken to act in accordance with the humanitarian provisions dealing with occupied territory contained in the Geneva Convention relative to the Protection of Civilian Persons in Time of War on a de facto basis, its official position is that this convention does not apply de jure in the West Bank and the Gaza Strip, because these areas are not "occupied territory" in the meaning of the Convention, since sovereignty in these areas never vested in Jordan and Egypt (see, e.g., the statement of Israel's Ambassador to the United Nations, A/32/PV 47, October 26, 1977). Israel has agreed, however, to defer any discussion of claims to sovereignty until the negotiations on the permanent status of these areas, as provided in Article V of the Declaration of Principles. In this context, the provision contained both in Article XXIII(5) of the Cairo Agreement and in Article XIII(3) of the Preparatory Transfer Agreement is significant: "Nothing in this Agreement shall prejudice or preempt the outcome of the negotiations on the interim agreement or the permanent status to be conducted pursuant to the Declaration of Principles. Neither Party shall be deemed, by virtue of having entered into this Agreement, to have renounced or waived any of its existing rights, claims or positions."
21. See Joel Singer, *The Declaration of Principles on Interim Self-Government Arrangements — Some*, 1 JUSTICE (Journal of the International Association of Jewish Lawyers and Jurists) 4–13, at 6 (1994).
22. Regulations annexed to the Convention Respecting the Laws and Customs of War on Land, signed at the Hague on October 18, 1907, 2 AM. J. INT'L L. (supp.) 90–117 (1908).
23. MORRIS GREENSPAN, THE MODERN LAW OF LAND WARFARE 223 (1959).
24. GERHARD VON GLAHN, THE OCCUPATION OF ENEMY TERRITORY 97 (1957).
25. Theodor Meron, *Applicability of Multilateral Conventions to Occupied Territories*, 72 AM. J. INT'L L. 542–557, at 549 (1978).
26. Id., at 550.
27. Israel signed the Convention on March 7, 1966 and ratified it on January 3, 1979. For the text of the Convention, see 660 U.N.T.S. 195; 25 K.A. 861.
28. The change in the attitude of the Committee became evident in 1987, when it wrote in its report: "Reference was made to the need to obtain some reporting from

[the occupied] territories in order to monitor the implementation of the Convention. In that context, it was pointed out that the Committee itself, at an earlier date, had decided that it was not competent to receive any information on the occupied territories as that might imply recognition of the legitimacy of the occupation. Several members expressed the view that the Committee should revise that decision ..." [A/42/18, at 119].

By 1992 the change in the Committee's attitude was complete. Its annual report stated that: "The Committee underlined that ... Israel's report needed to encompass the entire population under the jurisdiction of Israel. The report under consideration, which described the situation only within the State of Israel itself, is in that respect incomplete" [A/46/18, at 87–88].

29. Von Glahn, supra note. 24, at 211.

30. The Camp David Agreement referred to the Palestinian autonomous authority as "the self-governing authority" and as "the administrative council" alternately. In their written documents, the three delegations decided to use these two expressions in an abbreviated form, as follows: "the SGA(AC)."

31. This and subsequent documents referred to below in this section are unpublished materials contained in the files of the Israeli Ministry of Foreign Affairs.

32. Prof. Ruth Lapidoth, who was the Legal Adviser to the Israel Ministry of Foreign Affairs during these autonomy negotiations, summed up this point as follows: "It has been more or less agreed that the self-governing authority will have no competence with respect to external security and foreign relations but whereas Israel has held that it must retain these powers, in Egypt's opinion they should be suspended for the duration of the transitional period". Lapidoth, *The Peace Process*, in ISRAEL, THE MIDDLE EAST AND THE GREAT POWERS 197, 203 (Israel Stockman-Shomron, ed., 1984).

33. Paragraph 11 of the Peace Initiative, published in GUIDE TO THE MIDEAST PEACE CONFERENCE 82 (1991).

34. Article 3 of Annex II of the Declaration of Principles, entitled Protocol on Withdrawal of Israeli Forces from the Gaza Strip and Jericho Area.

35. Under General Assembly resolution 3237 of 22 November 1974, the PLO was invited to participate in the sessions and the work of the General Assembly and all international conferences convened under the auspices of the General Assembly as an observer. This resolution also stated that the PLO should be entitled to participate in the sessions and the work of all international conferences convened under auspices of other organs of the United Nations. A further General Assembly resolution, 3375 of 10 November 1975, called for the PLO to be invited to participate on an equal footing with other parties in all efforts, deliberations and conferences on the Middle East held under the auspices of the United Nations.

General Assembly resolution 43/177 of 15 December 1988 stated that, as of that date, "the designation 'Palestine' should be used in place of the designation 'Palestine Liberation Organization' in the United Nations system, without prejudice to the observer status and functions of the Palestine Liberation Organization, in conformity with relevant United Nations resolutions and practice."

It should be noted that the effect of resolution 43/177 was purely terminological and that it was specifically stated to be "without prejudice to [the PLO's] observer status." The status of the PLO at the United Nations is thus still that laid down in the resolutions passed in 1974 and 1975.

Nothing in the agreements concluded thus far between the PLO and Israel supports any change in the standing of the PLO either within the United Nations or in any other forum. To the contrary, the status of the PLO is intricately bound up with the status of the West Bank and the Gaza Strip. Any assertion by the PLO, therefore, that the status of these areas has changed, and that accordingly the status of the PLO in the United Nations should be changed, would itself be a breach of these agreements. In this regard, in Annex II, Article 6 of the Declaration of Principles, the parties agreed that: "Other than these agreed arrangements, the status of the Gaza Strip and Jericho area will continue to be an integral part of the West Bank and Gaza Strip, and will not be changed in the interim period." This principle also finds expression in the provision included in the final clauses of both the Cairo Agreement, Article XXIII (6), and the Preparatory Transfer Agreement, Article III (5), which states: "The Gaza Strip and the Jericho Area shall continue to be an integral part of the West Bank and the Gaza Strip, and their status shall not be changed for the period of this Agreement. Nothing in this Agreement shall be considered to change this status." In addition, a similar provision is included in the exchange of letters between Israel and the PLO, dated May 4, 1994, which was concluded in connection with the Cairo Agreement. These letters provide, in paragraph 5: "Neither side shall initiate or take any step that will change the status of the Gaza Strip and the Jericho Area pending the outcome of the permanent status negotiations." On the observer status of the PLO at the United Nations, see Opinion of the Legal Counsel of the United Nations on the Status of the PLO Office to the United Nations, dated 23 September 1982, reproduced in I.C.J. Pleadings, Applicability of the Obligation to Arbitrate under Section 21 of the United Nations Headquarters Agreement of 26 June 1947, at 94–97.

36. According to the records of the Israeli Ministry of Foreign Affairs, the PLO currently has some form of foreign representation in 88 countries, as follows:

Embassies or full diplomatic missions: Algeria, Angola, Bahrain, Bulgaria, Burundi, Cambodia, Chad, China, Congo, Cuba, Cyprus, Czech Republic, Djibouti, Egypt, Ethiopia, Gabon, Ghana, Guinea-Bissau, Hungary, India, Indonesia, Iraq, Jordan, Kazakhstan, Libya, Malaysia, Mali, Mauritania, Mauritius, Morocco, Mozambique, Namibia, Nicaragua, North Korea, Nigeria, Pakistan, Philippines, Poland, Qatar, Romania, Saudi Arabia, Sudan, Tanzania, Tunisia, Turkey, Uganda, Russia, Vietnam, Zambia, Zimbabwe, Yemen. General Delegations: Australia, Belgium, Germany, France, Holland, Italy, Japan, Luxembourg, Portugal, Spain, United Kingdom. Information offices: Argentina, Bolivia, Chile, Finland, Mexico, Panama, Peru, Sweden, United States. Nonresident representatives: Benin, Burkina-Faso, Denmark, Guyana, Mongolia, Vanuatu. Other: Austria, Brazil, Canada, Greece, Kenya, Madagascar, Nigeria, Switzerland, Thailand, Uruguay. As elaborated in n. 35 above, nothing in the Israel-PLO agreements justifies any change in the status of these offices. Moreover, any assertion by the PLO to the contrary would itself be a breach of these agreements.

37. PECDAR, established on October 31, 1993, is the PLO's central institution for managing the process of reconstruction and development in the West Bank and the Gaza Strip during the transitional period. For a description of PECDAR's work and structure, see THE INTERNATIONAL BANK FOR RECONSTRUCTION, EMERGENCY ASSISTANCE PROGRAM FOR THE OCCUPIED TERRITORIES 16–18 (1994).

38. This provision also has the effect of preventing the opening in the Gaza Strip and the Jericho Area of offices of international organizations. Thus, when, subsequent to the signing of the Declaration of Principles, the Secretary-General of the United Nations initiated the relocation of the headquarters of the United Nations Relief and Works Agency for Palestine Refugees in the Near East (UNRWA) from Vienna to Gaza, Israeli consent was required. Israel agreed to allow this relocation to take place in order to accommodate the requirements of both the Palestinians and of UNRWA. For details concerning the transfer of the UNRWA headquarters to the Gaza Strip, see Report of

the Commissioner-General of the United Nations Relief and Works Agency for Palestine Refugees in the Near East, 1 July 1993–30 June 1994, G.A.O.R. 49th Session, Supplement No. 13 (A/49/132) at 6.

39. ISRAEL. MIN. OF FOR. AFF., FOR. RELS., THE PLO AND THE PALESTINIAN AUTHORITY: PRACTICAL GUIDELINES FOR BRIEFING FOREIGN MISSIONS IN ISRAEL (1994) [internal paper].

40. This provision is analogous to the provision contained in Article 36(1) of the Vienna Convention on the Law of Treaties, 1969, which provides that "A right arises for a third State form a provision of a treaty if the parties to the treaty intend the provision to accord that right ... and the third State assents thereto. Its assent shall be presumed so long as the contrary is not indicated, unless the treaty otherwise provides." This convention does not apply to the Cairo Agreement, because Israel is not a party to the Convention and the PLO cannot be a party, since it is not a state. Nonetheless, the principle contained in this Article — that an agreement between two parties can contain provisions for the benefit of a third party — is clearly analogous to the situation envisaged in the Cairo Agreement, whereby the PLO may conclude agreements which are effectively for the benefit of the Palestinian Authority in certain specified fields.

41. In one instance, pursuant to the Cairo Agreement, a PLO official signed an agreement with an international organization adding to his title in the PLO a second title held by him in the Palestinian Authority. Israel insisted that the additional reference to the title in the Palestinian Authority be deleted. Similarly, Israel has insisted that, in agreements concluded between the PLO and third parties, the official signing the agreement on behalf of the PLO not add a title suggesting that this PLO official is also an official of the "state of Palestine." The assertion that such a state exists is negated by a host of provisions contained in the Declaration of Principles and subsequent Israel-PLO agreements, which establish autonomy, and not a Palestinian state, in the West Bank and the Gaza Strip, deferring the resolution of the final status question to the end of the five-year transitional period (Article V of the Declaration of Principles). Furthermore, Chairman Arafat, who, upon the declaration by the PLO in 1988 of the establishment of the "State of Palestine," assumed the title "President of Palestine," undertook to abstain from using this title in paragraph 4 of the exchange of letters dated May 4, 1994, accompanying the Cairo Agreement. This provision reads as follows: "When Chairman Arafat enters the Gaza Strip and the Jericho Area, he will use the title "Chairman (Ra'ees in Arabic) of the Palestinian Authority" or "Chairman of the PLO," and will not use the title "President of Palestine." The prohibition on using a title intended to convey an implication of statehood was clearly not meant to be limited to Chairman Arafat, but to extend to all PLO officials."

42. See supra notes 35 and 36 and the accompanying text.

43. Israeli Ministry of Foreign Affairs internal paper, supra note 39.

44. Id.

45. The "Lateral Roads" mean the three roads connecting the Israeli settlements in the Gaza Strip with Israel. Under Article IV(7) of Annex I of the Cairo Agreement, these roads were placed under Israeli security responsibility.

46. Israel Ministry of Foreign Affairs internal paper, supra note 39.

47. 1994, *S.H.* 1497, at. 85. All translations from the Law are unofficial.

48. Id., sec. 2.

49. Id., sec. 5.

50. Sec. 585, Public Law 103–306 — August 23, 1994 (108 Stat. 1656).

6

From Liberation to State Building in South Africa: Some Constitutional Considerations for Palestine

ADRIEN KATHERINE WING

I. INTRODUCTION

In May 1994, the world watched as South Africa elected its first democratic government after a bloody history of British colonialism, Afrikaner settler colonialism, and nearly 50 years of the racist apartheid policies of the National Party. An important aspect of this bold new experiment with democracy was the passage of one of the most progressive constitutions in the world. This article will discuss the various constitutional choices made as South Africa grapples with the transition from antiapartheid liberation struggle to democratic state building, and attempts to build a human rights state. Additionally, since the author has expertise with respect to Palestine as well, the paper will contain suggestions as to where Palestine might utilize the South African experience in its own transition process. In October 1997, the Palestinian Legislative Council (PLC) passed the Third and final Reading of the Basic Law. As of the time of this writing, it awaits President Arafat's signature. I hope that my comments might be considered if the Third Reading is not signed and undergoes further revisions. Additionally, my recommendations might have relevance when the PLC undertakes drafting a new constitution for the independent state of Palestine.

Over the years, numerous comparisons have been made between the liberation struggles of South Africa and Palestine. Many considered the African National Congress (ANC) and the Palestine Liberation Organization (PLO), both accredited United Nations General Assembly Permanent Observers, to be fighting variants of minority settler regimes. Military connections and strategic alliances between the enemies of the liberation movements, Israel and apartheid South Africa, were well documented.[1] While the historical, political, and legal differences are obviously many, certain similarities between the two cases are undeniable. Groups who felt themselves oppressed waged both nonviolent and violent warfare against their oppressors. The oppressed were not allowed to govern themselves and were subjected to military or emergency rule, with well-documented international human rights violations. In each society, attempts have been made to impose a fractionated bantustan solution, rather than a democratic one. In both places, liberation movements formerly branded as terrorist sat down to negotiate the transition of power. In both countries there has been the same fear articulated by South African Constitutional Court Justice Albie Sachs:

> [T]he elimination of [colonialism] does not guarantee freedom even for the formerly oppressed. History unfortunately records many examples of freedom fighters of one generation who become oppressors of the next. Sometimes the very qualities of determination and sense of being involved in a historic endeavor which give freedom fighters the courage to raise the banner of liberty in the face of barbarous repression transmute themselves into sources of authoritarianism and historic forced marches later on. On other occasions, the habits of clandestinity and mistrust, of tight discipline and centralized control, without which the freedom-fighting nucleus would have been wiped out, continue with dire results into the new society.[2]

South Africa appears to be avoiding this fate. The end result is becoming clear: majority rule in an independent democracy. The bantustan option was defeated. In Palestine, the end result remains to be seen.

While the unique aspects of these transitions make generalization a hazardous endeavor, there are points of fruitful comparison that might assist Palestinian decision makers. In order to put the South African experience in its proper historical context, the remainder of this section will discuss the apartheid legacy. The next section highlights certain textual features of the South African constitution, and discusses how these features might be considered in future versions of the Palestinian Basic Law.

A. Apartheid and Constitutionalism in South Africa

South African constitutions were continually reshaped to meet the needs of successive undemocratic and racist regimes. The country's legal structures incorporated the worst of the Western legal tradition while ignoring its safeguards against the abuse of power. The South African legal system is a "disease that grew and developed from what was effective government in Britain, given to the hard-won affirmation of individual rights, into a monster that eventually devoured justice itself when transplanted into colonial South Africa. In brief, the monster has two limbs: the unrestrained supremacy of Parliament and the constitutional denial of democracy, both of which resulted in an all-powerful racist rule."[3]

Although racism had been a part of white domination before 1948, apartheid ("apartness" in Afrikaans) as a legal system of racial segregation was instituted after the National Party came to power in that year. Apartheid affected every area of South Africon Mandela in 1990, an important aspect of those talks was the nature of the future constitution. The South African government's Law Commission[4] and the ANC's Constitutional Committee[5] proposed various draft constitutional provisions including a bill of rights, which had not previously existed in the constitution.[6] The Convention for a Democratic South Africa (CODESA) multiparty talks started in November 1991, and despite numerous problems, deadlocks, and acts of violence, culminated in the passage of an interim constitution by the outgoing apartheid parliament in November 1993.

This interim constitution was the result of the struggles of innumerable committed individuals combined with the leadership of the ANC and other groups. While representing a carefully negotiated compromise between oppressed and oppressors, the constitution provided a foundation for governance to begin overcoming the legacy of apartheid. The interim document laid the groundwork to help prevent the new government from copying its antidemocratic predecessors and engaging in repression of its opponents.[7]

On the other hand, there have been many complaints from progressive circles that the South African political and constitutional compromise was a sellout, entrenching white elite property interests.[8] The radical rhetoric of the apartheid-era ANC allied with the Communist Party was replaced with soothing tones of conciliation, resulting in a document that guarantees white private property rights in a capitalist economy. The Afrikaner dominated civil service were guaranteed their jobs in the new dispensation as well. Reparations for the years of apartheid would be handled in the form of the Truth and Reconciliation Commission. While the

Commission has the power to make recommendations to the President for granting reparations to victims, it also has the power to recommend pardons to even the most egregious human rights abusers, if their confessions before the Commission are viewed as legitimate.[9] Additionally a set of Constitutional Principles, negotiated between the parties, bound the newly elected parliament from revamping the interim constitution as it may have wished. The interim constitution was replaced by a permanent constitution, most of which took effect in 1997. This permanent constitution was the work of the 1994 democratically elected parliament, sitting as a constituent assembly for two years. It was approved in December 1996 after some changes mandated by the new Constitutional Court to bring it into compliance with the Constitutional Principles.

Now that the apartheid legacy has been summarized, the article next explores some of the textual features that the South African constitution that may have relevance for Palestine in the future.

II. CONSTITUTIONAL PROVISIONS

Constitutionalism has been defined as the process of "making the state into a *recht staat*, an *état de droit*, a state that is governed by its own public law. This kind of state is accountable; it has elements of legislative control or a monitoring supervision of the executive. The administration of justice is authorized through the judicial system."[10] In keeping with this principle, the South African constitution established legal structures for the express purpose of institutionalizing democracy in the country. The textual provisions are a potential source of inspiration for the PLC.

A. Parliament as Constitutional Assembly

One of the most important outcomes of the South African constitutional process was the decision to create a popularly elected parliament that would also serve as a constitutional assembly to draft a permanent constitution by year three of the interim period.[11] The Palestinian Basic Law could likewise provide that the PLC serve as a constitutional assembly to write the permanent governing document, not only the interim Basic Law. Sufficient time should also be allocated for comments by the public.

B. Supremacy of the Constitution

Article 2 of the South African constitution specifically states that the constitution is the supreme law of the land, and that any law or conduct which is inconsistent with its provisions is invalid.[12] This supremacy clause was considered essential for a society in which statutes wielded by evil men had been the reality of the abuse of power. It was also important due to the tension between the new democratic norms and the inegalitarian structures existent in all the previous legal layers, especially customary law of the various black ethnic groups.

Palestine faces a similar situation in terms of the need to validate democratic state building and constitutionalism. But the Third Reading has no supremacy clause. Article 6 states that all authorities are subject to the law, but does not make clear that all law should be subject to the constitution. This is critical for the same reasons as in South Africa. The pre-existing legal traditions are inegalitarian and there is no history of democratic leadership.

C. Separation of Powers

The South African constitution has an elaborate system of checks and balances to help ensure that the rule of law will eventually supplant the rule of men. For example, the South African President can be impeached by a two-thirds majority of the National Assembly for serious misconduct, or he can be removed by a vote of no confidence by a majority of the Assembly.[13] The Third Reading of the Basic Law does not provide for impeachment or removal of the President by a vote of no confidence. Thus the President remains in office for the duration of the Interim period, however long that is.

D. Judicial Review and a Constitutional Court

Article 98 of the South African interim constitution for the first time established a Constitutional Court appointed by the President and with the power of judicial review.[14] The creation of this court, separate from the predominantly white regular judiciary, was a priority of the ANC. A broad-based Judicial Services Commission was also created to recommend appointees to the bench.[15] These bodies will play an important role in preventing abuses by the judiciary.

Palestine should strongly consider establishing similar bodies, especially considering its regional context. In most Middle Eastern countries, the judiciary is subservient to the regime in power. However liberal the laws on the books may appear, and no matter whether they are based on the shari'a or on secular principles, the judiciary's effectiveness tends to be a function of the political style of the ruling party. Rarely is the judiciary able to contradict the policies of the executive branch or to transcend the limited role assigned to it by the political authorities. Palestinians will need to adopt safeguards to avoid reproducing these problems.

Like the apartheid-era judiciary, the Israeli-appointed judiciary that serves in the Palestinian civil courts of the Occupied Territories lost whatever legitimacy it may once have had. The PA, like the new South African government, faces the task of restoring the legitimacy of the judiciary. Judges need to be regarded as impartial and competent, rather than as political cronies loyal to the ruling faction. To this end, the Third Reading provides for an appointed judiciary with guarantees of independence and tenure.[16] A High Constitutional Court shall also be formed.[17] These measures will do much to enhance the judiciary's credibility, if they are respected by the Executive branch.

E. A Competent Civil Service

South Africa inherited a civil service that had assisted in the implementation of apartheid for 40 years and had incorporated blacks in only the most menial positions. Chapter 13 of the interim constitution provided for a Public Service Commission to ensure the development of an efficient, nonpartisan bureaucracy that makes services and job opportunities available to all citizens regardless of race. The Basic Law should adopt a similar approach. The Palestinian situation is complicated by the fact that there is an abundance of qualified individuals for the relatively few skilled positions in the civil service. Only an absolute meritocracy in the hiring, retention, and promotion of civil service employees can dampen the frustrations of those who will be denied jobs in the bureaucracy. A constitutional mandate for egalitarianism in the civil service would be useful measure to this end.

The current provision in the Third Reading merely states that "matters of civil service shall be regulated by law."[18] This wording is entirely too vague to prevent future cronyism and corruption.

F. Protecting the Public

South Africa under apartheid, like the rest of Africa, was not immune to governmental abuses of power which threatened the safety of the public. Chapter Nine of the South African constitution therefore established several government agencies to safeguard the public interest. The Public Protector is a type of ombudsman whose duty is to investigate government corruption.[19] This appointed official can act with or without a complaint. The Human Rights Commission is empowered to investigate complaints of human rights violations and issue recommendations to the government.[20]

Recognizing the special conditions confronting women, the constitution drafters included a Commission for Gender Equality which can make recommendations concerning legislation.[21] A Commission on Restitution of Land Rights was established to address the legacy of blacks' forcible dispossession from their land.[22] This body can investigate claims, draw up court reports, and mediate disputes. There is also a Commission for the Promotion and Protection of the Rights of Cultural, Religious, and Linguistic Communities, which addresses the interests of these groups.[23]

Since Palestine also has a history of government corruption, human rights violations, gender discrimination, and land confiscation, the PLC would do well to constitutionally empower agencies to address these issues. If such problems are ignored or if responsibility for them is assigned to existing bureaucracies, the status quo is likely to continue. The appointive nature of such commissions must be carefully scrutinized to ensure that qualified people are sought out.

G. Enshrining Constitutional Principles

Fear and distrust among the South African parties led them to agree upon a set of preliminary principles as a first step in the process of negotiating the transfer of power. These principles could not be changed by the interim parliament or derogated from in the permanent constitution, and the Constitutional Court had the power to reject any proposed legislation that was inconsistent with them. Among the principles agreed upon were a multiparty system, equality of opportunity, and a trilateral separation of powers.[24]

Because there is similar distrust between Palestinians and Israelis as well as among the various Palestinian factions, a set of constitutional principles would be a useful instrument in building consensus at an early stage in the permanent constitutional process. Agreement on the concept of secular multiparty democracy, for example, would assuage certain doubts, though Islamic fundamentalists might not accept the idea without guarantees of minority-party protections. The principles would then bind the Constitutional Assembly as it drafts the permanent constitution.

H. Repealing Laws

Schedule seven of both the interim and permanent South African constitutions list a number of laws that were repealed simultaneous to the passage of the constitution. These provisions in the interim constitution abolished most of the de jure legacy of apartheid. The Third Reading does not specifically repeal any law and permits existing laws to remain in effect unless they contradict the Basic Law.[25] The Palestinians should follow the South African example and repeal the laws that are part of the legacy of Occupation, especially the British Emergency Defense Regulations. The South African constitution only permits a State of Emergency to be called under very limited circumstances.[26]

Another advantage of specific repeal is that it would require a comprehensive review of the multilayered legal regime in force in the Occupied Territories, which contains elements of Islamic, Ottoman, British Mandate, Egyptian, Jordanian, and Israeli law. These laws need to be systematically evaluated and replaced over a period of many years, but repeal in the constitution would signal the centrality of this task.

I. Protecting Human Rights

The South African constitution provides basic civil and political rights to all South Africans for the first time. It guarantees such rights as freedom and security of the person; freedom of religion, belief and opinion, expression, assembly, demonstration and petition, association, movement and residence; political rights to form parties; and criminal procedural rights.[27] There are also specific rights to life and human dignity, while servitude and forced labor are banned.[28] To allay white fears of socialism, there are specific guarantees concerning private property.[29] The constitution also provides for some economic, social and cultural rights, including the right to a healthy environment, housing, a language and culture, education and the right to basic nutrition, health and social services.[30] Children's rights are specifically delineated as well.[31] The economic, social and cultural rights are not absolute. The ANC realized that the new government would not have the resources to guarantee these costly entitlements. With respect to the rights to housing, health care, food, water, and social security, the government's responsibility is limited. "The state must take reasonable legislative and other measures, within its available resources, to achieve the progressive realization of each of these rights."[32]

The equality clause deserves special mention because its protections are much broader than those found in the US Constitution. The clause prohibits discrimination on the grounds of "race, gender, sex, pregnancy, marital status, ethnic or social origin, color, sexual orientation, age, disability, religion, conscience, belief, culture, language and birth."[33] It also permits affirmative-action initiatives based on these categories.[34]

Most of the rights can be limited if a five-part test is met which includes an analysis of the following factors: the nature of the right; importance of the purpose of the limitation; the nature and extent of the limitation; the relation between the limitation and its purpose; and the less restrictive means to achieve the purpose.[35] Certain rights can not be derogated from, even in a state of emergency, and a table is provided listing those norms.[36] The Bill of Rights must be interpreted taking into account international law, and the judges may consider foreign law as well.[37]

The South African constitution's attentiveness to human rights concerns makes it an apt model for Palestine, where human rights have long been an issue. The South African experience also demonstrates that it is possible to approve a constitution that is more progressive in its legal provisions than prevailing cultural norms. For example, none of the traditional cultures of South Africa whether they be Black, Colored, or white, approve of homosexuality, yet the equality clause covers homosexuals, lesbians, bisexuals and transgendered individuals. Of course, protection for homosexuals is not likely to be granted in the Palestinian Basic Law at this time.

The PLC might consider following the South African example in terms of the economic, social, and cultural rights. Article 23 of the Third Reading states that "convenient housing is a right for every citizen. The National Authority shall endeavor to insure housing to whom does not have a dwelling." While the "shall endeavor" language is potentially limiting, the "progressive realization" language in the South African constitution is more precise. Similarly, Article 25 of the Third Reading states "work is a right for every citizen." Going far beyond Article 23, Article 25 then goes on to state, "It is the obligation and command undertaken by the National Authority to provide it for all those who are able." The PA does not have the resources to undertake this type of well-meaning obligation at this time.

The PLC should also follow the example of the South Africans with respect to environmental rights. Article 33 of the Third Reading restores a section that had been deleted from the First Reading. But the current provision is too brief, stating "A balanced, clean environment is one of the human rights. Preservation and protection of the Palestinian environment for present and future generations is a national responsibility." According to Article 24 of the South African constitution:

everyone has the right —

(a) to an environment that is not harmful to their health and well-being, and

(b) to have the environment protected, for the benefit of present and future generations, through reasonable legislative and other measures that —

(i) prevent pollution and ecological degradation;
(ii) promote conservation; and

(iii) secure ecologically sustainable development and use of natural resources while promoting justifiable economic and social development.[38]

The government has limited its obligation through the use of the term "reasonable," and Palestine could do the same.

1. Women's Rights[39]. Because women have historically suffered unequal treatment under civil law and custom, constitutional attempts to improve their position face special challenges. The South African constitution's broad commitment to gender equality is definitely worth considering for Palestine.

The black women in South Africa still face a double burden of discrimination: as a black person under the apartheid legacy, and as a woman in a patriarchal society. Constituting more than 36 percent of the population,[40] they remain the most oppressed group in the country.[41] Black women are subject to male domination under the law in marriage, guardianship, succession, contract, and property. They suffer disproportionately from the poverty and political exclusion experienced by the black population, since they bear the brunt of the frustration and aggression that their husbands are powerless to express elsewhere, which often manifests themselves in the form of rape or physical abuse.

Nelson Mandela set the tone for equality in 1991 when he called for the creation of a nonsexist state.[42] The permanent constitution makes clear that the Bill of Rights binds all natural and juristic persons.[43] The equality clause has been broadened to make clear that neither the state nor any natural or juristic person may discriminate on the grounds of sex or gender, which were in the interim constitution, but also pregnancy, marital status, or birth, all characteristics which disproportionately affect women.[44] The article on freedom of belief does permit for recognition of traditional marriages, as long as they are consistent with other provisions of the Constitution.[45] While everyone has the right to practice and enjoy the cultural life of their choice, this right too must be consistent with the rest of the constitution.[46] All of these caveats could limit women's rights. The legislature has already legalized abortion in the early stages, and the Constitutional Court has ruled that President Mandela did not discriminate unfairly against fathers when he pardoned all female prisoners with young children under 12.[47]

For Palestinians, the period after the *intifada* has been one in which gender issues have been as much in flux as other aspects of society. Many women's groups have lost much of their membership and many of their projects have failed. According to Taraki, "the new political culture is certain to marginalize women further, based as it is on old boy networks of patronage and clientelism."[48] Some new politically independent women's groups have sprung up with an emphasis solely on women's concerns. An important victory for the new women's movement occurred in 1995–6 when the Women's Affairs Technical Group was able to get rescinded an Interior Ministry directive requiring a male guardian's approval for issuing passports to both married and unmarried women. Other efforts include lobbying for the draft Basic law, preparing a mock parliament to influence family status and other legislation, and encouraging women to run in the upcoming municipal elections.

The Third Reading of the Basic Law contains an article stating that there can be no discrimination between Palestinians because of gender.[49] On the other hand, Article 4 states that Islam is the official religion, a clause added in the sixth draft, and present in all Arab constitutions. Since Islam sanctions the differential treatment of women, there is an inherent tension between these two clauses.

In addition to the equality and antidiscrimination clauses already present in the Draft Basic Law, Palestinian decision makers should adopt additional reforms. There should be a clause that discusses the need for affirmative action programs or other positive measures to improve the status of women. All these proposals may be expected to generate substantial resistance, which will have to be countered with arguments for the legitimacy of gender equality. Elsewhere, I propose three types of justifications for legal reform in this area: reinterpretation of the shari'a, compliance with international human rights norms, and the changes wrought in Palestinian society by the *intifada* and the current period.[50]

After the adoption of the Basic Law, the PA should take steps to follow Article 10 of the Third Reading, which requires the incorporation of international declarations that protect human rights. An important treaty to ratify will be the Convention on the Elimination of All Forms of Discrimination Against Women (Women's Convention).[51] This document is critically important because it covers the private sphere, where most women spend the majority of their time and where a large amount of discrimination takes place. The Convention contains 15 articles describing the areas in which states must take "appropriate measures" to safeguard women's rights, including the areas of education, health care, nationality, culture, family and personal status, legal and political activity, employment, recreation, and mortgages and other forms of credit. Affirmative action is permitted, but "shall be discontinued when the objectives of equality of opportunity and treatment have been achieved."[52] The PLC should consider adopting these provisions, especially those affecting the private sphere.

III. Conclusion

This article has attempted to draw lessons from the South African struggle for democracy and constitutionalism for the benefit of Palestinian decision makers. These lessons concerned the actual text of the South African constitution, which provides for: parliament as a constituent assembly, supremacy of the constitution, separation of powers, judicial review and a constitutional court, a competent civil service, protection of public safety, enshrining of constitutional principles, repeal of laws, and protection of human rights. With respect to women's rights, Palestine should consider South Africa's lead and overcome the legacy of sexism by expanding the equal rights provisions in the constitution.

South African and Palestinian leaders have shared much in the course of their respective liberation struggles. Government officials on both sides have much to learn from each other as they confront future challenges. South Africans and Palestinians should continue to engage each other in a mutually beneficial cross-fertilization of ideas as they attempt to plant the seeds of democracy in arid soil. Palestine should follow South Africa's approach to democracy and reject the bantustan solution to the current political impasse. If the attempts at democratization and constitutionalism are successful in both societies, they will become role models for their regions and for the entire world.

Notes

1. For discussion of these connections, see e.g. Robert Adams, ISRAEL AND SOUTH AFRICA: THE UNNATURAL ALLIANCE (1984), and Jane Hunter, ISRAEL'S FOREIGN POLICY: SOUTH AFRICA AND CENTRAL AMERICA (1987). Needless to say, many supporters of Israel deeply resented any comparisons to the apartheid regime.

2. Albie Sachs, *The Future Constitutional Position of White South Africa (1990)*, cited in Fitzgerald, *Democracy and Civil Society in South Africa: A Response to Daryl Glaser*, 49 REV. AFR. POL. ECON. 106, 108–109 (1990).

3. Charles Villa-Vicencio, *Whither South Africa? Constitutionalism and Law-Making*, 40 EMORY L.J. 140, 144–5 (1991).

4. South African Law Commission, Working Paper No. 25, Project 58 (1989) discussed in Villa-Vicencio, supra note 4, at 156. For discussion of the Law Commission and its findings, see John Dugard, *A Bill of Rights for South Africa: Can the Leopard Change its Spots?* 2 S. AFR. J. HUM. RTS. 275 (1986); Van der Westhuizern, *An Update on the Law Commission's Bill of Rights Investigation: An Interview with the Honorable Mr. Justice P.J.J. Oliver*, 4 S. AFR. J. HUM. RTS. 99 (1988); Eric Bjornlund, *The Devil's Work? Judicial Review Under a Bill of Rights in South Africa and Namibia*, 26 STAN. J. INT'L L. 391, 405–7 (1990); M.C. Jozana, *Proposed South African Bill of Rights: A Prescription for Equality or Neo-Apartheid?* 7 AM. U. J. INT'L L. & POL'Y 45, 72 (1991). For the actual text of the Law Commission's report, see 21 COLUM. HUM. RTS. L. REV. 241 & n.1 (1989).

5. The ANC Constitutional Committee discussion documents include African National Congress, *Constitutional Guidelines for a Democratic South Africa* (1989), reprinted in 21 COLUM. HUM. RTS. L. REV. 235 App. A (1989); ANC Constitutional Committee, *A Bill of Rights for a New South Africa* (1990) reprinted in 18 SOC. JUST. 49 (Spr.-Sum. 1991); ANC Constitutional Committee, *What is a Constitution?* (1990); African National Congress, *Constitutional Principles and Structures for A Democratic South Africa* 24 (1991); ANC Constitutional Committee, *A Bill of Rights for a New South Africa* (1992). For a discussion of the philosophy underlying the ANC's constitutional guidelines, see Albie Sachs, *Post-Apartheid South Africa: A Constitutional Framework*, 6 WORLD POL'Y J. 589 (1989). For a discussion of the text of the guidelines, see Hugh Corder and Davis, *The Constitutional Guidelines of the African National Congress: A Preliminary Assessment*, 106 S. Afr. L. J. 633 (1989), and Johan Van der Vyver, *Comments on the Constitutional Guidelines of the African National Congress*, 5 S. AFR. J. HUM. RTS. 133 (1989).

6. Rep. S. Afr. Const. Act 110 of 1983, Proc. 119 GG 9308, July 6, 1984. For a history of South Africa's various constitutions, see Winston Nagan, *South Africa in Transition: Human Rights, Ethnicity and Law in the 1990s*, 35 VILLANOVA L. REV. 1139 (1990); Johan Van der Vyver, *Depriving Westminster of its Moral Constraints: A Survey of Constitutional Development in South Africa*, 20 HARV. C.R.-C.L.L. REV. 291, 327–36 (1985); Basson and Viljoen, SOUTH AFRICAN CONSTITUTIONAL LAW (1988); gretchen Carpenter, INTRODUCTION TO SOUTH AFRICAN CONSTITUTIONAL LAW (1987); Boulle, CONSTITUTIONAL REFORM AND THE APARTHEID STATE (1984); D. Marais, SOUTH AFRICA: CONSTITUTIONAL DEVELOPMENT (1989).

7. For a more detailed discussion of the South African constitutional process by this author, see Adrien Wing, *Communitarianism vs. Individualism: Constitutionalism in Namibia and South Africa*, 11 WISC. INT'L L.J. 295 (1993).

8. Makau wa Mutua, *Hope and Despair for a New South Africa: The Limits of Rights Discourse*, 10 HARV. HUM. RTS. J. 631 (1997).

9. Promotion of National Unity and Reconciliation Act, No. Act 34 of 1995.

10. Young, *The Debate on Democratization in Africa*, in Thompson, THE US CONSTITUTION AND CONSTITUTIONALISM IN AFRICA 127 (1990).

11. S. AFR. CONST. (Interim Constitution, Act 200 of 1993) art. 68.

12. S. AFR. CONST. (1996 Constitution) art. 2.

13. Id., arts. 89 and 102.

14. For a discussion of these options, see Adrien Wing, Sonya Braunsweig, and Qais Abdel Fattah, *Judicial Review for Palestine*, Birzeit Law Center (1996); Ziyad Motala, *Independence of the Judiciary, Prospects and Limitations of Judicial Review in Terms of the United States Model in a South African Order: Towards an Alternative Judicial Structure*, 55 ALBANY L. REV. 367, 397 (1991). For a review of the shortcomings of judicial review, see Penuell Maduna, *Judicial Review and the Protection of Human Rights under a New Constitutional Order in South Africa*, 21 COLUM. HUM. RTS. L. REV. 73 (1989). Nelson Mandela has stated: "For South Africa, the idea of a Constitutional Court is quite revolutionary.... The issue of whether we need or want a constitutional court ... presupposes the acceptance of constitutionalism. Without constitutionalism we do not need a constitutional court." Speech delivered to delegates at a conference on a Constitutional Court for South Africa, Magaliesburg (Feb. 1, 1991), quoted in Fink Haysom, *Democracy, Constitutionalism, and the ANC's Bill of Rights for a New South Africa*, 18 SOC. JUST. 47 (1991).

15. SOUTH AFR. INTERIM CONST, supra note 12, art. 105.

16. Third Reading, supra note 1, art. 89.

17. Id., art. 94.

18. Id. art. 78.
19. SOUTH AFR. CONST., supra note 13, art. 182.
20. Id. art. 184.
21. Id. art. 187.
22. S. AFR. INTERIM CONST., supra note 12, art. 122.
23. S. AFR. CONST., supra note 13, art. 185.
24. A full list of the principles is found in Schedule Four of the interim constitution.
25. Third Reading, supra note 1, arts. 109, 110.
26. SOUTH AFR. CONST., supra note 13, art. 37.
27. Id. arts. 12, 15, 16, 17, 18, 21, 19, 35.
28. Id. arts. 11, 10, 13.
29. Id. art. 25.
30. Id. arts. 24, 26, 30, 31, 29, 27.
31. Id. art 28.
32. Id. art. 27.
33. Id. art. 9(3).
34. Id. art. 9(2).
35. Id. art 36.
36. Id. art. 37.
37. Id. art. 39.
38. For a proposal on environmental rights for the Basic Law, see Kevin Papp, *Environmental Constitutional Protection, Human Rights and the Eighth Draft of the Temporary Constitution for the Palestinian National Authority in the Transitional Period,* IOWA J. TRANSNATIONAL L. AND CONTEMP. PROB. 529–576 (1997). Mr. Papp is one of my research assistants.
39. This subsection draws from Adrien Wing and Eunice de Carvalho, *Black South African Women: Towards Equal Rights,* 8 HARV. HUM. RTS. J. 57 (1995) and Adrien Wing, *A Critical Race Feminist Conceptualization of Violence: South African and Palestinian Women,* 60 ALBANY L. REV. 943 (1997). For other articles on South African women, see Melissa Cole, *"Inthuthoko Means that We Are Going Forward"; Hearing the Voices of Domestic Workers in South Africa,* 2 COLUM. J. GENDER & LAW 61 (1991); Christine Venter, *The New South African Constitution: Facing the Challenges of Women's Rights and Cultural Rights in Post-Apartheid South Africa,* 21 J. LEGIS.1 (1997); Jacqueline Krikorian, *A Different Form of Apartheid? The Legal Status of Married Women in South Africa,* 21 QUEENS L.J. 221 (1995).
40. *See* Sharon Fonn, *Working Women's Health, in* WOMEN'S HEALTH AND APARTHEID: THE HEALTH OF WOMEN AND CHILDREN AND THE FUTURE OF PROGRESSIVE PRIMARY HEALTH CARE IN SOUTHERN AFRICA 20, 29 (Marica Wright et al. Eds., 1988). White women make up roughly 8 percent, Colored women 5 percent, and Indian women 2 percent of the population. Id.
41. See Celina Romany, *Black Women and Gender Equality in a New South Africa: Human Rights Law and the Intersection of Race and Gender,* 21 BROOK. J.
42. "Fighting Another Good Fight," *Los Angeles Times,* Dec. 9, 1991, at B4.
43. S. AFR. CONST., supra note 13, art. 8 (2).
44. Id. art. 9(3).
45. Id. art. 15(3).
46. Id. arts. 30, 31.
47. President of the Republic of South Africa, *Minister of Correctional Services v. John Philip Peter Hugo,* CCT 11/96.
48. Lisa Taraki, *Palestine: From National Liberation to Feminism,* 5(2) MIDDLE EAST POL'Y 173, 175 (1997).

49. Third Reading, supra note 1, art. 9.
50. PASSIA, supra note 1.
51. G.A. Res. 34/180, 34 UN GAOR Supp. (no. 710.46) at 193, UN Doc. A/34/46 (1979) (entered into force Sept. 3, 1981).
52. Id. art. 4. Special measures protecting pregnancy are allowed. As broad as the Convention is, it does not cover abortion, pornography, domestic violence, or marital rape.

7

Peace and the Political Imperative of Legal Reform in Palestine
George E. Bisharat

I. Introduction

The message I wish to convey is relatively simple: first, that an aggressive program of legal reform in Palestine[1] would contribute strongly to the successful conclusion of a just, and therefore, durable peace between Israelis and Palestinians; and second, that such a program of legal reform should be elevated to a primary concern on the list of international and U.S. policy objectives for the region from its currently low level.[2] Palestinians are far more likely to remain committed to the peace process when they are convinced that peace has brought tangible benefits to their lives. After nearly 30 years of strongly repressive Israeli military occupation, Palestinians in the West Bank and Gaza Strip have a deep yearning for democratic self-government, and their continued frustration erodes support for the peace process. Moreover, a stable, democratic Palestinian administration is, in the long run, a more reliable peace partner for Israel than one that is founded on personalistic ties to an aging, and possibly ailing, leader — Yasser Arafat.[3]

The impetus for this article has its roots in my experience within the last year consulting over the Palestinian Legislative Council's (P.L.C.) draft law on the independence of the judiciary, during which time I have met with elected council members, professional staff of the Council, representatives of the judiciary and executive branches, academics, and others. Part of my mission here is simply to bear witness to the hopes and desires of some of the people on the ground—hard-working, overburdened, and largely unrecognized Palestinians who are struggling against daunting odds to provide their people with an accountable government and a society governed by the rule of law.

The term "legal reform" is a broad one. Indeed, the scope of reform needed in Palestine is very broad, encompassing legal institutions, civil and criminal procedure, and many areas of substantive law.[4] I will not, however, address all aspects of the needed reform. Specifically, I will not discuss the necessity for substantive changes in the areas of corporate banking and commercial law,[5] even though such changes are necessary to stimulate local and foreign investment, which in turn are needed to counteract unemployment and the general economic deterioration in the Palestinian sector. Other symposium participants will address these topics with far greater expertise than I would.[6] More to the point, however, there are other areas of legal reform that have a greater capacity to directly enhance the peace process—namely, those that affect the human and civil rights of the Palestinians—and it is these areas on which I wish to focus.[7]

Legal reform is only one of many objectives that can and should be pursued in support of the peace process, and I do not for a moment imagine that it, alone, will insure a lasting peace. As the negotiations have proven so labored and their success is in no way guaranteed, we must exploit every avenue possible to advance the cause of peace. Moreover, legal reform is one important area in which progress is politically feasible, a feature that may distinguish it from other possible policy objectives that, in the abstract, seem to offer even more attractions.

My argument is laid out in eight sections, of which this introduction is the first. In the second section, 1 will outline the legal framework within which the Palestinian Authority[8]—the interim governing body established for the Palestinians in parts of the West Bank and Gaza Strip—operates. Third, I will identify a set of problems inherited by the Palestinian Authority in the administration of justice in the West Bank and Gaza Strip, and fourth, I will examine the efforts to address these problems already undertaken over the last few years. Fifth, I will describe a series of abuses perpetrated by the Palestinian Authority against the human and civil rights of the Palestinian residents under its rule. Sixth, I will analyze the political impact of the Palestinian Authority's abuses of power within the Palestinian community, particularly as it pertains to the peace process. Seventh, I will review the record of the U.S. policy and that of the international community vis-à-vis the development of the rule of law in Palestine.

Eighth, and finally, I will propose a set of specific policy recommendations that, if implemented, would begin to ameliorate the problems I have identified, and in so doing, would further the objective of reaching a just, durable peace between Israelis and Palestinians.

II. THE LEGAL FRAMEWORK

Since 1993, Israel and the Palestinians have signed a veritable blizzard of declarations, agreements, letters, annexes, protocols, notes for the record, and the like, which together total close to 1,000 pages of documents, including the recent Wye River Memorandum of October 23, 1998.[9] It may help us to step back from this maelstrom for a moment and be reminded of the broad outlines of the current peace process. Many of us remember the dramatic image of Yasser Arafat and the late Yitzhak Rabin shaking hands on the White House lawn under the approving eye of President Clinton. In broad contours, the agreement they had reached consisted of three major components.[10] First, Israel and the Palestinians exchanged "recognitions"—Israel recognized the Palestinian Liberation Organization (P.L.O.) as the representative of the Palestinian people, and the P.L.O. recognized the right of Israel to exist in peace and security.[11] Second, the two sides agreed in general terms to a phased withdrawal of Israeli troops and administrative apparatuses from parts of the West Bank and Gaza Strip—areas occupied by Israel in the 1967 Arab-Israeli War and ruled by military government ever since—and to the establishment in those places of an interim Palestinian self-governing authority.[12] Third, the parties agreed to continue negotiating the issue of sovereignty over the territories, as well as the related issues of the status of the city of Jerusalem, the rights of Palestinian refugees, the fate of Jewish settlers in the West Bank and Gaza Strip, and others.[13] All of these things were to unfold within a "transitional" period of up to five years, commencing with the date of the inauguration of the Palestinian self-governing authority. Final status negotiations were to commence no later than the beginning of the third year of the interim period.[14]

The first steps to implement the Accord were taken in May 1994, when Israel and the Palestinians concluded the Agreement on the Gaza Strip and Jericho Area.[15] A "Palestinian Authority" (P.A.) was created with powers and responsibilities over a range of civil matters delegated to it by the Israeli military administration,[16] though none touching on matters set for discussion in the final status negotiations. One important fact to underscore here is that the conclusion of this agreement on May 4, 1994, started the clock ticking on the five-year interim or transitional phase, which will come to an end on May 4, 1999. Shortly thereafter, in June 1994, Yasser Arafat arrived in Gaza from abroad to head up an interim administration comprised of 24 members.

In September 1995, the Israeli-Palestinian Interim Agreement on the West Bank and Gaza Strip,[17] often referred to as "Oslo II," was reached, which extended the jurisdiction of the P.A. into other areas of the West Bank. The Agreement divided the region into three territorial categories: A, B, and C. In Area A, composed of the larger urban areas of the West Bank, and including about 4 percent of its total land area, the P.A. assumed responsibility for public order and internal security. In Area B, consisting of West Bank villages, the P.A. took charge of public order and security for Palestinians, while Israel retained responsibility for security in order to protect Israeli nationals and to confront the threat of "terrorism." Areas A and B together contained about 68 percent of the population of the West Bank and 23 percent of its land. Most of the land was assigned to Area C, where civil authority was planned to be gradually ceded by the Israeli military government to the P.A., while Israel maintained complete control over security and order. Israel further maintained exclusive authority over external security and foreign affairs.

In accordance with this scheme, Israel began withdrawing its army from the major towns of the West Bank and, with the sole exception of the town of Hebron, this first phase of withdrawal was completed by the end of 1996.[18] Three further Israeli troop withdrawals were scheduled to occur in six-month intervals.[19]

Elections for the head[20] of the P.A. and for an 88 seat Legislative Council were then conducted on January 20, 1996.[21] In these elections, Yasser Arafat, Chairman of the Executive Committee of the P.L.O., received nearly 88 percent of the popular vote, and 50 members of his Fatah political party gained seats in the Legislative Council.[22] Under the Oslo II agreement, the Council, together with the head of the P.A., exercises both legislative and executive authority. However, under Article V of the Oslo II agreement, the Council is to exercise executive powers through a special committee named the "Executive Authority." This body is composed of the head of the Council, a number of ministers and department chiefs selected by the head from among elected members of the Council, and other nonelected persons from outside the Council whose number may not exceed 20 percent of the total of the committee.[23]

Beyond this, the relative powers of the executive, legislative, and judicial branches of the P.A. are minimally spelled out. As events have unfolded, it has become increasingly clear that the real decision-making power within the P.A. rests almost solely within the hands of Yasser Arafat and a small circle of advisors, while the P.L.C. has been largely marginalized and rendered ineffective.[24]

The latest round of agreements, reached in October 1998, at Wye River, Maryland, solidified an earlier commitment by Israel to conduct a further stage of troop withdrawals.[25] Israeli forces were to have pulled back from a further 13 percent of the West Bank, now part of Area C. Most of the ceded territory was slated to become part of Area A, under full P.A. control, which would have then constituted a little over 14 percent of the region, while a small area was to have become part of Area B, under shared Israeli-Palestinian security authority. In return, the Palestinians agreed to take further actions to annul specific clauses of the P.L.O. charter calling for Israel's destruction and guarantee Israeli security.[26]

Clearly, neither Oslo I nor Oslo II awarded sovereignty over the West Bank and Gaza Strip to the Palestinians. In fact, both parties to the Accords undertook not to engage in activities that prejudiced the outcome of the final status negotiations.[27] One might justifiably wonder, then, where does my call for legal reform fall within this framework? After all, fundamental changes in the structure of the legal system and the substantive laws governing community life are quintessentially a sovereign prerogative. Would Palestinian action in this field run counter to the spirit, if not the letter of the Oslo Accords? The clear answer is "no." The original Declaration of Principles contemplated the establishment of "independent Palestinian judicial organs,"[28] and provided that the Palestinian "Council" would have the power to legislate within its jurisdiction.[29] The Agreement on the Gaza Strip and Jericho Area further authorized the P.A. "to promulgate legislation, including basic laws, laws, regulations, and other legislative acts"[30] and the Oslo II Interim Agreement specifically assigned the administration of justice through an independent judiciary to the P.A.[31] There is little doubt, then, that the kind of legal reform I advocate is, in principle, entirely consistent with the Oslo Accords and the overall peace process.[32]

It is also important to point out that, although the precise international legal identity of the P.A. may be somewhat indeterminate, as a political matter, at least, there is little or nothing to prevent the insistence by outside parties that it abide by international human rights standards and work to implement the rule of law.[33] In the first place, such a requirement is written into the Oslo II Agreement, where both parties agree to "exercise their powers and responsibilities pursuant to this Agreement with due regard to internationally accepted norms and principles of human rights and the rule of law."[34] Secondly, both the P.L.O. during the period prior to the Oslo Agreements and the P.A. after these agreements have unilaterally committed themselves to the observance of international human rights principles on a number of occasions and in a variety of ways.[35] For example, a "Basic Law" passed by the P.L.C. and intended to serve as an interim constitution for the P.A. contains numerous articles committing the P.A. to respecting fundamental human and civil rights both as delineated in various international treaties and in more general terms.[36] Yasser Arafat, moreover, issued a decree establishing the Palestinian Independent Commission on Citizens' Rights, a quasi-governmental board charged with monitoring the performance of the P.A. and ensuring the compliance of public institutions with human rights principles.[37]

In sum, then, the legal framework established by the various agreements between Israel and the Palestinians virtually promises legal reform in the manner I will suggest below.

III PROBLEMS IN THE ADMINISTRATION OF JUSTICE IN THE WEST BANK AND GAZA STRIP

The P.A. inherited a staggering array of problems in the administration of justice in the West Bank and Gaza Strip. For the sake of simplicity, these problems may be summarized as follows: 1) the absence of legal unity between the two regions; 2) confused and antiquated bodies of substantive and procedural law; 3) weak and vastly under-resourced judiciaries; and 4) a fragmented, demoralized, and poorly trained legal profession.[38] Let us briefly examine each of these challenges.

A. Absence of Legal Unity

Although the two regions historically had shared a common legal legacy through both the Ottoman Turkish administration and under British mandatory rule, they followed divergent legal trajectories since the collapse of the British Mandate in 1948. The West Bank then fell under Jordanian administration, and following its annexation in 1950, its court system and substantive laws were gradually assimilated into those of Jordan, which, like most of the Arab World, followed the continental civil law system.[39] The Gaza Strip, on the other hand, fell under the administration of the Egyptian military government, yet was never annexed to Egypt. Instead, its legal system continued to operate relatively free from Egyptian interference, applying "Palestinian law," which had its roots in the common law-influenced British mandatory system.[40] Thus, the two systems came to employ different terminology, procedures, and substantive law administered through different institutions.

Why is this a problem? Why is it any more problematic, one might wonder, than each of the 50 states of the United States having its own legal system? The answer is that the West Bank and Gaza Strip constitute a geographically tiny area and are sites of an evolving polity and economy that face multiple challenges: political, economic, administrative, and otherwise. Under these circumstances, integration is virtually a condition for survival. It is both costly and unwieldy to maintain two distinct legal systems and legal disunity hampers the development of commerce and other aspects of intercommunal life between the two regions.[41] Further, the absence of an integrated legal system was never the free choice of distinct communities with regionally distinct identities, but rather the product of the Palestinians' loss of independence to two different occupying authorities. There is political symbolic value to legal unity as well, as it reaffirms the "oneness" of the Palestinian people.

B. Confused and Antiquated Laws

Already subject to multiple layers of law laid down by foreign authorities — Ottoman, British, and Jordanian — both the West Bank and Gaza Strip were placed under Israeli military administration following the June 1967, Arab-Israeli war and remained so until the enactment of the Oslo Accords. What was the fate of the legal systems of the two regions for nearly 30 years under Israeli rule? International law requires that an occupying power — that is, a state that comes into control of territory outside its boundaries in a time of war, as Israel did of the West Bank and Gaza Strip — maintain the legal institutions and substantive law in force on the eve of its occupation. Amendments to existing law are permitted only for reasons of military necessity or where such changes are mandated by the interests of the public.[42]

These principles were at least partially honored by Israel. Thus, the Gaza Strip and West Bank legal systems (or whatever remnants of them existed in the regions) resumed operations within one year of the 1967 war.[43] However, no efforts were made to unify their court systems or to reconcile their divergent procedural and substantive laws. Legislation enacted in Jordan following the 1967 war was not enforced in the West Bank because it was not in force on the eve of the occupation. Thus, the Israeli military governments established in the West Bank and Gaza Strip assumed all governing authority there, including powers of legislation.[44]

In time, the Israeli military government liberally exercised its legislative authority by enacting over 1,400 legal changes in the form of military orders in the West Bank and 1,100 in the Gaza Strip.[45] Many of these orders dealt with military and security matters, while others seemed patently targeted to protect Israeli interests and not those of the Palestinian residents of the region. For example, a series of military orders issued in the early 1980s forced Palestinian farmers to count and register all fruit trees, tomato plants, and eggplants, and obtain licenses to plant any new ones—a rather obvious measure designed to protect Israeli agriculture.[46]

Meanwhile, a means for assessing the Palestinian community's need for new legislation was never institutionalized and local Palestinian leaders remained perennially reluctant to seek legislative innovations from an occupying power whose legitimacy they refused to acknowledge. Thus, the law remained stagnant in many areas of importance to the Palestinians. The gulf in communication between occupier and occupied was compounded by the fact that the Israeli military government never consistently publicized its orders, such that the Palestinians, including lawyers, were at times totally unaware of the laws that governed them. [47]

The resulting situation "cause[d] confusion about governing norms, prevent[ed] consistent and timely adjudications of civil and criminal cases, and produce[d] serious gaps between the formal codes and actual practice. Related to the lack of uniformity, the substantive law [was] not harmonized sufficiently with emerging international standards of commercial law."[48]

C. Weakened Judiciaries

The third problem is weakened and impoverished judiciaries. By all appearances, the Israeli military government, for its nearly three-decade stewardship over the court systems in the Occupied Territories, devoted as few resources as possible to judiciaries without actually forcing their closure. By the mid–1980s, the courts were already suffering from inadequate staffing at all levels, corruption brought on in large part by pathetically inadequate salaries, repeated challenges to their independence from the Israeli military government, crumbling physical facilities, administrative inefficiencies, and a host of other maladies.[49]

Perhaps most importantly, Israel had set up a military legal system in the Occupied Territories composed of courts and other administrative tribunals. In time, this system usurped the jurisdiction of the indigenous courts of the West Bank and Gaza Strip in so broad an array of civil matters as to effectively marginalize them.[50] During the *Intifada*, the Palestinian uprising between 1987 and 1993, the Palestinian police officers charged with investigating crimes prosecuted in the local courts and executing their judgments, resigned en masse, causing the legal systems of the West Bank and Gaza Strip to all but cease to function.[51]

D. Fragmented Legal Reform

The fourth problem centers upon the fragmented, demoralized, and professionally enfeebled bar. The problem was most acute in the West Bank, where leaders of the profession made the fateful decision to boycott the courts upon their reopening after the 1967 war. The intent of the strike was to signal the profession's rejection of the legality of the Israeli occupation and, in particular, its annexation of the city of Jerusalem. Little thought was devoted at the time to the possible duration of Israeli rule but assumption *was* that it would *be short-term*. Eventually, a few lawyers resumed practice, as did some new graduates of law faculties, only to be ostracized by the strikers.[52] Thus, the strike, officially called off only in 1995,[53] not only split and marginalized the profession, but also deprived it of a generation of wisdom and mentoring, and thereby led the way for Israeli military officials to exercise the responsibilities formerly vested in the local bar association. This they did with the same degree of inattention to community interests as they did other matters.

Circumstances were a little less dire in Gaza. But even there, the influx of many new and poorly trained lawyers to practice greatly weakened the economic status of the profession, and with it the social and political standing of lawyers. In neither region was there a law faculty offering instruction in local law; aspirants to law practice either studied by correspondence or by traveling abroad where they received training in the systems of the host countries. In addition, in both regions the profession was essentially idled by the closure of the courts during the *Intifada*.[54] Needless to say, there was never a bar association that united the legal professions in the two regions. Together, these factors clearly exacted a toll on the professional competence of the bar.[55]

To recount, then, the P.A. inherited a legal system facing challenges in four key areas: 1) legal disunity; 2) confused and antiquated laws; 3) weak judiciaries; and 4) an enfeebled legal profession of questionable competence. Keeping in mind that the various components of a viable legal system for any state are generally accepted as: 1) independent judiciaries; 2) substantive and procedural laws that are responsive to community interests; and 3) a professionally competent legal profession, one can appreciate just how devastating these problems were to the Occupied Territories.

IV. THE ADMINISTRATION OF JUSTICE UNDER THE PALESTINIAN AUTHORITY

What, then, has the P.A. done to deal with the problems we have just identified? To their credit, Palestinian leaders quickly recognized the need to revive and unify the moribund legal systems in the two regions, and there was reason for optimism that genuine, meaningful changes might be rapidly achieved.[56] Most significantly, the P.A. developed, with assistance from Australia, a detailed plan for improving the administration of justice in the areas under its control.[57] Work also began on establishing a Basic Law that was intended to serve as an interim constitution for the P.A.

After considerable public and official debate, a draft law was passed by the P.L.C. in April 1997.[58] Though not a perfect document, the Basic Law, if enacted and, more importantly, observed would greatly advance the rule of law in the region.[59] To date, however, it hangs in limbo, awaiting the signature of Yasser Arafat, who has offered no public rationale for his failure to ratify the law.[60] As further events have unfolded, those reasons for early optimism have diminished rather than increased. Although modest progress has been achieved on some fronts, the overall performance of the P.A. exhibits a troubling diffidence and at times, outright contempt of the law. So let us examine the P.A.'s record in our four key problem areas.

A. Legal Unification

First, in the area of legal unification, depressingly little has been accomplished. Yasser Arafat issued a decree extending the jurisdiction of the High Court of Justice formerly sitting in Gaza to include the West Bank; however, it appears not to have been fully implemented.[61] Some steps to establish law commissions—one dealing with the reform and harmonization of civil procedure and the other doing the same with respect to criminal procedure—have been taken, but as of July 1998, neither commission had been fully staffed or fully operational.[62] New laws applicable to both regions, either in the form of decrees issued by Yasser Arafat, or legislation promulgated by the P.L.C. since 1996, have begun to establish a common corpus of law for the West Bank and Gaza Strip.[63] However, substantial distrust between these legal communities, each of which tends to push for unification on its own terms has, no doubt, hampered progress in this important area.[64]

B. Confusion in Laws

In the second problem area, confused and antiquated substantive and procedural laws, things have only become increasingly complex and confusing. There are, as I have already mentioned, new sources of legislation, in the decrees made by Yasser Arafat, and laws passed by the P.L.C., which add to the multiple strata left by previous administrations. There is also confusion as to the ongoing applicability of the Israeli military orders. On the one hand, the Oslo Accords specifically call for the continuing application of those orders. On the other hand, one of the very first proclamations of Yasser Arafat following his assumption of powers was that "the laws, regulations and orders which were in force prior to 5 June 1967 in the West Bank and Gaza Strip shall remain in force until unified."[65] Note the date — June 5, 1967, the day on which the Arab-Israeli war started — and it is the laws prior to that date that are to remain in effect. The later-issued military orders are therefore presumably excluded. This decree, widely reported in the region's Arabic press, was apparently Arafat's attempt to distance himself from the politically unpopular military orders without patently violating a commitment spelled out in the Accords. A later decree, however, stated that the laws in force in the territories as of May 19, 1994, would remain operative — including, one must assume, the Israeli military orders issued before that date.[66] It has also become clear since then that the P.A. views some military orders as still in force and has directly cited them as authorizing some of its actions.[67]

In addition, the P.A. has imported laws on criminal procedure that have no roots in local jurisprudence, but instead were applicable to the revolutionary courts of the P.L.O. outside the West Bank and Gaza Strip.[68] These rather unforgiving rules have been applied in special courts set up by the P.A. — about which more will follow — without any enabling legislation.[69] Not surprisingly, local legal practitioners have little or no familiarity with or even access to these laws and are at an obvious disadvantage in the courts that apply them.[70] Thus, the confusion mounts.

One positive accomplishment in this area should be noted. The P.A. Ministry of Justice contracted with the Bir Zeit University Law Center to, for the first time, tabulate, gather, and index all the laws in force in the two regions. This project, now complete, enables judges, lawyers, legislators, and others to at least undertake their respective obligations with a better awareness of the laws in force.[71]

C. Problems in the Judiciary

Let us now turn to the third challenge, the weak and under resourced judiciary, where the courts have faced repeated challenges to their independence from the executive branch. First, there has been no clarification of the rules regarding which body has the authority to select judges and what procedure governs their appointments. As a matter of practice, this power has been monopolized by Yasser Arafat, who, in a number of his appointments, has appeared to reward political loyalty over professional competence and knowledge of local rules and practice.[72] More troubling still is the fact that several judges have been dismissed or forced into resignation in retaliation for issuing judgments unfavorable to the government.

This apparently was the case with Chief Justice of the High Court in the West Bank, Amin Abd al–Salam, who received a resignation order one week after a High Court ruling ordering the release of a number of university students illegally detained by the P.A.[73] Moreover, Chief Justice of the Gaza High Court, Qusai al-Abadla, was forced to resign in early 1998, following the publication of an interview in which he criticized Minister of Justice, Freih Abu Medein,[74] for interventions in the judicial system contrary to law. On a number of occasions as well, P.A. officials have simply refused to enforce or abide by decisions of the West Bank and Gaza courts.[75]

Just as the integrity of the court systems in the West Bank and Gaza Strip were undermined by Israel's establishment of a parallel military legal system, so too have they now been undermined by the establishment of two new Court systems under the Palestinian Authority. The Security Court system adjudicates internal and external national security cases according to procedures elaborated for the P.L.O. revolutionary courts abroad.[76] The High Court for State Security, established in a decree by Yasser Arafat in February 1995, convenes specially at the behest of the executive authority — an obvious infringement of the principle of the separation of powers.[77]

The military court system ostensibly tries cases involving members of the Palestinian security services on matters arising out of the performance of their duties.[78] With the proliferation of security agencies, the number of persons subject to the jurisdiction of these courts is considerable.[79] Military court trials follow the same procedures that are required for the Security Courts. As we shall see below, these procedures are summary, deficient, and unfair, especially in those cases that have imposed the death penalty.[80]

The message conveyed by the existence and practices of the security and military courts is that the regular civil courts are simply not the locus of real power. Thus, Palestinian citizens often appeal to security personnel, rather than the courts, for the resolution of their disputes. Nor has the message of the powerlessness of the regular civil courts been lost on their own judges. The High Court, ostensibly the highest legal authority in the land, has several times declined to hear cases involving illegal detentions ordered by military courts, on the grounds that it lacks the jurisdiction to do.[81]

On the bright side, the P.L.C. passed a Law on the Independence of the Judiciary in late November 1998, which was subsequently given to Yasser Arafat for ratification. This law is of paramount significance given its potential to greatly strengthen the judicial branch of government. In its current form, however, the law continues to suffer from numerous deficiencies, and I am pessimistic as to whether the law will even be ratified, let alone exert the positive influence over the judiciary that it set out to establish.[82] Despite this pessimism, enactment of the law on the Independence of the Judiciary will figure prominently on my list of policy recommendations.

D. The Legal Profession

Lastly, let us turn to the status of the legal profession. Here, at least, we can say that some real progress has been made. Negotiations between the various organizations representing lawyers in the West Bank and Gaza Strip resulted in an agreement for the establishment of a founding committee for a new Palestinian Bar Association, encompassing both regions, in June 1997. Shortly thereafter, a decree by Yasser Arafat bestowed on this committee the powers of a bar association.[83] From these measures, the legal profession has at least the beginnings of an organization that can articulate the concerns of lawyers, assure the competence of new entrants to the bar, enforce discipline within the profession, and perform other similar responsibilities. In addition, legal education tailored more to local practice is now available in several local universities.[84] No doubt the benefits of these developments will become more readily apparent as time goes on.

Overall, however, the progress of the P.A. toward overcoming the problems in the legal system has been disappointing. Perhaps this assessment of the performance of a fledgling government facing challenges at nearly every level seems overly harsh and critical. The consequences, however, may be read in the P.A.'s rather dismal record in the area of respect for Palestinian human and civil rights. It is to that record that I now turn.

V. Abuses of Human and Civil Rights Under the Palestinian Authority

Let me first clarify the relationship between the problems in the legal system outlined in the prior two sections and the abuses of human and civil rights I am about to describe. It is not the case that the problems in the legal system simply cause the human rights abuses. Indeed, both the problems and the abuses may themselves share roots in deeper causes related to external pressures on the P.A., internal political challenges faced by its leadership, and the nature of the Palestinian political culture.[85]

The external pressures emanate from Israel and the United States in the form of repeated demands that the P.A. crack down on "terrorism" as a price for further Israeli military withdrawals from the Occupied Territories. As I go through this litany of abuses, keep in mind that U.S. officials have been fully cognizant of them and have acquiesced in them and even encouraged their commission. The internal challenges involve maintaining the legitimacy of the peace process and the political leadership that has pinned its fate to the success of that process and holding off the Islamist and leftist nationalist opposition to the Oslo Accords. These demands fall on a leadership accustomed to working within the framework of a revolutionary movement only minimally constrained by law.

Even so, deficiencies in the legal system encourage the abuses, while improvements in the legal system will undoubtedly foster, though not independently cause, advancements in the P.A.'s respect for human and civil rights.

One other important clarification: the security services, under the direction of the executive branch, is primarily responsible for most of the rights violations. The executive branch consists of the P.A. head, Yasser Arafat, his selected ministers, and other department chiefs. The P.L.C., in contrast, is now the most important forum for airing the dismay of the Palestinian community over abuses of citizens' rights by the executive authority. However, its many resolutions and recommendations to the executive branch regarding human and civil rights violations have been consistently ignored, reflecting, in part, the absence of a constitution or other legal referent that clearly defines the relative powers of the branches of government in the P.A.[86] Thus, as I detail the record of abuses under the "P.A.," I am primarily referring to its executive branch.

The record of human rights abuses highlights the following four areas: 1) illegal and arbitrary arrests and detentions; 2) torture and physical abuse of detainees; 3) unfair trials; and 4) violations of the freedom of press and public expression.

A. Illegal Arrests and Detentions

Arbitrary arrests without reference to the law are perhaps the most widespread of violations against human rights by the P.A. There are, of course, laws of criminal procedure in force in both the Gaza Strip and the West Bank that regulate seizures of persons.[87] While wanting in some important respects, these laws nonetheless impose either warrant requirements or, in exigent circumstances justifying warrantless arrests, postarrest review of one form or another.[88] The laws also establish standards and procedures for review of pretrial detention and provide for attorney and family visitation.

The P.A. has frequently engaged in wide-ranging sweeps, generally in the aftermath of an act of violence against Israelis by Islamist opponents of the peace process, in which hundreds, if not more, have been arrested without warrant, often on the basis of political beliefs and affiliations rather than any grounded suspicion of actual criminal responsibility. For example, following several suicide bombings in Israel in 1996, the P.A. arrested almost 1,100 suspected sympathizers of Hamas[89] and Islamic Jihad and detained them for periods far in excess of the law.[90] The Palestinian Human Rights Monitoring Group in 1997 documented 117 cases in which individuals were detained without charge and without trial for more than a year;[91] and in some cases, detention has lasted for more than two years.[92] In August of that same year, another Palestinian human rights group estimated the number of persons detained without charge or trial at between 200 and 300.[93] Many have been held incommunicado for lengthy periods as well.

No doubt a condition contributing to this particular kind of violation is the proliferation of security services under the P.A. As of 1997, at least 12 military branches have been operating in the region, employing as many as 30,000 to 50,000 individuals.[94] The problem is not only, or even chiefly, one of numbers. Few members of the security forces are professionally trained police officers. Most members are either former P.L.O. fighters who came to the regions with the P.L.O. leadership in 1994, or young *Intifada* activists, many formerly imprisoned by the Israelis, who were awarded appointments in return for service to the nationalist cause and, one may surmise, ongoing political loyalty to Arafat.[95] The duties and terms of reference of these many agencies are nowhere specified. According to Human Rights Watch, "[t]he various security agencies appear to be autonomous units whose duties are ill-defined and overlapping. They appear to be accountable to no one but President Arafat, and sometimes act in competition with one another."[96] Courts, moreover, have proven nearly powerless to halt these illegal and arbitrary arrests.

B. Torture and Abuse of Detainees

The character of the security agencies also plays a role in the second even more disturbing category of human rights violations committed under the P.A., namely torture and abuse of detainees. The first death of a detainee in the custody of the P.A. was that of Farid Abu Jarbu'a in July, 1994, shortly after the P.A. came to power in the Gaza-Jericho areas.[97] An autopsy revealed traces of violence on his body, later announced by the Palestinian Justice Minister to have been the cause of death.[98] By the end of 1997, an additional 14 Palestinians had died in P.A. custody under questionable circumstances.[99] Some certainly died of pre-existing health conditions, but in 1996 and 1997 at least 14 deaths were confirmed to have been directly caused by torture.[100] Numerous reports of physical abuse at less than lethal levels have led Palestinian human rights workers to conclude "[t]orture is a routine and everyday reality in the Autonomous Areas...."[101]

The forms of torture employed by Palestinian security officials include beatings both with and without weapons, positional abuse, hooding, exposure to extremes of heat and cold, sleep deprivation, burning with electric elements, cigarettes, or molten plastic, and threats and insults.[102] Detainees are often subjected to more than one of these forms of abuse. Some methods, for example, positional abuse, which often involves shackling the person to a child-sized chair in a painfully contorted position for periods of many hours, mimic techniques used by Israeli interrogators against Palestinian detainees and may have been learned by Palestinian security officers who had previously been tortured themselves.[103]

As one can imagine, the practice of torture has not gone unremarked within or outside the Palestinian community. Palestinian official response to the outcry has generally been to deny the widespread torture of detainees, while admitting its occurrence in isolated examples and, even less frequently, to investigate and bring to justice its perpetrators.[104] Yet the manner of those investigations and trials: hasty, summary, and rife with procedural inadequacies, [105] suggests a lack of will to systematically root out the causes of official torture and instead a desire to appease critics with "show" trials and public scapegoats.

C. Unfair Trials

Earlier I alluded to unfair trials, especially those conducted in either the Security Courts or in the military courts. Let me now spell out some of the procedural deficiencies of these courts. Between the first trial in the Security Courts in April 1995 and February 1997, some 57 additional cases were tried. According to Human Rights Watch:

> Trials have usually been held at night, Within hours of arrest, and have often lasted only minutes. Defendants have been systematically denied the right to be represented by independent counsel, bring witnesses, or appeal their verdicts. The judges presiding over these courts are military commanders who reportedly have no judicial experience, having served in neither the ordinary criminal nor the military courts. [106]

Although P.A. officials announced that these trials would be held in public, authorities have typically given no advance notice of the trials and suspects themselves have only learned of their impending trial upon their entering the courtroom. [107] Families of defendants have typically not been notified prior to trial, and some have learned of their loved ones' convictions by radio announcement after the fact.[108]

The shortcomings of a Security Court trial are mirrored in the proceedings of the military courts. Punishments meted out by both types of courts have not been trivial. Both, in fact, are empowered to enforce the death penalty, and a number of death sentences have been handed down between the two court systems.[109] None were carried out until August 1998, when two members of a Palestinian security service tried in military court for murder and assault against other Palestinians were executed by firing squad within four days of the alleged offense.[110] Other sentences that included many years of hard labor have also been imposed.[111]

D. Muzzling Freedom of Expression

Let us now turn to the fourth and last major category of human rights violations, limitations on the freedom of the press and public expression. The P.A. has repeatedly shown a deplorable readiness to stifle public opposition to the peace process or criticism of its performance.[112] It has done so through either temporary or permanent closures of newspapers, interference with their distribution, and harassment and arrest of journalists, human rights workers, and other critics of the government.[113] This is so, notwithstanding provisions of the Palestinian Press Law passed by the P.L.C., guaranteeing freedom of expression.[114]

Interference with the distribution of newspapers or their closure was particularly endemic in the first two years of P.A. rule. In May 1995, the East Jerusalem newspaper *al-Umma* ran a caricature of Yasser Arafat, earning it a warning from the Preventive Security Service (P.S.S.) (perhaps the largest of the Palestinian security agencies) against issuing that edition.[115] Although most of the copies were seized by the P.S.S., some had already been released. The paper then published a statement outlining and criticizing the behavior of the P.S.S.[116] Shortly thereafter, arson damaged the offices of *al–Umma* and its owner, who reportedly had also been threatened, subsequently shut down the paper.[117] Further, the largest Palestinian daily in the area, *al–Quds,* suffered a one-week shutdown after publishing a paid announcement by Hamas and interviewing a prominent Palestinian critic of the peace process.[118]

Harassment and detentions of journalists were also common during this period. In one of the best-publicized of these incidents, the editor of *al–Quds* received a call on Christmas Eve, 1995, instructing him to move an article describing a meeting between Yasser Arafat and the Greek Orthodox Patriarch from page eight in the paper to the front page.[119] Following his refusal, the Preventive Security Service personnel detained him for five days.[120] Many other journalists, up to 25 in the first two years,[121] suffered detentions, while others had been beaten, threatened, and insulted at scenes they had attempted to report, and had equipment, notes, and personal belongings destroyed or confiscated by security personnel.[122]

Such assaults on the freedom of the press have been less common recently, though they have not stopped completely. In late October, 1998, 11 journalists were briefly detained and their notes and videotapes seized, while they attempted to interview Sheikn Ahmad Yassin on the Islamist reaction to the agreement reached at Wye River.[123] Following the Wye River meetings and in a misguided effort to carry out the terms of the Memorandum, Yasser Arafat issued an "anti-incitement" decree that would punish not only incitement to racial discrimination and violence, but also incitement "to division" or "to breaching the agreement" reached between the P.L.O. and other states—in short, virtually any criticism of the policies and actions of the Authority.[124] The effect of all of this has been, predictably, self-censorship on the part of the Palestinian press. In the words of one prominent Palestinian journalist, Ghassan al–Khatib:

> The problem is that there is no respect for the law and because the judicial system is weak, there is nobody strong enough to challenge these acts. Therefore newspapers are afraid to write anything that might annoy the P.A. Instead, they count on WAFA, the official Palestinian news agency, for what they know is okay to print.[125]

Lawyers and human rights workers who have spoken critically of P.A. practices have also been targeted. By far the best-publicized of these cases is that of Dr. Eyad Sarraj, a medical doctor and former commissioner-general of the Palestinian Independent Commission on Citizens' Rights.[126] He was initially detained in December 1995, for allegedly "defaming" the P.A.[127] He was again arrested in May 1996, for "allegedly slandering the P.A.," after having described it as "corrupt, dictatorial, [and] oppressive" in a

New York Times editorial.[128] During this incident, he was detained for eight days.[129] He was released on bail, yet had never formally been charged. [130]

On June 10, 1996, Sarraj was re-arrested and charged with possession of hashish in his clinic office.[131] Several days later, Sarraj was brought before a State Security Court which extended his detention on the charge that he had assaulted a policeman while in custody. [132] After 17 days in custody, Sarraj was released on bail after signing a document committing him to "abide by the law when it comes to publishing anything to do with the authorities."[133] However, the trumped-up drug charges were never officially dismissed. [134] Variations on this experience have been endured by a number of other human rights workers and lawyers in the region. [135]

This is only a partial list of the abuses against human and civil rights perpetrated by the P.A. To be sure, they pale by comparison to the range and scale of abuses suffered by Palestinians under Israeli military government in its heyday. For example, the P.A. has never engaged in punitive home demolitions,[136] deliberate campaigns of politically motivated killings,[137] forced exile,[138] and land confiscations.[139] According to Israeli military sources, 83,321 Palestinians were brought to trial in military courts during the *Intifada*,[140] and more than 18,000 administrative detention orders were issued from the beginning of the uprising to November, 1997.[141] Even in the post–Oslo period, substantial numbers of Palestinians continue to be held in Israeli prisons.[142] In May 1998, the Israeli human rights group B'Tselem made claims that Israeli intelligence services detain and interrogate some 1,000 to 1,500 Palestinians per year and that an estimated 85 percent are tortured. [143]

Still, one may ask, "How have the Palestinians put up with all of this? Why haven't they engaged in open revolt against the P.A.?" They may yet, in fact, and that is precisely the danger that neglect of these abuses entails. So let us now turn to look at the political impact of these violations of Palestinians' human and civil rights, and, in particular, weigh their implications for the progress of the peace negotiations.

VI. The Political Impact of Human and Civil Rights Violations

The first thing to keep in mind in gauging the political impact of the P.A.'s human and civil rights violations is the broader historical context. Palestinians of the West Bank and Gaza Strip suffered many years under a highly repressive Israeli military government. At the same time, occupation brought the Palestinians into unprecedented proximity with Israeli society and government and thus, introduced them to a working democracy. While never under illusions about the fruits of this democracy for themselves, or even for their Arab relatives living within Israel and suffering discrimination there,[144] Palestinians in the Occupied Territories were, nonetheless, able to witness parliamentary elections and debates, a highly critical and relatively free press, open public debate and assembly, and an authentic, healthy court system.

Though the Israeli military government in the Occupied Territories was repressive, it was also in many respects a highly legalistic administration.[145] This allowed at least limited scope for legal opposition to military government practices, and, by the mideighties, a number of Palestinian human rights groups had cropped up which were schooled in the language and organizing tactics of the international human rights movement and protected somewhat from Israeli retribution by ties to that movement.[146] In other fields such as labor and womens' movements, health, agriculture, and education a number of nongovernmental organizations (NGOs) were developed to address the human and social needs of the Palestinian people that were not being addressed by the Israeli military government.[147] These NGOs were decentralized in leadership and stressed institutionalized internal governance rather than personalized politics. In sum, then, a dynamic Palestinian civil society had emerged that had an image of what a democracy, albeit a flawed one, was all about, one which had some modest experience with democratic practices and high aspirations, if not expectations, of democratic self-government under the incoming Palestinian administration.

The Palestinian political spectrum today is broadly composed of three main forces: 1) a mainstream nationalist center, led by Yasser Arafat's Fatah; 2) a leftist nationalist opposition, including the Popular Front for the Liberation of Palestine and the Democratic Front for the Liberation of Palestine; and 3) the Islamist opposition, associated with Hamas and Islamic Jihad.[148] While the relative weight of these three forces in the West Bank and Gaza Strip has varied over the last several years, largely in response to ebbs and flows in the peace negotiations, the mainstream center, with the establishment of a Palestinian state through the Oslo peace process the centerpiece of its agenda, has maintained preeminence. Support by the Palestinian public for the peace process has proven remarkably durable, and there has even been a Palestinian constituency in support of P.A. repression for those who have attempted to derail the peace process through dramatic acts of violence.

However, the undemocratic practices of the P.A. have disappointed the Palestinians and undermined their enthusiasm for the peace process.

How could it not be so? This is a community, after all, that had honed its knowledge of human rights principles and advocacy skills under Israeli occupation, conducted grass-roots organizing and international publicity campaigns against Israeli torture of Palestinians, and criticized the injustices rampant in Israeli military courts. What pain and humiliation Palestinians must feel, to now be subjected to the exact same abuses, even down to the details of the torture techniques, at the hands of their own government. A combination of disbelief and deep despair were palpable in the voice of one Palestinian human rights lawyer to whom I spoke in July 1998. He told me:

> You know, under the Israelis, when a client's family approached me, I would at least know where to go to find out his whereabouts. Now, with all of these different security services, I can't even begin my representation. I have no idea even where to start, who to ask, what prison to go to find my client. It is very, very bad — worse than it has ever been. [149]

As emotionally telling as this comment is on one level, it is factually inaccurate. To repeat: neither the range nor the scale of P.A. abuses of human and civil rights approaches that of the Israeli occupation authorities. That matters are perceived otherwise by my human rights lawyer friend, however, tells you something about the deep psychological hurt P.A. practices inflict — mocking as they do the high hopes for an accountable, democratic regime that Palestinians of the West Bank and Gaza Strip had developed.

If support for the peace process has been surprisingly constant, even in the face of this catalogue of abuses by the P.A., it would be a grave mistake to assume that it will necessarily continue. This is because the support has been contingent on two key factors: 1) the sense that the peace process is actually moving forward, even if incrementally, and has not become totally stalled — in other words, that the "end" justifying the otherwise objectionable "means" is ultimately not lost; and 2) the ongoing leadership of Yasser Arafat. In the words of Palestinian political scientist Khalil Shikaki:

> The key to continued Palestinian support for Oslo is Arafat himself. If he were to leave the scene, the pro-peace camp would be in grave trouble. Indeed, the main constituency for peace comes from Arafat's Fatah movement, [which] defers to his leadership, and sees him as the unchallenged leader of Palestinian nationalism. Arafat remains the most potent symbol of the Palestinian revolution. [150]

The peace process was momentarily resuscitated with the agreement reached at Wye River, but has stalled yet again with the Israeli cabinet's vote to suspend implementation of the agreement. Far more intractable, final status issues loom ahead. How long Yasser Arafat survives—he is widely reported to be in ill-health—is anyone's guess. It thus seems evident that institutionalizing the Palestinian leadership and investing the broadest segment of the Palestinian population as is possible with substantial interests in the negotiations, is a necessity for the survival of the peace process. We can ill afford to have the Palestinians wake up some day and find that, with their economy shot and their leadership corrupt and repressive, they have gained absolutely nothing from peace, and therefore, have absolutely nothing to lose in resorting to violence. It is for just that reason that U.S. policy responses to this situation, and so, too, those of other nations, have thus far been so disappointing. Let us now turn to those responses.

VII. U.S. AND INTERNATIONAL POLICY RESPONSES

In fairness, the United States, the European Union, and other international organizations or nations have not been totally neglectful of the problems discussed herein. In fact, an impressive number of groups and countries have offered technical assistance of a wide variety to what might be called "rule of law development" under the P.A. As of July, 1997, some 17 donors and ten United Nations agencies and programs supported legal development in the West Bank and Gaza Strip with a total committed budget of about $72 million.[151] U.S. support has been mostly channeled through U.S. aid to a number of nonprofit development organizations which have sponsored programs for judicial training, technical assistance in legislative drafting, Ministry of Justice staff development, and other similar activities.[152] Although it may be premature to judge the effect of these various efforts, the fact remains that little progress has been made in addressing the major challenges to the administration of justice that I identified earlier.

But my main criticism is not with the level or efficacy of support for the P.A. rendered at the technical level. Certainly, one could counsel — and I do counsel — that more such support be provided given the enormity of the challenges. But none of it is likely to be effective without shifts in policy at the highest political levels, because at those levels, the consistent message conveyed by American leaders to Palestinian leaders is one of tolerance, if not actual encouragement of P.A. abuses, and an indifference to the glacial pace of legal reform efforts. This has come about as U.S. policy makers have repeatedly pressured the P.A. to act decisively to quell anti–Israeli violence, virtually without regard to the human and civil rights of Palestinians.

For example, in March, 1995, during a visit to Yasser Arafat in Jericho, Vice President Al Gore "warned that the P.A. must control Islamic suicide bombers ..." and welcomed as "an important step forward" a commitment by Arafat to set up the State Security Courts.[153] After receiving Arafat's pledge of redoubled efforts to counter "terrorism," the Vice President announced an accelerated U.S. aid program of $65 million.[154] Later, on the eve of the first prosecutions in the State Security Courts, Vice President Gore again praised the courts saying: "I know there has been some controversy over the security courts. I personally believe that the accusations are misplaced and that they [the Palestinians] are doing the right thing and moving forward and that they must move forward now with prosecutions."[155]

In April 1995, U.S. officials voiced approval of scores of arbitrary arrests following two bombing attacks. State Department spokesperson Christine Shelly said, "We expect the P.A. to take this type of concrete action against those within its jurisdiction who seek to destroy the peace process through acts of violence and terror."[156] At the same time, President Clinton was reported to have appealed to Palestinian authorities to respond to attacks launched from areas under their jurisdiction with "strictpunishment."[157]

On August 5, 1997, Secretary of State Madeleine Albright commented that "[w]hat we would like is as robust a reaction to the terrorists as [Arafat] took in March 1996, where he undertook a series of very specific steps to deal with the terrorist threat," a supposed reference to the arrests and detention without charge of several hundred suspected Islamists and the "abrupt closing" of a number of charitable societies affiliated with Hamas.[158] The relentless pressure on the P.A. to contain "terrorism" continued through the run-up to the Wye River negotiations, as President Clinton again reminded the Palestinian leadership of the need to take all measures necessary to suppress attacks on Israelis.[159]

It is not that U.S. policy leaders are ignorant of the abuses committed by the P.A. in their anxiety to measure up to U.S. and Israeli demands. The State Department's Country Reports on human rights have reported such abuses annually since 1995.[160] The U.S. Central Intelligence Agency has also been actively engaged in facilitating intelligence transfers between Israeli and Palestinian security officials even before the more public and formal role assigned to it in the Wye River agreement.[161] It simply strains credulity to think that the excesses of the P.A. have gone unnoticed by American officials working in such intimate cooperation with Palestinian officials.

To be fully accurate, U.S. officials have not always turned a blind eye to P.A. excesses. There has been a markedly greater willingness to criticize the P.A. when the context was one other than the direct battle against anti–Israeli violence, such as the harassment or jailing of domestic critics of the P.A. The United States publicly criticized the detention of Palestinian-American television journalist Daoud Kuttab, who had broadcast sessions of the P.L.C. in which corruption on the P.A. had been discussed,[162] and intervened constructively in the previously mentioned case of Eyad Sarraj, the Commissioner General of P.I.C.C.R.[163]

In February 1997, U.S. Consul in Jerusalem Edward Abington decried the excessive numbers of Palestinian deaths in P.A. prisons, and stated "[s]ecurity is important but it can't come at the cost of human rights."[164] A welcome statement, to be sure. But if you were Yasser Arafat, recipient of these mixed signals from U.S. officials, to whom would you listen: Edward Abington or Al Gore, with $65 million in aid to offer, Madeline Albright, and President Clinton?

No one should question the right of Israelis to be free of violent attack, nor the obligation of the P.A. to strive conscientiously to protect that right. Yet Palestinians, too, are entitled to this right. They are entitled to protection from the abuses of the Israeli military government, where it continues to operate. They are entitled to protection from armed Israeli settlers, who have often initiated attacks on or retaliated against nonlethal attacks from Palestinians with lethal violence. They are entitled to protection from the abuses of the P.A. Ever solicitous of Israeli security, U.S. official statements have rarely focused on violations of Palestinian security, or worse, they have endorsed them. This inconsistency can hardly boost our claim to even-handedness in our oversight of the peace process.

As Abigail Abrash of the R.F.K. Memorial Center for Human Rights said:

> Neither the findings from these U.S. [rule of law] assistance initiatives nor the detailed accounts of human rights abuses and systematic problems contained in the U.S. State Departments country reports appear to have informed U.S. policy. The U.S. government has not demonstrated a credible human rights policy towards the region. [165]

The time has come to rectify this inadequacy.

VIII. Conclusion

So what might we do differently? Here are two general, and three more specific steps that can be taken to redress the problems in current U.S. policy toward P.A. abuses of human and civil rights.

1. U.S. policy makers should consistently communicate that suppression of violent opposition to Israel and the peace process cannot come at the expense of Palestinian human and civil rights. The P.A. must, as it has promised, abide by international standards and conventions for the protection of human rights in its treatment of persons under its jurisdiction. This message will really only be effective if it occurs at the top leadership level, starting where it matters most—with the President of the United States—and ending, again, where it matters most—with Yasser Arafat. This admonition is also likely not to be effective if it is only one-sided—that is, if it is directed only at the P.A. and not simultaneously at the Israeli government, which has continued to commit violations of Palestinians' human rights during the post–Oslo period.

2. Rule of law development programs for the P.A. should not only receive further funding, but also feature more prominently in policy discussions at the top leadership levels. Programs have already been targeted to address the four major problem areas previously identified. What is now needed is a sense of urgency, an acknowledgment that the success or failure of these efforts is not inconsequential to the peace process, and a redoubling of efforts to overcome some of the obstacles to the efficient administration of justice under the P.A.

These are the two general recommendations I would make. My third, fourth, and fifth more specific recommendations build on the recognition that international vigilance may not be effective and, as a matter of principle, should not be required to insure respect for human rights under the P.A. Rather, the United States, together with the international community, should nurture the development of an indigenous infrastructure that will ensure the vindication of basic rights for Palestinians. The first and most fundamental task here is the building of a strong, independent judiciary equipped with a body of law adequate to constrain abuses of executive power. Thus, I recommend:

1. The United States should insist that the P.A. abolish the State Security Courts, and offer new trials in regular courts to those previously convicted in the Security Courts system. The record shows that trials in these courts have regularly fallen below minimum standards of justice and the very existence of the courts imperils the integrity of the judiciary as a whole. Military courts should be brought into conformity with universal standards for fair trials and clear principles defining the persons over whom military courts have jurisdiction must be elaborated.

2. U.S. policymakers should strongly urge that President Arafat sign, and thus render effective, the Basic Law. The Basic Law enshrines fundamental principles of human and civil rights recognized and voted on by elected representatives of the Palestinian community. Further, the Basic Law provides guidance for police and government officials as to the legality of their conduct and offers local courts standards by which to review claimed abuses of government authority. The Basic Law also sets forth a legal referent for the relative powers of the three branches of the Palestinian government, in the absence of which, the Palestinian executive authority functions without check. No other law or laws currently in place in the West Bank or Gaza Strip provide a substitute for the Basic Law.

3. U.S. policymakers should strongly encourage the P.A. to prioritize the passage of a comprehensive, coherent law for the judiciary that lays the cornerstone for a truly independent third branch of government. Most crucially, this law must establish a system of judicial selection that ensures appointment to these pivotal offices solely on the basis of merit, rather than political fealty. The version of the law already passed by the P.L.C. is neither comprehensive nor coherent, nor is there any guarantee that it will be signed into law by Yasser Arafat. We cannot afford to be indifferent to the fate of this absolutely critical piece of legislation — rather we should follow its progress closely and do everything possible to see that the law accomplishes what it must to be effective.

It goes without saying that the mere passage of laws in and of themselves will not significantly alter circumstances on the ground. Indeed, the P.A. has often demonstrated its readiness to act with little or no regard for law whatsoever. Real implementation and respect for the laws passed must also be monitored and ensured.

More can and should be done. Yet these steps alone will give a tremendous boost to the morale of those Palestinians, mainly in the P.L.C., who are trying to establish an accountable, law-abiding government. It will also mean much to the Palestinian public, waiting, with fading hopes, for some tangible benefit from the peace process.

I will not predict an apocalypse in the event we fail to do what I recommend. Perhaps it will all be unnecessary, and, at the end of the interim period, we will all toast a new Middle East peace. Something tells me that this is not likely, however, considering the arduousness of the negotiations thus far over issues far less intractable than the ones that lie ahead. I suspect, instead, that we are in for several more years of painful work.

What I can say with confidence is that we will narrow our chances of reaching that elusive goal of peace if, in the meantime, we do not exploit every avenue, including the one of legal reform, to broaden the constituency for peace. As the principal overseer of the Middle East peace process it is our responsibility to do this; as the pre-eminent power in the world today, it is also our moral duty.

Notes

1. Although I join the international consensus in support of the right of the Palestinian people to national self-determination, I do not use the term "Palestine" to signal such support. No commonly accepted expression exists that describes the complex of laws and institutions needing to be reformed. "Palestine" is the term currently used by Palestinians to describe the entity that is now emerging in the region. I adopt this term without prejudgment as to whether this entity will ultimately gain recognition as a state or not. See generally Omar M. Dajani, *Stalled Between Seasons: The International Legal Status of Palestine During the Interim Period*, 26 DEV. I. INT'LL. & POL'Y 27 (1997) (discussing the national rights of the Palestinian people).

2. As one observer has put it, the challenge of creating a viable legal system in Palestine has been overshadowed by the "high politics" surrounding the Oslo peace process. See Glenn F. Robinson, *The Politics of Legal Reform in Palestine*, J. PALESTINE STUD., Sept. 22,1997, *available in* 1997 WL 10948373.

3. There has been much speculation in the press as to the status of Arafat's health. See, e.g., *Arafat's Tremors*, JERUSALEM POST, Nov.20, 1997, at 10; Marjorie Miller, "Arafat's Sickly Appearance Raises Questions About Health, Succession, Mideast: Palestinian Leader's Tremors Add to Concerns About Peace Process with Israel," LOS ANGELES TIMES, Nov.18, 1997, at A6.

4. See generally Hiram E. Chodosh & Stephen A. Mayo, *The Palestinian Legal Study: Consensus and Assessment of the New Palestinian Legal System*, 38 HARV. INT'L L.J. 375 (1997) (discussing the status of and proposing reforms to the Palestinian legal system).

5. For a discussion of these issues, see generally MAZEN B. QUPTY & JOHN L. HABIB, LEGAL ASPECTS OF DOING BUSINESS IN PALESTINE (1995).

6. See David P. Fidler, *Foreign Private Investment in Palestine Rejected: An Analysis of the Revised Palestinian Investment Law*, 31 CASE W. RES. 3. INT'LL. 293 (1999); see also Keith C. Molkner, *Legal and Structural Hurdles to Achieving Political Stability and Economic Development in the Palestinian Territories*, 19 FORDHAM INT'L L.J. 1419 (1996).

7. Public opinion polls suggest that Palestinian support of the peace process is undermined more significantly by undemocratic practices of the Palestinian Authority than by the deteriorating economic circumstances. See Khalil Shikaki, *Peace Now or llamas Later*, FOREIGN AFF., July-Aug. 1998, at 29, 38–40.

8. The Palestinians refer to the Palestinian Authority as "As-sulta al-wataniya alfilastiniya," or the "Palestinian National Authority." See *Palestinian National Authority* (visited Jan.20, 1999) <http://www.pna.org/>.

9. See Wye River Memorandum (Interim Agreement), Oct.23, 1998, Israel-Palestine Liberation Organization: 37 I.L.M. 1251 [hereinafter Wye River Memorandum].

10. The agreements were solidified as the Declaration of Principles (DOP). See Israel-Palestine Liberation Organization: Declaration of Principles on Interim Self-

Government Arrangements, Sept.13, 1993, 32 I.L.M. 1525 [hereinafter Declaration of Principles].

11. This was accomplished in side letters to the Declaration of Principles between P.L.O. chairman, Yasser Arafat, and Israeli Prime Minister, Yitzhak Rabin. See Letter from Yasser Arafat, Chairman of the P.L.O., to Yitzhak Rabin, Prime Minister of Israel (Sept. 9, 1993) and Letter from Yitzhak Rabin to Yasser Arafat (Sept. 9, 1993), reprinted in 1992/94 VIII PALESTINE YB. OF INT'L L. (AI-Shaybani Scc'y of Int'l L.), at 230-31. The recognitions are not, of course, fully reciprocal, as the P.L.O. recognized the right of Israel to exist as a nation while Israel only recognized the P.L.O. as the representative of the Palestinian people, without acknowledging the latter's rights to national self-determination.

12. The precise terms of the withdrawal, the structure, and jurisdiction of Palestinian self-government were left for further negotiations.

13. See Declaration of Principles, supra note 10, at art. V(3).

14. See id. at art. V(2).

15. See Israel-Palestine Liberation Organization: Agreement on the Gaza Strip and the Jericho Area, May 4, 1994, 33 I.L.M. 622 hereinafter Agreement on the Gaza Strip and the Jericho Area.

16. Annex II of the Agreement on the Gaza Strip and the Jericho Area, entitled a Protocol Concerning Civil Affairs, contains a list of 38 powers and responsibilities transferred from the Civil Administration of the Israeli military government to the Palestinian Authority. See Agreement on the Gaza Strip and the Jericho Area, supra note 15, at Annex II, art. II.

17. See Israel-Palestine Liberation Organization, Interim Agreement on the West Bank and the Gaza Strip, Sept.28, 1995, 36 I. L.M. 551 [hereinafter Oslo II].

18. See Dilip Hiro, *Israel-Palestine: Netanyahu's Untenable Position,* Inter Press Serv., Jan.16, 1997, available in 1997 WL 7073221. Israel refused to withdraw from Hebron following a series of suicide bombings in early 1996, perpetrated by Islamist opponents of the peace process, in which 59 persons were killed. See "Pulloutfrom Hebron Not Expected Until After Elections," *Jerusalem Post,* May 5, 1996, at 1, available in 1996 WL 4072316. While a subsequent agreement was reached for Israeli withdrawal from Hebron in January, 1997, Israeli troops remain in the town, ostensibly to guarantee the security of several hundred Jewish settlers who are ensconced in the middle of the otherwise exclusively Palestinian Arab town. See Rebecca Trounson & Marjorie Miller, "Netanyahu, Arafat Agree on Long-Stalled Hebron Pull-Out," LOS ANGELES TIMES, Jan.15, 1997, at Al.

19. See Hiro, supra note 18.

20. The term used in the agreement for the leader of the Council is the Arabic "ra'ees," which is translated as either "president" or "chairman." See ELIAS A. ELIAS & ED E. ELIAS. ELIAS' MODERN DICTIONARY ENGLISH-ARABIC 127, 566 (17th ed. 1970).

21. The number of representatives in the Council was originally fixed at 82. See Oslo II, supra note 17. ch. 1. art. W. Later the number was increased to 88 by an amendment to the Palestinian Election Law. See JERUSALEM MEDIA & COMMUNICATION CENTRE, THE PALESTINIAN COUNCIL 14 (2d ed. 1998).

22. See JERUSALEM MEDIA AND COMMUNICATION CENTRE, supra note 21 (providing a detailed report of the election results and noting that, of the 35 new members of the Council formally registered as "independent," many leaned toward Fatah).

23. See Oslo II, supra note 17,ch. 1, art. V.

24. The effect of Mafat's repeated snubs and neglect of the P.L.C. has been to rel-

egate that body to the role of "a powerless debating club." See *The Dilemma Facing Yasser Arafat,* 3 STRATEGIC COMMENTS, 1, 2 (Nov.1997). For example, after an inquiry in 1997 uncovered widespread corruption and mismanagement among his ministers, President Arafat stalled for over a year in presenting a new cabinet for P.L.C. approval. Finally, in August, 1998, President Arafat appeared before the P.L.C., delivered a speech focusing on the travails of the peace negotiations, and then announced that the entire previous government would remain in office, supplemented by eight new "state" ministers without portfolio. See Graham Usher, *Arafat's New Cabinet— "Back Me or Sack Me,"* MIDDLE EAST INT'L, Aug.21, 1998, at 3.

25. As noted above, this commitment was contained in the Oslo II agreement at Article I and timeline attached thereto. The Wye River Memorandum establishes a 12-week implementation schedule and also commits both parties to negotiate the terms of the third Israeli troop withdrawal provided for in Oslo II. See Oslo II, supra note 17, ch. 2, art. X; Wye River Memorandum, supra note 9.

26. See Wye River Memorandum, supra note 9, § II.
27. See Oslo II, supra note 17, at Preamble.
28. Declaration of Principles, supra note 10, art. VII(2).
29. See id. art. IX.
30. Agreement on the Gaza Strip and Jericho Area, supra note 15, art. VII, ¶ 1.
31. See Oslo II, supra note 17, ch. 1, art. IX, ¶6.
32. This is not to say, however, that specific types of legal reform could not violate the agreements as they currently stand.

33. As the P.A. is not a state, it is ineligible to become a party to international agreements, including those pertaining to human rights. An argument can certainly be made, however, that the P.A. is nonetheless a subject of international law and may be held accountable at least to abide by customary norms of international law in the area of human rights. See HUMAN RIGHTS WATCH/MIDDLE EAST, PALESTINIAN SELF-RULE AREAS: HUMAN RIGNTS UNDER THE PALESTINIAN AUTHORITY 39 (Sept. 1997) [hereinafter H.R.W.IMIDDLE E. REP.]; Eyal Benvenisti, *Responsibility for the Protection of Human Rights Under the Interim Israeli-Palestinian Agreements,* 28 ISR. L.REV. 297 (1994).

34. See Oslo II, supra note 17, ch.3, art. XIX. The commitment is reiterated in the Wye River Memorandum. See Wye River Memorandum, supra note 9, art. II, ¶ 4.

35. The P.L.O. attempted to become a signatory of the Geneva Conventions of 1949 and their additional protocols in 1977, but was rebuffed on account of its non-state status. See Paul Lewis, "P.L.O. Seeks to Sign 4 UN Treaties on War," NEW YORK TIMES, Aug. 9, 1989, at A5.

36. See THE PALESTINIAN BASIC LAW (Third Reading) (1998) (Palestine), translated by Saladin Al-Jurf [hereinafter BASIC LAW]. The text of the PALESTINIAN BASIC LAW is reprinted in the Appendix to this issue of the *Case Western Reserve Journal of International Law.* 31 CASE W. RES. J. INT'LL. 495 (1999). Article 10 of the Basic Law states: "1) Human rights and basic freedoms are necessary and an obligation of respect. 2) The Palestinian National Authority works without delay to incorporate international and national declarations and agreements which protect human rights." Id. art. 10. Other articles guarantee equality before the law, freedom from arbitrary search or detention, the right to a public and fair trial, freedom of conscience, and the like. See id. arts. 9, 11, 14, 18.

37. See Decree Number 59 (1993) (in Arabic). The Decree was published in the Official Gazette and became effective only in 1995.

38. See generally Chodosh & Mayo, supra note 4 (reviewing problems of legal development facing the Palestinian Authority); see generally Frederick Russillo,

Preliminary Judicial Systems Needs Assessment: The Autonomous Areas of Palestine and the Occupied Territories (Nov.1994) (unpublished manuscript on file with author) (outlining and proposing solutions that address the current deficiencies in the legal framework and judicial structure of the West Bank and Gaza Strip).

39. See generally E. Theodore Mogannam, *Developments in the Legal System of Jordan,* 6 MIDDLE EASTJ. 194 (1952) (discussing the post-1950 changes to Jordanian laws and the Jordanian judicial system).

40. See John Quigley, *Judicial Autonomy in Palestine: Problems and Prospects.* 21 U. DAYTON L. REV. 697, 704–05 (1996). See also ADAMA DIENG ET AL., THE CIVILIAN JUDICIAL SYSTEM IN THE WEST BANK AND GAZA: PRESENT AND FUTURE 14–15 (1994).

41. See "Keeping People in their Place," ECONOMIST, Sept. 12–18, 1998 at 48–53.

42. Article 43 of the Regulations Respecting the Laws and Customs of War on Land states:

The authority of the legitimate power having in fact passed into the hands of the occupant, the latter shall take all the measures in his power to restore and ensure, as far as possible, public order and safety, while respecting, unless absolutely prevented, the laws in force in the country.

1 PROCEEDINGS OF THE HAGUE PEACE CONFERENCES 629 (James B. Scott ed., 1920).

43. Several important changes occurred in the West Bank court system as a consequence of its separation from Jordan and Israel's annexation of Jerusalem: access to the Jordanian High Court of Justice in Amman was cut off and judicial power was transferred by Israeli military order to the West Bank Court of Appeals. The latter court, formerly sitting in Jerusalem, was, because of its annexation by Israel in 1967, transferred to the West Bank city of Ramallah, ten or so miles to the north. See generally GEORGE E. BISHARAT. PALESTINIAN LAWYERS AND ISRAELI RULE: LAW AND DISORDER IN THE WEST BANK, 56–60 (1989) (discussing the interaction between the Israeli military court system and the existing legal system in the Gaza Strip and the West Bank).

44. See PROCLAMATION ON LAW AND ADMINISTRATION, (PROCLAMATION No.2) (Isr.), reproduced in MILITARY GOVERNMENT IN THE TERRITORIES ADMINISTERED BY ISRAEL 1967–1980: THE LEGAL ASPECTS, 450–51(1982).

45. See ADAMA DIENG ET AL., supra note 40, at 39–40.

46. See BISHARAT, supra note 43, at 136.

47. See RAJA SHEHADEH & JONATHAN KUTTAB, THE WEST BANK AND THE RULE OF LAW, 43–44 (1980).

48. Institute for the Study and Development of Legal Systems, Palestinian Legal Study: The Restoration and Modernization of the Palestinian Civil and Criminal Justice Processes 23 (June 30, 1995) (unpublished manuscript, on file with author). Raja Shehadeh, a Palestinian lawyer practicing in the West Bank since the late seventies and a prominent commentator on Palestinian legal affairs, challenges the "commonly held misconception" that the existence of multiple layers of law in the West Bank and Gaza Strip in itself was a source of confusion, as local practitioners always had ways of determining which among the possible sources of law properly governed particular legal problems.

See RAJA SHEHADEH, FROM OCCUPATION TO INTERIM ACCORDS: ISRAEL AND THE PALESTINIAN TERRITORIES 74 (1997). It is perhaps more accurate to say that the existence of the various legal strata caused no confusion as long as there was a consensus within the legal community on the means for resolving potential conflicts of laws. But the Israeli military government has, on occasion, exploited ambiguity concerning the ongoing applicability of certain laws to its own advantage. This was notably true of the Defence Emergency Regulations, a set of Draconian measures enacted by the British during the Mandate period to suppress both Palestinian and Zionist paramilitary groups and nationalist activities. The Israeli military government has maintained that these regulations were never formally repealed either in the Gaza Strip or West Bank, while Palestinian lawyers, including Shehadeh, have argued that they were repealed by implication. The Israeli view is contained in UZI AMIT-KOHN ET AL., ISRAEL, THE "INTIFADA" AND THE RULE OF LAW 45–48 (David Yahav et al. eds., 1993). The contrary view is argued in RAJA SHEHADEH& JONATHAN KUTTAB, THE WEST BANK AND THE RULE OF LAW 24 (1980), and MARTHA ROADSTRUM MOFFETT, PERPETUAL EMERGENCY: A LEGAL ANALYSIS OF ISRAEL'S USE OF THE BRITISH DEFENSE (EMERGENCY) REGULATIONS, 1945, IN THE OCCUPIED TERRITORIES 45–47 (1989).

49. See generally BISHARAT, supra note 43, at 125–44 (discussing the general deterioration of the West Bank's formal court system); ADAMA DIENG ET AL., INTERNATIONAL COMMISSION OP JURISTS & THE CENTRE FOR THE INDEPENDENCE OF JUDGES AND LAWYERS, THE CIVILIAN JUDICIAL SYSTEM IN THE WEST BANK AND GAZA 38–52 (1994) (identifying main problem areas in the civilian court system in the West Bank and Gaza).

50. *Cf.* RAJA SHEHADEH, OCCUPIERS' LAW: ISRAEL AND THE WEST BANK 84–91 (1985) (describing how the power and jurisdiction increased for the military courts and decreased for the civil courts).

51. The formal court systems also faced competition from informal mediators whose judgments were made more quickly and, as a result, were perceived to be more effective than those made by the courts. See generally Adrien Wing, *Legal Decision-Making Durmg the Palestinian Intifada: Embryonic Self-Rule,* 18 YALE J. INT'L L. 95, 123–27 (1993).

52. See generally BISHARAT, supra note 43, at 145–61 (examining the disintegration of the legal profession in the West Bank); George E. Bisharat, *Courting Justice? Legitimation in Lawyering Under Israeli Occupation,* 20 L. & SOC. INQUIRY 399–402(1995) (describing and analyzing the effects of the West Bank lawyers' strike).

53. See RAJA SHEHADEH, FROM OCCUPATION TO INTERIM ACCORDS: ISRAEL AND THE PALESTINIAN TERRITORIES 162 n.7 (Ctr. of Islamic & Middle E. L. Book Series No.4, 1997).

54. See Lisa Haijar, Authority, Resistance, and the Law: A Study of the Israeli Military Court System in the Occupied Territories, 526 (1995) (unpublished Ph.D. dissertation, The American University) (discussing the migration of lawyers from the civil courts to the Israeli military courts).

55. See Chodosh & Mayo, supra note 4, at 380, 430–31.

56. See, e.g., Gary A. Hengstler & Richard L. Fricker, *Yasser Arafat: My Vision,* A.B.A. J., Feb.1994, at 46; Gary A. Hengstler, *Building a Rule of Law,* A.B.A. J., Feb. 1994, at 50; Gary A. Hengstler, *First Steps Toward Justice,* A.B.A. J., Feb.1994, at 52; Richard L. Fricker & Gary A. Hengstler, *From Military Rule to Civil Law,* A.B.A. J., Feb.1994, at 62.

57. Specifically, the plan addressed 1) the unification of existing laws governing the West Bank and Gaza Strip; 2) the improvement of court buildings and facilities; 3) the unification of judicial systems and procedures; 4) the standardization of prosecution procedures; 5) the development of computerized legal and judicial databases; and 6) the development of an independent forensic science capability. See RULE OF LAW STRATEGIC DEVELOPMENT PLAN (The Palestinian Authority Ministry of Justice ed., 1996) (this publication was prepared in part by the contributions of Australian International Legal Resources).

58. See Adrien Katherine Wing, *The Palestinian Basic Law: Embryonic Constitutionalism*, 31 CASE W. RES. J. INT'L L. 383 (1999); Palestinian Legislative Council, *Laws and Projects* (visited Feb.24, 1999) <http://www.pal-p.l.c.org/engiish/laws/laws.htm>.

59. For a critique of an early draft of the Basic Law, see Naseer Aruri & John Carroll, *A New Palestinian Charter*, 23 J. PALESTINE STUD. 5 (1994).

60. Matwan Kanafani, a spokesman for Arafat and P.L.C. member, suggested that Arafat' s refusal to sign the Basic Law is out of concern over the lack of input from diaspora Palestinians, whose interests Arafat represents in his capacity as Chairman of the Executive Committee of the P.L.O. See Larry Kaplow, "Arafat Vows Power-Sharing, Crackdown on Corruption," ATLANTA JOURNAL CONSTITUTION, Dec. 31, 1997, at A7. According to Kanafani, "He has a problem with (the Council) being part of the Palestinian people but not all of the Palestinian people." Id.

61. See SHEHADEH, supra note 53, at 152–53 (describing the High Court's extended jurisdiction). The Palestinian Independent Commission for Citizens' Rights reports that, as of December 1997, no effort had been made to unify the High Courts in Gaza and the West Bank. See PALESTINIAN INDEPENDENT COMMISSION FOR CITIZENS' RIGHTS, THIRD ANNUAL REPORT,79–80 (1997) [hereinafter PICCRJ].

62. See Interview with Ibrahim Sha'ban, Member of the Civil Law Commission, Jerusalem (July 16, 1998) (notes on file with author).

63. As Raja Shehadeh points out, however, none of the new laws have explicitly identified the region(s) within which they are to be effective and it is only by inference that they have been made applicable to both the West Bank and Gaza Strip. See SHEIHADEH, supra note 53, at 152–53.

64. See GLOBAL BUREAU CENTER FOR GOVERNANCE AND DEMOCRACY, JUDICIAL ADMINISTRATION PROJECT IN THE WEST BANK AND GAZA (Mar.1996), at 1–3.

65. SHEHADEH, supra note 53, at 149 (quoting text of Decision No.1 issued on May 20, 1994).

66. See id. at 139, 150 (stating that the Israeli government has not stopped issuing military orders in the areas still under its control).

67. See, e.g., The Palestinian Society for the Protection of Human Rights and the Environment, *PNA Carries out Forced Eviction in Jericho Using Israeli Absentee Property Law* (visited Oct.14, 1997) <http://www.birzeit.edullawe~reports/1994/nov_94.html>. In one case reported by LAW, the Palestinian Society for the Protection of Human Rights and the Environment, the P.A. evicted a tenant and his family from a rented home in the Jericho area via an administrative order through the "Department of Absentee Property," an agency established by Israel to administer lands and properties confiscated from Palestinians who were alleged to have been absent from the property during the 1948 War. See id.

68. See Mona Rishmawi, *The Actions of the Palestinian Authority under the Gaza/Jericho Agreements*, in THE PALESTINE NATIONAL AUTHORITY: A CRITICAL APPRAISAL 3, 7 (Center for Policy Analysis on Palestine, 1995).

69. See generally id. at 7–8 (describing the procedures used by the courts and law enforcement agencies in treating prisoners).

70. See id. at 7

71. See Interview with Dr. Camille Mansour, Director of Bir Zeit University Law Center, in Bir Zeit, Jordan (July 9, 1998) (notes on file with author).

72. Thus a former lawyer from Gaza who returned from forced exile was appointed Chief Justice of Gaza. See Rishmawi, supra note 68, at 7.

73. See H.R.W./MIDDLE E. REP., supra note 33. Abd al-Salam's predecessor in

that position, Kbalil Suwani, bad earlier suffered a similar fate. See Glenn E. Robinson, *Authoritarianism with a Human Face,* CURRENT HIST., Jan.1998, at 13, 16.

74. See Rachelle H.B. Fishman, Palestinian Human Rights Suffer from Official Corruption. 351 LANCET 425, 425 (1998).

75. See PICCR, supra note 61, at 77-90.

76. The Security Courts consist of a Misdemeanor State Security Court, a General State Security Court, and High Court for State Security. See id. at 81–82.

77. See id.

78. See id. at 83.

79. See Debrah Horan, "Palestinian Police Preside Without Law," HOUSTON CHRONICLE June 22, 1997, at 1.

80. See PICCR, supra note 61 at 82.

81. See, e.g., Amnesty International, *Palestinian Authority: Prolonged Political Detention, Torture, and Unfair Trials* (visited Feb. 5, 1999) <http:!Iwww.amnesty.org.uk/reports/palestine/index.html>.

82. The law had not yet been signed by the head of the P.A.—a condition for its enactment—as of February 15, 1999, nor was there any indication that a signature was forthcoming. Telephone Interview with Keith Schultz, Associates in Rural Development, in Ramallah, Jordan (Feb.15, 1999).

83. See *The State of Human Rights in Palestine II: the Judicial System,* PALESTINIAN HUM. RTS. MONITOR, Aug.1997, at 17; PICCR, supra note 61, at 79.

84. Bir Zeit University Law Center has established a Masters in Law program geared to educate graduates of foreign law schools in local law. See Interview with Dr. Camille Mansour, supra note 71. Jerusalem University now offers a four-year undergraduate program in law, which leads to a "license" degree authorizing its holders to enter local professional practice. See Interview with Ah Khashan, Faculty of Law Dean at Jerusalem University, in Jerusalem (July 16, 1998) (notes on file with author).

85. See generally Glenn E. Robinson, Authoritarianism With a Palestinian Face. CURRENT HIST. Jan.1998. at 13 (discussing the causes of the P.A.'s authoritarian politics).

86. See PICCR. Third Annual Report. supra note 61, at 55–58.

87. For an overview of criminal procedure in Gaza and the West Bank, see Palestinian Legal Study, supra note 48.

88. Gaza law requires postarrest review within 48 hours by magistrate; Jordan vests power of review in prosecutor. See id. at Attachment Eat 1, Attachment F at 3.

89. "Hamas" in Arabic means "zeal" and is the acronym of "harakat al-muqawima al-islamiya," or "Islamic Resistance Movement." See ZIADABU-AMR, ISLAMIC FUNDAMENTALISM IN THE WEST BANK AND GAZA: MUSLIM BROTHERHOOD AND ISLAMIC JIHAD 66 (1994). Hamas was founded in Gaza before the *Intifada,* while Islamic Jihad was founded during it, both with the goal of ending Israeli occupation and establishing an Islamic state in Palestine. See id. at 53, 66, 93, 103. Hamas is composed of a nonmilitary, administrative, charitable, and political wing, and a military wing which has launched a series of deadly attacks against Israeli soldiers and civilians. See id. at 67; AHMAD RASHAD, HAMAS: PALESTINIAN POLITICS WITH AN ISLAMIC HUE 7 (1993). Islamic Jihad is a purely politicomilitary organization which is also responsible for multiple lethal attacks against Israelis. *Cf id.* at 4–5; ABU-AMR, supra at 106–08.

90. See *Human Rights Under the Palestinian Authority: Hearing Before the Subcommittee On International Operations and Human Rights of the Committee on International Relations,* 104th Cong. 77(1996) (statement of Abigail Abrash, Director, Robert F. Kennedy Memorial Center for Human Rights) [hereinafter Abrash Hearing].

91. See PALESTINIAN HUMAN RIGHTS MONITOR, supra note 82, at 7-8.

92. See Avi Macbus, "Israel: Demands Foster Palestinian Police State," FINANCIAL TIMES (LONDON), Oct.21, 1998, Int'l at 5, available in LEXIS Market Library, Promt File.

93. See HUMAN RIGHTS WATCH, HUM. RTS. WATCH WORLD REP. 1998, at 340 (1998) [hereinafter H.R.W. WORLD REP. 1998].

94. See Horan, supra note 79. One of the salutary provisions of the Wye River agreement is the planned reduction of this number to no more than 30,000; even that number is large in light of the size of the population of the region.

95. See generally GRAHAM USHER, PALESTINE IN CRISIS: THE STRUGGLE FOR PEACE AND POLITICAL INDEPENDENCE AFTER OSLO, 65-67 (1995).

96. H.R.W./MIDDLEE. REP., supra note 33, at 9

97. See id. at 18.

98. See id.

99. See id

100. See SENATE COMM. ON FOREIGN RELATIONS & HOUSE COMM. ON INT'L RELATIONS, 105TH CONG., COUNTRY REPORTS ON HUMAN RIGHTS PRACTICES FOR 1997, 1481 (Joint Comm. Print 1997) [hereinafter COUNTRY REPORTS 1997].

101. *The State of Human Rights in Palestine III,* PALESTINIAN HUM. RTS. MONITOR, Dec.1997, at 4.

102. See Amnesty International, supra note 81, cb. 6. U.S. Dep't State, *Israel and the Occupied Territories Reports on Human Rights Practices for 1997* (Jan.30, 1998) <http://www.state.gov/www/global/human_rights/1997_hrp_report/Israel.html> (describing position torture used on Ahma Abu Hamed).

103. See Amnesty International, supra note 81. On Israeli torture techniques, see HUMAN RIGHTS WATCH/MIDDLE EAST, TORTURE AND ILL-TREATMENT: ISRAEL'S INTERROGATION OF PALESTINIANS FROM THE OCCUPIED TERRITORIES (1994).

104. See Deaths in Detention: A Pattern of Abuse, Illegality, and Impunity, PALESTINIAN HUM. RTS. MONITOR, Dec.1997.

105. H.R.W./MIDDLEE. REP., supra note 33, at 14-15.

106. Id.

107. See Amnesty International, supra note 81.

108. See id.

109. See, e.g., Rebecca Trounson, "Palestinian Brothers Executed 4 Days After Crime," LOS ANGELES TIMES, Aug.31, 1998, at A6.

110. See id.

111. Amnesty International, for example, reports that two Palestinian naval policemen were sentenced to 15 and 10 years' imprisonment with hard labor for causing an unintentional death. Their trial, including a half-hour recess, was concluded within two hours. See Amnesty International, supra note 81.

112. See H.R.W./MIDDLE E. REP., supra note 33, at 23, 28-30.

113. See id. at 24-35.

114. Although the Press Law also contains vague provisions barring the publication of articles that "may cause harm to national unity," it authorizes the confiscation of such articles. H.R.W./MIDDLEE. REP., supra note 33, at 24 (quoting Article 37(3) of the 1962 Basic Law of the Gaza Strip). For a thorough analysis of the impact of the Press Law on freedom of expression, see PALESTINIAN CENTRE FOR HUMAN RIGHTS, CRITIQUE OF THE PRESS LAW OF 1995 ISSUED BY THE PALESTINIAN AUTHORITY (1995).

115. See H.R.W./MIDDLE E. REP., supra note 33, at 24.
116. See id.
117. See id.
118. See id. at 24–25.
119. See id. at 25.
120. See H.R.W.lMIDDLE EAST REPORT, supra note 33, at 25.
121. See id.
122. See *The State of Human Rights in Palestine IV,* PALESTINIAN HUM. RTS. MONITOR. Jan.1998, at 17–21.
123. "During the Negotiations of the Israeli/Palestinian Peace and Security Agreement at Wye Plantation, the Palestinian Police Arrests Journalists and Prevents Them from Contacting the Political Opposition and Confiscates their Films and Tapes," Palestinian Hum.Rts Monitoring Group, Press Release, Oct.24, 1998 (on file with author).
124. See *Wye: A Charter for Human Rights Violations* (visited Feb. 3, 1999) <http://www.lawsociety.org/press/ 1998/oct_26.html> (containing severe criticisms of the Wye negotiations and agreement published by LAW in an October 26, 1998 press release).
125. H.R.W.IMIDDLE E. REP., supra note 33, at 26.
126. See id. at 32.
127. See id.
128. Anthony Lewis, "Darkness in Gaza," *New York Times,* May 6, 1996, at AlS.
129. See H.R.W.IMIDDLE E. REP., supra note 33, at 32–33.
130. See id. at 33.
131. See id.
132. See id.
133. Id. (quoting Eyad Sarraj. *Justice in Heavens,* open statement following his third release from prison, on July 15, 1996).
134. See H.R.W./MIDDLE E. REP., supra note 33, at 33.
135. Others detained include Raji Sourani, director of the Gaza Center for Rights and Law; Bassam Eid, a researcher for the Israeli human rights organization B'Tselem; and Muhammad Dahman, an activist in ad-Dameer (a prisoner support organization). See id. at 31–35.
136. See generally Dan Simon, The Demolition of Homes in the Israeli Occupied Territories, 19 YALE J. INT'L L. 1(1994) (providing a critical legal analysis of the Israeli home demolition policy).
137. See Elia Zureik & Anita Vitullo, Extrajudicial Killings: Israel's Latest War on the Intifada 20 (1992) (unpublished manuscript on file with author) (providing evidence of Israel's reliance on political killings and summary executions).
138. See B'TSELEM, 1987–1997 A DECADE OF HUMAN RIGHTS VIOLATIONS 26 (Jan. 1998).
139. See generally George Bisharat, Land, Law, and Legitimacy in Israel and the Occupied Territories, 43 AM. U. L. REV. 467 (1994) (arguing, in part, that Israel has expended a great deal of energy to construct a legal regime facilitative of land confiscations).
140. See HUMAN RIGHTS WATCH/MIDDLE EAST, TORTURE AND ILL-TREATMENT: ISRAEL'S INTERROGATION OF PALESTINIANS FROM THE OCCUPIED TERRITORIES 2 (1994).
141. See B'TSELEM, supra note 138, at 18.
142. At the end of 1997, the U.S. State Department reported that 3,565 Palestinians were imprisoned by Israel, of whom 382 were under administrative detention. See COUNTRY REPORTS 1997, supra note 100, at 1465.
143. See Press Release from B'TSELEM and ACRI, in Joint Report to the U.N.

Committee Against Torture: Israel Continues to Violate Convention Against Torture, (May 14, 1998) (visited Mar. 1, 1999) <http:I/www.btselem.or/PRESS/980514.htm>. Other forms of repression continue as well. See generally B'TSELEM, DEMOLISHING PEACE: ISRAEL'S POLICY OF MASS DEMOLITION OF PALESTINIAN HOUSES IN THE WEST BANK (Sept.1997) (describing Israel's policy of mass demolition carried out on Palestinian homes built without effectively available building permits).

144. See generally DAVID KRETZMER, THE LEGAL STATUS OF THE ARABS IN ISRAEL, 77–134, 175–79 (1990) (discussing overt, covert, and institutional discrimination against Arabs in Israel).

145. See BISHARAT, supra note 43. at 47–69 (discussing the dual character of the Israeli military government).

146. See generally George Bisharat, Attorneys for the People, Attorneys for the Land: The Emergence of Cause Lawyering in the Israeli-Occupied Territories, in CAUSE LAWYERING: POLITICAL COMMITMENTS AND PROEESSIONAL RESPONSIBILITIES, 453, 463–67 (Austin Sarat & Stuart Scheingold eds., 1998).

147. See generally GLENN E. ROBINSON, BUILDING A PALESTINIAN STATE: THE INCOMPLETE REVOLUTION 38–65,184(1997) (describing the rise of these organizations and the management of these organizations by the PNA).

148. See Shikaki, supra note 7, at 30–32.

149. Interview with Mazen Qupty, Mazen Qupty & Associates, in Jerusalem (July 14, 1998).

150. See Shikaki, supra note 7, at 41.

151. See *Rule of Law Development in the West Bank and Gaza Strip: Survey and Status of the Development Effort.* UNSCO, at 9 (1997).

152. See id. Annex One: Rule of Law Sector Support Table, at 31–40 (providing a detailed list of recent legal reform activities along with their respective implementing organization, donor, and budget).

153. Clyde Haberman, "In Jericho, Pledges of U.S. Aid and a Glimpse at Arafat," NEW YORK TIMES, Mar.25, 1995, at A2.

154. See "Arafat Promises Crackdown on Terror," PLAIN DEALER, Mar.25, 1995, at Al5.

155. "Gore Sees Palestinian Trials Starting Soon," REUTERS WIRE, Apr. 5, 1995, available in LEXIS, NEWS Library, REUNA File (providing the comments of Vice President Gore made in a public conference held at the Washington Institute).

156. "U. S. Endorses Arrests in Wake of Gaza Attack," AGENCE FRANCE PRESSE, Apr.10, 1995, available in LEXIS, NEWS Library, AFPFR File.

157. See id.

158. See The Israeli-Palestinian Peace Process, Remarks and Q&A Session at the National Press Club, Washington, D.C., (Aug. 6, 1997) (remarks of Secretary of State Madeleine K. Albright) (visited Mar. 1, 1999) <http://secretary.state.gov/wwwlstatements/ 970806.html>; H.R.W. WORLD REP. 1998, supra note 93, at 343.

159. See id.

160. See SENATE COMM. ON FOREIGN RELATIONS & HOUSE COMM. ON INT'L RELATIONS, 104TH CONG., COUNTRY REPORTS ON HUMAN RIGHTS PRACTICES FOR 1995 (Joint Comm. Print 1995); SENATE COMM. ON FOREIGN RELATIONS & HOUSE COMM. ON INT'L RELATIONS, 104TH CONG., COUNTRY REPORTS ON HUMAN RIGHTS PRACTICES FOR 1996 (Joint Comm. Print 1996); COUNTRY REPORTS 1997, supra note 100.

161. H.R.W./MIDDLE EAST REP., supra note 33, at 41.

162. See H.R.W. WORLD REP. 1998, supra note 93, at 341, 343.

163. See H.R.W./MIDDLE EAST REP., supra note 33, at 42. The arrest of Sarraj also stimulated interest by the U.S. Congress in the excesses of the P.A., which led to bearings before the House Subcommittee on International Operations and Human Rights of the Committee on International Relations in July, 1996. See *Human Rights Under the Palestinian Authority: Hearing Before the Subcomm. on Int'l Operations and Human Rights of the House Comm. On Int'l Relations,* 104th Cong. 1-3 (1996).
164. H.R.W. WORLD REP. 1998, supra note 93, at 343.
165. See Abrash Hearing, supra note 90, at 82-83.

8

Mandate Ways: Self-Determination in Palestine and the "Existing Non-Jewish Communities"

John Strawson

International law is not an innocent bystander in Palestine. For the Palestinians the 20th century became a century in which their identity as people was so assaulted that they saw the name Palestine wiped from the map.[1] At the same time, the legal right to self-determination that became so central in international law after the Second World War became so elusive for the Palestinians that they entered the 21st with their right to exercise it still contested. Contemporary international law is forged out of a conjoining of the European enlightenment and European colonialism and is stamped with all the traces of conquest, oppression and arrogance that signifies the West's triumphs. For the past 200 years, the West, through colonialism has made the world map and through its international law legitimized it. Palestine was allotted a special place at the end of colonial expansion through the Mandate system of the League of Nations. As a consequence of awarding the Mandate to Britain the international legal narrative becomes enmeshed with the British as they constructed Palestine as a colonial state.[2]

The British Mandate for Palestine has played a significant legal role in marginalizing the identity of the Palestinians and thus their right to self-determination. Eight decades after the Mandate gave effect to the wording of the Balfour Declaration, Palestinians, have been forced to argue for their identity and their attachment to the land during both the interim phase and the permanent status talks of the Oslo peace process.[3] This essay is a reflection on the way in which the Mandate text constitutes Jews as central and Palestinians as marginal in Palestine. The story which ensues is very much what a film producer might call a "back-story" which sustains the plot. Behind the well-known sequence of events and legal debates lies a story which gives them their life. These legal stories are contained in academic legal works, memoirs and other texts in which various actors in the drama give their version of events and, sometimes, explanations for their actions. Legal discourses disconnected from their back-stories nourish the idea that the law exists in some objective form above the fray of life.

In the Mandate Jews were awarded the right to a "national home" in Palestine whereas Palestinians were constituted as the "existing non–Jewish communities" whose "civil and political rights" may not prejudice the establishment of the Jewish national home. The Jews were presented as a singular people whereas the Palestinians were seen as disparate plural communities whose entire identity appears to be reliant on their not being Jews, but the Jewish Other. The Mandate while placing an obligation on Britain to prepare the people in the territory for self-government so reconstructed the peoples as to obscure this task. Self-determination in the context of the British Mandate became, not legal doctrine applicable to the people in a territory, but a *sui generis* form, which appeared to place an obligation on the mandatory to assemble the people, or at least a part of them and then prepare the territory for self-government.

In the five years between the issuing of the Balfour Declaration and the League of Nations granting Britain the Palestine Mandate the population of Palestine changed little. With a total population of about 745,000 in 1922, the Palestinian population stood at around 660,000 with an additional Jewish minority of about 83,000.[4] When General Allenby captured Jerusalem from the Ottomans in December 1917, the Jewish population numbered 77,000. The minority Jewish population nonetheless received the central attention and the "establishment in Palestine of a national home for the Jewish people" became an apparent primary obligation. The Palestinians appeared only to gain rights as a secondary consequence of this as the text announced "it ... [was] clearly understood that nothing should be done which might prejudice the civil and religious rights of the existing non–Jewish communities in Palestine." While 90 percent of the settled population of the country were merely existing non–Jewish communities, the scattered Jewish Diaspora (in reality "communities") is the singular specter which hangs over the British Mandate. The actual Jewish minority in Palestine is not addressed in its own right. The legal formulations of mandate open a legal narrative that continues to exercise an influence on the present day. In arguing for every inch of the West Bank in the interim redeployments and in the permanent status talks, the Palestinians have to insert their own legitimacy into the legal discourse.

Supporters of the Palestinian cause have frequently used legal arguments to sustain the political struggle for self-determination.[5] Although an understandable stance which attempts to wrap the political position in legal legitimacy it is in my view flawed. International law far from being an objective series of doctrines and institutions constitutes a discourse, which encodes power and which because of this, enthrones a particular series of Western legal values. In this account, the Palestinian people having been constituted in this particular way are framed within a legal order. Far from suffering breaches of international legal obligations they suffer from it. It was the Mandate and international law that provided the basis for the treatment of the Palestinians and the results of dispossession are entirely a consequence of its logical application. The problem for the Palestinians has been not a breach of international law but its imposition. Many works on international law and the Palestine issue make a strong case in arguing that there have been many breaches of humanitarian law associated with the use of force, the Geneva Conventions, the treatment of refugees.[6] On the central question, however, of the right of the Palestinian people to self-determination there is a tendency to overlook the discourse of international law.

Paul de Waart is one of the most eloquent counsels in defense of international law. He argues in his book, *Dynamics of Self-Determination in Palestine*,[7] that the international community through the United Nations, is in breach of its obligations to the Palestinian people because of the existence of positive international law contained within a series of "unilateral, bilateral and multilateral legal instruments."

> ... the Balfour Declaration, the League of Nations Mandate and the UN Plan of Partition ... formed the birth certificates of the right to self-determination of the Jewish People and the "non-Jewish communities" in Palestine.[8]

These "birth certificates" are highly problematic for the Palestinians. At the most elementary level the erasure of the identity of the Palestinians and their characterization simply as non–Jewish, far from being a birth certificates for self-determination appear more as death certificates. The problematic formulation is at one with the dominant Zionist discourse of the period that Palestine was "a land without a people."[9] The use of the term "communities" indicates a fragmentary population with a less than secure relationship to the land where they live. As the Zionist project developed, Zionism has had to come to terms with the actual Palestinian population; it has had to change the formula from a land without a people to a people with little attachment to the land.[10] While de Waart's motives in attempting to outline positive legal duties that the international community owe to Palestinians are entirely honorable, the results are highly problematic.

De Waart's view that the Balfour Declaration represents a legal instrument is an interesting observation as the instrument itself is contained in a letter from a government Minister (Balfour) to an individual (Rothschild) representing a political organization (the Zionist movement). The letter refers to a territory over which Britain had no legal or actual power at the time and is couched in typically English ambiguous terms. Indeed the introductory paragraph describes the purpose of the letter as a "declaration of sympathy with Jewish Zionist aspirations." In the well-known second paragraph the letter continues:

> His Majesty's government view with favor the establishment in Palestine of a national home for the Jewish people, and will use their best endeavors to facilitate the achievement of this object, it being clearly understood that nothing shall be done which may prejudice the civil and religious rights of existing non–Jewish communities in Palestine, or the rights and political status enjoyed by Jews in any other country.[11]

It concludes with a request to Lord Rothschild "to bring this declaration to the knowledge of the Zionist Federation." It reads very much like the letter it is rather than the legally sounding "Balfour Declaration." It is in fact a "declaration of sympathy" for certain aspirations. It is difficult to read this text as creating or giving rise to any legal obligations or legal rights. The term "national home" was in 1917, and is today, an undefined entity within international law. Failure to "use their best endeavors to facilitate the achievement of this object" could hardly trigger legal action even if the recipient of the letter had *locus standii* in international law. It is significant that Lord Roshschild was asked to bring the contents to the attention of the Zionist movement indicating that this was not a direct commitment to the Zionist movement itself. De Waart's arguments in favor of this text constituting a positive legal source which possibly gives rise to the legal rights of Jews and Palestinians appears rather weak at that level. The declaration itself should be taken at face value as a letter expressing a new political position of the British government. If anything it prefigures a legal development and within its careful sentence construction proposes a new dispensation for the territory.

The adoption of the Mandate for Palestine by the League of Nations is, however, a different question as it was at this point that a recognizable legal instrument of international law came into existence. However, the Mandate system and the League of Nations need to be placed within the colonial context. One of the proponents of the Mandate system, the South African Jan Smuts, had argued in 1918 that:

> The peoples left behind by the decomposition of Russia, Austria and Turkey are most untrained politically; many of them are either incapable of or deficient in the power of self-government; they are mostly destitute and will require much nursing towards economic and political independence.[12]

Smuts reserved a special place for Palestine in his memorandum as he argued that Palestine could not have an "autonomous regime where the consultation of the country on the question of the Mandatory State, is not formally possible."[13] For Smuts the difficulty in Palestine arose from its ethnic heterogeneity that required an outside administration to ensure order and fairness. Jan Smuts was a committed Zionist and had a background in the racial politics of South Africa, another country where the majority were prevented from exercising the right to self-government.

Through the issuing of the League of Nations Mandates, public international law confirmed its colonial nature and created the basis for legitimate rule by Europeans over non–Europeans with the former empowered to assess the advance towards civilization. As Smuts observed "the doctrine of self-determination of a nationality which was the guarding principle in the re-arrangement of Europe, could not be applied to the former colonies or the Arab countries."[14] This encoding in international legal discourse with a hierarchy of culture according to existing European values was applied to Palestine with a particular twist. Whereas De Waart makes much of the "sacred trust," which appears frequently in League of Nations texts, he misses the point that this was the "sacred trust for civilization" by which the League clearly meant "European" civilization." At the time this was fully understood by many of the participants in the drama. Among these was Norman Bentwich who wrote:

> Of the Palestine Mandate it may be said that, if the Mandate system has not been evolved for other purposes, it would have had to be created for the government of this little land.... For Palestine, by its history, its geography, its population, and its destiny, is an international country, and its well-being and development form in the nature of things, a sacred trust for civilization.[15]

As if to demonstrate that this narrative was centrally located within international legal discourse, the passage above forms part of a book based on the lectures which Bentwich gave at The Hague Academy of International Law while he was the Attorney-General for Palestine in 1929. The elaboration of British colonial legal approaches as an exposition of international legal discourse highlights those features of law which are, at best, a patronizing interest in achieving "well being and development." In this case the agency of progress is the colonial regime.

Norman Bentwich was undoubtedly the single most important legal character in the development of the early Mandate. As Legal Advisor and then first Attorney-General for the first decade he made some of the critical decisions and also used his position to influence international legal discourse and doctrine. As we shall see he was far more complex than merely a Zionist activists who gained a position of influence at a significant juncture. Bentwich was perhaps the most significant British official to elaborate the legal character of the term "national home." "It signifies," he said, "a territory in which a people without receiving the rights of political sovereignty, has nevertheless, a recognized legal position and the opportunity of developing its moral, social and intellectual ideas."[16] These had significance for the operation of the Mandate, particularly at the level of building representative institutions:

> In Syria and Iraq the Mandatory was obliged to work with representatives of the people to draft an organic law on self-government. In Palestine there is no such obligation: but the Mandatory is directed to place the country under such conditions as will secure the development of self-governing institutions, and to encourage local autonomy. On account of the peculiar responsibility there could not be at once the institutions of self-government; but the process was to be developed by stages. It was obviously necessary, in order to fulfill the policy of the Jewish National Home, that the Mandatory should retain at the outset full powers of legislation and administration, since it was to be expected that the majority of the population would not be willing to give effect to the obligation assumed by the Mandatory towards the minority.[17]

Bentwich's argument for the special character of Palestine as opposed to the other examples, one French Mandate and the other British, is marked when set against his own explanation of class A Mandates which applied to all three as "territories detached from Turkey populated by civilized peoples that, it was thought, were unable to stand by themselves."[18] Indeed Bentwich was apparently enthusiastic about the novel features of the Mandate system which introduced two new features into international law: (1) "a national system of government under international law" and (2) "a system of guardianship of peoples similar to that of the guardianship of individuals of minor persons."[19] In Palestine these features of the Mandate do not apply. One of the elements that cannot stand alone or requires guardianship was not fully in place which was a sizeable Jewish population. However, the way in which Bentwich expresses this is with reference to the existing Jewish minority, as if the majority Palestinian population might frustrate that minority from developing its moral, social and intellectual ideas. As he explains:

> The principle of self-determination had to be modified because of the two national selves existing in Palestine; and the majority Arab population could not be allowed to prevent the fulfillment of the Mandate in relation to the minority Jewish population. It was observed by General Smuts, when he advocated the Mandate system, that "there will be found cases where, owing chiefly to the heterogeneous character of the population and their incapacity for administrative co-operation, autonomy in any real sense would be out of the question and the administration would have to be undertaken to a very large degree by some external authority. This would be the case, at any rate for sometime to come, in Palestine, where the administrative co-operation of the Jewish minority and the Arab majority would not be forthcoming.[20]

Bentwich's reliance on Jan Smuts is all the more interesting as Smuts wrote these words long before the Mandate system was established in his 1918 proposals for the program of the League of Nations.[21] The knowledge that the majority population would not accept that their right to self-government through representative institutions should be limited by the policy of the Jewish national home was at least an honest acceptance of a colonial viewpoint. However, Smuts' argument that the peculiarities of Palestine's situation was due to a heterogeneous population is special pleading as is clear when compared to Bentwich's own comparison with Iraq. In Iraq there were far more Jews than in Palestine and indeed the Jewish community dominated the commercial life of Baghdad[22] although this presented no special problem to the Mandatory. Indeed Iraq was more complex still as the population mix of Shi'a, Sunni and Kurds as well as Jews and a significant Christian community should have placed it in the same category. In fact Iraq was if anything forcibly united and under the guidance of Gertrude Bell, a Hashemite Monarch installed and form of guided Parliamentary system introduced. Smuts, like Bentwich, a Zionist, saw things differently not because of the population mix but rather because of the Zionist plan. It is interesting however that the essentialist arguments about ethnic divisions were deployed.

The concept of the Jewish National Home was seen by Bentwich as requiring a specific form of legal and political dispensation:

> Palestine is designed to be a bi-national country; and could not be placed under a form of national government in which the people of one nationality would dominate people of the other. The trustee therefore, has, for a time to secure fair treatment and justice for the two nationalities, till the two have come to understand one another better.[23]

This spelling out of the binational character of the entity that would result from the Mandate was an important clarification. The Palestinians were presented with a blueprint for the future of their society on the basis that there were two nationalities with equal rights to self-determination within the same territory. One of the tasks of the Mandate power was to oversee the development of good relations between these two peoples. This view was popular in British government circles since the Balfour Declaration. Herbert Samuel, destined to be the first British High Commissioner, had outlined aspects of this policy in November 1919:

> The immediate establishment of a complete and purely Jewish state would mean placing a majority under the rule of a minority; it would therefore run counter to the first principles of democracy, and would undoubtedly be disapproved by public opinion of the whole world.[24]

That immediate prospect was however delayed only as long as conditions could mature sufficiently to turn the country into a "purely self-governing commonwealth under the auspices of an established Jewish majority."[25] Samuel was coy as to how this majority might come about although he was insistent that there "can be no questions of despoiling men of their land ... hindering the exercise of religion ... or depriving any portion of the population of their full civil rights."[26] However, he continued, this state of affairs would not arrive until "Palestine becomes a state in which all its inhabitants are helped to attain a higher standard of civilization,"[27] and that at that moment the Arabs would "find that far from being prejudiced their position is improved."[28] From these statements the thinking of the British becomes clearer as Zionism became part of the civilizing mission. It is striking how Samuel saw the Palestinians not as a people with rights to self-determination but rather as individuals with rights to be protected, as individuals to be improved by civilization. These individuals stood to gain entry into Western civilization as individuals through the agency of a Jewish majority establishing the projected self-governing commonwealth.

A decade later Bentwich was able to reflect upon the means that were being used to achieve these ends. Writing of the role of the British he says:

> The part of the government has been to remove any disabilities that existed in Ottoman legislation; to furnish the country with a system of law and administration which is suitable to a progressive population; to open the doors to immigration so far as to agricultural and industrial development of the country; allow for the absorption of newcomers; to encourage fiscal and customs measures; to give facilities to Jewish Public bodies to develop their own system of education and cultural activities, and to facilitate the organization of the Jewish people as a national community.[29]

The nice reference to a "progressive population" was confirmation of Samuel's aim of civilization and may not just be a code for the Jewish population. The other policy objectives are clear enough. The Jewish majority would be developed through immigration and absorption. These "newcomers" were very much part of the modernizing project of developing new legal and fiscal systems. The role of the state for Bentwich was clearly a liberal one that created the general conditions for progress and development. The legal framework legitimized immigration — Jewish immigration — and fostered the development of the Jewish national community. Within this framework the organizations of Jewish (or Zionist) civil society would be able to undertake the transformation of Palestine. As he said:

> ... the functions of acquiring land for Jewish settlers, the organization of agricultural colonization, the establishment of new industries, the foundation of schools, higher colleges and a university, have been carried out by the Zionist organization and other bodies concerned with Jewish settlement.[30]

Thirty-five years later Bentwich asked himself, "What was the permanent legacy of the British Mandate in Palestine?"

> In the first place, the system of law and order, the rule of law – which embraced protection of the individual against the official — and the actual legislation of the Mandatory government. But there was more than thirty years of progressive administration which revolutionized the conditions of a backward Ottoman province.[31]

It is not surprising that law was the great achievement of the Mandate according to its most prominent legal official. His assessment even with the perspective of time saw the role of law as a progressive modernizing influence overcoming the backward Ottoman system. It is interesting too that he focused on individual rights within the new modernizing system. The Bentwich of the post–Israel period does seem to have become more reflective. "It was natural for the Arabs," he wrote,

> to fight against a policy which denied them the right of self-determination proclaimed as one of the principles of the new international order. Nor was it to be expected that they would support on humanitarian grounds the creation in this little land of a home for persecuted Jews, particularly when the Christian powers of Europe and America were not prepared to receive Jewish immigrants.[32]

In an ironic comment he observed that Palestinian Arabs "were also Zionist in wanting Zion as their national home."[33] Bentwich did grasp that individual legal rights achieved by the Mandate had not survived to protect Palestinians who remained in Israel after 1948. "The conditions of the Israeli Arabs" he writes "are not yet those of genuine equality, and in certain respects remain unsatisfactory."[34] He was at his most eloquent when writing about the 1956 Kafr Qassim massacre:[35]

> The trial brought home to a part of the Israelis the feeling of guilt of the congregation. They had passively adopted the idea that Arabs were inferior human beings whose property and even whose life, could be taken in the supposed interests of Israel's security.[36]

This appeared in a chapter devoted to the "Israeli Arabs" and although sensitive to the individual human rights, it seems somewhat naïve from the legal architect of the Palestinian disaster. His acceptance of the designation Israeli Arab is instructive too. Bentwich and his wife were quite wistful as they contemplated the Israeli reality prior to 1967. Looking out at the old city of Jerusalem from the then Israeli enclave on Mount Scopus, Helen Bentwich wrote:

> I take one last lingering look at the old city. I think of the thousands of Arabs, many of them friends of old, now leading wasted lives in the refugee camps on the other side of Jerusalem. And despite my deep admiration for the achievements of Israel, I feel infinitely sad as I remember the Jerusalem where I once lived and the hopes that I had then for a peaceful and united Palestine.[37]

Norman Bentwich looked back to 1918, a time when, he said, "a bi-national Palestine, which would ultimately be an Arab-Jewish Commonwealth seemed possible."

These benign reflections were, however, a consequence of the legal narrative of the Mandate and the British legal practices under it. As one reads the Mandate one cannot but be struck by the main references to individual human rights and the principle of nondiscrimination. Article 2 provides for "safeguarding the civil and religious rights of all the inhabitants of Palestine irrespective of race and religion." Article 14 providing for the freedom of conscience underlines this in stating that "no discrimination of any kind shall be made between the inhabitants of Palestine on the grounds of race, religion or language." Under article 22 three official languages, English, Arabic and Hebrew, are guaranteed equal status, and article 23 recognizes as official holidays the holy days of each community. These individual legal rights are undoubtedly seen by the British as modernizing the legal situation in the country compared to that which existed under the Ottoman system. However, under the guise of modernization and the provision of these rights the collective legal identity of the Palestinian Arab population was undermined. The fact that the Arab identity of the Palestinians was only alluded to when providing for language equality is noteworthy. All other references to nondiscrimination were generally posed, but no particular race identified. The coy use of the expressions, "inhabitants of Palestine," "each community," "such communities" pepper the text as testimony to the expert use of the English legal euphemism. Alone of the identified communities stand the Jews.

Ronen Shamir in his subtle analysis of British Mandate law and nationalism in the Zionist context argues that the role of the British colonialism has been omitted from the Zionist story. Within the main Zionist story the Jewish community of Palestine battles against the Arab presence and the British occupier. Shamir demonstrates that the colonial regime played a major role in defeating the Arab national risings of the 1930s and in fact left a legal system and a modern state for the Israelis to inherit.

> Too little attention as been given to the basic fact that the British, aided by their colonial experience elsewhere, created and installed a functioning state in Palestine; a rather advanced web of administrative apparatuses and governmental departments, a sound infrastructure and, of course, a fully developed, ready to use legal system.[38]

In this account of the development of the Israeli legal system the role of the British has remained deliberately obscured so as not to interfere with the essentialist and historic Zionist narrative.[39] Nevertheless current Israeli and Zionist narratives do contain much on the Balfour Declaration and the Mandate as legitimizing sources for the establishment of the state. The reliance on these, and especially the Mandate, indicates the significant role attached to international law in the Zionist story. While there is, as Shamir argues, a silence over the role of the British regime in constructing the state and law within, there is a conscious recognition of international law as part of the foundational discourse. The text of the Mandate appears in the collection of reference documents on the Israeli Foreign Ministry home page on the Internet reflecting this public admission. It is perhaps equally significant that the Order-in-Council for Palestine of 1922 does not appear in this collection. It was the Order-in-Council which gave effect in English Imperial law to the Mandate. Amongst its key provisions is article 46 which stipulated the legal sources that were to govern the courts and by implication the regime as a whole. This legal evidence of a colonial regime in Palestine is conveniently absent. The Mandate, complete with the conferment of a right to a national home on the Jewish people — the only identified people in Palestine — remains a central instrument.

There is, in some Israeli quarters, an obsessive legalism in attempting to argue the case against the right of Palestinians to a fully sovereign and independent state.[40] The phrasing of the Mandate usefully fits with the dominant Zionist construction of the Palestinians as either absent or, if present, tentatively so. The Palestinian presence and attachment to the territory is never the equivalent to the Jewish presence or of the Jewish character of the land. As in the Mandate the Palestinian Arab population are cast as semidetached in their own country. This approach informs the legal negotiations in the Oslo process. Uri Savir's account of the negotiations makes depressing reading for those who were hoping for major changes in attitudes. Two years into the process Savir commented about the interim agreement, eventually signed in September 1995, "few understood that if we could not treat the Palestinians with respect as equals, across the full spectrum of relations, they would repay us in kind in the fields where we were interdependent."[41] As the Israeli chief negotiator he should be in a good position to know.

The creation of the Palestinian Authority in 1994 literally put Palestine back on the map after 46 years of absence and created a new legal entity albeit suspended somewhere between autonomy and statehood. The re-emergence of a Palestine for the Palestinian people begins to remedy the lack of legal identity of a territory and a people. There appears to be a legal symmetry in the precarious legal personality of the Palestinian Authority in 1994 and the character of the "national home" for the Jewish people in 1922. Both are novel features within international legal discourse and doctrine. Whereas the "national home" was represented through the Jewish Agency, the Palestinian Authority has, through the implementation of the interim agreement, acquired an elected President and elected Legislative Council. Nevertheless, despite this apparent symmetry it is far from clear that the Palestinians have moved from the margins of Palestine.

The central place accorded to the Jews within the Mandate has been bequeathed to Israel in the language of the Oslo accords. The Mandate succeeded in creating a new legal entity, a national home, and placed obligations on the Mandatory to transform this into some reality. The problematic character of the national home concept was due to its uniqueness in international law. Indeed it remained undefined. The absence of the Jewish people from the territory further complicated the situation. The Jewish Agency represented both the Jewish minority in Palestine and symbolically represented an authority that could represent the Jews who were yet to come. This Hegelian sense of becoming that was acquired by the Jewish Agency is another difference with the Palestinian Authority. The basis of the Palestinian Authority is limited to representation of the Palestinians living in Palestine not the majority of the Palestinians who live as refugees outside. The Cairo Agreement is careful to limit to the character of the Palestinian Authority. The Israeli negotiators, perhaps unconsciously, wanted to frame the Palestinian Authority so that it did not have that potential of representation. The Oslo time-frame made that possible as the issue of refugees was to be discussed in the permanent status talks, and thus this and the other permanent status issues were not within the jurisdiction of the Authority. In articles IV and V of the Cairo Agreement the Palestinian Authority is constructed as an entity which deals with "territorial, functional and personal jurisdiction" within the areas limited by the agreement (and at that time certain parts of Gaza and the Jericho area). The jurisdiction of the Authority is entirely bound up with the withdrawal and subsequent redeployment of the Israeli forces and thus only extends to the Palestinians living in the designated areas. The Palestinian Authority was not intended to be a representative of the Palestinian people in the way in which the Jewish Agency was able to place itself in as a universal representative of the Jewish people wherever they were.

The legal discourse of assigning the marginal place to the Palestinians has thus remained present during the Oslo process negotiations. The structure and language of the texts no longer sees the absence of a named party, the Palestinians, but rather re-encodes the relationship by more ambiguous means. Under the Oslo Agreements Israeli withdrawal and redeployment from territory has not only been protracted but has been conducted by unilateral action of the Israelis, ensuring that withdrawals and redeployments are consistent with their national and security interests.[42]

Israeli redeployments from the West Bank were at the center of much of the disagreement over the implementation and in many ways were the most important actor, as the return of land occupied in 1967 was the critical part of any agreement. The Interim Agreement is studiedly ambiguous in the way it talks about these redeployments. Under Articles X (2) and XVII (8) the text outlines the terms of the redeployments. These read:

> Further redeployments of Israeli military forces to specified military locations will commence after the inauguration of the Council and will be gradually implemented commensurate with the assumption for public order and internal security by the Palestinian police, and to be completed within eighteen months of the inauguration of the Council... [X(2)].
>
> The Council's jurisdiction will extend to cover West Bank and Gaza Strip territory except for issues to be negotiated in the permanent status negotiations, through a series of redeployments of Israeli military forces. The first phase of the redeployment of Israeli forces will cover populated areas in the West Bank – cities, towns, refugee camps, and hamlets ... and will be completed prior to the eve of the Palestinian elections. Further redeployments of Israeli military forces to specified military locations will commence immediately upon the inauguration of the Council and will be effected in three phases, each to take place after an interval of six months, to be concluded no later than eighteen months after the inauguration of the Council. [XVII(8)].

These provisions appear to place an obligation on Israel to redeploy forces in three phases over a period of 18 months from the inauguration of the Palestinian Legislative Council. However, there are two key issues which are not dealt with. The first is how much territory is to be redeployed from and the second is who makes this decision. The drafters had been careful to omit any definite article before either "West Bank" or "Gaza Strip," and by placing the word "territory" immediately afterwards underlines that redeployments are not from the West Bank and the Gaza strip but merely from some of those territories. The drafters were cute in using the definite article before West Bank only when specifying redeployment from the population centers which were defined in the maps which accompanied the agreement and where areas A amounted to 3 percent of the territory. It is also clear that the deft drafters make the process appear almost an objective process, with the use of the words like "will commence," "to be completed," and "will take place." By omitting all reference to the agency of such actions, Israel silently occupies the decisive ground making its own decisions about the amount of the territory. It is noteworthy that while Oslo 1 provided for the withdrawal of Israeli forces from Gaza and the Jericho area (article V(1)) all subsequent pull-backs of Israeli forces become "redeployments" (article XIII). This slippage from withdrawal to redeployment further underlines the fragile character of the process. Whereas a withdrawal appears as a permanent act, a redeployment has a more temporary flavor to it. The language of the legal text endows the Israeli side with an active power while the Palestinians appear passive at the margins. When the one clear commitment of these articles was broken and redeployment was not completed within 18 months of the inauguration of the Palestinian Legislative Council (that would have been by September 1998) the Israelis managed to lure the Palestinians to further talks on implementation which became the Wye Plantation Agreement. The then Prime Minister, Benjamin Netanyahu, did not implement it and was defeated in the May 1999 elections. The new Labor Prime Minister, Ehud Barak, instead of carrying out the agreement to implement an already agreed-to obligation succeeded in obtaining more discussions, this time on how to implement the Wye Agreement which became the Sharm Al Sheikh Agreement. Each time it appears that the Israelis are positioned in an active center with the Palestinians at a passive periphery.

The slow and drawn-out process of negotiations is not merely a question of timing. Through the years since the 1993 agreement, Israeli governments have continued the policy of establishing Israeli settlements in the occupied territories and have even agreed to allow some illegally (according to Israeli legal lights) established settlements to remain. Settlement activity has seen a significant increase in the number of settlers in occupied land from about 120,000 in the West Bank and Gaza in 1993 to about 160,000 in 2000 – excluding the several hundred thousand settlers in equally occupied East Jerusalem. However, as serious has been the road-building program throughout the West Bank, which has created an Israeli network of roads, which link the Israeli settlements and largely bypass Palestinian towns and villages. These roads have created a virtual Israel in occupation, which allows Israelis an illusion that they are in Israel traveling to Hebrew named towns because they never have to gaze upon Palestine or Palestinians. Unless, that is, they want to literally look down. Looking down on Palestine is an activity for the Israeli settlers and their visitors as the settlements have been built on hills and the roads which now criss-cross the West Bank are generally at the same higher levels – for security reasons. The settlements and their network of roads add the impression of the transient character of the Palestinian people. At the same time the actual theft of land and the re-use of that land for Israeli purposes complicates the issue of withdrawal or deployment by the Israelis and the permanent status of the territories. Whereas colonialism most often enframed the colonized within their intellectual system, the Israelis have attempted to frame the Palestinians physically within Israel.

The international legal discourse on self-determination of peoples has developed entirely as a response to resistance to colonialism. The development of the legal doctrine is contained in a series of United Nations General Assembly Declarations made between 1960 and 1970.[43] Essentially the provisions of these resolutions and the way in which they have been interpreted by the International Court of Justice[44] have secured the principle that a colonial regime constitutes a denial of self-determination. However, despite the frequent use of the term self-determination of peoples, international law has failed to define the term people. It is also noteworthy that self-determination has been defined not positively but negatively; thus, certain types of regimes are seen as contradicting the right. The legal discourse's lack of a positive definition of a people played a negative role for the Palestinians. Between 1948 and 1967 the United Nations appeared to construct the Palestinians as a refugee community, rather than as a people entitled to the right to self-determination. Despite the provisions of the partition plan in resolution 181 (1947)[45] of the General Assembly the United Nations, the rest of the international community appeared to lose interest in the Palestinians as a people. For a brief moment, that resolution, whatever its consequences, had legally bestowed a Palestinian Arab identity on the majority of Palestine's population. However, with the creation of the State of Israel, absorption of the West Bank into Jordan[46] and the Egyptian occupation of Gaza, that moment ceased. Only a protracted struggle after the 1967 Israeli occupation of the West Bank and Gaza were the Palestinians able to insert their identity as a people into legal discourse and place the issue of self-determination upon the agenda. In 1974 the United Nations General Assembly finally adopted Resolution 3236 (XXIX) which recognized the Palestinian people as people with the right to self-determination. By this time the Palestinians were now absent from much of what had been Palestine in 1922. A further complicating factor was that the vast majority of the Palestinians living in the West Bank in 1974 were still Jordanian citizens.[47] In any event it would be another two decades before an Israeli government would be able to deal with, at least, some of the implications of this in the Oslo Agreements.

International legal discourse's reconstitution of the identity of the Palestinian people is as significant as its undermining of it through the Mandate. However, as we have seen, as the Palestinians attempt to re-inscribe themselves within the international legal order, they are forced to deal with the consequences of previous constructions of themselves. The attachment of successive Israeli governments to the previous images marked the current process. While the Palestinians have made their reappearance and the Palestinian Authority has acquired gradually more control of the map, to the Israeli authorities, the Palestinians do not yet appear as other peoples. The privileged and central position of Israel remains as successor to the Jewish National Home. The interests of the Israelis encapsulated in the term "security" dominate the discussion. In the Hebron Agreement, for example, 400 Israelis are able to control the center of a city with a population of some 100,000 Palestinians. Israeli settlers in the West Bank have been able to dictate the scope of the redeployment of Israeli forces in the same manner on the grounds of protecting Israeli security. Only in the late 1990s was the Israeli political establishment able to contemplate a Palestinian state. This state, however, is imagined as having its sovereignty curtailed by limiting its ability to have international alliances or an army of its own. In some versions, such a state will not have control over its own natural resources such as water or even over its airspace.

The discursive images of international legal discourse have played a part in nourishing Israeli images of its Palestinian other. It might be argued that since Palestine and the Palestinians have been returned to the geographic and legal map that international law, and with it the international community, have made restitution for past omissions. However, it has been the international community that has stood and applauded the signing of the legal agreements of the Oslo process although none of them specify that their aim is the achievement of self-determination. Within the Oslo agreements the Palestinians are enframed within a process of negotiating an outcome with the Israelis. The Palestinians have nonetheless taken significant steps in developing their own legal narratives through using the institutions of the Palestinian Authority, debating a Basic Law,[48] creating law schools,[49] and in elaborating a new legal system. In a sense the Oslo process offered the Palestinians the possibility of struggling for self-determination through institution building. Through this development a new departure in the law story of the Palestinians developed too.

In law schools around the world students of international law are often asked the question "is international law, law?" This positivist question diverts them and us all from the real question "is international law, international?" The question of Palestine and international law highlights the answer to the question in our postcolonial world.[50] International law and its discourse derive from the colonial period and have a postcolonial reality. If international law is to become international it must become a discourse which includes the peoples and their legal cultures which were excluded by colonialism. It is with the excluded started to wrestle for a presence within the discourse that the process can begin. However, the dominant forces within the international legal community must participate too. The Palestinian cause must serve as a terrible lesson of how colonial and postcolonial international law can be complicit in injustice. To learn that lesson requires a reconstruction of international legal discourse. For the "existing non-Jewish communities" in Palestine this cannot come too soon.

Notes

1. See EDWARD W. SAID, THE POLITICS OF DISPOSSESSION: THE STRUGGLE FOR PALESTINIAN SELF-DETERMINATION 1969–1994 (1994).

2. See especially RONEN SHAMIR, THE COLONIES OF LAW: COLONIALISM, ZIONISM AND LAW IN EARLY MANDATE PALESTINE 6–29 (2000).

3. The central legal texts of the Oslo process are: Israel-Palestine Liberation Organization Declaration on Interim Self-Government Arrangements, September 13 1993, 32 I.L.M. 1525 (1993); Israel-Palestine Liberation Organization Agreement on the Gaza Strip and the Jericho Area May 4 1994, 33 I..L.M.622 (1994); Israeli-Palestinian Interim Agreement on the West Bank and the Gaza Strip, September 28 1995, 35 I.L.M. 650 (1996). There are four other additional texts which implement aspects of these agreements, the Hebron Agreement (January 1997), the Wye Plantation Agreement (October 1998), the Sharm al Sheikh Agreement (September 1999), and the Protocol on the Safe Passage Between the West Bank and the Gaza Strip (October 1999).

4. Supra note 2, at six, the source being the Peel Commission, 1937.

5. There is an entire body of work on this issue see for example W. F. BOUSTANY, THE PALESTINE MANDATE, INVALID AND IMPRACTICABLE (1936); HENRY CATTAN, PALESTINE AND INTERNATIONAL LAW: LEGAL ASPECTS OF THE ARAB-ISRAELI CONFLICT (1976); MUSA E. MAZZAWI, PALESTINE AND THE LAW: GUIDELINES FOR THE RESOLUTION OF THE ARAB-ISRAELI CONFLICT (1997).

6. See for example GEORGE EMILE BISHARAT, PALESTINIAN LAWYERS AND THE ISRAELI RULE OF LAW: LAW AND DISORDER IN THE WEST BANK (1989); INT'L L. AND THE ADMIN. OF OCCUPIED TERRITORIES: WEST BANK AND GAZA, 1967–1987 (Emma Playfair ed., 1992) and EYAL BENVENISTI, THE INT'L L. OF OCCUPATION (1993).

7. PAUL J.I.M. DE WAART, DYNAMICS OF SELF-DETERMINATION IN PALESTINE: PROTECTION OF PEOPLES AS A HUMAN RIGHT (1994).

8. Id., 54.

9. See NUR MASALHA, THE EXPULSION OF THE PALESTINIANS AND THE CONCEPT OF "TRANSFER" IN ZIONIST POLITICAL THOUGHT 1882–1948 (1992).

10. For recent example of this see especially BENJAMIN NETANYAHU, A PLACE AMONG THE NATIONS: ISRAEL AND THE WORLD 329–357 (1993).

11. The Balfour Declaration, November 2, 1917 in the reference documents section of <http://www.israel.org/mfa>.

12. JAN SMUTS, THE LEAGUE OF NATIONS: A PROGRAMME FOR THE PEACE CONFERENCE 3 (1918).

13. Id., 5.

14. Id., 4.

15. NORMAN BENTWICH, THE MANDATE SYSTEM 21 (1930).

16. Id., 24.
17. Id., 27.
18. Id., 12.
19. Id., 17.
20. Id., 27–28
21. Supra note 12.
22. See DAVID FROMKIN, A PEACE TO END ALL PEACE: CREATING THE MODERN MIDDLE EAST 1914–1922, at 450 (1989).
23. Supra note 15, at 28.
24. HERBERT SAMUEL, ZIONISM: ITS IDEALS AND PRACTICAL HOPES 2 (1920). This was a speech delivered on November 2 1919, the second anniversary of the Balfour Declaration.
25. Id.
26. Id., 3.
27. Id.
28. Id.
29. Supra note 15, at 34.
30. Id.
31. NORMAN AND HELEN BENTWICH, MANDATE MEMORIES 1918–1948, AT 221–222 (1965).
32. Id., 22
33. Id., 23.
34. NORMAN BENTWICH, ISRAEL RESURGENT 168 (1960).
35. In October 1956 47 Palestinian villagers of Kafr Qassim were murdered by Israeli troops who were allegedly enforcing a curfew imposed on the villagers while many were still working in the fields. Eventually 11 officers were found guilty. One Major Malinki who was sentenced to 17 years for the murder of 47 people served only three years before being pardoned; he then gained a key security post at the nuclear installation at Dimona. See NUR MASALHA, A LAND WITHOUT A PEOPLE: ISRAEL, TRANSFER AND THE PALESTINIANS 1949–1996, at 21–35 (1997).
36. Id., 180.
37. Supra note 31, at 226.
38. Shamir, supra note 2, at 11.
39. For another Israeli attempt to come to grips with the British origins of Israel's law see: Asaf Likhovski, *In Our Image: Colonial Discourse and the Anglicization of the Law of Mandatory Palestine*, 29 ISRAEL L. REV. 291–359 (1995).
40. This remains true today, but was especially the case during the Premiership of Benjamin Netanyahu (1996–1999): see John Strawson, *Netanyahu's Oslo: Peace in the Slow Lane*, 8 SOUNDINGS 49–60 (1998).
41. URI SAVIR, THE PROCESS: 1,100 DAYS THAT CHANGED THE MIDDLE EAST 216 (1999).
42. For discussions on the Oslo process see THE ARAB-ISRAELI ACCORDS: LEGAL PERSPECTIVES (Eugene Cotran and Chibli Mallat eds., 1996) and RAJA SHEHADEH, FROM OCCUPATION TO INTERIM ACCORDS: ISRAEL AND THE OCCUPIED TERRITORIES (1997).
43. See Declaration on the Granting of Independence to Colonial Peoples and Territories, UN General Assembly Resolution 1514(XV) and its accompanying GA Resolution 1541(XV); the common article 1 of the two International Covenants on Human Rights (1966); and the Declaration on Principles of International Law Concerning Friendly Relations and Co-operation among States in accordance with the United Nations Charter, UN General Assembly Resolution 2625(XXV).

44. See Namibia Case, 1971 I.C.J. 16; and the Western Sahara Case, 1975 I.C.J. 12.

45. For an interesting review of this resolution 50 years afterwards see Walid Khalidi, *Revisiting the UN Partition Resolution*, 28 J. PALESTINE STUD. 5–21 (1997).

46. On this issue see AVI SHLAIM, THE POLITICS OF PARTITION: KING ABDULLAH, THE ZIONISTS AND PALESTINE, 1921–1951 (1988).

47. See ALLAN GERSON, ISRAEL, THE WEST BANK AND INTERNATIONAL LAW (1978).

48. See John Strawson, *Palestine's Basic Law: Constituting New Identities Through Liberating Legal Culture*, 20 LOY. L.A. INT'L & COMP. L.J. 411–432 (1998).

49. The work of Birzeit University's Institute of Law is particularly significant in this respect. In developing the data base of laws in force at the end of each period of occupation in the 20th century, launching a Masters program, and engaging in teaching, research and training projects with the legal profession, it has started a process in which law can be a conscious vehicle of liberation.

50. For a discussion of law and postcolonialism in a variety of situations see LAWS OF THE POSTCOLONIAL (Eve Darian-Smith and Perter Fitzpatrick eds., 1999).

9

Palestine and the United Nations
by Neri Sybesma-Knol

Introduction

The title of this contribution really covers two different subjects. On the one hand there is the manner in which the world organization has sought to deal with the problems concerning the former mandated territory which it inherited from its predecessor, the League of Nations. This has traditionally consisted of aid programs developed to alleviate the plight of the Palestinian refugees, as well as of a series of resolutions, by both the Security Council and the General Assembly, addressing various aspects of the Middle East conflict. These resolutions now constitute the accepted legal framework within which solutions for that conflict are to be worked out. On the other hand, however, there has been the ongoing process of recognition by the United Nations, first of the existence of a "Palestinian People," of its identity, its inalienable rights and its standing in international relations, as it was represented by the Palestine Liberation Organization, and later of the recognition of a potential "State of Palestine." Over the years, and more specifically from 1974, when the PLO was granted observer status by the United Nations General Assembly, representatives of the Palestinian people have acquired access to UN fora in various ways.

For the sake of clarity we will first briefly refer to history and the British Mandate, because we consider them to be the legal foundation of the UN's involvement and of the various United Nations resolutions with regard to the question of Palestine. As these will most certainly also form the subject of analysis in other contributions to this volume, we will limit ourselves to a general overview of the most important resolutions and decisions, followed by a listing of the United Nations bodies established to implement them, and the activities of these bodies.

In our opinion, however, history and the Mandate also present the legal foundation of a formal recognition of the Palestinian identity by the United Nations, and of its admission to UN fora. Our next subject will then be the question of the "standing" of the Palestinian people, of the Palestine Liberation Organization, and later of the State of Palestine, in the United Nations. We will trace the developments, analyze the possibilities for participation provided by the status of observer in UN fora, and discuss the practical implementation by the Palestinian representatives.

I. THE HISTORICAL BACKGROUND

A. Zionism and the Balfour Declaration

It is difficult to determine the beginnings of the "Question of Palestine"[1] as it is now included every year in the agenda of the UN's General Assembly, but it is maintained that it coincides with the emergence of the Zionist movement during the second half of the 19th century. The re-establishment of a Jewish State, in Palestine, was its primary project. While until the First World War the expansion of Zionism and its impact on the situation in the Middle East had not been impressive,[2] during the war years the leaders of the Zionist Movement campaigned energetically for recognition by the British Government when it became clear that under a "mandate system" which was supposed to be instituted after the war, Great Britain would be charged with the mandate over the territory of Palestine.[3]

In January 1917, Jewish leaders submitted to the Foreign Office an official memorandum of proposed policy in Palestine: the "Outline of Program for the Jewish Resettlement of Palestine in Accordance with the Aspirations of the Zionist Movement." Its main points were that the Jews in Palestine were to be recognized as a Nation, and to be given every freedom (civic, national, political and religious), as well as the right to purchase land and to immigrate.[4] The Memorandum led on November 2, 1917 (after the approval and support of President Wilson had been secured), to a declaration of support for the Zionist Movement by the British Foreign Office. It came to be known as "the Balfour Declaration," because it was laid down in a letter of James Balfour to Lord Rothschild: "His Majesty's Government view with favor the establishment in Palestine of a national home for the Jewish people and will use their best endeavors to facilitate the achievement of this object, it being clearly understood that nothing shall be done which may prejudice the civil and religious rights of existing non–Jewish communities in Palestine...." While Arab leaders expressed their doubts about the feasibility of this plan, they were appeased with promises of independence following the end of Ottoman rule in the area.

The authority of the British Government to act in this matter, and thus the legality of the Balfour Declaration, has been disputed. However, the fact is that its principles became official British policy and were taken over by the League of Nations in the text of the Mandate Agreement over Palestine, concluded with Great Britain in 1922. In our opinion there can be no doubt that the Mandate Agreement over Palestine, as concluded between the League of Nations and Great Britain, was a valid agreement under international law, and recognized as such by the international community of States. As we will see, the International Court of Justice has had ample opportunity to confirm the obligations of the Mandatory Powers as well as of the international community ensuing from the various Mandate Agreements.

B. The Mandate

All of the mandates over the former Turkish possessions, as specified in Article 22,4 of the League Covenant, were to be A-mandates. This meant that the territories in question, unlike other territories under the mandate system, had reached "a stage of development where their existence as independent nations can be provisionally recognized...." Nevertheless, a certain period of tutelage, and more specifically the rendering of administrative advice and assistance, was considered necessary, until such time as they would be "able to stand alone...." For according to Article 22 the real meaning of the mandates was, for one or the other of the mandatory powers to "ensure the well-being and development of the peoples inhabiting the mandated territories" as "a sacred trust of civilization."

This was confirmed by the International Court of Justice in its 1971 Advisory Opinion on the Legal Consequences of the Continued Presence of South Africa in Namibia (South West Africa) notwithstanding Security Council Resolution 276 (1970). The court clearly confirmed its earlier (1948) analysis of the mandate where it stated that "It is self-evident that the 'Trust' had to be exercised for the benefit of the peoples concerned, who were admitted to have interests of their own and to possess a potentiality for independent existence on the attainment of a certain stage of development: the mandates system was designed to provide peoples 'not yet' able to manage their own affairs with the help and guidance necessary to enable them to arrive at the stage where they would be 'able to stand by themselves'...."[5]

All of this led the court to several conclusions:

    tutelage was meant to be temporary;

    the well-being and development of the peoples concerned formed a sacred trust of civilization;

    the eventual goal of this process is "independent" existence in one form or another;

    the tutelage was to be exercised by the mandatories on behalf of the League of Nations;

    whereas the international community, as formerly represented by the League of Nations, is now embodied in the United Nations, it is the United Nations, and more specifically the General Assembly, that has inherited the duty and the right to protect and ensure the rights of the peoples of the former mandated territories. The Court therefore confirmed the right of the General Assembly to take decisions on the mandate over South West Africa, and on the future of the territory.

Every one of these conclusions, it is maintained, is evidently applicable to the situation in Palestine.

C. The Special Case of Palestine

However, in the mandate over Palestine, some exceptional circumstances came to play a major role. In the text of the Preamble to the Palestine Mandate Agreement, several references to the Balfour Declaration are to be found, such as ... that the Mandatory Power should be responsible for putting into effect the declaration originally made on November 2nd 1917 ... and ... whereas recognition has thereby been given to the historical connection of the Jewish people with Palestine and to the grounds for reconstituting their national home in that country...."

On the other hand, the Mandate also explicitly repeats the Balfour Declaration's guarantees with regard to the rights of the Arab population where it provided "... it being clearly understood that nothing should be done which might prejudice the civil and religious rights of existing non–Jewish communities in Palestine...." The question of who is then to be considered "the people" in the context of the mandate over Palestine is not easily answered. In any case, the duality of the mandate, and increasing Jewish immigration into the territory, soon became the cause of deep and divisive conflict. Violence erupted almost immediately.

Great Britain, as the mandatory power, had to try to reconcile the conflicting duties of the mandate: on the one hand to assist in the establishment of a Jewish national home (a Jewish state?), and on the other hand to safeguard the rights of the existing non–Jewish communities in Palestine, the Arab population. Already in 1924, the League's Permanent Mandates Commission[6] concluded that this policy gave "rise to acute controversy: it does not afford entire satisfaction to the Zionists, who feel that establishment of a Jewish National Home is the first duty of the Mandatory Power," and, on the other hand, was "rejected by the Arab majority, which refuses to accept the idea of a Jewish National Home and regards it as a menace to its traditional patrimony."[7]

In 1936, a Palestine Royal Commission, under Lord Peel, came to the conclusion that the mandate was impossible to fulfill. It recommended that the mandate should from then on be limited to Jerusalem and the Holy Places and that the rest of Palestine should be divided into a Jewish State and an Arab State, both to be given immediate independence. The Jewish community were in principle in favor of the plan because it would mean recognition and eventually nationhood, but the Arab leaders would not hear of it. Waves of violence broke out.

The Peel plan having been found unworkable, Arab and Jewish leaders were summoned to London for talks, but negotiations stranded, mainly on issue of Jewish immigration. As the British representative argued before the Mandates Commission: at the time of the Balfour Declaration, there were in Palestine 80,000 Jews and 600,000 Arabs; in 1939 there were already 450,000 Jews. The strength of the Jewish community could not be measured in numbers alone: "it is skillful and self-confident; it is disciplined; it has an economic power which makes its position in the county decisive."[8]

A new plan for Palestine was designed and in the form of a "White Paper" put before the Permanent Mandates Commission that considered it during the summer of 1939. Under the new plan, Jewish immigration would be restricted to 75,000 persons a year, limiting the Jewish proportion to one-third of the total population for a period of five years. Thereafter, Jewish immigration would be dependent upon Arab consent. Jewish rights to build land would be restricted. Independence was foreseen within ten years. The Mandates Commission unanimously rejected the white paper: while it found that the Balfour Declaration had been "a political error" and "an absurdity," and had proved to be unworkable, a plan that in practice nullified the mandate would be unacceptable. The British were to continue to exercise the mandate as it stood and maybe reconsider the possibilities of the Peel partition plan.

For both Jews and Arabs, the outbreak of the Second World War initially meant a truce in their conflict over Palestine. Nevertheless, two important developments took place during that period: Jewish extremists refused to accept this "truce" and from 1942 onward launched terrorist attacks against the British. Later the Jewish cause gained worldwide support and sympathy because of the holocaust and of the often tragic circumstances of would-be immigrants turned away by the British authorities. Also, official Jewish organizations began to look more and more to the United States for support for their case. In May 1942, the American Zionist Association, meeting in New York, adopted a program, calling for a Jewish state in the whole of Palestine, with unlimited immigration, and for the creation of a national Jewish army; it was later endorsed as the official policy of world Zionism.[9]

D. The End of the Mandate

After the War the situation deteriorated rapidly. British relations with Arabs as well as with Jews continued to worsen. A 1948 British proposal to divide Palestine into Arab and Jewish provinces, with local autonomy, and Britain remaining to administer the territory for another five years under the Trusteeship regime of the United Nations (the successor of the mandate system of the League), was rejected by both groups. The British government then decided to bring the problem before the United Nations. It requested that the question of Palestine be placed on the agenda of the next regular session of the General Assembly, and that a committee would be set up and a special session of the assembly would be convened to make preparations for the consideration of the problem. The (first ever) special session of the assembly convened on April 28, 1947. Items on the agenda were, at the request of Great Britain: "constituting and instructing a special committee to prepare for the consideration of the question of Palestine at the second regular session," and at the request of other (Arab) States: "The termination of the mandate over Palestine and the declaration of its independence."

The proceedings of the special session were wrought with procedural questions as to which nonmember states and which nonstate entities were to be heard; in the end both the Jewish Agency for Palestine and the Arab Higher Committee, as well as several Arab States, were given the opportunity to present their case.[10] At the recommendations of its First Committee, the assembly set up the United Nations Special Committee on Palestine (UNSCOP). UNSCOP started its investigations in June 1947; its conclusions were, in a majority proposal, that the mandate be terminated, and that independence be granted, "in Palestine," on the basis of partition with economic union, following a transitional period under United Nations responsibility. The proposal was adopted by the General Assembly, as Resolution 181 (II), at its Second Session, on November 29, 1947. On May 14, 1948, the United Kingdom relinquished its mandate over Palestine and completed the withdrawal of its troops.

II. United Nations Resolutions on the Question of Palestine

A. The Partition Resolution

Resolution 181(II) had set out in detail the delineation of the boundaries between the two states and Jerusalem and the steps to be taken prior to independence; it provided for the end of the mandate and the progressive withdrawal of the British troops; it set up a UN Palestine Commission to carry out the decisions taken and called upon the Security Council to oversee the implementation. It should be noted that both UNSCOP proposals had included basic conditions concerning human rights, including full protection for the rights and interests of minorities, and full equality for all citizens with regard to political, civil and religious matters. However, while the Jewish Agency, dissatisfied as it was with certain elements in the resolution, nevertheless decided to accept it, the plan was never accepted by the Palestinian Arabs and by Arab states. They invoked the principle of self-determination as laid down in the UN Charter, and generally contested the legality of any plan or recommendation providing for the dissection, segregation or partition of Palestine.

It is interesting to note here that there had been a second, minority, proposal of UNSCOP that provided for the establishment of a unified Palestinian State in the territory, under an Arab majority government. While this plan was never adopted, the General Assembly nevertheless had set up a subcommittee to look into it. It was this subcommittee that submitted a proposal that the assembly, before recommending any solution to the problem of Palestine, would request from the International Court of Justice an advisory opinion on eight legal questions connected with, or arising from, such a decision. Those questions together encompassed most of the legal arguments presented by the Arab states, and included such issues as the right of the indigenous population to determine its future constitution, the validity of the Balfour Declaration and its consistency with Article 22 of the Covenant, the duties of the mandatory power, and the competence of the United Nations to make recommendations on the future of the territory without the consent of the population.

Two proposals to submit these questions to the court, as well as later similar proposals relating to the legality of the proclamation of the State of Israel and its admission in the United Nations, or to the status of Palestinian refugees, were all defeated in the General Assembly.[11] In all of those cases, the proposals were rejected with very small majorities. While a large number of delegates seemed to favor referral to the court, others had committed themselves too much to the cause of a Jewish state to want to take the risk of a negative, or even a balanced, opinion of the court.

It may well be that the Court would not have been able to indicate just solutions for the problem of Palestine, which was one of the most difficult, volatile and emotional issues that the UN was ever called upon to deal with. No opinion reaffirming the legality of an independent Jewish state in the territory would have been acceptable to the Arab world. On the other hand, it would have been unacceptable to many Western countries if the court had questioned that legality. Nevertheless, it is maintained here that, if the court had had the opportunity (and the courage) to deal with the fundamental legal issues at an early stage, it would have helped tremendously to clarify the positions of third states, even when it could not have prevented or stopped violence.

The advisory opinions in the South West Africa cases have convincingly contributed to an international consensus on the illegality of the South African presence in the territory. Never after have there been discussions on the legal issues, or on the legal status of Namibia. Maybe the same could have been realized with regard to the Palestine question, where the legality and the meaning of decisions of 55 or 45 years ago continue to be questioned.[12]

B. UN Concern for Refugees:
General Assembly Resolution 194 (III)

The partition resolution divided Palestine into eight parts, ensuring that a minimum number of Jews would be left in the Arab state; within the boundaries of the Jewish State, however, there remained some 497,000 Arabs, as against 498,000 Jews. In the course of the hostilities that followed the establishment of the State of Israel in May 1948, parts of the territory that had been earmarked for the establishment of a Palestinian State also were brought under Israeli control; as a consequence, more than 726,000 Palestinians (half the indigenous population of Palestine) fled to the only parts of Palestine remaining outside Israeli control: the West Bank and the Gaza Strip.

At its third regular session the General Assembly dealt for the first time with the problem of the refugees, in the context of the ongoing conflict in the Middle East. In resolution 194 (III) it tried to deal first of all with the problem of immediate relief and assistance, and set up the first organizations to that effect: a United Nations Relief for Palestinian Refugees, and later the United Nations Relief and Works Agency for Palestine Refugees in the Near East (UNRWA). On UNRWA more below.

However, Resolution 194 also addressed the more fundamental aspects of the refugee question: it provided for the establishment of a three-member "Conciliation Commission for Palestine" which was to continue the functions of the United Nations mediator for Palestine, Count Folke Bernadotte. Following suggestions laid down in a report prepared by Count Bernadotte before he was assassinated in Jerusalem in September 1948, the Assembly stated "... that the refugees wishing to return to their homes and live at peace with their neighbors should be permitted to do so at the earliest practicable date, and that compensation should be paid for the property of those choosing not to return and for the loss of and damage to property which, under principles of international law or in equity, should be made good by the Governments or authorities responsible...."

At the time, the principle of the right to return seemed not even to be at issue: the central problem appeared a question of practical implementation. However, over the years, the return of the refugees has continued to pose serious problems on two accounts: on the one hand Israel's unwillingness to accept such large numbers of non–Jews within its borders, and on the other hand the unwillingness of the Palestinians, and often the impossibility, to permanently resettle in neighboring Arab countries. Millions of Palestinian refugees, and of persons displaced as a consequence of the 1967 war, still remain in refugee camps.

The General Assembly has, in an uninterrupted series of yearly resolutions, constantly reaffirmed the fundamental principles of Resolution 194, and there is little doubt now about its legal significance.[13] The issue is lately getting renewed and urgent attention, since the ongoing peace talks seem to be leading to the establishment of a State of Palestine, and some kind of negotiated settlement, in the near future. Refugees fear that in the course of the negotiations a "deal" will be struck on the refugee question. Individual refugees then stand to lose their rights as established under Resolution 194: the right to return to their ancestral homes and villages or (many villages having been destroyed and the land used for Israeli settlements) at least their right to compensation.

It should be noted that of course Resolution 194 does not apply to those Palestinians who were forced to flee their homes in the wake of the 1967 war. They are not legally considered to be "refugees," but are qualified as "persons displaced as a result of the June 1967 and subsequent hostilities." In any case, their "right to return to their homes or former places of residence in the territories occupied by Israel since 1967" has also been confirmed by the General Assembly in yearly resolutions.[14]

C. The 1967 War and Security Council Resolution 242

The Suez crisis, from the moment of the nationalization of the canal by Egypt, caused renewed hostilities between Israel and neighboring countries. A United Nations peacekeeping force, the United Nations Emergency Force (UNEF), was sent to oversee the cease-fire called for by the General Assembly. However, when in 1967 the Egyptian Government requested the withdrawal of UNEF from its territory, and UNEF 1 was disbanded, hostilities broke out again. By the time a cease-fire had been reached, called for this time by the Security Council, Israel had occupied Egyptian Sinai, the Gaza strip, the West Bank (including East Jerusalem), and parts of the Syrian Golan Heights.

Later that year, on November 22, 1967, the Council adopted Resolution 242 (1967) whereby two principles were set out for a peaceful settlement of the Middle East conflict: the "withdrawal of Israel armed forces from territories occupied in the recent conflict," and the "termination of all claims and states of belligerency and respect for and acknowledgment of the sovereignty, territorial integrity and political independence of every State in the area and their right to live in peace within secure and recognized boundaries free from threats or acts of force." The resolution was accepted by Egypt, Israel and Jordan, but rejected by Syria and strongly criticized by the Palestine Liberation Organization, because the terms of the resolution presupposed the recognition of the State of Israel. While the international community has from the beginning considered Resolution 242 to be the cornerstone of a just and durable peace in the Middle East, it has taken the Palestinians long years to change their interpretation of the legal situation and to be able to recognize the existence of a State of Israel. Only in the nineties, direct negotiations could begin on this basis.

On the other hand, there has been an ongoing discussion on the meaning of the words "from territories": did it mean all of the territories occupied by Israel? There seems to be general agreement on the fact that the land conquered in the course of the 1948 hostilities, even when not included in the "Jewish part" of the partition plan of Resolution 181, could now be considered as part of the territory of the State of Israel, but that the territories occupied in 1967 remain "occupied territory" in the international legal sense. When in the early seventies it became clear that Israel was considering a policy of settlement of the Palestinian and other Arab territories occupied since 1967, and the construction of Jewish settlements had begun, the Security Council in 1979 declared that Israeli policy and the settlements "had no legal validity and constitute a serious obstruction to achieving a comprehensive, just and lasting peace in the Middle East."

There can be no doubt as to the views of the international community on this matter; the Security Council has constantly pointed to the illegality of the settlements and in general of the acts of the occupying regime, as well as of the Israeli policy and laws with regard to Jerusalem. The council as well as the General Assembly have declared that "Israel's decision to impose its laws, jurisdiction and administration on the Holy City of Jerusalem is illegal and therefore null and void and has no validity whatsoever."

D. Resolution 2535 (XXIV) of the General Assembly

In 1969, a remarkable change of terminology occurred in UN discussions and documents. Until then, Palestinians always had been referred to as "refugees," but in Resolution 2535 (XXIV) of December 10, 1969, the General Assembly for the first time specifically and formally recognized the rights of the Palestinian People:

> ... Recognizing that the problem of the Palestine Arab refugees has arisen from the denial of their inalienable rights under the Charter of the United Nations and the Universal Declaration of Human Rights,
>
> *Gravely concerned* that the denial of their rights has been aggravated by the reported acts of collective punishment, arbitrary detention, curfews, destruction of homes and property, deportation and other repressive acts against the refugees and other inhabitants of the occupied territories,
>
> [the General Assembly] *Reaffirms* the inalienable rights of the Palestinian people.

In 1970 the General Assembly, while reasserting its previous demands for Israeli withdrawal from territories occupied in 1967, for the observance of the right to return of the refugees, and for the cessation of violations of human rights in the area, advanced in Resolution 2672C (XXV) the central position of the Palestinians in the Middle East situation in the following words:

> ... *Recognizes* that the people of Palestine are entitled to equal rights and self-determination, in accordance with the Charter of the United Nations; *Declares* that full respect for the inalienable rights of the people of Palestine is an indispensable element

in the establishment of a just and lasting peace in the Middle East.

For the first time in more than 20 years the General Assembly had formally recognized the existence of a Palestinian national identity. The logical consequences for the assembly of that recognition, and the question of who was to be regarded as the representative of the Palestinian entity, we will discuss below.

E. Resolutions and Comments of United Nations Human Rights Bodies

1. The United Nations Commission on Human Rights. The Human Rights Commission of the United Nations was established in 1946 as a Functional Commission of the UN Economic and Social Council. It is currently composed of 53 States. Its mandate was, in the early years, restricted to standard-setting: it prepared such momentous international legal texts as the Universal Declaration on Human Rights (1948), the Convention on the Elimination of all Forms of Racial Discrimination (1965), the UN Covenants on Civil and Political Rights and on Economic, Social and Cultural Rights (1966), the Convention on the Elimination of all Forms of Discrimination against Women (1980), the Convention on Torture (1984), and the Convention on the Rights of Children (1989).

However, from 1968 on, the commission began a tradition to also openly discuss human rights situations in the world, during its yearly sessions in Geneva. These discussions have traditionally been highly political in character, but attract much attention from the media and from interested human rights NGOs. While at this moment almost no country is exempt from criticism in the commission, the policy of apartheid of South Africa and the Israeli policies with regard to the Occupied Territories have been heavily criticized from the beginning. In yearly resolutions, most recently those of April 2000, the commission has strongly condemned Israeli policy with regard to the Occupied Territories, reaffirmed the right to self-determination of the Palestinian people, including the option of a state, expressed grave concern at the continuing Israeli settlement activities, noted with great concern the continued Israeli refusal to abide by the various United Nations resolutions with regard to the question of Palestine, and condemned the continued violations of human rights in the Occupied Territories. It should be noted that all of these resolutions were adopted either with quasi-unanimity or with a clear majority.

2. The Committee on Racial Discrimination. The Committee on Racial Discrimination, composed of 18 experts, was set up under the Convention on the Elimination of all Forms of Racial Discrimination, of 1965. The committee receives individual communications on violations of the convention, and considers periodic reports on the national situation, prepared by the government in question. In its "concluding observations" of March 19, 1998, on the combined seventh, eighth and ninth reports of Israel (UN Doc. CERD/C/294/Add.1,) the committee reiterated its "view that the Israeli settlements are not only illegal under contemporary international law but are an obstacle to peace and the enjoyment of human rights by the whole population in the region...." The same comment was given on "actions that change the demographic composition of the occupied territories," the denial of Palestinians to return and possess their homes in Israel, the demolition of Arab properties in East Jerusalem, inhuman and degrading interrogation procedures with regard to people of Arab origin, and in general the inequality of treatment under the law of the Arab minority.

3. The United Nations Committee on Human Rights. The Human Rights Committee of the United Nations was set up under the Covenant on Civil and Political Rights, adopted in 1966. It is composed of 18 experts, specialists in international human rights law, and serving in their personal capacity. The committee receives communications of states and of individuals on violations of the covenant and discusses national periodic reports. Israel is a party to the covenant, but has not ratified the First Optional Protocol which provides for the right of individual complaint, nor has it accepted the possibility of interstate complaint laid down in Article 41.

In its "concluding observations," dated July 28, 1998, on the first Israeli report (UN Doc. CCPR/C/81/Add. 13), the committee expressed its deep concern that Israel "continues to deny its responsibility to fully apply the Covenant in the Occupied Territories," and lists a large number of apparent difficulties with regard to the implementation of the Covenant, such as "deeply imbedded discriminatory social attitudes, practices and laws against Arab Israelis," violations of the freedom of movement for the Palestinians, and the fact that under the "guidelines for the conduct of interrogation of suspected terrorists" authority may be given to the security service to use "moderate physical pressure" to obtain information. The committee is also "concerned at the preference given to the Jewish religion in the allocation of funding for religious bodies, to the detriment of Muslims, Christians, Druze and other religious groups".

4. The Committee on Economic, Social and Cultural Rights. The UN Committee on Economic, Social and Cultural Rights was set up under the Covenant on Economic, Social and Cultural Rights to receive and discuss national periodic reports. In its comments on the initial report of Israel (UN Doc. E/1990/5/Add.39) in November 1998, the Committee, while welcoming a recent health insurance law, and the recent establishment of an Authority for the Advancement of the Status of Women, nevertheless expresses great concern on several questions. Discrimination, employment policy, the question of "closures," the permanent residency law, land use and housing, a second class status for non–Jewish citizens, and gaps in the educational system are all points of concern.

And then there is the question of land ownership. The Status Law of 1952 authorizes the World Zionist Organization/Jewish Agency and its subsidiaries including the Jewish National Fund to control most of the land in Israel. "[T]he Committee takes the view that large-scale and systematic confiscation of Palestinian land and property by the State and the transfer of that property to these agencies, constitute an institutionalized form of discrimination because these agencies by definition would deny the use of these properties by non–Jews." The committee therefore "urges the State Party to review the status of its relation" with these agencies.

III. UNITED NATIONS BODIES ESTABLISHED TO DEAL WITH THE QUESTION OF PALESTINE

A. The United Nations Relief and Works Agency for Palestine Refugees in the Middle East: UNRWA

As we have seen, after the establishment of the State of Israel and the hostilities which followed, the United Nations General Assembly has had to try to deal with the plight of the Palestinian refugees in several ways, to find solutions for their status, resettlement or return.

In the first place, however, attention had to be given to the question of immediate emergency assistance for the almost 750,000 people who had fled to areas held by the Arabs. Most of them went to the West Bank, others to the Gaza Strip, Jordan, Lebanon, Syria, or further on. UN aid began in November 1948, when the General Assembly authorized the advance of $5 million for relief, appealed to member states to contribute to a special fund and requested co-operation from the UN agencies. On December 1, 1948, an operation, United Nations Relief for Palestine Refugees (UNRPR), was set up on the basis of voluntary contributions from several member states. When hopes for the immediate return of the refugees faded, more lasting arrangements had to be made. The task of UNRPR was taken over by the United Nations Relief and Works Agency for Palestine Refugees in the Near

East (UNRWA), established by GA Resolution 194 of December 8, 1948.[15] Its mandate has been regularly extended, most recently to June 30, 2002.

UNRWA started its work on May 1, 1950 from headquarters in Beirut; it was led by a director, now a commissioner-general. Its activities are concentrating on providing basic health and educational facilities in 648 elementary and preparatory schools, eight vocational training centers, and 122 health centers in 59 refugee camps. All of this is financed from UNRWA's General Fund, made up of voluntary contributions. Separate project funds are allocated to training and infrastructure development. Over the years, however, donor contributions to the general fund have remained below expectations. With the UNRWA registered refugee population's demographic increase mounting, general fund expenditure has declined and the agency has had to cope with perennial financial problems. At its 25th session, the General Assembly set up a working group on the financing of the activities of UNRWA; in yearly resolutions, the assembly has continued to ask for financial support.

Over the years, UNRWA's original program and activities have also had to be adapted to new political developments: first as a consequence of the 1967 war, which caused new waves of persons to flee their homes, this time as "displaced persons"; and then, in relation to the 1982 Israeli invasion of Lebanon, where a difficult emergency operation for the Palestinians had to be set up. As a consequence, both in 1967 and in 1982, the functions of the agency were widened to include humanitarian assistance, as far as practicable, and on an emergency basis, to other displaced persons in serious need of immediate assistance.

More recently, the new context created by the signing of the Declaration of Principles on Interim Self-Government Arrangements by Israel and the PLO, and subsequent implementation agreements, has had major consequences for the activities of UNRWA, which now are geared towards the development of economic and social stability in the territories rather than to emergency relief. In support of the peace process, the agency started its Peace Implementation Program to upgrade infrastructure, create employment and improve living conditions in refugee communities throughout its area of operations. In this it co-operates closely with the Palestinian Authority. Also, the headquarters of the agency have been relocated in Gaza.

B. The United Nations Truce Supervision Organization: UNTSO

The fighting that followed the proclamation of the State of Israel in 1948 ended after several weeks through a truce called for by the Security

Council. The truce went into effect in June and was to be supervised by the United Nations Mediator, Count Folke Bernadotte, together with a three-member Truce Commission, and with the assistance of a group of international military observers which came to be known as UNTSO, the United Nations Truce Supervision Organization. The first group of observers, 31 each of the three members of the Truce Commission (Belgium, France and the United States) were immediately deployed in Palestine and some of the Arab countries.

Despite the efforts of the mediator and the presence of UNTSO, renewed fighting in the area broke out in July. Thereupon the Security Council, deciding that the situation in Palestine constituted a threat to the peace and invoking Chapter VII of the Charter, ordered a cease-fire. Between February and July 1949 separate armistice agreements were signed between Israel on the one hand, and Egypt, Jordan, Lebanon and Syria on the other. In this context, new assignments were given to UNTSO, which became an autonomous operation, under the command of a chief of staff. Its headquarters are in Government House, Jerusalem. UNTSO is financed from the regular budget of the UN. In the process of the general streamlining of United Nations operations its personnel was reduced from 298 in 1990 to 153 in April 2000.

The UNTSO, as well as other UN military observers, were and remain unarmed. They operate with the consent of the parties, and are dependent on their co-operation. They have no power to prevent violations of the truce, or to enforce decisions; nevertheless, their presence often may have a deterring effect. In some cases UNTSO observers have been able to play a role in helping to end hostilities, as in the 1967 war, or in monitoring critical situations, as in and around Beirut, in 1982. UNTSO observers have also frequently been drawn on as a reserve of experienced personnel to be employed in the setting up of other observer missions, in the Middle East as well in other places such as Angola, Haiti, Iraq-Kuwait, and Bosnia.[16]

C. The Committee on the Exercise of the Inalienable Rights of the Palestinian People

The UN Committee on the Exercise of the Inalienable Rights of the Palestinian People was established by the General Assembly in 1975. It was originally composed of 20 member states chosen by the General Assembly, but later enlarged to 23 members. Its annual reports are considered by the General Assembly, but are also transmitted, by the Secretary-General, to the Security Council. The members of the council have sometimes met the recommendations of the committee with skepticism, and the United States has in the past pronounced a veto on it. Criticism concentrated on the fact that the reports were unbalanced because they only concern the rights of the Palestinian people.

D. The Division for Palestinian Rights of the Secretariat

Following the affirmation of the inalienable national rights of the Palestinian people and the establishment in 1975 of the committee, the General Assembly recognized the need to better inform the public on all aspects of the question of Palestine. A Special Unit on Palestinian Rights was established in the secretariat to assist the committee, and to prepare studies and publications. The unit, now the Division for Palestinian Rights, is part of the Department of Political Affairs of the UN secretariat. The program of work of the division has been constantly extended and now includes the organization of seminars and regional symposia, liaison with interested NGOs, and the organization of staff training programs for the Palestinian Authority. It prepares regular publications and press communiqués on the question of Palestine and on developments in the peace process.

In accordance with a mandate given by the General Assembly in 1991, the division established a website, the UN Information System on the Question of Palestine (UNISPAL) and has been gradually developing it. Its main objective is to provide users with full-text documents of the UN system relevant to the question of Palestine and the Arab-Israeli conflict in the Middle East. It now lists more than 3,000 documents.

E. The Special Committee to Investigate Israeli Practices Affecting the Human Rights of the Palestinian People and Other Arabs of the Occupied Territories

The special committee was established in 1968; it reports to the General Assembly on the current situation in the occupied territories with regard to such aspects as Israeli settlements, the applicability of the Geneva Convention Relative to the Protection of Civilian Persons in Time of War, and the right to return of the Palestinian refugees. The committee is composed of three member states appointed by the President of the General Assembly.

The members of the committee are not in a position to conduct inspections on the spot. Rather, their annual report presents specific data as contained in a summary of relevant articles appearing in the newspapers

Ha'aretz and the *Jerusalem Post* published in Israel, and articles appearing in the *Jerusalem Post* published in the Occupied Territories. The report is considered annually by the General Assembly

IV. The Palestinian Presence in the United Nations

A. The UN's Recognition of Palestinians as a People, and of the PLO as Their Authentic Representative

As we have seen above, it was only in the early seventies that the question of Palestine was put on the agenda of the General Assembly again and that the assembly recognized the existence of a Palestinian identity. At its 29th session, in 1974, the assembly recognized the Palestine Liberation Organization as the authentic representative of the Palestinian People, and invited it to participate in its deliberations on the question of Palestine in its plenary meetings (GA Res. 3210 (XXIX). At the same session, the assembly reaffirmed the inalienable rights of the Palestinian people in Palestine, emphasizing that their realization was indispensable for the solution of the conflict in the Middle East (GA Res. 3236 (XXIX). The assembly also invited the PLO to participate, in the capacity of observer, in its sessions and its work and in all international conferences convened under its auspices; it considered that the PLO was similarly entitled with regard to all international conferences convened by other organs of the United Nations (GA Res. 3237 (XXIX).[17]

B. Observer Status for the PLO

1. The Admission of Observers in the United Nations. Establishing working relations with non–United Nations entities has always been of high priority for the organization. Relationships with nonmember states have been set up almost from the beginning, when nonmember Switzerland established a permanent observer mission at headquarters. In the case of sovereign states, this does not normally pose any diplomatic difficulties: the Secretary-General is officially notified of the event. Over the years, a number of states have followed the example of Switzerland; most of them have now become members of the UN. At this moment only Switzerland and the Holy See maintain observer missions at headquarters.

The situation is different in the case of other entities that want to "observe" the United Nations, and participate in its activities. In that case, an official decision of the General Assembly is required, stating the purpose and the modalities of the observer relationship. There are several categories. In the first place, there are: "Intergovernmental Organizations which have Received a Standing Invitation to participate in the Sessions and Work of the General Assembly." Under this heading the most important regional organizations, such as the Organization of American States, the League of Arab States, the Organization of African Unity, were initially invited. At this moment, however, the list of these observers has grown to some 30 organizations, concerned with all aspects of international cooperation. It provides interesting proof of the ever-widening scope of United Nations activities.

The second category, under the heading "Other Organizations that Have Received a Standing Invitation to Participate in the Sessions and Work of the General Assembly," is composed of the national liberation movements recognized by the Organization for African Unity and the Arab League respectively. For years representatives of those movement had been regularly invited to the United Nations to participate in the discussions of the "Committee on the Implementation of the Declaration on the Granting of Independence to Colonial Countries and Peoples" of specific interest to them, and some had established relationships with other relevant United Nations bodies until, in 1974, they were accorded official observer status by the General Assembly. At the peak of the decolonization period some 17 liberation movements had a standing invitation to participate in UN-discussions related to their specific interests and problems. The PLO belonged to this category.

A third category has more recently been added to the list. They are the International Committee of the Red Cross, the International Federation of Red Cross and Red Crescent Societies, and the Sovereign Military Order of Malta.[18]

2. Access and Modalities for the Participation of Observers in the Work of the Organization. Among the most important facilities granted to invitees of the United Nations is the arrangement for access to the host country and to headquarters. These arrangements are laid down in the respective headquarters agreements, concluded between the organization and the host countries. In principle, the host country is under an obligation to grant the appropriate visas.

Access of observers to United Nations organs has never been systematically regulated, but takes place on the basis of countless ad hoc decisions, taken by presiding officers whenever the question posed itself. Nevertheless, certain rules have been developed.

With regard to the General Assembly; nonmembers have access to the main committees in the discussion of items with which they are particularly concerned. Access to the plenary has been extremely rare. Occasionally, there have been addresses by important personalities, such as the Pope. Intergovernmental organizations have been granted access to the main committees on the basis of the relevant resolutions and decisions. Liberation movements have in-principle access to the main committees to participate in discussions of particular interest to them.

With regard to the Security Council, Articles 31 and 32 and Rule 37 of the Provisional Rules of Procedure of the Council provide for the participation of a nonmember State in the debate, if it is a party to a dispute under consideration. Rule 39, on the other hand, permits the council to invite "persons, whom it considers competent for the purpose, to supply it with information or to give other assistance in examining matters within its competence." This frees the council from any obligation to pronounce itself upon delicate questions such as whether the matter under discussion is a "dispute," or whether the invitee represents a "state." Also, it has permitted the council to invite representatives of intergovernmental organizations to participate in discussions, and has been invoked on numerous occasions to enable leaders of liberation movements to address the council on matters of particular concern to them.

As to the ECOSOC system, opportunities for participation are quite extensive — The Council has repeatedly invited observers. The Rules of Procedure of the Functional Commissions provide for extensive modalities for participation of nonmember states, intergovernmental organizations and liberation movements. Finally, the regional commissions of ECOSOC have traditionally played a pioneering role in the admission of observers; more often than not, nonmember states, intergovernmental organizations and liberation movements have realized their first access to the United Nations by way of participation, or membership, in these commissions.

As to United Nations conferences, the convening resolutions of UN organs usually determine the guest list. Normally, all states, as well as all observers admitted to participate in the work of the General Assembly, are invited.

3. The Participation of the PLO, Successes, Difficulties, and Developments. There is no need to say that many of the decisions on admittance to observership have been highly political decisions. We have argued in the past how the admission of an observer implies a certain degree of recognition by the international community of sometimes disputed entities. Thus, the admittance of certain organizations such as the European Communities in 1974, or certain liberation movements, also in 1974, or of the International Federation of Red Cross and Red Crescent Societies in 1994, have been subject of heated debate and protest from some quarters. It should not come as a surprise that this was also the case with the PLO, and that each step of the way to more complete recognition and to better forms of participation has been difficult.

Nevertheless, the modalities for participation by the PLO have from the beginning been quite substantive, and were expanded over the years: Chairman Arafat was invited to address the assembly plenary, the first time ever for a representative of a nonmember state. In December 1975, the Security Council decided that a representative of the PLO was to participate in its debate, "with the same rights of participation as are conferred when a Member State is invited to participate under rule 37" (of the Provisional Rules of Procedure of the Council). After that, Palestinian representatives have been able to take part in the council's debate on numerous occasions. From 1994 on, the council has invited them to participate "in accordance with the rules of procedure and the previous practice in this regard," which meant that a request for participation was no longer subject each time to a separate vote.[19]

At its 30th session, the General Assembly called for the invitation of the PLO to participate "on an equal footing with other parties in all efforts, deliberation and conferences on the Middle East that were held under the auspices of the United Nations." In 1988, the General Assembly decided that the PLO was entitled to have its communications issued and circulated as official documents of the United Nations.

When on November 15, 1988, the Palestine National Council proclaimed the State of Palestine this act was formally acknowledged by the Assembly; it was decided that, effective as at December 15, 1988, the designation "Palestine" should be used in place of the designation "Palestine Liberation Organization" in the United Nations system.

An important diplomatic victory was booked in 1994, when the assembly decided that Palestine, together with member and nonmember states, was to participate in the Special Commemorative Meeting of the General Assembly at the occasion of the fiftieth anniversary of the United Nations, and to be included in the list of speakers.

It cannot be denied, however, that sometimes there have been serious difficulties. In 1988, a crisis arose in UN-US relations because of the refusal of the United States to grant a visa to Chairman Yassir Arafat to enter the US in order to attend the 43rd session of the General Assembly. The reaction of the assembly was swift and clear: it decided, without prejudice to normal practice, to consider item 37 of its agenda, the "Question of Palestine," in plenary at the United Nations office in Geneva during the period December 13–15, 1988. Chairman Arafat addressed the assembly in Geneva.[20]

On March 2, 1988, the Assembly had already formulated a request for an advisory opinion of the International Court of Justice on another aspect of the host country's obligations under the UN-US Headquarters Agreement: the decision of the US Senate to close the offices of the PLO in Washington, D.C. and in New York. The court was never called upon to address the underlying legal questions and limited itself to the conclusion that there indeed existed a "dispute" on the application and interpretation of the Headquarters Agreement. Nevertheless, it may be deduced from the text of the advisory opinion that there could not be any question about the legality of the PLO's permanent mission and about the duty of the United States not to interfere with its activities.[21]

4. The Present Modalities of Participation by Palestine in the Work of the UN. In 1997–98, the General Assembly was once more persuaded to "upgrade" the status of Palestine vis-à-vis the United Nations and to confer additional rights of participation on Palestinian representatives to a unique and unprecedented level, somewhere in between member states on the one hand, and other observers on the other. A draft resolution, sponsored by Indonesia and cosponsored by 23 other States[22] was put before the General Assembly in December 1999. During the preceding months, the Palestinian side had actively worked for its adoption. A memorandum on "Observer Status at the United Nations and Endeavors to Achieve Full Participation of Palestine in the Work of the Organization" was prepared and distributed, and intensive consultations took place with the European, Latin American and Arab Groups.

On July 7, 1998, the Assembly then adopted Resolution 52/250, entitled Participation of Palestine in the Work of the United Nations, by an overwhelming majority: 124 votes in favor, four against, and 10 abstentions.[23] One of the surprising elements in the vote was the unanimous positive vote of the 15 members of the European Union; while the EU, in intensive negotiations with the Arab Group and with the Palestinian delegation had succeeded in "watering down" the text, its eventual unanimous support added dramatically to the political significance of the resolution.

At present, and as established by the secretariat on the basis of Paragraph 1 of Resolution 52/250 of July 7, 1998, the Status and Modalities of Participation for Palestine are the following:

1. The right to participate in the general debate of the General Assembly. In order to be inscribed in the list of speakers, the Permanent Observer Mission of Palestine will be invited to submit preferences of date and meeting within the period of the general debate of a regular session.

2. Inscription on the list of speakers. Without prejudice to the priority of member states, Palestine has the right of inscription on the list of speakers under agenda items other than Palestinian or Middle East issues at any plenary meeting of the General Assembly, after the last member state inscribed on the list of that meeting. In the plenary meetings of the assembly, the established practice concerning the inscription on the list of speakers under the agenda item "Question of Palestine" has continued. Under agenda items on Palestinian and Middle East issues, Palestine is inscribed on the list of speakers in the order in which it signifies its desire to speak. On all other issues, Palestine has the right to be inscribed on the list of speakers at any meeting of the plenary after the last member state inscribed on the list for that meeting.

3. The right of reply. The right of reply is accorded by the presiding officer, in the order in which Palestine signifies its desire to make a reply.

4. The right to raise points of order related to the proceedings on Palestinian and Middle East issues. The right to raise points of order does not include the right to challenge the decision of the presiding officer, or the right to rise to a point of order made in connection with the actual conduct of voting. Decisions on points of order are made immediately, by the presiding officer, according to the rules of procedure of the assembly. Palestine may not appeal such a decision.

5. The right to cosponsor resolutions and decisions on Palestinian and Middle East issues. Palestine may cosponsor draft resolutions or draft decisions under agenda items concerning Palestinian and Middle East questions, but may not be the sole sponsor. Action on such resolution or decision may only be taken upon request of a member state.

6. The right to make interventions. The right to make interventions used to be subject each time to a precursory explanation by the president. Now the president, at the beginning of each session of the General Assembly, will indicate that Palestine's participation in that session will take place in accordance with resolution 52/250; after that there will be no precursory explanation prior to any intervention by Palestine in the session.

7. Seating. Palestine is seated immediately after nonmember states and before intergovernmental organizations and other observers. In the General Assembly Hall, it occupies three seats as well as the three seats immediately behind.

8. The Blue Book. The Blue Book, "Permanent Missions to the United Nations," now lists Palestine under a new category III: "Entities having received a standing invitation to participate in the sessions and work of the General Assembly and maintaining permanent observer missions at Headquarters."

9. The right to vote. Palestine does not have the right to vote, including voting in elections. It may neither submit its own candidacy for any election or appointment nor submit the names of candidates.

Thus, small but politically significant changes have since taken place in the position of Palestine in UN.

In November 1998, Mr. Arafat addressed the General Assembly plenary under agenda item "General Debate." It was the first time that an entity that was not a member state participated under that item.

There were no restrictions with regard to speaking order.

Seating arrangements for Palestine are now the same as for Member States.

Palestine cosponsored 21 resolutions during the 53rd session of the General Assembly.

The listing of Palestine in the Blue Book under a new heading of entities "Maintaining Permanent Observer Missions at Headquarters" means a change in that formerly the word "office" was used with regard to the Palestinian presence in New York.

At the request of the mission, the title of "ambassador" is now used in conjunction with "Permanent Observer for Palestine."

It is impossible in this context to go into a full account of the many and varied activities of Palestine's permanent observers in United Nations bodies and at UN conferences. However, the Permanent Observer Mission now maintains a website, where detailed information on interventions, relevant resolutions, documents, and daily activities may be found.[24]

V. Conclusions

Since 1948 the United Nations had not been able to adequately address the admittedly multifaceted and volatile conflict over Palestine. UN membership appeared too deeply divided on the question to be able to agree on just and equitable solutions, and impose them on the parties to the conflict. Until the time when an enlarged membership demanded a new approach, the question was dealt with only as an "emergency situation," and the fundamental issues were not even touched upon. Meanwhile the situation has continued to deteriorate.

Only from the early seventies onwards has the organization been able, albeit at first with narrow majorities, to formally pronounce itself on the basic questions of legality and equity, and of the fundamental rights of the peoples concerned. Since then, such points of view, however outspoken (some have said biased) they were, have collected ever more support, until quasi-unanimity now has been reached on the most fundamental issues. Most importantly, the organization has made it possible for all parties to the conflict to be heard.

Nevertheless, the United Nations has so far not been able to play a decisive role in bringing about a durable peace in the Middle East. Negotiations, between Israel and neighboring countries, and later between Israel and the PLO, have always taken place outside the UN context. The beginnings of the "peace process" were brokered by third states in the traditional fashion of open or quiet diplomacy. With regard to that process the United Nations has been forced into a limited role of endorsing developments elsewhere, such as the convening of the Peace Conference on the Middle East in Madrid in 1991, and the signing of the Declaration of Principles on Interim Self-Government Arrangements by Israel and the PLO in 1993, as well as subsequent implementation agreements. In addition, the organization did only reaffirm a number of principles considered crucial for the achievement of a final settlement, such as the principle of "land for peace," and the implementation of all UN resolutions, including Security Council Resolutions 242 (1967) and 338 (1973), which form the basis of the ongoing peace process.

While the assembly has repeatedly recognized that the United Nations should have been able to play a more active and expanded role in that process than has been possible so far, it cannot be denied that the attention given by the organization to a continued discussion of the basic issues underlying the question of the Middle East has contributed significantly to the start of the negotiations towards a final settlement. In particular the fact that the texts of the relevant United Nations resolutions are recognized as a valid legal basis for such a settlement should help to find solutions for the numerous and difficult outstanding issues.

Notes

1. There is of course a flow of literature on the subject. We point here to: UNITED NATIONS, THE ORIGINS AND EVOLUTION OF THE PALESTINE PROBLEM, PART I, 1917–1947 (1978) and PART II, 1947–1977 (1979), and subsequent UN publications. For an interesting analysis of the similarities in the acquisition of international legal status by the Jewish Agency for Palestine and the PLO, respectively, *see* Robert Fisher, *Following in Another's Footsteps; the Acquisition of International Legal Standing by the Palestine Liberation Organization*, 3 SYRACUSE J. INT'L L. & COM. 221–253 (1975).

2. Jewish immigration to Palestine had been limited, certainly up to the First World War.

3. During the First World War, a debate on the future of the German colonies and the Turkish possessions in the Middle East had already started between advocates

of simple annexation, and proponents of a system of administration by "individual European States under the supervision of an International Commission" as was outlined in 1917 in a memorandum of the British Independent Labor Party. The idea was taken over by the British Government in 1918, and later put before the Imperial War Cabinet of the Commonwealth Governments by General Smuts of South Africa. At the Paris Peace Conference, a compromise solution, with varying degrees of control by the administering Governments, was worked out. Eventually it was incorporated in the Covenant of the League of Nations, Article 22.

4. ABBA EBAN, MY PEOPLE: THE STORY OF THE JEWS 345 (1968).

5. 15 I.C.J., at para. 46.

6. The Permanent Mandates Commission of the League of Nations was a body of experts with no decision-making authority but with enormous influence. The Commission members, elected by the Council, acted in their personal capacity. Their recommendations to the League Council were never disregarded.

7. Fifth session of the Permanent Mandates Commission, Report to the League Council, 5 League of Nations O.J. C661, CPM 207 (1924).

8. Statement of Malcolm McDonald before the Permanent Mandates Commission, as described in ELMER BENDINER, A TIME FOR ANGELS: THE TRAGICOMIC HISTORY OF THE LEAGUE OF NATIONS 324 (1975).

9. This program, known as the Biltmore Program (the meeting took place in the Biltmore Hotel in New York) was based on proposals by the then head of the Executive Committee of the International Jewish Agency, David Ben-Gurion.

10. For a detailed discussion of the proceedings, see 1946–1947 U.N.Y.B. 276–303 and UNITED NATIONS, THE ORIGINS AND EVOLUTION OF THE PALESTINE PROBLEM, 1947–1977, at 5 (1978).

11. See MICHLA POMERANCE, THE ADVISORY JURISDICTION OF THE INTERNATIONAL COURT IN THE LEAGUE AND THE UN ERAS 248–249 (1973) and LELAND GOODRICH, EDVARD HAMBRO AND ANNE SIMONS, CHARTER OF THE UNITED NATIONS: COMMENTARY AND DOCUMENTS 564 (1969) for a detailed history of these events.

12. See Neri Sybesma-Knol, The Status of Observers in the United Nations 266–267 (1981) (unpublished Ph.D. dissertation, University of Leiden) and the literature quoted therein.

13. Id. at Chapter X, note 30. It was noted that "The Arab view towards resolution 194 has always been ambiguous: sometimes they regard it as a legal nullity, and at other times as the source of the right to return of the Palestinian refugees. These refugees themselves also see it as the legal basis of that right. But the Palestinian organizations have always considered the resolution, in connection with the founding of the State of Israel, as illegal," quoting Kurt Radley, *The Palestinian Refugees: the right to return in International Law*, 72 AM. J. INT'L L. 586–614 (1978). In our opinion, the right to return has been firmly established by the uninterrupted series of United Nations resolutions and decisions referring to it. Recent events and decisions on the return of refugees and compensation, as in Central and Eastern Europe, also appear to confirm this.

14. The texts of the respective resolutions may be found in the relevant official UN documents, and in the yearbooks of the United Nations. Recently, full texts of resolutions may be found on the UN website: <http://www.un.org/Docs>.

From a legal point of view, it is interesting to note that the basic resolutions on Palestine are now routinely adopted with quasi-unanimity: only Israel and the United States, sometimes joined by Micronesia, vote against.

During the 1999 session of the General Assembly the following votes were recorded:

Res. 54/ 37, "Jerusalem," 139–1–3.
Res. 54/ 41, "Special Information Program on the Question of Palestine of DPI," 151–3–2.
Res. 54/ 42, "Peaceful Settlement of the Question of Palestine," adopted without a vote.
Res. 54/ 69, "Assistance to Palestinian Refugees," 155–1–2.
Res. 54/ 70, "Working group on the Financing of UNRWA," adopted without a vote.
Res. 54/ 71, "Persons displaced as a result of the June 1967 and subsequent hostilities," 154–2–2.
Res. 54/ 72, "Offers by Member States of grants and scholarships for higher education, including vocational training, for Palestinian refugees," 158–0–1.
Res. 54/ 73, "Operations of UNRWA," 154–2–1.
Res. 54/ 74, "Palestinian refugees' properties and their revenues," 154–2–2.
Res. 54/ 75, "The University of Jerusalem 'Al Quds' for Palestine Refugees," 155–2–1.
Res. 54/ 77, "Applicability of the Geneva Convention relative to the Protection of Civilian Persons in Time of War, of 12 August 1949, to the occupied Palestinian territory, including Jerusalem, and the other occupied Arab territories," 154–2–1.
Res. 54/ 78, "Israeli Settlements in the occupied Palestinian territory, including Jerusalem," 149–3–3.
Res. 54/ 79, "Israeli practices affecting the human rights of the Palestinian people in the occupied Palestinian territory, including Jerusalem," 150–2–3.
Res. 54/ 116, "Assistance to the Palestinian People," adopted without a vote.

15. *See* UNITED NATIONS, BASIC FACTS ABOUT THE UNITED NATIONS 40, 96, 172, 255–256 (1998) and more specific UN publications and reports.

16. For an extensive overview of United Nations peacekeeping activities and military observer missions, *see* UNITED NATIONS, THE BLUE HELMETS: A REVIEW OF UNITED NATIONS PEACE-KEEPING (1996). On UNTSO *see id.* at 17–32.

17. For general and historical discussions on the status of observers in the United Nations, *see* RUSSELL JAY, UNITED NATIONS OBSERVER STATUS: AN ACCUMULATION OF CONTEMPORARY DEVELOPMENTS (1976); ERIK SUY, 2 THE STATUS OF OBSERVERS IN INTERNATIONAL ORGANIZATIONS 79–179 (1978); NERI SYBESMA-KNOL, THE STATUS OF OBSERVERS IN THE UNITED NATIONS (1981); Neri Sybesma-Knol, *The United Nations Framework for the Participation of Observers, in* THE INTERNATIONAL LEGAL STATUS OF TWAIWAN IN THE NEW WORLD ORDER 167–189 (Jean-Marie Henckaerts ed., 1996); Neri Sybesma-Knol, *The Continued Relevance of the Participation of Observers in the Work of the United Nations, in* INTERNATIONAL LAW, THEORY AND PRACTICE IN HONOUR OF ERIK SUY 371–394 (Karel Wellens ed., 1998).

18. With regard to the important question of liaison with nongovernmental organizations, or "civil society," an extensive system of consultation was set up with the Economic and Social Council, under Article 71 of the charter.

19. *See* Neri Sybesma-Knol, *The Status of Observers, supra* note 17, at 288–291, for a discussion of the procedural difficulties and discussions accompanying the first invitation of the PLO to the Security Council. While any of the permanent members could have prevented that, the decision to hear the PLO was considered a procedural one, not involving the veto.

20. For an authoritative legal analysis of the question, *see* W. Michael Reisman,

The Arafat Visa Affair: Exceeding the Bounds of Host State Discretion, 83 AM. J. INT'L L. 519–527 (1989).

21. *See* Erik Suy, *Recht und Praxis der Amtssitzabkommen*, 3 VEREINTE NATIONEN 82–86 (1988). Already in 1982 the Legal Counsel of the United Nations had elaborated on various legal aspects of permanent observer missions; see opinions no 32 (Scope of privileges and immunities of a Permanent Observer Mission to the United Nations), 33 (Privileges and immunities accorded to the representatives of intergovernmental organizations which have acquired observer status at the United Nations on the basis of a standard invitation issued to them by the General Assembly), and 34 (Question of what constitutes under the Agreement between the United Nations and the United States of America regarding the Headquarters of the United Nations, an invitation to the Headquarters of the United Nations requiring the Host State to grant admission to the invitees), 1982 U.N.Y.B. 205–210.

22. Afghanistan, Algeria, Bahrain, Bangladesh, Comoros, Cuba, Djibouti, Egypt, Guinea, Jordan, Kuwait, Malaysia, Mauritania, Oman, Qatar, Saudi Arabia, Sudan, Tunisia, United Arab Emirates, Viet Nam and Yemen.

23. Against: the United States, Israel, Micronesia and the Marshall Islands; abstaining: Bulgaria, Congo, Honduras, Liberia, Malawi, Paraguay, Poland, Rumania, Rwanda and Zambia.

24. <http://www.palestine-un.org/mission>.

10

From Ostracism to a Leading Role — Spain's Foreign Policy Towards the Middle East Since 1939

JUAN BAUTISTA DELGADO

I. INTRODUCTION

The international position of a state is said to be determined by its characteristics and by the structure of international society of each period.[1] Thus, it is usually claimed that a state does not have the foreign policy that it desires but somehow that which the other states allow it to have. Spain's foreign policy between 1939 and 1975 was determined internationally by the special nature of the Francoist regime and externally by the Second World War and its consequences, which opened up a new era in international relations. Therefore, in this study more remote historical precedents will be left aside.

Spain's foreign policy towards the Middle East was of a singular nature under Franco, which made it unique within the framework of Western Europe, of which it is a part geographically and culturally speaking. Ten years were to pass from the democratic restoration in 1975 for the normalization of Spain's international relations with Israel to take place when diplomatic relations were established in January 1986. From then on, and coinciding with Spain's membership of the European Community (EC) in the same year, this country has played an important role as the prime mover of important diplomatic initiatives which led to the organizations of events such as the Madrid peace conference in 1991 and the Euro-Mediterranean Conference in Barcelona in 1995.

The aim of this essay is to analyze Spanish diplomatic actions in the Middle East from a dual perspective, namely political and diplomatic, both of which need to be examined in order to appreciate the issue as a whole. Firstly, the characteristics and determining factors of Spain's foreign policy in general and in particular in the Middle East will be examined. This will help to understand the reasons behind certain choices made by Spain's diplomacy. Secondly, Franco's policy in the region will be carefully assessed before going on to the democratic period which started in 1975 and will bring us up to present times, when Mr. José María Aznar is preparing for his second conservative government after gaining an absolute majority in the latest general elections of March 2000. This will be followed by a strictly legal examination of Spain's stance on Middle East issues leading to a series of final reflections.

II. Characteristics and Determinants of Spanish Foreign Policy

A. Geohistorical Determinants of Spanish Foreign Policy

Spain's particular historical evolution, which goes far back in time, was determined by several facts, each with a different interpretation[2]:
- Its geographical position in the Western Mediterranean and its separation from the rest of Europe by the Pyrenees.
- Its complex cultural make-up, with Islamic, Christian and Jewish influences.
- Its position as a great imperial power in the American continent from the late 16th century until the 19th century.
- Its technical and scientific backwardness, leaving it outside the European industrial revolution of the 18th and 19th centuries.
- Its political isolation from Europe until well into the 20th century.

As Roberto Mesa noted, Spain's international relations have been historically determined by three constant and unchanging factors: firstly, the geopolitical situation of the Iberian peninsula between the Mediterranean sea and the Atlantic ocean, as well as Europe and Africa, make it fundamental to the working of the strategic military system of the West; secondly, Spain's economic dependence on the United States and industrial Europe; and thirdly, the casual but relevant fact that General Franco's dictatorial regime died with him. The pact between Franco's political heirs and the democratic forces gave rise to a democratic Spain whose political transition was made possible by, among other factors, setting aside all the outstanding problems of the time. This agreement procedure was ambiguously known in Spain as "consensus" and affected both domestic and foreign policy.[3]

B. A Public Opinion Indifferent to International Affairs

Spain's foreign policy has been traditionally alienated from the great national debates, a fact which has been blamed on its eminently complex nature, leaving it in the hands of experts. This in turn results in the exclusion of public opinion and the building of an area of competence reserved for those experts, not only of arcane knowledge but also of the decision-making process.[4] From the above, one can derive three singular aspects of its public opinion perception of foreign affairs concerning Spain's national interest. This is a legacy of Franco's regime which determined significantly the main lines and options of Spain's foreign policymakers. Rafael Grasa has outlined these determining factors[5]:

- A public opinion of a singular nature within the context of the Western bloc, taking into account: a) its total lack of appreciation of the Soviet threat; b) a strong anti–Americanism, a result of its vague awareness of the United States support of the dictatorship; c) unlike other European countries, the feeling that they owe nothing to the United States for the liberation from fascism; d) a widespread identification of "Europe" with democracy, modernity and progress, which explains the unanimous approval of the membership of the European Economic Community.
- The belief by the main governmental players of the Franco regime that the biggest threat was internal, namely subversion and opposition to the regime.[6]
- A strong split among the Armed Forces, political parties and public opinion with regard to the decision to join NATO after Franco's death.[7]

Besides the influence of the legacy of the Franco regime, the appreciation of the Spanish national interest is affected by the intertwining of foreign security and defense policies that took place in Spain during the transition from dictatorship to democracy.

C. Spain and the Middle East

The Spanish diplomat Jorge Dezcallar, who was the director for many years of the Department for Africa and the Middle East of the Spanish Foreign Affairs Ministry, states that Spain has always paid special attention to the problems in the Middle East for different reasons.[8] Firstly, Spain is aware that the situation in that area affects its own security. There have been four wars in the last 50 years (1948, 1956, 1967 and 1973), the invasion of Lebanon and the *Intifada*, not to mention the more recent problems, such as the Iran-Iraq war, the annexation of Kuwait, Scud missiles over Israel and the Lebanese powder keg. Secondly, the Middle East is a permanent source of instability and in its territory is stored one of the largest military arsenals in the world today. In the Middle East lies the source that feeds the expansion of Islam in two ways: ideological (Iran) and economic (the Gulf States). An Islamic ideology is spreading from east to the west throughout the southern rim of the Mediterranean and coming dangerously near Spanish territory. Finally, Middle East security affects Spain's own security because it is an area of primary strategic importance for Europe and for Spain itself due to Spain's dependence on the region for its energy supplies.

Besides these reasons, the situation in the Middle East has been of historical interest to Spain since the Mediterranean has always been considered a key element of its foreign policy, together with Europe and Latin America. Finally, it is important not to lose sight of the fact that the Middle East is by far the area where most Spanish arms and ammunitions exports are concentrated.[9]

III. Spanish Foreign Policy Towards the Middle East

A. Phases of Franco's Foreign Policy (1939–1975)[10]

Any critical reference to Franco's foreign policy needs to be clarified beforehand.[11]

Firstly, it was an activity which was the exclusive competence of the head of state; i.e., an area of public policy in which General Franco always maintained a direct and particular interest. He shaped it both in terms of strategic orientations and operative implementation in a personal and decisive way.

Secondly, it was an activity almost exclusively reserved for the competent organs of the Administration. Thus, in a regime which denied all civil liberties and where all criticism was forbidden, the checks and balances of civil societies that normally affect the development of foreign policy did not exist. Of course, Parliament did not fulfill its functions of control of the executive that are proper in democratic regimes.[12]

Thirdly, under Franco's dictatorship, foreign policy hardly provoked informed public debate. The press was constantly manipulated and until the 1960s it was subjected to rigorous censorship leaving a great deal of documental evidence in the archives of the Spanish Ministry of Foreign Affairs.[13]

B. Franco and His "Traditional" Enemies: Communists, Freemasons and Jews

According to Jose Mario Armero, Franco was always obsessed with the idea that there was a conspiracy between Freemasons and Communists. In all his speeches, he blamed this conspiracy for the precarious political situation in Spain. Freemasonry was to blame for the decadent situation and was always seeking ways to sabotage the country. This conspiracy was generally thought to be in the hands of foreigners who did not want the prosperity of the homeland and who conspired with Spanish elements, even with the Communists themselves, to achieve this aim.[14]

This myth regarding Freemasonry has echoes of Hitler's attitude towards the Jews, whom Franco sometimes included in his accusations, referring in the official national propaganda to the Jewish-Masonic-Moscovite conspiracy, a mix that causes hilarity from today's perspective.[15]

Franco always put himself forward as an authentic defender of Western civilization against his "traditional" enemies: Freemasonry, Communism and Judaism. However, his political pragmatism and his political survival instincts, led him to a series of concessions.[16] Thus, as far as Jews are concerned, the regime took an ambiguous stance during the Second World War.[17] The General tried to improve the political climate by making use of some isolated actions—but never a general policy—in favor of the Sephardic minorities in the occupied Eastern European countries during the Second World War. In accordance with this, Spanish diplomats managed to help many Sephardic Jews to escape from Greece and from other German-occupied Balkan countries by issuing them with Spanish passports.[18]

Once the Second World War had finished, Franco tried to obtain the support of the Jewish communities and, with that purpose in mind, gave some extremely cordial interviews, among which stands out the one with the noted journalist from The *New York Times*, Sulzberger. After the signing of the agreements with the United States in 1953, the regime made a series of concessions and several synagogues were given permission to open. Nevertheless, the regime never recognized the State of Israel, although this was mainly due to the fact that in the postwar years Israel never showed the slightest interest in being recognized by a discredited regime, such as Franco's, which had always displayed such fierce anti–Semitism in the past. This hostility towards Israel and estrangement from the Jews in the postwar years helped Franco to draw up his pro–Arab policy and the visits by Arab dignitaries in the 1940s made up for the absence of Western public figures, who reproached Franco for, among other things, his anti–Semitism.

C. Franco and the Arab Countries

The regime pursued tenaciously one international goal: its own survival after the defeat of the Axis and its recognition and gradual normalization of relations in the international arena. However, as this failed to occur with the countries of the region, it was forced to adopt substitution policies.[19] Regarding foreign policy, the regime adopted a sometimes cynical pragmatic philosophy contrary to the official rhetoric and based on imperial aspirations and nationalist affirmation in the face of European rejection. With this in mind, Ambassador Armengod claims that Franco's substitution policies were partly a result of this internal contradiction caused by Spain's inability to find its place in Europe.[20]

The Arab countries, which Franco boasted he knew so well, were the object of his attention and relations were handled with special care, although the results were not always fruitful for Spain. However, they fulfilled the role of feigning a minimum of external credibility for the regime. The pro–Arab dialectic of successive Franco governments created a permanent stance that was very difficult to overcome even after Franco's demise.[21] The visits of Arab heads of state were used as a way of presenting General Franco as a statesman whose opinion was heard by prominent figures from other continents. This policy was maintained invariably for years and only towards the end of the dictatorship was the nuance of supporting the Arab countries in their "rightful" claims put forward. Paradoxically, those claims were also directed towards the Spanish overseas possessions in Africa. The Arab world pressed for Spain's withdrawal from the Equatorial Guinea, Ifni (an enclave in Morocco) and the Western Sahara, which were in general terms carried out abruptly and, in the latter case, without any real guarantees for the native population to exercise their right to self-determination. Morocco's independence itself was achieved as a result of mistaken Spanish policy, without any preconceived plan and in a state of pure abandonment.[22] Those ties of "traditional friendship" of the days of the dictatorship consisted mainly of correct diplomatic relations between governments on the same ideological wavelength, but never of a drawing together of peoples. Parallel to the pomp and ceremony of the diplomatic visits and official statements, Spanish public opinion had a stereotypical view of the Arab world very similar, if not identical, to that which was current in European countries.

To sum up, Franco's "traditional friendship" with the Arab countries proved to be a hollow cliché, without content.[23] However, although there was a lot of pomp and propaganda surrounding these diplomatic relations, the regime knew how to profit from them. Thus, at the time of the embargo against Franco, the Arab countries turned out to be useful for his foreign policy.[24] In any case, the pro–Arab policy of the regime proved to be a heavy burden for Franco. The regime was forced to give its continuous support to the Arabs during their successive conflicts with Israel, although most of the U.S. military supplies to the latter passed through Spain. Arab diplomacy was always hostile towards Spain regarding the problem of the Spanish enclaves and territories in Northern Africa (Ifni, Western Sahara, Ceuta, Melilla, Chafarinas Islands and the Rocks of Alhucemas, and Velez de la Gomera). To make matters even more complicated, when the last government of the dictatorship, led by Carlos Arias Navarro, surrendered the Western Sahara to Morocco and Mauritania as a result of Arab pressures, Spain earned the enmity of Algeria, which undertook a harassment campaign in the Canary Islands through radio programs and terrorist attacks by the now defunct independence organization MPAIAC,[25] led by Antonio Cubillo.

D. Franco's Foreign Policy Towards the State of Israel

Historically, the lack of diplomatic relations between Spain and Israel was due to the understandable stance of the new Israeli state towards the Franco regime. When the British mandate ended on May 15, 1948, the National Council for a Jewish State announced to the UN that it would become the provisional government of Israel. This communiqué was based on the resolution 181 (II), of November 29, 1949, which included a partition plan of Palestine with the establishment of independent Arab and Jewish states. The authorities of the new State of Israel sent a note to every country in the world with two exceptions: Western Germany and Spain. Israel's rejection of Franco's Spain was logical.[26] The creation of the State of Israel owed a great deal to the first waves of immigration from Central European countries and the Tsarist Empire, made up of people fleeing autocracy, particularly after the failure of the liberal Russian Revolution of 1905. This must be considered together with General Franco's alignment with the Axis powers during the Second World War and the memory of the expulsion of the Jews from Spain by the Catholic Kings Ferdinand and Isabel back in 1492.[27] With such historical precedents and population structure, it was not surprising that the new state of Israel maintained an intransigent attitude towards General Franco's regime. From then until the end of the dictatorship Spanish-Israeli relations can be described as "negative symmetry": when one wanted diplomatic relations, the other refused and vice versa. In 1949 Spain offered Israel the establishment of diplomatic relations; "not just now," was the Israeli reply.[28]

On May 16 of that year an event took place which left a profound mark on Spanish diplomacy and was to condition relations between both countries for many years: the Israeli vote in the UN against the lifting of the diplomatic boycott of Spain and the stern speech made by the Israeli representative, Abba Eban, who made clear that the main reason for the negative vote was the association of the Francoist regime with the Nazi-Fascist axis.

In the 1950s it was in Israel that voices were heard asking for the establishment of relations but these attempts failed because Spain had already set out its position towards the Arab countries. This was due purely to pragmatic reasons: Spain needed Arab support for the operation which would lead to Spain's integration in the UN and its emergence from diplomatic isolation. Fernando Morán, a veteran diplomat who became minister of foreign affairs in the first Socialist government of the 1980s, explained later that thanks to Arab support, the US operation to integrate Spain into the UN in 1955 was made possible (this time Israel voted in favor).[29] Therefore, from 1948 to 1955, there was manifest hostility by Israel towards Franco. From 1955 to 1970, successive Israeli attempts to establish relations with Spain failed since the international context had changed as a result of the Cold War and Madrid had already defined its position regarding Arab countries; and it had achieved the recognition of its status by the United States and was no longer so interested in establishing relations with Israel.[30] Finally, from 1970 to 1975, the Israeli approaches continued, having as an objective the establishment of consular and official contacts, but not full diplomatic relations.[31] The diplomatic pressure from the Arab countries and the need of Spanish diplomacy to count on their support in international forums in such thorny issues as decolonization of Western Sahara, the so-called "African identity" of the Canary Islands and the future of the Spanish enclaves in Northern Africa, were to be the determining factors of Spain's attitude towards Israel for many years.

Regarding the issue of whether anti–Semitism was present in Franco's policy towards Israel, there are differing opinions, and although this cannot be categorically stated to be the case, there is no doubt that there was animosity and prejudice in certain parts of the Administration.[32]

IV. THE RESTORATION OF DEMOCRACY AND THE NORMALIZATION OF SPANISH EXTERNAL RELATIONS: THE ESTABLISHMENT OF DIPLOMATIC RELATIONS WITH ISRAEL

A. The Middle East Policy of the First Post-Franco Government

The historical period which followed Franco's demise is characterized by two events: the restoration of the Bourbon monarchy and the beginning of a process of democratic reconstruction. In 1969 Franco chose Juan Carlos de Borbón, the grandson of King Alfonso XIII, to succeed him as head of state. When Franco died in 1975, Juan Carlos came to the throne as King Juan Carlos I. Almost immediately the King initiated a process of transition to democracy that within three years replaced the Francoist system with a democratic constitution. King Juan Carlos I confirmed the existing government, whose president was Carlos Arias Navarro. During Navarro's term in office, there was an attempt to establish diplomatic relations with Israel. This initiative was approved by the then Minister of Foreign Affairs, José María de Areilza. Nevertheless, he was not able to take it forward due to the inertia of Spanish Arab policy and the short period of time that he remained in his post.[33] According to the Spanish government, there were at that time some important factors which determined the future establishment of diplomatic relations with Israel: a) it was a matter which fell into the exclusive responsibility of the Spanish government and any interference or pressure whatsoever would be considered unacceptable; b) this event would only take place when it could have some positive outcome for the peace process in the area; c) Israel should hand over the territories occupied in 1967; d) Israel should recognize the Palestinians' right to self-determination. Therefore, diplomatic relations with Israel were not established. With reference to this matter, Mr. Areilza fell back on the usual clichés. He claimed that the Israeli question should be considered within the framework of the United Nations stance, which recognized the state of Israel, and he also said that the time would come when a channel would be found through which diplomatic relations could be established. However, at the same time he added that Spain respected the spirit and letter of the resolutions adopted by the Security Council and the General Assembly of the United Nations on the need for a withdrawal from all the occupied territories, and went even further than resolution 242 of the Security Council. He also spoke up in defense of Palestinian human rights and their legitimate right to a homeland, which was more or less what General Franco said in many of his speeches.

B. Spain's Middle East Policy During the First Government of Prime Minister Adolfo Suárez

The governmental crisis of 1976 ended with Carlos Arias Navarro's resignation and Adolfo Suárez's appointment as Prime Minister. Mr. Suárez was interested in foreign policy and was well aware of its importance, but he had no clear idea of international relations or of the role that Spain should play in the world. On July 7, 1976, the composition of the new government was revealed. The foreign affairs portfolio went to Marcelino Oreja Aguirre, a professional diplomat. In declarations to Spanish National Radio, he stated that, in general terms, Spain's foreign policy would remain unchanged.[34] Mr. Oreja's term in office can be divided into two different periods. The first from July 1976 to June 1977, when the first democratic elections took place in Spain, can be defined as nondemocratic since there was no parliamentary scrutiny of his policy. Nevertheless, his personal democratic spirit was beyond any doubt. The second period goes from June 1978 until September 1980, when he became a member of the first democratically elected government.

Mr. Oreja, through successive statements, laid out the general lines of the foreign policy of his government. He outlined three main areas: Europe, Latin America and the Arab world. Regarding the latter, he said: "The just causes of the Arab nation will always find in the Spanish government all the support which their rightful claims demand. Spain can offer its technological potential and can boost trade with the Arab world. In the cultural field, our geographical proximity to the Arab world and the common aspects of our history make it impossible to put back further the solid development of our exchanges and, of course, of Arab studies in Spain. I mean by all this that we are putting forward common action of great importance." This important statement came as a result of the energy crisis and its impact on Spain's trade balance. The notion of being good neighbors and friends, having a common history and so forth, had not prevented Spain from being treated as a second-class trade power.

When public opinion gradually realized that Spain's pretended privileged friendship with the Arab countries was a failure, Spaniards understood that international affairs were governed by some rules that have little to do with supposed historical links. Franco's foreign policy had also insisted on ignoring the existence of the State of Israel and the official propaganda had made it clear that this was the fault of Israel. However, the real nature of these clichés was betrayed by two events: firstly, Arab terrorism which hit Spain during those years; and secondly, the awareness that despite all the links that apparently united Spain with the Arab countries, it was considered as a colonial power which retained some enclaves on the African continent against the will of their population and neighbors.[35] This Arab stance had been adopted collectively and showed itself to its full extent during the Western Sahara decolonization process. Since then, it was clear that the Arab countries considered France, the United Kingdom, Germany or Italy much more important for their interests than Spain, even though this country had not established diplomatic relations with Israel and continued stating through successive governments its support for "rightful Arab claims" and the Palestinian cause and its legitimate representative, the PLO.

In spite of the change in Spain's public opinion, which had been caused, as we have seen, by the Arab stance towards Spain during the Western Sahara crisis and had put an end to 40 years of official rhetoric, Mr. Oreja followed the line of his predecessors due, in his own words, to "Spain's age-old links with the Arab countries," which made Spain "deeply conscious of their concerns,"[36] and gave rise to "a special commitment towards them and our friendship." Finally, Mr. Oreja insisted that "our support of the lawful claims of the Arab nations remains unchanged and I take great pleasure in proclaiming so." [37]

Notwithstanding this firm position, the issue of the establishment of diplomatic relations with Israel was expected to be solved in the short term. Prime Minister Adolfo Suárez was initially in favor of this but, according to Armero, as time went by, Mr. Suárez found reasons to freeze this issue, probably because of the influence of his pro–Arab advisers.[38] His Minister of Foreign Affairs, Marcelino Oreja, was also probably in favor of the establishment of relations but his civil service background may have prevailed over the politician and imaginative statesman in him.[39] In the United Nations he repeated the arguments in favor of a withdrawal from the territories occupied by Israel, and in an interview with a New York newspaper he even cited as a reason for the nonexistence of diplomatic relations with Israel some sort of diplomatic slight towards General Franco.[40] As we have already mentioned, the conditions demanded by Mr. Oreja for the establishment of relations were the withdrawal from the occupied territories, the creation of a Palestinian homeland and a peace agreement in the area, that is to say, leaving the solution of the relations with Israel in the hands of third-parties, not of Spain and Israel.

C. The "Unión de Centro Democrático" Governments (1978–82)

The first legislative elections in Spain since 1936 took place on June 15, 1977. The triumph was for Adolfo Suarez's "Union of the Democratic Center" (UCD). The main goal of the new Parliament was to draft a new constitution, which was ratified by referendum on December 6, 1978.[41]

Marcelino Oreja remained in the position of Minister of Foreign Affairs in the first democratically elected government. His second term in office took place in the now democratic Spain with political parties, freedom of press and a Parliament elected by universal, direct and secret suffrage. After 40 years, Spain's foreign policy was again submitted to the control of the legislative power and a free press.

On July 11, 1977, the new government's political manifesto was announced. On foreign policy, the target was the normalization of relations with all countries in the world.[42] The government reiterated its policy of friendship with the Arab world, whose rightful causes they claimed to share. The government's stance on the Middle East crisis became more and more radical and it aligned itself with the "hawks" of that time who rejected any agreement between the Arab countries and Israel. This meant that from then on it was no longer merely a question of insisting on the old concepts of friendship and support for the rightful causes. On October 2, 1978, Mr. Oreja declared before the General Assembly of the United Nations that the only way to peace hinged on the enforcement of the UN resolutions and the recognition of Palestinian national rights. That meant that Spain was now aligned with the front that was against the agreement that had been reached in Camp David between Egypt and Israel.[43] The following year Mr. Oreja expressed himself in similar terms before the world forum. A great number of statesmen who visited Spain at that time proclaimed their support for the Arab cause through joint communiqués.[44] The leading articles of most of the official press and television news broadcasts advocated the absolute need for an Arab-Israeli agreement on the grounds of resolutions 242 and 338 of the United Nations.

More important than this was the approval given to the PLO to set up an official bureau in Madrid and the visit made by the President of its executive council, Yasser Arafat, from September 13 to 15, 1979. Once in the capital of Spain, Mr. Arafat stated: "We know that we have close relations with the government and the people of Spain and we cannot forget that Spain has not yet established relations with Israel." When the Spanish Prime Minister, Mr. Suárez, warmly embraced Mr. Arafat, who was clad in his famous guerrilla uniform, this caused great consternation, even among Mr. Suarez's closest allies.[45]

The deep crisis the UCD was undergoing marked its end as a political party. Successive ministerial changes proved to be fruitless and all these circumstances influenced Mr. Suárez's decision to resign from the presidency of the government and the party that supported him. The candidate for new Prime Minister was Leopoldo Calvo Sotelo, who was chosen with the agreement of large sectors of the UCD. During the vote of confidence session on February 23, 1981, there was an attempted coup that failed spectacularly.[46] The fact that this extremely serious crisis was successfully overcome strengthened all the Spanish constitutional institutions and consolidated the so far faltering democracy. Foreign policy should have also been reconsidered and given a new impulse, but those expectations gradually vanished. Mr. Calvo Sotelo then did a volte-face on foreign policy, which became more defined and clearly pro–Western, leaving aside any temptation of divergence from such policies. The new minister of foreign affairs was José Pedro Pérez Llorca, who remained in his post for 22 months. His term in office was merely one of transition, leaving to the following government the resolution of the outstanding international issues.

There were real possibilities with this government of tackling the question of the establishment of diplomatic relations with Israel. In fact, Mr. Pérez Llorca was in favor, but passiveness soon set in. Spain's Foreign Affairs' vice-secretary had regular meetings with Samuel Haddas, who was Israel's ambassador to the World Tourism Organization, with its headquarters in Madrid. Haddas was Israel's "de facto" representative in Spain. The negotiations seemed to be progressing until it was announced that Moshe Dayan was to visit Spain on a tourist visa, when he was really coming to attend some cultural events organized by the Spanish Israelite community. Mr. Pérez Llorca's reaction was very negative. The Prime Minister, who had criticized the former Prime Minister's embrace with Yasser Arafat, seemed to be inclined to break with the anachronism which constituted the lack of relations between Spain and Israel. This opportunity to put an end to more than 40 years of misunderstandings was let slip due to Mr. Pérez Llorca's reaction following the events in Lebanon and the massacres in the refugee camps of Shabra and Shatila.[47]

Despite the good intentions of the members of the different governments during this period, it was clear that the process of establishment of diplomatic relations with Israel would not reach a satisfactory conclusion with the UCD. The reasons were the fear of the Arab world's reaction in the form of a possible oil embargo and the breaking of diplomatic relations, together with the influence of some advisers close to the main decision centers.

D. *The Socialist Governments (1982–96)*

In November 1982, after the general elections of the previous month, Felipe González was elected Prime Minister with the support of his parliamentary group, the PSOE (Partido Socialista Obrero Español [Spanish Workers' Socialist Party]) which had obtained an absolute majority in Congress. The new president had a good knowledge of international affairs, but was undoubtedly more interested in solving domestic problems. Foreign policy seemed to be exclusively in the hands of the Minister of Foreign Affairs, Fernando Morán, whose diplomatic background ruled out any unexpected initiative. His appointment was received with certain objections by conservative factions and the US Department of State.[48] Armero thinks that international affairs and the making of Spain's foreign policy suffered from lack of planning again during this period. Nevertheless, the success of the Socialist governments to round off outstanding relevant international missions must be acknowledged.[49]

The foreign policy of the different Socialist governments continued to be something in which other cabinet members, with no connection with the Foreign Ministry, intervened. Even some members of the Socialist Party Executive seemed to feel that they were entitled to become directly involved in certain international issues. The Prime Minister himself and his staff had also intervened directly on some of them, although the character of some ministers allowed them to act by themselves. In any case, the drawing up of foreign policy was as poorly defined as during the previous administrations and despite the work of the Ministers of Foreign Affairs (Fernando Morán, Fernando Fernández Ordóñez, Javier Solana and Carlos Westendorp) it remained the exclusive domain of certain people or institution, independently of other political and social groups.

The Socialist Party's 1982 manifesto only spoke of trying to encourage good diplomatic and friendly relations with Middle East countries. The establishment of diplomatic relations with Israel was neither among the 100 electoral commitments made for the first legislature nor in the "Ten Points on Peace and Security" (Decálogo) outlined by the Prime Minister Felipe González before the Congress of Deputies on October 23, 1984.[50] However, from the beginning Felipe González was well aware that Israel remained a problem still to be resolved.[51] According to Julio Feo (González's staff secretary), the Prime Minister also knew that Jewish communities from different countries through their respective lobbies would press for the establishment of relations with Israel and that the Arab countries would be against this, but, in the end, they would accept this as inevitable.[52]

Fernando Morán thought that the establishment of full diplomatic relations with Israel would depend on two factors: the self-determination of the Palestinian people and any possible Spanish contribution to the peace process in the region. Despite this, the will to settle this question was clear for the Socialist leaders and the right moment for it had to be found. Some rumors from Socialist circles close to the Minister of Foreign Affairs blamed the Tsahal raids in southern Lebanon for making the establishment of relations difficult. The negotiations with the European Community for Spanish membership brought new determining factors to this issue. It was suspected that some EC countries would press the Spanish government to normalize relations with Israel. Some even thought that the ratification of the adhesion agreement might be blocked in the parliaments of some EC countries through motions put forward by political parties which did not understand the reasons for the nonexistent relations between Spain and Israel.[53]

The first news that the time of the establishment of relations was coming was given by Bettino Craxi, to whom Felipe González hinted that the issue would be settled in 1986.[54] The Spanish Minister of Foreign Affairs, Fernando Morán, thought that this issue could have some very interesting consequences for his country, namely an increase in the Sephardic community's influence in Israeli society and politics.[55] In fact, Mr. Morán was not enthusiastic about the establishment of relations with Israel, despite his contacts in Spain and abroad with the relevant personalities in the Jewish world. However, he waited for the right time and in exchange demanded some inexplicable concessions. He failed to understand that it was only a formal act, because relations existed "de facto" and the repercussions were not damaging for Spain. Rather it was an artificial problem which affected the principle of universality that was meant to govern Spain's external relations.[56] All this meant that it was to be his successor, Francisco Fernández Ordóñez, who took the final step towards normalization of relations with Israel.[57]

After the governmental crisis in July 1985, Mr. Morán resigned and was replaced by Francisco Fernández Ordóñez, whose stance on this issue was in tune with that of the Prime Minister and his staff.[58] When Mr. Fernández Ordóñez arrived at the ministry he found a difficult problem pending on his agenda. As well as the usual reasons for postponing an agreement with Israel, now the addition of Spanish demands and the fear of a possible wave of terrorist attacks were making things ever more complicated.

Moreover, the civil servants in the ministry were more in tune with the opinion of the former minister. Nevertheless, there was a shift on this issue in August 1986 thanks to the personal intervention of Juan Antonio Yáñez.[59]

As the negotiations were taking place, the Spanish Prime Minister from the outset set about preparing all his counterparts in the Arab world for the event. In turn, the Minister of Foreign Affairs started what might be termed "a campaign of information and awareness" through which he informed his Arab colleagues of his government's stance on the issue[60]; it was called "Operation ERDEI."[61]

On January 10, 1986, the Minister of Foreign Affairs summoned all the Arab ambassadors accredited in Madrid. He informed them that in the near future Spain would establish relations with Israel and handed each ambassador a letter signed by the Prime Minister. The joint communiqué by which relations were established was signed in the Hague on January 17. Shimon Peres, who had just started a visit to Holland, met Felipe González on Sunday, January 19. First, they held a meeting with the Dutch Prime Minister and later there was a press conference of the Israeli and Spanish Prime Ministers alone.

The very day of the establishment of diplomatic relations, the Spanish government issued a statement in which it made clear that relations with Arab countries would remain linked to "the traditional policy of friendship and solidarity with the Arab world, which has close links with Spain for historical and cultural reasons." The Spanish government rejected the resort to threat or the use of force to obtain territorial gains, which would never be recognized. The government offered itself as a mediator to seek a fair and lasting peace to the Middle East conflicts in international forums and acting from within the European Community.

Armero states that the negative repercussions of this event were minimal.[62] Iran and Kuwait recalled their ambassadors, who returned to Spain some time later. The Minister of Foreign Affairs, Francisco Fernández Ordóñez, informed the Foreign Affairs Commission of the Congress that the decision had been adopted at a time when tension in the Middle East seemed to be low. The fact that Spain had become a member of the EC on January 1 also influenced this decision. Some precautionary measures were taken, such as the official recognition of the PLO bureau in Madrid and the trip by Mr. Fernández Ordóñez to Syria, both of which took place in August 1986. The Spanish minister went on to visit Israel in September.

Regarding Spain's relations with the Middle East countries under the Socialist governments, they were deeply influenced by the establishment of relations with Israel and there were no remarkable divergences from the policies of former governments. The visits and interviews with Arab dignitaries continued without these excellent relations involving a greater Spanish cultural or economic presence in the Middle East. Despite this, Armero thinks that during the Socialist legislatures there was an ideological rapprochement with Arab countries. This was not simply the result of ideology since it would be more than debatable to say that the Arab Socialist parties were closer to the Spanish Socialist Party doctrine than the Israeli Labor Party. Therefore, the aforementioned author deduces that one should wonder whether the reasons were more the sum of prejudices whose origins lay in the clandestine times of the dictatorship and the clear-cut US support for the State of Israel.[63]

E. *The Conservative Governments (1996–)*

The much-anticipated victory of the conservative Popular Party in the general elections on March 3 brought about a major shift in Spanish politics during 1996 after 13 years of Socialist rule. Prime Minister José María Aznar López appointed a Cabinet, which took office in May. It reflected the range of his party's views—from Thatcherite free-marketers to more paternal, state interventionists in line with traditional Spanish conservatism.[64] Abel Matutes, a Spanish banker from the Mediterranean island of Ibiza and former EC commissioner, was chosen as minister of foreign affairs. The Aznar government maintained the outgoing Socialists' stance on the Arab-Israeli conflict. This coincided with the EU line: a call for the parties in the conflict to prevent not only violence but also tense situations which could cause it. The principles of the conservative government's Middle East policy remained unchanged although with different nuances when new situations arose. Spain spearheaded the EU's position on this matter, and in the declaration of Luxemburg the active involvement of the Spanish diplomat Jorge Dezcallar was decisive.[65]

During this period Spain continued with its bilateral contacts and with a few slight changes maintained the previous government's stance. During the official visit of the former Israeli Prime Minister Benjamin Netanyahu to Spain in 1998, the Spanish authorities demanded that the Israeli government allow the distribution of Spanish aid to the Palestinians, which had been held up at Israeli ports. On the occasion of a tour of the Middle East in June 1998, Prime Minister Aznar reiterated the Spanish position based on four points: the respect of the UN resolutions, the peace agreements, the territorial integrity and security of the states of the region, and the rights of the Palestinian people. The nuances mentioned above were that the Spanish Prime Minister supported US mediation and offered its capital Madrid as the venue for a new peace conference (the Madrid II proposal).[66] Another example was Prime Minister Aznar's meeting with the president of the Palestinian National Authority, Yasser Arafat, in which the Spanish leader managed to avoid committing himself on the settlements policy of the Israeli government and on the proclamation of a Palestinian state.

Despite the fact that as a result of Yasser Arafat's visit to Madrid in November 1998 to present the Wye Accords and ask for Spain's support for the peace process, Madrid asked Israel to fulfill its compromise and respect the principle of "peace for territories," a change in tone can be detected — suggesting a tacit move towards the US positions.

V. Spain's Current Official Position Regarding the Arab-Israeli Conflict

Since the establishment of diplomatic relations with Israel, Spain has been accepted as a mediator by both parties in the conflict, the Arab-Palestinians and the Israelis.[67] Madrid made it clear from the outset that it wanted to contribute to the search for peaceful and negotiated solutions and to bring a Mediterranean perspective to Brussels.[68] The aim was for the EC to pay more attention to the problems on its Southern border, since the "Magna Carta" of the EC on the Middle East, the Declaration of Venice,[69] was at that time already six years old (June 8 1980) and, in the opinion of the Spanish government, it needed to be updated. Therefore, when Spain took over the EC Presidency in January 1989, the government decided to focus particularly on Middle East problems and thus it was announced from the start.[70] The objective was to profit from the "window of hope" that had been opened by the Palestinians following their National Congress in Algiers in November 1988, the start of the dialogue between the US and the PLO, and Mr. Arafat's statements in Geneva and Paris in which he renounced terrorism and declared the Palestinian National Charter to be outdated. The ratification of the Algiers agreement during the summit of the Arab League markedly strengthened the strategic shift of the Palestinian leaders. So, the Spanish presidency became involved alone in a policy of contacts with all the involved parties through constant trips and visits. The result of these conversations was a large working document where divergences and points of contact between the parties were analyzed. This document was drafted by the State Foreign Policy Office for Africa and the Middle East, translated and given to all the EC partners. Its conclusions constituted the basis for the so-called "Madrid Declaration on the Middle East," which was approved by the European Council on June 27, 1989, after heated negotiations. This declaration meant, on the one hand, the updating of the Venice Declaration[71] and, on the other hand, a convergence between the position taken by Spain and that of the EC. For the Spanish government, this was the fulfillment of its commitment to bring a Mediterranean perspective to the heart of the EC. Therefore, it is in the Madrid Declaration and in the unilateral statement of January 17, 1986, which coincided with the establishment of diplomatic relations with Israel, that the nucleus of the Spanish position on the Arab-Israeli conflict and the Palestinian question can be found. According to them, Spain's stance reads as follows in general terms.[72]

1. Israel has the right to existence and security within internationally recognized borders. This security must be internationally guaranteed. The Palestinian people have legitimate rights, among which figures self-determination with all its consequences. Spain will not prejudge the outcome of this process and will accept the will of the Palestinians.

2. The peaceful solution to the Palestinian problem demands the conciliation of the Israeli right to security with the rights of the Palestinians to justice and self-determination. If the terms of this equation prove to be incompatible, the problem cannot be solved by peaceful means.

3. Spain favors a negotiated solution between the parties on the basis of Security Council Resolutions 242 and 338, which stipulate the exchange of peace for territories.

4. Spain does not recognize the Israeli annexations carried out since 1967 (Eastern Jerusalem, the West Bank, the Gaza Strip and the Golan Heights). Therefore, it has constantly and repeatedly called for the withdrawal of the Israelis from such territories.

5. Spain does not accept Israel's declaration of Jerusalem as its capital. The free access to this city must be always guaranteed to everyone.

6. Spain rejects the Israeli policy of settlements in the occupied territories. These settlements are illegal and should be dismantled as a first step towards the devolution of the territories mentioned above.

7. Spain rejects terrorism in all its forms and does not accept that terrorist attacks can be used as a means to achieve political goals.

8. The PLO is the legitimate representative of the Palestinian people and has the right to take part in the peace process negotiations.

9. Spain expresses permanent concern for the fate of the Palestinians living under Israeli occupation and states that the fourth Geneva Convention on the Protection of Civil Population is applicable to the Israeli occupied territories.

10. Spain is willing to contribute, and indeed is contributing, to the

cause of peace and to economic development in the Middle East, both internationally and from within the European Union. As long as peace remains a goal, Spain will contribute to the improvement of the living conditions of the inhabitants of Israeli occupied territories with a worthy cooperation program.

11. Spain will try to encourage an improvement in relations between Israel and its neighbors while recognizing that this will not be easy as long as the Palestinian problem remains unsolved.

12. Spain is against the equation zionism-racism made by the United Nations General Assembly and rejected the Arab boycott against Israel.

13. Israel must withdraw from the area it occupies in Southern Lebanon in fulfillment of resolution 425 of the UN Security Council.

The status of Jerusalem is the most complicated issue for the Spanish government.[73] According to Abel Matutes, its position is clear and based on International Law. Spain does not recognize the annexation of East Jerusalem by Israel in 1967. Thus, and as set out in the Florence Declaration of the EU of June 21 and 22, 1996,[74] the solution to the problem of Jerusalem is not the exclusive competence of Israelis and Palestinians but a question in which the international community has something to say, and its voice must be taken into account. The problem not only involves finding a suitable solution to the religious problem concerning the guarantee of free access to the holy sites of the three monotheist religions, but also ensuring that its political dimension is equally answerable to criteria of international law. However, it is clear for the Spanish government that the solution to the Jerusalem issue should embrace the rightful aspirations of the Palestinian people.[75]

Regarding the conflict in Lebanon, the Spanish government declared itself to be strongly committed to independence, territorial integrity and sovereignty of Lebanon in accordance with the terms of resolution 425. Its stance on the issue of the Israeli settlements in the occupied territories, including Jerusalem, has always been firm and clear and coincides fully with the EU's line, as can be seen in many statements.[76]

As to the peace process, Mr. Aznar has recently stated that the EU, aware of the challenges and the great danger which it is facing, has issued numerous statements which encompass the basic elements of the Spanish position. For the Spanish Prime Minister, the EU must increase its political influence in accordance with its economic commitment without undermining the US role as mediator. In effect, the EU should play a complementary role. This task has been undertaken by the European special envoy in the region, the Spanish diplomat Miguel Angel Moratinos, and consists of bringing the parties to accept a code of conduct, to abstain from unilateral actions and to facilitate economic cooperation: in brief, to reestablish a climate of trust which will enable final negotiations to be entered into concerning the big issues (borders, Jerusalem, refugees) in such a way as to achieve a definitive agreement.

In President Aznar's words, the bilateral relations with the countries of the region are more than optimum. Spain is one of the leading aid donors—if not the first—to the Palestinian National Authority, and the EU is also an important collaborator. It is no coincidence that Mr. Arafat visited Spain twice in 1998. Israel is Spain's first trading partner in the region and has also been active in the promotion of other political and cultural events, such as the opening of a new Cervantes Institute (Spanish cultural institute). The former Prime Minister of Israel, Benjamin Netanyahu, was also in Spain twice that year and Egypt is an economically and politically privileged partner for Spain as well.

VI. CONCLUSIONS

Spain's foreign policy under Franco was determined by the singular nature of the regime itself. Apart from the controversy concerning the existence or not of systematic planning of Spanish foreign action during this period, the fact is that General Franco implemented a substitution policy using Arab countries' friendship as proof of an alleged international recognition of his isolated regime. The Francoist alignment with Arab countries and the systematic support for their claims within the UN,[77] backed by official propaganda, mirrored the anti–Semitic nature of the doctrine on which it was founded and contrasted with the belligerent position of the Arabs in favor of the decolonization of Spanish territories in Northern Africa at that time. During this period, Spain's policy towards the Middle East suffered the consequences of anachronism: the nonrecognition and isolation of Israel and the supposed benefits from the traditional Spanish-Arab friendship did not ever become more than an exchange of pompous official visits and mutually flattering but hollow declarations.

The period which started after Franco's demise in 1975 did not see great changes as far as relations with the Middle East countries were concerned. The center-right governments which ruled Spain until 1982 did not alter policy towards Israel: this was due to a mythical pro–Arabism, inertia, fear and prejudices, as well as the perception by Spanish diplomacy that political and economic interest might be damaged.[78]

From 1981, after the failed military coup in Spain, there was a pro–Western shift in Spanish foreign policy as well as in the Socialist leaders who came to power in 1982. The establishment of diplomatic relations with Israel in 1986 was the logical conclusion of the process of normalization that Spain underwent in the international sphere. Spain, which had followed traditionally the UN stance on Middle East issues, adhered to the EC position after its membership in 1986, both of which gave continuous support to the Palestinian claims.

It is evident that since the establishment of diplomatic relations with Israel, Spain has improved its standing in the Middle East and its diplomacy has made an effort, both bilaterally and within the EU framework, to find a peaceful and negotiated solution to the Arab-Israeli conflict. Initiatives such as the Conference on Security and Cooperation in the Mediterranean and the priority that Spain gave to this issue during its presidency of the EU are proof of this. Its role was reinforced by the selection of Madrid as the venue for the peace conference of 1991, which gathered for the first time since 1949 Arabs and Israelis around the same table. This choice meant the recognition of a more balanced policy towards both parties in the conflict.[79] The celebration of the Euro-Mediterranean conference in Barcelona in 1995,[80] the decisive intervention of Spain in the negotiations on the establishment of diplomatic relations between Israel and Mauritania,[81] and the choice of the Spanish diplomat Miguel Angel Moratinos as special envoy of the EU for the Middle East, show the important role that Spain is playing in the region.

Spain is a medium-size power on a world scale;[82] however, it is playing an important role in the diplomacy of the Middle East. This is due to the links of friendship with the Arab countries and a gradual rapprochement with Israel that has made it a valid and trustworthy mediator for both parties. Thus, Spain is also the leading country within the EU on this question; its membership, while diminishing Spanish autonomy has undoubtedly moderated[83] the country's stance on this issue. Nevertheless, one must not lose sight of the fact that the leading role of peace negotiations in the region belongs to the United States of America. This means that Spain must continually adjust its intervention to those of the North Americans, always aware of its secondary but not unimportant role. Therefore, Spain must continue to implement much more active diplomatic actions, both politically, economically and culturally. The near future may be decisive in finding a negotiated solution to put an end to many years of war. Spain cannot be absent from any negotiations that affect the Mediterranean, both for historical reasons and immediate economic and geopolitical interests. Nevertheless, to achieve this, an effort must be made to improve the drafting of Spanish foreign policy, which, unfortunately, still lacks an overall and well- defined plan of action.

Notes

1. On Spain's world position, see Miguel Herrero de Miñón, *España en el mundo*, in ENTRE DOS SIGLOS. REFLEXIONES SOBRE LA DEMOCRACIA ESPAÑOLA 3–26 (Lamo de Espinosa Tussell & Pardo de Esinosa Tussell eds., 1996).

2. See ROBERTO MESA, DEMOCRACIA Y POLÍTICA EXTERIOR EN ESPAÑA 121–122 (1988).

3. Id., at 66–67.

4. Id. at 77.

5. See *Evolución de la percepción de las amenazas a la seguridad en España*, 26 REVISTA CIDOB D'AFFERS INTERNACIONALS 65–76 (1993). This text can be found on the internet at <www.cidob.es/castellano/Publicaciones/Afers/26.html >.

6. This explains several phenomena regarding the armed forces which are a legacy of the Franco regime: their instinctive anti-Communism, their poor technical training, the deployment of elite troops around the capital Madrid (the paratroop Brigade) and not at the borders, and the overmanning both of soldiers and officials to such an extent that 60 percent of the Defense Department budget was assigned to personnel costs.

7. In fact, a good many who were in favor of joining pleaded reasons other than those of security: to guarantee EEC membership or the loyalty of the armed forces in order to avoid a possible coup d'état.

8. *El conflicto de Oriente Medio y la política de España*, in UN NUEVO ORDEN DE SEGURIDAD PARA ORIENTE MEDIO 97–98 (A. Marquina ed., 1991; *España ante el problema palestino*, 19 POLÍTICA EXTERIOR 13 (1991); *La política exterior de España (política española hacia los países árabes)*, in EL MEDITERRANEO Y EL MUNDO ARABE ANTE EL NUEVO ORDEN MUNIAL 104–105 (D. García Cantús ed., 1994).

9. Figures from the 1980s taken from VICENC FISAS, LAS ARMAS DE LA DEMOCRACIA 33 (1989).

10. From the end of the Spanish Civil War in April 1939 until November 1975, Spain was ruled by General Francisco Franco. The principles on which his regime was based were embodied in a series of Fundamental Laws passed between 1942 and 1967. These laws declared Spain a monarchy and established a legislature known as the Cortes. Yet Franco's system of government differed radically from Spain's modern constitutional traditions and it was, in fact, a dictatorship, see *"Spain" Encyclopædia Britannica Online.* <http://members.eb.com/bol/topic?eu=115200&sctn=1> .

11. See Angel Viñas, *La Politica exterior del Franquismo*, in LAS REACIONES INTERNACIONALES EN LA ESPAÑA CONTEMPORÁNEA 115 (1989).

12. Under Franco, the members of the Cortes (parliament), the "procuradores," were not elected on the democratic principle of one person, one vote but on the basis of what was called *organic democracy*. Rather than representing individual citizens, the procuradores represented what were considered the basic institutions of Spanish society: families, the municipalities, the universities, and professional organizations. Moreover, the Cortes did not have the power to control government spending, and the government was not responsible to it. The government was appointed and dismissed by the head of state alone, see *"Spain,"* supra note 10.

13. Id.

14. *See* JOSÉ MARIO ARMERO, LA POLITICA EXTERIOR DE FRANCO 44 (1978).

15. Franco's obsession with Masons and Jews is paradoxical considering his family background. Franco was the second son of an old seafaring family, who came on

the father's side from Andalusia and had provided navy officers in El Ferrol (Galicia) for six generations without interruption. Franco's parents did not make for the ideal couple. His father, Nicolas, an officer in the quartermaster corps of the Spanish Navy, was a good professional who retired with the rank of vice-admiral. Even though the stories concerning his fondness for drinking and gambling might be exaggerated, he was not an ordinary navy officer. He was an agnostic and freethinker who mocked the conventional morals of his times. He was a very resolute and vehement man who raised his son quite harshly. He considered the piety and Catholic morals of his wife to be somewhat naive and unimaginative, and they became for him more and more disagreeable as the years went by. Of all his children, the father seemed to have shown less fondness for the compulsive and reserved Francisco Franco, whose personality resembled more that of his mother. Despite this, it seemed that Franco had a normal and not specially unhappy childhood, although he showed the same lack of fondness towards his father

The persistent rumors regarding Franco's supposed Jewish forbears seem to be unfounded. However, it should be remembered that during the 15th and 16th centuries proportionally more Jews were assimilated into Spanish and Portuguese society than in any other European country throughout their history. A significant part of Spanish and Portuguese population has some remote Jewish ancestors and, if this were the case for Franco, his situation would not be very different from that of millions of Spaniards, see STANLEY PAYNE, FRANCO. EL PERFIL DE LA HISTORIA 8-10 (1993). The attitude of Franco's father towards his son never improved. Even after the Civil War, he continued to call his son "inept" and insisted that the very idea of his son as a "great leader," as was repeated on a daily basis on the government-controlled press, "was a joke." Don Nicolás was pro–Jewish and hated Hitler, whom he thought would destroy or enslave Europe. He thought that his son's anti–Masonic mania was absurd: "What would my son know about Masonry? It is an association of great and honorable men and, of course, very superior to him in wisdom and openness of spirit." See PILAR JARÁIZ FRANCO, HISTORIA DE UNA DISIDENCIA 59–60 (1982).

16. There are different opinions as to the meaning of Franco's anti–Semitism. Contrary to widespread belief that it was mere rhetoric for the benefit of the ally of the moment, Agustín Ramón Rodríguez Ovide believes that it was an ideology deeply rooted in the regime's doctrine; see RAICES, nº 22, at 14–18 (1995). On Spain's involvement in the issue of the assets of the Holocaust victims, *see* Enrique Múgica Herzog, *España y el oro nazi*, 12 POLÍTICA EXTERIOR 5–22 (1998). The report of the Spanish Research Commission on Third Reich gold transactions during the Second World War ("Report on Nazi Gold R.D. 1131/1997, 11 July") can be downloaded from the website of the Spanish Ministry of Foreign Affairs: Monetary Gold, <www.mae.es/mae/oro2gm/oromonetario/default.html>; Report on Spanish insurance companies, <www.mae.es/mae/oro2gm/seguros/seguros.html>; Spain and the pillaging of European art collections during the Second World War, <www.mae.es/mae/oro2gm/arte/arte.html>.

17. See FEDERICO YSART, ESPAÑA Y LOS JUDIOS EN LA SEGUNDA GUERRA MUNDIAL (1973); HAIM AVNI, ESPAÑA, FRANCO Y LOS JUDIOS (1982); CHAIM U. LIPSCHITZ, FRANCO, SPAIN, THE JEWS AND THE HOLOCAUST (1984); ANTONIO MARQUINA-GLORIA INÉS OSPINA, ESPAÑA Y LOS JUDIOS EN EL SIGLO XX (1987); DIEGO CARCEDO, UN ESPAÑOL FRENTE AL HOLOCAUSTO. ASI SALVO ANGEL SANZ BRIZ 5000 JUDIOS (2000). On the actions of Spanish diplomats, see <www.mae.es/holocausto/Default.htm>.

18. Many Jews succeeded in escaping over the Pyrenees border, though it has been said that in many cases it was due not so much to the Spanish generosity but more to the bribes paid to the Spanish official guarding the frontier posts. However, one of

the most outstanding Jewish personalities, the German philosopher Walter Benjamin, was denied entry into Spanish territory in 1940; faced with being handed over to the Gestapo by the Spanish police authorities, the philosopher preferred to cut his veins with a razor blade, shedding his blood with that of other intellectuals, over the already widely discredited reputation of the Franco regime.

19. The regime's foreign policy towards the Arab countries can be seen as the clearest example of what could be called "substitution functions" in the general scheme of the external action of a certain country. See FERNANDO MORÁN, UNA POLÍTICA EXTERIOR PARA ESPAÑA: UNA ALTERNATIVA SOCIALISTA 18–20 (1980).

20. See foreword to the book LA POLÍTICA EXTERIOR ESPAÑOLA EN EL SIGLO XX, at 13 (1994).

21. See ARMERO, supra note 13, at 54–55.

22. Morocco's independence — in its formal sense — reveals the Spanish head of state's peculiar behavior when he put in motion all his propaganda machinery and mass mobilization in order to turn one of the worst moments for Spanish foreign policy into an apparent triumph. Neither the Parliament, the National Council nor the Official State Gazette mention the end of the Spanish Protectorate in Tangier. Faced with possible criticism, Franco decided to make that date a new "Victory Day," similar to the day commemorating the end of the Civil War, with the Sultan Mohamed V parading through the streets of Madrid surrounded by flags and with the applause of the crowds. It was a national holiday as Franco had ordered. Some time later these loose procedures of granting independence at the last moment were to create big problems for Spanish residents of the former colonies and to strain relations with the Arab countries, which shows that the repeated claim that he knew those states well was false and that Spanish friendship with them was not very reliable.

23. See Felipe Sahagún, *España frente al Sur*, in LA POLÍTICA EXTERIOR ESPAÑOLA...; see supra note 20, at 237–278; MESA, supra note 2, at 162, 235.

24. In 1973, with the Yom Kippur war, Spain was not among those countries blockaded by the Arab league, although the Spaniards, like the rest of the world, had to pay for the rise in oil prices.

25. "Movimiento para la independencia del archipiélago canario" (Canary Islands Independence Movement).

26. See RAANAN REIN, FRANCO, ISRAEL Y LOS JUDÍOS, CSIC, Chap. 2 (1996). M. ESPADAS BURGOS, FRANQUISMO Y POLÍTICA EXTERIOR 178 (1987).

27. See M. Espadas Burgos, id. at 178.

28. See Shmuel Hadas, *España e Israel: Quinientos años después*, 30 POLITICA EXTERIOR 196 (1992–93).

29. Id. Fernando Morán was a main artificer of Spain's Arab World policy.

30. The minister of foreign affairs, Fernando María Castiella, even stated that "the lack of diplomatic relations with Israel gives us prestige before the Arabs." In the early 1960s, any visit or activity in Spain by Jewish personalities or organization was described by the authorities as "part of a perfectly-orchestrated Jewish-Israeli plan." However, the Franco government helped Jewish emigration from Morocco in the early 1960s, most of which went to Israel. Later, the Spanish government intervened in the Six-Day War in 1967 in favor of Egyptian Jews, enabling them to emigrate. At the same time, the Franco's executive carried out a virulent anti–Israeli campaign supporting the Arab countries, see HADAS, supra note 28, at 197.

31. For an analysis "in extenso" of the Spanish-Israeli relations during Franco's era, see J.A. LISBONA, RETORNO A SEFARAD. LA POLÍTICA DE ESPAÑA HACIA SUS JUDÍOS EN EL SIGLO XX, chaps. 6–12 (1993); REIN, supra note 26; MARQUINA and OSPINA, supra note 17, chaps. 4–7.

32. See LISBONA, id., at 108–111, 141–142, 177–180, 271–274; HADAS, supra note 28, at 198.

33. See HADAS, supra note 28, at 198.

34. See JOSE MARIO ARMERO, LA POLÍTICA EXTERIOR DE ESPAÑA EN DEMOCRACIA 41 (1989).

35. Id. at 61.

36. Declarations made to the French Magazine *L'Express*, and published by the Spanish newspaper ABC, Oct. 26, 1976, at 41.

37. Speech made to the General Assembly of the United Nations on September 27, 1976.

38. Najib Abu-Warda claims that the Prime Minister made the condition that an Arab country first recognise Israel and that Israel, in turn, should hand back the territories occupied in the 1967 war, see *Las transformaciones del mundo árabe y sus consecuencias en las relaciones hispano-magrebíes* in *La política exterior española en el siglo XX ...*, supra note 20, 303–334, at 311.

39. During conversations that Armero had with the Minister, Mr. Oreja always displayed an immutable list of reasons which made the establishment of relations impossible. Some were of historical nature, others related to the political situation at that time, such as the oil embargo by the Arabs; others were diplomatic, such as the lack of definition of borders with Israel or the conversations which led to the Camp David agreement, *Política exterior de España en democracia,* supra note 34, at 62.

40. Id.

41. The Spanish people approved with an 88 percent majority the new Constitution, which defines Spain as a Parliamentary Monarchy.

42. When the constitution was ratified, full diplomatic relations already existed with all states except Israel, Albania and North Korea.

43. Id. at 131–132.

44. For instance, the ones issued on the occasion of the visit of the Iraqi vice-president, Senegal's president Leopold Sedar Senghor or Sudan's president, Gaafar el Numeyri.

45. Id. at 133.

46. A group of Civil Guards burst into the Congress and held the Deputies as hostages while the general-in-chief of one of the country's military regions supported the coup by ordering his troops to occupy Valencia. The decisive intervention of the King aborted the attempted coup, and the Spanish defended their democracy. This event further weakened the government and the party in power.

47. Id. at 150.

48. Id. at 153.

49. Id.

50. See SAHAGUN, supra note 23, at 244 and JULIO FEO, AQUELLOS AÑOS 445 (1993).

51. The Six Day War and the tragic dimensions of the Palestinian issue were the events that aroused Spanish public opinion labout the Arab-Israeli conflict. Since then, solidarity with the Palestinian people has been a constant demand for Spanish popular movements and also for Spanish diplomacy to such an extent that, as mentioned below, for adhesion to the EC, some of its members demanded that Spain recognize Israel. As that condition coincided with the goal of democratic Spain of normalizing relations with the rest of the world, the problem was not so much the recognition or not of the State of Israel but how and when this would be done in such a way as to suffer the fewest possible reprisals from the Arabs. See MESA, supra note 2, at 162, 238.

52. See FEO, supra note 50, at 445.

53. FEO says that the pressure of the pro–Israeli lobbies was "in crescendo" in the different European Parliaments as the ratification of Spain's joining of the EC came closer. In particular, Spain anticipated problems with the Dutch Parliament. The Spanish Prime Minister decided to take the bull by the horns and discussed the issue with Ruud Lubbers, the Dutch Prime Minister, and promised him that it would be settled soon after Spain's joining the EC. On the other hand, the Arab countries were not granting Spain any preferential treatment at that time and, as mentioned below, by the end of 1985 Spain had become the second country in Europe most affected by international Arab and Islamic terrorism, id., at 446.

54. By the middle of December 1984 the Israeli Labor Party member Mija Jarish and the person in charge of the relations with Spain in the Israeli Labor Party, Aaron Barnea, were invited to attend the XXX PSOE Congress as observers. Shimon Peres sent a verbal message to Felipe González with them: diplomatic relations had to be established immediately. This could have been a political triumph for Peres against the Likud. Mr. González asked them to assure Mr. Peres that diplomatic relations would be established during that legislature, see FEO, id. at 446. The principle according to which the establishment of relations was a question not linked to whichever party was in power was a criterion which was underlined from the beginning of the negotiations of the Spanish Socialist government with the Israeli authorities. This was disclosed by José Antonio Yáñez — Director of the International Department of the Spanish Prime Minister's Office — when he told two important leaders of the Likud — Rony Milo and Eliahu Ben Eliassar — that Spain would not freeze the issue only because their party was in power and that neither would it be settled automatically if the Labor party were in government. Yáñez insisted that it was not a party matter but rather an issue for their peoples, regardless of who was in power at that time. See FEO, id.; MORAN, *España ...*, supra note 19, at 180. Nevertheless, there seems to be no unanimity on this point as, according to MARQUINA and OSPINA, during a meeting in Madrid of the International Socialist in 1983, Israel Gat, head of the International Department of the Israeli Labor Party, stated that if the Labor Party were to win the elections that were to take place in Israel on July 23, 1984, the recognition on behalf of Spain would occur immediately, see supra note 17, at 322–323.

55. See MORAN, *Una política exterior ...*, supra note 19, at 189–190.

56. As a Socialist Senator since the first legislature in 1978, Morán defended the principle of universality of Spain's international relations. However, as far as Israel was concerned, he always claimed that the establishment of relations would depend on this country's will to negotiate with the Palestinians. Morán was always sympathetic to the Arab causes to such an extent that when he was appointed Minister of Foreign Affairs of the first Socialist government he was vice-president of the Spanish-Arab Friendship Association and member of the Euro-Arab Cooperation Parliamentary Association.

57. At this point, it is necessary to point out an observation made by a key player in Spain's foreign affairs, the lawyer José Mario Armero: there has probably never been an issue in Spain, an international issue, with which Spanish public opinion had been so impatient. To the age-old sympathy of the Spanish people for the people of Israel and their struggle, which seemed to remind them of David against Goliath, had to be added the task which the Israeli diplomat Shmuel Haddas was carrying out in Spain. He spent days and nights talking with all political parties, journalists and businessmen all over Spain. Many outstanding Spanish personalities visited Israel, more or less publicly, and cultural and scientific ceremonies were organized in Spain. In fact, the relations were already full and it only lacked formal ratification and the appointment of ambassadors. On Haddas' activities see his article cited supra note 28; MAARIV,

Dec. 10, 1986; FERNANDO MORÁN, ESPAÑA EN SU SITIO 177–178 (1990); José Antonio Lisbona, supra note 31, at 333–338.

58. Francisco Fernández Ordóñez had stated publically several years before that the establishment of relations with Israel was indispensable, see GACETA ILUSTRADA, May 9, 1986.

59. After Mr. Fernández Ordóñez had informed Julio Feo of the need to speed up the process of establishment of relations with Israel, the latter recounts that the Prime Minister organized a meeting with them and with Juan Antonio Yáñez. Mr. González told the Minister that Julio had passed on his concerns to him and wanted the Minister to know what was really going on with the issue. Felipe González explained to him that there had always been an open channel between his Office and that of the Israeli Prime Minister. He explained the President's Office strategy to them and also why he preferred that the issue continued to be dealt with from his office: on the one hand, the risk of leaks would be smaller and, on the other hand, it was a way of undermining Itzhak Shamir, who was a conservative, whereas Shimon Peres was a member of a brother party. Francisco Fernández Ordóñez seemed to be pleased with the news of the meeting and he understood and supported the Prime Minister's reasons for the issue to be handled by both Prime Ministers' staffs and not their own Ministries of Foreign Affairs. See FEO, supra note 50, at 449.

    i. The principle of universality was one of the secular goals of Spain's foreign policy.

    ii. This did not mean the approval of Israel's internal or external policy, and Spain was to maintain its policy of condemnation of the Palestinian occupied territories.

    iii. This measure was to be adopted to put an end to an anachronism in a country which was closely linked with the EC, of which Spain was to become a member in the near future.

    iv. Spain wanted to make clear its firm will to continue defending in international forums its well-known stance in defense of the rightful Arab causes and, particularly, the legitimate claims of the Palestinian people and their right to self-determination.

    iv. The Minister informed all his counterparts that the decision would be adopted by the first semester of 1986.

60. "Establecimiento de relaciones diplomáticas con el Estado de Israel" (Establishment of diplomatic relations with the State of Israel").

61. The operation turned out well because at that time Yemen was experiencing problems, Libya was involved in a conflict with the United States and Great Britain, Iran and Iraq were at war, and favorable winds were beginning to blow from Moscow. The King and the government of Spain had done a good job preparing, informing and explaining the position to the most relevant Arab countries. This was without doubt made easier by the fact that Egypt had established relations with Israel in 1979 and it had signed an agreement on military cooperation with Spain worth more than $1 billion at the beginning of the '80s. The support of Tunisia, Morocco and the oil-producing Gulf States was also decisive. Even so, the key to the success of the operation probably lay in Spain's firm commitment to grant the PLO bureau in Madrid embassy status and to defend the interest of the Palestinians and the Arabs before the EC. See SAHAGUN, supra note 23, at 258–259.

62. Many Socialist Party members, close to the Prime Minister and the Vice-President, did not hide their sympathy towards the Arab world and against Israel. The President's Office staff, as well as many of the party advisers, were and are still fervent supporters of the PLO. Therefore a shift in Spain's relations with the countries of the

region was very unlikely. See ARMERO, supra note 34, at 220. This may have been the reason for the Spanish government claims that they always experienced difficulties in finding "the right time" for the establishment of diplomatic relations with Israel and made great efforts to prevent any protest from the Arab countries or objection from the most radical wing of the PSOE, headed by the pro–Palestine vice-president of the government, Alfonso Guerra, who had supported in 1982 the demand to expel the Israeli Labor Party from the Socialist International due to the invasion of Lebanon. See REIN, supra note 26, at 333. The anti–Israeli tendency originates from the end of the sixties when the support for the Palestinian struggle became an important reference in the world of revolutionary symbols of the Spanish left, whereas Israel began to be seen as an instrument in the pay of the United States of America in the Middle East. See MORAN, *España ...*, supra note 57, at 171; MESA, supra note 2, at 238.

63. See YEAR IN REVIEW 1996: WORLD-AFFAIRS, *Encyclopædia Britannica Online*, <www.eb.com>.

64. It is important to point out that this official remained in his post after the change of government.

65. See Elvira Sánchez Mateo, *La política exterior española en 1998*, 1998 ANUARIO FUNDACIO CIDOB, <www.cidob.es/castellano/Publicaciones/Anuarios/98sanchez.html>. On the Madrid II proposal, see CONFERENCIA DE PRENSA DEL PRESIDENTE DEL GOBIERNO, DON JOSÉ MARÍA AZNAR, Y DEL PRIMER MINISTRO DE ISRAEL, BENJAMÍN NETANYAHU, Madrid December 3, 1996, <www.la-moncloa.es/interv/presi/p.0312960.html>, CONFERENCIA DE PRENSA DEL PRESIDENTE DEL GOBIERNO, DON JOSÉ MARÍA AZNAR, Y DEL PRIMER MINISTRO DE ISRAEL, BEN JAMÍN NETANYAHU, March 5, 1998, <www.lamoncloa.es/interv/presi/p.0503981.html>CONFERENCIA DE PRENSA DEL PRIMER MINISTRO DE ISRAEL, BENJAMIN NETANYAHU Y DEL PRESIDENTE DEL GOBIERNO, JOSÉ MARÍA AZNAR, Jerusalén, June 29, 1998, <www.la-moncloa.es/interv/presi/p.2906980.html>.

66. Above all on the celebration of the Madrid Conference on the Middle East in October 1991, see Ehud Gol, *Quinientos años y diez mas*, ABC, Jan., 17, 1996, at 16; DEZCALLAR *Un nuevo orden de seguridad ...*,supra note 8, at 99.

67. On January 17, 1986, the day of the establishment of relations with Israel, Spain included the following paragraph in "The Hague Declaration": *Spain trusts that with its membership of the EC it can contribute more actively to open the way to a fair, global and lasting solution to the conflict and will spare no efforts in achieving these goals.* See JORGE DEZCALLAR, LA COOPERACION POLITICA EUROPEA Y EL PROCESO DE PAZ EN ORIENTE MEDIO 14 (1990).

68. See MIGUEL ANGEL BASTENIER, LA GUERRA DE SIEMPRE, PASADO, PRESENTE Y FUTURO DEL CONFLICTO ARABE-ISRAELI 195–196 (1999). This text can be found on the internet: <www.medea.be/en/index204.htm>.

69. The best proof that this last commitment was not made in vain was the intense work carried out by Spain during its presidency of the EC Council of Ministers in the first semester of 1989 to mobilize the Europeans in favor of a negotiated settlement to the Arab-Israeli conflict.

70. The Madrid Declaration revises the EC stance on the conflict, as set out in the Venice Declaration of 1980 and in dozens of communiqués made by foreign ministers; among these, the one which stands out is that of the February 23, 1987, which enshrines European support for an international Middle East peace conference. This text can be found on the internet: <www.pna.net/peace/mdrid_declare__1989_me.htm>.

71. See DEZCALLAR, *El conflicto de Oriente Medio ...*, supra note 8, at 100–101; *La política exterior de España ...*, supra note 8, at 104–105; *España ante el problema palestino*, supra note 8, at 13–14.

72. See Ramón Armengod, *Jerusalén y el proceso de paz de Oriente Próximo*, 54 POLITICA EXTERIOR 31–32 (1996).

73. See <http://ue.eu.int/es/summ.htm>.

74. *Comparecencia del Ministro de Asuntos Exteriores, Abel Matutes Juan, ante la Comision de Asuntos Exteriores del congreso, para explicar la posicion del gobierno en relacion con el proceso de paz en Oriente Proximo, a peticion del grupo parlamentario socialista (BOCG-Comisiones, núm. 66, 9–10–96)*, Actividad Parlamentaria, Comparecencias del Ministro de Asuntos Exteriores, 1996 REVISTA DE ACTIVIDADES, TEXTOS Y DOCUMENTOS DE LA POLITICA EXTERIOR ESPAÑOLA. <www.mae.es/mae/textos/OID/ATDPE/ATDPE1996/parlamentaria/comparecencias/Mae/028.htm>. In his statement, the minister declared that, as far as refugees were concerned, it was a problem which had not only obvious economic and political repercussions but also an undeniable human and social aspect because it affected directly the reunification of whole families who were separated by the Arab-Israeli wars, without going further into the issue.

75. The European Council declaration in Dublin of December 13, 1996, explicitly mentions the problem of the settlements. It says literally that this issue is undermining the trust in the peace process and describes them as being against international law and an important obstacle to peace; see <http://ue.eu.int/es/summ.htm >.

76. During the Franco regime, Spain voted in favor of resolutions 242 and 338. The movement of greatest rapprochement to the Palestinians probably took place in November 1974, when, in contrast with the abstention or negative vote of most Western countries' delegates, the Spanish delegation to the UN voted in favor of resolutions 3236 and 3237 of the General Assembly concerning the right to self-determination of the Palestinian people and the granting of observer status to the PLO. Until then, Spain had joined with all UN condemnations of Israel. See ABU-WARDA, supra note 38, at 309–310; MESA, supra note 2, at 239.

77. José María de Areilza in declarations to the Spanish journal INFORMACIONES, as reprinted by MARQUINA and OSPINA, see supra, note 17, at 313.

78. See Ehud Gol, *La Bar-Mitsvá de las relaciones hispano-israelíes*, DIARIO 16, Jan. 18, 1999, at 4.

79. See the bulletins of the Conference of the Spanish Centre for Peace Research in <www.cip.fuhem.es/mediterraneo/bol1.htm>, <www.cip.fuhem.es/mediterraneo/bol2.htm> and <www.cip.fuhem.es/mediterraneo/bol3.htm>. The text of the Declaration of Barcelona can be found on the website of the Spanish Centre of International Relations: <www.ortegaygasset.edu/ceri/euromediterranea/barcelona.html>.

80. See Ehud Gol, "España-Israel, del Cervantes a la alta tecnología," *La Razon*, Dec. 16, 1998, at 26.

81. See Jordi Palou, *El concepto de potencia media. Los casos de España y México*, 26 REVISTA CIDOB D'AFERS INTERNACIONALS 65–76 (1993). This text can be found on the internet: <www.cidob.es/castellano/Publicaciones/Afers/palou.html>.

82. Despite Spain's membership of the EU and the loss of independence of action concerning foreign policy which it involves, it continues to maintain different positions from those of its partners, something which reminds us of its old secular pro–Arab policy. Good proof of this was Spain's linking of the ratification of the Mediterranean Agreements—sponsored by the EU—to the progressive implementation by Israel of the Peace Agreements with the Palestinians and advances in this issue. In the same way, it was not until February 26, 2000, that Spain lifted its veto against Israel's membership of the European Group in the UN, after strong pressure from the US. Spain was the last country of that group to approve. See "España admite a Israel en el grupo europeo de la ONU tras ser presionada por EE UU," *El Pais*, Feb. 27, 2000, at 3.

Part II
Economic Issues

11

Palestinian Economic Development in the Era of Globalization
DAVID P. FIDLER
FADI G. HARB

I. INTRODUCTION

The Palestinian people have long dreamed of the day when they finally achieved statehood in the international system. Palestinians have struggled for decades to have their right of self-determination — a right recognized as fundamental in contemporary international law — vindicated. While the final status negotiations between the Palestinians and Israel have not, as of this writing, been completed, these negotiations seem to be progressing on the implicit assumption by *all* parties that the end result will be the creation of a Palestinian state. The final status negotiations seem to be, at the end of day, about delimiting the geographical scope of the new Palestinian state and defining the sovereign powers of that state.

This chapter focuses on what looms ahead for the new Palestinian state in terms of economic development. This forward-looking focus is not meant to underestimate the critical, yet still unresolved questions in the final status negotiations. For analytical purposes, we take the creation of a Palestinian state as an inevitable product of the tortuous peace process. Events may prove this position premature or terribly naïve, but we are interested in how the Palestinian state will pursue economic development in the era of globalization.

In talking about a Palestinian "state," we are using this term as it is understood in international law. States historically have been the primary subjects of international law, and international legal rules largely consist of principles that govern the relations among states. Central to the dynamic of international law is the concept of sovereignty. States are sovereign entities, meaning generally that they possess primary power over what happens over a specific territory and population. International law addresses how sovereignty may or may not be used in the international system. Any Palestinian state will, presumably, be a "state" as that term is understood in international law — it will have sovereignty over a territory and a people.[1] A question that Palestinian and Israel negotiators are facing in the final status negotiations, and that we are addressing in this chapter, is what will Palestinian sovereignty under international law mean?

One of the contentious issues currently being debated by international relations and international legal scholars and practitioners revolves around the impact of the processes of globalization on state sovereignty. Many writers have argued that globalization undermines state sovereignty because many global processes and phenomena erode state power and control. Other commentators claim that globalization is not destroying sovereignty so much as reshaping it in a form that resembles the way sovereignty operates in Western, liberal countries. As Palestinians emerge into statehood, these theoretical questions about globalization's impact on sovereignty become very relevant.

This chapter's focus on Palestinian economic development in the era of globalization reflects not only the structure of this book but also the emphasis given to economics in analyses of globalization. While globalization is not merely an economic phenomenon, economic forces and actors have received the lion's share of attention from experts trying to decipher the meaning of globalization for states and peoples. As Gordon Walker and Mark Fox observed, "[t]he key feature which underlies the concept of globalization and distinguishes it from internationalization is the erosion and irrelevance of national boundaries in markets which can truly be described as global."[2] The Palestinian state will emerge into an economic reality that differs substantially from what peoples emerging into statehood in the past have faced.[3] Palestinian economic development will face pressures and challenges from not only the particular nature of Palestinian self-determination but also the globalizing world with which the Palestinian state will have to come to grips.

No one familiar with Palestinian economic development since the signing of the 1993 Declaration of Principles would argue that the Palestinian economy is prepared for the rigors of globalization. This chapter aims, however, to examine this accurate but simplistic perspective by trying to identify how globalization challenges the future prospects for Palestinian economic development. We believe that this question is one of the most important questions facing the Palestinian people, and it deserves serious consideration by those interested in the fate of the Palestinians and of the region in which they live. Our analysis does not provide the final answer to this question because it is, in many respects, preliminary. Our intention is to help people involved in the future of the Palestinian state to think about the consequences of this state coming into being at this moment in history.

II. Economic Development in the Era of Globalization

Before concentrating on the Palestinian economy, this chapter's focus requires us to examine briefly the nature of economic development in the era of globalization. States have long pursued the goal of economic development; but, in different historical eras, strategies for achieving such development have varied greatly. The Palestinian state will emerge into the international system just as it continues through a historic shift in how states pursue economic development. During the Cold War, the international system experienced a great division between socialist and capitalist states on the best approach to national economic development. With the end of the Cold War, this great division has disappeared, leaving capitalism triumphant in the wake of Communism's collapse. This triumph has fueled the processes of globalization in powerful ways that will dramatically affect the economy overseen by the Palestinian state.

A. What Is Globalization?

"Globalization" has almost as many definitions as it has writers who have examined it.[4] Defining globalization is such a controversial and difficult undertaking because the act of definition is laden with normative consequences. Two different definitions of globalization will give the reader a flavor for the normative battleground globalization as a concept has become. Jan Aart Scholte defines globalization as "processes whereby social relations acquire relatively distanceless and borderless qualities, so that human lives are increasingly played out in the world as a single place."[5]

The theme of Scholte's definition is one of nascent human unity, human lives lived in a new, distanceless, and single world—a "global village."

Martin Khor sees globalization differently because he defines globalization as "what we in the Third World have for several centuries called colonization."[6] Khor's definition draws attention to globalization fostering inequality, domination, racism, and exploitation. If there is a global village, it is one in which, to borrow some searing words from Jean-Jacques Rousseau, we should "see unfortunate nations groaning under yokes of iron, the human race crushed by a handful of oppressors, a starving crowd overwhelmed with pain and hunger, whose blood and tears the rich drink in peace, and everywhere the strong armed against the weak with the formidable power of the law."[7]

We do not attempt to synthesize such disparate and irreconcilable definitions of globalization. Our definition is simplistic; but, for our purposes, we believe it appropriate and workable. As used in this chapter, globalization refers to processes or phenomena that undermine the ability of the sovereign state to control what occurs in its territory. So much of the literature on globalization focuses on what is happening to the state and to sovereignty that it seems logical to see the essence of globalization directly in its effects on state sovereignty. As Scholte has argued:

> The contemporary state is quite unable by itself to control phenomena like global companies, satellite remote sensing, global ecological problems, and global stock and bond trading. None of these things can be grounded in a territorial space over which a state might endeavor to exercise exclusive jurisdiction.... Alongside these material changes, globalization has also loosened some important cultural and psychological underpinnings of sovereignty. For example, as a result of the growth of transborder networks, many people have acquired loyalties that supplement and perhaps even override feelings of national solidarity that previously lent legitimacy to state sovereignty.[8]

The undermining of state sovereignty applies importantly in the economic realm and affects strategies for economic development. According to Roger Tooze, globalization produces a fundamental problem in studying international political economy: "the actual or potential structural mismatch between a formal state system based on territory (i.e. nation states) and an economic system that is increasingly non-territorial and globalized...."[9] This structural mismatch poses challenges for states that want to pursue economic development, particularly developing states.

During the Cold War period, many developing countries adopted economic development strategies premised on the idea that governments could control and direct economic activity. This movement reached its climax with the adoption of the New International Economic Order (NIEO) in the United Nations in the early 1970s. The NIEO had two basic goals: (1) to allow developing countries to regain economic sovereignty by reducing the power and influence of nationals and corporations from developed countries in the economies of developing countries[10]; and (2) to increase the power and influence of developing countries in the international economic system.[11] NIEO-inspired economic policies often involved expropriation of foreign-owned property, restrictions on foreign investment, restrictions on imports from developed countries, and centrally planned development of industrial or manufacturing capabilities. The NIEO approach to economic development, along with related socialist concepts of economic development, was premised on the assumption that governments of states could still control economic activity within their respective territories. Under this assumption, there is no structural mismatch between sovereign states and economic activity.

In the era of globalization, the dominant strategies for national economic development recognize that economics has become nonterritorial and globalized. NIEO principles of economic development now lie with Communism, on the ash heap of history. As Tooze argued, "[i]f we now have a 'global' economy ... the ability of the state to achieve its objectives is, at the very least, challenged and, depending on the extent of 'globalization', may be severely reduced."[12] In this environment, the dominant strategy for economic development comes from liberalism or neoliberalism, which "provides the ideological basis for globalization and has become the unquestioned 'common sense' of the world economy."[13] High-profile protests in Seattle at the World Trade Organization ministerial meeting and in Washington, D.C. at the annual meetings of the World Bank and the International Monetary Fund in 1999 and 2000 respectively, indicate that liberalism's hegemony in the era of globalization is not unquestioned; but these protests did little to weaken the grip of liberalism's dominance in connection with strategies of economic development.

It is within this period of liberal dominance that the peace process has painfully moved to the point where a Palestinian state is no longer unthinkable. As part III of this chapter demonstrates, the strategy for Palestinian economic development designed during the peace process bears the clear imprint of liberal economic and political thinking. This strategy was, therefore, crafted with the rigors of globalization in mind.

B. Economic Development and Globalization

Before looking at the Palestinian experience with economic development in the 1990s, a brief overview of the liberal "common sense" of the global economy is needed to outline the basic structure of economic development thinking in the era of globalization. The importance of liberal economic thinking to globalization is difficult to understate. Thomas Friedman has argued that:

> The driving idea behind globalization is free-market capitalism — the more you let market forces rule and the more you open your economy to free trade and competition, the more efficient and flourishing your economy will be. Globalization means the spread of free-market capitalism to virtually every country in the world. Therefore, globalization has its own set of economic rules — rules that revolve around opening, deregulating and privatizing your economy, in order to make it more competitive and attractive to foreign investment.[14]

Substantively, three principles characterize the prevailing liberal perspective on economic development and activity in the global era: (1) national market liberalization; (2) integration with global markets; and (3) market-supportive legal rules and political institutions. In this section, we briefly describe these three principles of liberal economic development strategy.

1. National Market Liberalization. In the post–Cold War period, concerted efforts have been made all over the world to liberalize national markets as part of economic development policies. This strategy is exactly the opposite of what many socialist and developing countries pursued during the Cold War — heavy government involvement in the economy and restrictions on the freedom of private enterprises and individuals. NIEO-based economic policies were, by and large, disasters for economic development in the developing world, disasters which paralleled the economic and human toll socialist approaches to economic activity exacted in Eastern Europe and the Soviet Union. To liberalize the productive powers of private enterprise and individual entrepreneurs, economic development policies had to scale back government involvement in the economy and create space in which private parties could freely negotiate their own transactions in the market. Key tactics in the market liberalization of national economies were (1) privatization of state-owned economic assets; and (2) deregulation of the economy to lift the burdens of government interference from the productive capabilities of private enterprise.

2. Global Openness. Linked with national market liberalization was reorienting economies to be open to international trade and foreign investment. As suggested above in section A, globalization blurs traditional distinctions between the national and the international economy. To thrive in the era of globalization, national economies could no longer follow the

NIEO hostility toward economic interdependence with other countries and peoples. Global openness would be reflected in export-oriented economic growth (contrasted with NIEO import-substitution policies) and in attempts to attract and keep foreign investment (contrasted with NIEO animosity toward foreign-owned assets and foreign investment). In addition, much of globalization feeds off technological advances, such as computer and information technologies. The only way for a state to utilize such technological progress for national economic development is to be open to what is happening technologically elsewhere in the world. Such technological openness also means that the ability of the state to control the use of new technologies is reduced, which means that the new technologies provide companies and people with enormous opportunities to become connected with the rest of the world.

3. Legal and Political Infrastructure. National market liberalization and global economic openness do not occur, and are not maintained, without proper legal rules and political institutions to sustain globalization-sensitive economic development. Economic development strategies for the globalized world need a certain kind of "enabling environment" provided by legal and political systems. Reform of legal and political systems has become a hallmark of liberal economic development strategies, exemplified in "rule of law" initiatives[15] and "good governance" programs of international organizations such as the World Bank and the IMF.[16] Important in this context was the mounting international campaign to mitigate or eliminate corruption as a feature of economic activity in many developing countries.[17] Harmonization of legal rules to facilitate global business transactions also played a key role in reshaping legal systems for the rigors of globalization. These efforts at legal and political reconstruction for economic development purposes tie into the larger debate that developed during the 1990s in international legal circles about an emerging human right to democratic governance.[18]

C. Liberal Economic Development and Its Political and Cultural Consequences

Seeing liberal economic development strategies as the "common sense" of the global economy masks to some extent the profound political and cultural consequences such common sense causes in many regions of the world. As Tooze observed, "[t]he ending of the cold war and the internal collapse of most of the centrally planned economies has led to the 'triumph' and spread of one form of political-social-economic organization: modern capitalism."[19] Under this dynamic, the world moved in the direction of political, economic, and cultural or civilizational homogenization that raises many difficult questions. Simon Murden, for example, observed:

> The process of globalization had major implications for cultures. The dilemma that emerged right across the world ... was the extent to which engaging with the world market economy threatened existing patterns of culture and social order.[20]

Directly in the path of the cultural juggernaut of liberalism is Islamic culture, or Islamic civilization. Samuel Huntington characterized the tension between the West and Islam in this way:

> The underlying problem for the West is not Islamic fundamentalism. It is Islam, a different civilization whose people are convinced of the superiority of their culture and are obsessed with the inferiority of their power. The problem for Islam is not the CIA or the U.S. Department of Defense. It is the West, a different civilization whose people are convinced of the universality of their culture and believe that their superior, if declining, power imposes on them the obligation to extend that culture throughout the world. These are the basic ingredients that fuel conflict between Islam and the West.[21]

Palestinians find themselves on the cutting edge of this conflict because they are a culture influenced by Islam trying to thrive in a globalized world. Economic development strategies have deeper consequences for the Palestinians because of these cultural or civilizational tendencies, as suggested by the power and influence wielded in Palestine by Islamic groups such as Hamas.

III. Making the Palestinian Economy: From the Declaration of Principles to the Present

A. The Oslo Strategy for Palestinian Economic Development

The obstacles facing Palestinian economic development were widely recognized well before the 1993 Declaration of Principles launched the peace process between Israel and the Palestinians. George Abed wrote in 1990 that "[i]t is clear that Israel's occupation of the West Bank and Gaza, even if it were to end soon ... , will leave the emerging Palestinian economy burdened by colossal handicaps and distortions."[22] Israeli domination of the occupied Palestinian territories from 1967 created numerous structural deformities in the Palestinian economy, including "deformation of its manpower development and deployment; isolation from its natural, Arab markets; suppression of industrial development; neglect of infrastructure (roads, communications, power); and the design of its infrastructural facilities for serving Israeli rather than Palestinian needs."[23] Radical restructuring and development would be needed to liberate the Palestinian economy from its debilitating dependence on Israel. Abed described one of the crucial items on the agenda of a future Palestinian state:

> The success of the development program would depend critically on the system of economic management to be introduced into the new Palestinian society. This in turn will be shaped by the outcome of certain fundamental decisions regarding the organization of the society itself (e.g., the extent of state interference in economic affairs, the degree of openness of the economy, basic economic legislation concerning taxation, property rights, and so forth). All indications point to the development of an economic system that allows a dominant role for the private sector and for the price mechanism in the allocation of resources. The exchange and trade system, except for certain transitory arrangements, will have to be virtually free of controls.[24]

A few years after Abed's analysis the same issues confront the makers of the peace process between Israel and the Palestinians. The leaders, diplomats, and experts who crafted the peace process demonstrated a keen awareness that the success of the peace process depended upon, among other things, the economic development of the areas to be under Palestinian self-rule.[25] The World Bank conducted, for example, a comprehensive evaluation of the economic situation in the Palestinian areas prior to the signing of the Declaration of Principles.[26] In the words of one commentator, the World Bank report "makes gloomy reading."[27] The World Bank identified serious infrastructure problems with the economies of the Palestinian areas that would have to be remedied through significant economic reform and the assistance of international aid and private investment.[28] Although the World Bank recognized the need for public assistance from the international community, it emphasized that the long-term economic viability of the Palestinian areas would depend on the success of the private sector,[29] including foreign private investment.[30]

Those crafting the peace process constructed a specific strategy for Palestinian economic development to ensure that the process included economic opportunities for the Palestinian people. The Oslo strategy for Palestinian economic development involved four pillars: (1) international aid; (2) continued close Israeli-Palestinian economic relations; (3) foreign investment; and (4) Palestinian access to foreign markets.[31] These elements formed an interdependent and complex approach to Palestinian economic development. International aid was intended to assist the Palestinians in building a modern economic infrastructure that would lay foundations to attract foreign investment. Close economic arrangements between the Palestinians and Israel would, in the short term, give Palestinian labor and goods access to Israeli markets. In the long term, it would allow the Palestinian Territories to integrate into the regional economy. Foreign investment would be attracted by Palestinian access not only to the Israeli market but also to regional and other international markets, as the Palestinian Territories could serve as an export platform. Thus, Palestinian access to other markets besides Israel was critical to the development of the private sector generally and the inflow of foreign investment specifically.

The mechanisms designed to implement this Palestinian economic development strategy were an international aid program, the Protocol on Economic Relations between Israel and the Palestinian Liberation organization (Economic or Paris Protocol),[32] and the creation of an "enabling environment" of political and legal reforms to promote private-sector development in the Palestinian Territories.

1. International Aid Program. Less than a month after the signing of the Declaration of Principles on September 13, 1993,[33] 47 countries attended the Conference to Support Middle East Peace and pledged approximately U.S.$2 billion in aid over a five-year period to support the development of the Palestinian economy and the transition to Palestinian self-rule.[34] Central to this international aid program "was that such aid would be primarily used to build the economic infrastructure necessary to encourage private investment in the Palestinian Territories."[35]

2. Economic Protocol. The Economic Protocol established the framework for Palestinian economic relations with Israel and the rest of the world for the interim period. The Economic Protocol laid down the structure for the movement of goods and labor between Israel and the Palestinian Territories and for Palestinian trade with the rest of the world. Essentially, the Economic Protocol created a free trade area between Israel and the Palestinian Territories, a modified customs union based on Israeli customs duties and rules, and the opportunity for the PA to open foreign markets for Palestinian exports. Under the Economic Protocol, Palestinian goods were to move freely into the Israeli market.[36] Such access to the significant Israeli market "promised to eliminate the discriminatory treatment suffered by Palestinian goods during the period of occupation."[37]

The Economic Protocol did not, however, provide for free movement of labor between Israel and the Palestinian Territories. It merely states that both parties "will attempt to maintain the normality of movement of labor between them," but each determines "the extent and conditions of the labor movement into its area."[38] Israeli control over Palestinian labor flows into Israel, combined with Israel's policy of systematically reducing the level of Palestinian employment in Israel, heightens the importance of the development of the Palestinian private sector, which would need to absorb growing numbers of Palestinian workers.

The modified customs union established in the Economic Protocol subjected Palestinian imports to the Israeli customs regime,[39] with the exception of certain products that could be imported at tariff rates set by the PA.[40] Thus, Israeli customs rules and practices would largely drive Palestinian imports. Although during the Economic Protocol negotiations the Palestinians pushed for a free trade arrangement that would allow them to set their own tariffs on imports, Israel wanted a customs union to avoid recognizing Palestinian borders as would be required under a free trade arrangement.[41] The political positions of the two sides led to the modified customs union, a compromise that "borrows certain elements of both a common market and a free trade area agreement."[42]

As for Palestinian exports to markets other than Israel, Oslo II granted the PA the authority to negotiate agreements with States and international organizations to open foreign markets for Palestinian goods.[43] For the Palestinian private sector to develop, greater access to world markets would be needed, and such access "would also help attract foreign investors who might be interested in the Palestinian Territories as an export platform."[44]

3. Enabling Environment. When the Declaration of Principles was signed, it was clear the Palestinians had much work ahead creating the appropriate political and legal environment to encourage and assist private-sector development. Decades of occupation left the Palestinian political and legal systems ill-prepared for facilitating a modern, market economy.

The World Bank stressed in 1993 that many policy, legal, and institutional reforms were needed in the Palestinian Territories "in order to create a climate conducive to sustainable economic and social development."[45] Central to creating the proper enabling environment for private-sector development are transparent, modern, and efficient legal, regulatory , and institutional rules and processes.[46] Thus, legal reform and credible political institutions to implement the law are critical to the development of a modern Palestinian economy.

B. Breakdown of the Oslo Strategy for Palestinian Economic Development

Immediately after signing of the Declaration of Principles, optimism about the future of the Palestinian economy prevailed. As the World Bank observed, "[a] low-cost, well-educated work force with a strong entrepreneurial tradition, anticipated privileged access to markets (in Israel, the rest of the Middle East, and Europe), a Palestinian diaspora that is ready and able to provide investment funds, and committed support from the international community give the West Bank and Gaza appreciable economic potential."[47] Events have shattered this optimism as the Palestinian economy has suffered since September 1993. The July-August 1998 issue of the *Palestine Economic Pulse* captured the misfortune of the Palestinian economy as follows: "[t]he once optimistic future for Palestine's economy with its rich human resource base, its strategic geopolitical location and religious significance, envisioned by many and documented in many literary sources ... has faded into oblivion."[48] In mid–June 1998, the U.S. Undersecretary for Economic, Business, and Agricultural Affairs referred to the condition of the Palestinian economy as a crisis.[49] Research published by the World Bank and the Palestine Economic Policy Research Institute in 1999 listed the following as serious problems that have plagued the Palestinian economy since the signing of the 1993 Declaration of Principles: (1) declining standards of living; (2) high and increasing levels of poverty; (3) excessively high and widely fluctuating unemployment rates; (4) sharp deterioration in employment in Israel and low absorption of returning labor; (5) decline in per capita incomes; and (6) a dramatic fall in trade.[50] None of the elements of the Oslo strategy for Palestinian economic development has been achieved, which threatens the economic pillar of the peace process. The early fears that economic deprivation in the Palestinian Territories would affect attitudes towards the peace process find empirical support in the fact that "most West Bankers and Gazans actually blame their economic difficulties on Oslo."[51]

1. Problems with International Aid. Table 1 below shows the level of donor aid commitments and disbursements from 1994 through the first half of 1999. These numbers do not, however, indicate the many problems that have prevented international aid from having the anticipated impact on Palestinian economic development envisioned at the beginning of the peace process.[52] Controversies about delays in the distribution of aid have dogged the relations between the PA and the donor community.[53] Much of the international aid intended to jump-start the reconstruction of the Palestinian economic infrastructure has been diverted to keeping the PA afloat and funding emergency employment programs.[54] The United Nations, Office of the Special Coordinator in the Occupied Territories (UNSCO) reports that from 1994 to 1997 approximately 64 percent of donor aid went to support the PA budget, while only 36 percent went into public investments.[55] In 1998, more disbursed aid, 49 percent, was directed to public investment largely because the PA experienced its first balanced budget in this year.[56]

Table 1: Disbursements as a Percentage of
Donor Commitments to the PA, 1994–
First Half of 1999 (in nominal U.S.$)

Year	Commitments	Disbursements	Ratio
1994	819,225,000	515,313,000	62.90 percent
1995	638,222,500	416,719,000	65.29 percent
1996	888,047,000	536,822,900	60.45 percent
1997	620,143,000	485,791,000	78.34 percent
1998	654,601,000	330,069,500	50.42 percent
1999 (QI and QII)	524,412,600	174,040,360	33.19 percent
Grand Total	4,144,651,100	2,458,755,760	59.32 percent
Annual Average, 1994–1998	724,047,700	456,943,080	63.11 percent

Source: UNSCO, Report on the Palestinian Economy, Autumn 1999

The positive trend of how more international aid is being spent on public investment is counterbalanced by a declining level of disbursed aid. UNSCO reports that "the level of donor disbursements in 1998 was about one-third below the 1994–1997 average."[57] UNSCO attributes the falling level of aid disbursements to a number of factors, including (1) donor uncertainty about the peace process and the slow implementation of the Oslo Accords and the Wye River Memorandum; (2) increasing oversight by donor agencies of the use of aid; (3) difficulties experienced in building consensus between donors and the PA on priorities for the use of aid; (4) problems encountered because of the relative inexperience of PA agencies and the fragmented legal system; (5) failure of the PA to commit its own funds to public investment; (6) the slow pace of legal and institutional reforms that would encourage more private involvement in infrastructure development; and (7) actions taken by Israel that hamper public investment projects.[58]

UNSCO is worried about the downward trend in public investment produced by the reduced levels of donor disbursements that continued from 1998 into 1999.[59] UNSCO and experts continue to emphasize the importance of public investment and the role aid has to play in rebuilding Palestine's economic infrastructure,[60] but the evidence suggests enormous challenges remain. Thus, "[t]he interdependence between public aid and private investment, identified by the World Bank and the donor countries as the key dynamic of economic development for Gaza and the West Bank, has not yet been established."[61] While perhaps necessary given the shocks the Palestinian economy suffered from border closures during the peace process, the historical diversion of aid funds into PA budget support and other short-term consumption expenditures has meant that the "opportunity to lay the foundations for sustained medium-term economic growth is being lost."[62]

2. Problems with the Economic Protocol. The Economic Protocol's free-trade arrangement under which Palestinian goods were to move freely into Israeli markets has, from the Palestinian perspective, collapsed because of Israeli border closures and other security measures.[63] The border closures created severe disruptions in Palestinian trade, leading "to export market losses and disruption in the domestic supply of goods and services linked to imports."[64] Border closures have also created havoc for Palestinian labor flows into Israel, disrupting income flows from Israeli-source earnings.[65] The border closures, in response to political violence, pitted Israel's need for security against the Palestinian need for economic development.[66] According to the *Palestine Economic Pulse*, attempts to find solutions to this basic clash of interests largely proved to be a "dialogue of the deaf."[67] The adverse economic impact of Israeli border controls and restrictions remained great in the first half of 1999. According to UNSCO, because of Israeli border policies, "Palestinian public agencies and private businesses, as well as international agencies, continued to experience significantly higher transaction costs, time delays and lost productivity due to restrictions on personnel and goods at border crossings."[68]

Leaving aside the border problems, the modified customs union arrangement in the Economic Protocol has not worked well for the Palestinians.[69] Palestinians complain that Israeli nontariff barriers adversely affect Palestinian exports to Israel.[70] In addition, the instability of the business climate in the Palestinian Territories has encouraged many Palestinian businesses to import products "under the name of an Israeli intermediary, and in so doing, deprive the PA of revenue which it is rightfully due."[71] Frustration with the Economic Protocol has also arisen because the modified customs union imposes on the Palestinian economy tariff costs higher than those the PA would likely charge if it had control of Palestinian import policy .[72] Palestinian businesses and consumers pay higher prices for many imports because of high Israel tariff rates, while facing greatly restricted access to Israeli and world markets because of border closures, nontariff barriers, and the lack of Palestinian trade infrastructure. Given all these factors, it is hardly surprising that the nature of the Israeli-Palestinian economic relationship structured in the Economic Protocol is being critically questioned.[73] Access to the lucrative Israeli market promised in the Economic Protocol aimed at attracting private investment,[74] but the failure of the access to materialize in any significant way has deterred private investment in the Palestinian Territories.

While the PA has been active in negotiating trade arrangements and agreements with other states,[75] Palestinian exports to world markets have not increased substantially because such exports have been dependent on Israeli ports and thus have been subject to the same problems as exports to Israel.[76] This continuing need for Israeli trade access and infrastructure produces the situation that "the complex maze of documented trade agreements and mechanisms ... have in practice done little to change its economic dependence on Israel."[77] While work has progressed on the completion of an airport and seaport in Gaza,[78] to date this progress has not materially altered the Palestinian economy dependence on Israeli trade infrastructure for imports and exports. Foreign investors have not, therefore, had much reason to view the Palestinian Territories as a stable export platform for accessing markets in Europe, the Middle East, and elsewhere. The stunted condition of Palestinian exports to world markets detrimentally affects overall Palestinian private sector development. As Diwan concluded, "the WBGS [West Bank and Gaza Strip] economy will not be able to grow in a sustainable fashion unless it manages to increase substantially its export of goods and services."[79]

3. Problems with the Enabling Environment. Finally, the enabling environment considered central to developing the Palestinian economy has not materialized politically, economically, or legally. Widespread corruption has severely "tarnished the PA and further hurt prospects for Palestinian economic development."[80] After an internal audit revealed that PA corruption and mismanagement wasted approximately U.S.$326 million, or 40 percent of the PNA's annual budget, the Palestinian Legislative Council put pressure on Arafat and his council to clean up the PA. In June 1998, Arafat "agreed to reshuffle the PNA Ministerial Cabinet accused of corruption, and appealed to the Palestinian Legislative Council ... to delay its proposed no-confidence vote."[81] While the PA has moved to put an end to the widespread corruption, the corruption scandal further deepened the concerns of foreign companies (buyers and investors) about the Palestinian Territories as a place to do business. Moreover, the scandal constituted a manifest failure by the PA to create and maintain the proper political enabling environment for private-sector development.

Economically, the PA's public statements about its desire to promote a free market economy clashed with its "practice of creating trade monopolies for itself."[82] The PA has established import monopolies on a number of products.[83] The PA trade monopolies are not secretive matters as "[c]oncerns about the attempts by the PA to monopolize sectors of the Palestinian economy are commonplace among investors and groups trying to facilitate the peace process and Palestinian economic development."[84] The Israeli director of the Israel-Palestinian Center for Research and Information (IPCRI) has argued that PA monopolistic behavior "will strangle the private sector and delay or prevent economic development."[85] In the wake of the corruption scandal, the PNA has moved to reorganize or privatize government economic enterprises[86]; but the monopolies, like the corruption scandal, have hurt the development of an enabling environment for Palestinian economic development.

The need for legal and regulatory reform identified in 1993 as critical for private-sector development remains an obstacle to Palestinian economic development. Five years after first identifying the need for legal and regulatory reform, the World Bank still maintained that "the business environment suffers from confusing commercial legislation and a lack of public sector regulatory institutions."[87] In its latest *Report on the Palestinian Economy*, UNSCO argued that "the still weak legal and institutional environment — particularly from the point of view of foreign capital — constitute continuing obstacles to investment in the Occupied Palestinian Territory."[88]

While efforts have been made by the PA to address the needs for legal reform, these efforts have not always been successful. The Palestinian Investment Law is a case in point. Despite the central importance of foreign investment to the Oslo strategy for Palestinian economic development, the original and the revised Palestinian Investment Law have been criticized by intergovernmental and academic experts as inadequate.[89] Similar concerns have been expressed about the Palestinian telecommunications law[90] and the laws to regulate the industrial estates within the Palestinian Territories.[91] The Palestinian Stock Exchange has been operating without an adequate regulatory framework or securities law.[92] Impediments regarding basic commercial and property laws must be addressed to create an attractive environment for private-sector investment.[93] While international organizations, governments, and nongovernmental organizations are working with the PA on legal reform,[94] much work remains in creating the proper legal enabling environment for private-sector development.

Larger legal issues also complicate Palestinian economic development. For example, Arafat has not approved the Palestinian constitution — the Basic Law[95] — although it has been approved by the Palestine Legislative

Council.[96] While Arafat's failure to sign may be related to the lack of progress in the peace process and the anomaly of enacting a constitution when the PA does not even control its own borders,[97] the absence of this fundamental law adds to the legal vacuum businesses perceive in the Palestinian Territories.[98] It also contributes to concerns about the PA's lack of respect for human rights, prominently documented in a critical report by Amnesty International.[99] The Wye Memorandum also highlighted PA human rights problems by providing that "the Palestinian Police will exercise powers and responsibilities to implement this Memorandum with due regard to internationally accepted norms of human rights and the rule of law, and will be guided by the need to protect the public, respect human dignity, and avoid harassment."[100] Legal experts have also examined abuses of human rights by the PA.[101] To date, the "rule of law" does not characterize Arafat's or the PA's governance of the Palestinian economy or people.

4. Problems with Private Investment in the Palestinian Territories. All these factors have combined to create low levels of private investment, both domestic and foreign, in the Palestinian Territories. Domestically, most of the private investment has been channeled into residential housing,[102] a type of investment that "has lesser impact in terms of increasing the productive capacity of the economy."[103] The World Bank noted that "[p]rivate investment over the 1994 to 1997 period (excluding housing, which does not expand productive capacity) averaged a low 8.75 percent of GDP."[104] The World Bank estimates that, in 1996, gross investment in residential housing amounted to 14 percent of GNP, while gross investment in machinery and equipment totaled 7 percent of GNP.[105] The International Monetary Fund estimates that private investment levels of 15 percent to 20 percent of GDP are needed for tangible economic growth.[106] In its latest *Report on the Palestinian Economy*, UNSCO commented with concern that "non-construction private investment in the Palestinian economy has continued to lag behind."[107]

Foreign investment in the Palestinian economy has also been very low. UNSCO noted "the very low level of new foreign company registrations and approved foreign investment projects" as indicators of a lack of foreign investor interest in the Palestinian economy.[108] In the first six months of 1999, only one new foreign company registered with the PA, and foreign investment projects made up only 14 percent of investment projects approved under the Palestinian Investment Law, suggesting "that planned new foreign investment remains limited in the Palestinian economy."[109] Evidence of the lack of foreign investor interest in the Palestinian economy can also be found in the rise and fall of Builders for Peace, a nonprofit organization established by the Clinton administration, after the signing of the Declaration of Principles, to encourage foreign investment in the Palestinian Territories. Organized in the optimistic days of the post–Declaration period, Builders for Peace closed its doors in August 1997 because the investment climate in the Palestinian Territories was inhospitable to foreign investors.

In addition, the highly touted industrial zones to be established in Gaza and the West Bank,[110] which were intended to attract foreign investors, have captured the interest of mainly local Palestinian business, Israeli companies, and some Palestinian diaspora groups.[111] Israeli actions also seem to be undermining the potential of the Palestinian industrial zones as "Israel currently plans to develop an industrial estate on confiscated Palestinian land in the West Bank in Kufr Qumran near Nablus."[112] This Israeli move seems "to undermine the whole purpose" of the Gaza industrial estate.[113]

C. Summary on the Current Condition of the Palestinian Economy

The Oslo strategy for Palestinian economic development involved four pillars: (1) international aid to stimulate investment in public infrastructure; (2) close economic relations with Israel to provide Palestinians with access to the lucrative Israeli economy and to Israeli trade infrastructure; (3) access for Palestinian exports to foreign markets beyond Israel; and (4) attracting significant foreign investment to help the private sector become the engine of Palestinian economic growth. The latest UNSCO *Report on the Palestinian Economy* gives some indication of how the Oslo strategy has fared. UNSCO highlighted a number of significant worries about the current Palestinian economy, including (1) the downward trend in public infrastructure investment produced by reduced levels of international aid disbursements; (2) stagnation in Palestinian exports ; (3) stagnation in domestic private investment; (4) very low levels of foreign investment; (5) a still weak legal and institutional environment for private-sector investment and development; and (6) political uncertainties about the peace process.[114]

These problems indicate not only how comprehensively the Oslo strategy for Palestinian economic development broke down but also how unprepared the Palestinian economy is for economic development in the era of globalization. National market liberalization, integration with global markets, and development of market-supportive legal rules and political institutions are not principles one would associate with the existing situation in the Palestinian economy. In many respects, the breakdown of the Oslo economic development strategy results from the structural dependence of the Palestinian economy on Israel combined with deteriorating political relations between the Palestinians and Israelis because of political violence and difficulties in the peace process. In other respects, however, the retrogression and stagnation of the Palestinian economy flows from matters within the control of the PA, such as political and legal reforms needed to achieve national market liberalization, to encourage global openness, and to build market-friendly legal and political systems. While it is reasonable to argue that the structural dependence of the Palestinian economy on Israel is, to a large extent, currently beyond the control of the Palestinians, the difficulties this structural dependence has created have been exacerbated by actions and omissions of the PA and the PLO.

In Part IV, we explore how the Palestinian public and private sectors can make progress in preparing the Palestinian economy for development in the era of globalization. While we will discuss actions the Palestinian public sector should take, our emphasis will be on how the private sector has to take the lead in forcing economic, legal, and political change if the Palestinian people are to see economic development as part of the globalizing world.

IV. Preparing the Palestinian Economy for Development in the Era of Globalization

Many Palestinians in the public and private sector recognize the ill-preparedness of the Palestinian economy for the rigors of globalization. With the prospect of a Palestinian state looming on the horizon, this lack of preparedness for economic development bodes ill for the near and medium term of the Palestinian people. The creation of a Palestinian state will force Palestinians to confront harsh questions about what their sovereignty will mean if their economy continues to be structurally disadvantaged and politically mismanaged. Palestinians who are actively engaged in thinking about Palestinian economic development in the era of globalization have begun to construct a substantive and procedural paradigm to guide the Palestinian economic development in the future. In part IV, we describe this emerging paradigm and reflect on its prospects for building more economic opportunity for Palestinians.

The substantive and procedural paradigm being constructed to guide

Palestinian economic development in the era of globalization is the product of an initiative called the Palestinian National Trade Dialogue Project (NTDP). The NTDP was created in response to concerns and ideas put forth by the Palestine Trade Center (Paltrade), a private-sector group established in 1998 to promote the development of Palestinian trade. One of Paltrade's most serious concerns since its establishment has been the absence of effective mechanisms and dialogue between (1) members of the Palestinian private sector, and (2) the Palestinian private sector and the PA in connection with the development of Palestinian economic policy.[115] Paltrade created the NTDP to provide a more effective way for the Palestinian private sector to voice its concerns and work more productively with the PA on economic development policy. The PA's Ministry of Economy and Trade supports the NTDP, and the World Bank and the Palestinian Economic Council for Development and Reconstruction (PECDAR) have funded the NTDP through the Technical Assistance Trust Fund.[116] Paltrade has identified five strategic objectives in creating and implementing the NTDP: to (1) reduce fragmentation and enhance dialogue within the private sector; (2) identify and prioritize private-sector interests; (3) articulate private sector positions and recommendations regarding key policy issues; (4) create a dialogue between the private sector and the PA; and (5) support cooperation between the private and public sectors.[117]

The NTDP is an interesting development for two major reasons. First, it is a Palestinian private-sector initiative. This is important because, since the peace process began in 1993, economic development policy has been dominated by a top-down intergovernmental and governmental process, led by international financial institutions, such as the World Bank, important donor countries, such as the United States, and the PA. The NTDP represents Paltrade's conclusion that economic policy formulation and implementation to date has not been sufficiently informed by the Palestinian private sector — the very sector that is supposed to be the long-term engine of Palestinian prosperity. In other economies, the private sector has been the leader in preparing governments and populations for the challenges and opportunities presented by the processes of globalization. The problems of Palestinian economic development during the peace process have revealed that "the Palestinian private sector is fragmented, often lacking organizational mechanisms to articulate their interests and requirements for growth, with the exception of a few industry associations."[118] The NDTP asserts that, in the future, economic development policy must be made with the Palestinian private sector having a stronger, unified voice on the direction of the Palestinian economy. While the PA has consulted the private sector in its past efforts, the participation by the private sector has not been rigorous enough for the needs of making Palestinian economic development policy. Paltrade is arguing for a stronger "bottom-up" approach to economic development policy in the era of globalization to balance the primarily "top-down" status quo approach of the PA, donor governments, and international financial institutions.[119]

Second, the NTDP — as a private-sector initiative — presents and advocates strongly for the liberal strategy for economic development discussed earlier in this chapter: (1) liberalization of national markets; (2) integration with other economies and the global marketplace; and (3) building the appropriate legal and political infrastructures to support Palestinian companies in their pursuit of global opportunities and profit. This liberal strategy has, of course, been important to debates about the economic future of Palestine for many years. In discussing the economic viability of a Palestinian state in 1990, George Abed argued that "the development of an economic system that allows a dominant role for the private sector and for the price mechanism in the allocation of resources" was very important for the future of the Palestinian economy.[120] Free-market capitalism was also the dominant model used by the World Bank and donor governments in their advice to the PA during the peace process. [121] The liberal strategy for economic development is also at the heart of Paltrade's NDTP initiative. In one of the papers commissioned by the NDTP, Salah Abdelshaffi argued that the economic philosophy of the Palestinian economy in the era of globalization must allow the private sector to play the fundamental role in economic development activities,[122] which is consistent with the prevailing liberal strategy driving economic development globally today.

The NTDP reflects a commitment by members of the Palestinian private sector to accept, without significant changes, the liberal strategy for economic development for the era of globalization. Paltrade and the NTDP represent the conclusion of many Palestinians that free-market capitalism provides the only viable path for raising living standards. Paltrade does not seem to be interested in searching for a Palestinian "third way." Paltrade is pushing hard for Palestine to don what Thomas Friedman colorfully called the "Golden Straitjacket":

> When your country recognizes this fact [i.e., free-market capitalism is the only viable alternative left], when it recognizes the rules of the free market in today's global economy, and decides to abide by them, it puts on what I call the Golden Straitjacket.... To fit into the Golden Straitjacket a country must either adopt, or be seen as moving toward, the following golden

rules: making the private sector the primary engine of its economic growth, maintaining a low rate of inflation and price stability, shrinking the size of its state bureaucracy, maintaining as close to a balanced budget as possible, ... eliminating and lowering tariffs on imported goods, removing restrictions on foreign investment, getting rid of quotas and domestic monopolies, increasing exports, privatizing state-owned industries and utilities, deregulating capital markets, making its currency convertible, opening its industries, stock and bond markets to direct foreign ownership and investment, deregulating the economy to promote as much domestic competition as possible, eliminating government corruption, subsidies and kickbacks as much as possible, opening its banking and telecommunications systems to private ownership and competition and allowing its citizens to choose from an array of competing pension options and foreign-run pension and mutual funds. When you stitch all of these pieces together you have the Golden Straitjacket.[123]

The policy recommendations flowing from the NTDP process follow the prescriptions of the liberal strategy for economic development in the era of globalization, or the Golden Straitjacket: promote private sector development, reduce the size of the PA, reduce the PA's budget deficits, attract foreign investment, increase exports, so on.[124] Promoting adoption of the Golden Straitjacket is not a new idea in connection with Palestinian economic development, but perhaps the NTDP process represents the first concerted effort on the part of the Palestinian private sector to push for the liberal strategy of economic development. The PA has used free-market rhetoric, but its behavior reveals that its leadership never seriously bought into the need to put on the Golden Straitjacket.

Paltrade is not naïve about the ramifications of following the course prescribed by liberal development strategy. Nassar Nassar, Chairman of the Board of Directors of Paltrade, put the harshness of Palestine's economic future into perspective when he argued:

In many ways, Palestine is still an infant economy. Obviously, we can neither prevent nor resist globalization. We will pay a price. There will be a cost and parts of the economy could be crushed by the globalization process. The small and medium-sized businesses are particularly vulnerable, as they are not ready to enter the international markets. We do not have many cosmopolitan companies that are prepared to face such competition. We are not opposed to globalization, but we need to prepare ourselves.[125]

One of the implications of Paltrade's emphasis on adopting the liberal strategy for economic development is that Palestinians cannot hesitate to put on the Golden Straitjacket and continue to wear it, even when it hurts. Certainly, there will be pain that the PA will have to handle if the move toward a free-market economy is to be sustainable. Donning the Golden Straitjacket could produce opposition from within the private sector as the shock of exposing industries to the rigors of global markets generates private-sector demands for protectionism. The PA will also have to face the challenge many countries face today: how to redistribute income to deal with poverty, unemployment, rural development, public housing, education, and health services without unnecessarily reducing the private sector's ability to create economic growth. Economic pain and social dislocation are still very much part of the Palestinian economy's future, even after Palestine begins to pursue seriously economic development along liberal lines.

While the NTDP is presented as a public-private partnership in Palestinian economic development, the private sector's tempered enthusiasm for the liberal strategy to economic development might not be equally shared by the PA. After all, as part III demonstrated, the PA's performance since 1993 has not been a model of free-market behavior. Recommendations on PA reform flowing from papers presented under NTDP auspices sound very familiar to anyone familiar with the advice rendered to the PA by the World Bank and donor governments since 1993. Whether the PA, and particularly the top leadership group, are serious about putting on the Golden Straitjacket remains an open question. Arafat's leadership depends on retaining maximum power and flexibility for him, political features that the liberal framework for economic development does not respect. Friedman notes that the Golden Straitjacket has very important consequences for the power of politicians and governments:

> As your country puts on the Golden Straitjacket, two things tend to happen: your economy grows and your politics shrink. That is, on the economic front the Golden Straitjacket usually fosters more growth and higher average incomes—through more trade, foreign investment, privatization and more efficient use of resources under the pressure of global competition. But on the political front, the Golden Straitjacket narrows the political and economic policy choices of those in power to relatively tight parameters.[126]

What Paltrade is pushing in the NTDP has, thus, profound political implications for the PA, and especially for Arafat's authoritarian style of leadership. The Golden Straitjacket would require the PA to adopt and implement transparent laws and regulations that meet international standards in the economic, commercial, and financial areas because the continuing absence of a unified, internationally competitive legal framework is incompatible with the liberal strategy for economic development. "Rule by Arafat" would have to be replaced by the "rule of law" under the Golden Straitjacket. In addition, the liberal strategy for economic development would also affect the policy freedom of any constitutionally empowered legislative body that may come into existence with a Palestinian state. The political implications of the NTDP strategy extend well beyond the end of the Arafat era.

There are signs that the PA is moving more aggressively in the direction demanded by the Golden Straitjacket. First, Paltrade believes that the success of the NTDP initiative results not only from its private-sector energy but also from the support from the Ministry of Economy and Trade. Paltrade and the Ministry of Economy and Trade see the NTDP as a true partnership, and both believe that such a public-private partnership is crucial for pushing Palestinian economic development plans forward.

Second, in January 2000 President Arafat established the Palestinian High Council for Development (Development Council), which is a ministerial-level body that has the mandate to develop the financial and administrative systems of the PA that support economic development and to strengthen the principle of transparency in how the PA deals with the economy. The Development Council will work with the Palestinian Investment Promotion Agency on stimulating foreign investment into Palestine and will oversee and complete privatization of the PA's commercial activities as part of Palestine's economic development strategy. President Arafat has also approved the establishment of a development fund for Palestine. The Development Council is responsible for managing all direct and indirect investments of the development fund and will be advised by both public- and private-sector advisors.

Third, the Ministry of Economy and Trade is trying to prepare the PA for Palestine's application to the World Trade Organization (WTO). Such an application is, of course, dependent on Palestine achieving statehood; but the efforts underway at the Ministry of Economy and Trade to prepare a Palestinian application for WTO membership is a powerful sign that the PA is trying to fit itself for the Golden Straitjacket of market liberalism and for adherence to the international legal regimes that form part of the fabric of the Straitjacket. Not only would WTO membership for Palestine help it improve its trade relations with Israel but it would also signal to the world that Palestine is willing and able to compete with other countries under the international rule of law enshrined in the WTO.

Paltrade's push for the Palestinian version of the Golden Straitjacket confronts perhaps the most difficult problem facing Palestinian economic development in the era of globalization: the Israeli Straitjacket. The NTDP is encouraging more analysis and debate about how a Palestinian state's economic relations with Israel should be structured,[127] but it remains unclear what the final status negotiations will produce. As part III demonstrated, Israeli economic policies and national security behavior have wreaked havoc on, and continue to hurt, the Palestinian economy (see Table 2).

Table 2: The Continuing Costs of the Israeli Straitjacket

Type of Impediment	*Description of Impediment*	*Costs to Palestinian Economy*
Border Closures	Israel closes the borders between itself and the areas under Palestinian control, and prohibits all Palestinians from entering Jerusalem who do not hold a Jerusalem ID, or a special permit from Israel	Closures and prohibitions lead to lost wages, cause declines in exports and imports, increase transportation and other operational costs, deter foreign investment, and fragment the Palestinian market between the West Bank and Gaza
Permits	Israel requires travel, work, and vehicle permits for all Palestinians traveling (1) from and to the West Bank and Gaza, and (2) within the West Bank between Palestinian controlled areas and Israeli-controlled areas	Permits dramatically limit the freedom of movement of goods and people to and from the West Bank and Gaza and increase the costs of transportation and operation to Palestinian businesses
Restrictions on Investors	Foreign investors wishing to visit the West Bank or Gaza require either a visiting permit or visa from Israel	Foreign investors, especially those from Arab countries, have trouble getting such permits, and the requirement to have one increases the costs of trying to do business in Palestine
Application of Israeli Military Law	Israel continues to apply military law as it did during the occupation	The nontransparent application of military law raises the risks and costs for domestic and foreign investors
Restrictions Applied Industrial Zones	Israel refuses to allow Palestinian industrial zones to operate as	These restrictions on Palestinian industrial zones limit the potential

Type of Impediment	Description of Impediment	Costs to Palestinian Economy
	agreed and as they need to do to boost economic growth	that such zones have to stimulate economic development, particularly in exports and foreign investment
Restrictions on Land Registration	Israel applies land use and authorization controls for all areas not classified as "Area A" in the Interim Agreement	Land use restrictions hamper the ability of cities and industrial estates to grow
Trade and Border Crossing	All normal movements of goods and people across borders is controlled by Israel and is subject to "security checks"	Israeli control of the borders means increased transportation costs, increased time to deliver goods, and often the destruction of perishable products such as fresh-cut flowers and agricultural products

Source: *Study on Impediments Imposed by Israel on Palestinian Economic and Commercial Activities*, by the Palestinian Economic Council of Development and Reconstruction, Palestinian Team to the Multilateral Negotiations, and the Private Sector and Investment Unit of Orient House, January 1997.

Most Palestinian private-sector leaders believe that the Palestinian state will remain economically dependent on the Israeli economy for many years to come. How will Israeli economic hegemony in the region affect Palestine's adoption of the Golden Straitjacket? The Palestinian private sector also does not pretend that Israeli security concerns will vanish when a Palestinian state comes into being. How will Israeli national security concerns affect Palestine's adoption of the Golden Straitjacket? Palestine's adoption of the Golden Straitjacket faces problems that do not affect other developing countries in the same extreme degree. Paltrade does not have any easy answers to the problems created by the Israeli Straitjacket, except to hope that increased input by the Palestinian private sector into the final status negotiations will yield results more conducive to free-market economic development in the state of Palestine. To follow the rules of the Golden Straitjacket will require the Palestinian state to have control over its own borders with Israel and control over the flow of goods into and out of Palestine. The Economic Protocol's hybrid free-trade agreement and customs union arrangement will have to be replaced by a straight free-trade agreement between Palestine and Israel. But more trouble looms ahead for the Palestinian economy if Israel fears the economic and national security implications of a Palestine dressed in the Golden Straitjacket.

For this trouble to be mitigated, Israel has to perceive that the Palestinian Golden Straitjacket is actually better for its economy and national security than the continued application of the Israeli Straitjacket to the Palestinian economy. After all, the Golden Straitjacket would impose on the PA policies, rules, and institutions that would make it a safer, more stable neighbor than the current seething, poverty-stricken territories Palestine represents. Thus, the degree of willingness on the part of the PA to don the Golden Straitjacket may influence Israeli perceptions of the threat posed by Palestinians. Here again the Palestinian private sector has a huge role to play because it must be the engine of reform from the Palestinian side. Perhaps the "bottom-up" approach to economic development the NTDP is trying to foster will provide a mechanism for convincing Israel to loosen and then ultimately discard the hated and harmful Israeli Straitjacket.

Paltrade's push for adoption of the liberal strategy for economic development also raises cultural issues for Palestinians. Many critics argue that globalization promotes cultural homogenization throughout the international system on the basis of Western norms, values, and practices. Globalization, many assert, erodes traditional and non–Western cultures, such as Islamic culture, by forcing open markets, politics, and laws to adopt Western forms of economics, government, and law. The NTDP does not expressly discuss the cultural difficulties that the Golden Straitjacket approach to Palestinian economic development may cause for Palestine. One reason for this may be that Palestinian culture, for various reasons, is already open and exposed to the cultural effects of globalization. Average Palestinians have access to satellite television and access to the Internet, and they are using both in increasing numbers, which is a reflection of acceptance rather than rejection of the instrumentalities of globalization. The openness of Palestinian society is also affected by Palestinians from the diaspora who are returning from living in Western societies for many years. These Palestinian returnees bring with them a desire to have an open and free society. Palestinian culture has also been influenced by its proximity to Israel, which proximity has built into Palestinian society a need to know what is happening in the world and to learn from other countries what works politically, economically, and legally. Fears that Islamic groups, such as Hamas, will lead efforts to prevent Palestinian society from being corrupted by Western, cultural imperialism in the form of globalization exist but are exaggerated. Hamas is a political organization that works primarily to end Israel's occupation of Palestine. While it is influenced by traditional Islamic teachings and practices, Hamas is not representative of Palestinian culture or society. Palestinian culture should not be simplistically considered an "Islamic culture" because it is more textured and nuanced than this label can communicate. This reality means that the Palestinian cultural response to globalization will be a complex process that produces neither abject capitulation to the norms and values of the West nor complete rejection of Western, cultural imperialism.

V. Conclusion

The eventual creation of a Palestinian state will mark the end of the Palestinian people's long-suffering journey to self-determination. The poor condition of the Palestinian economy combined with the challenges the processes of globalization pose for all states and peoples today mean that the creation of the Palestinian state will only be, to steal a phrase from Winston Churchill, the end of the beginning as far as where self-determination will lead the Palestinian people politically, economically, legally, and culturally. The sovereignty of any Palestinian state will be extraordinarily constrained by the confluence of Israeli security concerns and the workings of globalized markets. Many Palestinians in the private sector believe that Palestine has no option other than donning the Golden Straitjacket of liberal economic development with all its political, legal, and cultural consequences. The major unanswered questions are whether (1) the PA and the political leadership of Palestine have the foresight to implement seriously and urgently the liberal strategy for economic development; (2) Israel will have the wisdom to encourage the Palestinian state to embrace serious liberalization as a method of securing peace and prosperity in the region; (3) the Palestinian private sector is up to the challenge of leading the Palestinian economy out of the morass into which it has fallen during the peace process; and (4) the Palestinian society is ready for the culturally challenging times globalization has in store for it. The answers to these questions will determine what sovereignty under international law will mean for the Palestinian people.

Notes

1. See IAN BROWNLIE, PRINCIPLES OF PUBLIC INTERNATIONAL LAW 70–77 (5th ed. 1998) (discussing the legal criteria for statehood in international law).
2. Gordon R. Walker and Mark A. Fox, *Globalization: An Analytical Framework*, 3 IND. J. GLOBAL LEGAL STUD. 375, 380 (1996).
3. We are thinking here about the new states created in the process of decolo-

nization during the Cold War period. These new states emerged into an international system radically different from the one states are experiencing today.

4. See, e.g., Alfred C. Aman, Jr., *An Introduction*, 1 IND. J. GLOBAL LEGAL STUD. 1, 1 (1993) (noting that globalization "means different things in different contexts"); and Benedict Kingsbury, *The Tuna-Dolphin Controversy: The World Trade Organization and the Liberal Project to Reconceptualize International Law*, 5 Y. B. INT'L ENV. L. 1, 4 (1994) (noting that " '[g]lobalization' may have many different meanings").

5. Jan Aart Scholte, *The Globalization of World Politics*, in THE GLOBALIZATION OF WORLD POLITICS: AN INTRODUCTION TO INTERNATIONAL RELATIONS (J. Baylis and S. Smith eds., 1997), at 13, 14.

6. Quoted in Scholte, supra note 7, at 15.

7. Jean-Jacques Rousseau, *The State of War*, in ROUSSEAU ON INTERNATIONAL RELATIONS (S. Hoffman and D. P. Fidler, eds., 1991), at 33, 42-43.

8. Scholte, supra note 7, at 21.

9. Roger Tooze, *International Political Economy in an Age of Globalization*, in THE GLOBALIZATION OF WORLD POLITICS: AN INTRODUCTION TO INTERNATIONAL RELATIONS (J. Baylis and S. Smith eds., 1997), at 212, 219.

10. Resolution on Permanent Sovereignty over Natural Resources, G.A. Res. 1803, U.N. GAOR, 17th Sess., Supp. No. 17, at 15, U.N. Doc A/5217 (1962); Charter of Economic Rights and Duties of States, G.A. Res. 3281, U.N. GAOR, 29th Sess., Supp. No. 31, at 50, U.N. Doc. A/9631 (1974) [hereinafter Economic Charter]. Article 2 of the Economic Charter sets forth a comprehensive summation of this goal. Id. art. 2, at 52.

11. This goal is embodied in the Economic Charter in the form of various rights and duties designed to provide developing countries with preferential treatment in the international economic system. See generally Economic Charter, supra. For example, Article 13(1) of the Economic Charter states that every state has "the right to benefit from the advances and developments in science and technology for the acceleration of its economic and social development." Id. art. 13(1), at 53. Article 14 of the Economic Charter states that the duty to cooperate in promoting expansion and liberalization of world trade means that states should:

> [T]ake measures aimed at securing additional benefits for the international trade of developing countries so as to achieve a substantial increase in their foreign exchange earnings, the diversification of their exports, the acceleration of the rate of growth of their trade, taking into account their development needs, an improvement in the possibilities for these countries to participate in the expansion of world trade and a balance more favorable to developing countries in the sharing of the advantages resulting from this expansion.

Id. art. 14, at 53.

12. Tooze, supra note 11, at 221.

13. Id., at 227.

14. THOMAS L. FRIEDMAN, THE LEXUS AND THE OLIVE TREE: UNDERSTANDING GLOBALIZATION 9 (Rev. ed. 2000).

15. See, e.g., Thomas Carothers, *The Rule of Law Revival*, FOREIGN AFF. , Mar./Apr. 1998, at 95.

16. See, e.g., WORLD BANK, GOVERNANCE: THE WORLD BANK'S EXPERIENCE (1994); INTERNATIONAL MONETARY FUND, GOOD GOVERNANCE: THE IMF'S ROLE (1997).

17. See OECD Convention on Combating Bribery of Foreign Public Officials in International Business Transactions, Dec. 17, 1997, at <http://www.oecd.org/daf/nocorruption/20nov1e.htm.>

18. See, e.g., Thomas M. Franck, *The Emerging Right to Democratic Governance* 86 AM. J. INT'L L. 46 (1992); Gregory H. Fox, *The Right to Political Participation in International Law*, 17 YALE J. INT'L L. 539 (1992); BRAD R. ROTH, GOVERNMENTAL ILLEGITIMACY IN INTERNATIONAL LAW (1999); and DEMOCRATIC GOVERNANCE AND INTERNATIONAL LAW (G. H. Fox and B. R. Roth eds., 2000).

19. Tooze, supra note 11, at 226.

20. Simon Murden, *Cultural Conflict in International Relations: The West and Islam, in* THE GLOBALIZATION OF WORLD POLITICS: AN INTRODUCTION TO INTERNATIONAL RELATIONS (J. Baylis and S. Smith eds., 1997), at 374, 377.

21. SAMUEL P. HUNTINGDON, THE CLASH OF CIVILIZATIONS AND THE REMAKING OF WORLD ORDER 217–218 (1996). For an argument that the West is imposing a new "standard of civilization" on the world through international law, see David P. Fidler, *A Kinder, Gentler System of Capitulations? International Law, Structural Adjustment Policies, and the Standard of Liberal, Globalized Civilization*, 35 TEX. INT'L L. J. 387–413 (2000).

22. GEORGE T. ABED, THE ECONOMIC VIABILITY OF A PALESTINIAN STATE 17 (1990).

23. Id., at ix.

24. Id., at x–xi.

25. See David P. Fidler, *Foreign Private Investment in Palestine: An Analysis of the Law on the Encouragement of Investment in Palestine*, 19 FORDHAM INT'L L. J. 529, 531 (1995) (noting that "[m]any believe that Palestinians who see no improvement in their standard of living or find no economic opportunities as a result of the peace process will question the wisdom of making deals with Israel and perhaps support forces that oppose the peace process"); Odin Knudsen, "Beyond the Israeli Election: Bringing Forth a Sustainable Palestinian Economy," *Palestine Economic Pulse*, May-June 1996, at 21 (former Resident Representative in World Bank's West Bank and Gaza Mission arguing that without economic development "the Palestinians will become more impoverished, breeding more resentment and hostility towards Israel").

26. See 1–6 INTERNATIONAL BANK FOR RECONSTRUCTION AND DEVELOPMENT, DEVELOPING THE OCCUPIED TERRITORIES: AN INVESTMENT IN PEACE (1993) [hereinafter WORLD BANK REPORT].

27. Edmund O'Sullivan, "Putting Palestine Back to Work," *Middle East Economic Digest*, Oct. 1, 1993, at 2, 3.

28. 1 WORLD BANK REPORT, supra note 28, at 13.

29. Id.

30. Id., at 15.

31. See David P. Fidler, *Peace through Trade? Developments in Palestinian Trade Law During the Peace* Process, 38 VA. J. INT'L L. 155, 156–57 (1998) (describing these four fundamental elements of the Oslo economic strategy for the Palestinian Territories).

32. Protocol on Economic Relations between the Government of the State of Israel and the P.L.O., Representing the Palestinian People, 33 I.L.M. 696 [hereinafter Economic Protocol], in Interim Agreement on the West Bank and Gaza Strip. Sept. 28, 1995. Isr.-PLO., 36 I.L.M. 551, 639 [hereinafter Oslo II].

33. Declaration of Principles on Interim Self-Government Arrangements, Sept. 13, 1993, Isr.-PLO 32 I.L.M. 1525 [hereinafter Declaration of Principles].

34. See Fidler, supra note 27, at 533–34.

35. Id. at 534 (citing Deborah Zabarenko, "Global Meeting Set to Raise $2 Billion for Mideast," Reuters. Oct. 1, 1993, available in LEXIS. Nexis Library, CURNWS File).

36. See Economic Protocol, supra note 34, arts. VIII(1), IX(1). The movement of

Palestinian agricultural products is subject to Israeli veterinary and phytosanitary measures and certain quotas to be phased out by 1998. See id. art. VIII(2)–(10).

37. Fidler, supra note 33, at 162.
38. Economic Protocol, supra note 34, art. VII(I).
39. Id. art. III(1).
40. See id. arts. III(2), III(4), III(10).
41. See Ephraim Kleiman. *The Economic Provisions of the Agreement Between Israel and the PLO*, 28 ISR. L. REV. 347, 354–55 (1994).
42. Id. at 355.
43. Oslo II, supra note 34,. art. IX(5)(b).
44. Fidler, supra note 33, at 162–63.
45. 1 WORLD BANK REPORT, supra note 28, at 17.
46. See id. (discussing the legal and regulatory framework).
47. World Bank, *West Bank and Gaza* (visited Mar. 29. 1999) <http://www.worldbank.org/html/extdrl/offrep/mena/wb&g.htm>. See also DEVELOPMENT UNDER ADVERSITY: THE PALESTINIAN ECONOMY IN TRANSITION (I. Diwan and R. A. Shaban, eds., 1999), at 15 ("With the signing of the Declaration of Principles in September 1993, there were high hopes for a quick resumption of economic growth. These expectations were based both on the presence of strong structural advantages in the Palestinian society and economy, and on the fact that for a variety of reasons, growth had remained below potential prior to the onset of the peace process").
48. "The Paris Protocol Gridlock ... What Next?" *Palestine Economic Pulse*, July-Aug. 1998, at 2, 3.
49. See id. at 2; see also Jawad Naji, "From the Editor," Palestine Economic Pulse, Sept.-Oct. 1998, at 1, 1 (citing the Undersecretary's argument that "peace between Israelis and Palestinians would never take hold unless accompanied by 'jobs and economic security'").
50. Radwan A. Shaban, *Worsening Economic Outcomes Since 1994 Despite Elements of Improvement*, in DEVELOPMENT UNDER ADVERSITY: THE PALESTINIAN ECONOMY IN TRANSITION, supra note , at 17, 20–26.
51. Khalil Shikaki, *The Politics of Paralysis II: Peace Now or Hamas Later*, FOREIGN AFF., July-Aug. 1998, at 29, 42. For data on Palestinian public opinion on economic issues, see Shaban, supra note 52, at 18–19.
52. For a description of the evolution of the international aid program for Palestine, see Ali Khadr, *Donor Assistance,* in DEVELOPMENT UNDER ADVERSITY: THE PALESTINIAN ECONOMY IN TRANSITION, supra note 49, at 143, 143–149.
53. See Fidler, supra note 27, at 541 (discussing Palestinian concerns over the aid program); and Khadr, supra note 54, at 149 ("The donor effort has been criticized for falling short of fulfilling its promise, with delays in committing funds and sluggish performance in implementing projects being the rule rather than the exception").
54. See World Bank, *West Bank and Gaza Update, First Quarter 1998*, (visited Feb. 24. 1999) <http://www.palecon.org/update/mar98/contents.html> (noting that negative political and economic events in the peace process "have thwarted donors' intentions and often impaired the most efficient use of their resources" and that "[d]onor assistance was redirected from intended investment to consumption-oriented, non-investment support aimed at mitigating the negative impact of these shocks"); and Khadr, *Donor Assistance,* supra note 54, at 149–152.
55. UNSCO, *Report on the Palestinian Economy, Autumn 1999* (visited May 1, 2000), http://www.arts.mcgill.ca/MEPP/unsco/palecon99/000.htm.
56. Id.; and UNSCO, *Report on the Palestinian Economy, Spring 1999* (visited May 1, 2000), http://www.arts.mcgill.ca/programs/policsci/faculty/rexb/unsco-sp99/part1.html.

57. UNSCO, *Report on the Palestinian Economy, Autumn 1999,* supra note 57.
58. Id.
59. Id.
60. UNSCO, *Report on the Palestinian Economy, Autumn 1999,* supra note 57; Kahdr, *Donor Assistance,* supra note 54, at 152–153.
61. Fidler, supra note 27, at 543.
62. Khadr, *Donor Assistance,* supra note 54, at 152.
63. Ishac Diwan, *International Economic Relations: Access, Trade Regime, and Development Strategy,* in DEVELOPMENT UNDER ADVERSITY: THE PALESTINIAN ECONOMY IN TRANSITION, supra note 49, at 84, 86 ("Instead of the expansion expected under the Economic Protocol, trade flows have collapsed in recent years"). For an economic assessment of the impact of border closures on the Palestinian economy during the peace process, see Radwan A. Shaban, *The Harsh Reality of Closure,* in DEVELOPMENT UNDER ADVERSITY: THE PALESTINIAN ECONOMY IN TRANSITION, supra note 49, at 45–65.
64. Id. at 50.
65. See id.; and Fidler, supra note 33, at 163–67 (discussing the havoc wreaked on the Palestinian economy by border closures).
66. See "Palestinian-Israeli Economic Relations," *Palestine Economic Pulse,* May-June 1998, at 4, 4 ("For Palestinians, the primary issue of free access to import and export markets collides with the central Israeli concern of security at all levels of debate"); Mel Levine, *Palestinian Economic Progress Under the Oslo Agreements,* 19 FORDHAM INT'L L. J. 1393, 1406 (1996) (arguing that the Israeli-Palestinian situation "is a classic political/economic conundrum").
67. *Palestinian-Israeli Economic Relations,* supra note 68, at 4. But see Wye River Memorandum, Oct. 23, 1998, Isr.-PLO, 37 I.L.M. 1251, art. III (renewing processes to work on economic development in parallel with security issues).
68. UNSCO, *Report on the Palestinian Economy, Autumn 1999,* supra note 57, at Part F.
69. For an analysis of the Economic Protocol, see Diwan, *International Economic Relations: Access, Trade Regime, and Development Strategy,* supra note 65, at 84–96.
70. See Fidler, supra note 33, at 166 (discussing Israeli nontariff barriers on Palestinian exports).
71. "The Paris Protocol Gridlock ... What Next?" supra note 50, at 3. The PA loses such revenue because under the Economic Protocol, customs duties paid on products destined for the Palestinian Territories are to be paid to the PA. Economic Protocol, supra note 34, art. III(15). The use of Israeli intermediaries means that goods really destined for the West Bank or Gaza are marked as Israeli imports, meaning the tariff payments go to Israel rather than the PA. The payment of such tariff revenues to the PA "is fundamental to the revenue performance of the PNA." "Development in Palestine: A New Direction," *Palestine Economic Pulse,* May-June 1996, at 2, 2. The practice of using Israeli intermediaries has resulted in the loss of "tens of millions of dollars of revenue" by the PA. Keith C. Molkner, *Legal and Structural Hurdles to Achieving Political Stability and Economic Development in the Palestinian Territories,* 19 FORDHAM INT'L L. J. 1419, 1448 (1996); see also Naji, supra note 51, at 1 (noting in late 1998 that "[m]onies lost to the Israeli treasury in this respect are estimated to have cost the PA some $350 million per annum"); and Diwan, *International Economic Relations: Access, Trade Regime, and Development Strategy,* supra note 65, at 87 (analyzing the tax leakage problem).
72. Fidler, supra note 33, at 167; Diwan, *International Economic Relations: Access, Trade Regime, and Development Strategy,* supra note 65, at 88 (noting that "the Israeli

trade regime has several disadvantages compared to an ideal regime chosen independently by the WBGS").

73. See. e.g., *Palestinian-Israeli Trade Relations: Free Trade Area or Customs Union?* 1 PALESTINE ECON. POLICY RESEARCH INST. 1 (Nov. 1996) (M.A.S.) (visited Sept. 8, 1998) <http://www.palecon.org/masdir/notes/freetrade.html> (reporting on economic forum debating optimal trade regime for Palestinian Territories); Fidler, supra note 33, at 188 (arguing that "the free trade area plus customs union arrangement needs to be replaced with a straight free trade agreement between the Palestinians and Israel"); "Palestinian-Israeli Economic Relations," supra note 68, at 4 (reporting on exchange of views at seminar on Israeli-Palestinian economic relations); "Political Separation and Economic Integration," *Palestine Economic Pulse*, May-June 1998, at 5 (reporting on economic integration ideas of Shimon Peres); "The Paris Protocol Gridlock ... What Next?" supra note 50, at 2 (analyzing the Economic Protocol); Joe Saba, "The World Bank on Palestinian Competitiveness," *Palestine Economic Pulse*, Sept.-Oct. 1998, at 3, 3–6 (recounting a recent speech by World Bank Resident Mission Director for the West Bank and Gaza arguing that the Economic Protocol and its application hurt Palestinian competitiveness); Diwan, *International Economic Relations: Access, Trade Regime, and Development Strategy,* supra note 65, at 93–95 (analyzing which trade regime with Israel would be best for the Palestinian economy).

74. Diwan, *International Economic Relations: Access, Trade Regime, and Development Strategy,* supra note 65, at 92 (noting that "the major goal of WBGS trade policy is to attract investment into the economy").

75. Id. at 88 (noting that the PA has signed ten bilateral trade agreements with other countries).

76. Id. at 89 (noting impact on Palestinian trade of lack of Palestinian trade infrastructure).

77. Jawad Naji, "From the Editor," *Palestine Economic Pulse*, Mar.-Apr. 1998, at 1.

78. Diwan, *International Economic Relations: Access, Trade Regime, and Development Strategy,* supra note 65, at 91 (discussing the Gaza airport and port and the problems their development has faced.)

79. Id. at 95.

80. Fidler, supra note 33, at 184–85 (discussing PA corruption and its effects on Palestinian economic development) (citing Neil MacFarquhar, "The Sullen Love: As Gaza Stagnates, Arafat is Blamed as Well as Israel," *New York Times*, Aug. 16, 1997, at 1). After investigating PA corruption. David Hirst of the *Guardian* newspaper concluded in April 1997 that Arafat "and his coterie of unofficial economic 'advisors' have thrown up a ramshackle, nepotistic edifice of monopoly, racketeering and naked extortion which merely enriches them as it further impoverishes society at large." David Hirst, "Shameless in Gaza," *Guardian*, Apr. 21, 1997, at 9.

81. "Economic Diary," *Palestine Economic Pulse*, July-Aug. 1998, at 15, 15.

82. Fidler, supra note 33, at 183.

83. See Hirst, supra note 82, at 9.

84. Fidler, supra note 33, at 183.

85. Id. at 183 (quoting Letter to President Clinton from Gershon Baskin, Israeli Director of the Israel-Palestinian Center for Research and Information, Apr. 4, 1997 (on file with author); see also Saba, supra note 75, at 4–5 (analyzing the detrimental economic consequences of the development of "Palestinian public or semi-public monopolies" for importing goods).

86. See Saba, supra note 75, at 6 (urging PA to privatize the public and semi-public enterprises dominating importing).

87. World Bank, *West Bank and Gaza,* supra note 49; see also Saba, supra note 75, at 4 (World Bank official arguing in September 1998 that Palestinian economic development is still hindered by the "[c]ontinued lack of development of the legal infrastructure for business").

88. UNSCO, *Report on the Palestinian Economy, Autumn 1999,* supra note 57, at Executive Summary. See also Osama Hamed, *Private Investment,* in DEVELOPMENT IN ADVERSITY: THE PALESTINIAN ECONOMY IN TRANSITION, supra note 49, at 69, 70 (arguing that "[t]he present legal environment needs significant improvement to attract investors").

89. See, e.g., Hamed, *Private Investment,* supra note 90, at 70–71 (discussing flaws in the present Palestinian investment law); David P. Fidler, *Foreign Private Investment in Palestine Revisited: An Analysis of the Revised Palestinian Investment* Law, 31 CASE W. RES. J. INT'L L. 293 (1999) (critically analyzing the revised Palestinian Investment Law); *The Legal Framework for Business in the West Bank and Gaza Strip,* MAS POL'Y NOTES 3 (Sept. 1996) Palestine Economic Policy Research Institute (MAS) <http://www.palecon.org/masdir/notes/framework.html> (discussing critical comments of Joseph Battat of the World Bank on the original Palestinian Investment Law); World Bank, *West Bank and Gaza,* supra note 49 (arguing the PA "should give early attention to passage of a new investment law"); Fidler, supra note 27, at 529 (providing a critical analysis of original Palestinian Investment Law); David P. Fidler, *Economic Development, Foreign Investment and the Peace Process: Recent Events Make Revision of Palestinian Investment Law Even More Critical,* MIDDLE E. EXECUTIVE REP., Nov. 1996, at 8.

90. See Sam Bahour, "Telecommunications Regulations ... Competency is a Must," *Palestine Economic Pulse,* May-June-1998, at 13 (stating that "[a] serious review of this Law ... is urgently needed. In its current somewhat antiquated form, it lacks the necessary provisions for the dynamic challenges facing the global telecommunications sector).

91. See Ezra Sadan, *Industrial Parks in Territories Controlled by the PA* (visited Mar. 5. 1999) <http://www.ipcri.org/ind.html> (reporting that potential investors are worried about incomplete legislation).

92. See "The PSE — Ahead of Its Time," *Palestine Economic Pulse,* May-June 1998, at 11 (noting that "[r]egulation is also still a serious problem").

93. See Saba, supra note 75, at 4 (noting the need to improve Palestinian tax, judicial, commercial, and property laws).

94. See, e.g., World Bank, *West Bank and Gaza Update, Second Quarter 1998* (visited Sept. 8, 1998) <http://www.palecon.org/update/jun98/operations.html> (reporting on World Bank's U.S.$5.5 million Legal Development Project that "aims at assisting the PA in modernizing the legal framework and increasing the efficiency and predictability of the judicial process" and on World Bank's specific efforts on insurance, securities, mortgage, tax, mutual funds, and competition law reform). On Palestinian legal reform generally, see Hiram E. Chodosh and Stephen A. Mayo, *The Palestinian Legal Study: Consensus and Assessment of the New Palestinian Legal System,* 38 HARV. INT'L L. J. 375 (1997); and George E. Bisharat, *Peace and the Political Imperative of Legal Reform in Palestine,* 31 CASE W. RES. J. INT'L L. 253 (1999).

95. See THE PALESTINIAN BASIC LAW (Third Reading) (1998) (Palestine), translated by Saladin Al-Jurf [hereinafter BASIC LAW]. The text of the BASIC LAW is reprinted in 31 CASE W. RES. J. INT'L L. 495 (1999). For an analysis of the BASIC LAW, see Adrien Katherine Wing, *The Palestinian Basic Law: Embryonic Constitutionalism,* 31 CASE W. RES. J. INT'L L. 383 (1999).

96. Julian Borger, "The Shadow of the Hawk," *Guardian,* Aug. 17, 1998, at 2

("Arafat has so far withheld his signature from a basic law that would provide the [PA] with a constitutional structure"); Wing, supra note 97, at 403 (noting that the "final version [of the BASIC LAW] remains on President Arafat's desk").

97. See also Wing, supra note 97, at 403–404 (stating that she "was told the principal reason for his refusal to sign is that the Basic Law establishes checks and balances that would fill the constitutional vacuum and end the legal possibility of governance by executive fiat").

98. See Deborah Horan, *Israeli and Palestinian Investors Are for Peace*, Inter Press Serv., Feb. 2, 1998, available in LEXIS, News Library, CURNWS File (noting concerns of businessmen about the lack of a basic law and the condition of laws governing commerce).

99. AMNESTY INTERNATIONAL, PA: PROLONGED POLITICAL DETENTION, TORTURE, AND UNFAIR TRIALS, AI INDEX: MDE 15/68/96 (1996); see also Fidler, supra note 33, at 185–86 (discussing human rights abuses of PA).

100. Wye River Memorandum, supra note 69, art. II.C.4.

101. See, e.g., Bisharat, supra note 96, at 274–283 (analyzing human rights abuses by the PA in four areas: (1) illegal and arbitrary arrests and detentions; (2) torture and physical abuse of detainees; (3) unfair trials; and (4) violating freedom of press and public expression).

102. UNSCO, *Report on the Palestinian Economy, Autumn 1999*, supra note 57 (noting that construction activity is "the main component of private investment" in the Palestinian economy). For analysis of private investment in housing in Palestine, see Hamed, *Private Investment*, supra note 90, at 73–77.

103. World Bank, *West Bank and Gaza Update, First Quarter 1998*, supra note 56; see also United Nations Office of the Special Coordinator in the Occupied Territories, *UNSCO Report on Economic and Social Conditions in the West Bank and Gaza Strip* (Spring 1998) (visited Sept. 8, 1998) <http://www.arts.mcgill.ca/mepp/unsco/unqr.html>, at 6 ("Residential construction has been and remains the main type of private investment in the WBGS").

104. World Bank, *West Bank and Gaza, 1st Quarter, 1998*, supra note 56.

105. See id.

106. See *Palestine Special Report*, MEED WEEKLY SPECIAL REPORT, July 17, 1998, available in LEXIS, News Library, CURNWS File (citing IMF analysis of Palestinian private investment).

107. UNSCO, *Report on the Palestinian Economy, Autumn 1999*, supra note 57.

108. Id.

109. Id.

110. See Hamed, *Private Investment*, supra note 90, at 71–72 (describing the Gaza Industrial Estate).

111. See World Bank, *West Bank and Gaza*, supra note 49 (noting that surveys indicate that the initial tenants of the Gaza industrial zone "will come mainly from existing enterprises in Gaza, and some West Bank, Israeli, and overseas Palestinian groups"); see also Fidler, supra note 33, at 180–81 (discussing problems that have plagued the industrial zones concept).

112. *Political Separation and Economic Integration*, supra note 75, at 5.

113. Id.

114. UNSCO, *Report on the Palestinian Economy, Autumn 1999*, supra note 57, at Executive Summary.

115. Palestine Trade Center, *National Trade Dialogue Project (NTDP)* (visited May 8, 2000), <http://www.paltrade.org/paltrade.htm>.

116. Id.

117. Id.

118. Id.

119. Paltrade's NDTP initiative does not mean that the governmental and intergovernmental entities involved in trying to foster Palestinian economic development did not recognize the importance of the Palestinian private sector. What Paltrade's initiative does suggest, however, is that such recognition from governments and international organizations remained theoretical and that mechanisms for effective input from the Palestinian private sector were never really constructed.

120. ABED, supra note 24, at xi.

121. Fidler, supra note 27, at 534, ftn. 18.

122. Salah Abdelshaffi, *The Identity of the Palestinian Economy in the Face of Globalization*, summarized in Paltrade, *National Trade Dialogue Project*, supra note 117.

123. FRIEDMAN, supra note 16, at 104–105.

124. Paltrade, *National Trade Dialogue Project*, supra note 117.

125. *Interview with Mr. Nassar Nassar*, 5 PALTRADER 1 (April 2000).

126. FRIEDMAN, supra note 16, at 105–06.

127. See, e.g., Samir Abdullah, *Prospects for Final Status Economic Relations with Israel*, summarized in Paltrade, *National Trade Dialogue Project (NTDP)*, supra note 117 (analyzing three choices regarding future trade relations with Israel: economic separation, a free-trade agreement, and a customs union).

12

Legal and Structural Hurdles to Achieving Political Stability and Economic Development in the Palestinian Territories
KEITH C. MOLKNER

INTRODUCTION

The following essay was written in an attempt to condense into a few pages various observations and impressions resulting from nearly 30 months of continuous involvement in economic and legal aspects of the Middle East peace process. Ninety-five percent of it was written immediately before the renewal in February 1996 of terrorist bombings in Israeli cities and the subsequent prolonged closure of the Palestinian Territories. Following these events, certain changes were added to the text in an attempt to address the tragic loss of life and the current precariousness of the peace process.

The essay was originally composed in a spirit of cautious optimism, recognizing the seriousness of the hurdles before the Israeli and Palestinian peoples, but believing in their dedication to putting decades of tragic conflict and suffering firmly behind them. The later additions, however, were written during a period of sadness and anxiety. As this book goes to print, none can tell how deeply the peace process has been damaged. The decision to publish the essay in spite of the present difficulties was therefore not easy. Nonetheless, irrespective of the fluid political situation, the basic underlying realities and interests remain the same. Hopefully, the discussion in this essay of specific hurdles to stability and development will be of some use to those who, sooner or later, will have to find solutions to these problems.

I. PARAMETERS OF THE PROBLEM

The current Middle East peace process is built, in large part, on two sea changes in the psychology of conflict that has plagued the region for decades: Israeli recognition of Palestinian aspirations to self-determination and Palestinian recognition of the legitimacy of the Israeli State. In recent years, bilateral and multilateral negotiations between Israel and the surrounding Arab states have introduced important additional elements, such as: full peace with Jordan; active ties with Morocco, Oman, and Qatar; lower intensity but important ties with several other Arab states in North Africa and the Gulf; and ongoing peace talks with Lebanon and Syria. These other developments, however, were made politically possible by means of mutual recognition on the part of Israel and the Palestinian Liberation Organization ("PLO"). Furthermore, continued improvement in Arab-Israeli relations will remain dependent on future progress in Israeli-Palestinian rapprochement. Thus, successful implementation of the agreements on Palestinian self-rule is critical to a comprehensive and durable Middle East peace.

The successful implementation of Palestinian self-rule, in turn, relies on two major criteria: the establishment of stable and effective governance, and real economic growth that is rapid, profound, and sustained. Leaders both within and without the region have repeated that if it is to succeed, the peace process must deliver real and visible improvements in the lives of ordinary people. In the case of the Palestinians, this primarily means that disorder, violence, and wide-scale poverty must cease.

As the institutions of Palestinian self-government have evolved, it has become increasingly apparent that the principal challenge for Palestinian decision-makers will be to establish structural and legal bases for the emergence of a civil society and a dynamic economy. Only by creating a new environment that protects individual liberties and encourages entrepreneurial activity will the current process enable the Palestinian people to reap the benefits of peace. The hurdles that confront Palestinian decision makers in this regard are considerable, and may be divided into two groups. First, Palestinian leaders must recognize and resolve the "structural" challenges reflected in the political and economic realities imposed by current events. These include the peace process with Israel, the creation of the Palestinian National Authority ("PNA"),[1] and the more recent creation of the Palestinian Council.[2] The second group of hurdles facing Palestinian authorities are legal. These challenges embody the legal fallout of the region's tumultuous recent history, which has resulted in an awkward amalgam of laws derived from legislation enacted under the auspices of various rulers who have controlled the West Bank and Gaza (collectively, "Palestinian Territories") at different periods during this century. This essay addresses both groups of hurdles, structural and legal, in turn.

II. STRUCTURAL HURDLES

The structural hurdles to development have unfolded in lockstep with the establishment of Palestinian self-government. The optimism among Palestinians during late 1993, when Israel and the PLO signed the Declaration of Principles on Interim Self-Government Arrangements,[3] cooled as it became apparent that Palestinian aspirations for full independence, democratic government, and economic prosperity would not occur immediately. Contrary to popular expectations, the end of Israeli military rule over Gaza, Jericho,[4] and, later, other West Bank cities[5] did not automatically lead to an improvement in economic life or the establishment of a genuine rule of law. In fact, the changes led to new economic, political, and administrative problems.

A. Economic Problems

The most dramatic of the structural problems facing Palestinian decision makers is the painful economic transition currently under way. Unemployment has risen sharply since the early months of the peace process, approaching 60 percent in Gaza alone. Over 100,000 Palestinians who formerly worked in Israel found themselves jobless as the Israeli Government implemented its policy of "separation" between the two peoples.[6] The results for the Palestinian economy have been devastating.

Initially, Palestinian leaders hoped that new enterprises would be initiated in the areas under Palestinian self-rule, providing alternative sources of employment. The shortage of capital in the Palestinian economy, however, made it imperative that Palestinian leaders attract substantial investment by diaspora Palestinians[7] and other foreign investors. Unfortunately, such foreign investment has yet to materialize. Thus, while many new companies have been registered, comparatively few factories and other job-creating enterprises have been established.

In addition to unemployment, the Palestinian economy suffers from restrictions on the movement of Palestinian goods into Israel. While Israel and the PLO signed a customs union agreement nearly two years ago providing for free movement of industrial goods and most agricultural produce,[8] the Israeli security closures constitute a formidable barrier to the entry of Palestinian goods. Not only has this nontariff barrier resulted in largely one-way Israeli-Palestinian trade, it has also interfered with Palestinian exports to third markets and hampered commerce between Gaza and the West Bank.

Finally, the financial and banking sectors of the Palestinian economy are only now emerging from 27 years of marginal existence. Arab and foreign banks existing in the West Bank and Gaza prior to the 1967 Arab-Israeli War were closed by Israeli Military Order shortly after the entry of Israeli forces. Direct financial links to the Arab world were severed and Palestinians came to rely on gray market providers of financial services, such as money changers and money lenders.[9]

Following the signing of the Declaration of Principles, several Jordanian and Palestinian banks quickly moved to open or reopen branches in the West Bank and Gaza. Presently, about 12 banks operate over 50 branches in the Palestinian Territories, roughly a 500 percent increase in institutional coverage since September 1993.[10] Furthermore, total deposits increased tenfold from 1993 to 1995.[11] Despite this dramatic expansion, the Palestinian banking sector continues to be characterized by poor regulation and insufficient service. Lending remains heavily constricted and conventional wisdom attributes this, in part, to bank-facilitated capital flight. Moreover, the lack of a central check clearance facility and the prevalence of dishonored checks seriously impede the development of an efficient system of payments. The larger effect of such problems is an insufficient harnessing of domestic financial resources for the development of the Palestinian economy.

B. Political Problems

While the economic problems described above exert the strongest direct effect on the majority of Palestinian individuals and families, the problems that attract the greatest attention of foreign governments, international media, and the Palestinian leaders themselves, are essentially political. These problems implicate the central question of the peace process: will the Palestinian leadership be able to provide political stability and maintain its internal legitimacy while simultaneously fulfilling its obligations to Israel and concluding further Israeli-Palestinian negotiations? For the peace process to succeed, the answer must be affirmative.

The Palestinian leadership has been walking a political tightrope ever since the negotiations known as the "secret Oslo channel"[12] became publicly disclosed. Historically, the PLO strove to be a broad-based national organization that, although dominated by Fatah,[13] was willing to accommodate all movements dedicated to the "liberation" of Palestine. Since the Fatah leadership undertook, on behalf of the PLO, to recognize Israel and to foreswear the use of violence, however, a rift has opened in Palestinian society between "moderates" who support working towards Palestinian statehood within the framework of transitional autonomy, and "extremists" who reject any negotiated solution that concedes maximalist Palestinian claims. The Palestinian leadership thus finds itself under pressure both from Israel and the West, particularly the United States, to crack down on extremists and from a substantial portion of its own constituency to renounce the new partnership with Israel and the United States.

The conflicting political pressures that Palestinian leaders face are well-illustrated by the issue of the Palestinian Covenant.[14] The Covenant, essentially the PLO's charter, calls for the destruction of Israel and implicitly rejects a peaceful solution to the conflict. Israeli Prime Minister Yitzhak Rabin made the renunciation of these provisions a precondition to Israeli recognition of the PLO and the signing of the Declaration of Principles.[15] Accordingly, on September 9, 1993, PLO Chairman Yasser Arafat wrote a letter to Prime Minister Rabin declaring these articles inoperative and undertaking to make the necessary changes in the covenant. Despite repeated demands by Israel and the United States that the changes be made, however, and despite repeated promises by Chairman Arafat to do so, the covenant remains unchanged.[16]

Failure to amend the covenant revealed the precarious position of the PNA, at least prior to the elections of January 20, 1996.[17] Political reality dictated that the PNA satisfy minimum Israeli expectations, particularly with regard to the prevention of violence against Israelis, while preserving a demeanor of dialogue and national unity that included, rather than excluded, the Islamicists and other members of the emergent opposition. When a series of bus bombings in Israeli cities in late 1994 and early 1995 nearly brought the peace process to a standstill,[18] however, it became increasingly problematic for Palestinian leaders to speak in English of peace and coexistence while continuing to speak in Arabic of *jihad*.[19]

Following the repeated spectacle of Palestinian police arresting large numbers of suspects after each terror strike against Israel and then releasing them a few days later,[20] the PNA acted to assert its authority. Various tactics were used to put an end to instability and violence. Attempts were made to coopt, marginalize, intimidate, or incarcerate opponents of the regime. Special closed courts were established to try "security offenders" under military procedures without providing proper defense counsel.[21] Journalists, newspaper editors, and human rights activists who spoke out found themselves unemployed or, in some cases, jailed.[22] In one case, *Al-Nahar*, a major Palestinian newspaper with an "errant" editorial policy, was closed for an extended period.

The Palestinian elections were optimistically expected to presage the arrival of a new period of democratization and political calm. Generally, the populace deemed the elections a success. The voting, which was monitored by large numbers of local and international observers, was by most reports orderly and fair.[23] Yet, the fact that Hamas[24] and other opposition movements boycotted the election, and that heavy-handed tactics were used to promote favorable press coverage of Fatah candidates and suppress opponents,[25] revealed the limits on stability and genuine democracy in the nascent Palestinian political system. Despite such concerns, however, in the immediate aftermath of the elections, it was generally thought that the new council would enjoy greater popular legitimacy than the unelected authority which preceded it. Well-wishers hoped that this expanded legitimacy would lead to greater freedom of action regarding relations with Israel, increased internal stability, and heightened respect for the rule of law.

Tragically, the Palestinian political system and the peace process itself were subjected to a devastating shock before the council had ever convened. The recent bombings of Israeli busses and a street corner by Hamas terrorists in late February and early March, 1996,[26] resulted in an indefinite cessation of Israeli-Palestinian talks and a protracted closure of the Palestinian Territories.[27] Support for the peace process has fallen dramatically among both Israelis, concerned for their security, and Palestinians, suffering from the effects of the closure.[28] It remains to be seen whether the Palestinian political leadership will be able both to recapture Palestinian popular support for the peace process and convince Israel that it is doing all it can to break the terrorist infrastructure and contain extremism. It also remains to be seen whether the Palestinian leadership will continue to have Israeli partners in peacemaking following the Israeli general elections in May, 1996. Support among the Israeli public for the peace process has fallen dramatically, as have the chances for reelection of Prime Minister Shimon Peres.[29] Chairman Arafat and the Palestinian leadership have come under tremendous pressure to dissolve the infrastructure of terrorist groups inside the Palestinian Territories. Meanwhile, the Israeli Government has declared that if Arafat fails to do so, Israel will. In the wake of the bombings, Chairman Arafat banned all armed groups inside Palestinian-controlled territory and committed his regime to confiscating their weapons and arresting their hardcore members. Action by the Palestinian security forces to fully implement these commitments will probably result in serious armed resistance. Failure to take meaningful action, however, will, in all likelihood, permanently doom the peace process.

C. Administrative Problems

In addition to the economic and political problems discussed above, Palestinian development also faces hurdles engendered by administrative problems. These structural problems affect the quality of daily administration by Palestinian officials of the territories under their jurisdiction. As a result of these problems, Palestinian governance is less efficient and effective than it would otherwise be.

One source of inefficiency stems directly from the interim structure of the peace process. This structure is based on a gradual transfer of power and responsibility from the Israel Defense Forces ("IDF") to a Palestinian Interim Self-Government Authority over a five-year transitional period, followed by the negotiation of a final settlement.[30] While the history of mutual mistrust may have made this formula a tactical necessity designed to gradually build confidence on both sides, it is nonetheless extraordinarily difficult for Palestinian decision makers to embark upon long-term planning in the absence of a final status agreement. In particular, Palestinian leaders and officials are presently in the awkward position of administering the powers and territories under their jurisdiction without assurance concerning what the final extent of these powers and territories will be. Thus, they are uncertain whether Palestinian self-rule will ultimately take the form of an independent state, a confederation with Jordan, or some other, as yet undisclosed, arrangement.

Additional administrative problems derive from the geographic division of the territories under Palestinian self-government into two major territorial units: the West Bank and the Gaza Strip. Prior to the implementation of Palestinian self-rule, the West Bank and the Gaza Strip had functioned as two distinct administrative units since the 1948 Arab-Israeli War.[31] This long separation continues to have important consequences for the administration of the territories under Palestinian self-government. For example, the court systems of the West Bank and the Gaza Strip remain separate and distinct, each governed by its own rules and procedures. While the PNA took some steps to harmonize the two judicial systems under the administrative framework of its Ministry of Justice, it remains unclear how or whether the two systems will ultimately be unified.

Still more important, as will be discussed below, two separate legal systems exist in the Palestinian Territories. Whereas the legal system of Gaza derives from English common law, the legal system of the West Bank is based on the legal tradition of Jordan, which is heavily derived from civil law. That Palestinian officials must currently administer two different legal systems further contributes to the administrative complexity of Palestinian self-governance.

Administrative difficulties such as these are considerably heightened by the noncontiguous geography of the West Bank and Gaza. It is often difficult or impossible for Palestinians, including public officials, to get permission to cross Israeli territory in order to move between the two territories. Various plans have been discussed regarding creation of a safe passage through Israel for travelers moving between Gaza and the West Bank. None of them, however, have yet been put into action. Furthermore, those parts of the West Bank that are currently under various forms of Palestinian self-rule, commonly referred to as Areas "A" and "B," are themselves noncontiguous. Thus, passage between them, while not as difficult as passage between the West Bank and Gaza, still involves travel through the Israeli-controlled portions of the West Bank, known as Area "C."[32] Lastly, an additional impediment to efficient and effective administration is the fact that while the Palestinian Council has jurisdiction over civil affairs in both Areas "A" and "B" in the West Bank, PNA police can operate only in Area "A."[33]

A final set of administrative problems stems from corrupt practices within the PNA. Stories abound concerning individuals who have exploited their positions within the PNA for personal gain. While these stories may well be exaggerated, it generally appears that the PNA has suffered from a certain level of corruption. Among other allegations, it has been credibly reported that certain Israeli companies have successfully employed improper financial inducements to gain monopoly positions with respect to the import of certain goods into the Palestinian market. One may hope that the newly elected Palestinian Council will be able to disclose and reduce, or eliminate, such corrupt practices.

III. Legal Hurdles

The present legal structures in the Palestinian Territories also constitute a major hurdle to development. As noted above, the existence of two separate legal systems for Gaza and the West Bank constitutes a source of inefficiency that hampers economic development. Furthermore, not only are the legal systems of Gaza and the West Bank inconsistent with one another, they are also each internally disharmonious.

The internal disharmony of the Gaza and West Bank legal systems stems from the fact that each system is constructed from a confoundingly complicated body of diverse legal sources. The laws of Gaza are comprised of British Mandate ordinances, as amended and supplemented by Egyptian and Israeli military orders. The laws of the West Bank, in contrast, are comprised of Jordanian statutes, as amended and supplemented by a different set of Israeli military orders. In addition, the legal systems of the West Bank and Gaza both contain a residue of Ottoman law in certain legal fields, as well as new enactments by the PNA. Thus, inconsistency between the laws of the West Bank and Gaza is aggravated by the internal disharmony and complexity of the two legal systems.

Furthermore, the British and Jordanian ordinances and laws that comprise the statutory basis of the legal systems in Gaza and the West Bank, respectively, are also generally anachronistic. The British ordinances are entirely comprised of pre–1948 laws, while the Jordanian laws date from before June 1967. These laws often embody legal thinking and terminology that are outdated and unsuited for modern economies. Additionally, many of these laws have been amended by cumbersome Israeli military orders that are often insufficiently hospitable to commercial and other economic activity.

While thousands of military orders were promulgated by the Israeli military authorities in the West Bank and Gaza beginning in 1967, they have never been fully compiled and consolidated. Furthermore, a significant number of military orders and policy directives have not even been made available outside the IDF and the Civil Administration.[34] Thus, a certain level of legal uncertainty exists in the West Bank and Gaza regarding the laws in force. Finally, because the amendments by military order were generally drafted to serve the needs of Israeli security rather than Palestinian development, several of the military orders amend laws in a manner that renders them overly burdensome and restrictive.

The disharmony, uncertainty, and confusion associated with the legal systems in the West Bank and Gaza have resulted in various concerns on the part of international investors and business interests regarding the legal vacuum in the Palestinian Territories. Despite such problems, however, the legal system functions surprisingly well on a day-to-day basis. Business is conducted successfully and routinely in the West Bank and Gaza. Palestinian courts operate under well-established procedures and adjudicate a wide variety of commercial cases. In addition, alternative mechanisms for resolving disputes are frequently employed and carry the force of cultural tradition behind them. These mechanisms include mediation, conventional arbitration, and traditional practices of conciliation known as *Sulha*.[35]

The primary legislative challenge presently before the newly elected Palestinian Council is to review the body of laws in the West Bank and Gaza and to identify priority areas for legal reform. Such reforms should be built on the existing legal structures to which Palestinians are accustomed, but should eliminate harmful anachronism, incongruity, and irrationality. By thus modernizing and harmonizing commercial legislation in an organized and well-considered fashion, the Palestinian Council will be able to systematically eliminate the existing legal hurdles to economic development.

The remainder of this essay briefly surveys three legal fields that the Palestinian Council is likely to address in the near future: investment law, banking law, and tax law. Each of these fields currently presents various hurdles to economic development.

A. Investment Law

As mentioned above, local and foreign investment in the Palestinian economy is one of the foremost requirements of Palestinian economic growth. This was recognized early on in the peace process, as evidenced in an annex to the Declaration of Principles, which calls for Israeli-Palestinian cooperation in the creation of a "Financial Development and Action Program" to encourage international investment in the region.[36] While such a cooperative program has yet to be established, the PNA placed considerable emphasis, almost from the date of its inception, on the creation of a new Palestinian investment law.

At the time of the Israeli withdrawal from Gaza and Jericho and the creation of the PNA, the legal structure in place for encouraging investment in the West Bank and Gaza was disharmonious, confusing, and inadequate. This legal structure consisted of a 1967 Jordanian law,[37] two Israeli military orders,[38] and a set of policy directives issued by the Israeli Civil Administration in the West Bank.[39] These laws, orders, and directives relied on discretionary decision making and heavy administrative control while granting insufficient incentives and legal guarantees to investors. The PNA earmarked the replacement of this legal structure with a modern, unified investment law representing the first commercial law reform.

A drafting period of several months ensued during late 1994 and early 1995 that saw the preparation and circulation of a number of draft Palestinian investment laws. Ultimately, the final draft was submitted by the

PNA Ministry of Economics, Trade, and Industry to Chairman Arafat and the PNA Council of Ministers. Following its approval of the draft, the PNA promulgated the Law on the Encouragement of Investment ("Investment Law") on April 29, 1995.[40]

The Investment Law sets forth a new legal structure for the encouragement of investment and revokes all prior inconsistent legislation. For the time being, however, the law has entered into force only in those areas of the West Bank and the Gaza Strip that fall within the legislative jurisdiction of the Palestinian Council,[41] specifically, the Gaza Strip (excluding Israeli settlements and the IDF base) and Areas "A" and "B" of the West Bank. According to the law, the council's jurisdiction is to be extended over 18 months to the remaining Area "C" territories, except for those areas that are linked with issues to be negotiated in the "final status talks."[42] Concurrently, the Israeli military orders and Civil Administration directives concerning investment will remain in force throughout the interim period in all areas not transferred to the jurisdiction of the Palestinian Council.

The Investment Law represents a major improvement over the earlier laws, military orders, and directives in force in the West Bank and Gaza. The law is marred, however, by several features that, in effect, constitute obstacles to the creation of a legal structure that will be genuinely attractive to investors. These legal hurdles fall into three basic categories: the investment law's guarantees and protections for investors, incentives, and the administrative framework.

1. Investor Guarantees. The Investment Law provides several guarantees of the rights of investors, including prohibition of expropriation, guaranteed national treatment of foreign investors, and free repatriation of profits and capital.[43] One problem with these guarantees, however, is that their terminology and language is not fully consistent with internationally accepted legal usage. By thus deviating from standard international language, the Investment Law engenders a lack of clarity regarding the interpretation of the guarantees. The Investment Law poses a second problem related to the guarantee of investor rights in its provision stating that Palestinian investors will be given a "priority" in the purchase of tax-exempt fixed assets from other investors.[44] While it is unclear from the Investment Law how this priority is to be implemented, it appears to compromise the guarantee of equal treatment of foreign investors. A final problem is that while the Investment Law gives Palestinian Courts jurisdiction to adjudicate investment disputes,[45] it fails to make reference to the option of using independent arbitration or various international dispute resolution mechanisms in appropriate cases. As foreign investors often have greater confidence in such mechanisms than in local courts, the Investment Law would be more encouraging to such investors if it included a statement recognizing the right of investors to make use of such mechanisms where agreed upon by the disputants or where called for under international agreements.

2. **Incentives.** The incentive structure created by the Investment Law consists of exemptions from income taxes and dues for a specified number of years.[46] The Investment Law provides for both "regular exemptions" (fixed term) and "exceptional exemptions" (discretionary term). The Investment Law also establishes the Higher Palestinian Agency for the Encouragement of Investment ("Agency"), which is responsible for administering the exemptions. Only investment projects which have been approved by the Board of Directors of the Agency ("Board") may receive exemptions.

The major shortcoming of this incentive structure is its reliance on excessive exercise of discretion by the Agency and the Board. Generally, under the Investment Law, investment incentives should "to the extent possible be automatically granted, directly linked to the type of activity to be encouraged and equally extended"[47] to foreign and local investors alike. Under the Investment Law, however, applications for exemptions are to be approved or rejected on what is essentially a discretionary basis. While the Investment Law provides that the Board must state reasons for its decision on an application,[48] it does not provide clear and binding criteria to be used in reaching the decision. Furthermore, the Investment Law fails to provide firm guarantees against arbitrary actions that alter the status of exemptions after they are granted. As a result of such reliance on open-ended discretionary decision making, the Investment Law fails to provide an incentive structure that is rational and predictable.

3. **Administration.** The framework for administering the Investment Law is centered on the board of the agency. The board is comprised of 15 members, each of whom serves a three-year term.[49] The primary functions of the board include carrying out the business of the agency, deciding on applications for exemptions, and suspending or revoking exemptions for violations of the law.[50]

The major problem regarding this administrative framework is that the board appears to be less a professional body of impartial civil servants than a collection of disparate, potentially competing political interests. Thirteen of the 15 members of the board are political appointees selected by the Chairman of the PNA. Furthermore, only one of the members is a full-time employee of the agency. This highly politicized administrative structure creates the potential that political interests and institutional biases of members stemming from their activities outside the agency will unduly influence the board's decision making. This potential could undermine investor confidence in the impartiality of the administration of the Investment Law.

A related criticism of the administrative framework created by the Investment Law concerns the fact that the general tone and emphasis of the Investment Law seem to be placed on administration as a tool of bureaucratic control rather than a means of efficient and liberal treatment of investment. This tone and emphasis is exemplified by, inter alia, the failure of the Investment Law to provide a mechanism for challenging a rejection of an application for benefits. Furthermore, while the Investment Law does provide a right of appeal in the case of investors whose exemptions are suspended or revoked by the agency, the appeal must be made directly to the Chairman of the PNA.[51] This type of mechanism for direct appeal of administrative disputes to the chief executive is highly irregular and further reflects the Investment Law's tendency towards heavy administrative and political control.

While these legal hurdles represent genuine obstacles to the encouragement of investment in the Palestinian economy, the promulgation of a uniform Palestinian investment law represents a substantial step forward in the creation of a modern Palestinian legal infrastructure. It should also be remembered that the Investment Law represents the first achievement of Palestinian commercial law reform. Moreover, problematic features of the Investment Law can be corrected by enacting amendments as the commercial law reform process continues to develop. The inauguration of the newly elected Palestinian Council may create opportunities for specialized legislative review and, where necessary, amendment of legal enactments promulgated by the PNA prior to the elections. If this is the case, the Investment Law would be an obvious candidate for such review.

B. Banking Law

The emergence of a strong banking sector in the Palestinian Territories is one of the primary prerequisites for economic development. The large-scale return of Palestinian and foreign, mostly Jordanian, banks to the West Bank and Gaza over the last two and one half years is a positive development that has already had a pronounced effect on savings patterns. Previously limited to using Israeli banks, money changers, or various informal financial institutions, Palestinians now have access to modern banks located in all the cities and major towns of the West Bank and Gaza. The expansion of the banking sector, however, has highlighted the inadequacy of the present banking laws and engendered several new problems.

The banking laws presently in force in the West Bank and Gaza are outdated and incomplete. The most important banking statute in effect in the West Bank is the Jordanian Banking Law of 1966.[52] Its equivalent in Gaza is the British Mandate Palestine Banking Ordinance of 1941.[53] While numerous Israeli military orders have directly or indirectly amended the banking law in the Palestinian Territories, many of them were never given effect or enforced.[54] In fact, the volume and disorganization of the military amendments has rendered it at times difficult to determine precisely what the current law requires. This complicated legal structure constitutes a serious hurdle for regulators, the banking sector, and the entire financial infrastructure of the Palestinian economy.

Efforts to reform the legal structure as it applies to the banking industry must address three major types of problems currently afflicting the banking sector. First, as the newly established Palestinian Monetary Authority[55] ("PMA") has not yet fully developed its licensing and supervisory capacities, banks are operating in the Palestinian Territories with a minimum of regulatory oversight. Second, despite the dramatic increase in the number of operating banks, the provision of essential banking facilities, such as lending and checking services, remain well below required levels. Third, and finally, Palestinian businessmen and economists have raised serious concerns that foreign banks are exporting Palestinian deposits to finance lending operations abroad, precisely at a time when the Palestinian economy is suffering from an acute shortage of capital.

These problems figure prominently in the effort currently under way to reform the banking laws and regulations in the West Bank and Gaza. It remains uncertain whether this effort will ultimately result in a total unification of the banking laws of the West Bank and Gaza, or whether the harmonization will be more limited and gradual. In any case, modernization of banking and related laws is a high priority of the PMA. Such reforms are particularly necessary with respect to four legal fields: licensing, supervision, system of payments, and lending.

1. Licensing. The Bank of Israel was responsible for licensing banks in the West Bank and Gaza from June 1967 until the May 1994 signing of the Economic Protocol. The Economic Protocol provided for the creation of the PMA as the licensing authority for banking activities in the Palestinian Territories. The PMA was formally constituted by an executive decree issued by Chairman Arafat in January 1995.

Once the Israeli-Palestinian peace process opened the way for Arab and foreign banks to return to the Palestinian Territories, Jordanian banks quickly moved to assume a dominant position in the region. Since the PMA did not come into being until 1995, and since Israel and Jordan had already concluded a memorandum of understanding on banking cooperation by December 1993, Jordanian banks applied to the Bank of Israel for licenses to open branches in the Palestinian Territories until the PMA was established. The PNA subsequently agreed with the Jordanian Government that the PMA would retroactively approve licenses issued to Jordanian banks by the Bank of Israel during this period. Most of the banks presently operating in the Palestinian territories are, therefore, operating under conditions set forth in the licenses issued by the Bank of Israel prior to the cancellation of its supervisory role in the Palestinian Territories.

The PMA is now in control of bank licensing in Gaza and Areas "A" and "B" of the West Bank. However, it is not yet fully staffed and is operating in an atmosphere of a regulatory vacuum. The PMA is not yet in a position to properly evaluate the necessary qualifications of owners and managers of banks applying for licenses to operate in the Palestinian Territories. Nor has it established regulatory guidelines for evaluating applications in light of the economic needs of the Palestinian Territories. Further institutionalization of the PMA and development of legislation and regulations promulgated by the Palestinian Council and the PMA, respectively, are fundamental requirements if bank licensing procedures in the Palestinian Territories are to move beyond the present interim arrangements.

2. Supervision. The PMA recently established a banking supervision department responsible for monitoring the proper operation, stability, solvency, and liquidity of banks operating in the Palestinian Territories. The PMA has successfully enlisted a number of qualified supervisors with experience acquired in various Arab and Western countries. The level of professional competence of these supervisors is generally thought to be quite high. However, the supervision department is presently operating without an established regulatory structure.

The banking laws currently in force in Gaza and the West Bank fail to articulate the responsibilities and powers of a supervisory authority. The British Mandate and Jordanian statutes provide no basis for the imposition of prudential regulations and the carrying on of "on-site" inspections by a supervisory authority. Furthermore, the need for such regulation and inspection is particularly great, because the absence of a lender of last resort for Palestinian banks, as opposed to Jordanian or other foreign banks operating in the Palestinian Territories, has created considerable uncertainty regarding their stability, solvency, and liquidity.

Presently, Jordanian and other foreign banks operating in the Palestinian Territories continue to be supervised by their respective home supervisory authorities. These home authorities generally act as a lender of last resort for those banks falling under their supervisory responsibility. For example, Jordanian banks, which account for a large majority of deposits in the Palestinian Territories, are supervised by the Central Bank of Jordan, which not only monitors the banks but also protects them through its role as lender of last resort. Thus, Jordanian and foreign banks are, at least objectively, more secure than local Palestinian banks. This situation places Palestinian banks in a disadvantageous position that will continue until the PMA is more thoroughly established, both in terms of financial resources and regulatory authority.

3. System of Payments. Checks are written in the Palestinian Territories in Israeli sheqels, Jordanian dinars, and U.S. dollars. No central clearing house system exists for the Palestinian territories. Checks clear in different ways depending on the currency in which they are denominated. Inefficiencies in check clearance have impeded the more widespread dissemination of checks as a means of payment.

While sheqel-denominated checks can be efficiently cleared through the Israeli central clearance system in Tel Aviv, dinar-denominated checks are generally cleared bilaterally between local banks. This practice can be inefficient and burdensome, since each local bank must credit and debit separate accounts with a growing number of other banks, and must separately assess the credit of each of these banks. Dollar-denominated checks are cleared on a collection basis, for instance, through an actual transfer of money rather than through the crediting and debiting of accounts, a procedure that is slow and relatively expensive. The establishment of a central clearing facility for dinar checks would improve efficiency. However, any such facility would have to be closely coordinated with the Central Bank of Jordan.

The presentation of checks without adequate backing funds on account ("bad checks") further compromises the acceptance of checks as a means of payment. The large volume of bad checks written in the Palestinian Territories constitutes a significant problem, and the original banking statutes in effect in the West Bank and Gaza fail to provide a mechanism to deter this practice. An Israeli military order provides for restrictions to be placed on a checking account in the event of repeated check-bouncing on any given account.[56] However, this order has been largely ignored by banks in the Palestinian Territories. Thus, an important priority of Palestinian banking law reform should be to create an effective legal mechanism to enforce coordinated restriction, or other penalties, against offenders.

4. Lending. The volume of financial lending by banks in the Palestinian Territories is well below the needs of the market and the resources of banks. Most banks operating in the West Bank and Gaza are over liquid, in some cases maintaining loan-to-deposit ratios of only 20 percent. Furthermore, the majority of lending carried out by banks in the Palestinian Territories is reputedly in the form of small-scale overdraft facilities, which account for 86 percent of all lending by Palestinian banks.[57] Worse still, it is widely believed that foreign banks are facilitating capital flight by transferring Palestinian deposits to more attractive markets in Jordan and elsewhere. Whether or not this is the case, the low level of lending in the Palestinian Territories constitutes a grave hurdle to development of the Palestinian economy.

The primary impediment to lending in the Palestinian Territories has been the inability of banks to enforce secured lending agreements through the court system. There is no collateral lending law in Gaza, and the Jordanian Collateral Lending Law of 1953, currently applicable in the West Bank, is outdated and in need of replacement. Furthermore, during the period of Israeli occupation, Palestinian courts refrained from issuing foreclosure judgments against defaulting debtors, as execution of the order would require cooperation with the IDF. Additionally, the strong Palestinian social taboo against evicting an owner from his land may continue to make foreclosure difficult or impossible in cases where real property is put up as collateral. Finally, the absence of a modern land registration system in the West Bank and Gaza poses further obstacles to the use of real property as security for collateral lending.

While Palestinian courts can now rely on the Palestinian police to enforce foreclosures, the procedures for doing so have not yet been tested. A modern Palestinian collateral lending law clarifying these procedures would substantially alleviate the concerns of banks regarding judicial enforcement of collateral loan agreements. Such legislation should harmonize the foreclosure procedures in Gaza and the West Bank, provide safeguards for defaulting debtors, such as a generous notice provision and a right of debtor redemption, and include language that can be incorporated into collateral lending contracts stating that the bank may exercise the foreclosure option if the debtor fails to redeem the loan within the notice period. Concurrently, a somewhat more interventionist approach could be used to directly address the problems of over liquidity and capital flight by issuing regulations requiring reasonable loan-to-deposit ratios.

C. Tax Law

The establishment of an efficient taxation system is a third prerequisite for Palestinian economic development. The present tax laws, derived from disharmonious, anachronistic statutes amended by a cumbersome body of military orders, pose serious hurdles for both Palestinian taxpayers and tax collectors. These hurdles include burdensome rules and procedures, a lack of legal clarity, and excessive discretionary powers granted to the tax authorities. Furthermore, the exercise of tax powers by the Palestinian Council is far more restricted by agreements with Israel than those powers exercised with respect to investment law, banking law, and other commercial law fields. The rules governing Palestinian tax powers were first established in the Economic Protocol and were subsequently reconfirmed in a slightly modified form by the Interim Agreement. These rules and restrictions have engendered additional hurdles to Palestinian economic development.

Under the Interim Agreement, the tax powers exercised by the Palestinian Council are divided into two classes of taxes: indirect taxes and direct taxes. The Interim Agreement provides that the Palestinian and Israeli tax administrations will each levy and collect all indirect taxes in their respective areas of jurisdiction. Such indirect taxes include a value added tax ("VAT"), a purchase tax, and an import tax. At present, the areas under the responsibility of the Palestinian tax authority include Gaza (excluding Israeli settlements and the IDF base) and Areas "A" and "B" of the West Bank. Area "C" will continue to fall under the responsibility of the tax departments of the Israeli Civil Administration until such time as these areas are transferred to the Palestinian Council in accord with the Interim Agreement.

The Palestinian Council is similarly empowered to levy all direct taxes on economic activities in the areas under its administration, as well as on economic activity by residents living in areas under the responsibility of the Israeli tax administration. Direct taxes include an income tax on individuals and corporations, a property tax, a municipal tax, and fees. However, under the August 1994 Agreement on the Preparatory Transfer of Powers and Responsibilities,[58] the Palestinian tax authority is empowered to tax income earned by Palestinians and foreigners anywhere in the West Bank, except for settlements and IDF areas. Thus, while the Palestinian Council is responsible for levying direct taxes on all residents of Gaza (excluding Israeli settlements and the IDF Base) and Areas "A" and "B" of the West Bank, it may also levy income tax on all non–Israelis earning income in Area "C" (excluding Israeli settlements or IDF areas).

The PNA established an income tax department and a VAT department shortly after it came to power in 1994. During the first year of Palestinian self-rule, inaccurate reporting by taxpayers was rampant and resulted in low revenue. These difficulties primarily arose as a result of a lack of trained personnel and poor coordination with the outgoing Israeli Civil Administration tax departments. For example, very few trained Palestinians were available to perform the tasks previously discharged by Israeli tax officers, particularly assessment and investigation. In addition, the Palestinian tax departments commenced their operations in Gaza and Jericho without any taxpayer files, despite the fact that the Civil Administration had maintained a sophisticated computerized taxpayer file system.

Following the transfer of tax powers in the West Bank, the Palestinian tax departments sought to avoid the problems they had experienced in Gaza and Jericho by initiating close cooperation with Israel regarding personnel training and computer services. Over 200 Palestinian tax officers were hired and sent to participate in specialized training courses established through cooperation with the Israeli tax departments. Furthermore, the PNA contracted the services of SHAM, the Israeli company providing tax-related computer services to the Israeli Government. The efficiency and resources of the Palestinian tax departments have thus dramatically improved since the early days of self-rule.

Despite the improvements in the institutional capabilities of the Palestinian tax departments, the actual tax laws and policies continue to create serious hurdles for both revenue collection and economic development. Furthermore, other hurdles have arisen as a result of the implementation of various Israeli-Palestinian agreements regarding coordination of tax policy and cooperation in the area of tax administration. The most important hurdles are apparent in three spheres of taxation: income taxation, VAT and purchase taxation, and import taxation.

1. Income Tax. The current income tax laws in the Palestinian Territories are problematic for four reasons. First, as in other legal areas in the region, the tax laws in the West Bank and Gaza are not uniform. The disharmony between West Bank and Gaza tax law seriously complicates compliance and revenue collection for both taxpayers and tax administrators. Second, the income tax statutes are out of date. In Gaza, the relevant statute is the 1947 British Mandate Income Tax Ordinance,[59] while in the West Bank it is the 1964 Jordanian Income Tax Law.[60] Third, both the tax regime and tax enforcement are made dauntingly complex by the numerous amendments issued by the Israeli military Governments in both territories between 1967 and 1994, as well as by amendments issued by the Egyptian military Government in Gaza between 1948 and 1967. Many of these military orders are poorly drafted and ambiguously worded, creating a lack of legal clarity and inviting excessive interpretive discretion by the tax authorities. Fourth, in addition to these basic problems, the tax laws contain provisions that constitute specific hurdles to development.

The most crucial of the specific obstacles to development engendered by the tax laws have been the inordinately high income tax brackets and rates that the Israeli military government established prior to the transfer of tax powers to the Palestinian Authority. For example, the highest tax bracket in the Palestinian Territories during the period of Israeli military rule was 55 percent. By comparison, in Jordan the highest tax bracket is currently 45 percent and in Israel 48 percent. Moreover, during the period of Israeli military rule, West Bank and Gaza taxpayers faced the highest rate of taxation if their income exceeded the approximate equivalent of US$16,000. By comparison, under current Israeli law, taxpayers do not reach the highest tax bracket until their annual income surpasses the approximate equivalent of US$30,000.

Additional specific hurdles to Palestinian economic development are posed by the required prepayment of income tax. Under Israeli military orders, taxpayers must prepay estimated income taxes based on payments from previous years. This requirement constitutes a burden for taxpayers, generally, and for small businesses, in particular, as it presumes these individuals and entities enjoy a steady cash flow and ready access to credit when, in fact, they often do not. Consequently, many Palestinian businesses operate in the informal sector, evading taxes and fostering inequities between firms that are capable of operating informally and those that are not.

The Palestinian tax authorities are well aware of the problems of the current tax laws. Certain regulatory changes have already been made to ease the most burdensome procedures and rules regarding tax brackets and rates. Furthermore, an effort is now under way to unify and modernize the income tax laws of the West Bank and Gaza. Palestinian authorities have relied on the assistance of international tax and legal experts to this end and a draft Palestinian income tax law may be prepared in the near future.

2. VAT and Purchase Tax Rates. VAT and purchase tax rates have been specially addressed in Israeli-Palestinian negotiations. The interdependence of the two economies, formally linked through the customs union agreement, argues for coordination of certain aspects of tax policy and administration. Thus, Palestinian-Israeli agreements have established special guidelines regarding VAT and purchase tax rates. As a practical matter, these guidelines restrict the freedom of the Palestinian Council to set VAT and purchase tax rates independently of Israel. While harmonization of VAT and purchase tax rates between the two economies provides certain theoretical macroeconomic benefits, the limits on independent PNA policy formulation exact a definite economic cost.

The Interim Agreement provides that the Palestinian and Israeli tax administrations will each levy and collect VAT and purchase taxes in their respective areas of responsibility. According to the agreement, the purchase tax rates in both jurisdictions will be identical for both locally produced and imported goods.[61] The sole exception from this rule permits the Palestinians to determine their own purchase tax rate on motor vehicles.[62] The Palestinian VAT rate, however, may be set 1 percent to 2 percent lower than the Israeli rate.[63] The Interim Agreement also establishes that businesses under the Palestinian tax authority's jurisdiction may not be exempt from VAT if their annual revenue exceeds US$12,000.[64] Finally, the Interim Agreement provides rules for the clearance of VAT revenues between the Israeli and Palestinian VAT departments.

The arrangements for VAT clearance have raised several problems for the Palestinian tax authority. By the terms of the Interim Agreement, the Palestinian VAT department is to receive the VAT paid by Palestinians purchasing goods or services in the Israeli economy. Similarly, the Israeli VAT department is to receive the VAT paid by Israelis in the Palestinian economy. In order to expedite clearance of Palestinian and Israeli VAT claims, it was agreed that a special unified invoice must accompany every transaction between Palestinian and Israeli businesses.[65] The VAT department of each side is to distribute the invoices to businesses that sell goods and services to clients from the other side. Upon receiving payment for the goods or services rendered, the seller must issue an invoice specifying the amount of VAT paid. The invoices must then be used to establish VAT clearance at monthly meetings between representatives of the two VAT administrations.[66] Clearance claims are to be settled within six days of each monthly meeting, through the issuance of a payment by the administration with the net balance of claims against it.[67]

Given the per capita income of the Palestinian Territories, the minimum permissible VAT of 15 percent is an unusually high rate. Purchase taxes are also probably higher than they would normally be, in the absence of a commitment to match Israeli purchase taxes. The PNA agreed to harmonize its VAT and purchase taxes with Israel as a necessary condition for free access to the Israeli market for Palestinian goods. However, nonimplementation of free-trade commitments as a result of the security closures has meant that Palestinians are, in effect, paying the price of the customs union without enjoying its benefits. In addition, the Palestinian VAT department has expressed concern that Israel has not acted to implement the VAT clearance arrangements. According to the Palestinians, many Israeli companies selling products to clients in the Palestinian Territories are neither provided with invoices, nor even made aware of their existence. Furthermore, in the absence of sufficient logistical support, the Palestinian VAT department has been unable to monitor the movement of Israeli goods into the Palestinian territories. Thus, the Palestinian VAT department, which expects to be owed between US$100 million and US$150 million on annual VAT clearance with Israel, is presently in a weak position to enforce compliance with VAT rules and to secure its interests through VAT clearance procedures.

   3. Import Tax.   The essence of the customs union established between Israel and the PNA is a harmonized import and customs policy. With respect to external trade, Israel and the Palestinian Territories are treated as one economic entity. The goal of the customs union is to prevent leakage of low-tariff imported goods from the Palestinian Territories into Israel. Thus, according to the Interim Agreement, Palestinian import taxes must generally be set no lower than the Israeli import taxes on equivalent goods.[68]

   However, the Interim Agreement provides three lists of goods for which Palestinian import taxes may be set independently of the Israeli tax rates. Goods on the first two lists may be imported to the Palestinian Territories in quantities agreed upon by the two sides, according to the needs of domestic consumption in the Palestinian market.[69] Any such goods imported to the Palestinian Territories in excess of the agreed-upon quantities are subject to import taxes set no lower than the corresponding Israeli import taxes.[70]

   The third list comprises basic food items and other goods required by the Palestinian economic development program that may be imported in unrestricted quantities subject to independently established Palestinian import taxes.[71] Finally, imported motor vehicles may also be taxed at a rate set independently of the Israeli customs rate.

   The Interim Agreement also establishes a procedure for the clearance of revenues from all import taxes and levies between Israel and the PNA. The clearance of revenues is based on the place of final destination.[72] Thus, import taxes collected on goods in Israel's territorial sea or in airports and destined for the Palestinian territories are to be credited to the Palestinian customs administration. Revenue clearance is to be effected within six working days from the date the import taxes are collected.[73]

   The first major problem with the scheme for import tax harmonization established by the Interim Agreement is that, as with VAT and purchase tax rates, the Palestinian customs rate is probably higher than it otherwise would be, in exchange for a nonimplemented free-trade relationship with Israel. The second, and more serious, problem is that the restrictions on the PNA's ability to independently determine its own import policy substantially weakens its capacity to negotiate favorable trade terms with third countries. Due to these restrictions, the PNA is not in a position to offer favorable access to its domestic market as a quid pro quo for reciprocal access to a given foreign market. Thus, the PNA is largely dependent on Israeli trade policy to open foreign markets to Palestinian products. This situation is particularly unfortunate because the foreign markets that most interest Palestinian exporters are often countries with which Israel has little or no trade.

The third, and final, problem concerns import tax revenue clearance. Because high-volume Israeli importers can generally obtain lower unit costs and shipping rates than Palestinian importers, Palestinian businesses often prefer to import through Israeli firms. Furthermore, Palestinian businesses often prefer to use Israeli importers in order to avoid costly delays resulting from security checks. Thus, a large quantity of goods destined for the Palestinian Territories arrive at Israeli sea and airports marked as imports to Israel. Import taxes collected on these goods by Israeli customs officials, therefore, accrue to the Israeli treasury rather than the Palestinian treasury. Palestinian tax officials estimate that tens of millions of dollars of revenue, if not more, is being lost annually on this basis.

The hurdles deriving from the income tax, VAT, purchase tax, and import tax systems in the Palestinian Territories are doubly significant. Not only do these hurdles place costly burdens on entrepreneurs and other taxpayers, they also result in low public revenue with untold consequences for the stability of the current political system. Reform of tax laws and policies, including those deriving from agreements with Israel, is, therefore, essential to ensuring an environment that is favorable to economic development and political stability.

CONCLUSION

The Middle East peace process has moved mountains since the September 1993 signing of the Declaration of Principles. Most of the Palestinian inhabitants of Gaza and the West Bank are now living under the authority of a democratically elected Palestinian Council. The IDF has departed from almost all Palestinian cities. Several Arab and Muslim states have opened diplomatic relations with Israel or initiated diplomatic and economic contacts. Business leaders throughout the region are joining forces to engage in joint ventures, trade, and other forms of economic cooperation. However, for the Palestinians, the process of building a free, prosperous, and stable society is far from complete.

The structural and legal hurdles to achieving economic growth and political stability in the Palestinian Territories represent a tremendous challenge to the Palestinian people. These hurdles cannot be overcome easily or quickly. In surmounting them, the Palestinians will require considerable support from fellow Arabs, technical and financial assistance from the United States and Europe, good faith and cooperation from Israel, and, most importantly, resolve and determination from their own people to make peace and self-determination succeed. In solving the structural and legal hurdles to national development, the Palestinian leadership can be truly effective only if the Palestinian people organize the mechanisms of civil society, develop positions on contemporary issues, and voice their opinions at every level of public policy formulation.

The 20th century has seen the emergence and development of a Palestinian national consciousness that arose in a context of protracted suffering and dispossession. With the implementation of self-government after so many decades of disenfranchisement, the Palestinian nation is now at a crossroads. It can choose the rule of law, democracy, and peace, or it can choose poverty, anarchy, and conflict. The recent resumption of terrorist attacks against Israel during late February and early March, 1996 is, therefore, of the gravest possible concern. Not only do such attacks result in the loss of numerous innocent lives and feed the vicious cycle of violence and retribution, they threaten the very foundations of the peace process by calling into question the ability and commitment of Palestinian society to contain its radical elements. It is thus of inestimable importance that Palestinian society and its political leaders make a strategic decision to identify the cessation of all violence and terrorism as a primary national interest, and move decisively to quell them.

The Palestinian future is not written in stone. In fact, the Palestinians probably now have more control over their collective fate than ever before in their history. Furthermore, the level of Palestinian control over the course of their national life is continuing to rise. The Palestinians are now in a position to make difficult choices concerning the direction of their national future.

As they begin tackling the numerous hurdles to achieving political stability and economic growth, they carry a profound responsibility. Their choices will disproportionately affect the fortunes of larger nations and the entire region. It has long been said that the Palestinians are the key to peace in the Middle East. It is also often said that the Middle East is the lynchpin to ensuring the stability and peace of the world. Thus, the success of the Palestinians in surmounting the hurdles before them is a matter of truly global concern.

Notes

1. The Palestinian National Authority refers to the interim self-rule authority created upon Israeli withdrawal from Gaza and Jericho in the summer of 1994. See Michael Kelly, "In Gaza, Peace Meets Pathology," *New York Times*, Nov. 27, 1994, § 6 (Magazine), at 56 (discussing formation of PNA).
2. The Palestinian Council, or *Al-Majlis Falistini*, in Arabic, is the legislative body elected by Palestinian voters on January 20, 1996.
3. Declaration of Principles on Interim Self-Government Arrangements, Sept. 13, 1993, Isr.-PLO, 32 I.L.M. 1525 .
4. The end of military rule in these areas took place following the withdrawal of Israeli troops from Gaza and Jericho under the Agreement on the Gaza Strip and the Jericho Area. Israel-PLO Agreement on the Gaza Strip and Jericho Area, May 4, 1994, Isr.-PLO, 33 I.L.M. 622 .
5. The end of Israeli military rule took place following the redeployment of Israeli troops outside West Bank cities under the Israeli-Palestinian Interim Agreement on the West Bank and the Gaza Strip. Israeli-Palestinian Interim Agreement on the West Bank and the Gaza Strip, Sept. 28, 1995, Isr.-PLO (on file with the Fordham International Law Journal).
6. Separation, or *hafrada,* in Hebrew, was first put forward as the response of the Government of Prime Minister Yitzhak Rabin to the terrorist attacks by Palestinian extremists attempting to torpedo the peace process by conducting suicide bombings in Israeli cities. The practical effect of this policy was the initiation of "security closures" during which Palestinians were not allowed to pass the checkpoints into Israel. It was resurrected by the Government of Prime Minister Shimon Peres in response to the even worse suicide bombings of early 1996.
7. See Joel Brinkley, "Comment by Baker Angers Shamir," *New York Times*, Mar. 3, 1990, at AS (discussing Palestinian diaspora).
8. Cairo Agreement, supra note 4, annex N, 33 I.L.M. at 696; Interim Agreement, supra note 5, annex V. The Protocol on Economic Relations Between the Government of the State of Israel and the PLO Representing the Palestinian People was signed as a separate agreement in Paris, but was subsequently attached to the Gaza/Jericho Agreement as Annex IV. A revised form of the Economic Protocol was later included in the Interim Agreement as Annex V. For purposes of this essay, "Economic Protocol" refers to the original agreement as signed in Paris. References to the newer version refer to the Interim Agreement.
9. Two Arab banks, the Bank of Palestine and the Cairo Amman Bank, were licensed to reopen in the 1980s, but the services they provided remained inadequate. Indeed, it was common for no interest to be paid on savings deposits and lending was woefully scarce. By 1998, these two banks operated only 13 branches for the entire West Bank and Gaza Strip.
10. PALESTINIAN ECONOMIC POLICY RESEARCH INSTITUTE, PALESTINIAN BANKING SECTOR STATISTICAL REVIEW xii–xiv (1995) [PEPRI].
11. Id.
12. See Serge Schmemann, "Killing of Bomb 'Engineer' Unites Palestinian Factions," *New York Times*, Jan. 10, 1996, at AS. The "secret Oslo channel" refers to Israeli-Palestinian talks that were held quietly in Norway and resulted in the Declaration of Principles. Id. The channel's existence became public knowledge in early September 1998. Id.
13. Fatah, or "victory," is the dominant faction headed by PLO Chairman Yasser Arafat.

14. The Palestinian National Charter, reprinted in THE ISRAEL-ARAB READER 366, 366–71(Walter Laquer & Barry Rubin eds., 4th ed. 1984).

15. See Steven Greenhouse, "Mideast Accord: In Washington; Twist to Shuttle Diplomacy: U.S. Aide Mediated by Phone," *New York Times*, Sept. 25, 1995, at A1 (discussing inception of Declaration of Principles).

16. See Tzachi Hanegbi, "A One-Sided Peace," *New York Times*, Mar. 6, 1996, at A21 (discussing covenant and Arafat's refusal to amend it).

17. See "Arafat Sets Jan. 20 as the Date for First Palestinian Elections," AP, Dec. 14, 1995, at A12 (discussing elections and role of PNA and Palestinian Council).

18. See Serge Schmemann, "Bus Bombing Kills Five in Jerusalem; 100 Are Wounded," *New York Times*, Aug. 22, 1995, at A1 (discussing impact of bombings on elections).

19. *Jihad* is the Islamic term for holy war.

20. See Steven Emerson, "High Noon for Arafat," *New York Times*, Oct. 20, 1994, at A27 (reporting on release of Hamas operatives one day after their arrest).

21. See Clyde Haberman, "Arafat's Police in Gaza Widen Crackdown on Muslim Radicals," *New York Times*, Apr. 12, 1995, at A1 (discussing closed courts).

22. Id.

23. See Serge Schmemann, "Arafat Backed in First Voting by Palestinians, *New York Times*, Jan. 21, 1996, at A1 (declaring overall success of elections).

24. Hamas refers to the largest and most active Palestinian extremist group. In Arabic, Hamas is an acronym for "Islamic Resistance Movement."

25. See "Arafat Backed in First Voting," supra note 23, at A1 (discussing boycott); Joel Greenberg, "Palestinians Trying Out Elections, Warts and All," *New York Times*, Jan. 18, 1996, at A10 (discussing tactics used to suppress opponents).

26. See Serge Schmemann, "Bombings in Israel: The Overview; 2 Suicide Bombings in Israel Kill 25 and Hurt 77, Highest Such Toll," *New York Times*, Feb. 26, 1996, at A1 (reporting on aftermath of bombings).

27. Id.

28. See Serge Schmemann, "Bombing in Israel; Israeli Rags Rises as Bomb Kills 19, Imperiling Peace," *New York Times*, Mar. 4, 1996, at A1 (reporting on effect of bombings on Israelis and Palestinians).

29. See Serge Schmemann, "The Trials of a Peace Seeker — A Special Report; Terrorism Forces Peres from Brink of Triumph," *New York Times*, Mar. 10, 1996, at A1 (analyzing effect of violence on peace process and Peres Government).

30. The Declaration of Principles articulates the transfer of power, while the Cairo and Interim Agreements implement it.

31. The West Bank was occupied by Jordan in 1948 and annexed in 1951, whereas the Gaza Strip came under Egyptian occupation in 1948 but was not annexed. Israel occupied both territories in 1967 but preserved their administrative separation by appointing one military commander for the West Bank and another for the Gaza Strip.

32. Interim Agreement, supra note 5. Area "A" is comprised of the eight Arab cities of the West Bank: Bethlehem, Hebron (where only part of the city is under Palestinian self-rule), Jenin, Jericho, Kalkilya, Nablus, Ramallah, and Tulkarm. Area "B" is comprised of smaller towns and villages in which Palestinian jurisdiction encompasses civil affairs, but in which Israel is responsible for internal security. Area "C" consists of the Israeli-controlled remainder of the West Bank, including rural areas, military zones, and Israeli settlements.

33. Interim Agreement, supra note 5.

34. The Civil Administration was the administrative and civil affairs apparatus of the Israeli military government in the West Bank and Gaza. It was dissolved in Gaza

upon the withdrawal of Israeli forces and its jurisdiction in the West Bank is now limited to Area "C" territories.

35. *Sulha* is a traditional method of conflict resolution embedded in centuries of Arab tradition. According to this method, a dispute is brought before one or more respected community leaders or elders who mediate the dispute and reconcile the parties. The decisions are generally treated with respect and compliance.

36. Declaration, supra note 3, annex III, 32 I.L.M. at 1537–40.

37. Jordanian Temporary Law No. 1 for 1967: The Encouragement of Capital Investment Law.

38. The Encouragement of Capital Investment, Military Order 1055 of 17 June 1991 (Gaza District) (Isr.); The Encouragement of Capital Investment, Military Order 1342 of July 7, 1991 (Judea and Samaria) (Isr.)

39. The Encouragement of Investment Act (as amended 21 November 1991); Civil Administration of Judea & Samaria (Judea and Samaria); Unnumbered Directives on The Encouragement of Foreign Investment.

40. Law on the Encouragement of Investment, reprinted in David P. Fidler, *Foreign Investment in Palestine: An Analysis of the Law on the Encouragement of Investment in Palestine,* 19 FORDHAM INT'L L.J. 529, 603–10 (1995) .

41. Interim Agreement, supra note 5, art. 18. Article 18 reads, "The Council has the power, within its jurisdiction as defined in Article 17 of the Agreement, to adopt legislation." Id.

42. Interim Agreement, supra note 5, art. 17. The relevant final status issues are settlements, Jerusalem, and borders. Declaration, supra note 4, art. 5, 32 I.L.M at 1526. Final status talks are slated to begin in the Spring of 1996 and to last no more than three years.

43. Investment Law, supra note 40, arts. 9, 18, at 606, 608.

44. Id. art. 16, at 608.

45. Id. art. 20, at 609.

46. Id. art. 1, at 603. "Dues" are defined as customs duties and purchase taxes on machinery, equipment, and raw materials. Id.

47. *Guidelines on the Treatment of Foreign Investment,* 7 ICSID REV.: FOREIGN INVESTMENT L. J. 302 (1992).

48. Investment Law, supra note 40, art. 13, at 607–08.

49. Id. art. 3(2), at 604.

50. Id. arts. 5, 11–17, at 605, 606–08.

51. Id. art. 19, at 609. In Arabic, the term for chairman, *Raees,* is also often translated as President.

52. Jordanian Temporary Banking Law No. 94 of 1966.

53. Palestine Mandate Banking Ordinance No. 26 of 1941, published in THE PALESTINE GAZETTE No. 1134, Supplement No. 1 (Oct. 9, 1941).

54. The Bank of Israel often simply applied the Jordanian and British Mandate statutes in supervising Palestinian banks, despite the existence of superseding military legislation.

55. Cairo Agreement, supra note 4, annex IV, art. IV(l), 33 I.L.M. at 703; Interim Agreement, supra note 6, annex V. art. W(1). The Palestinian Monetary Authority ("PMA") acts as the central financial institution within the PNA. Id.

56. Israeli Military Order Regarding Checks Without Coverage, No. 1024 (Judea and Samaria) of 1982.

57. PEPRI, supra note 10, at XV.

58. Agreement on Preparatory Transfer of Powers and Responsibilities, Aug. 29, 1994, Isr.-PLO, 34 I.L.M. 455 (1995) (done in Cairo, August 19, 1994).

59. Income Tax Ordinance No. 13 of 1947 (British Mandate), published in The Palestine Gazette, No. 1568, Supplement No. 1, (Mar. 20, 1947).
60. Hashemite Kingdom of Jordan Income Tax Law, Law No. 25 (1964).
61. Interim Agreement, supra note 5, annex V, art. 6.
62. Id. art. 3.
63. Id. art. 6. Currently, the Israeli value added tax ("VAT") rate is 17 percent.
64. Id.
65. Id.
66. Id.
67. Id.
68. Id. art. 3.
69. Id.
70. Id.
71. Id.
72. Id.
73. Id.

13

Palestinian Economic Progress Under the Oslo Agreements
MEL LEVINE

FOREWORD

The essay that follows was written in January 1996, prior to the shocking series of terror bombings that killed over 60 innocent Israeli citizens and permanently maimed scores of others. These cowardly acts of hatred over a nine-day period have brought the peace process itself to its knees, rendering the economic concerns expressed in this essay trivial by comparison. I was dissuaded from my inclination to leave the essay unpublished, however, because of my affection and admiration for Yitzhak Rabin, to whom this text is dedicated, and because I still believe that Palestinian economic development is in Israel's best interest. I was persuaded that the lessons I have learned since devoting myself to that end two and one half years ago are worth sharing. It is presented in the unedited form in which it was written prior to the current crisis, which has shaken me as deeply as it has all others who had the privilege of knowing Yitzhak Rabin, of admiring the natural decency of his leadership, and of sharing his courageous vision of the future.

INTRODUCTION

To frame this essay in a manner that will reflect the author's perspective, I want to emphasize that I am one of two copresidents of Builders for Peace — a nonprofit organization created by leaders of the American Arab and Jewish communities first to foster and facilitate American private-sector investment in the newly autonomous West Bank and Gaza, and secondly, to assist in promoting broader regional economic integration. The organization's founders initiated this agenda in response to a challenge issued by President Clinton and Vice President Al Gore on the occasion of the 1993 Rabin-Arafat signing ceremony on the White House South Lawn. The fact that the founding Board members, indeed the copresidents, of Builders for Peace represent the traditionally diverse interests of those two communities symbolizes a remarkably broad endorsement of the concept. This essay assesses progress under the Oslo Accords toward Palestinian economic development based on the Builders for Peace experience to date.

Beyond American Jews and Arabs, Palestinian private-sector development is supported by Democrats, Republicans, Palestinians, and Israelis, and by the spectrum of disparate interests within each of those entities. Before accepting my position with Builders for Peace, I met with Prime Minister Rabin, who assured me that his vision of regional peace and Israel's security included the betterment of Palestinian conditions and urged me to do all I could to lead that agenda forward. Shimon Peres has echoed the same theme on numerous occasions with the belief that "a dollar invested in the West Bank or Gaza is two dollars invested in Israeli *security*." The Palestinian Authority and the Government of Israel have appointed official liaisons to Builders for Peace both to symbolize their endorsement and to facilitate the process where possible. The U.S. Government has provided modest operating funds in support of the effort out of its foreign assistance budget. The World Bank, the Departments of State and Commerce, the U.S. Trade Representative, the U.S. Trade and Development Agency (TDA), the U.N. Development Project (UNDP), the U.S. ambassadors and consuls general in the region, and the U.S. Congress have all been consistent supporters of the mission.

Individually and collectively, each has endorsed the general proposition that private-sector Palestinian development is not just a worthwhile end in itself, but also a precondition to the success of the peace process. The concept has now had two and a half years to germinate since the Declaration of Principles[1] and the historic Rabin-Arafat handshake, however, and the attentive observer has a right to ask how well Palestinian private-sector development is progressing in the real world. The answer is of course more complicated than the question, but the following generalizations are permissible: (1) the diplomatic agenda has moved forward more rapidly than the economic agenda; (2) a number of the economic benefits presumed to be forthcoming with the 1993 breakthrough are only now beginning to materialize, and most remain hypothetical; (3) impediments that would appear inconsistent with the mission's widespread, high-level support have plagued many committed investors; and yet (4) there is documentable progress in several key areas that provide a solid basis for hope.

I. Economy of the Palestinian Territories

Economic and demographic data on the newly autonomous Palestinian territories reveal both the self-evident urgency for private sector development and the realism that imbues its advocates. Not surprisingly for a region whose political status has been so tumultuous for so long, any such data are somewhat speculative. Moreover, because border restrictions still inhibit free movement between Gaza and the West Bank, it is necessary to describe them separately in order to present a useful picture of the economic challenge. The combined population of these territories is roughly 2.3 million — about the same as St. Louis — with 35 percent of it in Gaza, making it one of the most densely populated pieces of real estate on earth. Additionally, the Palestinian population is growing at a rapid 3 percent in West Bank and 3.3 percent in Gaza. The September 1995 "Oslo II" Agreement[2] gave self rule to 99 percent of the Palestinian population within 27 percent of the West Bank's 5,800 square kilometers. Two hundred of Gaza's 340 square kilometers received autonomy under Oslo I[3] in May 1994.

The West Bank's purported per capita annual income of US$1,700 is twice that of Gaza and roughly 10 percent of Israel's. The overall Palestinian gross national product (GNP) of US$3 billion is smaller than that of several Caribbean islands. The 380,000 strong combined labor force, at least 50 percent of which is ostensibly unemployed, is growing by about 10,000 per year. Because of the birth rate, 65 percent of the Palestinian population is under the age of 15. Over 20 percent of the GNP is earned outside of Palestinian territory. The second largest source of jobs, after agriculture, is Israel, whose Palestinian borders open and close somewhat randomly in response to perceptions of the terrorist threat. A spate of terror bombings after the 1993 Declaration of Principles[4] led to an Israeli policy that formally allowed approximately 30,000 married Palestinians over the age of 30 to work in Israel. This was down from 80,000 in earlier years, but the new policy also excluded the tens of thousands who are typically allowed to enter for day labor in Israeli's "grey economy."

The Palestinian territories have never been a state. Prior to the late 20th century Egyptian, Jordanian, and Israeli governance of these lands, Palestine was a part of the early 20th century British Empire. The British, of course, acquired it as spoils of World War I from the Ottoman Turks, whose oversight predated the modern notion of sovereign statehood. The population now commonly known as Palestinians has, therefore, never governed itself independently and has struggled more than most to sustain its identity, culture, and traditions. Ironically, however, Palestinian administrative skills are routinely credited for the economic and commercial coherence of many surrounding Arab states and Gulf Emirates, and their diaspora population of 3 to 3.5 million has been among the most commercially successful everywhere it has gone, especially in the United States. It is to this remarkably resilient, resourceful, well-educated[5] pool of "human capital" that proponents of Palestinian economic growth frequently point. Indeed, sectors like industry and tourism are natural outlets for the expression of any such pent-up Palestinian commercial energies. To the extent that the absence of self-rule has stifled growth in these areas, the new Palestinian autonomy agreements may indeed point to a significant Palestinian economic growth potential.

There is also recent historical evidence in favor of this proposition. Prior to the 1987–93 Palestinian uprising known as the *Intifada*, the economy and living standard of the West Bank and Gaza grew dramatically. For example, according to the World Bank, between 1970 and 1980: (1) per capita gross domestic product (GDP) doubled; (2) primary and secondary school enrollments grew by over 50 percent; (3) life expectancies increased by five years (and by another five over the ensuing seven years); (4) infant mortality declined by a third; (5) the number of households with electricity more than doubled; and (6) the number with safe water tripled. Between 1968 and 1980, the average annual increases in GDP and GNP were 7 percent and 9 percent respectively due to integration with, and, yes, dependence on, Israel and the regional economic boom. Furthermore, Palestinian economic growth continued even after Israel's economy slowed in the mid–1970's as skilled workers found employment in the Gulf countries and provided remittances that offset weaknesses in Israel's oil-dependant system.

Nor was this growth restricted to the upper echelons of the Palestinian labor market. On the contrary, unskilled labor played a significant role in Palestinian growth and brought with it a demonstrable reduction in poverty. It is true that job creation during this period took place almost exclusively outside the West Bank and Gaza, but the data demonstrate the levels of economic progress that are possible if political conditions permit economic relationships throughout the region.

As the regional boom crested in the early 1980s, however, the frustration of rising Palestinian expectations began to take its toll. Between 1980 and 1987, real GDP growth fell to 5 percent and export growth stagnated. This decline — exacerbated by the *Intifada*, intensified by disrupted economic relations with Israel, and accelerated by the resultant strikes and border closures— has still not been reversed. Merchandise exports in 1991 brought in 37 percent fewer dollars than in 1987 as the Israeli regulatory regime restricted the movements of goods and people. None of this was improved, of course, by the Palestinians' official and psychological support for Iraq in the 1991 Gulf War.[6] Besides the immediate restrictions wrought by this existential danger to Israel during the Gulf War itself, Iraq's defeat brought a termination of reliable Palestinian employment in Kuwait and throughout the Gulf.[7] Workers who once provided a steady flow of remittances to their homeland now began returning there themselves in quest of employment, while diminished consumption in the West Bank and Gaza were exacerbating economic decline.

Ironically, 1991 might one day be viewed as the turning point in recent Palestinian economic history. The defeat of Saddam Hussein, following on the heels of the West's victory in the Gold War, put Israel in the most secure position she has enjoyed in her brief history as a modern state. This unequivocal reality put Israel in a political position from which she could afford to take greater political risks. Prodded by U.S. diplomacy leading to the 1991 Madrid Conference,[8] physically and psychologically exhausted by the burdens of the occupation and the *Intifada,* and restructured politically by the Labor Party's victory in 1992, Israel took the bold and controversial steps that led to the Declaration of Principles,[9] which has guided Israeli-Palestinian negotiations since it was announced to an unsuspecting world in 1993.

Sentiments that underpinned the *Intifada* clearly represent a powerful influence in the West Bank and Gaza to this day, and Israel's current security requirements will not allow its political leaders to permit the open-border commercial environment that the Palestinian business community seeks. But Israel is in the midst of a throttle-to-the-wall economic boom of her own today, and the six-member Gulf Cooperation Council[10] lifted the secondary boycott on companies that do business with Israel in September 1994.[11] These developments, in conjunction with the peace process, have opened up vistas of a new regional economy based on previously unlikely relationships throughout the Middle East. If this agenda unfolds in a systematic manner, regional powers like Egypt, Saudi Arabia, and the Gulf countries could come together with Israel in a trade regime that ideally suits Palestinian purposes. While such regional commercial harmony remains hypothetical, the diplomatic process has come further than most expected before 1993, and the Palestinians have demonstrated — at various times both at home and abroad — an extraordinary level of business prowess. It is for these reasons that supporters of the peace process look hopefully toward private-sector development as both a stimulant to, and a consequence of, progress in the Israeli-Palestinian relationship.

II. Palestinian Commerce Under the Oslo Process

Participants in the Palestinian-Israeli dialogue continue to relearn that business has a pace and direction of its own that can be neither assured nor prohibited by the surrounding politics. Just as Palestinian businessmen have found ways to produce and trade at times despite political barriers, no political formula can by itself orchestrate the rhythms of investment, risk, market response, trade, and profit. Political conditions are neither irrelevant to nor determinant of these undertakings, but the experience to date has reminded us that what they can do is create an environment in which unseen hands are allowed to assess, strive, fail, learn, maneuver, and, if the time and place are right, succeed. The architects of peace understood from the outset that the material fruits of their labor had to become apparent in the everyday lives of the Palestinian people in order for progress at the negotiating tables to settle in "on the street," but, alas, their rhetoric all too often exaggerated the extent to which diplomacy could engineer such an outcome.

Thus, the photogenic "handshake" in September 1993 was followed promptly by an International Donors Conference where the representatives of 43 states, hosted by the U.S. State Department, outbid one another in the euphoria of the moment, pledging upwards of US$2.5 billion toward "reconstruction of Palestinian infrastructure." In the ensuing two and one half years, the donors have spent less than one third of that amount, and what has been spent has gone largely to covering the Palestinian deficit, the recurrent costs of Palestinian administrative overhead, and a Palestinian police force that constitutes 2 percent of the population. The United States alone pledged US$500 million over five years: US$125 million from the Overseas Private Investment Corporation (OPIC) in the form of financing for private-sector U.S. investors, and $375 million by way of the U.S. Agency for International Development's (USAID's) conventional foreign assistance.

The OPIC largess, of which less than one million dollars has changed hands in the first 30 months, was touted as precisely what was needed to liberate the dormant energies of Palestinian entrepreneurship. Private-sector investment in an era of declining foreign assistance budgets would export the best of what the United States had to offer. Market instincts would move investment, not philanthropy, into the parts of the economy where it was most needed. It would not only move more quickly than foreign assistance, but the profit incentives behind it would create permanent jobs in response to the spirit of the Palestinian market, and nurture the seeds of market behavior from which pluralism springs naturally rather than being imposed from on high.

The handshake proved to be a memorable photo-op, but the agreements it yielded have hardly generated a Palestinian economic renaissance. Oslo I encompasses a generic Declaration of Principles, signed in September 1993, and a more formal instrument of implementation that was signed eight months later in Cairo.[12] Sandwiched between them was a set of economic terms and conditions, signed in Paris in April 1994,[13] which became an appendix to the Cairo document. Collectively, these instruments granted limited economic autonomy to the dusty hamlet of Jericho, near the Allenby bridge to Jordan, and to 60 percent of the Gaza strip, 50 miles and two Israeli borders away along the Mediterranean coast. A Palestinian-Israeli "customs union" was formed by the Paris Economic Agreement, but it included no provisions for passage between Gaza and the West Bank, and no special arrangements for moving products in or out of either location by way of Israel, which controlled access to both.

A series of terror bombings throughout Israel by Palestinian opponents of the peace process not only made it unnecessary for Prime Minister Rabin to publicly justify Israel's retention of border controls, but made it politically untenable to lift them. Indeed, they tested the very strength of his commitment to the process in the face of the domestic political anxieties. Rabin's commitment, which proved so unshakable that it ultimately cost him his life, kept the process together throughout the two years of Oslo I's tumultuous reign. Indeed, as the average Palestinian seemed to support the terror more than the Oslo I, Rabin and then Foreign Minister Peres knew better than anyone that Palestinian economic growth would provide desperately needed support for the risks they had undertaken.

As internal political tension dominated the implementation of the agreement on both sides, and prolonged the negotiation of Oslo II's expanded autonomy provisions by over a year, questions about the nature and extent of investment became quite secondary. Thus, throughout that period, the closure of Israel's borders to the newly autonomous territories became a nearly requisite response to the persistent security threat regardless of the economic consequences.

Through various base-building efforts in the United States and the Middle East region during these difficult times in the process, Builders for Peace discovered a broad interest in the West Bank and Gaza from across the spectrum of the U.S. business community. Indeed, several investors moved forward and placed capital at risk in the territories despite the uncertainties in the wake of the agreements.

During the Oslo I period, two substantial West Bank housing projects were built and sold with exclusively private U.S. capital. One of them, a solid U.S. joint venture with a local Palestinian partner, has stayed in place, finishing one project while planning the next. Contrary to initial expectations, however, the American is neither Arab nor Jewish. Similarly, neither is the family from Youngstown, Ohio that opened a precast concrete factory in Gaza in 1995. Nor is the Salt Lake City man who has completed an impressive TDA-sponsored feasibility study for the placement of a U.S. crude oil refinery in Gaza to service the local petroleum and asphalt markets.

There is no shortage of interest on the part of Palestinian-Americans in bringing their success back to Gaza and the West Bank, but the primary incentive for investment is based on market principles, not ethnic sentiments. The fact that investment moved slower than negotiators had hoped, while disappointing, is unsurprising. The market merely dictated the same caution in business investment that the negotiators are experiencing with regard to the future status of Jerusalem, Hebron, the settlements, the refugees, the borders, and the creation of reliable, safe passage between Gaza and the West Bank. Both are saying the same thing: "wait and see."

But a "wait and see" attitude is more than many experts would have dared to forecast had they foreseen the turmoil that accompanied Oslo I's implementation. Violence from the opponents of peace on both sides exceeded the expectations of many. The difficulties of collecting many donors' pledges, and of World Bank coordination of what was contributed, were hardly anticipated after the October 1993 Donors Conference at the State Department. The seemingly routine nature of border closures in the absence of safe passage within the Gaza–West Bank–Israel customs union was part of no one's thinking during the halcyon days when investment opportunities were initially highlighted. Finally, the shocking murder of Yitzhak Rabin capped one of the most tumultuous periods in the history of Israeli-Palestinian relations.

III. PROSPECTS FOR ECONOMIC CHANGE UNDER OSLO II

To ask why economic progress was as slow as it was under Oslo I misses the point, because few would have predicted that the political process itself could survive such turmoil. Yet two events that demarcated the transition from Oslo I to Oslo II demonstrate the readiness of both sides to move forward. First, the prompt, relatively uneventful redeployment of Israeli troops from many West Bank Palestinian population centers took place more smoothly than anyone had a right to expect, in some cases without even generating headlines. Secondly, on January 20, 1996, 80 percent of one million eligible Palestinian voters traveled long distances and waited hours to participate in the first democratic election in Palestinian history.[14] While acknowledging the historic achievement this represents, however, it is important that the right lessons be learned from it. It would be wrong, for example, to conclude that these two events, both fostered by Oslo II's expansion of West Bank autonomy, manifest unbridled approval of the process as it has unfolded to date.

The Palestinian election exhibits a Palestinian leadership selection process more democratic than any in the Arab world save perhaps precivil war Lebanon. Many candidates who opposed Arafat's handpicked nominees won on January 20, and several Hamas-dominated areas of Gaza featured turnouts as high as 90 percent.[15] The Carter Center and the National Democratic Institute, which jointly sponsored a delegation of 40 election observers from 11 countries, acknowledged that the election had its share of irregularities, but concluded that overall, "the Palestinian people had an historic opportunity to choose their leaders ... and did so with enthusiasm and a high degree of professionalism."[16]

Despite stagnant economic realities that persisted throughout Oslo I's implementation, architects of the process can rightly claim that it bought time for the Palestinian Authority to establish itself while fashioning the first self-governing apparatus in Palestinian history. But the "no free lunch" axiom applies as well, because the time bought was purchased at the expense of other urgent priorities. The appropriate reaction should be a sigh of relief rather than self-congratulations. Yes, the election suggests an encouraging degree of pragmatism and moderation on the part of the Palestinian people. The election-redeployment experience provided sufficient near-term gratification to offset temporarily the frustration surrounding unemployment, inaccessible borders, a burgeoning youth population, disappearing job prospects in Israel and the Gulf, and soaring birth rates in a patriarchal culture rife with unemployed fathers. Does this mean that the man on the Palestinian street, who presumably needed to see real benefits from the peace process in his everyday life, simply knew better and expected less? When compared to how fulfilling an American would find the experience of voting while unemployed, such a testimony to Palestinian faith and hope would be good news indeed.

Thus, we must avoid the impulse to delude ourselves about what has and has not been vindicated. If investors and donors continue to "wait and see" throughout the Oslo II implementation, as they did during the two years it took to negotiate it, Palestinian pragmatism and moderation will be in for a long and frustrating test. Oslo II's implementation will take place during final status negotiations that, for good reason, were delayed until now. A governing authority has been legitimately elected, but it now must govern in an area where boundaries are still to be determined, where sovereignty still resides elsewhere, where issues related to the first *Intifada* remain unresolved in the minds of most, and where the most intractable issues that have divided the parties will be on the table. One axiom of the development literature that I cited in my July 1995 testimony before U.S. Senator Hank Brown's Near East Subcommittee[17] is worth recalling in this regard. From Iran in 1979 to Tiannamen Square to the fall of Communism, it is seldom oppression *per se* that causes revolution but normally the sustained failure to satisfy rising expectations.

Thus, those who worked so diligently to elevate Palestinian expectations after Oslo I should not be misled as to what has been achieved. The election itself expressed Palestinian expectations of a better life. It is, therefore, not Oslo I as implemented, but Oslo II as the Palestinians expect it to be implemented, that was endorsed by the elections—much like Benjamin Franklin's characterization of second marriages as the triumph of hope over experience. So while the parties are busy negotiating Oslo III— the "final status" of Jerusalem, Hebron, refugees, settlements, and boundaries—and while the Israelis are engaged in a historic election of their own, they should take a hard, honest look at what has stood in the way of Palestinian economic progress, because that is how the Palestinian people will be measuring the governing skills of the leadership they have temporarily empowered to represent them.

IV. Impediments and Solutions

Realistic observers will learn quickly that there is plenty of blame to go around, which leads to finger pointing among traditional adversaries. Palestinians tend to cite Israeli border and port procedures, point-of-entry harassment, and other business-as-usual practices that reflect a mismatch between policy at the rhetorical level and practice at the street level. The Israelis, in turn, point to the Paris Economic Accord as the agreed terms of commercial relations and to their own legitimate security concerns as the basis of their policies on border access. Similarly, investors who are ready to begin putting businesses in the region, of whom there is no shortage, express frustration about: OPIC's seemingly impossible terms for loan qualification, the resultant absence of private sector financing sources in a high-risk region, the void in formal Palestinian commercial law, the undocumented restrictions they invariably encounter at Israeli ports, and the absence of any long-term infrastructural road map in public sector Palestinian planning. None of these is without merit, but an official response to economic difficulties cannot begin with finger-pointing. Parties should grant, from the outset, that there is much that each of them can do to improve the investment climate. It would be inappropriate in this format to offer an exhaustive listing of impediments that have been documented, but a cursory review of the broad categories and of processes for their resolution is worthy of brief discussion.

A. Israeli Practices

By far the most widely discussed category of impediments involves the difficulties associated with Israeli-Palestinian borders. One illustrative example involves a successful manufacturer of furniture in South Carolina who wants to compete for European markets. Gaza's geographic proximity and labor costs could put him in an ideal position to do so. He studied the market and its costs and arranged for land and a business partner in Gaza, but his business plan calls for him to import a container of raw materials and export a container of finished product every day. This requires routine movements of goods in and out of Israeli ports, across Israel, and across the Gaza border, in both directions. He promptly discoveries that Gaza's borders are not traversable on a reliable enough basis to pursue the risk. His plans are now on hold because, without reliable ingress and egress, he can neither establish himself as a reliable supplier to the new markets nor make payments on an enabling loan. OPIC and others provide political risk insurance, but it does *not* cover border closings to which Israel, as shall be noted below, has no current practical alternative in her search for security. There are additional examples that parallel this case, and comparable cases involving extant manufacturing operations in Gaza, restrictions at the Rafah checkpoint with Egypt, diversions of trucks 40 kilometers south from Rafah to Netzama (Israel), unloadings and reloadings from Palestinian to Israeli trucks and vice versa, burdensome documentation for tariff and duty allocations, the unreliability of Jordan River crossings, and the denial of free access to Palestinian products in Israel itself. Another entire genre of impediments derives from the absence of safe passage between Gaza and the West Bank, which restricts even non-export-oriented Palestinian producers to a fraction of their potential markets. Since there is enough commercial risk associated with investing in the West Bank and Gaza without these additional financial burdens and delivery uncertainties, no one will build a factory there while these conditions persist. From a trade and investment standpoint, manufacturing is one of the more logical near-term sources of large-scale indigenous Palestinian employment; human resource skills are among the few obvious assets that Palestinians can offer for near-term relief from their economic plight; and exports are the only means to bring new money into these depressed regions.

However, the challenges these complaints present to Israel cannot be assessed on exclusively economic grounds. The prospect of Palestinian trucks moving freely through Israel, or even into the West Bank and Gaza from other neighboring states, constitutes a clear and present danger to Israeli security. The peace process itself has been placed in serious jeopardy many times since 1993 because of terror activities far less threatening than trucks, and terrorists have used trucks everywhere from Beirut to the World Trade Center to Oklahoma City in recent years to deliver large explosives to random targets. No one will find a workable solution to the border access problem by ignoring or denying this reality, or by seeking solutions outside its framework. It is a classic political-economic conundrum. The Palestinian leadership will find no solution to its economic crisis without recognizing legitimate Israeli concerns in this area.

Indeed, the border issue brings the Peres Government, as it did the Rabin Government, face to face with core principles that brought the process to this point. The current government, like its predecessors, embraces the political, economic, and moral obligations associated with Palestinian self-rule and economic autonomy in principle, but it has insufficient confidence in its negotiating partner's capacity to offset the accompanying risks. The border problem shines a bright light on this contradiction. It is analogous with U.S.-Soviet Cold War negotiations when national security constraints could be accepted only under strict verification regimes. Then as now, verification was too often cited as both the enabler and the delimiter of the substance of negotiations, because no amount of verification provisions can bridge the chasm of distrust when national security is at stake. The best the sides can do under such circumstances is to endure one another's limitations through partial measures until it becomes apparent that compliance is in the genuine self-interest of both parties rather than an externally enforced regime of constraints. If this proves to be untrue, then the process has greater weaknesses than those associated with border procedures.

The Israelis could accelerate this confidence-building process in two ways. The first is to demonstrate convincingly that any burdensome border controls and port procedures that are in place are there solely for security purposes and not to create or preserve foreign trade advantages or domestic market controls. They could do this by bringing Palestinian business representatives and political counterparts into a process, perhaps informally, perhaps with American or European commercial and security experts as third parties. It would probably have to be done at a subofficial level so that no one's national security policies appear to have been marginalized or subordinated to outside interests. Secondly, they could take a hard, open-minded look at creative procedures that have been attempted already, some of which are now in place. For example, the Israelis themselves operate special "convoys" on a routine, scheduled basis to transport Palestinian goods to Israeli factories and distributors who rely on Gazan suppliers. Police inspections and escort patrols are provided so that interruptions are rare and delivery schedules can be met. These are no doubt expensive and logistically difficult exercises for the Israeli security system, but it demonstrates that creative solutions are possible.

Other potential solutions, of course, involve the construction of Palestinian ports, international funding for additional Israeli inspection facilities, and rapid, off-hour escort procedures that expedite Palestinian containers to and from destinations without recurring unloadings and reloadings. Experts should also closely examine the availability of efficient inspection technologies that might speed and simplify the border crossings. The United States has inspectors on the ground at Russian missile production facilities who routinely distinguish between permitted and prohibited strategic missiles that vary by centimeters while they are housed in containerized launchers in railcars. Western COCOM[18] inspectors until recently prohibited shipments to Eastern Europe if they included items as small as haircombs. Impregnable "tags" can be used to certify inspected trucks at the loading end so that their cargoes need not be transferred and reinspected en route to a predetermined destination.

Realism dictates that both sides must enter a quest for creative solutions with an honest acceptance of one another's core requirements. This means that the Palestinians must accept, as a minimum, that "free movement" is not exclusively, or even primarily, an economic issue, and that the Israelis must accept the presence of a determined economic partner and competitor on their doorstep. Good faith may or may not follow, but without these going-in positions on both sides, it is prohibited.

B. Palestinian Practices

The second category of impediments involves confusion and ambiguity in Palestinian administrative procedures. One American completed a TDA-sponsored feasibility study a year ago for a US$40 million crude oil refinery, that would not only be a profitable operation in Gaza, but would also generate up to US$100 million per year in revenues for the Palestinian Authority and provide 1,500 jobs. The investor plans widespread Palestinian public ownership with emphasis on service station owners. But so far he has not been able to get the Palestinian Authority's go-ahead to build the plant. U.S. officials at all levels routinely advocate the project in meetings with Palestinian leaders. The answer is always different, but never yes or no.

Without a doubt, the absence of established, systematic Palestinian decision making structures on foreign investment has prevented projects that would otherwise be in place, employing Palestinians and bringing revenues into the West Bank and Gaza. Some will argue that this is unsurprising in light of their centuries of inexperience with self-rule. Others will point out that pre-election governing procedures by an authority negotiating for its survival is not the venue on which to judge its day-to-day administrative performance. But the Palestinian leadership's style of carefully crafted ambiguity in these matters, combined with what is clearly a highly centralized decision-making apparatus, leaves the Palestinian Authority wide open to accusations ranging from exclusion of undesirable foreigners to outright corruption. Builders for Peace has seen no documentary evidence of these administrative processes, and U.N. and World Bank counterparts have consistently said they are nonexistent. U.S. foreign assistance transfers can withstand the most intrusive auditing standards, including end-use certifications, and U.S. investors operate in an accountable, transparent manner in all commonly known investment undertakings in the region. So there may be no basis for such characterizations, but in the absence of open and accountable procedures, neither is there a basis on which to refute them, which leaves little room for investors to measure the associated risk.

As a result, projects that would otherwise now be employing Palestinians and fostering an environment for follow-on market development are beyond the scope of rational planning. Construction goes forward in areas where infrastructural plans are unknown or nonexistent. Highly professional bids for large scale projects that would be funded privately or by donor countries languish without selections. Infrastructure projects like power, waste water, telecommunications, and road construction, which would regularize domestic conditions and simplify further planning, remain neither approved nor disapproved.

As we move from the implementation of Oslo I to the implementation of Oslo II, the assets to improve these trends are in place. An elected authority is now available from which to staff ministries and delegate authority to expert levels. A law encouraging foreign investment[19] has been crafted in accordance with internationally recognized language and structures.[20] Competent advisory services are readily available through U.S. funding, as well as a competent array of nongovernmental and private volunteer organizations. The new Palestinian Authority will have its hands full for the coming year as it strives to expand beyond the small slices of territory it now governs in the West Bank and Gaza and to justify the mandate it has been given by its constituents, but it will have to demonstrate its competence to a broader international audience if it expects to reward its people's confidence with a diverse array of international investors.

Professor David Fidler's pioneering scholarly work[21] and Keith Molkner's excellent analysis of the Palestinian Foreign Investment Law[22] probably document all of the strengths and weaknesses of the terms of the law that can be identified in the absence of case law. The problem with legal analysis in the absence of case law is that it is only through implementation that a society's cultural values and traditions actually give life to a new commercial regime. Chairman Arafat has said time and time again that he favors "free markets." But until Palestinian businesses and foreign investors are able to pursue their own commercial instincts, no one will know what these words actually mean. Arafat has been criticized repeatedly for his over-centralized role in Palestinian business creation, but such criticism is somewhere between premature and unfair because he is only now in a position to assemble a legitimately elected array of ministerial positions, and to delegate the authority appropriate to their portfolios. Decentralization will bring its own bureaucratic procedures, which, especially at the outset, are unlikely to be more decipherable than at present. Yet it is clear that decentralized, nondiscriminating, court-enforced rule of law is an essential missing ingredient to Palestinian participation in the global economic arena.

C. U.S. Practices

A third category of impediments involves shortcomings in the U.S. government's own widely advertised investment support services. An American investor actually opened a precast concrete plant in Gaza in

1995, leasing equipment from an Israeli bank that had foreclosed on a pre–Oslo buyer, and servicing the burgeoning residential construction "boom." This investor secured a US$1 million loan, which is the first and only loan OPIC has made to date for the West Bank and Gaza. Another investor worked with OPIC for a loan to build a large hotel in Gaza for over a year before concluding that OPIC's terms defeated the economic viability of the project. Interestingly enough, that investor appears to have secured private-sector financing through foreign sources under far less onerous terms, but we will not know for sure until the spring of 1996. Other cases demonstrate that these examples are unique. In each case, the investors are seeking alternative financing, and may well succeed, but it has taken time to discover the nature of OPIC's terms while these projects languished.

OPIC is a unique agency of the U.S. government with a challenging charter. On one hand it is an instrument of U.S. foreign policy with a responsibility to support private-sector investment with financing and risk insurance in developing countries. On the other hand, OPIC must operate as a bank that actually returns a profit to the U.S. Treasury on a year-to-year basis. Under Ruth Harkin's skilled leadership the agency returned a record profit in 1994 and expected to exceed that accomplishment in 1995. If all of OPIC's decisions emanated from their status as an arm of U.S. foreign assistance, it would duplicate the efforts of the USAID. On the other hand, if all it was guided by were return-on-investment interests, it would be no different from a private bank.

OPIC must find a balance between these often conflicting characteristics of its identity, emphasizing one or the other or both as conditions permit. The fact that Builders for Peace has often been frustrated with OPIC's criteria for finding that balance is no secret to our friends and supporters. Indeed, I have reluctantly seen it necessary to criticize OPIC staff policies publicly despite my high regard for OPIC President Ruth Harkin.

OPIC engaged in an aggressive public campaign throughout 1993 and 1994, calling U.S. and Palestinian attention to the US$125 million in financing that the agency intended to make available to investors in the West Bank and Gaza as a part of U.S. government policies in support of the peace process. U.S. officials routinely refer to a "US$500 million" U.S. contribution to the international donors effort, of which the OPIC pledge is 25 percent. As investors began bringing actual projects to OPIC's doorstep, however, lending terms that were not widely understood beforehand came to define a decidedly risk-averse set of preconditions. Principal among these is the policy whereby OPIC will only "lend against" businesses that are up and operating at their projected performance levels. Loans that support construction and early operations are available, but must be fully collateralized so that the U.S. government is not at risk until anticipated revenue flows have been under way for a specified period, normally a year. The effect of this policy, which places all of the start-up risk on the investor, is to exclude small-scale business persons, specifically, those who can meet the published requirements for 50 percent equity capital and various forms of operating reserves, but who need financial backing to complete the project. Business investment in the West Bank and Gaza is hardly a low-risk undertaking, but successful American entrepreneurs have demonstrated a willingness to go forward in the face of such risk if plausible financing is available. The absence of such support from conventional banks is presumably why an OPIC is needed in the first place.

Donor countries, all of whom would prefer to fulfill their pledge obligations through high-visibility, low-risk undertakings, compete with one another for the kinds of projects OPIC policies will support. Large scale infrastructure projects with virtually guaranteed revenue streams and midrange undertakings with large corporate assets behind them will have no trouble finding such support. But only OPIC can provide financing for those who need it most. For example, industrialization in the West Bank and Gaza is quite low—16 percent of Palestinian employment and eight percent of GDP. But it is the most plausible source of large-scale, near-term employment. Only 30 of the 4,200 industrial units in the West Bank and Gaza in 1990 employed 50 people or more, and the average number of employees was four. These "cottage industry" operations, which typify the successful businesses of many Palestinian-Americans as well, are the most logical targets for joint venture investments, in which American know-how and capital are joined with local Palestinian street sense. If investors had the capital on hand to undertake such ventures in compliance with OPIC's terms, however, they would not need financing. In short, its services work best for those who need it least, and vice versa. It may have been that early 1995 was simply how long it took for serious investors to begin seeking the support facilities OPIC had been heralding for the previous year or so, but its orientation toward the "for profit" side of their identity, as opposed to the "instrument of foreign policy" side, seemed to crystallize just after Congress changed hands at the end of 1994. A Congressional Research Service study in April 1995,[23] a *New York Times* article by House Budget Committee Chairman John Kasich calling for OPIC's privatization in July 1995,[24] and a spate of amendments to the Fiscal Year ("FY") 1996 Foreign Operations Bill marked OPIC as a target for abolition by the new Republican Congressional leadership. OPIC's protection from such action, ironically, derives from precisely the same logic that most convincingly calls for its privatization—the fact that it returns a profit to the government, which renders it "self-sustaining." In light of Israeli and Palestinian practices identified above as impediments to investment, OPIC risk aversion, which amounts to an aversion to investment in the West Bank and Gaza, is defended by many as well-advised. After all, policies that scrupulously protect the interests of the U.S. taxpayers ought to be among such an agency's highest priorities. But one of the principal benefits of U.S. investment in the region would be to reveal these and other impediments, to provide the case studies that are needed to identify and eliminate them. In the absence of foreign investment experience, the status quo interests that maintain many of these impediments will provide the only expert testimony as to their effect. In this sense, trails that need to be blazed through the morass of existing practices might prove to be comparably beneficial to the U.S. taxpayer. Policies that weight OPIC's criteria more toward U.S. foreign interests, and less toward self-sustaining return on investment, would help serve that purpose.

A second area in which U.S. policies as currently practiced impede Palestinian economic expansion is U.S. import policies toward Palestinian products. The U.S.-Israel Free Trade Agreement[25] (FTA) included the West Bank and Gaza on a de facto basis until the Palestinians achieved economic autonomy. No one intended for the Oslo agreements to penalize the Palestinians economically, but when the West Bank and Gaza were considered occupied territories they benefited indirectly from many of the labeling, tariff, quota, and product inspection benefits that the United States yields to a close friend like Israel. Indeed, attempting to compensate for this unintended consequence of peace, the U.S. government extended preferential tariff rates to Palestinian goods under the Generalized System of Preferences[26] (GSP) in early 1995. However, GSP excludes textiles and agricultural products, which are currently the Palestinians' most marketable products, and, moreover, Congress failed to reauthorize the GSP program for FY 1996.

Palestinians enjoy preferential trade advantages today with Israel and with the European Union, but they currently receive no statutory advantages with regard to the U.S. market. Legislation that would extend duty-free treatment to all Palestinian goods imported to the United States has been proposed by the Administration and approved by the House Ways and Means Committee. It now awaits the approval of the full House and Senate. As discussed, an export oriented industrial strategy is the most likely near-term solution to the Palestinian employment problem, and access to the U.S. market is a precondition to U.S. investment toward that end.

D. International Practices

The final category of impediments, which involves all of the parties, is the persistent difficulties they have had in attempting to create border industrial zones, which would address many of the impediments this paper has raised. Such zones would be constructed under specially agreed Palestinian and Israeli terms and operated under jointly approved but independently chartered authority. Located on the border, they would enjoy specially structured provisions for movements in and out, and thus might resolve many of the ongoing border difficulties as they relate to both manufacturing and exports. Their special legal status would "jump-start" development of commercial law by limiting its scope to the specific zone, and would enable infrastructure development to be targeted to within the zones' agreed parameters. The United States, which strongly supports the zones for their "quick-fix" potential, has expressed willingness to seek special provisions for tax-exempt access of these zones' products into the U.S. market, even if progress on Palestinian FTA status continues to be delayed. The Israelis and Palestinians agreed in early 1995, in principle, to create these zones on the Palestinian side of the border in the vicinity of Israeli commercial centers from which they can draw logistical support. Yet, the idea which is fully endorsed at the conceptual stage, is nowhere near a physical reality. This is apparently because the special security, legal, and commercial procedures that would be enacted by the parties for the zones have remained beyond the reach of negotiators to date.

As this seemingly ideal near-term solution slips away, both sides have begun looking for alternative solutions. The Israelis would build the zones on their own side of the border with special subsidies for investors who bring businesses there, and with provisions to enable the employment of Palestinians who are now unable to enter Israel. But the Palestinians are looking for more than just jobs out of these zones. Troubled by the "state within a state" status of border zones and reluctant to endorse Israeli-owned zones with Palestinian workers, many Palestinian leaders would prefer zones located on internal Palestinian territory in order to more fully exploit the benefits of foreign investment for their own infrastructure requirements. While the debate continues, a potentially lucrative target for investors languishes in the realm of unresolved issues.

CONCLUSION

The compelling need for private-sector Palestinian development, which essentially went unanswered throughout the period of Oslo I's implementation, cannot await the resolution of all final status issues at the political level. Indeed, the compromises and disappointments invariably associated with the give and take of diplomacy may necessitate more than ever some evidence of economic progress. It would be unwise for the architects of the political process to forget this, or to interpret the outcome of the Palestinian election as a reprieve from the obligations they have assumed in the economic realm.

Moreover, the economic issues, like the pending political issues, have remained unresolved for good reason. They go to the core of what self-rule and economic autonomy mean. To separate them from the political realm as if they were an unrelated category misses the point entirely. The economic impediments cursorily reviewed in this essay are the residue of political accommodations not yet achieved. They are central to any complete definition of the final status relationship. But coherent mechanisms for their resolution are not properly structured for consideration at the political level because they have been set aside from the formal proceedings. To elevate their relevance, to crystallize their core issues, and to enlighten negotiators, expert panels are needed beginning at the semiofficial and subofficial levels. These should include business and management specialists, as well the good offices of third-party American participants.

The most useful opening agenda item for consideration by such panels would be an examination of what stands in the way of progress on industrial zones. The immediate effects of manufacturing-based "export processing zones" on jobs and balance of trade cannot be achieved by other means. These border zones, which the World Bank views as "security islands," would certainly attract private investment in the form of Israeli-Palestinian, American-Palestinian, or American-Palestinian-Israeli joint ventures, many of which are now awaiting the arrival of such a systematic regime for investment. The fact that the parties have agreed in principle regarding the broad outlines of such zones means that conceptual issues that will delay other solutions have already been overcome. All of the problems associated with borders, ports, commercial codes, business licensing, and access to markets — problems whose details require definition to be sure — are subsumed under that broad conceptual umbrella. They are difficult issues, but a framework for their resolution is in place. The parties should focus intense, expert attention on them, with international support, firm deadlines, and clear objectives.

Palestinian interest in the more internally focused zones for targeted infrastructure development should also be explored with the supportive cooperation of their foreign counterparts. The Israeli Ministry of Trade has also expressed interest in developing zones on their side of the border — either independently or through the "mirror model" in parallel with a Palestinian zone — to absorb currently inaccessible Palestinian employment. If the Palestinians' internal "municipal industry complexes" were examined in the same context as these more unilateral Israeli models, the broad outlines of a compromise might begin to take form. Indeed, the two unilateral models operating "in parallel" might be able to benefit from the same ingress, egress, and transportation protocols even if both are not on the border. The Israelis are motivated by moral as well as economic incentives when considering the issue of Palestinian unemployment. The Palestinians are motivated by developmental as well as economic incentives, but are limited by political factors when it comes to Israeli-dominated economic structures. Confidence-building efforts that begin with a clear recognition of these parallel perspectives will discover much common ground.

The World Bank's well-established interest in industrial zones is further cause to move forward with this agenda. This commitment brings with it the Bank's good offices, technical expertise, and a degree of otherwise unattainable financial backing. The combination of the Bank's willingness to coordinate and channel donors' contributions in the form of guarantees to investors, and Israel's commitment to provide secure shipment routes to and from ports, overcomes many of the going-in problems that will burden other approaches. The Bank has estimated that US$200 million would be required for each park, of which US$20 million could come from donors, US$10 million from the Bank itself, US$20 million from the Palestinian Authority, and the remaining US$150 million from private investors. These numbers are entirely consistent with the level of interest that has been expressed in the American private sector.

The broader issues associated with Palestinian freedom of movement will require time, realism, and confidence building. Industrial zones are one way to begin that process at the private-sector level, but additional processes are needed as well. Palestinian producers whose economic potential has been limited by the occupation, must be allowed to outgrow their roles as suppliers for Israeli exporters and become exporters themselves. They must be allowed to compete with Israeli counterparts not just in foreign markets but within Israel itself. Without such an atmosphere of cooperation, which will take time to develop, Israel's own vision of a new regional economic order will be limited to annual showcase conferences and wishful rhetoric. It is true that the West's victories in the Cold War and the Gulf War were fundamental factors that enabled Israel's constructive role in the peace process, but it is Palestinian acceptance to date of Israel's political terms that has laid the groundwork for broader regional accommodation. That acceptance is fragile, but so is Israel's sense of security. Both should be treated with care by those who are charged with the responsibility of moving the process forward.

Notes

1. Declaration of Principles on Interim Self-Government Arrangements, Sept. 13, 1993, Isr.-PLO, 32 I.L.M. 1525 (1993).

2. As used in this paper, "Oslo II" is the Israeli-Palestinian Interim Agreement on the West Bank and Gaza Strip, Sept. 28, 1995, Isr.-PLO (on file with the *Fordham International Law Journal*).

3. As used in this paper, the term "Oslo I" encompasses: the Declaration, supra note 1, 32 I.L.M. at 1525; the Israel-PLO Agreement on the Gaza Strip and Jericho Area, May 4, 1994, Isr.-PLO, 33 I.L.M. 622; and the Protocol on Economic Relations between Israel and the PLO, which was later included as an appendix to the Cairo Agreement. Cairo Agreement supra, annex IV, 33 I.L.M. at 696.

4. See, e.g., Serge Schmemann, "Bombings in Israel: The Overview," *New York Times*, Feb. 26, 1996, at Al.

5. The Palestinian population has more college degrees per capita than any Arab state. 3 INTERNATIONAL BANK FOR RECONSTRUCTION AND DEVELOPMENT, DEVELOPING THE OCCUPIED TERRITORIES AN INVESTMENT IN PEACE 34 (1993).

6. See Stephen Franklin, "Banking on Peace in Mideast," *Chicago Tribune*, Jan. 30, 1994, at 1 (discussing economic repercussions of Palestinian support for Iraq in Persian Gulf War).

7. Id.

8. See David Hoffman & John M. Goshko, "The United States; Main Objective is to Keep Parties at Table," *Washington Post*, Oct. 30, 1991, at A32 (discussing Madrid Conference and U.S. role therein).

9. Declaration, supra note 1, 32 I.L.M. at 1525.

10. The Gulf Corporation Council (GCC) is a cooperative consisting of Bahrain, Oman, the United Arab Emirates, Qatar, Kuwait, and Saudi Arabia.

11. Norman Kempter, "Arabs Ease Boycott Linked to Israel," *Los Angeles Times*, Oct. 1, 1994, at A6.

12. Cairo Agreement, supra note 3, 33 I.L.M. at 622.

13. Economic Protocol, supra note 3, annex IV, 33 I.L.M. at 696.

14. Daniel Schorr, "Palestinians Voted for Their Own Participation," *Christian Science Monitor*, Jan. 26, 199, at 19.

15. See "Palestinians Vote for Democracy, But Will They Get It?" *The Economist*, Jan. 27, 1996, at 37 (noting that, in some areas, 90 percent of Palestinians voted and that many of Arafat's hand-picked candidates were defeated).

16. Press Release, "Preliminary Statement of Carter Center/NDI International Delegation to January 20, 1996 Palestinian Election," Carter Center & National Democratic Institute for International Affairs, Jan. 21, 1996, at 1.

17. Economic Development and U.S. Assistance in Gaza/Jericho, 1995: Hearing Before the Subcommittee on Near East and South Asian Affairs of the Senate Comm. on Foreign Relations, 104th Cong., 1st Sess. (1995) (testimony of Mel Levine) available in LEXIS, Nexis Library, Curnws File.

18. The Coordinating Committee for Multilateral Export Controls (COCOM)

served to keep Communist states from acquiring advanced Western technology by preventing export of such technology. After nearly 45 years, it was disbanded in 1994.

19. Law on the Encouragement of Investment, translated in David Fidler, *Foreign Private Investment in Palestine: An Analysis of the Law on the Encouragement of Investment in Palestine*, 19 FORD. INT'L L.J. 529, 603–10 (1995).

20. For a comprehensive analysis of this law, see Fidler, supra note 19.

21. See, e.g., id.

22. See, e.g., Keith Molkner, *Legal and Structural Hurdles to Achieving Political Stability and Economic Development in the Palestinian Territories*, 19 FORD. INT'L L.J. 1419 (1996).

23. Memorandum from Wayne M. Morrison, Analyst in International Trade and Finance, Congressional Research Service, to House Budget Committee (Apr. 11, 1995).

24. John R. Rasich, "Get Rid of Corporate Welfare," *New York Times*, July 9, 1995, at 15.

25. United States-Israel Free Trade Agreement, Apr. 22, 1985, U.S.-Isr., 24 I.L.M. 653, H.R. Doc. No. 61, 99th Cong., 1st Sess. (1985).

26. 19 U.S.C. §§ 2461–66 (1994).

Selected Bibliography

The literature on the legal aspects of "the Question of Palestine" and the Palestinian Arab-Israeli conflict is legion. What is offered here is meant to serve as a general opening guide upon which the interested researcher should build. Much of the relevant and appropriate literature can be culled from one of the bibliographies listed here; subsequently published material is indexed in the *Index to Legal Periodicals* and *LegalTrac*.

Sanford R. Silverburg. "An International Legal Bibliography on the Palestinian Arab-Israeli Conflict," *Denver Journal of International Law and Policy*, 10, no. 2 (Winter 1981): 263–278.

———. *The Palestinian Arab-Israeli Conflict: An International Legal Bibliography* (Monticello, IL: VANCE Bibliographies, August 1982) [P-1028].

———. "A Select International Law Bibliography on the Arab-Israeli Conflict," *Law Library Journal*, 72, no. 1 (February 1979): 12–20.

———. "A Selected International Law Bibliography on the Arab-Israeli Conflict," *Suffolk Transnational Law Journal*, 4, no. 1 (1980): 47–88.

Esther Mann Snyder. *Israel: A Legal Research Guide* (Buffalo, NY: William S. Hein and Co. Inc., 2000).

Some materials are out of print, albeit useful and should be consulted if available. I have in mind here such items as:

The Jewish Yearbook of International Law 1948 edited by Nathan Feinberg and J. Stoyanovsky (Jerusalem: Rubin Mass, 1949).

Revue de droit international pour le Moyen Orient, vol. 1, no. 1 (May/June 1951) to vol. 4, no. 2 (December 1955). Published at times by G. Maisonneuve (Paris) and A. Pedone (Paris).

Basic materials focusing on the general topic or specific contentious issues:

Eyal Benvenisti. *The International Law of Occupation* (Princeton, NJ: Princeton University Press, 1993).

George Emile Bisharat. *Palestinian Lawyers and the Israeli Rule of Law: Law and Disorder in the West Bank* (Austin, TX: University of Texas Press, 1989).

Bernard Botiveau. *L'État palestinienne* (Paris: Presses de Sciences Politiques, 1999). [La Bibliothèque du citoyen].

Stephen Bowen (ed.). *Human Rights, Self-Determination and Political Change in the Occupied Palestinian Territories* (Cambridge, MA: Kluwer Law International, 1997). [International Studies in Human Rights Series, no. 52].

Francis Anthony Boyle. *The Future of International Law and American Foreign Policy.* (Dobbs Ferry, NY: Transnational Publishers, Inc., 1989). (Chap. 5).

Henry Cattan. *Palestine and International Law: The Legal Aspects of the Arab-Israeli Conflict.* 2d ed. (New York: Longman, 1973).

Eugene Cotran and Chibli Mallat (eds.). *The Arab-Israeli Accords: Legal Perspectives.* (Boston, MA: Kluwer Law International [in association with the Centre of Islamic and Middle Eastern Law (CIMEL), School of Oriental and African Studies (SOAS)], 1996). [CIMEL Series no. 1].

Eugene Cotran and Adel Omar Sherif (eds.). *The Role of the Judiciary in the Protection of Human Rights* (Cambridge, MA: Kluwer Law International [in association with the Centre of Islamic and Middle Eastern Law (CIMEL), 1998). [CIMEL Series, no. 5]. Part II.

Paul J. I. M. de Waart. *Dynamics of Self-Determination in Palestine: Protection of Peoples as a Human Right* (Leiden: E.J. Brill, 1994).

_____. *The Legal Status of Palestine Under International Law* (Bir Zeit, Palestine: Bir Zeit University, Law Center, 1996).

La Dossier Palestine: la question palestinienne et le droit international (Paris: La Découverte, 1991).

Nathan Feinberg. *On the Arab Jurist's Approach to Zionism and the State of Israel.* (Jerusalem: The Magnes Press, The Hebrew University, 1971).

Alan Gerson. *Israel, the West Bank and International Law* (London: Frank Cass, 1978).

Giancarlo Guarino. *La questione della Palestina nel diritto internazionale* (Turin: G. Giappichelli, 1994).

John W. Halderman (ed.). *The Middle East Crisis: Test of International Law* (Dobbs Ferry, NY: Oceana Publications, 1969).

Israel in Lebanon: The Report of the International Commission to Enquire into Reported Violations of International Law by Israel During its Invasion of the Lebanon (London: Ithaca Press, 1983).

Journalism Under Occupation: Israel's Regulation of the Palestinian Press (New York: The Committee to Protect Journalists/ARTICLE 19, October 1988).

Majid Khadduri (ed.). *Major Middle Eastern Problems in International Law* (Washington, DC:American Enterprise Institute for Public Policy Research, 1972). [U. S. Interests in the Middle East Series].

Hans Köchler (ed.). *Legal Aspects of the Palestine Problem: With Special Regard to the Question of Jerusalem.* (Vienna: W. Braumüller, 1981). [Studies on International Relations, 4].

Ruth Lapitdoth and Moshe Hirsch (eds.). *The Arab-Israeli Conflict and its Resolution: Selected Documents* (Boston: Martinus Nijhoff Publishers, 1992).

Law and Courts in the Israeli-Held Areas. (Jerusalem: Institute for Legislative Research and Comparative Law, Faculty of Law, The Hebrew University of Jerusalem, January 1970).

League of Arab States. Secretariat General. *Israeli Settlements in the Occupied Arab Territories: An International Symposium* (n.p.: Dar al-Afaq al-Jadidah, [1985]).

W. Thomas Mallison. *The Palestine Problem in International Law and World Order.* (Burnt Mill, Harlow, Essex, England: Longman, 1986).

W. Thomas Mallison and Sally V. Mallison. *An International Law Analysis of the Major United Nations Resolutions Concerning the Palestine Question* (New York: United Nations, 1979). UN Doc. ST/SG/SER.F/4.

Musa E. Mazzawi. *Palestine and the Law: Guidelines for the Resolution of the Arab-Israeli Conflict* (Reading, Eng.: Ithaca Press, 1997).

John Norton Moore (ed.). *The Arab-Israeli Conflict* (Princeton, NJ: Princeton University Press [sponsored by the American Society of International Law], [1975]). 3 vols.

Emile A. Nakhleh. *The West Bank and Gaza: Toward the Making of a Palestinian State* (Washington, DC: American Enterprise Institute for Public Policy Research, 1979). [AEI Studies 232].

Issa Nakhleh. *Encyclopedia of the Palestine Problem* (New York: Intercontinental Books, 1999). 2 vols.

Jamal Raji Nassar. *The Palestine Liberation Organization: From Armed Struggle to the Declaration of Independence* (New York: Praeger, 1991).

National Lawyers Guild. 1977 Middle East Delegation. *Treatment of Palestinians in Israeli-Occupied West Bank and Gaza* (Washington, DC: National Lawyers Guild, 1978).

The Palestine Question: Seminar of Arab Jurists on Palestine, Algiers, 22–27 July 1967 (Beirut: The Institute for Palestine Studies, 1968).

Emma Playfair (ed.). *International Law and the Administration of Occupied Territories: Two Decades of Israeli Occupation of the West Bank and Gaza Strip, 1967–1987.* (New York: Oxford University Press, 1992).

John Quigley. *Palestine and Israel: A Challenge to Justice.* (Durham, NC: Duke University Press, 1990).

Seif A. El-Wady Ramahi. *International Law & The Palestine Question: An Analysis of its Legal and Political Dimensions.* (Tokyo: Biblio, 1979).

Yitzhak Reiter. *Islamic Institutions in Jerusalem: Palestinian Muslim Organizations Under Jordanian and Israeli Rule* (Cambridge, MA: Kluwer Law International [under the auspices of The Jerusalem Institute of Israel Studies], 1997). [Arab and Islamic Laws Series, No. 15].

Edward W. Said. *The Politics of Dispossession: The Struggle for Palestinian Self-Determination 1969–1994* (New York: Pantheon Books, 1994).

Yezid Sayigh. *Armed Struggle and the Search for State: The Palestinian National Movement, 1949–1993.* (New York: Oxford University Press, 1997).

Ronen Shamir. *The Colonies of Law: Colonialism, Zionism and Law in Early Mandate Palestine* (New York: Cambridge University Press, 2000).

Amos Shapira and Mala Tabory (eds.). *New Political Entities in Public and Private International Law: With Special Reference to the Palestinian Entity.* (Boston: Kluwer Law International, 1999).

Raja Shehadeh. *From Occupation to Interim Accords: Israel and the Palestinian Territories* (Cambridge, MA: Kluwer Law International, 1997). [Centre of Islamic and Middle Eastern Law (CIMEL), Series, No. 4].

Edward M. Siegel (ed.). *Israel's Legitimacy in Law and History* (New York: Center for Near East Policy Research, 1993) [Proceedings of the Conference on International Law and the Arab-Israeli Conflict, Sponsored by The Louis D. Brandeis Society of Zionist Lawyers, October 21, 1990, New York].

Julius Stone. *Israel and Palestine: Assault on the Law of Nation* (Baltimore, MD: The Johns Hopkins University Press, 1981).

United Nations Seminar on the Question of Palestine. *Question of Palestine: Legal Aspects: A Compilation of Papers Presented at the United Nations Seminars on the Question of Palestine in 1980–1986.* (New York: United Nations, 1991).

Mayir Vereté. *From Palmerston to Balfour: Collected Essays of Mayer Vereté* (London: Frank Cass, 1992).

Quincy Wright. *The Middle East: Prospects for Peace* (Dobbs Ferry, NY: Oceana Publications [for the Association of the Bar of the City of New York], 1969). [13th Hammarskjold Forum, Dec. 4–5, 1969].

F. Yahia. *The Palestine Question and International Law* (Beirut: Palestine Liberation Organization, Research Center, 1970).

Essential yearbooks and periodicals would include:

Arab Law Quarterly, vol., 1, pt. 1 (November 1985) to date.

Bulletin from the United Nations. Special Unit on Palestinian Rights, vol. 1, no. 1 (June 1978)–vol. 5, no. 5/6 (May/June 1982).

Israel Law Review, vol. 1, no. 1 (January 1966) to date.

Journal of Palestine Studies, vol. 1, no. 1 (Autumn 1971) to date.

Palestine & the UN: Monthly Bulletin issued by the Permanent Observer Mission of Palestine to the United Nations, vol. 1, issue 1 (Mid-October 1966–June 1978). [SER-BIB/SERLOC].

The Palestine Yearbook of International Law, vol. 1 (1984) to date, published by the Al-Shaybani Society of International Law (Nicosia, Cyprus).

Revue égyptienne de droit international/Egyptian Review of International Law, vol. 1 (1945) to date.

Yearbook of Islamic and Middle Eastern Law Volume 1, 1994 (1995) to date, published by Kluwer Law International (Cambridge, MA).

Unpublished Masters Theses and Doctoral Dissertations:

Abed-Rabbo, Samir A. "Might Does Not Make Right: International Law and the Question of Palestine." Ph.D diss., University of Miami, 1981.

Abuelghanam, Khaled Abdelkarim. "The Question of the Legitimacy of the Jordanian Presence in Palestine." Ph.D diss., Texas Tech University, 1992.

Buttu, Diana Nazic. "Reinterpreting Islamic Law: The Case of Divorce in Palestine." LL.M thesis. University of Toronto, Faculty of Law, 1996.

Forsythe, David Prevatt. "The United Nations and the Peaceful Settlement of Disputes: The Case of the Conciliation Commission for Palestine." Ph.D diss., Princeton University, 1968.

Funk, Chris D. "The Use of Terrorism as a Means to Create a Homeland for Stateless Refugees in the Middle East," Masters thesis, San Jose State University, 1991.

Gruen, George Emanuel. "Turkey, Israel and the Palestine Question, 1948–1960: A Study in the Diplomacy of Ambivalence." Ph.D diss., Columbia University, 1970.

Hyatt, David Mayer. "The United Nations and the Partition of Palestine." Ph.D diss., The Catholic University of America, 1973.

Al-Jubeir, Nail Ahmed. "The Legal Status of the Palestine Liberation Organization Under International Law." Masters thesis, The American University, 1987.

Kenny, Edward L. "The United Nations Handling of Two Territorial Questions: Palestine and Indonesia." Masters thesis, The American University, 1959.

Mansy, Thomas M. "Palestine in the United Nations." Ph.D diss., Georgetown University, 1956.

Oskoui, Barbara Joan. "Nationalism, Legitimacy, and Sovereignty: The Case for Palestinian Statehood." Masters thesis, San Jose State University, 1992.

Sankari, Farouk Ali. "The United Nations Truce Supervision Organization in Palestine." Ph.D diss., Claremont Graduate School, 1968.

van Aggelen, Johannes Gerrit Cornelis. " Conflicting Claims to Sovereignty Over the West Bank: An Indepth Analysis of the Historical Roots and Feasible Options in the

Framework of a Future Setttlement of the Dispute." D.C.L. diss., McGill University, Faculty of Law, 1989.

von der Hardt, Anya Aicha. "A Case for the Palestine Liberation Organization: Human Rights Violations in the West Bank and Gaza." Ph.D diss., The Union for Experimenting Colleges and Universities, 1987.

Organizations whose efforts include relevant publications:

Bir Zeit University
Institute of Law
P. O. Box 14
Bir Zeit
Palestine
http://www.lawcenter.birzeit.edu/
law@law.birzeit.edu

The Center for Policy Analysis on Palestine
2435 Virginia Avenue, N.W.
Washington, DC 20037
http://www.palestinecenter.org
jfcpap@palestinecenter.org

Centre of Islamic and Middle Eastern Law
University of London
School of Oriental and African Studies (SOAS)
London, England
http://www.soas.ac.uk/Centres/IslamicLaw/Materials.html

Al-Haq/Law in the Service of Man
P.O. Box 1413
Ramallah
Palestine
http://www.unipalgt.com/~alhaq

Institute for Palestine Studies
3501 M Street, N.W.
Washington, DC 20007
http://www.ipsjps.org/html/jpsl.html
jps@ipsig.org

Palestinian American Research Center (PARC)
Randolph-Macon College
P.O. Box 5005
Ashland, Virginia 23005
http://www.parcenter.org
parc@rnc.edu

Contributors

Sanford R. Silverburg is a Professor of Political Science and Department Chair at Catawba College, Salisbury, North Carolina

Joseph H. Weiler is Manley Hudson Professor and Jean Monnet Chair of Law, Harvard Law School, Cambridge, Massachusetts

Adrien Katherine Wing is Professor of Law, University of Iowa, College of Law, Ames, Iowa

John Strawson is Principal Lecturer in Law and in Law and Middle Eastern Studies, University of East London, England

Joel Singer is an associate with Sidley & Austin, Washington, D.C.

John Quigley is President's Club Professor in Law, College of Law, The Ohio State University, Columbus

Neri Sybesma-Knol is Professor of International Law, University of Brussels, Belgium

George E. Bisharat is Professor of Law, Hastings College of Law, San Francisco

David P. Fidler is Associate Professor of Law, Indiana University School of Law, Bloomington, Indiana

Fadi G. Harb is Manager, Membership Development Project, Palestine Trade Center (Paltrade), Ramallah, Palestine

Mel Levine was a U. S. Congressman from California from 1983 to 1993. He is currently a partner at Gibson, Dunn & Crutcher, Los Angeles

Keith C. Molkner is Director of Government and International Affairs, Global Commerce Zone Inc., Chicago

Juan Bautista Delgado is an international lawyer and a Lecturer at the Open University in Murcia, Spain.

Index

Abbas, Mahmoud 15
Abd al-Salaam, Amin 225
Abed, George 338–339
Abington, Edward 237
Abrash, Abigail 237
Abu Jarbu, Farid 229
Abu Mazen 15
Accord of Luxembourg 101
Achille Lauro Affair 175
Afghanistan 59
African National Congress (ANC) 200–201, 206
Al-Abadla, Qusai 225
Albright, Madeleine 236–237
Allon Plan 109
Apartheid 201, 204
Arab Higher Committee 40–41
Arab–Israeli Conflict 75–76
Arafat, Yasser 214–215, 217–219, 223–226, 228, 231, 233–34, 236–237, 291, 371
Armero, Jose Mario 303
Australia 21

Balfour Declaration 55, 76–77, 252, 254, 258, 261, 272–273
Barak, Ehud 265
Bell, Gertrude 257
Bentwich, Helen 255–260
Bentwich, Norman 255–260
Bir Zeit University Law Center 224
Bloc of the Faithful (*Gush Emunim*) 65
Blum, Yehuda 73–74, 78, 80
Brownlie, Ian 10
B'Tselem 232
Builders for Peace 395–396

Cairo Agreement 183–189, 191–192, 263
Camp David Accords 59, 128, 130, 175, 180, 182–183
Canada 21
Cattan, Henry 75–78, 80
China 21, 119
Civil Rights 227–235, 238
Clinton, William J. 237
Committee for the Elimination of Racial Discrimination 179
Convention for a Democratic South Africa (CODESA) 201
Convention on the Elimination of All Forms of Discrimination Against Women 209
Council on Foreign Relations 161
Cyprus 45

Dajani, Omar 163
Declaration of Principles (DOP) 19, 163, 169, 180, 182–183, 190–191, 218, 339–342, 369–373, 397–399
Democratic Front for the Liberation of Palestine 233
de Waart, Paul 253–255
Dezcallar, Jorge 301
Dinstein, Yoram 57

Eban, Abba 41
economic development: Gaza Strip 397–400; globalization 333–338; Oslo Accords 338–349; West Bank 397–400
economic protocol 340–345
Egypt 47
Egyptian–Israeli Peace Treaty 59

Index

European Common Market 58
European Convention of Human Rights 16
European Economic Community (EEC) 84–106, 116–117, 121, 124
European Union 21–22, 42, 235

Feinberg, Nathan 77
Fez Summit 58–59
Finland 22
Food and Agricultural Organization (FAO) 44
Franco, Francisco 299–300, 302; and Arab world 304–305; and Israel 305–316; and Middle East 307–316
Friedman, Thomas "Old Straitjacket" 351–358
Further Transfer Protocol 19

Gaza–Jericho Agreement 19
Gaza Strip 11, 19, 41, 43, 46–47, 49, 51, 59, 63–64, 70, 160, 163, 169, 174, 178–180, 183, 185, 190–191, 193–194, 214–215, 217–223, 225, 232, 234–235, 264–265, 373–375, 396, 405–406; and justice 219–222
General Agreement on Tariffs and Trade (GATT) 17, 161
Germany 22
Gerson, Allan 73
Gore, Al 236–237
Great Britain 22
Greenspan, Morri 178
Gush Emunim (Bloc of the Faithful) 65

Hague Academy of International Law 256
Hague Regulations 178
Hamas 233, 403
Hannum, Hurst 176
Hebron 66, 217
Hebron Agreement 9, 266
human rights 227–235, 238
Huntington, Samuel P. 338
Hussein, King 70
al-Husseini, Faisal 164

Interim Agreement 163, 264
International Convention on the Elimination of All Forms of Racial Discrimination 179

International Labor Organization (ILO) 44
International Law: belligerent occupation 46; *in statu nascendi* 10; *jus ex injuria non oritur* 79; *res nullius* 73; *restituti in integrum* 76; subjects 15–17; *terra nullius* 14
Intifada 208, 220, 222, 228, 232, 399
Iran 59
Islamic Jihad 233
Israel 41, 44, 46, 49, 59–68, 70–72, 75, 79–80, 83, 106, 108, 118, 174, 178, 236, 305; Armistice Agreement—Jordan 74; military government 220, 232–233; occupied territories 221–222, 227, 232–233; occupied territories—Jewish settlements 265; Palestine Liberation Organization (PLO) Agreement 190; "Trustee Occupant" 74
Israeli–Palestinian Interim Agreement 216

Jaffa 66
Japan 22
Jericho Area 183, 185, 187, 189–191, 193
Jerusalem 163–165, 190–193, 252; East 191, 265; West 74
Jewish Agency 49
Jordan 22, 47, 59–60, 70–71, 73, 117, 266
Jordan River 110, 125
Jordan Valley 109–110
Jordanian–Israeli General Armistice Agreement 74

Kelsen, Hans 24
al-Khatib, Ghassan 231
Klinghoffer, Leon 175
Knesset 49
Kuttub, Daoud 237

League of Arab States 11
League of Nations 14, 38–39, 55, 251–252, 255, 257
League of Nations—Permanent Mandates Commission 38–39
League of Nations Mandate—Palestine 55, 76–77, 273, 277
legal maxims—*nasciturus pro jam nato habetur* 10
Lillich, Richard B. 176
Lissitzyn, Oliver 16

Index

Madrid Conference 9
Mandela, Nelson 208
Memorandum of Understanding 181
Meron, Theodore 179
Mesa, Roberto 300
Mitterand, François 42
Monnet, Jean 87
Montevideo Convention 163, 175
Mubarak, Hosni 59

Netanyahu, Benjamin 265
The Netherlands 22
New York Times 231
Nongovernmental Organizations (NGO) 233

Oil Producing Exporting Countries (OPEC) 119
Orient House 164–165
Oslo Accords 224, 263; and economic development 400–404
Oslo I 218, 264
Oslo II 216–218
Oslo Process 266
Ottoman law 219

Palestine 10–15, 38–39, 41, 44–45, 47, 49, 51, 60, 63–64, 68–71, 76, 82–83, 106, 108, 117–118, 125; Bar association 226; basic law 160–161, 166, 199, 209, 239, 266; British Mandate 38, 76, 219, 251–252, 254–262; covenant 68–69, 76; Declaration of Independence 10, 42, 48, 164, 176; economic development 332–333, 369–370; economic development—banking law 379–383; economic development—investment law 376–379; economic development—legal aspects 376–379; economic development—Palestine authority (pa) 344–347; economic development—tax law 383–389; Egypt 38; entity 9; France 38; Great Britain 38; Greece 38; High Court of Justice 223; Italy 38; Jewish population 252–254, 257; legal reform 214–215; national self-determination 40, 72; National Trade Dialogue Project (NTDP) 350–358; nationalism 70; press law 230; Preventive Security Service (P.S.S.) 230–231; security courts 229–230, 236, 238; Switzerland 38
Palestine Bar Association 226
Palestine Liberation Organization (PLO) 10, 14, 16, 18, 20, 23–24, 41–42, 44–46, 48, 51, 58–59, 60, 64, 68, 71, 75, 80–81, 113, 117, 119–120, 127, 130, 160, 164, 166, 169, 174–176, 178, 183–189, 192–193, 200, 217–218, 224, 231, 271, 290–291, 369, 371–373; observer status—United Nations 288–290
Palestinian Authority (PA)/Palestinian National Authority (PNA) 11, 18–22, 24, 43, 160–161, 215–218, 165–166, 169, 183–187, 191, 193, 209, 215–217, 219, 222–227, 229–238, 262–263, 266–267, 371–373; and civil rights 227–235; and human rights 227–235; and justice 223–226
Palestinian Economic Council for Development and Reconstruction (PECDAR) 169, 184, 350
Palestinian Independent Commission on Citizens Rights 231
Palestinian Legislative Council (PLC)/Palestinian National Council (PNC) 19–20, 42–44, 47–48, 51, 160, 162–164, 199, 202, 207, 209, 214, 217–218, 223, 226–227, 262, 264
Palestinians 60–63, 67, 69, 76, 253, 266; refugees 266, 278–280
Popular Front for the Liberation of Palestine 233
Preparatory Transfer Agreement 189

al-Quds 231

R.F.K. Memorial Center for Human Rights 237
Rabin, Yitzhak 215
Rothschild, Lord 254

Sachs, Albie 200
El-Sadat, Anwar 59
Samuel, Herbert 258
Sarraj, Eyad 231–232, 237
Saudi Arabia 59
Savir, Uri 262
Schuman, M. Robert 86
Schuman Plan 92
Shaikai, Khalil 234

Shamir, Ronen 261
Sharm al-Sheikh Agreement 265
Smuts, Jan 255, 257
South Africa 22
Spain 22; Arab–Israeli Conflict 316–319; Arab world 314; Israel 307–310, 313, 315; Palestine Liberation Organization (PLO) 310, 314; United Nations 306; Yasser Arafat 310
Suárez, Adolfo: Middle East 308–310; Palestine 309; Palestine Liberation Organization (PLO) 309
Sweden 22

Truth and Reconciliation Commission 201–202

al-Umma 230–231
United Nations 11, 16, 3–40, 43, 49, 235; Charter 39–40, 73; Commission on Economic, Social and Cultural Rights 283–284; Commission on Human Rights 282–283; Commission on Racial Discrimination 282–283; Commission on the Exercise of the Inalienable Rights of the Palestinian People 286–287; Palestine Partition Resolution 55, 76, 79, 128; Relief Agency (UNRWA) 284–285; Secretariat—Division for Palestinian Rights 287; Security Council 41, 48, 50–51, 68, 75; Security Council—Resolution *242* 50–51, 68, 75, 280–281, 295; Security Council—Resolution *338* 295; Special Commission on Palestine (UNSCOP) 276–278; Truce Supervision Organization (UNTSO) 285–286
United Nations General Assembly 16, 19, 40, 43–44, 46, 48, 266; Resolution *52/250* 292; Resolution *181* 50, 266, 277, 305; Resolution *194* 278–280; Resolution *2535* 281–282; Resolution *2672* 281–282; Resolution *3210* 288;
Resolution *3236* 266, 288; Resolution *3237* 288; Special Commission on Palestine 40; Special Commission to Investigate Israeli Practices Affecting the Human Rights of the Palestinian People and Other Arabs of the Occupied Territories 287–288
United Nations Information System on the Question of Palestine (UNISPAL) 287
United States 23, 59, 67, 117, 214, 235–236; Central Intelligence Agency (CIA) 236; Memorandum of Understanding 181–182; Overseas Protective Investment Corporation (OPIC)—Palestine 400, 410–412; Palestinian Authority (PA)—human rights 235–240
USSR 48, 60, 119

Venice Declaration 21
Von Glahn, Gerhard 179–180

West Bank 11, 19, 41, 43, 46–47, 51, 61, 63–68, 70, 72–78, 108–109, 111–113, 117, 160, 163, 169, 174, 178–180, 183, 185, 190, 193–194, 218–223, 225, 232, 234–235, 263–266, 373–375, 396, 406; and Great Britain 74; and justice 219–222; and Pakistan 74
World Bank 415
World Trade Organization (WTO) 17, 161
Wright, Quincy 78
Wye River Meeting 231, 235–236
Wye River Memorandum 216, 218, 231, 235–236, 265

Yassin, Sheikh Ahmad 231

Zionism 65–67, 69–70, 76, 253–256, 258, 260, 261, 262, 272–273